P9-DEB-805

THE UNIVERSITY AND THE CHURCH

The University and the Church:
Essays in Honor of William Alexander Johnson

Copyright © 2008 by William Alexander Johnson
Hudson Books

All rights reserved. No part of this book may be reproduced (except for inclusion in reviews), disseminated or utilized in any form or by any means, electronic or mechanical, including photocopying, recording, or in any information storage and retrieval system, or the Internet/World Wide Web without written permissions from the author or publisher. All of the writers in this Festschrift have given their permission for inclusion in this publication.

For further information contact:

Hudson Books
244 Madison Avenue, #254
New York, NY 10016

The University and the Church:
Essays in Honor of William Alexander Johnson

LIBRARY OF CONGRESS CONTROL NUMBER 2005922643
ISBN: 0-9764459-7-2

To my dear friend, and dearst colleague Richard Seagraves (handwritten inscription)

THE UNIVERSITY AND THE CHURCH
ESSAYS IN HONOR OF WILLIAM ALEXANDER JOHNSON

Edited By
James Proud and Karl Johnson

Preface By
Warren Adler

Cover By
Will Barnet

Preface

Scholar, priest, writer, public speaker, athlete, opera performer: William Alexander Johnson has distinguished himself in so many fields, it is impossible to do justice to the many achievements, awards and honors of this true Renaissance man.

The oldest of seven children, Johnson was born in Brooklyn, New York, on August 20, 1934, to Swedish immigrant parents. His father was Charles Rafael Johansson, originally a merchant sailor from Sweden and later a house painter in New York City; and his mother, Ruth Augusta Anderson, was a housewife.

He attended the New York City public schools and received his B.A. from Queens College of the City University of New York. He graduated cum laude with academic concentrations in Philosophy and Psychology.

An accomplished athlete, he played baseball, football, soccer, and basketball, ran track, and earned six athletic letters in college.

Later concentrating his efforts in both scholarship and religion, he received his M.A. from New York University and his B.D. at the Drew Theological Seminary, the latter launching him on a second career path as an Episcopal priest. He has spent his entire professional life in the University and the Church.

He received his Ph.D. from Columbia University, his thesis exploring the Kantian influence on Schleiermacher. He also received a Doctorate from the University of Lund in Sweden, where his thesis explored "Nature and the Supernatural in the Theology of Horace Bushnell."

After further studies at the University of Basel in Switzerland and the University of Copenhagen, Johnson embarked on a long and distinguished dual career in academia and the Episcopal Church in America.

He has taught philosophy and religion at numerous colleges and universities, including Trinity College, Drew University, Princeton, Manhattanville and Brandeis University where, for 25 years, he held the Albert V. Danielsen Professorship in Philosophy and the History of Ideas as well as a professorship in Near Eastern and Judaic Studies.

Professor Johnson has also served as a visiting professor at universities in Tokyo, Copenhagen, Strasbourg, Guadalajara, Rome, the Gregorian University, Perth, Australia, Bryn Mawr College, MIT, NYU, UTS and the Theological College of Pangnirtung on Baffin Island in the Northwest Territories of Arctic Canada.

He is a canon at the Church of John the Divine in New York City.

In 1955, he married the former Carol Lundquist. They have three children and three grandchildren.

Professor Johnson is a member of the Century Association and the Lotos Club in New York, where his seminars on World Thinkers in Literature, Philosophy and Politics are in great demand.

He was very much involved in the Civil Rights movement in the 1950s and '60s, and was a "freedom rider" in Georgia, Alabama and Mississippi. He helped found the Student Non-Violent Coordinating Committee (SNCC), and marched in Selma.

The important intellectual influences in his scholarly work have been the philosophical perspective of the Anglo-American analytic tradition; theologically, he is strongly committed to the Luther-Barth Incarnational perspective. And therefore, as a consequence, he has attempted in his professional life to integrate the two, in what he believes is not a competitive intellectual enterprise.

He is author of 15 published books in the academic fields of philosophy and theology and has written more than 200 articles that have appeared in numerous scholarly publications all over the world.

He has also been the subject of a TV special on his experiences as a crew member on the liner *Stockholm* when it crashed with the *Andrea Doria* in 1956. One of his proudest accomplishments was to perform on the stage of the Metropolitan Opera in Manhattan, as *un popolo* (a supernumerary) in the operas *La Boheme*, *The Masked Ball*, *Tosca* and his favorite, *Aida*.

Everyone who has contributed an essay to this Festschrift has been closely associated with William Alexander Johnson in the University or the Church. They all represent significant associations in his life.

Warren Adler

Contributors

Warren Adler, Writer, New York

James Proud, Priest and Lawyer, Philadelphia

Karl Johnson, Writer, New York

Will Barnet, Artist, New York

Edward LeRoy Long, Jr., Professor, Drew Theological Seminary

Robert E. Seaver, Professor, Union Theological Seminary

Richard Shaull, Professor, Princeton Theological Seminary

Schuyler Brown, Professor, Trinity College, University of Toronto

Bertil Werkström, Archbishop and Primate, Church of Sweden

Gustaf Wingren, Professor, Lunds Universitet

Huston Smith, Professor, Syracuse University, MIT

James A. Carpenter, Professor, General Theological
    Seminary
James Carse, Professor, New York University
Owen C. Thomas, Professor, Episcopal Divinity School
Fred Sommers, Professor, Brandeis University
Peter Carnley, Archbishop and Primate, Anglican Church of
    Australia
Frank G. Kirkpatrick, Professor, Trinity College,
    Hartford, Connecticut
Benson Saler, Professor, Brandeis University
Nino Langiulli, Professor, Saint Francis College,
    Brooklyn, New York
Marvin Fox, Professor, Brandeis University
Glenn Tinder, Professor, University of Massachusetts
Gunnar Hillerdal, Rektor, Växjö, Sweden
Balfour Brickner, Rabbi, New York
Alan Mittleman, Professor, Muhlenberg College, Jewish
    Theological Seminary
Robert S. MacLennan, Former Pastor, Hitchcock
    Presbyterian Church, Scarsdale, New York
Michael Paley, Rabbi, New York
Krister Stendahl, Dean, Harvard Divinity School, Bishop
    of the Church of Sweden
David Birnbaum, Writer, New York
Moorhead Kennedy, Former Hostage in Iran, Writer,
    Maine

Robert Satter, Judge, Supreme Court of Connecticut

Paul Moore, Jr., Episcopal Bishop of New York

Harry Reynolds Smythe, Director, The Anglican Centre, Rome

John S. Nurser, Priest, Professor, Lincoln, Great Britain

Hans Klette, Professor, Lunds Universitet

Lars M. Gunné, Professor, Uppsala Universitet

Marvin Barrett, Writer, New York

TABLE OF CONTENTS

xiii

xiv

THE UNIVERSITY AND THE CHURCH

1

Prologues and Epilogues: The Intersection of Jurisprudence and Theology

James Proud

In the course of time, societies, like individuals, come to order themselves and set the rules of conduct by which the members must either live in community or be put away. The scope of this ordering touches on the disputes and issues of everyday life, the grist of humanity. It ranges from petty dishonesty in weighing and measuring to juvenile delinquency, to incest and adultery, and to kidnapping and murder. When formulated, such rules of conduct are placed in codes of laws that the members of the society are expected to know and obey. At first, such jurisprudence is relatively simple, but as the history of each society uniquely develops, the rules and laws become more extensive and complex. We live today in such an advanced society that it is hard to imagine a time when the laws were few and known to all.

But societies seek not only order. Many attempt to reach outside the real world of human conduct—of trade and com-

merce and domestic relations and criminal justice—to the ineffable, to the mysterious beyond in which their divinities dwell,
and to the holy places where those divinities may be found.
Such societies seek to be ordered by a divine plan and under
heavenly dispensation. And this is often expressed in their statutes of earthly governance. This form of theological reflection
not only gives special character and definition to the society
but often shapes and molds its jurisprudence.

There are numerous instances of this point of intersection
between jurisprudence and theology in the statutes and enact-
ments of early societies throughout the ancient world. Generally
found in the codal prologue or epilogue is an invocation of, an
address to, the patron deity. Also set forth at the beginning and
the end may be a description of the divine attributes. Next in
the prologue comes a recitation of the lawgiver's purposes and
motives and other good works—often construction projects—
dedicated to the godhead. Occasionally, there is a recitation of
the divine blessings and the curses that will come in this world
to the obedient and the disobedient. In remarkable ways now
lost to the modern imagination, such early legal systems reflected the dynamic interactive search for god and for social
order.

Uruinimgina's Reform Inscription (Lagash)

In the reform inscription (ca. 2350 B.C.E.) of King
Uruinimgina (sometimes rendered "Urukagina")[1] of the
Sumerian city-state of Lagash, there is a prologue dedication of
the laws to the patron god "Ningirsu, the foremost warrior of
Enlil," who was the executive god of the Sumerian pantheon.
After reciting the social ills besetting the people and before
enacting the reforms, Uruinimgina states, "When Ningirsu, the
foremost warrior of Enlil, gave the kingship of Lagash" to
Uruinimgina, the Ningirsu "set up for him the divine decrees
of former days," and Uruinimgina "held close" to the divine
injunctions laid upon him. The last reform law in the text

---

[1] Kramer, S.N. (1963) *The Sumerians: Their History, Culture and Character* (Chicago:
University of Chicago Press), pp. 317-22.

illustrates a jurisprudential-theological concern that continues to trouble us in our own day: "Finally Urukagina made a covenant with Ningirsu that a man of power must not commit an injustice against an orphan or widow."

The Lipit-Ishtar Law Code (Isin)

Although the law provisions of the code (1934 B.C.E.) of King Lipit-Ishtar,[2] who reigned over Sumer and Akkad from his city of Isin, are badly damaged, both the prologue and the epilogue are relatively intact. Declaring what he has been called by the high gods to do and what he has done, the king, not immodestly, states in the epilogue that, in accordance with the divine words, he has caused his realm "to hold to true justice" and that he has "abolished enmity and rebellion: made weeping, lamentations, outcries . . . taboo; caused righteousness and truth to exist; brought well-being to the Sumerians and Akkadians." In concluding, he observes that the stele, or stone monument, inscribed with the code is endowed with his blessings upon all who commit no evil deed regarding it, who do not damage his handiwork, who do not erase the inscription, and who do not write another name upon it: may such persons "be presented with life and breath of long days . . . may Enlil's bright forehead look down upon him." In similar terms, curses are invoked upon those who dishonor this godly work.

The Code of Hammurabi (Babylonia)

The law code of Hammurabi,[3] dating from about 1791 B.C.E., was in effect during the central reign of the Old Babylonian (Amorite) Dynasty. Its civil and criminal laws, arranged topically under 282 sections, touch on subjects as diverse as medical malpractice and wine sales. Of relevance here is the extensive listing in the prologue of the gods and goddesses of the Babylonian pantheon, together with reference to their cult

[2] Pritchard, J.B. (1969) ed. *Ancient Near Eastern Texts Relating to the Old Testament*, Third Edition with Supplement (Princeton: Princeton University Press), pp. 159-161.
[3] Ibid., pp. 163-180.

centers and temples. In five columns, consisting of over 290 poetic lines, King Hammurabi, the sixth of the eleven dynastic kings, claims the patronage of each of these divine beings and recites how he, "the god-fearing prince," has been named "to cause justice to prevail in the land, to destroy the wicked and the evil, that the strong might not oppress the weak, to rise like the sun over the black-headed [people], and to light up the land." He is, by divine grace, variously "the one who strides through the four quarters of the world," "the fiery wild-bull who gores the foe," "the lord adorned with scepter and crown," "the solicitous, the perfect one," "the wise one, the administrator; the one who plumbed the depths of wisdom." This divine patronage is similarly referred to in the five columns and over 480 lines of the epilogue. There, before pronouncing blessings and curses upon the obedient and the disobedient for ages to come, Hammurabi declares that "[t]he great gods called me, so I became the beneficent shepherd whose scepter is righteous . . . in my bosom I carried the peoples of the land of Sumer and Akkad; they prospered under my protection; I always governed them in peace; I sheltered them in my wisdom."

In contrast to the introductory and conclusory prolixity of Hammurabi's Code, the law code of Gortyn (Crete),[4] which dates from the middle of the Fifth Century, B.C.E., has a prologue of arresting brevity: "Gods!"

The Code of Manu (Vedic India)

The jurisprudence of Vedic India in the first millennium B.C.E. is collected in the Laws of Manu;[5] Manu, the archetypal "man," the Hindu "Adam," learned the laws from the Creator himself. Before expounding the sacred and civil institutes by which the duties of the castes are settled according to their order, all as ordained by the wisdom of the Self-existent godhead,

---

[4] Willets, R.F. (1967) ed. & trans. *The Laws of Gortyn.* (Berlin: Walters De Gruyter & Co.), p. 39.

[5] Bühler, G., trans. Manu, The Laws of Vol. 25 in *Sacred Books of the East,* ed. F. Max Müller (Reprint, Delhi: Motilal Banarsidas, 1964).

Manu first describes the creation in which "the divine Self-existent (Svayambhû–himself) indiscernible, (but) making (all) this, the great elements and the rest, discernible, appeared with irresistible (creative) power, dispelling the darkness."

The Code of the T'ang Dynasty

The earliest extant Chinese law code is that of the T'ang Dynasty,[6] and the received form of the code and its sub-commentary date from 624 and 653 C.E., respectively. Chinese law rested on the sixth century B.C.E. Confucian ideal of ordered virtue and social harmony. While Confucian teaching depended on no articulated theology, there were important underlying assumptions about divine models for earthly conduct. These appear, for instance, in the subcommentary to Code Article 5: "Anciently, the former wise kings imitated the models suspended in the heavens."

More than they were under Confucian teaching, however, the common people of early China were under the influence of the philosophy of Lao-tzu, the legendary contemporary of Confucius. At the heart of Lao-tzu's philosophy is the Way, the ultimate reality by which all things exist. The Way underlies the laws that insure the ordered harmony of existence, as seen in this passage from the *Tao*:

> There was something formed out of chaos,
> That was born before Heaven and Earth.
> Quiet and still! Pure and deep!
> It stands on its own and doesn't change.
> It can be regarded as the mother of Heaven and
>   Earth.
> I do not yet know its name:
> I "style" it "the Way." . . .
> Man models himself on the Earth;
> The Earth models itself on Heaven;
> Heaven models itself on the Way;

---

[6] Johnson, Wallace, ed. & trans. (1979) *The T'ang Code*, Vol. 1: General Principles (Princeton: Princeton University Press), p. 60.

And the Way models itself on that which is so on its own.[7]

From its western to its eastern regions, these texts are a sampling of the ancient world's quest for a divinely ordered jurisprudence, a theologically determined social compact. And we should expect to find this intersection of heaven-inspired civil governance nowhere else if not in the Covenant, Deuteronomic, and Holiness codes.[8] In fact, all three codes are rooted in divine order and direction. While their contents are variously referred to as "ordinances," "statutes" and "laws," these codes set forth not only civil legislation but also extensive cultic regulations. They provide rules of the festival calendars, of the manner of sacrifices, of the foods that may and may not be eaten, and of the priests and holy things. Most importantly, each code puts in primary place a version of the altar law for regulating the community's encounters with God. There can be no doubt that these codes are similar in nature and type to others of the ancient world and that before a light editorial hand had done its work, they, too, had their own invocatory prologues and epilogues. What the editors may have taken out, we cannot reclaim. What they have put in, we can identify.

In all of Israel's codes there are only three detectable editorial insertions, and each appears in the Covenant Code where it introduces either the entire code or everything following the altar law. The first two insertions, in separate clauses, constitute the code's opening phrase:

"The Lord said to Moses:"

This is the same formula that introduces each chapter (except the last) of the Holiness Code. It sounds like the rhetorical device of a careful author of an important legal, and written, composition. It does not sound like the opening attention-getting flourish of a law bard about to recite Israel's oldest law code directly to the assembled people.

---

[7] Lao-tzu, *Tè-Tao Ching*, trans. R.G. Hendricks (New York: Ballantine, 1989), p77.

[8] Covenant Code = Exodus 20:22-23:19; Deuteronomic Code = Deuteronomy Chs 12-26; Holiness Code = Leviticus Chs 17-26.

"Thus you shall say to the Israelites:"

This also is the same formula used in the beginning of each chapter (except the last) of the Holiness Code. In all cases it follows immediately after the first formula statement. And in each case it is the divine instruction telling Moses to whom he must address the law in that chapter, whether to "the priests, the sons of Aaron," or "to the people of Israel," or variants thereof.

In the Holiness Code this yoked pair of formula statements is used nine times to introduce a new article. It is an effective literary device for marking a change of subject. It would seem an ineffective device for an orator. Its insertion in the Covenant Code suggests that an editor familiar with the style of the Holiness Code was readying the Covenant Code for publication.

The third, and last, editorial insertion comes just after the altar law and introduces all the civil and cultic laws in the Covenant Code:

"These are the ordinances that you shall set before them:"

This clause echoes the opening phrases both of the prologue to the Deuteronomic Code—"These are the statutes and ordinances"—and of its epilogue—"This very day the LORD your God is commanding you to observe these statutes and ordinances." A similar phrase is used in over ten other places in the passages on the Law of Israel set in the Book of Deuteronomy (Deut 4:44-28:68), of which the Deuteronomic Code is only a part. Moreover, the Holiness Code makes use of the same Deuteronomic phrase nine times, all but the last referring to "my statutes and my ordinances." The usage made of this phrase in both Deuteronomy and the Holiness Code is integral to the texts; it is natural in the contexts. Its single use in the Covenant Code seems neither natural nor necessary; rather, it is a lead-in that an orator could do without.

After excising these slight editorial additions, what is left of the original Israelite prologues and epilogues?

1.   Although the *Covenant Code* appears to have no epilogue, it has a startlingly fresh prologue: "You have seen for yourselves that I spoke with you from heaven." The directness and brevity of the speech are novel when contrasted to the editors' formularies or to Hammurabi's much earlier grand catalogue of the Babylonian pantheon. In this, the code's original opening, God speaks directly to the people; the editorial insertions just noted make Moses the intermediary.

2.   The *Deuteronomic Code*, with no apparent editorial insertions, has its own prologue and epilogue, each freestanding yet corresponding to the other. The prologue is simple and direct: "These are the statutes and ordinances that you must diligently observe in the land that the LORD, the God of your ancestors, has given you to occupy all the days that you live on the earth." And the epilogue echoes forthrightly the contract between the LORD and his chosen people: "This very day the LORD your God is commanding you to observe these statutes and ordinances;" for, "Today you have obtained the LORD's agreement to be your God." And reciprocally, "Today the LORD has obtained your agreement: to be his treasured people . . . for him to set you high above all nations. . . and for you to be a people holy to the LORD your God, as he promised." Such a prologue and epilogue are typical of the others in the ancient legal literature we have been reviewing.

3.   And the last, the *Holiness Code*, also without apparent editorial manipulation, bears no trace of a prologue. But just as Hammurabi's Code centuries before concluded with blessings upon those who heeded his words and unspeakable curses upon those who ignored them, so the *Holiness Code* has an extended epilogue that sets forth blessings upon those who "follow my statutes and keep my commandments," and curses upon those who "will not obey me, and do not observe all these commandments." The epilogue also notes God's promise to remember the covenant with the people and their fathers if the accursed confess their iniquity.

What did the prologues and epilogues mean to the codifiers who wrote these codes, and to the governed who heard and

read them? Such invocations and such blessings and curses are
not written into the laws of our day, nor have they been for
some time. But between the earliest and latest texts quoted above
there is a span of some three thousand years, testimony that for
millennia the common belief was that the prologues and
epilogues had the power to produce their intended effect—to
bring divine power into the ordering of human affairs. This
testimony is the more impressive because not only did it span
so many eras, but it also spanned the entire world known to the
ancients. Such coincidences and synchronism were not just the
result of sharing ideas along trade routes. Rather, there evidently
was a perception, common to all, that the wholeness of life was
an interplay between heaven and earth, between this world and
the beyond, and the order and governance were fundamental to
all existence, both the seen and unseen. The idea is so poetic
that it is a poet who best expresses it. Here is Walt Whitman:

> A vast similitude interlocks all . . .
> All distances of place however wide,
> All distances of time . . .
> All souls, all living bodies though they be ever so
>   different . . .
> All nations . . . all identities that have existed or may exist . . .
> All lives and deaths, all of the past, present, future,
> This vast similitude spans them, and always has spann'd,
> And shall forever span them and compactly hold and
>   enclose them.[9]

Each invocation of otherworldly authority in the ancient
codes quoted above is grounded in belief in such an "interlocking
similitude." Uruinimgina referred to the "divine decrees of
former days" and Lipit-Ishtar to "true justice;" Hammurabi was
called "to destroy the wicked and the evil;" the Creator himself
taught the laws to Manu; and for the Chinese there were the
"models suspended in the heavens," and the Way on which
heaven itself was modeled. All speak of a true order, available for
the human community, commanded by a divine power which

---

[9] Walt Whitman, "On the Beach at Night Alone" (1856) from *Leaves of Grass*
(NY: Penguin, 1974), p. 169.

virtuous governors must invoke. All assume it is only through such power that true social, political, and economic peace and justice can be found.

This marriage of jurisprudence and theology is central to the Israelite codes and at the core of the belief that the laws they contain are divinely ordained. And yet, each invocation has a different underlying idea. The *Covenant Code* invocation—its prologue—aptly reminds Israel of the phenomena of sight and sound encompassing the lawgiving at Sinai: "You have seen for yourselves that I spoke with you from heaven." Divine intervention alone gives the law's narrator sufficient authority to remind the hearers that they owe total obedience to God's regulations for their community.

The prologue and epilogue of the *Deuteronomic Code*, however, invoke another concept—that for their diligent observance of "these statutes and ordinances," the people have obtained the LORD's agreement to be their God, to set them "high above all nations that he has made, in praise and in fame and in honor." In exchange for the people's obedience to him, he will treasure them. This notion of agreement, or contract, may have been borrowed from the treaties of peace and goodwill the Hittites negotiated with foreign powers. In these treaties the all-powerful Hittite monarch exchanged reciprocal promises of mutual protection and peaceful commerce if his authority was accepted by the ruler of another nation.

The epilogue of the *Holiness Code* is yet a third type, that of blessings upon the obedient and of curses upon those who "spurn my statutes, and abhor my ordinances" —such curses as "will make your sky like iron and your earth like copper."

Today, our codes of laws do not invoke divine authority for their grounding, and our lawmakers do not assume there is any interlocking order that spans and compactly holds and encloses all life, except, possibly, the order provided by civil government. We wonder that the ancients believed otherwise and even smile at their simple faith. They, in turn, may smile at our hubris.

2

The Vocation of Religiously Affiliated Higher Education

Edward LeRoy Long, Jr.

Historically, the relationship between religious and educational institutions has been both intimate and strained. They have shared many common features and purposes. Traditionally, both have been concerned with the nurture of persons in their wholeness; both have been concerned to understand reality as a gestalt and to develop conceptual understandings that help people to relate to that reality; both have been concerned to cultivate personal moral integrity and aim to contribute to public well-being. Both have lived according to mores and rituals that constitute a communal lifestyle rather than having existed merely to create a single product or standardized service. Often architectural similarities subtly reflect this kinship, as does ceremonial dress.

Both are corrupted when they become primarily profit driven; when they resort to coercive violence as a modality for getting people to do their bidding; or when they judge success by merely quantitative measures. Since both should be guided by a vision of integrity that transcends popular whims and fancies, both have, on occasion, been accused of being somewhat "other worldly."

11

It is not uncommon to think of the kinship between religious and educational institutions as one in which churches have played the parental role, colleges and universities the role of offspring. To be sure, across the years various religious bodies have officially established institutions of higher learning and in that sense have been the progenitors. And it certainly is true that ecclesiastical bodies have frequently founded educational institutions whereas few, if any, educational institutions have founded churches. But instead of thinking of the relationship of churches to educational institutions as one of parent to offspring, we may appropriately think of ecclesiastical and educational institutions (especially as they exist today) as siblings, having a common parentage in a commitment to human well-being. Thinking about ecclesiastical and educational institutions in this way suggests a somewhat different but no less important understanding of the relationship between them than does thinking of the relationship as one between parent and offspring. It enables us to recognize their common features but also to appreciate why rivalries and tensions sometimes develop between them and why both institutions legitimately think of themselves as defining their own reasons for being.

*

Faith and learning were once integrally related, the relationship of religious and ecclesiastical institutions quite naturally collegial. Most institutions of higher education in America once included religious instruction and religious observance as normal aspects of their pedagogical task. They did this because when they were established, religion was a well accepted aspect of the human enterprise and honored as a highly important ingredient in the search for human fullness. When institutions like Harvard, William and Mary, Princeton, and Yale were founded, it was simply assumed that the curriculum would include teaching about faith and morals and that the extra curriculum would involve activities such as attendance at chapel services. This was the case, not so much because some of these institutions were initially sponsored by ecclesiastical bodies (as, indeed several of them were) but because it was normal and customary to consider religion as crucially important for human life. The colleges founded by various denominations in the nineteenth century embraced this pattern as well and often legitimized the partnership between faith and learning with Scottish Common Sense philosophy. Even universities founded by state governments followed this same pattern until well into the twentieth century. This was possible because there was little felt tension between the expectations of religious fidelity and the expectations of scholarly effort. Faith and learning had not yet parted company.

Most of these institutions—especially those considered in the mainstream of America higher education—have undergone a massive change that has rendered the place of religion peripheral to their central agendas, indeed even suspect within the academy. The most common way to describe this transformation is to define it as a process of secularization. But it is too simplistic to think of this as signifying only the dropping of religious instruction from the curriculum and of required religious practices from the extra curriculum—although those consequences have indeed taken place. The changes involved have affected the fundamental quality of higher education itself. George Marsden has described the growing separation between faith and learning as constituting a loss of the "soul" of the university—a transformation of its very reason for being.[1] In their study of Church-related higher education, Manning Pattillo and Donald MacKenzie have contended that mainstream educational institutions underwent a transformation in which a broad humanistic learning compatible with the fundamental concerns of religion has been replaced by an intellectual climate dominated by science and in which concern for teaching of whole persons has been replaced by disciplinary specialization and research.[2] Mark R. Schwehn has characterized this change as a triumph of an academic specialization that begins in graduate school and which is the intellectual heir of

---

[1] George M. Marsden, *The Soul of the American University: From Protestant Establishment to Established Non-Belief* (New York: Oxford University Press, 1994).

[2] See Manning M. Pattillo, Jr. and Donald MacKenzie, *Church-Sponsored Higher Education in the United States: Report of the Danforth Commission* (Washington, D.C.: American Council on Education, 1966), especially chapter one.

Max Weber's call for universities to advance knowledge rather
than be concerned with the growth and nature of persons.[3] In
his history of the parting of the way between religion and higher
education, Douglas Sloan suggests that the separation between
faith and learning has become almost complete because the
theological perspectives of the mid-twentieth century (mainly
those of neo-orthodoxy) were inadequate for bridging the growing gap between the thought worlds of the churches and the
thought world of the academy.[4]

There has been a distinctive movement of reaction against
these consequences among a group of educational institutions
which have made the inculcation of religious doctrine central
to their reason for being. Although there are a handful of institutions with a long history of a specifically religious orientation
which have followed this pattern, some of the most highly
visible (and in many ways clearest) examples of this creedal/
doctrinal pattern are recent in origin.[5] Unlike the involvement
with religious faith present in the early years of the college and
university representative of the first pattern, this trend has developed in large measure to counter secularization. Moreover,
it has come about as a result of changes that have altered the
ways in which religious faith is embraced and practiced. For
instance, explicitly dogmatic assertions about the infallibility of
religious authority, whether in relationship to ecclesiastical office or sacred scripture, arose in the late nineteenth century as
defensive measures against intellectual challenges to religious
belief. When confessional stances making such claims are used to
define academic purposes, the result is the creation of learning
communities that differ from the main line institutions—even
from the main line institutions as originally founded. Instead of
thinking of faith and learning as natural partners, such reactive

---

[3] Mark R. Schwehn, *Exiles from Eden: Religion and the Academic Vocation in America* (New York: Oxford University Press, 1993), see especially chapter one.

[4] Douglas Sloan, *Faith and Learning: Mainline Protestantism and American Higher Education* (Louisville, Kentucky: Westminster John Knox Press, 1994).

[5] Some of the larger and better known (as well as heavily financed) institutions belonging in this category have been founded by media evangelists to reinforce their particular theological message.

strategies seek to make learning subservient to faith, the agenda of the academy hostage to religious dogma.

The term "Christian colleges" has come to be used as a way of distinguishing institutions that have moved in this direction. Although this term may include some institutions with long histories that do not manifest the reactive pattern being described, it nevertheless tends to raise suspicions among many educators who fear rigid confessionalism as a threat to intellectual inquiry. Moreover, many institutions representing the reactive pattern do not feel that the term "Christian college" is sufficiently clear in its meaning and therefore designate themselves "Bible colleges." Whatever the terminology, instead of including religion because it is a normal and important aspect of a holistic perspective on human life, this reactive pattern tends to think of religion as calling for an intentional struggle against the infidelity and immorality of a secular world, as providing an enclave of piety and morality that offers an alternative to the more prevalent trends of intellectual life and public practice. Instead of thinking of religious teaching as a normal aspect of the educational agenda, these institutions think of religious teachings as calling for allegiance to rigidly held doctrinal positions, some of which require the acceptance of ideas or concepts that stand in pronounced contrast to widely accepted academic thinking. Many of these same institutions also frequently enforce rules of student conduct involving conservative moral premises and (often) conventional middle class lifestyles.

Institutions that define their purpose in such reactive terms employ doctrinal tests in picking faculty and addressing intellectual issues. They are generally committed to the promulgation of a version of Christian faith that has emerged as a reaction to the forces of secularization. Intellectually, many such institutions demand acceptance of intellectual positions based upon faith commitments understood as alternative ways of knowing —for instance, favoring teaching of creationism in place of evolution. Hence, such institutions develop a separatist academic culture in which faith dogmas are controlling, although many of them have very demanding instructional regimens and expect high achievement from their students in pursuing the aims which they espouse.

Curiously, however, the way these institutions understand knowledge bears more affinities to the modernity they seem to decry than to the historic traditions they presume to embrace. They view religious faith as providing alternative propositional formulations of fact. It is quite telling that their form of orthodoxy is frequently called theological positivism, even as the most articulate forms of secular philosophy are called positivism. This is why they can treat creationism as a scientific fact just as much as secular biology might see the theory of evolution as a description of a natural process. Instead of looking at faith as a grounding for reflective understanding, they tend to conceive it as an alternative (or supplemental) form of propositional truth. The intellectual approach of these institutions can therefore be said to offer an inverted expression of a modern mindset, not an alternative understanding which appreciates the complexity of truth and the elusiveness of certainty.[6]

Moreover, these same institutions seem quite ready to accept and to encourage allegiance to many features of the contemporary world that are very much aspects of modernity. Although they would prohibit the teaching of Darwinian theories in the classroom, they generally either embrace without question (or openly defend) a free enterprise system that uncritically accepts social Darwinism as part of life. They are generally favorable to the military—many have ROTC programs—and frequently support a truculent nationalism that relies largely upon the use of force to implement policy. This is not historic Christian separatism at all, but the embrace of the most functionally questionable aspects of a contemporary secular cultural world—the very aspects of the world that can plausibly be regarded as the furthest removed from a biblically informed vision of human well-being.

★

---

[6] See Edward Farley, *The Fragility of Knowledge: Theological Education in the Church and the University* (Philadelphia: Fortress Press, 1988).

Nearly eight hundred[7] educational institutions in the United States continue to be associated by background or present stance with churches or other religious bodies, constituting well over twenty percent of the institutions of higher education in the United States today. These religiously affiliated institutions must wrestle with the divisive separation of faith and learning that has just been described. They do this in widely different ways.

Many are doing so by identifying with the secularizing trends that have so deeply affected main line higher education. A smaller number feels the tug of religious confessionalism in order to be identifiably religious. A small group in between is struggling (or should we say floundering?) to work out a viable identity that enables them to relate to a secular academic world without repudiating (as a goodly number of the institutions once found within this group have already done) their professed relationship to the ecclesiastical group from which they have sprung and with which they have long maintained something of a sibling relationship.

The plight of these religiously affiliated institutions is made more difficult because so many have been all but disowned by the religious bodies that originally supported them. Churches have become less and less interested in sponsoring higher education, not merely because of budgetary constraints, but because the relationship between faith and learning has become less and less a focus of concern of mainstream religious groups. The triumph of the therapeutic model of ministry, which thinks of the church as a center of psychological coping and spiritual healing, does very little to draw the attention of the rank and file member in the pew to the importance of higher education as an object of religious concern. Parishes have little difficulty

---

[7] It is, of course, difficult to know how many institutions are so identified. The number mentioned here is taken from the careful listing of *Church-Related Colleges and Universities* made by Joan Keeton Young in June 1994. (See Merrimon Cunninggim, *Uneasy Partners: The College and the Church* [Nashville: Abingdon Press, 1994] pp. 126-172). This is a sizable group and represents between a fifth and a quarter of all the institutions of higher education in the country, which number somewhere around 3,700. (See HEP 1995 *Higher Education Directory*, Mary Pat Rodenhouse, ed. [Falls Church, Va.: Higher Education Publications, Inc. 1995.])

understanding why they should sponsor counseling centers; they are less clear why they should sponsor campus ministries. They may (and quite rightly) understand why they should provide shelter and food for the needy, but they often see little reason to support educational institutions (except perhaps seminaries). Consequently a large number of church-related colleges are obliged to draw financial support and potential students from the same constituencies as do other colleges and universities and to gear their educational agendas toward the same objectives.

The apparent choice between religiously unproductive secularism and educationally suspect confessionalism must be transcended by creative searching for new and different ways of thinking about the calling of religiously affiliated colleges or universities. Such institutions may come to think of themselves as called to a special witness at a time when so much higher education seems disdainful of the church and so many churches are seemingly disinterested in the academic enterprise. This is a time which needs renewed attention to the importance of faith commitments in the pursuit of learning and the importance of learning for the enrichment of religious commitment. By considering themselves called to such a witness, educational institutions associated with religious groups may see their role as one of helping to overcome the inadequacies both of a learning that has ceased to appreciate the importance of belief and of a believing that has ceased to appreciate the importance of learning.

*

If religiously affiliated higher education takes seriously the situation in which it now finds itself, it may develop new outlooks and forge new practices that have important implications for higher education in general as well as for its own viability. The suggestions that follow are avenues for exploring this problem in new (albeit, tentative) ways; for doing something new, not recreating a past golden age. They suggest ways in which the religiously affiliated institution may transcend the dichotomy between secularization and doctrinal dogmatism so that learning and believing can be brought together, not further split apart.

a. Religiously related institutions may well take as a challenge the task of re-interpreting learning as a covenantal process in which all parties have both privileges and obligations, and which depends upon a set of commitments and practices that must be deliberately nurtured.

Whatever else may be true of higher education in our time, it faces a momentous challenge to help counteract a deep and persistent disinterest (if not indeed hostility) toward the learning process among those who attend colleges or universities in order to be merely certified rather than to embrace a unique set of values. The rise of consumer mentality seriously threatens the viability of much higher education, especially in a time when colleges are competing for students and are thus tempted to think of themselves as marketing a product rather than as being communities of unique commitment that involve acculturation into a special guild.

There is a good deal of contemporary attention being focused on the importance of teaching as a way of counteracting an excessive emphasis on the prestige value of research. Much of this attention to teaching is important, even long overdue. But some of this emphasis on teaching misses the major issue, as when expressed in a misguided demand for faculty to spend longer hours in the classroom or when it assumed that an award to a single good teacher-of-the-year will provide the incentive to improve teaching across the board. To emphasize faculty responsibility for teaching is not necessarily to embrace institutional responsibility for creating an exciting learning environment and cultivating the attitudes that enable persons to participate wholeheartedly within such a community. The religiously related institution must do more than merely jump on the bandwagon of a public clamor for more attention to teaching, even if (as may plausibly be the case) it has probably paid more attention to teaching all along than has the secular research university. The fundamental task of the academic community is not merely to teach subject matter content, but rather to inspire learning and to nurture those attitudes and commitments upon which it depends. One of the greatest barriers to learning in contemporary institutions of higher education is the failure of students to love and embrace the scholarly ideal, not the failure of faculty to convey information. In some cases this failure grows out of an anti-intellectual student culture in which the tendency abounds to get by with the least output of time or effort on studies, but in other cases it stems from a loss of the scholarly vision from the life of the institution as a whole.

To give learning due respect and concern requires deliberate and intentional cultivation. It may very well involve bringing about something analogous to the kind of changes and transformations in the orientation of the self that religious faith has long associated with conversion. This means that academic institutions must concern themselves not merely with the techniques that are required on the part of faculty to improve teaching, but with the conditions of commitment and involvement on the part of all parties to the pedagogical covenant that need to be embraced in order to make learning profound and meaningful. For example, it may require the rethinking of course evaluations that seem to treat the classroom as a kind of television production that students rate as consumers. These should be superseded by evaluations that focus attention on the mutual (or covenantal) dynamics that have hopefully been operative in a given classroom encounter so that students see themselves as jointly involved in determining the success of a course.

The zeal and ability to learn well is not a natural endowment that all those who gain admission to colleges or universities innately possess. It is developed through acculturation into a unique community that respects certain conventions, that cherishes certain mindsets, that is loyal to a set of commonly acknowledged values, and that involves a deep transformation of the self as a condition for its attainment. Although their present success at this task may not be better than that of higher education as a whole, religiously related higher education is in a position to understand what is involved in transformational renewal and to offer guidance for making such a *metanoia* a part of what it means to become involved in the learning process.

    b. Another way in which the religiously affiliated institution can bring an important perspective to the academic process involves the reconceptualizing of knowledge and extending the scope of scholarly interest.

    The contemporary academy faces a crisis of knowing. The hegemony of the scientific method that has been looked to as providing intellectual certainty for the modern university is presently under various clouds of suspicion. The intellectual heritage of the Enlightenment has been deeply challenged, not so much because religious dogmatism accuses it of heresy, but because a large segment of post-modern thinking recognizes its limitations and distortions. This challenge, appearing (at least most notably) in deconstructionism, offers both an opportunity and a set of dangers—but at least it is a movement from within the academic enterprise and not from outside the scholarly camp.

    Although it would be unwise for religiously affiliated higher education to jump on the bandwagon of deconstructionism as a solution to the faith/knowledge problem, there is a sense in which the contemporary ferment about the scope and reliability of knowledge opens a way for a kind of thinking often associated with theology to speak to the educational enterprise more cogently than has been the case for almost a century. Deconstructionism, for instance, provides a more adequate critique than it provides a constructive agenda; it is implicitly nihilistic rather than potentially foundational. Nevertheless, matters of epistemology are sufficiently under re-examination today—both to call for imaginative rethinking and to open the discussions about the foundation of knowing to perspectives that have been too readily closed out by a triumphalist secularism. This does not mean that faith affirmations will be readily heard or embraced, but it does mean that the foundational premises of all human knowing can be explored without prior restraints being imposed by a largely secular rationalism.

    The exploration of foundational issues constitutes a large part of what Gordon D. Kaufman has called "Critical Theology."[8] Kaufman contends that a particular kind of theological

---

[8] Gordon D. Kaufman, "Critical Theology as a University Discipline," in David Raymond Griffin and Joseph C. Hough, Jr, eds, *Theology and the University: Essays in Honor of John B. Cobb Jr.* (Albany: State University of New York Press, 1991), chapter two.

reflection, which he calls "critical theology," has a role to play in higher education. Such a theology is concerned not with asserting creedal or doctrinal positions, but with understanding the roles that beliefs and commitments play in human life. Critical theology stands in counter distinction to confessional theology, although Kaufman notes there has often been a critical element within confessional strands of the Christian tradition.

Kaufman seems to suggest that one of these ways of doing theology belongs in the university; the other, in the church. While this assignment of roles is plausible, the church-related college or religiously affiliated university ought not to be forced to adopt either option, but should be a place where genuine conversations are possible between these two ways of doing theology. The possibilities for utilizing theology in the service of understanding can be greatly enlarged if the conditions are possible for critical theology to dialogue with confessional theology. The critical theology most at home in the university can help to keep confessional theology from being understood as merely making assertions that have the status of objective information in the rationalist sense; the confessional theology most at home in the religious community can help to keep critical theology from dismissing faith commitments as little more than pious wishes.[9] Religiously affiliated institutions of higher education might prove to be the only places in which interaction between these two kinds of theology can take place, but the creation of such a possibility will require deliberate cultivation. This involves understanding how intellectual openness can relate to the commitments by which communities of faith define themselves, and also how the free exploration of ideas must take account of the loyalty to convictions that is the heart of much religion. Although the potential for tension is enormous, so also is the possibility for probing more deeply into the most fundamental issues of human existence than is likely if either an ideology of rationality or an ideology of confessionalism is controlling.

---

[9] On the balancing of these two thrusts, see Robert N. Bellah, " At Home and Not at Home: Religious Pluralism and Religious Truth," in *The Christian Century*, Volume 112, Number 13 (April 19, 1995), pp. 423-428.

It is important that this agenda not be made the sole responsibility of a department that teaches religion (or religious studies). Issues that involve the tension between the critical and the confessional stances arise in relationship to many disciplines, each of which is shaped by foundational assumptions that are historically shaped and embraced as axiomatic beliefs. Theological reflection, therefore, cannot be merely a scholarly specialty; it must be a broadly human undertaking. Theological issues are not the sole province of a group of experts who have made reflection upon a certain kind of reality their unique domain, but should be the concern of all those who wish to understand the meaning of human life on the deepest possible levels.

There are staffing implications to the embrace of this agenda. Colleges or universities that would earnestly undertake such foundational inquiry have a responsibility to choose as faculty members persons who are capable of dealing with the broad issues, albeit in relationship to their disciplinary specialties. This is a quite different requirement than testing for adherence to a particular set of dogmatic propositions; it measures breadth in scholarly and intellectual achievement, not conformity to particular conclusions. It honors astuteness, not merely correctness. It is concerned to find a particular kind of competence, not to avoid heresy. The capacity to understand and carry on this kind of intellectual activity is not found in every aspirant for faculty appointment (even in those applying for positions in the field of religious studies), but it can be discovered (if perhaps only rarely) among those seeking careers in higher education. It is the responsibility of religiously affiliated institutions to discover persons who have the requisite skills and bring them aboard, and once aboard to see that they are respected and duly encouraged to pursue such interests.

c. A third way in which the religiously affiliated institutions can offer a special witness to our time is by demonstrating the importance of a commitment to an ecumenically understood public welfare. The term ecumenical as used here signifies the whole known world, not merely church related activities, and the term welfare suggests a measure of broad human good and not merely a system of support for the needy.

There is an adage that speaks of knowledge as "being in order to goodness." That terminology suggests that the reason for education is to equip persons for service in society. In contrast, much higher education today proceeds on the assumption that knowledge is in order to itself. This attitude implies that knowing by itself is self-legitimizing or, more commonly, is a mere skill to be employed in self-serving satisfaction. Students may be more interested in how a degree prepares them for employment than in how the employment contributes to the edification and improvement of the widest possible public good.

It would be unfair to charge all secular higher education with nurturing self-serving concern for personal satisfaction and narrowly understood economic self-interest, and it would be presumptuous to claim that all religiously affiliated institutions are clearly effective in raising students' commitments to a broadly understood public good. There are academic institutions in both categories in which the idea of service is respected and in which groups exist that solicit the voluntary interest of students in undertaking worthy service projects. There may be no institutions that altogether lack pockets of such concern and commitment. But the academic professionalism characteristic of the modern university does not consider the cultivation of social commitment to be an essential part of its task. Being among "the best and the brightest" does not necessarily imply a sense of obligation to an ecumenical public welfare. The choices which students make as to where and in what ways they will use their knowledge and their skills after they graduate are not a focus of institutional concern or attention. Concern for the public good is simply allowed to drift somewhere out and beyond the parameters of institutional responsibility.

It will not do for the religiously affiliated college or university thus to ignore the consideration of such matters. Although it would be contrary to the very nature of the academic process to force students into any particular employment patterns or vocational obligations, it is not contrary to an educational ethos respecting the claims of the world, especially of the claims of the poor and of the oppressed in an ever widening world, to be highlighted within the educational process. Moreover, religiously affiliated colleges and universities can give preference in admission to those who look upon learning as a preparation for philanthropic commitments, honor alumni and alumnae whose lives exemplify service to others rather than extraordinary economic gain, and shape their institutional policies by standards of humanitarian commitment and ecological responsibility. Moreover, religiously affiliated institutions must examine the policy issues that arise in relationship to the pursuit of justice in the total community.

To do this requires resources as well as resolve. When the various religious bodies founded colleges in the nineteenth century they saw the support of colleges as a way to make a contribution to the public well-being of a society moving onto a frontier. They gave, sometimes generously, not so much to further their self-interest as religious groups, but to prepare people to serve crying needs. The needs in our time are much greater, involve a far wider geographical spread and a world-encompassing cultural challenge, and involve more momentous stakes. They require new levels of dedication and broadened understandings. Religious bodies with worldwide constituencies can bring unique perspectives to this process and should be asked to accept the challenge of supporting those institutions that prepare leaders to work on the far-flung frontiers of our time. Churches that, as do some of the major denominations, have more members in third world countries than in the United States, are in a position to counter perspectives often associated with narrow-minded nationalism. Ecclesiastical movements like the World Council of Churches provide a more inclusive community from which to view the world than is normally encountered in the public arena—though the churches of individual countries do, admittedly, often have difficulty raising the awareness of their members to the importance of such a perspective. Those religious bodies that take seriously their associations with persons of faith in other parts of the world can encourage and facilitate programs of outreach and concern that are intentionally devised to focus attention on the need to prepare graduates who are dedicated to overcoming the gap between economic privilege and economic oppression in our society and also the gulf between the first and the other worlds. Religiously affiliated institutions that are content to attract students who lack (indeed often resist) such a moral vision, or who seek to define their educational vision entirely according to the factors that are associated with the term "prestige," are failing to live up to one of the important aspects of their reasons for being.

★

In discussing church-related colleges, Merrimon Cunninggim has rightly argued that their fundamental obligation is to be colleges, to cherish the academic values of truth, freedom, justice and kinship.[10] I have elsewhere suggested that the health of higher education today depends upon orthopraxis, in contrast to calls for orthodoxy often associated with the confessional pattern or calls for orthognosis characteristic of the modern secular institution.[11] The three agendas suggested here would enrich and enhance the program that Cunninggim advocates by focusing on the practices that the academic institution must follow in bringing faith and learning together. These are not suggestions for creating pseudo-churches; they are suggestions for creating richer and more sensitive educational institutions in which religious faith and practice are rightly honored. To implement them wisely would make religiously affiliated institutions better as colleges and universities—perhaps even better than any institution can hope to be if it does not take such concerns seriously.

---

[10] *Uneasy Partners*, op. cit., p. 117.
[11] See *Higher Education as a Moral Enterprise* (Washington, D.C.: Georgetown University Press, 1992), especially chapter one.

3

Liturgical Leadership

Robert E. Seaver

In an essay about "The Language of Worship," Geoffrey Wainwright writes that, "...liturgy is essentially *spoken and heard.*" [1] He is writing about: "... a number of bipolar tensions between legitimate *desiderata* in liturgical language ..." [2], and he asks the question, "How are modern liturgical authors to master the relation between the written, the read, and the spoken word?" To which he immediately responds: "Poets, dramatists, and actors might help them." [3]

Indeed they can, say I. And it is with a desire to further the dialogue that Wainwright alludes to in response to his own question, that I intend to say some of the things that I have learned about liturgical leadership from the point of view of an artist. That is how I perceive myself. That is what I try to be. I am not a philosopher. Nor am I a scholar. I am a craftsman. I am a craftsman of the theater who is also a teacher (and sometimes an administrator), who also embodies sensibilities as a man of faith and hope.

---

[1] Cheslyn Jones, Geoffrey Wainwright, Edward Yarnold, S.J. (editors), *The Study of Liturgy* (New York: Oxford University Press, 1978), p. 472.
[2] Ibid., p. 471.
[3] Ibid., p. 472.

To get at the topic we will need to challenge, perhaps even cast off, some of our cherished notions of what it means to lead. Liturgical leadership viewed from the perspective of an artist is quite different from that of "running the show" or, for that matter, "playing the leading role." This is not to say that artists have no ego-involvement in their work. The many I know—including myself—certainly do. What I have in mind will become clear as I proceed. So, let us see how the artist might be of help to those of us who exercise liturgical leadership in Christian churches. I shall do this under several headings:

> the liturgical leader as artist;
> the liturgical leader as prompter;
> the liturgical leader as director; and,
> the liturgical leader as a person of faith.

Liturgical Leader As Artist

Seeing something in a new way is what art is all about. Artists see what most people barely look at. And artists turn the experience of what they have seen into paintings, musical scores, novels, dances and, of course, plays, showing us the funny, sad, impossible, idealistic, even the nasty side of ourselves. Ibsen, showing us what happens when truth is not faced; Pirandello, contrasting fiction and fact, probing the results of snap judgments and easy assumptions; Willy Loman declaiming, "It's not what you do, Ben, it's who you know and the smile on your face. It's contacts, Ben, contacts."[4] For those who have the eyes to see, Arthur Miller, in his play *Death of a Salesman*, explodes the big American lie of being well-liked, stripping away the mask so that Willy Loman can see that he has never been who he thought he was. And we, who enter into a performance of that powerful play, either as actor or as observer, find the key to the solution of the dramatic images which Arthur Miller evokes for us not in our heads but in our guts as we pour out our anguish in tears of pain over the loneliness and emptiness we find in our lives. That's strong stuff. But that is what artists do. Mr. Peachum, in

---

[4] Arthur Miller, *Death of a Salesman* (New York: Viking Press, 1949), p. 86.

Bertold Brecht's play, *The Threepenny Opera*, puts it succinctly: "Between 'giving people a shock' and 'getting on their nerves' there's a certain difference, my friend. I need artists. Only an artist can give people *the right sort* of shock."[5]

On the occasion of my retirement as a Professor of Speech and Drama at Union Theological Seminary (New York City), some of my associates gathered for a colloquy in my honor. One of my former students, now a pastor in a church in Massachusetts, told of an experience planning a service for Lent. The text was Luke 4—the temptation and fasting of Christ. Elizabeth, that's her name, had gathered several members of her congregation together and they sat in the church and "stared at the chancel: Wilderness, desert, dry, barren, hot, dead, dust. What was the text saying? Wilderness, forest, dark, lost, alone, loneliness. Yes, loneliness, that was it. The wilderness was loneliness. Without any hesitation we all agreed the wilderness was loneliness and the mood and the message of that Sunday was about loneliness. We wanted people to feel the loneliness Jesus felt."[6]

That is what art does. *When one talks about art one talks about experience.* One experiences something—the beauty of a flower, the dryness of a desert—and one searches for a way to put the intensity of that experience into a form that can be shared with another. A visual setting! A song! A story! A dance! An expression that might display something like the force of the original experience to those who have eyes to see and ears to hear. Something like communication takes place as a result of such making-believe (make-believing). Something is disclosed. Something that otherwise was not accessible becomes clear. One *feels* the loneliness the writer of the Gospel posed not only years ago in the early church but also for Elizabeth and her colleagues on that grey January day in Massachusetts in 1986.

It is also worth noting that the planning committee began by considering the space within which they would be working.

---

[5] Bertold Brecht, *The Threepenny Opera*, in *The Modern Theater, Vol. I* (Eric Bentley, ed.) (Garden City, NY: Doubleday/Anchor Books, 1955), Act I, Scene 3, p. 140.

[6] Remarks made by Elizabeth Wheeler at a colloquy in honor of Robert E. Seaver on the occasion of his retirement as Professor of Speech and Drama at Union Theological Seminary in the City of New York. May 13, 1986.

That is, they set about building a world in which people could make believe. They dispensed with the sanctuary furniture and added "a three-foot cross backlit in red—the color of passion, of danger. The color that says at once, 'STOP!' This spot is important. Be wary! Go no further without knowing where you are and what you may be in for. Now! Now that you are in this place, preparing to worship God."

Each of us has been creating spaces for years as we cope with the complexities of the world about us, spaces in which to live and breathe. W.H. Auden calls these spaces "secondary worlds," spaces where ". . . we can exclude everything except what we find sacred, important, enchanting."[7] Auden is speaking about art as something made—a world of literature, for example, or a world of architecture. Within these worlds one creates symbols of what really matters—books, homes, poetry, churches, theaters. And he is speaking about the artist in each of us— about each of us as makers. What is striking about the world which Elizabeth and her colleagues created was that they replaced the familiar setting with which they, and presumably their congregation, were comfortable with one that was harsher, more appropriate to spiritual discipline, a setting that suggested that which was painful, even disagreeable.

If, as liturgical leaders, we are witness to what Saint Jerome somewhere calls "the secrets of the heart," we will need to come to grips with artists and their powers of visualization and expression. And, if we are willing to discipline ourselves, they can teach us how to see. Then we will have acquired one of the trademarks of liturgical leadership. We will be *a believer who can be a make-believer.* With that, indeed as part of that, comes a faculty for serendipity—that "gift," Webster calls it," ...of finding valuable or agreeable things not sought for." Elizabeth expressed it this way: "In our quiet murmurings to one another, almost like a prayer, we received the message of the text and found the message of the day."[8] So a liturgical leader is something of an artist, a maker, a doer who creates worlds for making believe (make-believing). The trademark: *feelings* in the gut.

---

[7] W. H. Auden, *Secondary Worlds.* (New York: Random House, 1968), p. 52.

[8] Remarks made by Elizabeth Wheeler.

The Liturgical Leaders As Prompter

In Elizabeth's account of her Lenten planning session, she also remarked that ". . . the task of the pastor is not to make change but to permit it, to allow ideas to surface, to say 'Yes' to the folks and their visions."[9] How does one cue the laity into action? Consider the prompter as a model.

My former colleague Johann Hoekendijk, the distinguished Dutch theologian, says that:

> The layman [*sic*] is not a pastor's assistant, he is not an 'extension' of the pastor; nor is he a miniature clergyman [*sic*]. It is the pastor who is the servant of the layman. The aim of the pastor is to remind God's missionary people of their task. But he himself does not appear on the world-stage. The drama *(Laienspeil)* being played out there is a secular drama, in which he cannot take part. From time to time he may be permitted to act as producer, but mainly a prompter. Unfortunately the pulpit has very little resemblance to a prompter's box, and the man in the pulpit is all too visible.[10]

Let's play with Hoekendijk's notion of pastor as prompter. A theater prompter uses a prompt book. A prompt book is a record of the stage director's work. The book is organized for the purpose of guiding the play in performance. In theater, one often hears a prompter referred to as being "on the book." The prompter is part of stage management; sometimes as an assistant stage manager. Tyrone Guthrie, himself an eminent theatrical director, describes the prompter at rehearsal as "the whipping boy of actors . . . If they fail to give a prompt not merely at the moment when it is wanted . . . but the moment before, then there is hell to pay with compound interest."[11]

Intuition and tact are essential qualities of an efficient prompter. In *A Life in the Theater*, Guthrie relates an amusing moment when a prompter "spoke too soon." The actress, who

[9] Ibid.
[10] Johann C. Hoekendijk, *Die Zukunft der Kirchie und die Kirche der Zukun* (Stuttgart, 1965), p. 34.
[11] Tyrone Guthrie, *A Life in the Theater* (New York: McGraw Hill Book Co., 1959), p. 181.

Guthrie describes as "a fascinating, brilliantly clever and talented little woman," turned on the prompter "with blazing eyes":

> "Did you speak?"
> "Yes. I gave you the line."
> "Are you acting the part or am I?"
> "You are trying to, and you always dry up on that line."

What followed in Guthrie's description was one of those hideous moments that seem to go on forever, but actually is quite short. "For the assistant stage manager to address Dame Marie Tempest," writes Guthrie, "was like a corporal giving a back-answer to a field marshal, like a rowboat ramming the Queen Mary."[12]

But such is the work of the liturgical leader as prompter, if, that is, one perceives liturgy as an act of "making present in word, symbol, and sacrament the paschal mystery of Christ so that through its celebration the men and women of today may make a saving encounter with God."[13] I am taking worship as public performance seriously in the best sense of that word as the reenactment of an action involving the practical disciplines of setting, of clothing, of speech and movement, of all that gives an event "style," which John Henry Newman once described as "...a thinking out into language."[14] In this case into the languages of worship.

How does one do this when, in so many instances in churches, the liturgical leader is expected to give directions? "That's what they're there for!" Let's shift the focus a bit and look at the role of the liturgical leader as director.

The Liturgical Leader As Director

Tyrone Guthrie is an especially satisfying model as a director for our purpose. In the first place, he believes "that the purpose

---

[12] Ibid., p. 181.
[13] Jones et. al., *The Study of Liturgy*: see J.D. Chrichton, "A Theology of Worship," p. 16.
[14] Raymond Macdonald Alden, ed., *Readings in English Prose of the Nineteenth Century* (New York: Houghton-Mifflin, 1917), p. 439.

of the theatre is to show mankind (*sic*) to himself, and thereby to show to man God's image."[15] Next, I think his understanding of the task of the director in relation to the preparation of a play compares favorably with my view of the task of a liturgical leader in relation to the public worship of the congregation. Both help to bring their material to vigorous life. Guthrie says this about a director's role in preparing a play:

> He does not play the leading part. He does more.
> He interprets, shapes, guides, inspires the entire per-
> formance.[16]

This is what Hoekendijk is alluding to when he says, speaking of the pastor as prompter, ". . . he himself does not appear on the world-stage."[17] In churches, liturgical leaders who own this trademark will keep "love for one another at full strength" (I Peter 4:8, NEB) using whatever gift each one has received "in service to one another, like good stewards dispensing the grace of God in its varied forms" (I Peter 4:10 NEB).

Here is an account by Moss Hart, himself a distinguished man of the theater, writing about still another celebrated writer/ director, George S. Kaufman, and his skill in dispensing grace as he directed actors:

> He gave no lesson in acting nor did he use the power
> some directors wield to hold a cast helpless before him while
> he discusses his own interpretation of the playwright's
> meaning, or with becoming modesty performs each part for
> each actor in turn to show how easily it might be played to
> perfection with just a modicum of his own talent. Instead, he
> seemed to allow the actors to use him as a sounding board.
> He watched and listened and without seeming to impose his
> own preconceived ideas of how a scene should be played, he
> let each actor find a way of his own that was best for him; and
> slowly, with no more than a whispered word here and there,
> the scenes began to take on a directorial quality and flavor

---

[15] Tyrone Guthrie, *A Life in the Theater*, p. 349.
[16] Ibid, p. 137.
[17] Hoekendijk, *Die Zukunft*, p. 31.

that were unmistakably his.The sovereign motif of his direction seemed to be an artful mixture of allowing actors the freedom to follow their own instinctive intelligence and tastes, and then trusting his own ear for comedic values—an ear that had the unerring exactness of a tuning fork.With no directorial vanity ego of his own, he was able to indulge actors in theirs, and an actor's ego in the early days of rehearsal is like a blade of new spring grass that will grow and reseed itself if it is not mowed down too quickly by a power-driven lawn mower— the lawn mower in most cases being the overenthusiastic imposition of a famed directorial hand.[18]

From time to time we see these distinctive qualities of prompter/director that Hans Hoekendijk, Tyrone Guthrie and Moss Hart describe, in pastors, musicians, and other liturgical leaders in churches. Where have these people received their training? Webster describes prompting as "being ready and quick to act as occasion demands."There are no courses that I know of on "being ready" or "quick to act." How does one learn this?

One learns to prompt by prompting, just as one learns to direct by directing. By "apprenticing!" By doing *and failing* as well as by doing and succeeding.That is what learning a craft is all about—making something seem easy when it is not. Becom- ing a craftsman requires practice. Daily practice! Practice even when one is not expecting to preach a sermon or to play an instrument in public. Practice—the repetition of an action which leads to habits which are strengthened by daily exercise, which leads to fitness for action "as occasion demands." I am not talking only about general physical fitness. That is taken for granted. Bodies—especially bodies of those who propose to minister to others—must be kept in shape, in tune, ready for action. The fitness I am talking about is an inner vitality that comes from being "centered." It is the mixture of "caring" and "not caring" that T.S. Eliot wrote about in *Ash Wednesday*. It is then and only then, when we need no longer "mock ourselves with falsehood," "when our peace [is] in His will," when one is fully freed to be of service, that a liturgical leader can sit off toward one side as

---

[18] Moss Hart, *Act One* (NewYork Random House, 1959), p. 315.

George Kaufman did to observe, to listen critically, to give others their freedom to solve problems their way, trusting one's self—and the Holy Spirit—to be ready and resourceful for assistance as the occasion demands. Ready, that is, to be a "Life-giving Loser." The images Brian Wren conjures up in his hymn, "Name Unnamed," fit very nicely—

> "Maker of Rainbows"
> "Spinner of Chaos"
> "Weaver of Stories"
> "Nudging Discomforter"
> "Straight Talking Lover"
> "Midwife of Changes"
> "Woman of Wisdom"
> "Dare-devil Gambler"
> "Life-giving Loser"

These are the trademarks of an artist, of a prompter, of a stage director—

> Wounded and weeping
> Dancing and leaping
> Sharing the caring that heals and redeems.[19]

They are also the trademarks of the sensitive liturgical leader. It's not an easy position in which to be. I have in my time been one of those stage directors Moss Hart described. I liked to show how easily a scene or a moment might be played by an actor. And while there may be times when one can justify such disclosures, the approach is really questionable. What must be kept in mind is that letting an actor find her way takes time. As any collaboration takes time. And, moreover, the sort of collaboration that Hoekendijk and Guthrie and Hart are talking about assumes some highly disciplined players. But this is no reason to throw up stumbling blocks about depth of experiences and standards of performance. I have found that when I am

---

[19] Brian Wren, "Name Unnamed," from creative work by members of the *SFTS Summer Workshops in Music,* July 1986 (24.7.86) [Carol Stream, Ill.: Hope Publishing Co.].

fully centered, that is, free to be fully myself as a director, happy to be of service to the task at hand, I can serve another, no matter how young or inexperienced, helping her or him to "come out" and believe and make believe.

The Liturgical Leader As A Person of Faith

An article in *The Christian Science Monitor* caught my attention. The title read, "Shaker Design: Worship in Workmanship." The article was inspired by an exhibition of "Shaker household items, dolls, textiles, and graphic designs"[20] at New York City's Whitney Museum of American Art. In her article, Marilyn Hoffman mentioned an instruction of Mother Ann who founded "the United Society of Believers (or Shakers as they were later called because of their dance of worship)."[21] Said Mother Ann:

> whenever [the Shakers] put their hands to work, they also put their hearts to God.[22]

Here is the crucial trademark, isn't it? The one that points to the heart of liturgical leadership. The one that invites Mystery. The Mystery of the Spirit, as Elizabeth and her planning committee learned, "always full of surprises and laughter, and ready with a 'Yes.'"[23] In her lovely book, *Mystery and Manners,* Flannery O'Connor writes as follows:

> The fiction writer presents mystery through manners, grace through nature, but when he finishes there always has to be left over that sense of Mystery which cannot be accounted for by a human formula.[24]

How do those who know they are quite fallible and sinful, who know they live in an earthen vessel, reach maturity as a "liturgical leader"? We are called as artists and pastors perpetually

---

[20] Marilyn Hoffman, *The Christian Science Monitor,* Friday, June 27, 1986, p. 25.
[21] Ibid.
[22] Ibid.
[23] Remarks of Elizabeth Wheeler
[24] Flannery O'Connor, Mystery and Manners (Editors, Sally and Robert Fitzgerald). (New York: Farrar, Strauss & Giroux, 1969), p.162.

to open our eyes to new prospects of reality. They will require changes in our time-honored customs, while still exhibiting meticulous craftwork. Obviously each of us will need greater inner resources of courage and faith if we are to endure. What I find hopeful is that there are cheerleaders along the way who help us through the liturgy of work and worship to receive power for playing our part. Here is Eudora Welty on one writer's discovery:

> It is our inward journey that leads through time— forward or back, seldom in a straight line, most often spiraling. Each of us is moving, changing, with respect to others. As we discover, we remember; remembering we discover; and most intensively do we experience this when our separate journeys converge. Our living experiences at those meeting points is one of the charged dramatic fields of fiction.[25]

---

[25] Eudora Welty, *One Writer's Beginning* (Cambridge: Harvard University Press, 1984), p. 102.

4

The Redemptive Suffering of the Poor

Richard Shaull

As women and men who live in the modern era, we have been almost overwhelmed by the senseless suffering of millions of innocent people. To the suffering, destruction and death brought on by two World Wars, must be added not only the death of six million Jews in German concentration camps, but the possibility of a nuclear holocaust. And now, on top of all this, we are becoming aware of the suffering of the Third World poor and those who stand with them in their struggle for liberation.

What is breaking through to our consciousness, in an inescapable way, is the death, each year, of several million children, women and men from hunger and poverty. This has been going on for a very long time, even though we were unaware of it. More than this, alongside the suffering of those millions who die, is the daily suffering of one billion human beings who, because of poverty, are condemned to a subhuman existence that verges on death. Their lives become one long experience of dying. Thus, Gustavo Gutierrez dares to put alongside of Auschwitz those "equivalents of Auschwitz" which:

> Continue in the midst of the starvation of millions, the humiliation of races regarded as inferior, discrimination against women, especially women who are poor, systematic social injustice, a persistent high rate of infant mortality, those who simply "disappear" or are deprived of their freedom, the suffering of people who are struggling for their right to live, the exiles and the refugees, terrorism of every kind, and the corpse-filled graves of Ayacucho.[1]

Moreover, their suffering has another dimension to it: when they awaken to their situation, become aware of the causes of their suffering and dare to struggle to overcome it, they, as well as those from other classes who dare to take up their struggle for liberation, are often harassed and persecuted, arrested or "disappeared," tortured and killed. In Latin America, this is happening especially in Christian circles. Most of us here are well aware of the martyr's death of Archbishop Romero and of a number of priests and nuns; we may not realize that thousands of lay persons, with less visibility and support, have paid the same price for their participation in this struggle.

A group of political prisoners in El Salvador gave graphic expression to the experience of nameless thousands when they wrote:

> We are victims of the most cruel tortures, beaten and maltreated in every imaginable way: we have electric shocks applied to the tenderest parts of our bodies—genitals, soles of our feet, head, tongue, eyes, ears . . . We are suffocated by the "hood" . . . We have acids applied to our tissues, which eat away our flesh and cause terrible pain. We are hung in the air in various ways for long periods of time while being hit and beaten on different parts of the body. And we women, besides undergoing these tortures, are sexually humiliated in every possible way, having to put up with the worst violations by our captors who prey on our defenseless bodies like possessed beasts.[2]

---

[1] Gustavo Gutierrez, *On Job* (Maryknoll, New York: Orbis Books, 1987), p. 103.
[2] Quoted by Enrique Dussel, "The People of El Salvador: The Communal

Some Latin American theologians have spoken of this poverty and suffering in the Third World as something analogous to the fear of nuclear annihilation experienced so widely in the First World. And, we might add that, while this danger of a nuclear war can be greatly reduced, if not eliminated, by reasonable negotiations between the superpowers, there is no conceivable way that the suffering of the Third World poor can be significantly reduced by the actions of a few people or nations in the foreseeable future.

Faced with the immensity of this suffering, many Christians speak of a great pain deep inside of them that will not go away. And all of their experiences of the richness and joy of living are permeated by the sadness that this awareness brings daily.

However, First and Third World people tend to respond very differently to this reality and experience of suffering. We in Europe and North America are often overwhelmed by the irrationality of it all and may question whether it is possible to believe in God in the face of it. From the time of the Enlightenment, modern men and women have had the sense that they are abandoned in an absurd world, incapable of finding any rational explanation for what is happening around them. Rabbi Richard Rubenstein has given expressions to the anguish of many when he questions the possibility of believing in God after Auschwitz. Others declare that, if there is a God, this God must take the blame for this suffering. As one French writer put it, "I saw the Creator kindling his pointless cruelty, feeding the fires in which old men and children were dying."[3]

In many parts of the Third World, on the other hand, those caught in the midst of the most horrendous suffering often respond in a way that is quite different. They not only find it rich in meaning, they experience a new vitality and look hopefully toward the future. This is especially true in Latin America among Christians who not only declare in words, but also manifest in their lives, a new experience of the *closeness of God*. In the West, conscience is often made blind by its inability to give meaning to apparently arbitrary suffering; in Latin

---

"Suffering of Job," in *Job and the Silence of God*. Christian Duquoc and Casiano Floristan, ed. (New York: Seabury, 1983), p. 64.
3 Lautreamont, *Chants de Maldoror*, chant 2, strophe 3.

America, conscience is frequently awakened and stirred to sacrificial action by suffering.

When Pope John Paul II visited Villa El Salvador, on the outskirts of Lima, Peru, two residents, Victor and Isabel Chero, welcomed him with these words, by which they gave expression to a spirit I have found among the poor wherever I have traveled in Latin America in recent years:

> Holy Father, we are hungry, we suffer affliction, we lack work, we are sick. Our hearts are crushed by suffering as we see our tubercular wives giving birth, our children dying, our sons and daughters growing up weak and without a future. Yet despite everything, we believe in the God of life.[4]

Those who have suffered persecution and faced death because of their faith-inspired dedication to the struggle of the poor often speak of what that experience means for them in ways that we may find difficult to comprehend. Leonardo Boff tells of one priest in the northeast of Brazil who shared the suffering of the poorest peasants and, because of it, was attacked, arrested and tortured. He went about this work:

> ...with a joy not of this world, for there is a joy that the world cannot give—the joy of suffering for the people's cause, of sharing in the passion of the Lord, and of having hammered out one more link in the chain of historical liberation being forged by God through the intermediary of human effort, for the subversion of every unjust order that stands in the way of the reign of God.[5]

And, when Father João Bosco Burnier was murdered at a police station in the Amazon as he and Bishop Pedro Casadáliga protested against the torture of a prisoner, Casadáliga declared, "This is not a sad time but a beautiful Gospel time."

For the privileged as well as for the poor, this present suffering of the oppressed in their struggle for liberation has become the occasion for a new experience of the presence and grace of

---

[4] *Paginas* 68-69 (April 1985): 34.
[5] Leonardo Boff, *Passion of Christ, Passion of the World* (Maryknoll, New York: Orbis Books, 1987), p. 120.

God. In the midst of it, the privileged find a claim laid upon them; as they respond to it, they are met by God in that claim. The poor, on the other hand, are surprised by the presence of God as grace: the source of new life and hope, of sharing in community, even of joy. Both grasp, or are grasped by, the dynamic of this God's redemptive action in history and find themselves incorporated into it. In a life-and-death struggle, they discover what real life in the world is all about and have a taste of the richness of the divine life as well. For them, the Gospel has become, once again, amazing good news. As they receive and live it, in dialogue with their biblical and theological heritage, they find themselves perceiving their own faith, as well as what is happening in the world around them, in new ways.

As I have lived with them and listened to them, I have been fascinated by the insights emerging from their experience of suffering and theological reflection on it and have concluded that they may have something to offer to Christians in other parts of the world as well. Here, I would like to explore their thought as it is articulated around a number of specific issues. Their thought on these issues cannot, and should not be, systematized; it is only gradually finding expression in images, metaphors, and concepts appropriate to it. As the issues to be examined are closely related to each other, some of their central theses will be repeated in somewhat different contexts, but I have found no way to avoid this. I must also state from the beginning that I am here writing about a movement of thought with which I have been, at least peripherally, associated over the years. As I have drawn close to those who suffer, I have been convinced by their witness; my faith has been deepened and my thought transformed by this encounter. Thus, I find myself at times writing in the first person about what I am here examining.

Suspicions Regarding Some Western Approaches

Both Latin American liberation theologians and European and North American thinkers experience a profound anguish of mind and spirit in the face of the horrendous suffering around them. For the latter, this anguish tends to focus on the problem of finding any meaning in all of it, the problem of believing in

God in the midst of it, and thus of seeking a conceptual reconciliation of the misery of the world with the nature of God. In Latin America, however, this anguish is that of seeing and feeling the unjustified suffering of innocent poor, of valuing life and seeing it denied to so many. And this anguish leads to the compulsion to act to overcome this suffering by organizing human life on another basis—not on the basis of power which exploits and oppresses, but on the basis of empowerment of the poor. In this struggle against human sinfulness, God is not a problem to be explained, but an ally to be joined. God is known as a participant who takes sides in the struggle, "Emmanuel," God with us in all of it. This God is experienced by the privileged as a Claim laid upon them and by the poor as the Source of life and of hope for liberation.

We have here, I believe, two quite different approaches to the problem—and, along with this, two quite different *ways of thinking about it.* Those of us who have been surprised by this experience have found ourselves compelled to reflect on its meaning in new ways as we examine it in the light of Scripture and seek a language to express it. And, as we do this, we find ourselves looking more critically at Western theological approaches and raising a number of questions about them.

1.   If the God of the Bible is the God who hears the cry of the suffering poor and stands in solidarity with them, then we can understand the ways of God in the world as we live in this same solidarity with those who suffer. If Christ accomplishes our redemption through this solidarity, which leads to the cross, we can hope to know about that redemption only as we take up the cross and follow in his footsteps. Out of the reflection of those who live this way may come new and richer understanding.

This has been my experience, time and again, in the Base Communities or with the emerging leadership of the Church of the Poor. Those who commit themselves to the struggle of the poor, and risk their lives daily in it, often have a depth of understanding before which I can only remain silent. And those who follow the way of the cross speak of a realm of mystery and an experience of grace which expose the superficiality of my

perception. In their midst, I have some sense of what has led
Leonardo Boff to declare:

> The Western history of reflection on suffering, from the
> Job of the Bible to Carl Jung, is the story of the failure of all
> theoretical solutions, the history of the frustration of all
> concepts. Evil is not there to be understood, but to be
> combatted.[6]

And, as we combat it, we may grow in our understanding
of it.

From this perspective, we may also be led to question our
ability to arrive at truth by arranging concepts and developing
logically consistent patterns of thought; we will distrust one-
directional movement from abstract rational concepts to life.
And we may begin to judge whether something is true, not
because it corresponds to the divine nature as we conceive of it,
but because it leads to liberation in history and offers life to
those deprived of it. Affirmations of faith grasp us as truthful
when we live them out and come to know what they promise.
Along the road of obedience, we can expect to arrive at deeper
understanding.

2. For liberation theologians, the central reality they
confront is that of human suffering in the midst of injustice and
the imperative to overcome it. Their first and major responsibility
is to accept this claim laid upon them, respond to it, and engage
in building the reign of God. Their theological reflection thrives
in this context, in dialogue with the biblical story.

From this vantage point, there is something about the
Western intellectual's preoccupation with the problem of
meaning that arouses our suspicion. We suspect it is destined to
fail because it ignores this claim and thus operates outside the
realm in which greater understanding can come. As a product
of the Enlightenment, with its faith in the superiority of reason
and its yearning to liberate reason from all external authority, it
ends up becoming what Frederick Herzog calls "controlling
reason."[7] Rational beings, in charge of themselves and their world,

---

[6] Ibid., p. 17.
[7] Frederick Herzog, *God-Talk* (Maryknoll, New York: Orbis Books, 1989).

approach the *problem* of God from the standpoint of rational superiority. From this perspective, God can only be a problem or an unnecessary hypothesis. But, as contemporary events defy all canons of reason, obsession with the question of meaning focuses more and more on the threat of chaos. And even theologians, deeply concerned about injustice, agonize over "the dilemma of history as chaotic." Victims of the rational world they have created, they often seem strangely immobilized.

3.　As we sense the spiritual vitality of Christians suffering in the struggle for liberation, we are coming to the conclusion that the struggle of European and North American intellectuals with the question of suffering today should focus not so much on the problem of God as on the problem of Western bourgeois culture. It may well be that our inability to go beyond the dilemmas posed by Job's friends is due primarily to the spiritual insensitivity produced by a culture created and developed in the context of Western domination and exploitation. It is the culture of a people so obsessed with competition and striving for profits that they have little place for concern for the others in need or for justice. In this case, then, new understanding can only come as the result of conversion.

God as Claim: The Awakening of Conscience in the Face of Suffering

For me, one of the most important developments in recent decades in the religious scene in Latin America has been this new experience of encounter with and response to God. In intellectual Christian circles, our spiritual pilgrimage was very much affected by the discussion about secularization and "the death of God" in Western Europe and North America. Many of us struggled with the absence of any experience of God, the crisis of faith and the tendency among those most concerned about Christian presence in the world to leave the Church and abandon any hope of finding satisfaction for their spiritual longings.

And then, gradually, as a significant number of priests, religious women and lay persons began to move closer to the poor and share their lot and struggle, something unexpected happened: attention shifted from concern about the absence of God to the presence of a Claim that could not be ignored, an imperative from beyond oneself that was much stronger than an intellectual analysis of society. The struggle with questions of faith once again came to the fore. And, increasingly, those involved in these struggles found themselves speaking of a new experience of the presence of God.

As I have sought to understand the way this shift has occurred, something that Gustavo Gutierrez points out in his commentary on the Book of Job[8] makes a great deal of sense to me. In his struggle with the problem of suffering, Job experiences a similar transformation in outlook. He begins with his own suffering and his faith in God, insists on the injustice of this suffering and agonizes over God's relationship to it. But, after a time, he turns his attention to the suffering of others and remembers that authentic belief in God calls for solidarity with the poor in the struggle to overcome their suffering. God is on the side of the poor and demands of human beings that they do justice; thus, faith in God centers the attention of the believer on this struggle. The result of this shift, as Gutierrez perceives it, is that "now that he is bearing the lot of the poor in his own flesh, his talk of God becomes more profound and truthful. The point is that commitment to the poor provides firm ground for prophetic talk of God."[9]

In the midst of the suffering of others, Job comes to realize that God "delivers the afflicted by their afflictions, and opens their ear by adversity" (36:15). In his own suffering, Job is then open to a new manifestation of God; suffering becomes one mode by which God reveals God's self. As Job goes out from himself toward the poor, to share their suffering and help them, he also experiences their trust in God and shares their hope. Along this road, he comes to a new realization of the mystery of God, a God who cannot be contained in our limited categories, but who is known, above all else, as the God who hears the cry of the poor, who breaks the power of the wicked and opens the way to justice.

---

[8] Gutierrez, chap. 6.
[9] Ibid., p. 48

Many Latin Americans have found themselves moving—
or being moved—along a similar path as they have turned toward the poor and begin to share their struggle. In fact, some
theologians claim that a real breakthrough has occurred here in
the modern quest for God. In fulfillment of Dietrick Bonhoeffer's
prediction, made shortly before his death, a time has come when
Christians are once again speaking about God with a new and
powerful language which is also, as Bonhoeffer assured us it
would be, a shocking language. This God language, emerging
from the midst of the desperate suffering of the poor, speaks of
a spiritual pilgrimage, several elements of which merit consideration:

1.   The locus of this new encounter with God is not the
head, but the heart. Central to it is the awakening of conscience
rather than the search for meaning. This is the thesis developed
by Frederick Herzog on the basis of his own immersion in and
systematic reflection on liberation theology in his recent book.[10]
He traces the Western intellectual journey that ended up with
the "death of God," the product of a civilization that made God
the explanatory principle of the universe and hoped to arrive at
God by making use of the logic and categories of philosophy.
But, claims Herzog, this whole process was destined to fail, not
only because it was dominated by "controlling reason," but also
because it was seeking God in the wrong place. We are thus free
to realize today that this process says much more to us about the
crisis of Western culture than about God. Or, as Herzog puts it,
"the God of the Western head-trip is dead."[11]

The Latin Americans, on the other hand, find themselves
addressed in the midst of poverty and injustice. A claim is laid
upon them. They sense a power impacting them from beyond
"in the pangs of conscience and the comfort of conscience."[12]
They recognize, with St. Paul, the law "written on their hearts,"
to which "their conscience also bears witness" (Rom. 2:15). In
this situation, the most important thing is not to try to find the
right answers, but to wake up. And, with awakened conscience, the

---

[10] Herzog, chap. 1.
[11] Ibid., p. 62.
[12] Ibid., p. 70.

heart committed to the poor experiences the "reality of God as Christians try to build the Kingdom of God."[13]

Along this path, Christians not only have a sense of God underneath them and beside them, before them and behind them, but they are preeminently grasped by the God *ahead of them*: God present in the justice-struggle, calling human beings to follow God's movements for human liberation through history. Consequently, obsession with the *problem* of God gives way to captivation, and those who are caught up in the struggle with God experience new vitality and a sense of empowerment as well as of direction.

In this context, the issue that emerges is not that of atheism, but of idolatry. Those who are unwilling to respond to the divine claim laid before them in the other, the victim of injustice, are often compelled to create their own gods and worship them. Only by thus sacralizing their own values and institutions— ascribing a divine value to them—can they resist the divine claim in conscience and thus sustain their world as it stands under divine judgment. And, in a society influenced for centuries by Christianity, the supreme idolatry resides in using the name of the Christian God to sacralize a society based on exploitations and oppression. No wonder that theological conceptualization related to this God is incapable of facing or dealing with God's presence in the midst of the suffering of the poor.

2.   Those who accept the divine claim laid upon them often discover that the poor, in the midst of their suffering, witness powerfully to the reality of God and God's presence in the midst of life. How often those living in solidarity with the poor, even priests and nuns, have spoken to me of the renewal of their faith and of experiences of conversion, gifts mediated to them through those to whom they have ministered. And they speak of simple, but amazing, things: the willingness of desperately poor people to give the little bit of food they have to others who have none at all; their spirit of solidarity; their willingness to risk almost certain death in their struggle for life; the spirit of joyfulness and of hope in the most representative situations.

---

[13] Ibid., p. 60.

In some strange way, those who live in this way point to a Source beyond themselves and speak quite naturally of all this as a gift from God. And those who receive this gift often perceive not only their own spiritual barrenness, but also the possibility of moving beyond it. Thus, Gustavo Gutierrez can say that "only if we know how to be silent and involve ourselves in the suffering of the poor will we be able to speak out of their hope" and receive it as a divine gift to us. Only if "we take seriously the suffering of the innocent and live the mystery of the cross amid the suffering but in the light of Easter" can we go beyond the "windy arguments" of Job's friends and become more attuned to the mystery of the divine.[14]

The most compelling witness to this experience of the presence of God among the suffering poor of which I am aware comes from a French Dominican priest, Dominique Barbe, who lived for twenty years in the *favelas* of São Paulo. In his book, *Grace and Power*, this amazing reality shines through from beginning to end. He expresses what it means for him most succinctly in these words:

> God moves with more ease and feels more at home in the middle of the *favelas*, under the viaducts, and in the poor districts, than in the rich quarters; because God finds there something that corresponds to the divine nature: love. God's name and power are revealed more easily there than elsewhere. God's grace is *felt*. Therefore it is easier for a human being to undergo a spiritual experience and to acquire faith.[15]

In our academic circles, I have often found that we get so bogged down in our attempts to arrive at a rational under-standing of the suffering around us that we are unable to act; we assume that, only after resolving our intellectual problems, will we be in a position to respond. Among the poor in Latin America, something quite different occurs. Awakened conscience responds, becoming involved in the struggle for justice, and, along this road of obedience, new possibilities for understanding open

---

[14] Gutierrez, p. 103.
[15] Dominique Barbe, *Grace and Power* (Maryknoll, New York: Orbis Books, 1987), p. 22.

before it. Thinking, situated in a heart committed to the poor (Herzog) and sensitive to the witness of the Spirit moving in their midst, leads to a dynamic response. Those surprised by the presence of the divine experience new motivation and empowerment. They find themselves oriented toward the future, daring to dream of a new era of justice and peace. No longer at home in Egypt, they rebel against the injustice around them and embark on an Exodus. And, as they face the suffering that comes with solidarity with the poor, they realize that Christ shares that suffering and that they share in Christ's suffering. They witness to, and in some way participate in, the struggle to establish God's reign of justice in the world. Thus, historical existence is perceived as a constant struggle to create conditions for a full life for those to whom it has been denied, to liberate the oppressed, and their own lives take on meaning and purpose in relation to it.

3. This experience opens up new horizons for thought as it strives to deal with the problem of suffering and God's relation to it. The theologian is no longer the detached observer, but, rather, someone called to move out of self-centeredness into an immediate commitment to the poor, to helping those who suffer. And, as he/she does this, perception changes. For Gutierrez, this step marks a turning point in Job's quest: "Job sees that commitment to the poor puts everything on a solid basis, a basis located outside his individual world, in the needs of others who cannot be ignored." And to do this "is to find a way to God" and to speak about God once again in the midst of suffering.[16] Questions about suffering are set in the context of real anguish about it as well as the sense that God wills injustice and is present in the struggle to overcome it. Thus, anguished questioning and trust are somehow combined.

This approach is expressed dramatically in Psalm 22, the opening lines of which were used by Jesus on the cross to express his sense of complete abandonment by God: "My God, my God, why hast thou forsaken me?" In this psalm, the writer agonizes over his own extreme suffering ("all my bones are out of joint;

---

[16] Gutierrez, p. 48

my heart is like wax . . . my strength is dried up like a potsherd, and my tongue cleaves to my jaws," vs. 14-15) and persecution for the cause of justice ("a company of evildoers encircle me; they have pierced my hands and feet . . . they stare and gloat over me," vs. 16-17) as well as the suffering of the poor around him. And yet, the psalm is a song of deliverance in which God is glorified for having saved a poor person from his attackers. This God has liberated the oppressed in the past; God "has not despised or abhorred the affliction of the afflicted" (v. 24). And this God can also be counted on to liberate them in the future: "The afflicted shall eat and be satisfied." Consequently, "those who seek God shall praise the Lord" (v. 26). This God cannot be fit neatly into our rational theological categories. We strive to understand; we come close to despair at making any sense of it all; yet, our experience of God's presence with us in the struggle leads us, at the same time, to live by trust.

Divine Power and the Empowerment of the Powerless

For those of us who are not victims of injustice, the discovery that the God of our faith is a God of justice who sides with the poor and wills the liberation of the oppressed may make it even more difficult for us to believe. How can we believe in the presence and power of a God in a world in which so many millions are desperately poor and exploited?

But, when we get closer to the suffering poor who are struggling for liberation, we are often amazed to find that they are not obsessed with this problem. They groan in the midst of their pain; they long intensely for a better day, but they are also captivated by an experience of the presence and power of God, raising them up and creating space for them to become Subjects. They may have no reasonable explanation of the reason they are suffering, but their attention is focused elsewhere—on the struggle for liberation and on God's call which creates a space for them and gives a special vocation to them in it.

This experience often leads them to turn to the Bible. Others who have been touched by their witness join them. And, in their re-reading of the Scriptures, they perceive something most of us have never seen. As we read the Old Testament especially, we are most aware of the imagery which speaks of an all-powerful God, Creator and Lord of the universe, who raises up and brings down nations and individuals as He chooses. They, on the other hand, are aware of another language about God, two dimensions of which we will examine here: (1) an undercurrent, even in the early history of the people of Israel, which affirms human beings over all that would keep them down, even God, and portrays God as One who takes the initiative in creating this space for women and men to become Subjects, and (2), the witness of Jesus, by his word, life and death, to the God who cannot be identified with oppressive power, but is supremely a God of love whose goal for history is the establishment of a kingdom in which the poor and marginal will occupy privileged positions.

1.   For Franz Hinkelmmert,[17] this undercurrent first surfaces in the story of Abraham, who feels compelled to sacrifice Isaac, his firstborn, in obedience to a command of God. In those times, this act was seen as central to the patriarchal system. By killing his son, the father sustains the sacral order of hierarchical domination which guarantees the stability of society and the authority of the past over the present and future. But God stops him. The Angel asks Abraham to assert his freedom over this sacred law and to break this circle of power of father over son. And, when he does this, God promises to multiply Abraham's descendents and to make him a blessing to all the peoples of the earth.

By this act, God encourages Abraham not only to open the way to freedom and the future, but also to establish a new relationship between father and son which would gradually transform radically the divine-human relationship as well. When Jesus addressed God as "Abba," he addresses God as a parent without authority, in a relationship of affection and mutual love. If God encourages this break, the symbolic world sustaining divine and human domination is shattered, opening the way for the emergence of those kept down by it.

---

[17] Franz Hinkelmmert, *La Fe de Abraham y el Edipo Occidental* (San Jose: DEI, 1989).

Job, in his anguish in the face of suffering, dares to question and stand up to God. He is compelled to affirm his innocence, to "remonstrate with God," to insist on his integrity to his dying day and thus question God's right to attack him. Job also lays before God the wretchedness of the poor and even asserts that "God remains deaf" to their cry. He has a sense that God will defend him and be his "avenger," but that the way of God in the world cannot be understood within the traditional logical categories of Job's friends. In the end, he recognizes that God has a plan which gives meaning to God's creative work and government of the world; he affirms God's greatness, but, as Gutierrez puts it, this "greatness of God is to be identified less with power than with freedom and gratuitous love—and with tenderness."[18]

For this audacity, Job is neither judged nor punished, but affirmed. And, as a result of this struggle, he arrives at a new awareness of the transcendence and freedom of the God present in the gentle wind and still small voice. Gutierrez concludes that this "mystery of divine freedom leads to the mystery of human freedom and respect for it." He writes:"God wants justice indeed, and desires that divine judgment reign in the world; but God cannot impose it, for the nature of created beings must be respected. God's power is limited by human freedom; for without freedom God's justice would not be present within history."[19]

Job goes even further. He not only dares to stand up to God and argue with God when plunged into suffering, but he also challenges the moral law, considered to be divine. In his struggle with God, he comes to know a Redeemer who lives. He finds a God who cannot be enclosed in a rational and moral order and thus should not be used to sacralize a legal system or a society. And, for this defiance, he is recognized and rewarded by God. Faith in this God frees men and women from bondage to such a system and tends to nourish the spirit of rebellion. In the words of Christian Duquoc, "The God of the Mosaic tradition is the defender of the oppressed precisely because he is not the regulator of order. Revolt, rising from the heart and

---

[18] Gutierrez, pp. 68–69.
[19] Ibid., pp. 77, 78.

directed at him, is more to his liking than the invocation of his power to ensure the policing of the world."[20]

Jesus carries all this much further. He defies those who represent the moral and rational order and identify God with it. Jesus flaunts the Mosaic law, considered to be sacred, daring to give priority to his own judgment and to the welfare of the neighbor in need. He stands with the oppressed and the excluded, against the law, when used against them, as well as the pretensions of religious and political leaders. He would pay the labourers hired at the eleventh hour as much as those who began early in the day and pardons the adulterous woman, rejecting the application of the legal penalty. And, when those who find security in the law use it against him, he is sentenced and killed under its rule. On the cross, the outcast Jesus witnesses to a God who cannot be enclosed in, or used to validate, such an order, a witness confirmed by this God in and through Jesus' resurrection.

This undercurrent, emerging early on in the history of Israel and reaching its culmination with Jesus of Nazareth, undermines all efforts to make of the God of Israel and of Jesus Christ a God who rules strictly over all human beings and demands their submission, thus sustaining a system of oppression and submission. If God encourages and rewards those who affirm their integrity and the cause of justice before God, and at the same time comes to the poor and stands with them against those who claim divine support for an unjust order, then the presence of this God and faith in this God are destined to contribute to a dynamic in history, encouraging the emergence of those at the bottom as subjects and protagonists in the struggle for the future.

In his history of the revolutions that have shaped our Western world, Eugen Rosenstock-Huessy calls attention to Michelangelo's painting in the Sistine Chapel in the Vatican in which God is creating Adam, "keeping in the folds of his immense role a score of angels. Thus at the beginning of the world all the divine powers were on God's side," while human beings stood naked and alone. But he then imagines a scene portraying the end of creation, in which, by God's design, all the spirits that had once

[20] Christian Duquoc, "Demonism and the Unexpectedness of God," in *Job and the Silence of God*, p. 86.

accompanied God have moved to the other side, thus helping and strengthening and enlarging him/her into the divine.[21] What Rosenstock-Huessy does not say here, but illustrates throughout this volume, is that this divine movement sustains a historical process which not only moves forward by means of revolutions, but also moves downward, toward the marginal and outcast, and raises them up.

2. In the Gospels, Jesus vigorously rejects the use of power to dominate and thus radically re-interprets God's way of bringing justice in the world. He shows great reluctance to use the title of Messiah and repudiates the idea, then associated with it, of a new King David who would restore the nation of Israel and reestablish the dynasty. In his time of temptation in the desert, he struggles against any desire to gain such power for himself or use it even for "righteous" ends. When John the Baptist sends his disciples to inquire of Jesus whether or not he is the hoped-for Messiah, Jesus responds by referring to the mighty works he has done on behalf of the poor and outcasts, but makes no mention of the judgment John preached. If the people of that time expected a Messiah who would intervene to destroy the unjust and resurrect the just, Jesus announces a new age, dominated by forgiveness and the power of the Holy Spirit.

When his disciples express their yearning for position and power, Jesus declares that, while "the rulers of the Gentiles lord it over them, whoever would be great among you must be your servant, and whoever would be first among you must be your slave" (Mt. 20:25-27). He then adds, "the Son of man came not to be served, and to give his life as ransom for many" (v. 28).

Time and again, Jesus confronts the powerful; he exposes the way the power to dominate works and undermines its legitimacy. He denounces as perverse any power that leads to oppression. At the same time, Jesus stands firmly with those who are marginalized or excluded, the victims of power. He takes up their cause and challenges the established order of power from the perspective of what it does to them. And, he announces the imminent coming of a kingdom, which comes as good news

---

[21] Eugen Rosenstock-Huessy, *Out of Revolution* (Norwich, Vermont: Argo, 1969), pp. 727-28.

to the poor because of the benefits they will receive in it. He thus declares that the transformation of the life of the poor is central to the messianic age. But its achievement will not come as the result of the use of oppressive power. "My kingdom is not of this world," he declares, thus insisting that it cannot rely on this type of domination even for righteous ends. Jesus gives himself to those on the margin. He raises them up and gives them a new place in the struggle for the future. Those who are powerless and have no place are called upon to envision and structure this new order. And Jesus, by becoming poor, living in solidarity with those at the bottom and choosing to die in their defense, dramatically shows the way to be followed in moving toward it.

Throughout the Gospels, what Jesus says and does is presented as the central event in a divine drama of redemption. In and through his life, death and resurrection, God is revealed; God's action on behalf of human beings is carried forward. Those who become Jesus' disciples are incorporated into this historical process. And Jesus' way of dealing with power which oppresses and dominates is presented as God's way in the world and as indicating the path to be followed by his disciples.

This comes through most clearly in the Gospel of John. Jesus declares that "the Son can do nothing on his own accord, but only what he sees the Father doing . . . As the Father raises the dead and gives them life, so also the Son gives life to whom he will" (5:19,21). In what Jesus has said and done, "the Father who dwells in me does his works" (14:10); "he who has seen me has seen the Father" (14:9). Consequently, Jesus' choice to be a servant rather than lord it over others expresses God's way, God's power, and the path to be followed by his disciples in obedience to God. Thus, Jesus states that, as their "Lord and Teacher," he has washed their feet, and, therefore, "you also ought to wash one another's feet" (13:14). And, as this choice of the path of servanthood leads directly to the cross, that cross becomes the supreme manifestation of what St. Paul called "the power of God and the Wisdom of God."

In Philippians, Paul spells this out most dramatically when he speaks of Jesus' emptying himself, taking the form of a slave, humbling himself to death, even death on a cross. And, this abasement of Jesus as servant is the reason for his being glorified as Lord; it is also presented as the example which those who participate in the Spirit should follow (2:5-11).

In the opening verses of the Book of Acts, the main question the disciples have for Jesus is: "Will you at this time restore the kingdom to Israel?" Will the power of the risen Christ establish a new structure of domination, rather than continue along the path of the suffering and servanthood? Jesus' response is simply that they will receive power, the power of the Holy Spirit, and "you shall be my witnesses . . . to the end of the earth" (v. 8). The Spirit, poured out upon a small band of poor, marginal, apparently powerless people, continues the movement of the servant Jesus toward life, love and justice. Those who are nobodies, who have no place in the world, are the chosen ones. On the day of Pentecost, they are empowered to speak; they are filled with the energy of the Spirit, enabling them to confront the powerful and break the hold of the forces of decay and death around them. They experience a new quality of life in community as they learn to share all and thus live the first fruits of the kingdom announced by Jesus.

Across the centuries, this New Testament witness has led some theologians to conclude that we have to do here with God who limits self in order to allow human beings to develop; a God who has not taken history and its future out of our hands; a God who does not impose a perfect ordering of human life, economic, social and political; a God who chooses the way of apparent powerlessness and of love to bring in the kingdom.

Women and men of faith, struggling for the liberation of the poor and oppressed in Latin America today, would hardly quarrel with this conclusion. But they might have some suspicions about it as the statement of detached observers, seeking a too rational solution to a theoretical problem, and, thus, somewhat off the mark. For them, theological reflection on their suffering in the struggle for liberation is becoming more and more a matter of articulating a new experience, an experience of the life-sustaining presence and power of God, raising them up and making them participants in the transformation of the world; an experience with at least these dimensions to it:

—The sense that this apparent weakness and self limitation on the part of God is the way by which the God of the poor creates space for them to find a new identity as worthy human beings, to participate in a process of Becoming—becoming Subjects of their own life and destiny—and to accept their vocation as agents of the Reign of God.

—The conviction that, if the divine redemptive process follows this pattern in history, then the poor and the marginal are the ones who can best understand it, keep it on track and sustain the struggle. In the words of Christian Duquoc, "The excluded person endures injustice and oppression in his/her flesh, and in doing so, bears witness to the necessity of a different society; this person does not dream of a seizure of power that would betray what was proclaimed in his/her cry of revolt as well as what is contained in the promise."[22] Those at the bottom are the ones who can imagine a logic that breaks with that of domination, and in their cry of hope, they postulate a different future.

—A clue as to why it is that so often the poor and those in solidarity with them have such a rich experience of the presence of God. They are the ones who are best able to perceive that God is not absent from the world, but hidden. Others look for God in the centers of worldly power, without realizing that they are looking in the wrong place. Those denied access to the power of the world and struggling for liberation are surprised by the closeness of God. They testify that the risen Christ, who in his earthly pilgrimage chose the way of the cross and was crucified outside the city, is present in the world on the margin. They know a Presence and Power working for the transformation of the world in and through the empowerment of those at the bottom.

—A new sense of the dynamic reality of the Holy Spirit as the continuation of God's struggle to overcome the powers of domination and violence along the line determined by the life, death and resurrection of Jesus Christ. Sustained by the gift of the Spirit, the poor know the presence in history of the power

---

[22] Christian Duquoc, *Messianism de Jèsus et Discrètion de Dieu* (Genève: Labor et Fides, 1984), pp. 727-28.

of the risen Christ, overcoming oppression and exploitation. In the midst of their suffering and in their apparent powerlessness they expose the sickness unto death of a violent system, challenge those who live by it to repent, and point to a life-giving alternative on the road to peace and justice. For this, they are hated all the more, more violently suppressed, and, living in the power of the Spirit, they also keep hope alive.

The Abundance of Grace among Those Deprived of Everything

When we take into account the conditions under which the poor struggle to survive, we may be inclined to think that their poverty makes them less than human. Just recently, a social worker, employed in a shelter for the homeless in Philadelphia, found herself unable to cite a single positive thing that she could praise in the lives of the people with whom she worked. In contrast to this, Latin American theologians are discovering, among the poor caught up in liberation struggles, a quality of life which they can understand only as a manifestation of God's grace. As one of them put it, many Latin American Christians have been graced by God and have been transformed into grace for others. And, frequently, those who have seen these fruits of the Spirit in the lives of the poor have also been spiritually reoriented by their witness.

Of these manifestations of grace, the most evident is the amazing *hope* to be found among the poorest, even in the most oppressive situations.

This hope is not something to be found everywhere among the poor, who are often apathetic. But, in my contacts with groups who have begun to struggle for liberation, especially those with a religious background, this spirit comes through loud and clear. In fact, it is often most evident in international meetings where the genuine hopefulness of Latin America may stand out in sharp contrast to the sense of powerlessness so often found among North American participants.

This hope is not a naïve optimism that ignores the power of oppressive structures. Rather, it emerges in the midst of that oppression, on the part of people subjected to it for centuries. They are all too aware of this reality and the structures that sustain it; they feel its power every day. At the same time, they are convinced that a change can and will come and that they have a part in it. Something that seemed so impossible for so long is becoming a historical possibility. And, as they struggle for it, they develop a new sense of their own worth as creatures of God, a new identity as human beings.

Along this road, something else frequently happens: a profound transformation is what is hoped-for. The have-nots often dream of a world in which they will know material well-being and have power. In the First World, our hope for the future is limited to keeping what we have. But the hope inspired by Christian faith among the poor yearns for a world in which poverty will be torn out by the roots and oppression will be overcome, the hope of moving beyond present conflicts toward a new era of greater justice and peace. Moreover, on this faith-inspired journey, the poor often find that their suffering deepens and intensifies their hope. As Jon Sobrino puts it, we have here "the great paradox: the cross generates hope."[23] This has been the witness especially for Christians in El Salvador: humble members of Base Communities, lay leaders of the popular church, priests, nuns and Archbishop Romero; women and men who have faced the most violent repression and often sacrificed their lives, all the while with a sure hope in the triumph of justice.

When we try to ascertain what makes possible and sustains such hope, the answer they give is simply: It is a gift from God to those well aware of God's presence in their midst. Sobrino, who has accompanied this process for many years, says, "God instills hope because God is credible, and God is credible because God is close to the poor."[24]

No less amazing is the fact that often, in the Base Communities, those most deprived are *willing to share* the little bit they have. We read in the Book of Acts how, on the day of Pentecost, "all who believed were together and had all things in common;

---

[23] Jon Sobrino, *Spirituality of Liberation* (Maryknoll, New York: Orbis Books, 1988), p. 168.
[24] Ibid., p. 167.

and they sold their possessions and goods and distributed them to all, as any had need" (2:44-45). We do not expect that to happen in the church today; yet, we frequently hear of families who share their last pound of rice with others who have nothing, or invite a homeless family to move in with them in their one room shack. Refugees returning to El Salvador from Honduras decide to work together to build their homes, clear and cultivate the land and share all they produce.

As they do this, something else frequently happens. Those who are practically outside of the market economy, denied access to the abundance of things being produced and daily bombarded by sales propaganda on the television screen and elsewhere, may refuse to be caught up into this mad drive to acquire and consume. They come to realize that, in a society with limited resources, the basic needs of the poor majority can be met only if this consumerism is overcome and people are able to direct their energies toward the production of what is most urgently needed by all and toward distributing what is available on the basis of need. As one commentator has put it: what is taking shape here is a vision of a new society aiming at "the transcendence of selfishness as the principal human activity."

I have also found, among those who are making the greatest sacrifices because of their solidarity with the poor as well as those who risk their lives every day in the most violent and repressive situations, a *tremendous sense of vitality and energy* that comes when men and women are willing to work together in the struggle for justice for the poor.

For the last several years, I have taken part in a Course in Theology offered at the Departmento Ecumenico de Investigaciones (DEI) in San Jose, Costa Rica, for the emerging leadership of the Popular Church in the Caribbean, Central and South America. Among the participants are a few priests and nuns, living and working with the Base Communities; young middle-class professionals who have chosen to dedicate their efforts to serving the poor and "the project of the poor;" Delegates of the Word working in isolated border areas in Nicaragua, who may be killed at any time by the Contras; or those who live under the violent expression in El Salvador.

Here are people who risk their every day, yet affirm the value of life. They bear heavy burdens, yet live in amazing freedom. They often find all their efforts for the transformation of church and society blocked by those in power, yet they look hopefully toward the future. When I am with them, I realize that those who do not have many of the things I consider important for a rich life are nevertheless teaching me the way to live.

The experience of grace which I find most astonishing is the *spirit of joyfulness* among those who suffer most and are most persecuted for the participation in the justice struggle. I have read many times the words of Jesus in the Beatitudes, declaring blessed those who suffer such persecution and calling them to "rejoice in the day and leap for joy" (Luke 6:22), but I never expected to see it happening. Thus, my shock when I find so many manifestations of it in the midst of liberation struggles in Latin America.

The most dramatic witness to this has come from priests and lay persons whose lives have been threatened, or who have been arrested and tortured, and some of whom have been killed. Suffice it here to mention the words of Archbishop Romero, spoken a short time before he was assassinated:

> Christians ought always to foster in their hearts the fullness of joy . . . I have tried it time and again, yes and in the bitterest hours of the worst circumstances, when calumny and persecution was at its wildest. I have felt the gladness of grafting myself onto Christ, my Friend, and have tasted the sweetness that the joys of this world cannot give. I have felt the joy of feeling myself intimately "God's"—a gladness beyond human comprehension.[25]

The poor in the Base Communities may not speak in such eloquent terms of their rejoicing in life, but that spirit manifests itself in many ways: when people get together in the evening to share their experiences of the day, to sing and to pray; in their popular fiestas and liturgical celebrations; when they welcome others who are standing in solidarity with them; when they are working together on common community projects, or when

---

[25] Quoted in *Sobrino*, p. 167.

gathered together to celebrate small victories or even to remember those who have fallen in the struggle. For a number of my North American associates, this experience has not only exposed the barrenness of our affluent lifestyle, but also pointed to a spiritual reality largely unknown to us.

The poor do not try to come up with explanations for this experience of life in the midst of suffering. They simply believe in God, dwelling in their midst with good news for them. Like Job, they protest against suffering, but do not curse God; they trust God because they are aware of God's presence and love as they cry out in their suffering and struggle to overcome it. They may not understand the reason a God of love permits such suffering, but they sense that this God hears the cry of the poor, wills to overcome injustice, and meets them on the cross. And, as they share in the sufferings of Christ, they trust that the Crucified One has risen, and they expect new life in the midst of death. They also believe that this path of the cross is the road to liberation for them. In this spirit, a group of Christians living in the midst of the suffering and violence of Central America prepared a confession of faith which they released on Easter Sunday, 1988, entitled *Kairos Central America*. In it, they declared that God was moving through their history and pointed to the "signs of the kingdom" they perceived around them.

I confess that contact with women and men who have thus been graced, while deepening my faith, also raises a number of disturbing questions to me. Is it possible that those who share the lot of the poor, and with them struggle for justice, are discovering something about what it means to be a human being that we have largely lost in our obsession with competition, personal advancement and consumerism? If we sense the absence of God today, could the reason be that, by turning away from the suffering and struggle of the poor and marginal, we have situated ourselves outside of the realm of grace? And, if we yearn for a new experience of the presence of Christ in our lives, do we have any other choice than to share Christ's suffering with and for the outcasts?

Moreover, as I move in this realm of the Spirit, I have a better appreciation of what Latin American theologians mean when they insist that the crucial issue having to do with faith in God today is not atheism, but idolatry. The quality of life lived in the struggle of the poor for justice and their witness to the presence of God exposes the destructive violence inherent in structures of oppression and the inhumanity of those who maintain them. Confronted by this spiritual reality and power, the wealthy and powerful tend to sacralize all that is being called into question and demonize those who are critical of it. In other words, they create idols, worship them and demand that others do the same. When this happens, the struggle for liberation takes on a spiritual dimension; the worship of idols must be met by the passion for justice on the part of those who have changed sides and are willing to give their lives for the transformation of society.

Martyrdom: The Affirmation of Life through Death

Christian involvement in the struggles for liberation of Latin America is producing an extraordinary number of martyrs. In some countries, thousands of peasant and urban poor, moved by their faith to act to improve their lot and struggle for change, have been brutally murdered or have "disappeared." At the same time, a small but significant number of bishops, priests, nuns and lay persons from the privileged classes have met the same fate. Thus far, this violent repression has contributed to the growth of the movement rather than breaking it. The death of the martyrs has brought new vitality to the church and strengthened the poor in their struggle; it has also led many to a more profound understanding and experience of their faith.

Once again, Christians are being killed because of what they believe and the way they live, because of their faith in a God who hears the cry of the oppressed, who wills their liberation and who calls men and women to join in this struggle. Out of his experience in El Salvador in recent years, Jon Sobrino reports:

> We must not ignore the widespread and surprising fact that many Christians freely give their lives in order that the

people may live; they give their lives with the kind of
generosity that requires human beings to abandon everything
and not shrink in the face of persecution, death and even
cruel torture.[26]

In many instances, this journey toward martyrdom has begun
with a decision to live with the poor in their communities,
encourage them to come together to talk about their suffering
and to read the Bible, and help them to learn to read, reflect on
their situation and begin to work together to meet some of
their most basic needs. When they discover, often to their surprise,
that their lives are in danger, they realize that Christian love
may mean not only giving of themselves to the poor, but also
giving up their lives. They also realize that those with power
and wealth in an oppressive system will do everything in their
power to preserve their privileged position, that their fear of
loss may lead them to irrational acts of violence, and that in the
struggle for liberation, the prophets, Jesus, and others across the
centuries have been harassed, attacked, and often killed.

At the same time, those who are poor and marginal find
that their faith opens their eyes to the situation in which they
are living, awakens in them a deeper longing for liberation and
leads them to get together with others to discuss what is
happening to them and why, to organize simple programs of
adult education, or to set up a soup kitchen, a child care program,
or small production cooperatives. When these small steps toward
self-reliance bring the threat of death, their newly-formed faith
communities orient and sustain them.

For both the privileged and the poor, an experience of
faith has led them to struggle for social change. When this brings
the risk of greater suffering and death, this faith sustains them.
At the same time, their experience of suffering leads them to
take the Bible and theological reflection more seriously, and, on
the road to martyrdom, they probe new depths of meaning in
that heritage. At the center of this process is the realization that
they are in a situation similar to that of Jesus of Nazareth, who
gave himself totally to the poor and marginal, shared their life

---

[26] Jon Sobrino, *The True Church and the Poor* (Maryknoll, New York: Orbis
Books, 1984), p. 181.

and suffering and brought them a message of hope. He also opposed, denounced and unmasked the rich and powerful, those in positions of dominance in the religious institution, in Jewish society and in the Roman world. For this, he was killed. And, as the poor and those who stand in solidarity with them today follow this same path, they not only come to a new understanding of Jesus' life and teaching, but also gain new perspectives on God's relation to those who suffer and on the outcome of the struggle for liberation. Here, I would like to call attention to several aspects of this:

1. Those whose lives are threatened simply because they have identified themselves with the poor, finding themselves in a position similar to that of Jesus of Nazareth, are in a unique position to understand the way Jesus lived and what he taught: his assertion that the supreme thing in life is to live for others, especially the poor and marginal, to be totally dedicated to them and to long passionately for the establishment of God's reign, in which their deprivation and oppression will end. And, as they explore new dimensions of discipleship and experience a special closeness to God, they demonstrate what human life can become.

I first perceived what this can mean while spending a week with a group of eight men and women, providing dynamic leadership for the Church of the Poor in El Salvador. All of them were working closely with the Christian Base Communities, many of whose members have been killed by the military or right-wing death squads. Several of their closest colleagues, even members of their families, had met the same fate. And they knew that they, too, could be killed at any moment.

At first, I was most amazed by their spirit of caring and sharing, of hope and of joyfulness, gifts of the Spirit of which I have spoken above. But soon something else caught my attention: the fact that they spoke so freely and in such a natural way about their trust in God and their sense of God's presence in their midst. By the end of the week, I came to the conclusion that those who have accepted death as the price they may have to pay for their solidarity with the poor can teach us something about life. They had found life by giving of themselves, without reserve, to others. In their situation, our petty struggles to gain a bit of prestige or power over others made little sense. Coming from quite different social and educational backgrounds, they were bound together as equals in a common struggle. I was especially struck by their sense of self-confidence: they knew who they were as human beings. And, facing the possibility of being assassinated at any moment, they knew the reason they were living. In the words of Jon Sobrino, several of whose colleagues in El Salvador have been killed and who has himself received a number of death threats, "Paradoxically, it is persecution that reveals to Christians what true humanity is and grants them a share in it."[27]

2.   The martyrs provide no rational answer to the question why the innocent suffer so much at the hands of evil-doers, but they do claim that, as they suffer because of their identification with the victims of injustice, they participate in the *divine* struggle to overcome evil.

As they face crucifixion, they perceive that the cross is God's way of meeting evil. God confronts injustice by entering into solidarity with the pain of the poor of the world and precisely *in this way* acts to bring about their true liberation. Leonardo Boff affirms this clearly when he says: "God is not indifferent to the pains of the victims of history. Out of love and solidarity, God becomes poor, is condemned, crucified and murdered . . . because God does not wish to impoverish and crucify other human beings."[28] Those who face death because of their faith in Christ grasp what Saint Paul meant when he said that Jesus Christ chose to become a servant, even unto death, and that the Crucified have been exalted by God. They thus trust that, in following this same path in imitation of Christ, they also participate in some way in that victorious march.

Whether or not they come up with such theological reasoning, the martyrs witness to the mystery of the Cross of Christ. Death does not mean defeat; martyrdom contributes to liberation, giving life and strengthening hope for the future.

They also enrich our understanding of the mystery of human freedom. For, alongside the freedom of human beings to oppress,

---

[27] Sobrino, *Spirituality of Liberations*, p. 60.
[28] Boff, p. 32.

kill and destroy, they demonstrate that this same freedom makes it possible for us to love, to take the suffering of others upon ourselves, to struggle against the destructiveness of life to the point of death, and to know the richness of life that emerges out of death. In communion with them, the cross, which has been a stumbling block or was seen as foolishness, becomes once again, for us as it was for Saint Paul, "the power of God and the wisdom of God" (1 Cor. 1:18). With them, we may grasp what Paul meant when he spoke of "being given up to death for Jesus' sake, so that the life of Jesus may be manifested in our mortal flesh" (II Cor. 4:11); they confirm that, dying, we live and having nothing, we possess everything (II Cor. 6:9, 10).

3. Living with those who face death because of their faith in God and their commitment to the struggle of the poor, I am most astonished by the fact that this type of suffering breeds hope. The martyrs communicate a sense that they have tasted a quality of life that cannot be blotted out by violent death. They create a climate of love that often captivates others; they somehow proclaim that the struggle for justice is well worth the price they are paying. More than this, they help to keep alive the belief that social transformation can and will occur. Leonardo Boff captures this spirit when he says that they live "the reality of a new world of brotherly and sisterly communion, a world of the reign of God over everyone who is willing to be converted to it," and this new world "is so real, so true, so fulfilling, that no death, however violent, no torture, however inhuman, is experienced as destructive suffering."[29]

Surrounded by this witness of the martyrs, faith in the resurrection, on the part of the poor and those whose struggle with them, is renewed. This faith is not a matter of general victory over death, but confidence in the victory of the downtrodden and crucified victims of history. They are the ones for whom the promise of Jesus in John's Gospel is fulfilled: "In the world you have tribulation; but be of good cheer, I have overcome the world" (16:33). And thus, as Sobrino observes, "the scandalous lot of the servant of Yahweh, of Jesus crucified,

---

[29] Ibid, 231.

of the first, persecuted Christian community, recurs ever and
again in our day, evoking Easter and the Easter experience."[30]

4. For many years, I have been captivated by what Saint
Paul has to say about the death and resurrection of Jesus Christ
as the pattern, not only for the Christian life, but for life itself.
As a white male, enjoying a position of security and relative
privilege and power within an oppressive and destructive society,
I have known about both the pain and the joy of following this
route. Time and again, I have discovered that we are indeed free
to let go of what we most cherish, to die to our past, and, in so
doing, to be surprised by resurrection, by new possibilities of
meaning and fulfillment we did not know existed before. I have
also become convinced that in certain historical situations,
institutions and societies can be renewed and move toward the
future only as they follow this same path.

The experience of the martyrs in Latin America has
confirmed my belief that we are here dealing with the central
reality of the Gospel and the good news it offers. But they also
point to dimensions of this reality which I, at least, have only
begun to fathom.

Their confrontation with death exposes the superficiality
of our middle class way of life, even of many of our death
experiences. The brutality and viciousness of the violence which
those in power often perpetrate against those who challenge
them make us more aware of the depth of evil manifested by
the principalities around us. At the same time, the martyrs help
us to realize that sclerotic societies moving toward death are
usually incapable of re-creating themselves. This can happen
only as prophetic minorities envision and live for a new order
and demonstrate that they are willing to die, not only for the
victims of the established order, but also for those who would
destroy them. In places where the poor constitute the vast
majority of the population, as in some parts of Latin America,
some theologians speak of an entire people suffering for the
sake of a new society. The martyrs, whether individuals or
communities of the poor, who accept this suffering in the spirit
of the Servant, keep alive the hope for liberation.

---

[30] Sobrino, *Spirituality of Liberation*, p. 60.

"With Their Stripes We Are Healed"

In the course of my exploration of our theme, "The Redemptive Suffering of the Poor," an unexpected shift has occurred. When I began, I was preoccupied with the horrendous suffering of the poor and the question of theodicy. But I have generally come to realize that the poor compel me to turn my attention toward *my* situation and to be more concerned about the question of ethics. The focus shifts from the ways of God with the world to our way of life—or death.

The poor who struggle for liberation and those who stand in solidarity with them accept the suffering that goes with it and testify that God is very close to them; they also demonstrate a quality of life we rarely find elsewhere. Moreover, the life they live tends to provide a violent reaction on the part of those who are trying desperately to protect themselves from suffering through the security that comes from possessing land and wealth and gaining power over others. When their security is threatened, they resort to violence to preserve their wealth and power.

In the ensuing conflict, we have vividly portrayed two contrasting ways of life. On one hand, we have individuals and communities who assume that they can have life only as they deprive others of it. They spend their energies struggling to gain more and more possessions at the expense of others. They strive for even greater power which they get by denying it to others. They attempt to establish stability and peace through violence and repression. On the other hand, we have individuals and communities who choose to find life along the road of service to those in need. They are willing to renounce the power of domination in order to empower others, and work for stability and peace by struggling for justice for all. They soon learn that, to give life to others, they must be willing to give up their own lives.

As I have lived in these more extreme situations among people forced to choose between these two options, I have realized that they raise fundamental questions from life and history for me—and for my world—as well as for them. And, in turning anew to the words and actions of Jesus presented in the

Gospels, I have come upon a number of things which speak directly to the problem and also call for a decision on my part.

Dietrich Bonhoeffer's reference to Jesus as "the man for others" points in the right direction, but does not go far enough. In the Synoptic Gospels, Jesus is portrayed as the one who is *for the marginal people,* those who have few possessions, no place in society and no security. He identifies with them, sharing their lot as the one who "has nowhere to lay his head." Moreover, he is in their midst as a servant. Rather than exercising power over them, he humbles himself in order to create space for them to become more fully human. In his solidarity with them, he confronts those who would exercise power over them or keep them in bondage and undermines all their attempts to claim divine authority for their oppressive power. In this struggle to give life to those to whom it is denied, he chooses a path leading to his own death. At the same time, he claims that they are the privileged ones, those to whom the reign of God belongs.

Jesus makes it very clear that anyone who would follow him is called to live as he did. More than this, he declares that this giving of self in order to give life to those deprived of it is the only road to real life. And, he presents this option in the most uncompromising terms: If anyone asks for your coat, give him your cloak as well; "Give to him who begs from you, and do not refuse him who would borrow from you" (Mt. 5:42). Those who would follow Jesus, giving themselves as he gave of himself, can do so only if they break all ties: with their possessions, as the rich young ruler is asked to do; with their work, as those who left their boats or their positions as tax collectors; even with their families and with themselves. He also demands a complete restructuring of all power relationships: rather than ruling over others, as the Gentiles do, his disciples are called upon to live as servants, as Jesus did.

In the Gospel of John, this way of life is described by one word, "love," which means nothing less than giving of self and laying down life for others, following Jesus' example. Put in the sharpest possible terms, those who would save their lives by living to self will lose them. Only those who lose their lives in service to others can find life: "Unless a grain of wheat falls into the earth and dies, it remains alone; but if it dies, it bears much fruit" (Jn. 12:24).

Who is going to live this way and participate in this redemptive process moving toward the Reign of God? Not the wealthy, nor the powerful, nor those in high positions. Jesus chooses his disciples from among the poorest, even subversives like the Zealots, and sends them out to announce the good news to the poor. And he thanks God, who has "hidden these things from the wise and understanding and revealed them to babes" (Lk. 10:21). After the resurrection, the Holy Spirit empowers the lowly, who are willing to share all that they have with the others. In this context, it makes sense to speak of the poor as those to whom the reign of God belongs.

The New Testament does something more than present this way of life as the way Jesus lived and taught. It claims that, in doing this, Jesus is exhibiting God in the world, making God visible. As Arthur McGill points out in his fascinating study of suffering, "The power and life present in Jesus are not simple aspects of his human being, but belong to God. Jesus is the presence of God himself in the human sense. 'In him,' Paul writes, 'the fullness of God was pleased to dwell' (Col. 1:19)." Therefore, in his self expenditure and his teaching about it, "Jesus is not telling men how to reshape their lives. He is telling them what their lives become when they participate in God's own life, in what the New Testament calls 'eternal life.'" [31]

In other words, God's own love is present in the world in Jesus. The essential mark of God's divinity is this self giving of God to Jesus and through Jesus to those in need. What is most central in the life of Jesus is his willingness to receive all from God and to give of himself totally, even to death, to those in need, especially the poor and marginal. And authentic human life is that which participates in this divine life, available to those who are "born not of blood nor of will of the flesh . . . but of God" (Jn. 1:13).

If God gives so graciously and Jesus lives the divine life as he receives all from God, then we can relate to God and find

---

[31] Arthur C. McGill, *Suffering: A Test of Theological Method* (Philadelphia: Westminster Press, 1982), p. 59.

authentic human life only as we recognize our neediness and are willing to receive life as a gift every day. And, if Jesus, by his life, reveals to us a God who wills to give of self for the poor and marginal, then we taste of this divine life as we, receiving all from God, give all to those among whom God is present. Living in this milieu, we are no longer compelled to strive constantly to possess. Rather, we find life as we discover the way to let loose of what we have, and give of ourselves and of what we most need, in order that others may have life. We experience abundant life, not as we exercise power over others, but as we participate in the empowerment of others. And, as we live this quality of life in community, we envision a new ordering of life in the world that is capable of transforming our historical existence in the direction of the coming reign of God.

When we become more fully aware of the radicality of Jesus' way of life, we cannot escape the questions: Who can hear and respond to such a message? Who are in such desperate need that they may be willing to open themselves totally to God's grace and receive life as a gift? Who are able to see that life does not consist in striving to have more and more? Who are open to the possibility of giving of themselves what they need in order that others may live? Who is aware that the power of domination destroys life, even of those who wield it? Who dare to find life as they empower others? As I ponder these questions, I come to understand better what is happening in the Christian Base Communities and the reason, when I am with them, they give me life and strengthen my faith that social transformation is possible.

For Jesus, this way of life led to the cross. The same fate awaits those who struggle for justice for the poor today. But the New Testament affirms that Jesus, precisely in following this path toward crucifixion, reveals the power of God, the power by which God rules the world. Confronted by signs of imminence of his death, Jesus declares, in John's Gospel: "Now is the judgment of this world, now shall the ruler of this world be cast out" (12:31). According to McGill, "If the power of God reveals itself in and *as* Jesus," then "the distinctive mark of God's power is service and self-giving, and in this world such power belongs only to him who serves."[32]

As we pointed out earlier, those who share the sufferings of Christ with and for the oppressed often share this conviction. They are convinced that their struggle for liberation is connected to God's redemptive process in history. Thus, they trust that the giving of self in solidarity with the oppressed and in response to the God who gives is the source of life for the world. They see that the laying down of life for the victims of injustice contributes to overcoming injustice, that such love exposes evil and conquers hate. They understand that the resurrection represents the *victory of the crucified*. It thus exposes the pretenses, the destructiveness and the futility of the exercise of oppressive power. At the same time, it strengthens their hope that the thousands of little crucifixions in which they participate will contribute to the liberation of the oppressed of the world. When those who live by such faith become martyrs, they invite all of us to choose this same path of self-giving in order to share in Christ's victorious struggle to give life to those to whom it has been denied.

As I move among those who live by this vision and willingly pay the price of following it, I cannot avoid coming to the conclusion that our American way of life stands in striking contrast to it. I realize that our economic and political structures are not only in line with, but support, those that cause the suffering of the poor in the Third World. I also realize that those who suffer in the struggle for liberation are convinced that these structures produce death—for us as well as for them. And I know that their witness contributes decisively to the awakening of my conscience, with the burden it lays upon me.

This realization first broke through to many of us during the war against Vietnam. It has now been brought much closer to home by what our government has been doing in Central America, as we allow ourselves to see the way our involvement there contributes directly to the growing impoverishment of the people, the death of thousands and the uprooting of hundreds of thousands of El Salvador and Guatemala. Or when we see what has been and is being done to disrupt the economy and

---

[32] Ibid., pp. 60, 63.

overthrow the government of Nicaragua, which is attempting to break out of this vicious circle of poverty, oppression and violence.

This awareness has been heightened in recent years as we see what is happening here at home, in our own society: the mad struggle of those who already have wealth and power to further enrich themselves; the continued obsession with production and consumption, without regard for the exhaustion of natural resources or the destruction of the environment; the failure of our society to respond to the needs of the homeless, the lack of hope on the part of poor youth in our urban ghettoes, or the crisis in medical care, to mention only a few of the urgent problems staring us in the face and getting worse each year.

In our awareness of all this, we frequently tend to feel powerless, to be immobilized and to lose hope. And then, in and through our contact with those who suffer in Central America and elsewhere, something unexpected may happen to us. Through their eyes we are able to see that there is another way, which leads to life. In their poverty, they witness to a reality of grace available to us as well. In their weakness, their hopefulness may convince us that change is possible in our society. And they, by their struggle, set in motion a process by which not only their world, but ours, can be transformed. With their stripes, we may be healed.

At the height of the Reagan era, I was part of a group of fifteen women and men from various church agencies who were profoundly disturbed by what our government was doing to the poor in this country. We met to explore the ways we could respond to that challenge. As we talked with each other, we discovered, to our surprise, that almost all of us had lived and worked for a number of years in Asia, Africa or Latin America, or among poor and marginal people here at home. And we realized that it was as a result of living and working with them that our understanding of what was happening had been radically changed. Through them, our faith had been deepened. In solidarity with their struggle, our hope for the future had been renewed.

In one country after another in Latin America today, I find that growing numbers of young people from the middle and upper classes, even those who are more progressive in outlook, have little hope that life in their countries will improve. In the face of deepening economic and political crises, they look for ways to emigrate to North America or Western Europe. But, while this is happening, those who are so poor that they are outside the market economy are striving to create a new quality of community life as they share the little they have. Those excluded from the capitalist productive system are laying the foundation for a new economic order, based on local and regional self-reliance. Those excluded completely from the exercise of public power are learning to empower each other and are struggling for a re-ordering of power in society from the bottom up. They thus challenge and render obsolete political structures in which power flows from the top down, as is now the case both in Western and in Marxist-Leninist societies.

In contact with them, those of us who are not poor may be challenged to change sides and share in their struggle. But, as has happened frequently among those in Christian circles who have chosen to stand with the poor, we begin to realize that the initiative for the creation of a new future is now passing into their hands. They are the ones who have the vision of a radically transformed society and are willing to give their lives for it. They are becoming, as we say in Latin America, "the new historical subject," in partnership with whom we, too, may find a place as we are transformed by our association with them.

In conclusion, I would like to refer again to Eugen Rosenstock-Huessy, a German-American social philosopher and lay theologian, whose thought has had a great deal of influence over me in recent years and who first pointed me in this direction. The fact that he developed such a perspective during and immediately after World War I is all the more fascinating for me. Convinced as he was at the time that all major institutions in Germany were essentially bankrupt, he decided that he would have to look to the margins of the established order to find those prepared and willing to undertake the formidable task of creating a new society. Thus, he declined attractive offers from the government, the university and the church, because he knew that these institutions were incapable of carrying out what he called "the one thing necessary" at that time. He turned instead to the industrial workers and to the unemployed whom he perceived to be, for that time and place, the "human fulcrum" for dealing creatively with social questions. They, in their position of marginality and in their suffering, were the ones capable of envisioning a new world for all and struggling for it.

In an effort to understand better what he observed, Rosenstock-Huessy spent a number of years studying the history of the West and concluded that the unique factor in its development, the source of its dynamic energy and creativity, was a series of revolutions. On the basis of this insight, he wrote *Out of Revolution,* a history of the development of the West through its revolutions. This study confirmed his belief that the vision and energy for the re-creation of society always come from below. As he put it, "The mother country of the revolution is immune to the next one;" "Revolutions break out in the most backward country in relation to the previous revolution," and "salvation comes from where nobody expects it, from the depraved, from the impossible."[33]

He was able to perceive that, in history, time and time again, a particular portion of the human race, among those at the margin, assumes the burden and promise of a new ordering of society, for the sake of all. Through their passion and the price they pay in blood, they are capable of jarring humankind out of its historical groove, rallying past and future against a rotten present. Thus, they reorient us in time. They lead us to a mountaintop from which we are enabled to get a new perspective on what is happening around us.

Rosenstock-Huessy also was convinced that the inspiration for this revolutionary approach came from the Hebrew and Christian Scriptures and that those who participate in such movements coming from below make possible the revitalization

---

[33] Eugen Rosenstock-Huessy, *Die Hochzeit des Krieges und der Revolution* (Wurzburg: Patmos, 1920), p. 285.

of the church. For they are the ones who participate in "the death and resurrection of the Word;"[34] they make possible the "retranslation of the Holy Spirit in new forms of utterance,"[35] they open the way for "the penetration of the Cross into more and more fields of human existence."[36]

The poor and those who struggle with them for liberation today are part of a cloud of witnesses who keep faith alive and give life to the world. Rather than seeking to avoid suffering or find the right explanation for it, they take suffering into themselves. And in doing so, they catch a vision of a world beyond and are graced with strength to struggle for it; they provide us with an opening into the future and deepen our understanding as well.

---

[34] Eugen Rosentstock-Huessy, *The Christian Future* (New York: Harper, 1966), p. 128.
[35] Ibid., p. 243.
[36] Ibid., p. 165.

5

Liturgy and the Role of the Worshipper

Schuyler Brown

My introduction to the Prayer Book Society of Canada came about in an unusual way. Back in 1989 my wife called my attention to the fact that I was mentioned by name in the Society newsletter: "As a Toronto theologian, Schuyler Brown, put it, we have got to understand that all this business of trying to find out what the authority of Scripture intended is altogether the wrong orientation."

I wrote immediately to the Society to protest such an allegation, since I had never made any such statement. In due course, through the good offices of Kenneth Scott, a "correction" appeared, which concluded: "We apologize for this error." Readers of the newsletter were referred to an article of mine in New Testament Studies on "reader response criticism," or the role of the reader in Biblical interpretation.

This article is the starting point for my remarks today. I think that Biblical studies and liturgical studies have a common problem to which a consideration of the role of the reader, in one case, and of the role of the worshipper, in the other, may provide a solution.

Both of these areas of theological study use the historical paradigm. In Biblical studies this is called the historical-critical method. In liturgical studies the history of Christian worship is of paramount importance. Now the advantage of the historical paradigm is its supposed objectivity, and objectivity, of course, is the ideal of all academic pursuits.

But in the case of the Bible and liturgy, objectivity, however important, is not enough. For it leaves out the factor which makes the Bible sacred scripture, and which makes liturgy the worship of God. This missing element is the effect that the Bible and the liturgy have on the reader and the worshipper respectively.

It is in the illumination and transformation of the believer that scripture and worship achieve their purpose as means of divine grace. Without a consideration of the effect of scripture and liturgy on the believing subject, the objective, historical study remains incomplete, at least as far as the Church is concerned. Of course, if scripture and liturgy are pursued as purely academic disciplines, this subjective dimension might be considered irrelevant.

Since the worshipper is the one who experiences liturgy, the worshipper should also have a role in the evaluation of liturgy. That is why I am concerned about the exclusively theological focus of the evaluation process for the Book of Alternative Services. The result of this theological emphasis is to exclude most lay people from any effective contribution to the debate concerning how they will worship God.

Those who love the Book of Common Prayer often have no formal theological education or else have completed their theological training many years ago, before the current liturgical debate began. Therefore, Prayer Book supporters who are drawn into theological discussion of the new service book are often judged by theological and liturgical experts to be misinformed, simplistic, unsophisticated, or reactionary. But this is only because the theological focus of the debate makes it impossible for such persons to express their reactions to the new services in a natural and spontaneous way.

The limited focus of the evaluation process thus creates a "lose-lose" situation for us. If we abstain from participating in the debate because of our lack of theological expertise, we seem ineffectual; if we do participate, despite our lack of expertise, we may look ridiculous, at least to the other side.

I think the questionnaire distributed by the Evaluation Commission is omitting some very important, non-theological questions. The underlying assumption seems to be that since the BAS has been produced by liturgical experts, the only reason for not having it replace the Prayer Book would be if it could be shown to be heretical. A 450 year old tradition of Anglican worship is implicitly dismissed as irrelevant, and the spiritual attachment of countless life-long Anglicans to this tradition is ignored. But surely the fruits of the spirit which Prayer Book worship continues to produce deserve to be given as much consideration as the rational, historical arguments of liturgical experts.

In the words of Ignatius of Loyola, "It is not abundance of knowledge that fills and satisfies the soul but rather an interior understanding and savouring of things." Does any particular form of worship "fill and satisfy the soul"? Does it communicate "interior understanding" and spiritual relish? The Evaluation Commission's questionnaire provides no opportunity to answer such questions, even though it includes "experience" as one of the criteria for liturgy.

Of course, I am not faulting Professor Webster's subcommittee for carrying out the task assigned to them. But, as far as I know, the Evaluation Commission has not assigned anyone to investigate the non-theological aspects of our liturgical crisis, including the issues of the process itself, and this has left a serious lacuna.

A recent book by a Roman Catholic liturgist provides the sort of "view from the pew" which is exceedingly important but which is ruled out by our evaluation process: "In the old days, before all the changes, I used to go to Mass and it seemed like prayer, at least most of the time. Now I go and spend a good deal of time looking at my watch. Something's missing in the new liturgy. It doesn't seem so holy anymore." I wonder how many Anglicans may have had similar experiences with our new rites. If their reactions are expressed at all, they can be easily dismissed because they are not couched in the theological language which constitutes the professional jargon of the clergy.

John Henry Newman once wrote an essay on *Consulting the Faithful in Matters of Doctrine.* Today there is great interest, at least in Roman Catholic circles, in the place of "reception" by the faithful in forming doctrinal consensus. It seems to be that these concepts of "consultation" and "reception" have an obvious application to the process of liturgical renewal.

It is true that the 1549 Book of Common Prayer was simply imposed upon the English people, causing a riot in Cornwall. But I think this would be a most unfortunate precedent for the Anglican Church of Canada to follow in the last decade of the 20th Century.

Now I do not want to imply that there has been no consultation of the faithful in the process by which the BAS has been introduced to the Church. Each parish will have its own story to tell. Undoubtedly, there are parishes where the faithful have been consulted sincerely and without manipulation, and where their reactions have been duly noted and acted upon.

But I am sorry to say that there are also parishes whose rectors have such an exalted sense of their own leadership role in liturgical renewal that any hesitation or misgiving on the part of the faithful has been dismissed as "obscurantist" or even "pathological." After a while, those who have not jumped enthusiastically on the band-wagon are made to feel that they no longer belong, and when such persons have finally withdrawn from the parish, then a consensus statement on liturgical policy can be proudly announced.

In the Report of Dean Abraham's BAS/BCP Dialogue Group to the College of Bishops, he stated: "The process of liturgical renewal has, in many cases, been inadequate and insensitive, and needs to be changed, where necessary, so that an open dialogue about liturgy may be achieved."

For an open dialogue about liturgy to be possible, and for a resolution of the present impasse to take place, each of the three interested groups must be able to make its own contribution to the discussion, and in its own way. Professional elitism and the disenfranchisement of those who have not mastered the technical lingo should have no place in the Church. These three interested groups are the liturgical scholars, the clergy, and the whole people of God. (Of course, a particular individual may belong to one, two, or all three groups.)

Academic scholarship, whether in the area of scripture or in the area of liturgy, is of obvious importance to the Church. Such scholarship originates in the university, and that is where it primarily belongs. However, since the university represents the rationality of our society and culture, the Church can only ignore academic scholarship at its own peril. In the 2nd Century, Tertullian posed the question: "What has Athens to do with Jerusalem?" I would reply: Not too much, perhaps, but surely something.

However, the Church should not be over-awed by the specialized and sometimes quite narrow competence of the liturgical scholar. Such scholars, like any other academic group, owe their allegiance, first and foremost, to the professional guild to which they belong. The shared assumptions of a group of colleagues may make it difficult for them to appreciate or even acknowledge the views of those who come from a different place and have a different perspective.

Moreover, liturgical scholars who are active in composing modern liturgies have a vested interest in promoting these liturgies and in stressing their superiority to what has gone before. If someone is trying to sell me a new washing machine, I do not expect him to extol the virtues of the old model, which I already have. But what is in the interest of the liturgist is not necessarily for the good of the Church.

The second interested group is the clergy. Rectors, we know, have the canonical responsibility for ordering divine worship in their parishes. However, I do not see how this responsibility can be understood so broadly as to include the right to suppress the official service book of the Church. I am distressed when I hear of cases where rectors have used their authority to divide and polarize their congregation, and to make life-long Anglicans feel like unwanted strangers in their own Church.

I think of Paul's efforts to bring together the factions within the Church of Corinth. He implores his Christians to show respect and consideration of each other, and he warns them that those who boast in their superior knowledge should take care lest this knowledge destroy a brother or sister for whom Christ died (I Cor. 8:11). How different from the cynical attitude we sometimes encounter in our own Church, that disaffected Anglicans will eventually accept what is being imposed upon them since they have nowhere else to go.

The third interested group is the whole people of God. Their contribution is particularly precious because it is so different from that of the first two groups. Liturgical scholars use the language of Church history; the clergy use the language of theology. Both of these languages are forms of rational discourse. The faithful, by contrast, have the experience of worship. For the clergy, who must organize and orchestrate the liturgy, week after week, the actual experience of worshipping God is often mixed with distractions and pre-occupations. I always look forward to the holidays, when I can worship incognito as a simple actor in the liturgical drama, without having to be director and producer as well.

The faithful are more concerned with how worship is experienced than with whether it conforms to some 4th-Century liturgical prototype or to some contemporary theological theory. The faithful are therefore more sensitive to those affective, non-rational dimensions of worship which serve as the vehicle of divine grace. Remember Ignatius: "It is not an abundance of knowledge that fills and satisfies the soul."

The way people react to divine worship is as complex and mysterious as the way people react to sacred scripture. All we can say for sure is that these reactions are quite diverse. After eleven years in this diocese, I have the impression that there are strong and, at times, passionate attachments among the laity to both service books. It is impossible to say which group of laity is in the majority, since the Church has never conducted a referendum on liturgical preference, and parish surveys, for reasons that I have already given, are unfortunately suspect.

So why not start the great debate on liturgy with these passionate personal attachments, rather than with arguments about history and theology, in which only the experts can participate, and which are often inconclusive? You tell me what you love about liturgy, and I will try to do the same.

This would be in accord with Paul's exhortations, to which I have referred, and it would be more illuminating than a meaningless exchange of insults: "You're stuck back in the 16th century!" "You're soft on scripture!"

The Anglican way seeks to be tolerant of diverse approaches. If we can apply this tolerance to differences in worship, perhaps, in time, something truly wonderful may emerge, something which will surpass any of the liturgical options presently available.

The Prayer Book Society is primarily a lay movement. As such, you provide an important balance in the Church at a time when authoritarianism and clericalism are on the rise. For you remind us all that, although we are an episcopal Church, the obedience of faith is finally owed only to God and to God's holy word.

6

Kristenhetens Framtid och Gudsbilden

Bertil Werkström

När jag här och nu försöker formulera några tankar över ämnet: Kristenhetens framtid och Gudsbilden, gör jag det som en hyllning till William Alexander Johnson för hans gärning som universitets-professor och kyrkoman. Jag känner ytterst få som I likhet med William A. Johnson så engagerat och helhjärtat ägnat sitt liv både åt kyrkan och universitetet. (Ett annat exempel skulle kunna vara vår gemensamme lärare Gustaf Wingren.)

William A. Johnson har insett att det finns ett nära och viktigt samband mellen universitet och kyrka. –Universitetets moder är ju krykan, med dess utbildningsbehov. Men å andra sidan kan man säga att vad vore kyrkan utan universitetet och dess fostran och utbildning av forskare, lärare och präster. –Det är detta samband William A. Johnson har sett och det är därför han så helhjärtat ägnat sitt liv åt båda. Han har kanske också sett att kristenhetens framtid är avhängig av hur Gudsbilden tolkas och översätts till ett begripligt språk av kyrkan, dess anställda och frivilliga medarbetare. För detta tolkningsarbete behöver krykan ständig hjälp av teologer och forskare vid universitetet.

Universitetets forskare måste också ständigt och på olika sätt arbeta med Gudsbilden och de skilda tolkningsförsök som gjorts genom kyrkans historia.

Här finns alltså en ömsesidighet i relationen universitet och kyrka och deras respektive arbete med Gudsbilden. –Sedan har naturligtvis kyrkan ett särskilt intresse av kristenhetens framtid, som kanske inte delas av universitetet och dess forskare.

Efter denna inledning vill jag nu reflektera något över Gudsbilden. Det begrepp jag först vill lyfta fram är outgrundligheten.

Gud är outgrundlig.

Vi har genom kyrkans historia smyckat våra kyrkor och andaktsrum och också våra hem med symboler och bilder, som velat tala till oss om Gud. De har fungerat som ikoner, himmelske fönster mot evigheten, mot Gud själv. Trots dessa bilder måste vi ständigt påminna varandra om att Gud är outgrundlig och hemlighetsfull, ett mysterium. Därför blir alla försök att med ord eller bilder säga något om Gud bara trevande försök att visa på några sidor av Guds väsen.

I sitt avskedstal säger Jesus: "Detta har jag sagt er i bilder. Det kommer en tid, då jag inte längre skall tala i bilder utan med klara ord låta er veta allt om Fadern." (Joh. 16:25) Vi får alltså löftet om kunskap en gång, men vi är ofta alltför benägna att tala och handla som om det redan vore uppfyllt. Man kan också fråga sig varför så många kristna kommer med det ena anspråket efter det andra på att just de förstått Faderns identitet bättre än andra? Varifrån kommer alla dessa barnsliga behov av att först inmuta och sedan monopolisera sanningen?

Gudsblid och tillbedjan.

I förordet till Edmund Schlinks ekumeniska dogmatik skriver en katolsk professor, Heinrich Fries: "Vi kristna får inte längre betrakta varandra som om vår egen kyrka vore mittpunkten, utan vi måste erkänna att vi kretsar som planeter tillsammans med de andra runt solen Kristus och att vi får vårt ljus från honom." Ekumenisk teologi, som aldrig kan baseras på något slags minsta gemensamma nämnare utan endast på ett maxi-

mum av genomtänkt kristen teologi, måste innehålla starka inslag
av doxologi. Utan doxologi är ingen gemensam lära om Gud
möjlig i kristenheten. I doxologin återspeglar Guds härlighet.
Men lovprisningen görs inte som om Gud äras först genom
denna, tvärtom tillskriver doxologin Gud den ära och härlighet
som han redan har. Men Guds tilltal och handlande med oss
kan inte lämnas utan gensvar.

Gudsbilden och treenigheten.

Vi behöver ständigt aktualisera treenigheten, i våra respektive
kyrkor men också och inte minst i de ekumeniska samtalen och
i ekumeniska gudstjänster.

Bibeln har mycket att saga om Fadern, Sonen och Anden,
men den har igen utvecklad treenighetslära. Den trinitariska
bekännelsen kom till stånd för att slå vakt om den bibliksa
gudstrons enhetlighet och mångfald. Från de rika gudsbild enligt
vilken Gud är treenig, hämtar den allmänneliga kyrkan sitt
mönster för en ekumenisk grundhållning.

Det finns naturligtvis oändligt mycket mer att saga om
Gudsbilden, men hur mycket vi än försöker uttrycka vem Gud
är, vad Gud är, kan vi ändå aldrig mer än antyda Guds storhet
och rikedomen i hans väsen. Men detta visar ju också på det
faktum att här finns mycket att göra både för kyrka och universitet
var för sig och i samverkan.

Så till den andra delen av ämnet för minst bidrag till
hyllnings-skriften: *Kristenhetens framtid.*

Också här måste jag av naturliga skäl bli mycket kortfattad.

Till hjälp och utgångspunkt för mina tankar över detta ämne
väljer jag en psalm av den geniale svenske teologen och prästen
Olov Hartman. De tre första stroferna i den psalmen slutar med
orden: vet vi vem Gud är; vet vi vad Gud är, vet vi var Gud är.
Förklaringarna till dessa slutord ges i texten: "För att Du inte
tog det gudomliga dig till en krona, vet vi *vem* Gud är. –För att
du lydde fram till det yttersta döden på korset, vet vi *vad* Gud är.
–För att du nedsteg hit till de plågade, hit till de dömda, vet vi
var Gud är."

Det talas ofta om att kristenheten befinner sig vid en
skiljeväg. Antingen går vägen mot fortsatt avkristning i vårt

samhälle eller också går den mot en ny och djup andlighet. Om vägen går mot en ny andlighet och öppenhet, inleds denna process med en väckelse, som uppstår inte bland de starka och friska, inte bland dem som är mitt uppe i sin yrkeskarriär. Väckelsen kommer att börja, tror jag, bland de unga, bland de sjuka och handikappade, bland de av samhället marginaliserade. —Orsaken till att det kommer att bli så är att när Jesus blev människa bland människor, så var det just dessa grupper han vände sig till och sökte upp. Det var också av dem han blev mottagen med öppna armar. Det var hos dem den första kristna tron började spira och växa för att sedan spridas ut över världen. Om kristenheten har en framtid, och det har den naturligtvis om Gud vill, så har den en framtid genom en väckelse i dessa grupper i vår kyrka, i vart samhälle.

Till kristenhetens framtid hör en inriktning, som innebär en ökad uppslutning kring dem som lider i världen, för att inte lidandet ska behöva bli större än nödvändigt utan bli buret tillsammans med andra. Jag tror också att det kommer att bli ett ökat engagemang för fred och rättvisa, för att inte våldet och orättvisorna ska behöva bli störe än nödvändigt. Till kristnehetens framtid hör också ett engagemang för de fattiga, de nedersta, för dem som inte själva kan föra sin talan, och som därför blir bortglömda och föraktade, så att inte förtryckett, orättvisorna och föraktet ska behöva bli större än nödvändigt.

När Gud skulle säga sitt avgörande ord till mänskligheten, som hade vänt honom ryggen, lät hand det ta formen av ett nyfött människobarn. När Gud skulle ge oss ett hoppets och segerns tecken, lät han det bli ett avrättningsredskap. Han har alltid överraskat oss med gärningar och tecken, som ser ringa ut, som är svåra att känna igen. Men genom likande tecken och gärningar kan vi människor föra den kristna tron vidare och medverka till att kristenheten får en framtid.

Liksom kyrka och universitet hör samman, som jag tidigare framhållit, så finns det ett samband mellan Gudsbilden och kristenhetens framtid. Utan ständig nytolkning av Gudsbilden har kristenheten ingen framtid. Universitetet och dess forskare kan analysera och kartlägga hur Gudsbilden har tolkats genom kyrkans historia och hur detta överensstämmer med Jesu budskap och gärning. Forskarna kan också systematiskt sammanställa och typologiskt jämföra olika tolknings-modeller. Men det måste tillkomma kyrkan och dess medarbetare att utifrån detta material gora ständiga nytolkningar, där bilder och symboler från en gången tid ersätts eller omformas, så att människor i dag känner igen Gud i den verklighet de lever och rör sig.

7

Att Bli Människa

Gustaf Wingren

Enligt det budskap som våra bibliska skrifter förmedlar är detta att bli "frälst" exakt detsamma som att, äntligen, *bli människa.* Anledningen till att denna helhetssyn på vad mänsklighet är har gått förlorad för oss, är bl.a. att vi har förlorat detta som var den självklara förutsättningen för den äldsta kristna kyrkan, nämligen att *hela Bibeln är en enda enhet från* Första Mosebok till Johannes Uppenbarelse. Jag skall här dra tre linjer genom hela Bibeln, tre linjer som—alla tre—handlar om samma sak, *att bli människa.*

Alla tre linjerna börjar i skapelseberättelsen, fast på helt olika punkter i skapelseberättelsen (Gen. 1., Gen. 3., Gen. 11) och alla tre slutar i Nya testamentets senare del breven (Uppenbarelseboken).

Först ett ord om vad som menas med "skapelseberättelse." Naturvetenskapens kritik av teologins tal om "skapelse" har medfört, att vi numera bara räknar 1 Mos. 1–2 som skapelsetexter. Det bibliskt korrekta är att se de första *elva* kapitlen som ett stort enhetligt sammanhang, de handlar alla om *hela mänskligheten,* inte om Israel. Gamla testamentet är Israels heliga bok och denna bok inledes med berättelsen *före* Israels utkorelse, som börjar i Gen. 12:1–7, löftet till Abraham, löftet om ett särskilt *land* på jordklotet. Gen. 1–11 handlar däremot om *hela* jordklotet och om *alla* människor.

Nu tar vi, rakt igenom Bibeln, de tre linjerna, var för sig. Den första linjen handlar *om det mänskliga språket.* Människorna är de enda varelser som inte vid inbördes möten förstår varann. Fåglarna förstär varann, varifrån de än kommer, detsamma gäller fyrfota djur och vattnets varelser. Hur kan denna särställning i elände förklaras? Därom berättas det i Gen. 11:1–9, "Babels torn." Poängen är människors maktbegär, att "göra sig ett namn," "bygga ett torn som når upp till himlen." Precis samma poäng, människans maktbegär, hennes önskan att "nå upp till himlen" och alltså lägga beslag på Guds plats i universum, kommer vi att möta på var och en av linjerna—alla tre skildrar människan såsom urspårad på just denna punkt.

Om vi fortsätter på det språkliga spåret, så gäller den allmänna regeln, söm vi skall stöta på flera gånger, att Nya testamentets händelser innebär läkning av den skada som människan släpar på. När Abraham utkoras i Gen. 12, heter det ju: "I dig skall alla släkten på jorden varda välsignade" (1 Mos. 12:3). Detta löfte upprepas ordagrant i Gal. 3:8 av Paulus, när han argumenterar för att alla hedningar bör beredas plats i Jesu Kristi församling, de är "Abrahams barn," heter det (Gal. 3:7). På det språkliga planet yttrar sig detta nya barnaskap i det tungomålsunder, som Apostlagärningarna 2 berättar om.

Pingstens språkunder är en begynnande läkning av den skada som drabbade mänskligheten vid raserandet av Babels torn. Pingstens poäng är att alla *förstår* vad apostlarna säger då de förkunnar om Kristus. "Är de inte galileer allesammans, dessa som nu talar? Hur kan då var och en av oss höra sitt eget modersmål talas? Vi är parter, meder, elamiter, vi kommer från Mesopotamien, Judeen och Kappadokien, från Pontos och Asien, från Frygien och Pamfylien . . . vi är kretensare och araber— ändå hör vi dem tala på vårt eget språk om Guds stora gärningar" (Apg. 2:7–11).

I och med pingsten och kyrkans födelse på jorden har läkningen av människans skada börjat. Men bara börjat. Ännu suckar skapelsen, den ropar i ångest och väntar på sin slutliga förlossning (Rom. 8:18–25). När fulländningen kommer, när all synd och skada är borta och skapelsen äntligen är *hel* igen, då ljuder lovsången inför tronen och inför Lammet, och den sjunges av "en skara som ingen kan räkna," "en skara ur alla folkslag och stammer och folk och tungomål" (Joh. Upp. 7:9-12). Detta är den definitiva läkningen av skadan från Babels torn, en läkning som påbörjades på den första pingstdagen i Jerusalem. Nu har evangeliet nått ut till jordens alla hörn och blivit hört av alla människor.

Detta var det första spåret, det gällde en särskild punkt i människolivet, språket. Det förefaller oss primitivt att tänka på detta sätt—och det *är* primitivt. Men vad som inte är primitivt är det bakomliggande grundmönstret i kristen tro: att bli frälst, det är helt enkelt "*att bli människa;*" det är inte ett religiöst tillägg till det mänskliga, utan det är att bli av med en skada som tynger oss alla.

Jag vill här, på tal om primitivitet, göra ett litet inskott innan vi lämnar det språkliga ämnet. Det envisa fasthållandet vid mässan på latin, mot alla försök att införa modersmålet i gudstjänsten, har bl.a. sin grund i denna orimliga föreställning: latinet är nu början på det framtida himmelska språket, lovsången i det eviga livet. På denna punkt är det Martin Luther som står för mänsklighet, Luther och Olavus Petri—och Grundtvig.

Vi går nu över till linjen nummer två genom hela Bibeln, talet om människan såsom *avbild*, "avbild av Gud." Även nu börjar vi i Genesis, denna gång i kapitel 1, det välkända och ofta missbrukade stället: "Gud sade: låt oss göra människor till vår avbild, till att vara oss lika; och må de råda över fiskarna i havet och över fåglarna under himmelen och över boskapsdjuren och över hela jorden" (1 Mos. 1:26). Vi vet alla hur detta ord har tolkats: människan har av Gud fått herraväldet over hela skapelsen och över djuren. Därav har mycket djurplågeri och framför allt den oerhörda miljöförstöringen fått gudomlig legitimation.

Jag vill påminna om att den bit av Genesis som handlar om hela mänskligheten och om människans förpliktelser gentemot skapelsen består av elva kapitel, inte bara av två. Berättelsen om Noa och om floden säger vad Gud menade när han skapade människan till sin avbild (1 Mos. 6:13 – 8:22). När livet är hotat åligger det människan att ta hand om hane och hona av alla djur och sörja för att alla arter av djuren får överleva. Detta är den bibliska innebörden i skapelsen till "Guds avbild": människan skall bete sig som Gud—och Gud älskar det som han har skapat. Hur kan det komma sig att denna—helt klara—innebörd i skapelseberättelsen har gått förlorad? Ja, det beror inte bara på Bellman och hans melodi "Gubben Noa var en hedersman," som ju har utplånat allt allvar i vårt tal om Noa. Den verkliga förstörelsen i varje europeiskt tal om skapelsen ligger ända nere i medeltiden och i dess bruk av grekisk filosofi. För Platon och by gnistan i sitt innersta hade hemortsrätt i den gudomliga världen. Den stora klyftan gick för grekerna mellan ande och materia, och djuren ingick i "materia." Begreppet "skapelse" hade i detta sammanhang ingen funktion alls.

Noa var i Bibeln viktig, i den medeltida skolastiken blev han betydelselös. Och detta fel reparerades aldrig i den annars så bibeltrogna reformationen. Femtonhundratalets konflikter handlade om evangeliets predikan, mässoffret, påvemakten och klostret. Man måste gå ända ner till 100-talet för att finna en riktig *biblisk* tolkning av termen *avbild* (eikon, imago). Och då finner vi genast samma mönster som vi nyss mötte på det språkliga spåret, alltså först Genesis, sedan, rakt genom Bibeln, över till den nytestamentliga brevdelen. Med andra ord: först skapelsen (och skadan i skapelsen) sedan frälsningen, som är identisk med skadans läkning, inte ett "religiöst" tillägg till det mänskliga.

Efter 1 Mos. 1:26-28 följer Kol. 1:15, ordet om Kristus såsom "den osynlige Gudens avbild." Människan är skapad *till* Guds avbild, Kristus *är* Guds avbild. Man kan säga: vi människor är skapade till Kristus. Han är nämligen den första helt friska människan i historien, han är "Människosonen," den förste som till 100% levde för *andra* människor och inte alls till sitt eget gagn—därför kunde döden inte behålla honom. Efter uppståndelsen på tredje dagen lever han, nu och i evighet. Så lyder den irenaeiska läran om *recapitulatio*, skapelsens återställelse.

Recapitulatio pågår i detta *nu* och avslutas först efter vår kommande död, i det eviga livet. Om detta handlar allt det som säges om dopet och om Anden. Här vimlar det av utsagor om vår förvandling till avbilder av Kristus, vår formning till likhet med honom. Detta betyder att vi blir *mänskliga*: han är ju Guds avbild och vi är ursprungligen skapade till Guds avbild, en skapelse som vi, i vårt maktbegär, har förstört (jfr fotnoten till 2 Kor. 3:18 i 1981 års svenska översättning). Redan före sin död talar Jesus om sin väntade korsfästelse som ett svårt "dop" som han måste genomgå (Luk. 12:50). När smäleken sedan slår om i uppståndelsen på tredje dagen, är detta dop något som hans lärjungar vill få del av; alltså börjar döpandet i vatten omedelbart efter den första pingstdagen (Apg. 2:41). Om detta dop säger sedan Paulus, att vi på det sättet dör bort från synden och—redan här i vardagen—uppstår till ett rättfärdigt liv (Rom. 6:3-19). Slutet på detta blir, att vi kommer att förvandlas till likhet med Kristus (Fil. 3:20-21) eller med andra ord "bli hans sons avbilder" (Rom. 8:29, även 2 Kor. 3:18). Samma grekiska ord, eikon, tas gång på gång i bruk.

Termen ifråga, eikon, är skapelseberättelsens term, använd om syftet med människans skapelse (1 Mos. 1:26-27). Det var detta syfte som inte förverkligades; maktbegäret hos Adam förstörde allt—och det hebreiska ordet "Adam" betyder just *människa*. Tack vare inkarnationen, "människoblivandet," kunde skapelseverkets mål ändå till slut uppnås. Även vårt spår nummer två, med begreppet "avbild" i centrum, drar alltså tvärs igenom hela Bibeln.

Detsamma gäller i ännu högre grad den tredje och sista linjen, också den med start i Genesis. Här kretsar allt kring sådana storheter som frestelse, prövning, kamp, hunger, nöd, varvid allt koncentreras kring konsten atta bevara enkel *mänsklighet*, ja, på visst sätt: konsten att kunna förbli fattig. Lockelsen är att sträva efter en himmelsk, övermänsklig nivå, maktbegärets lockelse, precis som Babels torn på det första, det språkliga spåret.

Vad människan frestas till, det är att "bli såsom Gud" (1 Mos. 3:5). Likheten mellan denna "ädla" vision av makt och drömmen om Babels torn är tydlig, "att göra sig ett namn och bygga ett torn som räcker upp till himmelen" (1 Mos. 11:4). I båda fallen berättar Bibeln om en mänsklig skada som nu tynger oss alla, språkförbistringen, förgängelsen, döden.

Slående är den starka accenten på exakta paralleller till Adams frestelse i Genesis, när Nya testamentet berättar om läkningen av skadan. Jesus frestas i öknen och han frestas just till att bete sig som Gud (Matt. 4:1-11, Luk. 4:1-13). Att förvandla stenar till bröd, den näring som hela jorden behöver, är en gudomlig skapelsenhandling, och det är till att utföra detta under som djävulen försöker locka Jesus. Men parallellen med Adams frestelse går mycket längre än så. Adam frestades att äta av trädets frukt och en liknande djävulsattack blev Jesus utsatt för—han var ju hungrig efter en lång fasta.

Men det märkligaste är som sagt den specifika form som Jesu avvärjande av djävulens angrepp får: tre gånger frestas Jesus, tre gånger understryker han att han är en enkel *människa* utan några gudomliga anspråk. Människan skall leva av Guds ord (Matt. 4:4), hon får inte sätta Gud på prov (Matt. 4:7), ja, hon får inte tillbedja något annat än Gud (Matt. 4:10). Segern över djävulen i öknen består i detta: ingenting händer. När Adam frestades i lustgården, då hände det något, och det var detta som var människans nederlag, döden.

På visst sätt återvänder ökenfrestelsen när Jesus hänger på korset och pöbeln ropar: "Om du är Guds Son, hjälp då dig själv och stig ner från korset!" (Matt. 27:40). Återigen består segern i att ingenting händer. Tyst, utan svar, dör den korsfäste. Vad han gör, det är att bedja för soldaterna som genomför korsfästelsen (Luk. 23:24) och att lova en plats i paradiset för brottslingen på sidokorset (Luk. 23:43). Han gör alltså ingenting alls till sitt eget gagn, han tänker uteslutande på de *andra*. Denna utblottning är seger; därför har Gud upphöjt honom över allting och givit honom namnet över alla namn (Fil. 2:4-11).

Konsekvensen för den kirstna etiken finner vi i den strikt genomförda nytestamentliga förmaningen för vardagslivet. Att icke hämnas en oförätt, att vända andra kinden till, att uthärda förtal osv. Även här kan vi numera tycka, att mönstren blir väl primitiva, exempelvis i förhärligandet av martyriet säsom den högsta mänskliga livsformen på jorden. Säkert är, att det ideal, som Jesu offerdöd framkallade i den unga förnkyrkan, har haft en socialt och politiskt omskapande effekt i Europa, en effekt som vi ännu idag smakar frukterna av.

Till slut en kommentar till det nu flera gånger använda uttrycket "rakt genom hela Bibeln." När vårt allmänna tema lyder som det gör, *att bli människa*, kan ett sådant uttryck mana fram en föreställning om en mycket lång tidrymd, från världens tillblivelse till slutet på mänsklighetens historia. Långa bibliska perspektiv av det slaget framkallar hos oss moderna behovet av en "avmytologisering," helt i onödan. Bibeltexten skökter om sin avmytologisering själv, på egen hand, utan vår hjälp. Jag skall exemplifiera min tes med ett par bibliska satser om två olika "dagar," dels skapelsedagen, dels yttersta dagen.

Skapelsemyten talar om Adam (=människan) såsom danad av jord från marken (1 Mos. 2:7 och. 3:19). Författaren till Jobs bok visar lojalitet mot det traderade mytiska språket, han talar till Gud och sager: "Tänk på hur du formade mig såsom lera" (Job 10:9), "Jag är danad av en nypa lera" (Job 33:6). I själva verket har Job lika god kunskap om människans tillblivelse inne i kvinnans sköte som en normal svensk av idag har. Job beskriver i detalj, hur mannens säd utgjutes därinne och hur fostret därefter långsamt tillväxer.

Men det handlande subjektet i kvinnans livmoder är fortfarande Gud Skaparen: "Du utgöt mig såsom mjölk och såsom ostämne lät du mig stelna. Med hud och kött beklädde du mig, av ben och senor vävde du mig samman" (Job 10:10-11). Detta innebär att skapelsedagen inte är en dag på årtusendens avstånd. Min skapelsedag är den tidpunkt då jag blev till inne i min moders kropp. Om det händelseförloppet handlar skapelseberättelsen i Första Mosebok. Att tänka så är att följa Job, alltså att tänka *bibliskt*.

Nu går vi över till den andra dagen, "Yttersta dagen." På flera ställen talar Nya testamentet i mytologiska termer om den sista dagen i världens historia, kropparnas uppståndelse, samlingen av alla folk, räkenskapen inför Guds domstol. Så gör även Paulus, ingenting i myten subtraheras (se exempelvis 1 Kor. 15:12-28, Rom. 14:10-12). I själva verket vet Paulus att vårt kroppsliga liv slutar den dag då vi dör. Dödsdagen är den yttersta dagen, ett direkt och omedelbart möte med Jesus Kristus. De andra människorna, som nu lever runt omkring mig, de lever då fortfarande i sina kroppar, men jag har, tack vare döden, fått komma fram—jag är redan hemma.

Härom finns det mycket tydliga ustagor hos Paulus; jag nämner här två av dem. Filipperbrevet ger oss en målande bild av de många arbetsuppgifterna på jorden—den annalkande döden framstår som en förlust, eftersom så mycket är ogjort. Men å andra sidan vore det gott att nu få dö, att "bryta upp och vara hos Kristus, det vore det allra bästa" (Fil. 1:23). När annars det eviga livet efter domen genomgående skildras såsom obruten gemenskap med Kristus, att vara hemma hos honom, är det tydligt, att dödsdagen här innebär direkt inträde i evigheten. Ännu klarare är utsagan på det andra stället, i 2 Kor. 5:8: ". . .flytta bort från kroppen och få vårt hem hos Herren."

Detta innebär att yttersta dagen är en dag helt nära, inte belägen i ett avlägset fjärran—den är helt enkelt dödsdagen för var och en av oss.Vårt tema, att bli människa, och vårt på tre olika linjer utspridda material, rakt igenom hela Bibeln, rycker på detta sätt in i centrum av vår egen existens.Vi har varit med om skapelsedagen—vi är ju födda hit till jorden—och vi kommer att uppleva den yttersta dagen, ganska snart.Vi har några korta ögonblick på oss idag.

Om vi använder tiden rätt, blir vårt liv till gagn för *andra.* Använder vi tiden fel, har vi oavbrutet, fram till döden, tillgång till syndernas förlåtelse. Så talar Evangelium. Av allt vad bibelboken säger är detta det viktigaste, Evangelium.

8

Doing Theology in the Global Village

Huston Smith

Faced with the daunting (perhaps even pretentious) scope of my title, I feel the need to lower my anxiety with a disclaimer. I did not chose that title; Professor Sinha will bear me out that he assigned it to me. I did, though, accept his assignment, and the only reason that I have been able to come up with derived from the story of the man who on, encountering a cactus patch, stripped off his clothes and jumped in. When his friends pulled him out and asked for an explanation, all he found in him to say was that it seemed like a good idea at the time.

Like David Riesman's "the lonely crowd" and John Kenneth Galbraith's "conventional wisdom," Marshall McLuhan's "the global village" has proven to be one of the durable oxymorons of our century. Its general meaning is obvious, but what properties of a village is the world assuming? Two. Its institutions are weaving into a single social fabric, and a global mindset is emerging. I shall consider theology's responsibilities to these parallel developments successively.

I. Ethics in a Global Setting

Institutionally the world is becoming village-like in that its technology, finance, and communications are interlacing to become a single social network. *Technology* is globalizing because everyone wants its goods and services. *Finance* is globalizing as multinational conglomerates merge and weave the economy into a single internally responsive system. (When I asked my editor recently who owns HarperCollins, he said he wasn't sure, but he hears that it is someone in Hong Kong who may give one hour a year to checking in on this corner of his financial empire.) And *communication* is globalizing as television, the Information Superhighway and the World Wide Web of cyberspace feed peoples everywhere the same images and information.

As social ethics is not my field, I have little to say as to what the theological response to the (apparently unstoppable) merging of these three institutions should be. The best I can do is target some of the problems this amalgamation is engendering, which social ethicists must grapple with.

Those who pin excessive hopes on *technology* must continue to be reminded that if man cannot live by bread alone, still less can he live by gadgets, but something new has now entered the picture. "Every technological innovation," Anna Harrison pointed out in her Presidential address to the AAAS several years ago, "regardless of how great its positive impact on society, also has a negative impact which is sometimes unknown and sometimes suppressed." When DDT, the wonder drug of agricultural technology, was discovered, no one could have known or thought about its effect on birds' eggs. When nuclear power appeared, the problems of radioactive waste were partly unknown, and partly simply ignored. The automobile introduced fantastic mobility, but no one foresaw the pollution it would cause, or the way it would destroy the extended family and create sexual anarchy. It takes about thirty years now for the social consequences of a major technological innovation to manifest themselves. What are the odds that at some point they will catch up with us in irreversible ways?

In *finance* the overriding problem continues to be poverty, and Bernard Williams has made an interesting observation on the point. Speaking as both a classicist and a philosopher, he tells us that our assumption that the classical Greek philosophers condoned slavery is mistaken. With the exception of Aristotle, who entered a limp rationale, they thought it was awful. They just couldn't see how civilization was possible without it. Their attitude toward it was like ours is toward poverty. No one likes poverty, but we can't figure out how to get rid of it.

Among the proposals for ameliorating it I naturally have my preferences, but my confidence in their specifics takes second place to my conviction that more harm than good will come if we give unqualified allegiance to any detailed program. One of the enduring legacies of Karl Popper's *The Open Society and Its Enemies* is its argument that attempts to change the world completely and globally for the better by way of a preconceived ideology can only lead to totalitarianism. Instead of such holistic engineering—Popper's term—he argued for a gradual approach: an effort to improve incrementally the institutions, mechanisms, and techniques of human coexistence by remaining constantly in touch with experience and its feedbacks. Changes should be made according to what proves to be effective, rather than by prescriptions that assume we understand history and know everything we need to know about changing it for the better. Theologians can add to Popper's argument here their realization that in some deep-lying way human nature is flawed, from which it follows that political platforms will always to some extent be skewed to their devisers' self-interest; Reinhold Neibuhr's detailings of this point in his *Moral Man and Immoral Society* make it as important a study in social ethics as our century has produced. To think that we can make an end run around the human heart and, in the face of its clamorings, achieve the Kingdom of Heaven externally by revamping social institutions is to overlook the fact that the Kingdom is first and foremost an interior affair. Short of the eschaton, its arrival in the world will be in proportion to, and a function of, its arrival in human hearts. This doesn't counter the importance of social action, but it does insist that if such action is to be fruitful it must proceed on the understanding that "there never was a war that was not inward" (Marianne Moore).

As for the *informational* side of the global village, the chief problem that is emerging is that the quantity of information is obscuring our sense of what is important. This becomes clear if we compare the global village, water-logged by information, to an unlettered tribe. When the members of such a tribe gather around their campfire in the evening, everything the tribe knows —from the medicinal power of plants which their ancestors discovered through generations of trial and error, to the great orienting myths that give their lives meaning and purpose—is contained in the heads of its members. It stands to reason that trivia would not long survive in the spare space. Important information would be kept alive through repeated rehearsal, but trivia would fall by the wayside through disuse. The information revolution destroys this focus. It is not only that ever shorter sound bites cause sensation to upstage even information, let alone knowledge and wisdom. The companion problem is that global awareness shows villagers that their own metanarratives are not the only ones. Relativism enters, and certainties are eroded.

It stands to reason that theology has things to say about these social problems and their like, but I have already disclaimed more than a layman's knowledge of what they might be. So, leaving that important side of the global village to ethicists such as Michael Tai and Brian Wiebe, I will proceed to the side of my topic where I feel more at home: the global ethos that is emerging and how theology might respond to it.

II. Theology and the Global Ethos

Traditionally, when people wanted to know the Big Picture or ultimate nature of things they turned to their sacred texts; or if they were primal peoples, to the great orienting myths that their ancestors bequeathed to them. Since modern science arose, however, Westerners have looked increasingly to it to tell them what things are like. An intellectual historian has estimated that already a hundred years ago more Westerners believed in the periodic table of chemical elements—those elements really exist! —than they believed in any of the distinctive things the Bible speaks of. The reason for the shift is obvious. Modern science can prove its theses through controlled experiments. A moment's reflection on how much those theses have changed our world will convince anyone that they have a firm grip on the way nature works. This about-face from scripture to science has worked heavily against theology's overview. In his *Understanding the Present: Science and the Soul of Modern Man*, Bryan Appleyard asks us to imagine a missionary to an African tribe. Conversion is slow work until a child comes down with an infectious disease. The local medicine men are summoned and do their best work, but to no avail. The child's condition steadily worsens until the missionary administers the penicillin she thought to bring with her, whereupon the child recovers.

With that single move, Appleyard concludes, it's all over for the tribe's traditional culture. Elijah has challenged the priests of Baal, and has won. "Elijah" is science here, and its victories continue both at home and abroad. Stephen Carter reports a discernible increase in America's culture of disbelief in the last twenty years alone. "There is less respect for religion, less of an appreciation of it as an important force that can genuinely be the motive force in people's lives without being somehow a symptom of something neurotic."

How should theology conduct itself in a global village in which religion is increasingly on the defensive? I will propositionalize my proposals. They are heavily opinionated and, eschewing nuances, I shall state them categorically to make the issues stand out as starkly as possible.

1. Theology should recognize scientism as its principal enemy.

Science deserves no reproach, but scientism goes beyond the findings of science to assume that the scientific method is the only reliable (or at least most reliable) road to truth, and that the things science deals with are the most fundamental things that exist. In slipping into these assumptions, it turns into a religion that challenges traditional, orthodox ones to the core. Rarely is its position stated. It proceeds surreptitiously, by innuendo and surmise, and this makes it difficult to combat. If it came out into the open, the arbitrariness of its premises would become apparent and it would cease to be the problem that it is. It would be wrong to blame scientists; the proportion of them who are taken in by it is no greater than in the population at large.[1] No individuals or groups are responsible. It is the marvels of science and its technology that have made scientism the working assumptions of our era.

2.   In addition to the foregoing marks of scientism, theologians should be aware of its inherent imperialism.

The imperialism is not calculated, so again blame is out of place; but the imperialism proceeds anyway and Spinoza helps us to see why. Everything, the Blessed Spinoza taught, possesses an inbuilt *conatus*, a propensity not just to maintain itself but to enlarge its domain until it runs into something that stops it. This holds for institutions as well as organisms; and as there is nothing currently strong enough to stop science, it crests into scientism. I have already pointed out that many scientists as individuals recognize scientism for what it is, but two things keep going on. From the inside, loyalty to their profession pressures scientists to exaggerate their abilities in the public eye, for this brings both prestige and funding. Concomitantly, from the outside the public at large virtually requires scientists to behave that way, for the world is always in need of salvation, gods are salvation's agents, and science is the current god. So scientists are not allowed to point out that their competence covers only the physical world. They must pronounce on the whole of things, for a restricted god is not God at all. "The Cosmos (understood as what cosmologists deal with) is all that ever was or ever will be," Carl Sagan declaims;[2] and at the conclusion of *A Brief History of Time*, Stephen Hawking speculates on science's end: a set of equations which, because they could implicitly account for everything that ever happened or ever could happen, would be a Theory of Everything. In *Darwin's Dangerous Idea*,[3] cognitive scientist Daniel Dennett asserts flatly that Darwinism—"as se-

---

[1] John Polkinghorne's assessment of the matter is as clear-eyed as one could wish to find: "Science's greatest success is purchased through the modesty of its ambition, restricting the phenomena it is prepared to discuss to those of an impersonal, and largely repeatable, character," *The Faith of a Scientist* (Princeton, NJ: Princeton University Press, 1994), p. 5.

[2] Carl Sagan, *Cosmos* (New York: Random House, 1980), p. 4.

[3] Daniel Dennett, *Darwin's Dangerous Idea* (New York: Simon & Schuster, 1995).

cure an idea as any in science," he claims—shows conclusively that mind derives from "mindless, purposeless forces," rather than (as theologians had supposed) the other way around.

It would be a mistake to dismiss spokesmen like these as extremists, for—superstars that they are—they do more to shape the public image of science than their reasonable counterparts do. Bryan Appleyard, whom I have already cited, summarizes this second of my points as follows: "Spiritually corrosive, burning away ancient authorities and traditions, science has shown itself unable to coexist with anything."[4]

3.   Theology should expose its enemy for the paper tiger that it actually is.

Stripped of science's prestige, which it battens on but has no right to, scientism hasn't a leg to stand on. The astounding power of science to probe the workings of nature gives it zero credentials for pronouncing on the whole of things, unless one assumes that nature *is* the whole, which begs the question.

Nothing would do more to restore society's respect for theology than a clear recognition of this point, so I shall address it head on with an expanded syllogism.

a.   Science is our sacral mode of knowing.
b.   The crux of science is the controlled experiment.
c.   We can control only what is inferior to us.
d.   Conclusion: Science discloses only our inferiors, from which God is excluded by definition.

No science course or textbook ever informs us of beings that are superior to us in the traits we most prize, including intelligence, wisdom, and compassion; for as far as science can make out, the human species is the noblest thing in existence. And it is clear why science must so conclude, for it cannot see beyond us when it comes to values. To mount a controlled experiment of the sort that gives science authority to speak, one must know what the relevant variables are; and if grander beings than we exist—angels? God?—their variables elude us in the way those relating to human consciousness elude the

---

[4] Bryan Appleyard, *Understanding the Present: Science and the Soul of Modern Man* (New York: Anchor Books, 1994), p. 9.

sniff tests of dogs. Our superiors, if they exist, dance circles around us, not we them.

Obviously, that science cannot speak to God's existence doesn't prove that he does exist. It does, though, leave the question wide open. For as the saying goes, absence of evidence is not evidence of absence.

4. Recognizing that universities are scientistic and hence secular to the core, seminaries should stop tailoring their theologies to academic styles of thought.

At his inauguration a recent president of Johns Hopkins University, Steven Muller, made a pithy statement that speaks tomes. "The trouble with today's university," he said, "is that it is rooted in the scientific method, and the trouble with the scientific method is that it cannot deal with values." Strictly speaking, Muller should have said that it cannot deal with intrinsic and normative values, for it can deal with descriptive and instrumental ones. With that qualification, however, he could have gone on to list five other things it cannot deal with: existential meanings, teleology, qualities as distinct from quantities, invisibles that are not strictly entailed by the behavior of visible objects in the way electromagnetic fields are entailed, and (as many previous points noted) our superiors.

That is the huge omission: virtually our entire lived world. Yet the social (self-styled human) sciences ape the methods of the natural sciences in the hope of approximating their success. In doing so they leave the larger part of our humanity unaccounted for. Robert Bellah tells the story:

> The assumptions underlying mainstream social science are positivism (the assumption that the methods of natural science are the only approach to valid knowledge); reductionism (the tendency to explain the complex in terms of the simple and to find behind complex cultural forms biological, psychological or sociological drives, needs and interests); relativism (the assumption that matters of morality and religion cannot be judged true or false, but simply vary with persons, cultures and societies); and determinism (the tendency to think that human actions are explained in terms of 'variables' that will account for them). The upshot is that what social scien-

tists teach and write undermines all traditional thought and belief.[5]

Even the humanities feel the methodological suction of science's Black Hole. To speak only of religious studies, Marcus Borg reports that "to a large extent, the defining characteristic of biblical scholarship in the modern period is the attempt to understand Scripture without reference to another world because in this period the visible world of space and time is the world we think of as 'real.'"[6]

Arthur Green describes the consequence for Jewish Studies as follows:

> The emergence of Wissenschaft brought forth the bifurcation between the study of Torah as a religious obligation and the forging of scholarly research into a surrogate religion of its own. We are forced to 'bracket' for the purpose of teaching and research our faith in God. The methods by which religion is studied in the University are those of history and philology (in the humanities) and anthropology, psychology, and sociology (in the social sciences). Their impact has been to discount Torah as a divine creation. A scholar who submitted an article to the *Journal of the American Academy of Religion* or the *Journal of Biblical Literature* assuming that Scripture was quite literally the Word of God would be a laughing stock.[7]

In *The Soul of the American University*, George Marsden sums up the situation by saying that in five short generations, American universities have gone from "Protestant establishment to established non-belief." Given this switch, it is ironic to find seminaries routinely importing university styles of thought; but psychologically the move is understandable. Mainline seminaries ring the universities, whose greater prestige causes seminary

---

[5] Robert Bellah, in the *National Institute of Campus Ministries Journal*, Summer 1981, pp. 10-11.
[6] Marcus Borg, "Root Images and the Way We See," in *Fragments of Infinity* (Dorset, U.K. & Lindfield, Australia: Prism/Unity, 1991), p. 38.
[7] Arthur Green, in *Tikkun*, I. 1, 1968.

professors to look up their closest university counterparts and hope that they will consider theology, too, to be a respectable intellectual endeavor.[8]

Proceeding to content, our century has witnessed Heidegger shaping Bultmann and New Testament studies, Whitehead spawning process theology, Darwin inspiring Teilhard and the theology of hope, Marx prompting liberation theology, multiculturalism and Political Correctness powering feminine theology, and the just-mentioned "established non-belief" requiring Death-of-God theology. Influences of these sorts have been so routine that they have turned seminaries into subcultures for breeding new religions, William Abraham of Southern Methodist University argues. As these religions are mostly fathered by the secular university, it is not surprising that they are theologically anemic. Changing the subject (without notice) from cosmology to metaphysics, Bultmann argued (spuriously) that the collapse of the pre-Copernican three-story universe retires ontological hierarchies as well; but is Heidegger's Being (that this left him with) a match for the God of the Bible or the *ens perfectissimum* of medieval theology? If, as existentialists would have us believe, to objectivize is to be inauthentic, what does this do to our thoughts about God as he exists in his own right? Both Whitehead and the theology of hope historicize God and turn him into something that in ways is "not yet"—in this account God did not create time; he is caught in its net. John Cobb says we should "accept without hesitation or embarrassment the distinction between ultimate reality and God,"[9] and Teilhard's notion of Christ as "the term of evolution" upsets God's alpha-omega balance and makes meaning turn on the fate of nature. If science's actual findings required such diminishings we would have to put up with them, but they do not. The influences rise from universities like vapors, beclouding theological vision.

---

[8] George Marsden, *The Soul of the American University* (New York: Oxford University Press, 1994). Page Smith covers much the same ground in his *Killing the Spirit,* (New York: Viking, 1990).

[9] John Cobb, "Can a Christian Be a Buddhist, Too?" *Japanese Religions,* December 1978, p. 11.

I did not include feminine and liberation theologies in the losses I just listed because they have religious as well as academic roots and do good as well as harm. Their objectives are admirable, but their strategies raise serious questions. Thomas Ogden of Drew University thinks that a version of political correctness he calls "ultrafeminist" has vitiated theological institutions,[10] but I will withhold judgment on that and confine myself to what feminism is doing to language. Turning "hierarchy" and "patriarchy" into dirty words seriously affects the religious future.

"Hierarchy" was originally one of the noblest words in language, holding out (as it does etymologically) for power that issues from holiness. The eclectic left redefines the word to mean the exact opposite: oppressive, abusive power. To do so it resolutely closes its eyes to the fact that hierarchies can empower as well as oppress. A loving family with small children is an empowering hierarchy, as is a well run classroom. The paradigm of a benevolent, empowering hierarchy is God's relation to the world: "God became man that man might become God." Without worthy hierarchies we have no one to look up to. We are stripped of empowering role models.

As for "patriarchy," whether there have ever been other than patriarchal societies is unclear; definitions enter, and prehistory remains pretty much prehistory. Even if there have been, however, the enduring historical religions were for the most part patently fashioned by men—God's workings don't figure much in feminist accounts. So if patriarchy is bad, so are its products, the religions it fashioned. Intended or not, this is the message of feminist and liberation theology that falls on public ears which are poorly tuned to nuances and qualifications. Whether the mainline churches can survive this broadside remains to be seen, for beginning with the family, tradition turns on respecting one's elders who have given us life, and historians are reporting that no generation has regarded its heritage as reproachfully as ours

---

[10] Thomas C. Ogden, *Requiem: A Lament in Three Movements*, (Nashville: Abingdon Press, 1995).

does.[11] Some words that Walter Lippman penned a half-century ago echo ominously here.

> Socialization has to be transmitted from the old to the young, and habits and ideas must be maintained as a seamless web of memory among the bearers of the tradition, generation after generation. If this does not happen, community will break down into factional wars and the new generation will be faced with the task of rediscovering, reinventing, and relearning by trial and error most of what it needs. No one generation can do this.[12]

That injustice exists, and probably always has, is not in dispute and gives us our marching orders. The lines of causation, though, are tangled and obscure. We are back with Karl Popper's counsel: it is safer to work for specific immediate objectives than to pour energies into ideologies that presume to understand the complicated forces that went into the making of earlier societies and the way the world works. Such ideologies convince less by logic than by the violent voicing of partially legitimate causes. History does not inspire confidence in their long range effects.

Up to this point I have focused on problems. It's time for the good news: theology's opportunity.

5.   Amidst the bewilderment that almost everyone feels today, theology has the answer people are waiting to hear.

I say this because theology is the custodian of the wisdom traditions of humankind. Not everyone in them is wise. Modern science has retired their cosmologies, and their social blueprints—master/slave and gender relationships, e.g.—need to be reviewed in the light of changed circumstances and our continuing search for injustice. But on the nature of ultimate reality and the way human life can best be comported in its context, there is nothing outside the abiding religions that rivals their truth.

---

[11] For documentation, see Richard M. Weaver, *Visions of Order: The Cultural Crisis of our Time* (Bryn Mawr, Penn.: Intercollegiate Studies Institute, 1964/1995): "I do not find any other period in which men have felt to an equal degree that the past either is uninteresting or is a reproach to them."

[12] Walter Lippmann, *The Public Philosophy,* (Boston: Little, Brown & Co., 1955).

Currently, we are in the best position we have been in for four centuries to recognize this fact. For though scientism is still with us, frontier thinkers now recognize that science cannot provide a worldview and "leaves the problems of life completely untouched," as Wittgenstein pointed out. Seeing this is what, philosophically, has moved us from the modern into the postmodern era, but postmodernism is in no better position to compete with the wisdom traditions because it rejects worldviews in principle. More concerned with justice than with metaphysics—"society is the magic word of our times," George Will reports—postmodernism dismisses metanarratives on grounds that they "totalize," and thereby marginalize minorities.[13] This leaves theology without serious metaphysical rivals. *Carpe diem*; seize the day! Some think that differences among the world's religions make it inappropriate to speak of theology in the singular in the global village, but I find a common conceptual spine underlying them all: the Great Chain of Being.*

My *Forgotten Truth* is devoted to a cross-cultural discussion of that spine, but here I can only mention its pivotal point.[14] There is an alternate reality to the one we normally experience and expand through science. It is momentously better, more powerful and more real than our quotidian world, and the chief reason the mainline churches are losing ground is that scientism and the academy have loosened their grips on it, leaving them with no clear alternatives to the liberal intellectual ethos of our day. They continue to use the word "God," but what is the cash

---

[13] For an elaboration of this point, see my essay, "The Religious Significance of Postmodernism," *Faith and Philosophy*, July 1995.

* In revising the lecture from which this essay derives, it has occurred to me that Professor Sinha may have asked me to talk about the global village because of the pluralism the phrase suggests and the problems pluralism pose for theology. As it happened, however, my thoughts turned instead to scientism because if theologies the world over do not rise to its challenge, the problem of how they should relate to one another may take care of itself of their disappearing from history. Those who want my thoughts on religious pluralism will find them touched on in "Bubble Blown and Lived In: A Theological Autobiography" (*Dialog*, Vol 33, No. 4, pp. 274–279), and presented in greater detail in my *Introduction to Frithjof Schuon, The Transcendent Unity of Religions* (Harper Torchbook, 1975/Quest Books, 1984).

[14] Huston Smith, *Forgotten Truth*, (Harper, San Francisco, 1976/1992).

value of that word when it is injected into a world that is basically vectored by Darwin, Marx, Nietzsche, Freud, and the Big Bang?

That world is too small for the human spirit. To the degree that the mainline churches accept it, their parishioners will go elsewhere. In North America today, this means going to conservative churches (fundamentalist, evangelical, or Pentecostal), to Asian religions, or to New Age enthusiasms, all of which *do* challenge the naturalistic outlook of mainstream intellectuals.

9

Science and Theology: The Unstable Détente

Huston Smith

I. Thesis

Against the prevailing assumption that "the warfare between science and theology" (to resurrect W. E. H. Lecky's phrase) is a thing of the past, I propose to argue that if this is true it can only be because science has won the war. Only an exhausted theology, one about to sink into the sands of science like a spent wave, could fail to sense the enormous tension between its claims and those of a scientific world view.

There is, of course, a sense in which no tension exists or ever has existed. As truth is one and religion and science are both concerned with it, in principle they must be partners. But that is principle only—*de jure,* not *de facto.* For the partnership to work we would need to see clearly the inherent limitations of science and keep them in sharp focus. But we do not see these limitations, largely (I suspect) because we do not want to. Because science augments our power and possessions, we would like to think that it has no cutoff point; that its present limitations are provisional only, and that in time it would break out of them to service our complete selves in the way it now services our bodies. So we encourage it to expand, and count on its doing so. Mostly we want its technological fallout, but we want its theory too. For science* derives from the controlled experiment, and as that is as close to proof as we can get, a scientific world view would be one we could whole-heartedly believe. It would be true.

It happens, however, that a scientific world view is impossible. This does not mean that we are a long way from having such a view, rather that we never will have one—it is impossible in principle, a contradiction in terms. For "world" implies whole and science deals with part, an identifiable part of the whole that can be shown to be part only—most of this paper will be devoted to this showing. Again, it is crucial to see that this is not a temporary limitation but one that is built into science's very nature. To hope for a world view from science is like hoping that increasingly detailed maps of Illinois will eventually produce the ultimate map of the United States.

Three times before I have walked up to this point, approaching it from different directions to try to see precisely where the boundaries of science lie. Here, I propose to tell these sallies together—that the *OED* defines "sally" as "rush of besieged upon besiegers" makes the word poetically exact. But because I shall be riding this issue hard, devoting most of my space to it, I should say why I see the limits of science as at once the most important point we need to be straight on in relating science to technology and concomitantly the one we have yet to see clearly.

It seems to be agreed that a defining feature of modernity is loss of transcendence.[1] The sense of the sacred has declined; phrases like "the death of God" and "eclipse of God" would have been inconceivable in earlier days. No doubt readers will

---

* Unless otherwise qualified, "science" in the English-speaking world has come to denote modern science as epitomized by the natural sciences and, to avoid confusion, should be kept to this meaning. It is in this sense that the term is used in this essay.

[1] "If anything characterizes 'modernity,' it is loss of faith in transcendence, in a reality that encompasses but surpasses our quotidian affairs." From a review of Facing Up to Modernity, by Peter Berger, in *The Chronicle of Higher Education,* 9 January 1978, p. 18.

agree, in addition, that this is a real *loss*; fading of the belief that we live in an ordered universe which is related to other, unseen realms in a total harmony cannot but have serious consequences. That people now believe less in theologies generally is one thing,[2] but we must note too that the content of the theologies they are now offered have been diluted. It has been toned down to fit better with our prevailing, largely secular, mindset.

This last is the most controversial point I shall make, and it may be mistaken though I do not think so. As Section Three will be devoted to it, I hurry on here to ask: If our age *is* theologically on the defensive, what drove it into the corner? Many things, one can assume, but it seems clear—so clear that the point will not be argued here—that its chief assailant has been modern science. Science has spawned an outlook whose chief features are *naturalism* (the view that nothing that lacks a material component exists and, that in what does exist, it is its physical component that has the final say), *evolution* (generalized as the belief that the more derives exhaustively from the less, the higher from the lower), and *progress* (the centering of hope on a this-worldly, historical future). If we match these planks against the platform that issues from revelation, we get the following line-up:

Epistemology:	Science (the scientific method)	Revelation
Ontology:	naturalism	supernaturalism (transcendence)
Efficient cause:	evolution	providence
Final cause:	progress	salvation

Were we mentally capable of keeping the lefthand column in its place there would be no problem, but the triumphs of science have been too impressive to allow this. Method has mushroomed into metaphysics, science into scientism, the latter defined as the drawing of conclusions from science that do not logically follow. I do not charge this against science, nor its votaries whom I regard with a blend of gratitude, affection, and awe; the last thing I wish to do is paint them in the guise of

---

[2] "There is no doubt that in developed societies education has contributed to the decline of religious belief." Edward Norman, *Christianity and the World Order* (New York: Oxford University Press, 1979), p. 6.

white-coated bad guys. Scientism is a mark of our times, one we are all victims of and responsible for: in Descartes' fall, we sinned all. As there is no space here to trace its workings piecemeal, I propose to strike at the root. Through the three demonstrations of science's limitations alluded to, I hope to expose the delusion that our prevailing, predominantly secular outlook is scientific by showing that no inclusive outlook can be such. If this strategy succeeds, it will show that theology need cater to our prevailing styles of thought only if it wishes. Nothing in the way of evidence requires that it do so.

II. The Limits of Science

A. First Demonstration. In *Forgotten Truth: The Primordial Tradition,*[3] I noted that though science is not monolithic, its distinctive way of getting at truth—the scientific method— gives it a defining thrust which can be visualized as follows:

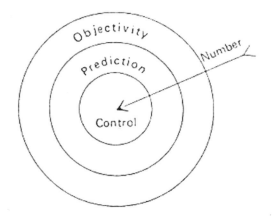

No knowledge deserves to be called scientific unless it is objective in the sense of laying claim to intersubjective agreement, but we move closer to science proper when we discover the truths that enable us to predict, and closer still when we reach

[3] Huston Smith, *Forgotten Truth: The Primordial Tradition* (New York: Harper & Row, 1976).

truths that facilitate control. Each move we make toward the circle's center finds our knowing meshing increasingly with mathematics, numbers being (as we say) the language of science.

The achievements of this probe for truth have been so dazzling that they have blinded us to the fact that they proceed from an extremely restricted kind of knowing. There are four things science cannot verify:

1. Intrinsic and Normative Values

Science can deal with instrumental values, but not intrinsic ones. It can tell us that smoking damages health, but whether health is better than somatic gratification it cannot adjudicate. Again, it can determine what people *do* like, but not what they should like. Opinion polls and market research are sciences, but there cannot be a science of the *summum bonum*.

2. Purposes

Science must concede purposes to human beings, and by inference perhaps to other animals as well, but it must try to explain these in terms of things that originate without purpose; behaviorism is so intuitively improbable that it would not have advanced were it not the most scientific approach to human behavior. To introduce intentions into explanations is anthropomorphic, and anthropomorphic explanations are the opposite of scientific ones. "The cornerstone of scientific method is . . . the *systematic* denial that 'true' knowledge can be got at by interpreting phenomena in terms of final causes—that is to say, of 'purpose'"[4]

3. Ultimate and Existential Meanings

Science is meaningful throughout, but there are two kinds of meaning it cannot interpret. One of these is ultimate meaning (what is the meaning of it all?[5]), while the other type is existential (the kind we have in mind when we say something is meaningful). There is no way science can force the human mind

---

[4] Jacques Monod, *Chance and Necessity* (New York: Random House, 1972), p. 21.
[5] A laser is splendid for cutting; useless for putting things together. Science has something of this character.

to find its discoveries involving; the hearer always has the option to shrug his shoulders and walk away. Unable to deal with these two kinds of meanings, science "fails in the face of all ultimate questions" (Jaspers) and leaves "the problems of life . . . completely untouched" (Wittgenstein). "Only questions which cannot be answered with scientific precision have any real significance" (E.F. Schumacher).

4. Quality

This is basic to the lot, for it is their qualitative components that make values, meanings, and purposes important. Qualities, however, being subjective, refuse to step into even the initial, "objective" ring of science's concentric circles as I have diagrammed them, nor do they follow its arrow of number. Certain qualities (such as colors or sounds) have quantifiable substrates (electro-magnetic waves of varying lengths), but quality itself is unmeasurable. Euphorometers have been attempted, but without success, for two pains do not add up to one that is twice as painful, and half a happiness does not make sense. Science's inability to deal with the qualitatively unmeasurable leaves it dealing with what Lewis Mumford calls a "disqualified universe."

This account of what science cannot investigate is resisted, but not (as far as I have been able to discover) because it is untrue. All that would be required to show that it is untrue would be a counter-example—a single instance in which science has produced precise and provable knowledge concerning a normative value, a final cause, an existential or global meaning, or an intrinsic quality. Considering the importance of these four domains for human life—for three hundred years we have all but held our breath waiting for science to close in on them —the fact that it has made no inroads whatever would seem to be a clear indication that science is not made for their kinds of inquiry.[6] Appeals to the infancy of science only obscure the issue by postponing the question of whether its advances can possibly fill in the lacunae. The answer is no; the change from

---

[6] An issue of the *Scientific American*, 243 (January 1981), confirms this nonprogress with respect to qualities. Its article by Jerry Fodor on "The Mind-Body Problem" espouses functionalism as the most promising current approach to understanding mental states and operations, but concedes that "the functionalist account does not work for mental states that have qualitative content" (122).

classical to relativity physics was momentous, but it did not move physics a whit closer to the untended areas. And we can see why it did not. For science to enter the domains it has thus far eschewed it would have to relax the demands for objectivity, prediction, control, and number from which its power in quantitative domains derives. We are free, of course, to turn science in this new direction if we want to, but we must realize that every step toward humanizing the enterprise will be a step away from the effectiveness it has so far manifested. For to repeat, it is precisely from the narrowness of its approach that the power of science derives. Our choice is between an effective and restricted science, or one that is ample but does not enable us to control the course of events much more than do art, religion, or psychotherapy. What is not possible is to have it both ways.

B. Second demonstration. Whereas the preceding demonstration sought to show how barren a scientific world view would have to be, disclosing perhaps as much of reality as an X-ray negative discloses of a human self, this second one[7] notes that it would also be stunted—or better, truncated. It would reveal about as much of the world as we would see if we were standing before a window whose shade was almost completely drawn. The ground outside the window would be visible, but trees and birds and clouds and mountains would be obscured.

The reasoning behind that statement runs as follows:

World views arise from epistemologies which in turn are generated by the motivations that control them. In the seventeenth century, Europe hit upon an epistemology (empiricism, the scientific method[8]) that augmented its control dramatically—over nature to start with, but who knew where such control might eventually reach? This increase in power pleased us to the point that we gave this way of knowing right of way. And with that move the die was cast with respect to a world view. Empiricism proceeds through sense knowledge, and that which connects with our sense is matter. I do not say that the world view this epistemology has generated is materialism (the view

---

[7] Anticipated in my "Excluded Knowledge: A Critique of the Modern Western Mind Set," *Teachers College Record* 80 (February 1979) and worked out in detail in "Beyond the Modern Western Mindset, " ibid., (May 1981).

[8] I am not overlooking the rational, mathematical component in science, but the crucial role of the controlled experiment gives empiricism the edge.

that nothing but matter exists), for our thoughts and feelings are, on the one hand, too conspicuous to be denied, and on the other, too different from what we experience matter to be, to be reduced to it. It is safer to dub our world view naturalism, defining this (see Section One) as the view (a) that nothing that lacks a material component exists, and (b) that in what does exist the physical component has the final say. That at the level of quantum mechanics this component seems to be "dematerializing" has not shaken our naturalism because matter (however we define it, however ghostly it may seem) remains what we can get our hands on and control. The problem lies deeper than willfulness—wanting to have our way with nature—for even our search for disinterested truth is drawn to naturalism and empiricism. Control includes, importantly, the controlled experiment, and this (more than any other form of validation) inspires confidence.

Now comes the point, the kind of world (view) the will to control can generate. Again let me characterize it negatively. *An epistemology that aims relentlessly at control rules out the possibility of transcendence in principle.*[9] By transcendence I mean something superior to us by every measure of value we know and some that elude us. To expect a transcendental object to appear on a viewing screen wired by an epistemology that is set for control would be tantamount to expecting the melody as well as the lyrics of a song to issue from a printout typewriter. We can "put nature to the rack," as Bacon advised, because it is our inferior; possessing (in the parts we can get at, at least) neither mind nor freedom, these parts can be pushed around. But if things superior to us exist—extraterrestrial intelligences superior to our own? Angels? God?—these are not going to fit into our controlled experiments.[10] It is they who dance circles around us, not we them.

---

[9] That modern epistemology so aims was documented in "Excluded Knowledge" (see footnote 7). I shall not reproduce the evidence I there assembled, it will be enough to repeat Ernest Gellner's summary verdict in his *Legitimation of Belief:* "We have become habituated to and dependent on effective knowledge [read: knowledge that enables us to control], and have bound ourselves to this kind of genuine . . . What . . . this . . . compulsion . . . amounts to is in the end simple: if there is to be effective knowledge or explanation at all, it must [pass the test of empiricism and mechanism], for any other kind of 'explanation' . . . is *ipso facto* powerless" (London: Cambridge University Press, 1974), pp. 206-207.

Naturalism's exclusion of things superior to nature combines with its discovery that within nature the superior comes after the inferior, and (to a yet undetermined extent) can be controlled via its inferior components, leaves it no option regarding etiology. Accounting must proceed from inferior to superior, from less to more. Chronologically and developmentally the more comes after the less; causally it comes out of the less, the only other determining principle allowed being chance.[11] In biology (with Darwin) higher forms come after and out of the lower; in sociology (with Marx) the classless society comes after and out of class struggle; in psychology (with Freud) the rational ego comes after and out of the irrational id. Even when the higher has appeared, the thrust is to understand and interpret its workings in terms of the lower. The name for this mode of explanation is, of course, reductionism, and the growth of the scientific world view can be correlated with its advance. For Newton, stars become machines. For Descartes, animals were machines. For Hobbes, society is a machine. For Le Mettrie, the human body is a machine. For Pavlov and Skinner, human behavior is mechanical.

C. Third demonstration. If the preceding demonstration showed that a scientific world view cannot rise above ourselves in the sense of providing a place for anything that is superior to us, this final check on its limitations shows that it cannot even accommodate ourselves. For scientific knowledge is theoretical whereas the bulk of human understanding is practical.[12] Practical understanding cannot be accommodated to theoretical knowledge.

Scientific knowledge is theoretical in that it consists of identifiable elements that are systematically related, and this differentiates it sharply from practical knowing—knowing how to

[10] Human beings must be kept in the dark if they are to be subjects for controlled experiments in regions where they are free. But transcendental subjects, if they exist, cannot be kept in the dark. By definition they know more than we do.

[11] William Pollard has spotted this appeal to chance as the Achilles' heel of scientific reductionism. It being a point at which things happen for which science has no explanation, it is a promising point at which to look for traces of providence. See his *Chance of Providence* (New York: Charles Scribner's Sons, 1958), and "Critique of Jacques Monod's Chance and Necessity," *Soundings* 53 (Winter 1973): pp. 433–445.

ride a bicycle, say, or how to swim. In these latter cases our knowledge proceeds in almost total oblivion of the components involved—muscles, nerves, cells, and the like—and their coordinations. It is a "knowing how," rather than a "knowing that."

Another way to put the difference is to say that theoretical knowledge is context-free whereas practical understanding is not. Once we consciously identify something our minds can isolate it from its context. In looking at a vase I cannot separate my sensation of blue from the vase, but once my mind tells me that the vase *is* blue, though the copula purports to join blueness to vase, in a far more fateful way it disjoins the two. For I can now think blueness without vase and this frees me to move it around my conceptual world at will. In abstracting—extracting—blueness from vase, cognition makes it context-free.

Science capitalizes on this freedom from context and tries to show us a contextless world, a view that is not affected by even the fact that it derives from our human angle of vision. And when it goes on to try to understand human beings (through the social sciences) this goal continues. It searches for behavior-ingredients that are invariant—the same regardless of their context—and the lawful relations those exhibit. The theories that summarize these relations currently take the form of formal models in which the facts are context-free, elements, or attributes, or features, or information bits, and the model is a computer program or flow chart showing how such elements are combined to produce complex individual or social behavior.

That these models, be they in structuralist anthropology, cognitive psychology, or decision analysis, have succeeded no better than their predecessors in enabling their practitioners to predict practical behavior, or to develop a unified theory of man that compares in any way to the unified view of nature that undergirds the physical sciences, should not surprise us. We should expect this failure for, to return to the nub of this third

---

[12] Martin Heidegger appears to have been the first to work out this difference clearly. My own account of it, which I only summarize here, appears in my "Four Cultures," *The Syracuse Scholar* 1 (April 1981), but that account is itself heavily indebted to Hubert Dreyfus's more comprehensive treatment of the matter in his "Holism and Hermeneutics," *The Review of Metaphysics* 34 (September 1980).

demonstration, most human knowledge is not theoretical but practical, and even theoretical knowledge rides on a practical base. Practical knowing can no more be separated from its context (to become available to abstract theory) than knowing how to swim can be separated from water. Through cultivated body-responses, the "tentacles" of our swimming skill grip the physical world like a root-system, and in social skills it is the same, the difference being only that here the context is a background of shared beliefs and practices which we internalize through imitation. Social skills, such as how far to stand from a conversational partner depending on age, sex, status, and purpose, embody a whole cultural interpretation of what it means to be human, what a material object is, and (more generally) what counts as real. Heidegger, Merleau-Ponty, and Wittgenstein have shown this convincingly. I believe that this inherited background of practices can never be spelled out in a theory to be fed into a computer. This is so, first, because it is so pervasive that we cannot stand outside it to make it an object of analysis; but even more because in the last resort it is not composed of cognitive features such as beliefs and assumptions at all, but rather of habits and customs, the sort of subtle skills which we exhibit in our everyday interaction with things and people—what Michel Foucault calls micro-practices. No one has the slightest idea how to construct formal rules for the skills involved in swimming or speaking a language, let alone those embodying our understanding of what it means to be a human being and live a human life.

III. Theological Compromise?

That was a long section, so let me reiterate its point. Believing that the decline in our sense of transcendence is a loss, and that the chief reason for the decline has been the rise of a rival outlook presumed to be scientific, it is important to show that the supposition is mistaken. Lacking space in this essay to show point by point where the error enters, I am critiquing the notion of a "scientific world view" itself; I have presented three lines of argument that converge in the conclusion that there can be no such thing. When we find someone writing that "science is the measure of all things, of what is that it is, and of what is not that it is not,"[13] we can know automatically that scientism, not science, is speaking.

But now comes the touchy part. Of the five postures Richard Niebuhr showed the church to have assumed toward culture in the course of its history—against it, of (or with) it, above it, paradoxical toward it, and with design to transform it[14]—we are clearly in a "with culture" phase. Vatican II formalized this for Roman Catholicism and Bultmann's victory over Barth is a weathervane for Protestantism. But if our culture is riddled with scientism—the problem being, as Victor Frankl puts it, not that the scientists are specializing, but that the specialists are generalizing—in being *with* culture, the church runs the danger of scientific rub-off.

There is no way to insure against this danger, but the guidelines, at least, seem clear. It goes without saying that theologians should respect the proven findings of science, and can continue to affirm as they have, in the past two decades especially, that:

> Scientists are no less blessed with *human virtues* than the rest of us. Their work does not pull against their idealism, good will, and natural piety (Harold Schelling, William Pollard, Ian Barbour).
>
> Their *intellectual virtues* are not mechanical—limited to logic and linear thinking. Great science requires as much imagination, inspiration, and "art" as any other creative endeavor (Abraham Maslow, Michael Polanyi).
>
> Equally, as institution, science is as *fallible* as other social efforts. False starts, blind alleys, in-house vendettas and outright mistakes plague it as much as they do the church (Thomas Kuhn, Watson's *The Double Helix,* and again Polanyi).

The commonalties, however, should not be allowed to obscure the distinctiveness of scientific knowing, and the limited character of the conclusions that can issue from that distinctiveness.

---

[13] Wilfred Sellers, *Science, Perception, and Reality* (New York: Humanities Press, 1963), p. 173.

[14] Richard Niebuhr, *Christ and Culture* (New York: Harper & Row, 1956).

The first of these two dividing, rather than reconciling, tasks is currently complicated by a move within the philosophy of science itself that slurs the difference between scientific and other ways of knowing. Because at advanced levels the components of science are not tested against experience one by one but only as a whole via theories, it is now generally accepted that scientific facts are theory laden. In verifying a theory we move in a circle from hypothesis to data, data to hypothesis, without ever encountering any bare facts which could call the whole theory into question. From this now-recognized holistic character of science—the point, to repeat, that its facts, like most others, have to be "interpreted" in the light of the systems in which they appear[15]— this new thrust concludes that science does not differ in kind from other self-contained systems of thought such as common sense, or even witchcraft. Paul Feyerabend's *Against Method* pushes this claim to anarchist extremes, but its basic point, which can be tracked back to Pierre Duhem in the last century, appears in varying degrees in the writing of N.R. Hanson, Willard Quine, and Richard Rorty.

We can agree that science is holistic. However, the theoretical character of its holism, which gestalts explicitly identified, context-free components, still differentiates it from other kinds of holism. This was the burden of the third demonstration in the preceding section. The difference must be kept in mind. For if we lose sight of the distinctive, restricted way science goes about knowledge we will think that its findings harbor more implications for theology than they logically can.

As these implications slope toward naturalism, evolution[16] and progress, if we insist on drawing them—or, what is more

---

[15] It is interesting to find the word "hermeneutics," and names like Heidegger and Hans-Georg Gadamer, now surfacing in the philosophy of science.

[16] I use the word to refer not to the proven facts of biology and the fossil record, but to the theory (assumed to be established by those facts) which claims that natural selection working on chance mutations adequately accounts for how we got here. No major theologian I know is currently challenging this doctrine—"the most influential teaching of the modern age," as E. F. Schumacher calls it—leaving it to Billy Graham and fundamentalist creationists on the one hand, and concerned laymen like Schumacher himself and secularists like Arthur Koestler on the other, to expose this "crumbling citadel," as Koestler calls it. See Arthur Koestler, *Janus: A Summing Up* (New York: Vintage Books, 1979), pp. 165-192; E. F. Schumacher, *A Guide for the Perplexed* (New York: Harper & Row, 1977), pp. 111-116; and my own *Forgotten Truth*, pp. 126-142.

common, if we lower our guard, in which case they are sure to enter undetected—theology will suffer. I think I see this happening. I say this tentatively. Kennett Roshi of Mount Shasta Zen Abbey once remarked that he was working on a new *ko'an*, "I could be wrong," and I would like to have that apply to the balance of this section.

So numerous are the theological innovations of modernity that one wonders if, at some unconscious level, they may not be fed by the assumption that as scientific knowledge is cumulative, all knowledge should be.[17] Be that as it may, when I scan the content of these innovations, what I mostly see is loss—loss that has been suffered, not from the proven facts of science, but from vapors that rise from them like steam, obscuring our sight. (1) Personalism concludes that we must relieve God of either his omnipotence or his goodness. (2) Bultmann's demythologizing rides the dismantling of pre-Copernican pictures of the physical universe to dismantle in fact the Great Chain of Being. If only because of what Heidegger (from whom Bultmann draws) will not permit us to *say*, on pain of inauthentic objectivizing, I do not see his Being as a match for either the Living God of the Bible or the *Ens perfectissimum* of medieval theology. (3) The Theology of Hope historicizes Christian expectations and introduces development into God, who in ways is "not yet." (4) Teilhard de Chardin's notion of Christ as "the Term of evolution" upsets his Alpha/Omega balance and makes meaning turn on the fate of nature.

(5) As I was myself weaned on Process Theology, I shall give it three paragraphs, beginning with loss. It deprives God of ultimacy, reserving that for three inexplicable givens: creativity, eternal objects, and the structure of actual occasions.[18] It rules

---

[17] For my part, I find it is more likely that our forefathers—less harried by life's accelerated pace, less deluged and distracted by avalanches of information, less insulated from illness, death, and nature generally—had the theological edge. I find what Anselm said of St. Augustine, that he understood Moses far better than we can, altogether plausible.

[18] "The direction is to accept without hesitation or embarrassment the distinction between ultimate reality and God, and to recognize that the God of the Bible . . . is a manifestation of ultimate reality—not the name of that reality" (John Cobb, "Can a Christian Be a Buddhist, Too?" *Japanese Religion* [December 1978]: 11).

out the possibility of a concrete, timeless perfection; only abstract entities (eternal objects) are eternal. And it replaces subjective human immorality with an objective version in which we are remembered by God; the traditional teaching that we must all one day awaken from life's dream into other dimensions in which the lie shrivels, the fiction is destroyed, and all deceptions are swept away, is done away with. On what authority, save the naturalism to which Process Theology is beholden? We can at least be clear, this essay has argued, that science doesn't force that naturalism on us.

Process theologians themselves, of course, do not see these revisions as losses, for to them classical theism is incoherent. Had their notion of coherence ruled at Nicea and Chalcedon, the Creeds could not have come down to save us as they have. Or to approach the point from a contemporary angle, is there any "incoherence" in classical theism—many are charged—that does not have its analogy in the paradoxes of quantum mechanics, and cannot, with deep discernment, be brought under Niels Bohr's claim that, whereas the opposite of a small truth is false, the opposite of a great truth is another great truth?

I was not myself conscious of the loss in this "up-dated"[19] Christianity until, seeking to expand my horizons through the study of world religions, I came (first) on the Vedanta, whereupon I found that my interest in Process Theology dropped markedly, and with it my interest in Christianity until I discovered that its classical expressions include everything of importance I had discovered in the Upanishads. Why, then, is this loss—Process Theology—being inflicted on Christians? (That is a strong charge. I keep repeating to myself, like the Jesus Prayer, "I could be wrong, I could be wrong!") Because—I answer from introspection, it being a part of my former self that I am trying to understand—theologians saw in Whitehead the prospect of reconciling religion with modern science. This is a chancy move. As Jeremy Bernstein observed in his review of Fritjiof Capra's *The Tao of Physics,* "to hitch a religious philosophy to a contemporary

---

[19] Schubert Ogden claims that Process Theology has achieved "something like a Heideggerian 'dismantling' (Destruktion) of the history of philosophical theology," *The Reality of God* (New York: Harper & Row, 1963), p. 48.

science is a sure route to its obsolescence, [for] the science of the present will look as antiquated to our successors as much of the nineteenth-century science looks to us now."[20]

Whitehead's philosophy of organism, focusing on its doctrine of prehensions, was modeled on, and thereby powered by, the most sophisticated science of its day; it followed carefully Einstein's prescription, required by his relativity theory, that as no coherent concept of an independently existent particle is possible, reality should be regarded as constituted of fields whose localized pulses do not end abruptly but spread to arbitrarily large distances with decreasing force. As this banished the spectre of clockwork mechanism, which for three hundred years had haunted theology with its view of the world as constituted of entities which are outside of each other in the sense that they exist independently in different regions of space (and time) and interact through forces that do not bring about any changes in their essential natures, it was a thrilling synthesis—I speak for myself; I felt it. But science keeps moving, and it now appears that the unified field theory Einstein had hoped for is not going to happen short of another paradigm change, which would carry us beyond Einstein and Bohr, and therefore beyond Whitehead. Relativity and quantum theory proceed for such opposite premises that it seems impossible for either to accommodate the other.[21] "What is probably needed," David Bohm writes,

> is a qualitative new theory, from which both relativity and quantum theory are to be derived as abstractions . . . The best place to begin is with what they have basically in common. This is undivided wholeness. Though each comes to such wholeness in a different way, it is clear that it is this to which they are both fundamentally pointing.[22]

---

[20] Jeremy Bernstein, review of *The Tao of Physics,* by Fritjof Capra, in *The American Scholar* 48 (Winter 1978-1979): 8.

[21] Relativity theory requires continuity, strict causality, and locality. Quantum theory requires non-continuity, non-causality, and non-locality.

[22] David Bohm, *Wholeness and the Implicate Order* (London: Routledge & Kegan Paul, 1980), p. 176.

Undivided wholeness sounds more like God's simplicity (in its technical medieval sense) than like the time-involved creativity and discrete eternal objects Whitehead took for ultimates.

IV. Science as Symbol

It is possible that the preceding section was squandered in what Freud called "the narcissism of small differences," though I do not think so. In any case, although I have exhausted the space allotted me, I do not want to end without noting that there is another side to the science/theology question, one that is very different and filled with possibilities that counter the pitfalls I have dwelt on here. If, instead of rummaging through science for direct, literal clues to the nature of reality, we could outgrow this fundamentalism and read science allegorically, we would find sermons in cloud chambers. That the deeper science advances into nature the more integrated it finds it[23] lends resonance to (though it does not prove) the faith-claim that the same holds for being as a whole: God, who is all in all, is likewise One. Or again, that science has found reality in its physical aspect to be incomparably more majestic and awesome than we had supposed[24] suggests—it does not prove—that if we could see the full picture we would find its qualitative depths to be as much beyond what we normally suppose as science has shown its quantitative ones to be.[25]

And remember, we are speaking of lightyears.

---

[23] Matter and energy are one. Time and space are one, time being space's fourth dimension. Space and gravity are one: the latter is simply space's curvature. And in the end, matter and its space-time field are one, matter being a local deformation of the spatio-temporal medium.

[24] "No literary imagination could have invented a story one-hundredth part as fantastic as the sober facts that [science has] unearthed" (Fred Hoyle, *The Nature of the Universe* [New York: New American Library, 1950], p. 128).

[25] Chapter Five of my *Forgotten Truth* is devoted to the symbolic power latent in our science today.

10

Notes for an Empirical Theology

James A. Carpenter

These notes are discursive, with no attempt to assess the
features of religious life and thought in anything more than a
fragmentary way, or to subject any one of them to an individual
and isolated analysis. They might better be called musings than
notes, musings on matters that others have mused on more fully
and fruitfully.[1] I have set them down in my own way because I
felt impelled to do so.

My principal concern is with some basic commonalities of
experience, things we know and feel that have about them some
measure of empirical verification, together with their interrela-
tion and bearing on religious understanding. The term empirical
as used here is more inclusive than its traditional grounding in
knowledge available through the five senses. While remaining

---

[1] See Alfred North Whitehead, *Modes of Thought* (New York: Macmillian, 1938),
p. 219; *Adventures of Ideas* (New York: Macmillian, 1922), p. 226, and especially
Process and Reality (New York: Macmillian: 1929), p. 248 ff. Whitehead develops
his view of emotion in various places but with great consistency. It entails that
the whole complexity of experience is either derived or modified from the
direct feeling of emotion from the body. But in the case of human beings,
emotion is never bare emotion; it is emotion interpreted, integrated and
transformed into higher categories of feeling.

sensational—all knowledge is sensational in that it is accessible only through sensate functions—empiricism includes emotion or feeling as developed in Whitehead's process thought, as that which is primordial in all experience, the underbelly of the mind.[2]

Within the sphere of emotion and feeling, certain experiences occur that have the quality of "senses," the sense of purpose, hope, value, beauty and freedom, which is foundational to them all. To them must be added yet another, the sense of evil. These senses are as empirical as sight and hearing. Though perhaps more intractable, they are ineluctably experienced, deeply felt realities.

To claim that the purpose we experience in our daily lives has no purpose beyond itself is already to have purposed that this is the case. We are purposeful beings—full of purpose—and we do nothing—except actions resulting from bodily mechanisms—without purposing it. Purpose is integral to knowledge: we know what we have purposed to know within the vast possibilities open to us. We must select some few, using the freedom we sense and know that we have. Purpose is among the most crucial givens of our activity and thought.

It is similarly so with value. We purpose that we have value. The deconstructionist values the deconstruction of normative values, sometimes with the purpose of reconstructing them, showing their fragility or doing away with them. The criminal mind values criminality, its daring and seductive thrill, together with whatever presumed good that might derive from it. To value is a human propensity that amounts to a sense as palpable as touch, and almost as immediate.

To hope is another "sense," deeply connected with the sense of purpose and also with the sense of freedom. To hope is to look toward an accomplishment, whether a change of fortune,

---

[2] Our freedom has been subjected to a lot of bad raps in recent times, perhaps chief among them is the notion that freedom is simply a conditioned reflex, the outcome of the impact of neurons upon each other. While the impact of neurons is no doubt at work, there must be a little something more involved. One is after all free to hold this reduction of freedom or free to hold another view thought to be more in keeping with the empirical evidence of the experience of freedom.

of feeling or of change in social ills. Hope can be conservative as well as prospective, as hope for a return of health or a past remembered well. But all hope involves purpose of some kind: to improve the conditions of life, remove obstacles to gain, or to best a rival, to name a few. And all hope involves value. Equally it involves freedom to select the value entertained.

The sense of beauty is somewhat less amenable to description, for beauty in a fundamental way is in the eye of the beholder. A rococo palace may be beautiful to its inhabitants but sheerly vulgar for those of more temperate tastes. *De gustibus non est disputadem* is an adage of wide application but there is something to be said beyond it. A look into the issue of order might help us find it, for order is one ingredient at least of beauty. A manicured lawn is no more ordered than a dirt yard kept carefully swept. A musical composition of Mozart, even at its most playful, is no less ordered than a meticulously constructed mathematical theory. All have order and order is at the basis of their beauty. Of course there is a certain beauty in disorder and disorganization, as in a disorganized person and that person's consequent activity. Disorganization is a defining characteristic of the person, which itself may be said to constitute a certain order, or at least a personal trait that might render that person interesting and charming, and perhaps alarming. However this may be, disorganized people tend to long for ordered lives. Many of them engage others to help them toward order, all the way from storage place organizers and interior decorators to plastic surgeons and psychiatrists.

There may not be a sense of order within us but I suspect there is something very close thereto, and if order, then beauty in its entertainment or inclusion of order. The sense of order like all other senses can be, and not unseldom is, misused. Examples spring to mind readily: the imposition of Teutonic order on those more mediterraneanly inclined, strictures of the religious right threatening those of more liberality of mind and the imposition of Soviet style principles on the artistic community. But withal order is an urgent matter for us. It will not do to speak of disorder as the real arena of life. If disorder were all we had, we should not speak of order. More fundamentally, we

have a world because there is order, and order because we have
a world (Whitehead).

The world is no doubt partly of our own making and
therefore relative to us, but the objectively real world is that
upon which we erect our sciences, philosophies and religions,
not only to combat the chaotic experiences we have of it but to
express our experiences of its ordered life and beauty. While the
threat of chaos is ever real, and not infrequently erupts in nature
and in personal and social life, order persists in interrelated
processes everywhere, not least in our own DNA structure.

Perhaps that is as good a point as any to speak of the function
of science or the sciences in a theology that essays to be empirical.
To begin, Whitehead observed that the sciences are refined
extensions of our senses. Their experimental tools take us beyond
our unaided senses and enable us to describe the interrelationship
of many actualities of the world more carefully and completely.
Against this view, Nicholas Wade has claimed that science is a
rational process in a largely irrational world.[3] Are rational
processes impositions upon the world? To some extent no doubt,
as conceded above. But do not these rational processes also
discern the "rationality" of the world in recognizable patterns
everywhere, processes that endure amidst change, upon which
the processes of the mind depend and without which they would
not exist? Is DNA a mental imposition on nature or rather a
discovery of an ordered process of nature which the mind
describes by means of rational processes? These questions beg a
rational decision based upon the available evidence. A whine
that the world is largely irrational flies in the face of much
evidence to the contrary and is itself a mighty abstraction.

It is certainly true, as Wade holds, echoing a common
conviction, that science as a rational process generates knowledge
of intrinsic value that binds together all races and cultures. But
again, does it generate values *ex nihilo*, apart from values that
pre-existed science for millions of years, waiting to be grasped

---

[3] In an otherwise breezily entertaining and informative article, "Learning
Disabled," *New York Times Magazine*, July 23, 1955, which concerns the
importance of teaching science in the lower schools, Wade is completely
convincing about this.

and named by us? At the most elemental level, there is the nutritional chain, without which there would be no knower to know. The human mind with its rational processes is not an isolate; it is interconnected with all else. The inventiveness of nature itself lies behind and conditions all the inventiveness of the sciences.

The scientific establishment more often than not speaks of itself as a separate enclave from all other human activities. The thing missed or dismissed is that the scientific bent is a dimension of humanity as such, at a prodigiously low level in most people perhaps, but nevertheless present and operative. In some few this bent rises to great feats of discovery and speculative theory, with multiple discoveries issuing from such theory. This would scarcely be possible, however, unless the drive toward science and scientific understanding were not an aspect of being human, something given to all of us, though again in extraordinarily different degrees and practical effectiveness.

It is often assumed too that the scientific enterprise is immune from the foibles and fallacies of other human concerns. This notion is being steadily eroded by reports of dishonesty, pettiness and thievery by practitioners in the scientific community. Most scientists, however, continue to be dedicated and, so far as may be, truthful. But modern science is a relatively young enterprise and is not as corrupted as more ancient ones. It is, we can only suppose, just as corruptible as the others. Time will tell but we may say now, on the basis of historical experience, that any endeavor to exempt itself from corruptibility is specious idealism. As a human effort it shares the ambiguity of all such efforts. Its vaunted purity is a myth or, better perhaps, a dogma, spawned through self-congratulation, hubris and its relative success. It is similarily so with religion

These observations are not meant to dampen the new rapprochement between science and religion and other human endeavors. Far from it. Still we cannot accept the scientific community's evaluation of itself any more than it accepts the self-evaluation of the religious and artistic communities. Its self-evaluation must be as critically assessed as it assesses others. If not, no real dialogue will be possible between them.

Science is important beyond estimation. The knowledge it affords makes for a great implementation of value. One such value, and a prime value at that, pertains to the sense of beauty. "What a beautiful theory" is a common cry of many scientists. Although ingredient to science, such cry is found in the whole spread of human experience. Scientific practitioners and theorists share it with the rest of us, for the joy of discovery is essentially human.

No mention of the sense of truth has been made directly. Yet the truth is that science, religion and art all strive toward the truth. Truth is purposed, hoped for, valued and evaluated out of freedom.

The role of science in empirical theology concerns the matter of attitude more than anything else, of openness to the scientific community and its deliverances. Not that scientific proclamations or "assured" results are to be taken as in any sense final or even approximate, but that the cumulative discoveries of science are always and everywhere to be taken into serious account. Not that all of us can comprehend the arcane language in which many of its dictums are cast, or even the dictum itself. But some of us can and these, though perhaps few, can render them relatively clear to the rest of us.

There can be no question but that science is a dominant influence of our time. But however dominant it is, other influences are dominating as well, commercialism for instance. The great shrine being built in Thailand to house Buddha's alleged tooth raises a further case in point. Thousands and thousands of people are consumed with fervor for the shrine, an empirical fact that cannot be dismissed as of no consequence whatever. While crass and questionable in the extreme (have no absurdities been promulgated under the banner of science?), it raises the issue of religion, of Buddhism in its world-wide impact, of Hinduism and Islam, of Judaism and Christianity in their varied and profound influence on the historical past, the present and almost certainly the future. True that religion must be placed under the sharpest scrutiny, its deep ambiguities called into account, the evils it has perpetuated immemorially acknowledged and the evils it is likely to bring in the future surmised; it is also and equally true that the purpose, hope, value, beauty and, yes, freedom it has engendered, the activity of moral and spiritual development it has inspired in untold individuals and whole societies must be taken into account also as plain empirical fact. Not to do so is to ignore the facts, at least half of them. So to whatever the degree the provenance of science has as an empirical theology, religious experience and religious communities stand as its basis.

There is quite probably a good deal of truth in the view that Western science is grounded upon Western religion, indeed most probable that it might not have arisen apart from the background and agency of biblical religion. However great the influence of the Chinese, the Enlightenment that emerged out of the late Middle Ages, the recovery of the legacy from the Greeks, the discovery of that of Islam and the chance and circumstances doubtlessly involved, nothing can obviate the interconnectedness of the rise of modern science with the Judeo-Christian-Islamic traditions of faith.

Like religion, science not only goes beyond the five senses, immensely so, it also deepens emotion, enlarges purpose, furthers hope and intensifies value and freedom. Science might be described as disciplined emotion, emotional response in confrontation with the mystery of the universe and a correlative yearning to investigate it, to render it intelligible and to secure the means for doing so. And after the intervening intellectual work and grinding attention to detail, there comes with successful result and exultant Hallelujah (no better expression has been found) an emotion of satisfaction and completion, however relative the result might prove to be. Such an emotion is hardly foreign to religion, though arrived at through somewhat different means.

As a human enterprise, science employs human capacities common to all of us.[4] Among the chief of these capacities is imagination. Without imaginative leaps of large scope, science could not proceed. The "shaping power" of the imagination

[4] Of the discussions of this matter, Bernard Lonergan, *Method in Theology* (New York: Herder and Herder, 1972), is among the best. See the first chapter especially, though many references to the subject are entered throughout.

(Coleridge) operates as surely and deeply in science as in poetry and religion. And all three share the capacity of being inspired and open to "revelation," whether by God, nature, the hidden recesses of the human mind itself, community pursuits and interests, or all of these forces in compounded impact. Science is a most spiritual enterprise. It exercises and expresses the human spirit as truly as religion and art, differing only in purpose and desired result. "Spirituality" is not an enclave indwelt solely by religious people. It pertains to all that is essentially human in endeavor and range (Tillich).[5]

Enough has been said to suggest the relation of science and religion and how deeply interfused they are. We have now to turn to the issue of issues, that of God. For my part the thing that most heavily redounds on my consciousness, and no doubt on my subconsciousness as well, is creative energy, immense and sprawled out everywhere. It is with these creative processes, local and cosmic and their constant interaction, where empirical theology best begins. The theology frequently said to begin with the message and ministry of Jesus does not in actuality or even scripturally begin here. The message and ministry of Jesus point beyond themselves to the God of Israel, Creator and Redeemer, the Holy One, in whom he put his trust. Jesus' message and ministry could have no ground or issue apart from this. Jesus mediates, focuses, intensifies and furthers his religious inheritance. He does not create it, he receives it, however remarkably creative his own life and work proved to be. The tradition has tended to separate creation and redemption, almost assigning them to different realms and to attend to redemption principally, having little and sometimes no regard for creation.[6] An empirical

---

[5] Paul Tillich, *Systematic Theology, III* (Chicago: University Of Chicago Press, 1963), pp. 21–30, has given us a search treatment of the dimension of the spirit of human life. I have found none better for brevity and scope.

[6] A notable example is Wilhelm Hermann, *The Communion of the Christian with God* (London: Williams and Norgate, 1903), p. 20, who asserts that we can no longer hope to find God by seeking him in nature: "We find God in nothing but Christ." A more modern statement of the same point of view is Alexander McKelway, *The Systematic Theology of Paul Tillich* (New York: Dell, 1964), p. 96: "Christian theology bases its knowledge of God entirely on his self-revelation in Jesus Christ." Instances are legion.

theology understands redemptive processes as aspects of the creative processes that are universally operative. Exclusive emphasis on redemption isolates religion from the world and renders it incapable of conversing with the world in its manifold interests and concerns. A greater concern with creation would help to remedy this situation, making dialogue with science, the arts and other human concerns more fecund.

Whitehead has observed that God has "secular functions" that are not of immediate interest to religious communities. One of these functions, crucial and all-encompassing in creation, might be described as the mathematical dimension of the world and within the divine life. It is of such magnitude that we might well infer that whatever God is, God is a supreme mathematician. The structures and processes of the world seem to indicate that this might well be so. Almost everything that we know and experience lends itself to mathematical interpretation. Numbers pertain to human activity as nothing else, from pagination in a book, measurements for a recipe, from the speed of light to the designation of God as one. The mathematical bent in us might be taken as a signal feature of the divine image in us, as emblematic, say, of the love of God in creative outreach. The Deists were not altogether wrongheaded. Through them the mathematical aspect of the world and, by inference, of God found firm ground in theology. The Romantic reaction did not erase it, though obscuring it by stressing strands of the tradition that were of more immediate religious interest. Some Romantics, however, strove to unify the two. Coleridge for example saw the universe as "an alphabet for infant minds," as the signature of God, at one with the biblical tradition and not against it.[7]

Theology today needs to attend to the "secular functions" of God energetically and focally. Empirical theology can be an agent in the endeavor. While this is so, theology needs to concern itself also and equally with the empirical realities of religious experience more than it has been wont to do.

---

[7] Samuel Taylor Coleridge, in *Notes on Henry More*, remarks that, "Any scheme of Christianity which does not arise out of, and shoot its beams downwards into the schemes of nature, but stands aloof as an insulated afterthought, must be false or distorted in all its particulars." See W.C.T. Shedd, ed., *The Complete Works of Samuel Taylor Coleridge* (New York: Harper), V, p. 113.

The religious impulse, like the scientific impulse, is as empirically verifiable an experience as any feature of the human life can be. The distinction between the two impulses is more indistinct than is often supposed. Both can be described as a sense or yearning toward the infinite, whether expressed in forms of worship or the urge toward an ever increasing knowledge of universal reality. The drive toward dogma in religious communities is not dissimilar to the drive toward finality of explanation in the scientific community. Although finality ever eludes both of them, each is in touch in some fundamental way with that which lies beyond them infinitely and to which they are intimately related.

An empirical reality that perhaps derives initially from the religious and philosophical communities but reaches far beyond them today into all communities is the cry for justice. All of us want it for ourselves and ever anon we want it for others less able to control their situation in life than we. Although in our own time the economic community extends enormous pressure on the multitudes to still the cry for justice, to render them helpless pawns in the game of superior kings and queens, few can completely escape from the feeling that things are not right with us, are not what they should be. This disquiet is a rumor of transcendence, of something beyond us, beyond the roll of the dice in the marketplace, a rumor and more than a rumor of judgment. Perhaps this is an instance of the impingement of the divine into human transactions. If we were simply reactive agents of commercialism without residue, why the feeling that things are not right and that they should be righted? But here again the present dominance of commercialism can dissipate the impulse toward justice, perhaps erase it and hold the erasure as a virtue. Commerce, however, is itself a virtue. Where would we be without it? But when made the virtue of virtues, the value beyond all others, those without the drive and wherewithal to pursue commercial virtue are lost in the backwaters of "the history of suffering" (Metz).

Yet the cry for justice, the demand for it, remains, never dominant but insistent everywhere and always, except perhaps for the totally insensitive. It remains for most if only in the form of pangs of a lingering guilt. But for the poor and needy—most of the world's people—the cry for justice goes on and on. Even those who have built great fortunes on the backs of the poor, as most fortunes are, desire more often than not, however self-aggrandizingly, to better folk, some folk at least, by establishing endowments for the arts and sciences, for furthering cultural life of mostly the few and perhaps, by fluke, for many. And further, even those who are completely cynical about the possibility of achieving justice remark on injustice and thus in some inchoate way entertain the notion that things could be better.

We feel prompted towards justice, somehow summoned to concern ourselves with it, though with widely varying levels of intensity, ranging all the way from Amos of old to modern industrial chieftains. This summons derives in part no doubt from the whole biological battle to survive but in the case of human beings that battle takes on a new dimension, a sense of being lured beyond ourselves—a lure that will not let us alone, discontenting us with things as they are and calling us, as it were, toward something more. This lure might be termed the divine spiritual presence working in our spirits. More traditionally, it might be called the "voice" of God. However ambiguously interpreted, the summons to justice seems clearly enough to have a note of unambiguousness attached to it. It is ingredient to our lives, to the way we are constituted, a part, we may say, of created reality and within created reality an activity of the all-enveloping divine creative energy.[8]

There is creativity in the moral realm of life as surely as there is creativity in the natural realm. While distinct, these realms of life are not separate from each other. Interconnectedness marks them at every turn and twist. Creative forces operate in all entities, forming one great creative enterprise. The local level of creativity is an instance of the cosmic level and the cosmic level is a magnification of the local level. These creative processes develop, then exhaust themselves, providing the ground for ever more and new processes to develop. This seems as incontrovertible as

---

[8] The cry for justice is raised to a very high pitch in Western societies but until recent history its pitch in Eastern societies has been very much muted. But when the cry becomes heard, as in India after Gandhi's work, the concern for justice becomes more evident and urgent.

our own birth and demise and the preparation they provide our progeny. Creative energy is surely within us but it just as surely transcends us in the natural processes that occur whether we will or not. These processes may be that—natural without remainder. But also and equally that may be involved in a creative power that sets the terms of their existence and affords them the freedom of their own development. That entities, analogously so with us, are relatively free to develop themselves, to realize their potentiality, the degree of their "freedom" vastly differing in respect to their status in the scale of being, seems to be in the order of fact. They cannot become, however, anything other than themselves, e.g., an earwig cannot become a cockroach any more than we can become anything but human beings. Limits are in place, directing limits. These limits to the development of species and a certain freedom to develop after their own kind—call it license if you will—all point to God, to divine creative energy everywhere and interminably operative. There is no way, at least for me, not to affirm the existence of God. While not an empirically established fact by a long shot, the affirmation has a great deal of empirical support.

Whether God is in the grip of the creative principle (Whitehead) or whether the creative principle is in God's grip, there is no way of knowing. Perhaps Origen was right to suggest that God is creative because God is God, that God could not be God apart from creativity and its issue. All manner of speculation has arisen around this point. A principal strand has it that God is complete in Godself and has no need of a creation. A pithy expression of this view is that God minus the world equals God; the world minus God equals nothing (Temple). Still, the idea that God is eternally creative is attractive. Empiricism cannot speak to this matter in a decisive way but if experience tells us anything it is that creativity surges through the universe as a first fact, giving rise to the supposition that creativity might indeed denote the prime characteristic of God.

However this may be, the tradition of faith has held that there is nothing outside of the sphere of divine creativity, which is productive of good only. This doctrine has led to a vast deal of difficulties for theology and to a vast deal of ingenuity of thought owing the existence of the manifold evils in the world, and decisively in human experience. The Isaiahic "poetical" view that God creates light and darkness and creates good and evil has rarely been systematically pursued, though Augustine and later Calvin especially gave thought to it in developing the doctrine of the divine inscrutability. Evils abound but we cannot know whether God is responsible for them because we cannot begin to grasp the mind of God or the infinite range of the divine action. In the case of Calvin there appears to be a covert admission that God in God's omnipotent power is pretty deeply implicated in evil. But, said he, silence on the matter is the appropriate theological response. Augustine quipped that hell was being prepared for people who raised such questions.

The theological habit has always been, and largely is still, to protect God from any implication in evil.[9] All sorts of attempts have been made and are being made to exonerate God from being the creator not only of good but evil alongside of the good. One such is that God is finite and can deal only imperfectly with the evils of a universe that seems to be infinite; another is that God is a moral force in history and removed somehow from the creative energies that universally clash and clang, and another yet is that God limits Godself, allowing evil in the interests of furthering a greater good, the development of creatures able to respond to divine outreach with relative freedom.

These are useful views that have the support of a number of strands of philosophical and theological thought. Certainly they have something to say for themselves but they do nothing to remove the manifest evils in the world we live in: evils in ourselves, evils in society and, as we perforce perceive them, evils in nature too. Our constant experience is of good and of

---

[9] The issue is whether a compaction of God into the mold of perfect goodness is too small to meet the realities of human life as we live it and have to live it. For us, as Yeats put it in *Crazy Jane*, "Fair and foul are near of kin/ and fair needs foul." This is always and everywhere our experience. Must not then our own conception of God be big enough to provision for it? In the tradition, God sends rain upon the just and the unjust and stops there. But if this is so, does not God send drought, plague, pestilence and famine upon the just and the unjust as well as rain?

evil. Without the experience of evil there could be no experience of good.[10] That seems to be our empirical situation, inextricably so. The creative processes of the world make for good and evil, not in equal measure perhaps but enough to be quite impressive. A sufficiently empirical theology can only raise the question whether God must not be responsible—ultimately—for both. In light of our own endless capacity to create good and evil, it might also have to raise the question whether that capacity betokens the image of God in us.

But the question of questions for us, however, is whether the God who creates both good and evil can be worshipped and served. Many, indeed most theologians would answer resoundingly in the negative, that it could not be so for a moment. There is much to be said for the view that God creates only good. It might be said on the other hand that this reflects an attempt to resolve the mystery of God, to render God amenable to human needs and purposes. Anyhow, the faith that God creates only good has always been "and in spite of faith," one never held without remainder, instanced perhaps most clearly in the tradition of Satan.[11] Another is found in popular religious experiences: "Why did God take my son away from me; why this terrible affliction?" Instances of this feeling could be multiplied indefinitely. While theologians have tried hard to deflect them, their success has not been complete, probably not even for themselves, much less for the many.

The ramifications of these matters do not in any way obviate what we have said of the divine lure toward beauty and truth or the divine summons toward justice. That evil in the world in all of its ominous complexity is addressable and is being addressed are experienced facts, facts that provide empirical evidence, we

---

[10] Evil intrigues us. As Philip Roth says so well in *Sabbath's Theatre*, "For a pure sense of being tumultuously alive, you can't beat the nasty side of existence." We cannot interest ourselves in a story that tells of goodness only. A snake in the garden is essential for a good story. The story of Jesus itself would lack interest without the Sadducees, the Pharisees and the Zealots with whom he disputed, the Romans who offhandedly crucified him and, too, without Satan and his legion of demons who tried to do him in.

[11] There is much current interest in the tradition of Satan. If Satan actually exists, however, he does so by "divine permission" as tradition has it, a softer way of saying by divine will and creation.

may say, for the presence and power of divine agency immanent in the world, and, because immanent, transcendent as well.

Let me end this piece with one more surmise among the many already made. One might wonder whether the divine interest in the world and in human beings could be sustained without the evils attending them. God's role in dealing with us would certainly be reduced—there would be much less to interact with. There would be no divine anger, judgment, forgiveness or summons. There would be divine love as that which creates and sustains life presumably, but love as empirically known among us entails anger, judgment of that which contravenes love; it induces forgiveness and issues summons. God's love no doubt is immeasurably greater than human love but is it totally different? We cannot think so if we believe that the love enacted in the life of Jesus accurately reflects the love of God. The love there set forth includes anger, judgment, forgiveness and summons.

11

The nth Messiah: A Note on Writing Gospels

James Carse

Gospel is the only literary genre unique to Christianity. Epistles, apocalypses, confessions, apologias, commentaries, sermons, sacred histories, and prayers are all found in traditions either prior to or independent of Christianity. Gospels are found nowhere but in Christianity.

To make this claim it must first be established that a literary work does not become a gospel simply because it is in some way about Jesus of Galilee. It is a genre that stands by itself, even though all of its known occurrences do indeed have Jesus as their focus. It is important to make this point because it must be seen that a gospel is not another literary form that happens to be about Jesus, as though it were a history, a memoir, an encomium adapted to some Christian end. There is something about a gospel that makes it exclusively available to followers of Jesus. For the same reason, there is something about Jesus that makes him an exclusive subject of gospels. To understand what a gospel is we must look at the figure of Jesus; to understand who Jesus is we must examine gospel as a singular literary phenomenon.

To give it the simplest possible definition, a gospel is a narrative account of the life and teachings of Jesus of Galilee. That this definition, though true enough, does not dispel the cloud of ambiguity surrounding the genre can be seen in the habit of Christians to speak of "the" gospel. The presumption here is that the gospels contain a single message or a unified portrait that can be abstracted from its language and stated independently. Oddly this presumption exists in spite of the fact that Christians have been notoriously unable to agree on just what "the" gospel is. In fact, Christian history can be understood as an unending disagreement of Christendom with itself over the proper understanding of "the" gospel. It might even be said that Christian history is the result of gospel's inherent ambiguities. In other words, if it had been possible to state "the" gospel, Christianity would have become a monolithic doctrinal community and as such doomed to expire with the rest of the world's ideologies. The core energy of the Christian tradition is the impossibility of finding the core meaning of its gospels. Its life is tied to a literary genre that requires its readers to interpret it even as it repels all interpretation.

The canonical gospels, if we consider Luke and Acts as a unified work, constitute more than half of the New Testament. The rest consists of epistles and a revelation. Epistolary literature was so common in the ancient world that letters were written and read as formal teachings. It is not surprising, therefore, that the letters of Paul and the other, largely anonymous, letters of the New Testament would have been preserved. Though they refer, sometimes obliquely, to issues specific to those addressed, they would not have been copied over and over with such precision had they been perceived as strictly occasional works. The apocalypse attributed to the unknown author, John, although not a common literary form among Christians, was common enough that its contemporary readers would not have been puzzled by its strangeness. The question then is why the gospels were preserved, especially when they conformed to no known literary tradition.

It is sometimes said that it is Paul as much as Jesus who has given shape to the Christian faith, that without Paul Christendom would have been very different. This is certainly true in part but the more telling question is whether Christianity would have existed without the gospels. Could Paul alone have given rise to a tradition of equal complexity and vitality? History cannot be played over by an alternative plot, so such questions can never have a definitive answer. However, there is a clue. We find it in the very fact that the New Testament has been established as a *canon*.

Just how and when the canon was agreed upon is not well known. We can say for sure that by the beginning of the fifth Christian century the publication of Jerome's Latin translation of the New Testament signaled an almost universal consensus on the contents of the canon. However, there is consensus on *why* the church felt it needed a canon: there was impassioned discord on many central doctrinal points, even to the divinity of Jesus himself. The issue was not which of these views was true but whose version of the truth was to be heard. It was a matter of competing authorities. The winning view in this competition had the intended result not of contributing to the ongoing conversation but of ending it.

The conversation didn't end, of course, but a principle of vast consequence was established: there is a Christian truth that excludes all others. It is, moreover, a truth that can be laid out in a body of teaching. That Christianity is largely a *theological* religion is the result of the establishment of a canon. Therefore, given the impulse toward theology among Christians, it is clear that Paul would be privileged as a teacher over Jesus. There is a theology of Paul. There is not a theology of Jesus.

If we think canonically, certainly Paul is the supreme teacher. It is his interpretation of the life and teachings of Jesus that becomes the rule for shaping Christian theology. There is some irony in this for Paul himself did not think canonically. There was for him no urtext according to which his doctrinal imagination had to shape itself. There was not another Paul to whom he could refer in disputes.

In returning to the prior question, why Christians took so quickly to the unfamiliar form of the gospel, we have to be careful not to introduce the principle of canonicity into our consideration. The gospels, in brief, did not (and do not) serve the function of establishing the truth once and for all. They are not arbiters of theological dispute. What then are they?

I have defined them as narrative accounts of the life and teachings of Jesus. The term narrative here has a special application. At the opening of his gospel Luke speaks of writing an orderly account of "those things that have happened among us." Typical of the other writers of the canonical gospels, Luke sees himself in the midst of an ongoing history. Though he looks back, and though he does indeed claim to be telling the truth, he is also telling a story that has yet to be finished. The Acts of the Apostles, the second half of his gospel, has no conclusion. There is no defining historical event that gives a singular meaning to the rest. The final chapter cannot be written, perhaps ever. John ends his gospel with the remark that if everything that has happened among us were written down it would fill more books than the world can hold. That is, the gospel is something that can never be told. It seems that essential to the definition of gospel is that it is the endless telling of that which it has not yet said.

Although these writers have been canonized, a more decisive rejection of the principle of canonization cannot be imagined. The canon as we have it has taken into itself a text that contradicts the very possibility of a canon. Indeed, from this perspective, even Paul now looks different. Instead of understanding the gospels through Paul's theology, it is now Paul whose theology seems as open ended as the gospels. It is not a theology that explains a closed history but floats on one unfinished, and unfinishable.

There is something about an unfinishable narrative that is manifestly disturbing. We know it is a story but we don't know what the story is. This is of course the way we experience our own lives. We live an unfinished narrative. The last chapter cannot be written for when it is we are no longer living it. When we see it this way it inevitably leaves us with a crisis of meaning. Because we can't see both ends of the course of our existence, it remains beyond evaluation. This is not a crisis the gospels resolve. On the contrary, it is a crisis the gospels stand in the way of resolving. It is also why the evangelists, in relating their accounts, cannot separate them from their own experience and the experience of their communities.

To highlight the peculiar character of gospel we can compare it to Virgil's *Aeneid*, a work roughly contemporary to the New Testament. It was Virgil's design to glorify the reign of his boyhood friend, Caesar Augustus. Although Augustus was still alive during the writing of the poem, Virgil nonetheless presented his allegory as a finished history. By telling the largely imagined story of the Trojan War hero Aeneas and his founding of Rome, Virgil has by implication declared that Augustus reigns over an empire whose story has ended. What is this but a vision of an eternal Rome? The gospel writers knew of no eternal human institution. Even the kingdom of God has an ambiguous temporal status: it is present only in the mode of having yet to come.

Given this unsettling feature of the gospel as a genre, we can see why it should be so frequently misread. By canonizing it, there is the hope that theological discourse can transform its bottomlessness into a scheme of certainties. By historicizing it, that is by putting its beginning and end in the past, we can see it as the portrait of an exemplary life, the emulation of which lays a certain meaning over our own existence. At the popular level Jesus is historicized as moral example, canonized as spiritual teacher.

If this were all the gospels came to they would have been long forgotten, surpassed by more relevant models, more commanding teachers. This bring us back to the peculiar nature of the genre. Gospel is not a history for, the end cannot yet be written into it. It is not a theological statement, for it is naked of doctrinal instruction. True, its focus is on the person of Jesus. True, the person of Jesus almost always has the status of messiah. But when we study the texts to arrive at a clearer understanding of who this person was and why it was thought he was the messiah, we come to the most alluring feature of gospel. It is infamously difficult, by wide agreement impossible, to develop a consistent portrait of Jesus from the existing texts. In fact, what we find is not Jesus but a great number of Jesuses.

To make it worse, if there is a plurality of messiahs in the canonical gospels, there is also a plurality of gospels outside the canon, many of them nearly included, others explicitly rejected, some ignored in the process of canonization. Fragments of about 35 gospels are extant; only one is complete: the Gospel of Thomas. Some scholars believe that there may be as many as 200 such works. Although this number will never be more than a guess, it is quite possible that writing gospels was the chief literary activity of Christians in the first two centuries after the death of Jesus. And each of these gospels presents a different Jesus. Why so many?

If the gospels are narratives of the unfinished histories in which the writers (and probably their intended readers) find themselves, they are at once personal and historical. As scholars have long known, each gospel bears the historical stamp of its author and its communal setting. If the writers wanted to tell the story of Jesus they could only tell it out of their own story. The Jesus each writer gives us is therefore a Jesus that makes sense of their own continuing journey. The one is a mirror for the other.

This seems to suggest that the gospel writers freely invented their material. Not so. Each of them either by direct statement or implication means to tell a story that is historically accurate. They are obviously aware that much of what they have heard cannot be true. Even so, their honest efforts to filter out all that is false leave us with irreconcilable accounts. The filters are themselves, of course, historical products.

The temptation here is, naturally, to work our own way through these manifold narratives to find the true Jesus that eluded his first and second century narrators. Roughly speaking, this has been done two ways. By assorted strategies of historical analysis, scholars have attempted to filter out the historically suspicious material and thus arrive at an irreducible core of words and events that can be ascribed to the real Jesus. If we think of this attempt as Protestant in spirit, the Catholic strategy has been not to validate the text by prying into its origins but by taking account of what has happened as a result of these first century events. The truth of the resurrection, by this method, is not to be found in the text but in the experience of Christians over the centuries.

Although they seem to come from radically different points of view, these two strategies have this in common: both imply that the faith rests on discoverable historical fact.

But if the history of the search for the historical Jesus has taught us anything it is that historical fact will continue to elude us. Just as each gospel writer stood in an irreducibly mirroring relation to Jesus of Galilee, so too does every reader. So too, indeed, did the contemporaries of Jesus, even his own disciples and friends.

More importantly, it is because historical fact eludes us that each new reading of the gospels will find a new Jesus. With each new Jesus comes a new way of conceiving the relation of the Christian community to the world. Because there can be no end of messiahs, each will be both a creature of the present age and a prophetic judgment on it.

I have argued that establishing a canon also established the principle that there is a discoverable truth that will serve to answer all our questions and end our quest for meaning. I have also argued that by including the gospels in the canon the church introduced into it a challenge to the very idea of canonization. Canonicity has the effect of giving theology primacy over gospel. Perhaps it is time to declare that neither has primacy.

This declaration is neither so radical nor original as it may sound. Paul, though he had very little to say about the life of Jesus, could not have written what he did without having a clear image of who Jesus was, what he did and what he said. In other words, his theology has a gospel imbedded in it. So, too, does every theology. It is therefore possible to read every theological work as a gloss on a presumed gospel.

In a sense, then, gospel writing never ceased. If there were scores, maybe hundreds, of gospels that were passed over in the process of canonization, there is no end of gospels haunting the theological tradition.

A modest proposal: bring the writing of gospels into the open. If writing gospels was a major literary activity of the first several centuries of Christendom, revive the activity. There need be no presumption that one is writing "the" gospel since such an authoritative document does not and cannot exist. As for the historical accuracy, every effort should be made to make one's gospel narrative as faithful to the circumstances of the time as possible. Since there is no way we can avoid mixing historical fact and imagination, let the imagination do what it can within acceptable historical limits. We need only look at the way in which the imagination of the evangelist John took a form astonishingly different from that of Mark. Just as a gospel is buried in every theology there is a theology buried in every gospel. As theologians are under no constraint to write a parallel gospel neither should a contemporary evangelist feel obliged to write a parallel theology. No matter. There will always be a theology at work in the writer's narrative construction. Neither should a modern writer be explicit in evoking the character of the present age for there is no way a gospel can be written except out of one's own contemporary setting.

Finally, let the gospel be its own prophetic assessment of the present age. The success of it as a gospel depends on avoiding every attempt to ideologize it. Even as Paul was unaware of the implied gospel in his work or as Luke was able to keep his narrative free of reference to contemporary issues, so should the modern writer respect the power of the gospel as a literary form to serve as its own prophetic voice.

12

Christianity and the Perennial Philosophy

Owen C. Thomas

I used to think that the main option in the West to the biblical religions, Judaism and Christianity, was naturalistic humanism. This is the worldview which affirms the uniquely human values of freedom, community, justice, equality, and so forth, in the context of a naturalistic philosophy, a metaphysic in which nature is the highest or broadest category. Now, I believe that this is no longer the case, and probably never was (except in the academy, and perhaps not even there). I am persuaded that the main option to the biblical religions today is what Aldous Huxley and many others call the perennial philosophy.

Huxley defines the perennial philosophy as "the metaphysic that recognizes a divine reality substantial to the world" and "the psychology that finds in the soul something similar to, or even identical with, divine Reality."[1] It has been exemplified in the West in Neoplatonism, the mysticism of the Pseudo-Dionysius, modern idealism, and such religious movements as Gnosticism, Rosicrucianism, Swedenborgianism, Theosophy,

---

[1] Aldous Huxley, *The Perennial Philosophy* (New York: Harper and Row, 1944), p. vii.

Spiritualism, and Christian Science, as well as imports from the East, especially Vedanta.[2]

It has also become an important school of thought led by such authors as Rene Guénon, S.H. Nasr, Jacob Needleman, Frithjof Schuon, and Huston Smith.

I

There is something of a consensus among interpreters that the world religions fall in to two main types, what Max Weber called the emissary and the exemplary types, and what Peter Berger has called the confrontation and interiority types. The first or emissary type is exemplified in the Jewish prophet, the Christian apostle, and the Muslim prophet; the second or exemplary, in the Hindu holy man, the Buddhist monk, and the Taoist sage. And the question is often raised and discussed about the relation between the two types of religion and whether or not a synthesis is possible.

It is usually assumed that Christianity generally falls within the emissary type and the perennial philosophy in the exemplary type. It would seem on the face of it that they represent quite distinct types of religious experience and religious tradition. But I want to suggest that Christianity has always in fact been a synthesis or amalgam, sometimes stable, sometimes unstable, of what I call biblical religion and the perennial philosophy.

I first became aware of this issue in the Forties through the neo-orthodox polemic against liberal theology and, in particular, against the elements in it of mysticism and idealism. In my graduate study, I did a good deal of work on the English Hegelians and especially on the debates between the absolute idealists and the personal idealists in which these issues figured. Then I began to notice that people from all walks of life were fascinated both intellectually and existentially by the perennial philosophy. I recall Reinhold Niebuhr once remarking that if a Christian theologian were invited to lecture at Columbia University, the philosophy department would be outraged, but if a Buddhist monk or a Hindu swami were invited, they would all purr like kittens.

---

[2] See the study of thirty-six contemporary groups of this type by Robert S. Ellwood in his book *Religious and Spiritual Groups in Modern America* (Englewood Cliffs, NJ: Prentice-Hall, 1973).

Then, several years ago, I participated in a group of theologians and psychiatrists in Boston assembled by Erich Lindemann. I discovered to my astonishment that the majority of the psychiatrists were rather disdainful of biblical religion but were quite fascinated with the perennial philosophy. In the Sixties, I noticed that much of the counter-culture movement was deeply informed by the perennial philosophy. Finally, I have often been surprised to discover that the operative faith of theological students and other Christians turns out to be some form of the perennial philosophy, that Christian people often assume that Christian faith and the perennial philosophy are the same thing. So, in a word, I have been continually impressed by the power and the pervasiveness of the perennial philosophy, and I continue to be curious about its relation to Christianity.

I want to approach this question by looking at the perennial philosophy and biblical religion as two ideal types, two heuristic constructs which may serve to organize certain historical data. By this, I mean that I will try to indicate the fundamental elements of each, not all of which, however, may be present in any particular example of them. In speaking of biblical religion, I am not referring to Judaism or Christianity in any of their specific forms, but rather to an ideal construct which may underlie any particular form of either of them. The same applies to my description of the perennial philosophy.

II

The ideal type of "perennial philosophy" is a religious worldview which, like all worldviews, involves a particular understanding of reality, including the divine, and the place of humanity in reality. It affirms that ultimate reality, the divine, is the nameless, ineffable One about which nothing else can be said except perhaps by negations. For example, it is not a person or personal. Then, there is the world, but its origin is obscure or problematic. In the Gnostic version of the perennial philosophy, the origin of the world is the result of a mythic accident or misunderstanding. In the Neoplatonic version, the world is the result of the emanation or overflowing of the divine substance, the reason for which is obscure. It is sometimes described as involuntary and sometimes as a reckless falling away from the One.

This means that the world is essentially divine, or, as Huxley puts it, the divine reality is substantial to the world. It also means that reality is ordered in a great hierarchy of levels of being stretching from the divine down through the spiritual, the psychic, and the organic, to the inorganic. This is a hierarchy of reality, power, and value. The higher or closer a level of being is to the divine, the greater its reality, power, value; the lower or farther from the divine, the lesser its reality, power, and value.

Humanity includes all the levels of being and, thus, is called a microcosm, the whole of reality in miniature. Humanity includes the inorganic, the organic, the psychic, the spiritual, and the divine. This means that the highest and essential level of human being is identical with the divine. The problematic character of the human situation is that the human spirit which is essentially divine is involved in the lower levels of being and as a result is confused, led astray, and forgets about its essential divine nature.

The way of salvation is for the human spirit to discover its true nature, to turn away from the lower levels of being, and to rise up until it is perfectly united with the divine in mystical union. This way of salvation is pursued in many different ways in the different versions of the perennial philosophy, but they usually involve some kind of asceticism or suppression of the bodily and the psychic through disciplines of meditation.

I pause to note that this is what many people believe Christianity is, especially people raised in the traditions of liberal Protestantism, Roman Catholicism, or Eastern Orthodoxy. The reason for this is that these traditions (and all other Christian traditions in varying degrees) are in fact syntheses or amalgams of biblical religion with various forms of the perennial philosophy.

From these fundamental elements of the perennial philosophy certain results tend to emerge. First, because of the monistic and hierarchical character of reality, individuality in general and human individuality or personhood in particular tends to become at least ambiguous in character, if not in actuality unreal or evil. The reason for this is that the more individuality or distinctness something has, the further it is from the divine, and thus the less reality, power, and value it will have. This is also indicated by the fact that the fulfillment of the individual is to become perfectly united with the divine in an identity in which there is no distinct individuality at all. Huston Smith puts it this way: "Only persons who sense *themselves* to be not finally real —*anatta*, no-self—will sense the same of the God of theism. And for them it does not matter that in the last analysis God is not the kind of God who loves them, for at this level there is no 'them' to be loved."[3]

A second tendency is that bodily life is viewed with suspicion. The reason is the same. Physical bodies are even further removed from the divine than the human psyche and they are, moreover, the source of human confusion and ignorance about its true nature, and thus are the source of evil. (Thus monism always tends to produce a dualism in regard to the body and the physical world.) Since human individuality and embodiment are the basis of human personal relations, human association and community become ambiguous, of little value, and subject to suspicion. Finally, since human history is the story of human communities and their relations, the significance of history becomes questionable. The significant movement of human life is not forward into the future in personal, communal, and historical development, but rather upwards out of bodily, communal, historical life in the direction of the divine.

The ideal type "biblical religion" has one point of agreement with the perennial philosophy, namely, the ultimate reality of the divine One. But even here there is a fundamental difference. In biblical religion, the divine is ineluctably personal and thus a differentiated or organic unity on the analogy of integrated human personhood, whereas in the perennial philosophy the divine One is absolutely simple and undifferentiated. Moreover, the divine in biblical religion is not nameless or ineffable, but has many names and must be spoken about.

Furthermore, the origin of the world is not obscure, but is understood to be the result of the divine will and action, namely, creation. This means that the world is not essentially divine, but rather creaturely, a kind of reality which is neither divine nor illusory, but contingent and real. There is a sense in which the created world is ordered in a hierarchy of levels of being, but

---

[3] Huston Smith, *Forgotten Truth: The Primordial Tradition* (New York: Harper and Row, 1976). p 52.

this is not a hierarchy of degrees of reality, but rather one of degrees of complexity and spiritual possibility.

As in the perennial philosophy, humanity includes all the levels of reality, with but one exception: humanity has no divine element, but is entirely creature. Furthermore, the problematic character of human life is not the involvement of humanity in bodily life, but is rather a matter of the perversity of the human will, of turning away from the divine will. The seat of the problem is in the human spirit, not in the human body. So, the way of salvation is the transformation of the will through the divine presence. The merciful and forgiving divine love draws the human will out of bondage into freedom.

From the fundamental affirmations of biblical religion, certain tendencies emerge which are the opposite of those of the perennial philosophy. In biblical religion, individuality in general and human individuality in particular are not ambiguous, but are affirmed as very good. The goal of individual fulfillment is not to be absorbed into the divine undifferentiated unity, but to live in personal communion with the divine and with one's fellow creatures. Accordingly, human bodily life is not to be turned away from, but is to be affirmed and will be transfigured in the fulfillment. (Thus a duality between creator and creature always tends to produce a monism of holism in regard to the body and the physical world.) Similarly, human personal relations and community are not seen as ambiguous, but rather as of the highest importance and value. Finally, therefore, history as the story of human communities and their relations is taken very seriously as the arena of human responsibility and the divine activity aiming at the fulfillment of all the creation.

III

These are the ideal types or constructs of the perennial philosophy and biblical religion. They have never existed in their pure forms as described. In any particular historical form of either one, the fundamental themes will be described in different ways and the tendencies mentioned will be modified accordingly. As I have suggested, Christianity has never existed as simply biblical religion, but has always been from the very beginning a mixture, amalgam, or synthesis of biblical religion with some form of the perennial philosophy. (Occasionally, the mixture has occurred with other types of philosophy, such as Stoicism. But most often it has been with some form of the perennial philosophy, which has been the dominant form of Western philosophy from Plato to Hegel.)

This amalgamating began in the Bible, and first in the Wisdom literature, and especially in the Wisdom of Solomon which was influenced by Middle Platonism, and also in the Gospel of John (although this is debated). It continued in Philo and the early Christian theologians, such as Clement of Alexandria, in whose writings the perennial philosophy was dominant. A real synthesis was achieved by such thinkers as Augustine, Bonaventure, and Aquinas; Psuedo-Dionysius represents the perennial philosophy in almost pure form. Very few theologians exemplify biblical religion in pure form, but Irenaeus, Calvin, and, on the Jewish side, Martin Buber come close.

A historical sidelight is that by the time of the Renaissance most people identified Christianity with the individual and world-denying aspects of the perennial philosophy, which we have noted above. So the Renaissance can be interpreted as the cultural manifestation of some of the individual and world-affirming themes of biblical religion, as seen, for example, in Renaissance humanism, Renaissance naturalism in art, the beginnings of modern science, and the emergence of a progressive view of history. These were seen as anti-Christian in character. Finally, since the Renaissance can in many ways be seen as the birth of the modern world, we have the strange reversal in which the modern world sees itself as an anti-Christian rebirth of classical culture, whereas it is in fact more the result of the culture working out of the fundamental themes of biblical religion. All of this can be seen as the result of the fact that Christianity was widely understood to be a form of perennial philosophy.[4]

---

[4] See, for example, Robert N. Bellah's description of Christianity as a rejection of the world in *Beyond Belief: Essays on Religion in a Post-Traditional World* (New York: Harper & Row, 1970), pp. 22–34. As against this interpretation, see Walter Zimmerli, *The Old Testament and the World*, trans. John J. Scullion (Atlanta: John Knox Press, 1976).

A continuing manifestation of the perennial philosophy since the medieval period can be seen in Romanticism. Denis de Rougemont has argued that Catharism, a religious movement based on the perennial philosophy with a Christian veneer, was the source of the tradition of courtly love which exalted the passion of Romantic love and looked down on marriage.[5] According to de Rougement, this tradition of Romanticism influenced many areas of Western culture, flowered in the Romantic movement of the last century, and emerged philosophically in German idealism, the main modern Western version of the perennial philosophy.

Today, we are experiencing a new Romantic movement which is also pervasively informed by the perennial philosophy.[6] Beginning with the youth culture movement of the Sixties and continuing down to the present in many religious and cultural manifestations, the new Romantic movement has influenced all of us and produced a new popularity for the many religious and philosophical groups which embody the perennial philosophy today.[7] As a result, many are drawn today to the perennial philosophy in these groups and also to the forms of Christianity in which the perennial philosophy is dominant, in particular the mystical traditions. Much of the interest in spirituality in the churches today grows out of the current Romantic movement and its grounding in the perennial philosophy. Also, many have argued that the new physics and the hallucinogenic drug experience both support the validity of the perennial philosophy,

---

[5] Denis de Rougemont, *Love in the Western World* (New York: Harper and Row, 1956).

[6] See the works of Theodore Roszak, *The Making of a Counter Culture* (Garden City: Doubleday and Co., 1969) and *Where the Wasteland Ends* (Garden City: Doubleday and Co., 1972).

[7] See the Ellwood study mentioned above and also his more recent work *Alternative Altars* (Chicago: University of Chicago Press, 1979). This movement was also partially informed by a revival of what Merold Westphal calls mimetic religion, exemplified in ancient Mesopotamian and Egyptian religion and marked by an affirmation of the goodness of nature as distinct. For history, see book, *God, Guilt, and Death: An Existential Phenomenology of Religion* (Bloomington, In: Indiana University Press, 1984).

especially in the form of Eastern mysticism. But this is hotly debated.[8]

IV

So, as I suggested at the beginning, the perennial philosophy seems to be the main option to Christianity today. This demonstrates the universal appeal and power of this tradition. The fundamental question emerges whether the authentic Christian tradition lies in biblical religion, in the perennial philosophy, or in a synthesis of the two. This raises the further question whether a true and stable synthesis of these two traditions is possible. Many students of religion have struggled with this question, but no consensus has emerged.[9]

Few theologians see this as a critical issue in theology. Earlier in this century, Karl Barth did see the issue and came down on the side of biblical religion. This is also generally true of the theologians in the tradition of political and liberation theology. Huston Smith sees the authentic Christian tradition to be squarely in the perennial philosophy. Some theologians engaged in the inter-religious dialogue have begun to explore the possibility of a synthesis of Christianity with Buddhism, which stands generally in the perennial philosophy tradition.[10]

Other interpretations of the relation of these two traditions from the point of view of one of them tend to explain away the other tradition or treat it as a lower level of understanding (Radhakrishnan and Buber are examples of this approach). But religious traditions of such widespread power and appeal can hardly be distinguished in terms of truth and error. They must both have a firm hold on some aspects of ultimate reality. Complementarity and synthesis seem to be the more appropriate

---

[8] For a critique of the former, see Ken Wilber, "Physics, Mysticism, and the New Holographic Paradigm," *The Holographic Paradigm*, ed. Wilber (Boulder, Col.: Shambala, 1982). For a critique of the latter, see R.C. Zaehner, *Mysticism Sacred and Profane* (London: Oxford University Press, 1957).

[9] See *The Other Side of God: A Polarity in World Religions*, ed. Peter Berger (Garden City: Anchor Press, 1981).

[10] See John B. Cobb, Jr., *Beyond Dialogue: Toward a Mutual Transformation of Christianity and Buddhism* (Philadelphia: Fortress Press, 1982).

way of understanding their relation. Needless to say, any synthesis would have to be carried out from the point of view of one of the traditions.

Paul Tillich is the main theologian in this century who has argued forcefully that the authentic Christian tradition lies in a stable synthesis of the two traditions. He has carried this out in his *Systematic Theology*, and I will conclude by indicating briefly how he does this.[11] Tillich's synthesis appears clearly at three main points in the system: God as being itself and personal, creation and fall as the transition from essence to existence, and the fulfillment as essentialization or the transition from existence back to essence. I will speak only of the first.

As I suggested above, the One of perennial philosophy is the ineffable, nameless, undifferentiated ultimate reality which is substantial to the world. The divine reality in biblical religion is the transcendent and immanent personal God who creates the world. Tillich synthesized these views by means of his ontology. In his three sets of polar ontological elements which characterize all of finite being, the key one in this connection is the polarity of individualization and participation. All of finite reality from the sub-atomic particle to the human being is informed by this polarity. On the human level, it takes the form of person and community. Since God is the ground of finite being, aspects of finite being can and must be used to speak symbolically of God. When the polarity of individualization and participation is applied to God symbolically, God is seen not as a person but as the ground of everything personal, not as the substance of all things but as the ground of all things. God is, thus, both the absolute individual and the absolute participant.

The human experience of the divine is informed by and varies according to this polarity of individualization and participation. Sometimes, as in biblical religion, it is nearer the individualization end of the polarity and is understood as a re-

[11] See *Systematic Theology*, 3 vols. (Chicago: University of Chicago Press, 1951–63), 1, pp. 174–78, 243–45. Others who have attempted such a synthesis are John A. T. Robinson in *Truth is Two-Eyed* (Philadelphia: Westminster Press, 1979), and George Rupp in *Beyond Zen and Existentialism* (New York: Oxford University Press, 1979).

lation to the personal God. Other times, as in the perennial philosophy tradition, it is nearer the participation pole and is understood as a participation in or union with God. But Tillich's point is that, according to his ontology, individualization and participation can be actualized only in relation to each other. There can be no pure individualization which does not involve participation, and vice versa. Therefore, the religious experiences of these two traditions are not entirely alien, but rather constitute complementary views of the divine reality.[12]

This, at least, is the implication of Tillich's synthesis. It is carried out primarily from the point of view of the biblical religion tradition. Other syntheses have been attempted on the basis of the perennial philosophy tradition. What I am suggesting is that Christianity, in line with its earliest formulations, should proceed to clarify its self-understanding as a synthesis of the biblical religion and perennial philosophy traditions, and thus broaden its appeal to those whose experience stands more in the latter tradition.

---

[12] See Paul Tillich, *The Courage to Be* (New Haven:Yale University Press, 1952), pp. 156-63. See also my elaboration of this thesis in "Tillich and the Perennial Philosophy," *Harvard Theological Review* 89:1 (1996).

13

What We Can Say About God

Fred Sommers

Most of us remember the story we heard as children about a little chicken who frightened all the barnyard folk with the report that the sky was about to fall. I think we all understood this story: Chicken Little was an alarmist who should have known better; any sensible chicken knows the sky won't fall. It won't fall because it is far too securely fastened to fall. I think this is what we thought at the time; certainly we made good sense of the concept of a falling sky. There was something absurd in the concept. Chicken Little was unduly frightened, but he was not mentally deranged.

I don't know at just what point we began to fail to understand the story of Chicken Little. Our concept of the sky has changed. The report that the sky is falling is no longer wildly implausible; it makes no more sense to us now than would a report that the equator has died, or that quadruplicity has finally drunk procrastination. The sky—we should now say—is not the *sort* of thing that either falls or fails to fall: it is not a physical object like the roof of a house; it makes no more sense to ask, say, for the weight of the sky than it makes sense to ask for the weight of the sunset.

The story of Chicken Little is only one example of a story which only children can understand. In this particular case the ontogeny of the concept recapitulates its phylogeny. For in the childhood of the human race, the sky was a vault or ceiling, and any ancient would have little qualms about the notion of a sky that falls or fails to fall. It is only in fairly recent times that the propriety of predicating *falling, weight,* and other similar physical properties of the sky could come into question.

The moral of this is clear. Sometimes philosophers grow wiser by pretending not to understand what they actually do understand. But just as often they grow wiser by actually failing to understand what they once thought they did understand. We thought we understood the story of Chicken Little; but now we know better—we really don't understand it. And we don't understand it because our conceptual scheme is more sophisticated than it once was. Given a crude concept of the sky, the story presents no conceptual problems. But given a corrected notion of the sky, we know the story to be meaningless.

The application of this moral to our topic is also clear. Our childhood concept of God—the concept of God that is *b'l'shon b'ne adam* (in human language)—allows for attributing to Him certain properties which later appear to us to be not merely false but senseless. We now do not say that God walked in the Garden, but neither did He fail to walk. God is not visible, but neither is He invisible as, say, an electron or a star of the 17th magnitude is invisible. God has neither body, nor does He have any bodily features. He has no extension, but, unlike a mathematical point, neither is He extensionless. Having de-materialized God to this extent, we no longer understand our childhood statements about Him. It is not that we have lost some conceptual capacity we once had. Rather, having corrected our notion of God, we find that what we once thought could be said of Him cannot be said of Him. Having gotten sophisticated we have lost a whole system of statements which once made good sense to us. Nor can we allow ourselves to *make* sense of these statements without sliding back to a primitive childlike conception of the divine.

Of course, we could make metaphorical sense of these statements. But a metaphorical walking or a metaphorical talking does not give us back statements about God's walking or God's talking. I suppose the metaphorical right arm of God corresponds to a metaphorical left arm, and the finger of the Lord is only one of ten analogical fingers; but none of these things is *physical*. Does it make metaphorical sense to say that God weighs a million pounds? A billion pounds? Is there only one metaphorical answer to the metaphorical question: How much does God weigh? If there is more than one, our metaphors are loose indeed. If there is only one answer, we had better drop the pretense of dealing in metaphors, admit that we haven't dematerialized God, and get down to the physics of the divine Body.

No, I think we must admit that whenever we take our predicates in the ordinary literal sense and use them to describe God, we no longer understand any statement that attributes to God a property which presupposes Him to be material. This does not mean we cannot attribute to him physical *agency*. Even an immaterial Being can have material effects. But it does mean that the statements attributing to God certain physical *states* or physical *properties* are meaningless statements. At least this is so for most of us who have accepted the consequences of reconstruing God as a non-material being. And this non-material conception of God is—I think—the standard one. It will repay us to pause for a moment to state what God is on this "standard conception." What can we say of Him, and what can't we say of Him?

We can't say of Him that He weighs or fails to weigh *n* pounds (for any number *n*), nor can we say of Him that He has rough or smooth texture. Nor can we attribute to Him any color, any shape, any location, any degree of malleability, density, viscosity, or motion. Thus we cannot say God is here, not here, or that He is in any state of motion, including the state of zero motion or rest. Indeed, just as we cannot attribute to Him any positive physical property, neither are we able to predicate any privation of these properties. Thus God is not weightless, not colorless, not shapeless; He neither has infinite mass nor negative mass nor zero mass. The point is that none of these predicates is predicable of Him; we cannot say things of God because He is not in the category of matter. A colorless bit of glass lacks color; it is in a state of privation with respect to the property of color. But God has no color, nor does He lack color; He is not that sort of thing. And being the sort of thing He is, we cannot say of Him what we can say of things that belong to the category of matter.

The standard conception of God as an immaterial Being or Spirit does not permit these predications or attributions. On the other hand, it does continue to permit us to say of God that He is merciful or merciless, vengeful or forgiving, rational or irrational, pleased or angry. In other words, having excised the material predicates, we are left with those attributions which pertain to God as a psychic, conscious, personal Being. What we can say of God pertains to Him as Spirit; what we cannot say of Him pertains to Him as bodiless spirit. I think this is a fair, if somewhat crude, summary of the standard conception of God insofar as it bears on the question of what is significantly sayable of Him. This shift from the anthropomorphic childhood conception of God as a *whole* person to that of a Bodiless Spirit is a concession to negative theology. The intelligent adult accepts *half* of the doctrine of negative theology. He is a negative theologian with respect to all material predicates; his theology is positive with respect to psychological predicates.

In what follows I shall show that this compromise position was rightly rejected by negative theology. In this context I mean by negative theology the thesis that nothing at all can be said of God in the sense that it is predicated of anything other than God. Thus if "kind" is to mean the same thing when predicated of God that it means when predicated of Florence Nightingale, then to say of God that He is merciful or kind is to say something meaningless. For negative theology it makes no more sense to say of God that He is merciful than it does to say of Him that He is brown or that He is round.

We have before us so far three views of the divine distinguished according to what we can say of the divine being. On the naïve view, everything predicable of a human being is predicable of the divine being; in the standard or sophisticated conception, all material predicates are unsayable of the divine being; and, finally, the negative theologian claims that nothing predicable of man is predicable of God. In what follows I shall have occasion to add other views to the aforementioned three alternatives. But mainly I shall be concerned with certain basic logical and ontological considerations that count for or against any particular view of the divine nature.

The difference between the naïve and sophisticated conceptions of God cannot fail to remind us of Descartes' theory that persons are ontologically composite entities, non-individuals that are composed of thinking and extended substances. Clearly any acceptable conception of God must be monistic. But in moving from the childlike conception of God as a whole person to the sophisticated conception of a non-material infinite spirit, the point of inflection is a natural moment for the Cartesian: it corresponds exactly to the psycho-physical dualism which is postulated in the Cartesian ontology of persons. This is no accident. I shall be arguing that Cartesian dualism is the natural ontology for the standard conception of God. I shall be arguing that one cannot consistently maintain a non-dualistic conception of man while maintaining at the same time the standard conception of God according to which we can say of Him that he is merciful but cannot say of Him that He is large or small or rough or smooth. Moreover, I shall argue that any non-Cartesian who denies materiality to God is logically forced over to negative theology.

It is time to state the conceptions of coherence which produce these results, and I hope the reader will bear with me while I turn to certain purely formal ontological principles, leaving for later a direct application of these principles to theology.

In the *Topics*, Aristotle asserts the theory that no term can be univocally predicated of things that belong to two different categories. For example, a knife and a musical note are things of different types or categories and this fact alone is sufficient to account for the fact that we cannot say of a knife that it is sharp and of a note that it is sharp and mean by "sharp" the same thing in both those statements. In the *Metaphysics*, Aristotle applies this principle to existence; he says that existence has as many senses as there are categories. This is Aristotle's famous thesis that we cannot univocally predicate existence of things in different categories, so that if we say that tigers exist and that the idea of justice exists we cannot mean the same thing by "exists" in both statements.

I wish to point out that this thesis along with one other very plausible thesis leads directly to negative theology. The second thesis is the theological dogma that God is ontologically *sui generis*, that He belongs to a category by Himself to which no other thing belongs. It follows immediately that nothing can be said of God in the same sense that it is said of any other thing. For all these other things belong to different categories, and all heterotypical predication is equivocal predication. This means, for example, that when we say of God that He exists, is merciful, is powerful and so forth, the terms predicated have different meanings than they have in ordinary use with other things. The view that nothing can be said of God that is said of anything else is precisely the view of negative theology. To call God merciful is nonsensical if by "merciful" we mean what we usually mean. We have already noted that equivocation offers no logical escape from a judgment of nonsense. For example, suppose we tried to save the statement "God is merciful" by pointing out that "merciful" does not mean what it usually means, or even by insisting that in this context the term is used in its "primary" meaning. (This is the Thomist doctrine of analogical predication.) This way of saving the significance of the statement carries with it the admission that in the original and ordinary senses of these words the statement is anyway nonsensical. Thus equivocation does not subtract from impredicability; it just shifts attention away from it. I *could* save the statement that Bertrand Russell is a prime number by pointing out that "prime number" in *that* statement does not mean the same thing as it means in "Seven is a prime number." But in thus saving the statement as a significant one, I must first make the admission that if "prime number" *does* mean the same thing in both statements, then it does not make any sense to predicate it of Bertrand Russell. So all attempts to save the significance of suspect attributions by equivocating terms predicated of God can get nowhere. This is why all analogical theories are illogical theories; there is no middle ground between univocity and equivocity and no way of repairing impredicability by multiplying meanings. For if the terms in their original meanings are impredicable, they remain impredicable.[1]

Negative theology is only an extreme example of the Aristotelian tendency to equivocate all predicates that are nominally predicable of God and other things. This position honestly accepts the consequences of the thesis that all heterotypical predication is necessarily equivocal along with the theological dogma that God is in a special category. For if we cannot say what we normally mean, we might as well admit that we cannot say what we mean. Negative theology is therefore an honest extreme. But I think also that it is a *reductio ad absurdum* of rational theology. To the question, "What can we say of God?", the negative theologian answers, "Nothing." If he is right, theology is — to use the Kantian characterization—"not a possible science."

Are we then—on these logical grounds—forced to accept negative theology? If the theory that all predication over different categories must be equivocal were correct, it would be difficult to see how negative theology could be avoided. For surely any rational theology must allow for the possibility that God is categorically unique. However, the logical theory is wrong; there are no compelling reasons to assume that things in different categories cannot have the same attributes. For example, if Sally Jones is interested in both men and mathematics—but more interested in men—then both men and mathematics have the characteristic of being interesting to Sally. Moreover, the term "interests Sally" as applied to both must be univocal; otherwise we could not say that Sally is *more* interested in one than the

---

[1] Analogical doctrines of the divine attributes suffer from the fact that no property may be literally predicated of God. In the normal case we literally predicate *P* of *a* and "analogically" predicate *P* of *b*. But we independently understand that b is because some other predicate, Q, *literally* applies to b. Analogical theories of the divine attributes illicitly trade on the normal use of analogy.

other. Equivocally applied, the term could not serve to make the comparison. Thus in the statements, "This man is rational," "This number is rational," the term "rational" is equivocally applied. Otherwise, we could use the term comparatively and say, for example, that this man is more rational than that number. Conversely, when the term *does* have a comparative use, it must be univocal. There are, indeed, *many* instances of things in different categories that are compared with respect to certain properties. We can, for example, compare events and material objects with respect to duration. Thus we can say that the sand in the upper half of an hour glass lasted as long as Lincoln's Gettysburg address. And here the term "lasted an hour" is predicated univocally of things in different categories, namely the sand and the speech. There is therefore no logical reason to say the same term cannot be univocally said of things of different types, no logical grounds for denying that the same attribute can be attributed to things in different categories. The logical argument for negative theology fails; it does not count against the possibility of saying of God what can be said of other things and of saying it univocally.

I have paid attention to this false logical theory because it has undoubtedly played a role in persuading some philosophers to accept negative theology as the only logically coherent possibility. It ought to be remembered that Maimonides, who adopted negative theology, was an Aristotelian, and that Aristotle clearly adhered to the doctrine that heterotypical predication must be equivocal. The doctrine, I say, is logically untenable. However, there are other formal considerations to which we must now turn. And these considerations provide sounder reasons for adopting a particular theological doctrine about what we can and cannot say of God.

I mentioned above that the naïve and sophisticated conceptions of God divided at a Cartesian point. And I should like to expose an argument implicit in the Cartesian dualism of mind and matter according to which persons are non-individuals. The argument itself is formally valid, whatever one might think of the truth of its premises or of the ontological doctrine of psycho-physical dualism in general.

The premises are these:

1) There are things of which it makes sense to say that they think or fail to think of Paris but of which we cannot say that they are five feet long or that they fail to be five feet long. An example of such a thing is the "I" of the "Second Meditation," the pure Ego, as yet not associated with a body. Let us call such things thinking substances.

2) There are other things of which it makes sense to say they are or fail to be five feet long but of which it makes no sense to say they think or fail to think of Paris. A piece of wax is an example of such an individual. Let us call things of this type material objects or extended substances.

These two premises establish that the features of Thought and Extension are *ontologically exclusive*. It follows that anything that has both thought and extension, anything of which it makes sense to say that it is five feet tall and that it thinks of Paris— such a thing cannot be an individual thing. Thus ordinary living persons are non-individuals, since of *them* we can significantly predicate determinations of the feature of Thought *and* Extension.

The formal outlines of this argument are clear. Once we establish that a pair of features is exclusive, it follows that any entity possessing both features is a non-individual. And one way of showing that a pair of features is exclusive is by showing that there are two things such that determinations of one feature apply to the first but not to the second while determinations of the other feature apply to the second but not to the first. Before applying this principle to the theological doctrine of attributes, let me take one other example as an illustration. The phenomenalist considers a material object, a bell, to be a collection of colors, shapes, sounds and other phenomenal data. In other words, for the phenomenalist the bell is not an individual but a composite entity. His argument for this position goes something like this:

1) There are things of which it makes sense to say they are red but of which it does not make sense to say they are noisy or loud. A color is such a thing.

2) There are other things of which it makes sense to say
they are noisy or loud but no sense to say they are red. A
sound is such a thing.

This establishes that colors and sounds have exclusive
features. It follows that anything of which it makes sense to
predicate both determinations is a non–individual. But it makes
sense to say of a bell that it is red and also that it is loud. We
conclude that the bell is not an individual but is a composite
thing possessing exclusive ontological features.[2]

We are now in a position to apply this principle in rational
theology. I shall make one assumption as a condition of adequacy
for any rational theology. An adequate conception of God must
be one in which God is not a composite being. This assumption
is more traditionally known as the dogma of God's Unity, His
Oneness. Rational theology finds a place for the divine within
an ontological scheme. In any ontology in which God is placed,
I shall assume that He is an individual and that He is not
constituted by other individuals. We have seen enough to know
that this condition may or may not be satisfied depending on
the other individuals assumed in the ontology. When it is not
satisfied for a given conception of God, then I shall vary the
conception, removing or adding ontological features in order
to satisfy the conditions of ontological coherence. In this
procedure I shall keep one thing fixed, the unity of God.

We proceed in the following way: We first say something
about the ontology in which we propose to locate God. This
ontology with which we start I shall call the "embedding
ontology." The notion of God that is consistent with that
ontology I shall call the theology of that ontology. Once we see
the relation of God to the other entities of the ontology it
becomes clear just what can be said of Him and what cannot.
(Of course whatever can be said of Him can also be said of
some other things in the ontology. For if it turns out that what
can be said of God is sayable of nothing else, then this is equivalent

---

[2] For discussion of the theory of ontological features, see the author's article
"Predicability" in *Philosophy in America*, ed. by Max Black, Allen and Unwin,
1965. See also, "Types of Ontology" in the *Philosophical Review*, Vol. LXXII,
No. 3, July 1963.

to the negative theologian's position that nothing can be said of Him. Nor—as we have noted earlier—does "equivocating" change matters.) Finally, we start with other embedding ontologies, repeat the process and make comparisons.

Let us for example suppose that the embedding ontology is non-Cartesian, and that the living human beings in the ontology are individuals and not composite. I shall call this conception of persons Aristotelian to distinguish it from the Cartesian dualistic conception. Let us further suppose that while it makes sense to say of a human being that he is thinking or failing to think about Paris, it does not make sense to say this of a material inanimate object such as a bit of glass. I do not think that this ontology is at all unusual. But now let us suppose that God is introduced into it and that He is construed according to the standard conception. He is therefore a being that has the feature of thought but not the feature of extension. If this is so, thought and extension become exclusive features of this ontology. For God has only thought but no extension, while inanimate matter has extension but no thought. Thus thought and extension are exclusive features that cannot be possessed by individuals. But by hypothesis they are both possessed by human beings, and human beings are individuals of the embedding ontology. The embedding ontology is therefore inconsistent with its theology.

Note that the source of our trouble is the introduction of the standard conception of God. For in the embedding non-Cartesian or "Aristotelian" ontology, Thought and Extension are *not* exclusive features; nothing is said about the possibility of a pure spirit that is disembodied. In the embedding ontology all those things that have thought also have extension. Given this ontology, it becomes impossible to conceive of God as a pure spirit. The standard conception of God cannot be located in this Aristotelian scheme of things. The question arises: How then *may* we conceive of Him?

Clearly, one way out is negative theology. According to negative theology, we do not commit ourselves to saying anything which pre-supposes God to have any feature whatsoever. In particular we do not commit ourselves to a conception in which God is a thinking thing. Thus we do not introduce into the

Aristotelian ontology the embarrassing assumption which we just saw is fatal to the standard conception. But perhaps we escape incoherence only to fall victim to silence. For the negative theologian does not so much achieve a theology that is consistent with the embedding ontology as he avoids one that is inconsistent with it.[3]

A conception of God that is entirely consistent with the non-Cartesian embedding ontology is that of the child. This is not surprising, since the naïve or childlike conception of God is entirely anthropomorphic; it introduces no new categories into the embedding ontology. God is a person; He possesses Thought and Extension. Of course, He differs radically in His determinations of these basic features. But like any other person, He has both Thought and Extension. As long as we stick to this theology we have not introduced anything that will lead us to consider Thought and Extension to be exclusive features. And if Thought and Extension are not exclusive features, then the principle of individuation we have been applying will not affect the status of persons as individuals.

The two theologies consistent with an "Aristotelian" ontology of persons are the naïve anthropomorphic theology and negative theology. It seems that anyone who is committed to the standard conception of God will have to avoid this non-Cartesian doctrine of persons. If they do so and begin with psycho-physical dualism there will be no difficulty. God is then categorically like the pure Cartesian Ego. Nor are there any individuals that have both the features of Thought and Extension. For Descartes persons are non-individuals, and indeed they must be ontologically composite since both God and egos

---

[3] The position of pantheism is diametrically opposed to negative theology, since, in one of its interpretations, all possible predications are *significantly* applicable to God as the single subject of all attributes. The position is derivable from the Aristotelian doctrine discussed above. For together with the assumption that existence is *univocally* predicable of, say, numbers and men, it will follow that numbers and men are in one category. The additional assumption that both are modes of a single substance makes this palatable. I have not discussed the pantheistic alternative in the body of the paper and have concentrated instead on those doctrines which distinguish between what can and what *cannot* be said of the divine nature.

possess Thought without Extension, while inanimate material bodies possess Extension without Thought, and this excludes the possibility that any individual of the ontology has both of these features. If, therefore, we revise the embedding ontology by accepting a Cartesian view of persons, we thereby omit "Aristotelian persons" as a category of individuals, and then the standard of God is easily locatable.

The question arises whether Cartesianism is the *only* way to save the standard conception. It is in fact not the only way. And I should like to point out one other possible revision of the embedding ontology that will allow for the standard conception.

We recall once more just how the standard conception requires the Cartesian dualism of persons. For suppose the standard conception is adopted and that we nevertheless assume that persons are individuals possessing both Thought and Extension. Then we have on the one hand God who is neither extended nor extensionless, who has neither the property nor its privation and therefore lacks the "feature" of Extension. And on the other hand we have *merely* material objects, inanimate bodies that lack the feature of Thought. But this contradicts our initial assumption that Thought and Extension are *not* exclusive features, i.e., that persons are ontological individuals possessing both Thought and Extension. For if an ontological *individual* possesses two features, those features are not exclusive.

Let us however stay with a non-Cartesian conception of persons and continue to assume that persons are ontological individuals. Let us also insist on retaining the standard conception of God.

God and persons are now categorically different, since persons have Extension while God does not.

We note immediately that in this ontology there can now be nothing that possesses Extension without also possessing Thought. This means that the so-called inanimate things cannot be devoid of the *feature* of Thought. We see then that an *animistic* conception of material objects is a coherent alternative to Cartesianism. In a non-Cartesian ontology embodying the standard conception of God, it must make sense to say of a stone that it thinks or fails to think of Paris. In such a scheme all objects have the feature of thought, and there is no categorical difference between persons and other physical objects. Since God, persons, and all physical objects possess thought, this ontology is thoroughly panpsychistic.

In sum, for anyone who begins with what I have been calling the "standard" theological conception of God as a bodiless spirit there are only two available ontologies: in the first, persons are construed as composite Cartesian beings; in the second, material objects are construed as animistic. Some reflection convinces us that no third alternative is available to the non-Cartesian who has denied extension of God. It is no wonder therefore that the medieval Aristotelians were attracted to negative theology.

We noted earlier that negative theology was the consequence of a false logical theory. But even if we reject the theory there are still good grounds for negative theology. The grounds in fact are as good as the grounds for avoiding Cartesian dualism, panpsychism, and the naïve anthropomorphic conception of God. Anyone who finds all three of these alternatives untenable will be forced to accept negative theology as the only remaining possibility.

Let me now summarize the results of the discussion. We have before us four doctrines. Negative theology is consistent with any ontology but is forced on anyone who rejects both Cartesianism and panpsychism while refusing to adopt an anthropomorphic conception of God. The anthropomorphic conception is likewise consistent with any ontology but is forced on anyone who rejects Cartesianism and panpsychism, while refusing to go to the extreme of negative theology. On the standard conception of God, God is a bodiless spirit. Two ontologies are consistent with it, Cartesian dualism and panpsychism.

It is interesting that the three positive theological conceptions have a certain symmetry. Cartesianism is in the center, and it provides no difficulties for the standard conception. If, however, we adopt an "Aristotelian" ontology that avoids psycho-physical dualism, then we have two extremes. We can, on the one hand, revise our notion of physical objects in the direction of animism. In this revision we give to all material objects the feature of

Thought, so that any extended substance is also a thinking substance. This is the solution of panpsychism. We can, on the other hand, give to God the feature of Extension, so that all things that have Thought have Extension. That brings us back to the naïve anthropomorphic conception of God, and in this solution, too, Thought and Extension are not exclusive features. The choice between panpsychism and anthropomorphism is forced only on those who reject Cartesian dualism. For only the non-Cartesian is embarrassed by the fact that Thought and Extension are exclusive features of an ontology containing a bodiless Spirit on the one side and inert matter on the other. The Cartesian is not so embarrassed, since persons are composed of two substances with exclusive features.

All four doctrines are coherent. This gives rise to the very natural question of choosing from among them the right doctrine. On this question I have little to say. But the following considerations must play a part in any adoption of a particular rational theology that meets the conditions of ontological coherence:

> 1) The naive anthropomorphic view requires the least tampering with the ontology of the ordinary man. In this ontology, persons are individuals and so are inanimate objects. Moreover, some things that can be said of persons cannot be said of inanimate objects; the common sense ontology is not animistic, at least it no longer is. While the ontology is philosophically attractive—and especially attractive to the Aristotelian—the theology of anthropomorphism is less so. I am inclined to favor it, however; it seems that medieval theologians were too hasty in their efforts to remove from God all traces of materiality. The price of this spiritualization is rather high, and it would certainly pay to take another look at a theology in which God belongs to the category of persons.

> 2) The Cartesian alternative is theologically attractive, philosophically less so. But here, too, the theological advantages of a God conceived of as a bodiless spirit may prove the worth of the ontological inelegance of psycho-physical dualism. Moreover, the Cartesian position has one advantage over other ontologies. It allows for a clear-cut notion of immortality. I have not discussed the ramifications for immortal spirits of

the coherent theological alternatives. But it should be noted that the naïve or anthropomorphic conception of God will require that immortal spirits are also material, so that it will make sense to ask how much they weigh, what color they are, and so forth. The Cartesian alternative requires no such view of immortality.

3) We have seen that the non-Cartesian who rejects a naïve theology must be animistic. The view is philosophically less respectable than some others. Undeservedly so, I think. The line between animate and inanimate matter is perhaps not a line that divides two categories of things but merely a line that divides two classes of things of the same category. Whether this alternative proves to be attractive is partly a matter of the way in which certain biophysical sciences develop, particularly the science of molecular biology. Also we already have in this century one example of a well-worked out panpsychistic metaphysics that avoids Cartesian dualism and adopts a version of the standard conception of God as a bodiless spirit. I refer to the ontology and theology of A. N. Whitehead. Panpsychism is an alternative that may become more attractive still. Certainly the arguments against it are hardly fatal to it, and they do overlook its considerable theological advantages.

4) Once again we come to negative theology. This is the doctrine which enjoins upon us a rational silence about those things of which we cannot speak. And I shall conclude this paper by finally taking this excellent advice.

14

John Henry Newman and the Demea Tradition in Anglican Theology

Peter Carnley

One of the more disastrous historical engagements of University and Church finally came to grief in 1858 when John Henry Newman returned to England from Ireland, his dream of establishing a Roman Catholic University in irretrievable tatters. The failure of the Irish bishops to support the venture with candour, and their apparent reluctance to deliver when it came to the promised reward of arranging to have Newman himself made a bishop, left him despondent, disillusioned and betrayed. Indeed, Newman's perceived disenchantment with the Irish hierarchy and general sense of alienation as a Roman Catholic inclined some to conclude that he was looking more favourably on his former experience as an Anglican. There were rumours in this period that he might even be thinking of a return to the Church of his baptism.[1]

---

[1] See Meriol Trevor, *Newman: Light in Winter* (London: Macmillan, 1962), pp. 215-6; Ian Ker, *John Henry Newman, a Biography* (Oxford: Clarendon Press, 1988), pp. 508-11.

Certainly, the years following the Catholic university debacle saw a gradual return to serious theological writing and a preparedness once again to put his own ideas on the line, something he had not done since converting to Roman Catholicism in 1845. Newman was troubled that as a Roman Catholic he did not have the influence and standing he formerly enjoyed as a theologian and writer, and could not make the positive contribution to the life of the Church that he had been able to make as an Anglican. What may not have been so apparent to Newman at the time was that he was beginning to re-engage with the fundamental themes of a theological tradition in which he had been formed in his Anglican days. For though he had changed his ecclesiastical allegiance in 1845, his basic theological stance remained much as it had ever been. From 1858 onwards salient elements of this fundamental theological orientation began to resurface and flower.

After withdrawing from Oxford to Littlemore after the publication of *Tract 90,* Newman endured a self-imposed suspension of the active exercise of priestly ministry and returned to a lay state for two years on the grounds that, if the Anglican bishops who persisted in 'mentioning' him in their pastoral charges would not allow him to entertain the interpretation of the Thirty-Nine Articles he had advanced in *Tract 90*, then he could not comply with the requirement to assent to them.[2] Given that assent to the Articles was necessary in order to function as a priest, Newman had painted himself into a corner. Clearly, this situation could not last indefinitely and finally he had little alternative than to move elsewhere. The writing of *The Development of Doctrine* furnished him with a rationale sufficient to help him over the intellectual hurdle posed by the need to revise his former views, though he showed little inclination to defend it or to answer the criticism of his reviewers. Thereafter his theological voice effectively fell silent for over a decade.

---

[2] *Apologia pro Vita Sua*, ed. Maisie Ward (London: Sheed and Ward, paperback edition, 1976), p. 124. After his last sermon in September, 1843, Newman voluntarily went into "lay communion," with "no Anglican oath, no clerical duty, no ecclesiastical administration."

Between 1846 and 1859, he neither engaged in theological controversy nor contributed to public theological discussion in any significantly creative way for, as he himself put it, upon his conversion to Rome the history of his religious opinions came to an end.[3] Thereafter he had no remarkably new theological ideas, and could not identify any notable alterations in his own religious beliefs, for he simply accepted the authoritative doctrinal positions of the Roman Catholic Church. Certainly, during this period, Newman does not appear to have felt any pressing need creatively to express theological ideas of his own systematic construction. He produced some pieces of an autobiographical kind that tended to be self-justificatory and polemical in nature, but he was otherwise preoccupied for a good seven years with the work of trying to get the proposed Catholic University off the ground. Apart from purporting not to have any new theological opinions of his own, in this early Roman Catholic period he was probably too busy to have any. Having become a Roman Catholic, his theological commitments were simply those of the Church to which he was prepared to give docile assent.[4]

This mood changed upon his return from Ireland in 1858. Now that he could no longer productively put his energies into establishing in Dublin a Roman Catholic equivalent of the Anglican Oxford that he had left behind, he began to express the desire to go back to his old studies, "and do something, if life is given me, more solid than I have done hitherto."[5] Despite his disclaimers about having any theological opinions of his own, he spoke of "how for years and years . . . I have wished to write on Faith and Reason—but the good time for it has never come." And even though in his despondency he lamented that he was now "too old; too weary, too weak, and too busy,"[6] something of his old terrier-like passion as a controversialist gradually returned;

---

[3] Ibid, p. 160.

[4] In the period 1846 to 1859, Newman published *Loss and Gain* (1848), *Difficulties and Anglicans* (1850), *The Present Position of Catholics* (1851), *Dublin Discourses* (1852), *Callista* (a novel, 1855), *Office and Work of Universities* (1856), and *Lectures and Essays on University Subjects* (1859). The period is not distinguished by any notable theological originality.

[5] *The Letters and Diaries of John Henry Newman*, ed. C. S. Dessain et al. Oxford: University Press, 1978-84), Vol. xviii, p. 547.

[6] Ibid, Vol. xix, p. 500.

it was not long before something of the intellectual energy of his theological youth commenced to flow once again.

Perhaps it is not surprising to find that, as he began to reconnect with his Anglican roots and to participate once again in overt theological discussion, many of his theological and ecclesial concerns were to run parallel with what were then live issues within Anglicanism. After his public confrontation with Charles Kingsley about the place of truth amongst Roman Catholic clergy, the writing of his *Apologia* necessarily led him to revisit the formative influences in his earlier Anglican life. Sections of the text were sent to his former acquaintances for them to read so as to verify his own memories. Not long after, in 1865, he met again with Keble and Pusey whom he had not seen since the parting of 1845. This physical reconnection was a tangible token of an intellectual re-engagement which had been slowly and silently developing since his return from Ireland seven years earlier.

In the 1850s, for example, synodical government was beginning to emerge in the Churches of the Anglican Communion, notably as a consequence of the pioneering work of the first Bishop of New Zealand, George Selwyn, who established a Synod for the Church of the Province of New Zealand as early as 1844. Building on initiatives taken by the Episcopal Church in the United States immediately after the War of Independence, Selwyn, as a Tractarian, was only too pleased to secure the freedom of the Church from State control by promoting constitutional autonomy. At the same time he embraced with enthusiasm the need to involve the laity in synodical structures. Not only in New Zealand, but within the Church of England itself from which he had come, Selwyn continued to exercise considerable influence. By the time of the first Lambeth Conference of 1867 he was the acknowledged authority on such matters; Selwyn it was who drafted the original Lambeth guidelines for synodical government that have since been followed in the Churches of the Anglican Communion. The subject of the role of the laity in decision making was a continuing issue in the context of these developments, with Newman's former Oxford Movement colleagues adopting divergent viewpoints with respect to the place of the laity in the Church. Pusey, for example, was happy enough to admit lay people to a share in the temporal affairs of the Church, such as the maintenance of buildings, the raising of finance and the like, but not in matters of doctrine.[7]

Given these debates about the role of the laity in the emerging synodical structures of Anglicanism, it is unlikely to be mere coincidence that, upon his return from Ireland, Newman himself became involved in a controversy that was the counterpart to these Anglican developments, but otherwise self-contained within the Roman Catholic Church. However, by publishing the tract *On Consulting the Faithful in Matters of Doctrine* shortly after his return from Ireland, Newman, whom Manning thought only ever to have been 'half-converted,' thereby brought down upon himself the wrath of the Roman Catholic hierarchy who judged him to be untrustworthy and unreliable. All this precipitated the famous charge of Monsigner Talbot in Rome that Newman was "the most dangerous man in England." Indeed, a certain sense of *déjà vu* did not escape Newman himself who felt with some melodramatic hand wringing that his brush with authority in the Church of England in 1841 was now being replayed in the Church of Rome.[8]

This tense exchange about the role of the laity within the Roman Catholic Church was 'overheard' in Anglican circles, as it were, and in this indirect way Newman contributed at one stage removed to the emerging more general Anglican consensus of the time concerning the legitimate role of the laity in the exercise of authority in the Church. Indeed, Newman's views

---

[7] Robert Gray, the Archbishop of Cape Town, who had called conferences in 1848 and 1851 to discuss synodical government, was in England to pursue the question in 1852. After a meeting with Pusey he recorded the following diary entry: "Talked also about Synods; found him alarmed at the readiness with which the whole Church was disposed to give power on points of doctrine to laity. Found he did not agree with the view that their assent should be asked in points of doctrine; regarded ancient precedents as complimentary, more than as involving privileges. Has a manuscript work on the subject ready for the press, but has lost it, having lent it to someone who has never returned it." *Life of Robert Gray*, ed. Charles Gray (London: Oxford and Cambridge: Rivingtons, 1876), Vol i, p. 358.

[8] See Meriol Trevor, op. cit., pp. 219-20.

on the importance of the reception of doctrinal definition by the laity and the need to consult the laity in doctrinal matters may be said to have found more favour within the subsequent history of Anglicanism and its developing synodical structures than within Roman Catholicism.

Almost at the same time, Newman picked up an interest in the theology of Henry Longueville Mansel, whose Bampton Lectures were delivered at Oxford in 1858 and given wide publicity.[9] Newman's return from Ireland coincided with their publication and he cannot have been unaware of the extensive interest they aroused—both the applause from contemporary orthodoxy and the religious press, and the spirited controversy, most notably, the heated public exchange between Mansel and F.D. Maurice.[10]

By contrast with Maurice, Newman found Mansel's views concerning the inscrutable mystery of God, and the limited capacity of human reason to achieve a knowledge of God, very congenial. Indeed, to a degree to which even Newman himself may not have been consciously aware, Mansel's Bamptons helped Newman to reconnect with his original Anglican theological underpinning, and perhaps more than anything else rekindled Newman's theological motivation for serious theological writing once again.[11] In a letter to Charles Meynell, who was Professor

---

[9] H.L. Mansel, *The Limits of Religious Thought* (London: John Murray): two editions were published in 1858 and two in 1859; a fifth edition in 1867 was reprinted in 1870.

[10] See F.D. Maurice, *What is Revelation? Letters to a Student of Theology on the Bampton Lectures of Mr. Mansel* (London: Macmillan, 1859) and Mansel's response *An Examination of the Rev. F. D. Maurice's Strictures on the Bampton Lectures of 1858* (1859). In a letter to Alexander Macmillan dated 1 September 1859 Maurice said: "If the religious world had not declared almost en masse in favour of Mansel I would not have written against him." By contrast the first bundle of reviews of his own reply to Mansel were "exceedingly unfavourable." See *The Life of Frederick Denison Maurice*, ed. by Frederick Maurice (New York: Scribners, 1884), Vol. ii, pp. 348-9. Maurice's fortunes were eventually to improve, however, at Mansel's expense.

[11] It is surprising that biographers and commentators show little interest in Newman's connection with Mansel. Meriol Trevor's otherwise exemplary biography does not so much as mention Mansel; Ian Ker's splendid *John Henry Newman, A Biography* (Oxford: Clarendon Press, 1988) likewise is entirely silent with respect to Mansel and Newman, perhaps because Ker's literary interest allows little inclination for the discussions of the Anglican antecedents of Newman's theology.

of Philosophy at Oscott College, the Roman Catholic Seminary near Birmingham, on 20 December 1859, Newman wrote: "I have read a good deal of Mansel's book, enough to show me that, as far as I may do so without risk of false doctrine or temerity, I agree with it."[12] Indeed, while he found objection with some of the things which Mansel said, his fundamental sense of agreement was so profound that Newman even felt that Mansel had drawn upon his own theological insights of a generation earlier. In signaling his agreement with Mansel's work, he went on to say, "It seems to me taken from my own Protestant teaching." Along with the letter to Meynell, Newman therefore enclosed a copy of his own *University Sermons* which contained some of the views which Mansel was alleged to have followed and which, said Newman, "I still hold."

The idea that Mansel's general thesis had been derived from the early Newman had in fact been suggested in a review of the *The Limits of Religious Thought* by Richard Simpson in *The Rambler* of December the previous year (1858), only weeks after Newman's retreat from Ireland.[13] Simpson had said that Mansel had in his lectures covered the very same ground as his "illustrious predecessor" Newman. Indeed, he mischievously went on to say that Mansel had "so diligently cultivated" and had reached "conclusions much alike" to the ideas of Newman and attained a "wonderful conformity" even in his phraseology to Newman's original work, but had omitted to mention his dependence upon Newman by name! Whether Newman would himself have come to the conviction that Mansel had based his lectures on his own original thought independently of Simpson's prompting is an open question.

In any event, in response to this, in the Preface to the third edition of *The Limits,* Mansel acknowledged the similarity of his thought with that of Newman, but protested that Newman's time at St. Mary's, Oxford, was nearly at an end when his own connection with Oxford began, and that he had had only the slightest acquaintance with the thought of Newman. What he

---

[12] *Letters and Diaries*, op. cit., Vol. xix, p. 256.
[13] Mansel was scholar (1839) and then tutor (1844) at St. John's College, Oxford.

did know of Newman's work did not strike him as having any bearing on his own argument.[14] *The Rambler* of July 1859, which Newman himself edited, quoted Mansel's disclaimer of direct dependence in the face of the similarities that Simpson had detected. Indeed, Newman said generously that Mansel's Preface to the third edition of *The Limits* had been a great surprise to him. It had given him much pleasure, a pleasure preceded by no pain, and it had not occurred to him that Mansel had deliberately passed him over.[15] Despite this, Newman continued in his letter to Meynell some months later to promote the suspicion that Mansel had drawn upon his own earlier work. The call to Christian humility not withstanding, Newman seems to have accepted the view that Mansel was simply derivative of himself.

In any event, and very importantly, Newman confessed to Meynell that, stimulated by the reading of Mansel's work, he was considering republishing the *University Sermons* with a new introduction designed to draw out the argument into 'propositions with something of system.' On 7 November 1859 he had already begun what was to remain in his lifetime an unpublished twenty-two page essay on the proof of the existence of God from a consideration of conscience,[16] the first of a number of false starts that eventually led to the publication in 1870 of *An Essay in Aid of a Grammar of Assent.*

What is patently clear is that during 1859 the reading of Mansel's Bampton lectures revitalized Newman's theological mind. It triggered his return to serious theological reflection and prompted him to pick up his abiding interest in an approach to religious knowledge understood as an awareness in faith of the mystery of God and an engagement with the Divine Will, not as a consequence of syllogistic reasoning, but through the operation of conscience. The importance of the contribution of Mansel in 1858-9 with respect to Newman's own subsequent theological output was enormous. Indeed, it led directly to the writing of what is arguably his most important theological work.

---

[14] *The Rambler*, December 1858, pp. 407-15. See especially p. 409.

[15] *The Rambler*, July 1859, pp. 247-248.

[16] Published in *The Argument From Conscience to the Existence of God*, ed. Adrian J. Boekraad and Henry Tristram (Louvain: Editions Nauwelaerts, 1961), pp. 103-25.

What seems to have escaped Newman at the time was that both he and Mansel were actually heirs to a common Anglican theological tradition. Indeed, Mansel was instrumental in re-connecting Newman with some very profound elements in a strain of characteristically Anglican theology of the eighteenth and early nineteenth cenutries, which flourished particularly at Oriel in Newman's formative years, and which Mansel himself succeeded in bringing to wide public attention once again in 1858.

For want of a better name this strain of Anglican theology may be called the Demea tradition, following the name of the fictitious but theologically representative character who is used by Hume in his *Dialogues Concerning Natural Religion* (1751+) to give definitive expression to it. Briefly put, the theological position articulated by Demea represents the theological stance of those who in Hume's day emphasized faith and revelation, the otherwise unknowable mystery and 'otherness' of God, and the essential dissimilarity between human and divine nature. Opposed to them were those who favoured a natural theology based on reason, which focused upon the apprehension of an alleged design in the material universe in order then to ground claims to a knowledge of the being and nature of the divine, an approach which entailed the essential similarity between the divine mind and human intelligence. This latter theological viewpoint of the party of "reason and evidence" is expressed in the *Dialogues* by Cleanthes, and in the historical context of the post-Newtonian world by physico-scientific theologians such as Ray, Boyle and Paley. It is a viewpoint that was very vigorously defended by George Berkeley.[17] Thus in the *Dialogues* Hume has Cleanthes argue from design in the universe to the similarities between divine and human intelligence.

> Look round the world: Contemplate the whole and every part of it: You will find it to be nothing but one great machine, subdivided into an infinite number of lesser machines ... The

---

[17] Berkeley may have provided Hume with the name Demea. As one who was unsympathetic with the fideistic negative theology of his day, Berkeley, in a passing reference to 'honest Demea,' takes the opportunity, somewhat unfairly, to make Demea represent those who are rigidly orthodox but afraid to think. See *Alciphron*, VII:27.

curious adapting of means to ends, throughout all nature, resembles exactly, though it much exceeds, the productions of human contrivance; of human design, thought, wisdom, and intelligence. Since ... the effects resemble each other, we are led to infer by all the rules of analogy, that the causes also resemble; and that the Author of Nature is somewhat similar to the mind of man; though possessed of much larger faculties, proportioned to the grandeur of the work, which he has executed. By this argument "a posteriori," and by this argument alone, do we prove at once the existence of a Deity, and his similarity to human mind and intelligence.[18]

In other words, because "like effects arise from like causes" an inference may be drawn from the created order to divine contrivance. In consequence Philo, the third contributing character in the *Dialogues*, and a skeptic, draws out with incisive critical probes the anthropomorphic implications of the design argument: "God has a mind like the human," said Philo. "I know of no other," replied Cleanthes. "And the liker the better," insisted Philo. "To be sure," said Cleanthes.[19]

By contrast, Demea defends "the adorable mysteriousness of the divine nature," for God is radically unlike humans, incomprehensibly sublime and unknowable as He is in Himself. This in turn entails both for Demea and Philo, but in a way that contrasts with the position espoused by Cleanthes, a certain agreement about the limitations of human reason. For example, Philo is made to say:

> Let us become thoroughly sensible of the weakness, blindness, and narrow limits of human reason: Let us duly consider its uncertainty and endless contrarieties, even in subjects of common life and practice ... who can retain much confidence in this frail faculty of reason as to pay any regard to its determinations in points so sublime, so abstruse, so remote from common life and experience?[20]

---

[18] David Hume, *Dialogues Concerning Natural Religion*, ed. Stanley Tweyman (London and New York: Routledge, 1991), p. 109.

[19] Ibid., p. 129.

[20] Ibid., p. 98.

In response to these words of Philo, Hume writes, "Demea seemed to imply an unreserved satisfaction in the doctrines delivered."[21] Indeed, Cleanthes has the problem of slipping perilously close to the idolatry of fashioning God in a human form, for "by representing the Deity as so intelligible, and comprehensible, and so similar to the human mind," says Demea, "we are guilty of the grossest and most narrow partiality, and make ourselves the model of the whole universe."[22]

In reaction to the rationalism of Cleanthes' position, and in a way that anticipates Schleiermacher, Demea's God is apprehended within the inner life of the religious subject:

> 'It is my opinion, I own,' replied Demea, 'that each man feels, in a manner, the truth of religion within his own breast; and from a consciousness of his imbecility and misery, rather than from any reasoning, is led to seek protection from that Being, on whom he and all nature is dependent.'[23]

Philo, apparently agreeing with Demea's fideism, asks ". . . is it necessary to prove what everyone feels within himself?" Nevertheless, Demea does not entirely reject a natural theology based on the evidence of the physical universe, but simply proposes the postponement of the teaching of it in favour of an early concentration on piety. Faith and piety, devotion and worship come first; only then does reason have a role as faith seeks further understanding.[24]

Cleanthes' rationalistic bent in turn finds what is referred to as the "rigid inflexible orthodoxy" of Demea all too mystical; such theologians are "mystics, who maintain the absolute incomprehensibility of the deity." [25] Indeed, noting a certain similarity between the negative theology of Demea and the skeptical position of Philo, Cleanthes expresses puzzlement by asking how mystics such as Demea "differ from skeptics and

---

[21] Ibid., p. 99.
[22] Ibid., p. 120.
[23] Ibid., p. 152.
[24] 'It is only as a science,' replied Demea, 'subjected to human reasoning and disputation, that I postpone the study of natural theology.' Ibid., p. 97.
[25] Ibid., p. 122.

atheists, who assert, that the first cause of all is unknown and unintelligible?"²⁶ In the polite name-calling of this passage the term "mystic" tends to acquire a pejorative sense, and Demea responds to the taunts of Cleanthes by saying, "anthropomorphite is an appellation as insidious . . . as the epithet Mystic." But Cleanthes persists: Demea theologians are "complete mystics . . . They are, in a word, atheists, without knowing it."

Philo, however, reveals that Hume was more sensitively aware of the orthdox pedigree of the Demea position: "You are honouring with the appellation of atheist," says Philo, "all the sound, orthodox divines almost who have ever treated of this subject . . ."²⁷ Nevertheless, Hume, who may have been perplexed as to how to handle the Demea position, chooses to assign centre stage to Cleanthes, and in the subsequent history of the critical discussion of the _Dialogues,_ it is in fact the design argument that has attracted most attention. Indeed, Hume's presentation of Demea is, if anything, somewhat thin, for he uses Demea to destabilize Cleanthes' approach to God by argument from design, but without really doing justice to the Demea position itself. This has meant that, in the history of philosophical theology subsequent to Hume, it has been almost wholly neglected.²⁸ As a consequence, the significance of the Demea tradition in Anglican theology in the eighteenth and nineteenth centuries

---

²⁶ Ibid. Anthony Collins provides an example of a thinker who prior to Hume had exploited the position assigned by him to Demea in a "freethinking" direction. See his _Disclosure on Freethinking_ (London, 1713). Though Collins claimed to be a sincere Christian, George Berkeley thought him to be a crypto-atheist.

²⁷ Ibid., 123. Not least amongst these is St. Paul himself in Romans 11:33: "O the depth of the riches and wisdom of God! How unsearchable are his judgments and how inscrutable his ways! For who has known the mind of the Lord, or who has been his counsellor?"

²⁸ One exception is J. Dye, "A Word on Behalf of Demea," _Hume Studies,_ 15, 1989, pp. 120-40. See also D.C. Stove, "Part IX of Hume's Dialogues," _Philosophical Quarterly,_ 28, 1978, pp. 300-9 and Donald E. Stahl, "Hume's Dialogue IX Defended," _Philosophical Quarterly,_ 34, 1984, pp. 505-7. Dye notes that Hume has Demea speak inconsistently as if "to make the reader wonder whether this character is supposed to think at all about the implications of the claims he espouses" (p. 121) and that Demea's small role in the _Dialogues_ suggests that "Hume does not take it all seriously."

and its absolute importance for an understanding of the theology of John Henry Newman has been almost entirely overlooked.

Newman had some acquaintance with the writings of David Hume. For example, he mentions in his *Apologia* having read Hume, and elsewhere discusses Hume on miracles. Whether he actually read the *Dialogues Concerning Natural Religion* cannot be explicitly and directly demonstrated, but it is hardly conceivable that anybody studying theology at Oxford in the first two decades of the nineteenth century could have avoided a serious reading of them.

Certainly, it is clear enough from his writings that Newman inherited the post-Humean suspicion of the argument from design which in the *Dialogues* is expressed by Cleanthes, but rendered problematic under the insistent scrutiny of Philo and Demea. Indeed, the approach to a belief in the nature and existence of God using reason on the basis of the evidence of the alleged design of the universe seemed to Newman singularly unconvincing. He saw clearly that observation of the universe with all its evil and distress could as easily lead to a belief in a God of whim, if not of a fiendish and vengefully punishing disposition, and certainly not necessarily to the God of moral goodness and truth of the Biblical revelation in Christ. In order to arrive at an awareness of the nature of God, Newman by contrast consistently favoured a negative natural theology and a more fideistic acknowledgment of the unknowable mystery of God, whose existence and nature is beyond the unavoidable anthropomorphisms resulting from rational inference from the design of the universe.

It is precisely at this point that Newman's theology displays an identifiable family likeness with that of Mansel. In a passage that is resonant of the character of Demea theology, Newman, in the *Grammar of Assent,* puts the alternative to an approach to God from design: Only "dim shadows of his Presence" may even be discerned "in the affairs of men;" "...He is specially a Hidden God, and with our best efforts we can only glean from the surface of the world some faint and fragmentary views of Him." [29]

---

[29] *An Essay in Aid of a Grammar of Assent* (1870), Image Books edition (Garden City: Doubleday, New York), 1955, p. 309.

It was as a consequence of his disenchantment with the approach to a knowledge of God using reason on the basis of the alleged design of the universe that Newman, following the initial impulse of Demea, turned to a more inward concentration of attention on an acquaintance with the Divine Will through the moral dictates of conscience. The last section of the *Grammar of Assent* picked up and developed the theme of conscience in a discussion of the relation of natural and revealed religion.[30]

To connect Newman securely with the Demea tradition, however, it is important to observe something of the formative influence upon him of both Richard Whately and Edward Copleston from the time he arrived at Oriel in 1822. It has often been observed that Newman's original religious conditioning by an evangelical family in Calvinism was very self-consciously abandoned in this period, though the dynamics of his transition to what might be described as a more "traditional Anglicanism" are not so well understood. This is precisely because commentators have failed to discern the growth to dominance of the Demea position in Newman's emerging theology under the tutorship of both Copleston and Whately.

Copleston, who became a Fellow of Oriel in 1795 and Provost in 1814, was in place when Newman arrived on the scene, though he was somewhat removed from Newman, but Richard Whately, who was also a Fellow of Oriel until his marriage, became Newman's close friend and mentor.[31] Indeed, as Principal of Alban Hall, Whately employed Newman as Vice Principal and theological tutor, and Newman was often in the

---

[30] In reply to Mary Holmes, who wrote to Newman after reading the first part of the *Grammar of Assent*, Newman said he was anxious to hear her views of the last hundred pages, which contain his essential concern about an approach to God through conscience that he hoped lay people might understand. See M. Trevor, *Newman: Light in Winter*, p. 486.

[31] Edward Copleston (1776-1849), after having been Fellow (1795), became Provost of Oriel in 1814, and held in plurality appointments as Bishop of Llandaff and Dean of St. Pauls from the following year. Richard Whately (1787-1863) was Fellow of Oriel (1811), then Vicar of Halesworth (1822) and Principal of Alban Hall (1825), until he became Archbishop of Dublin in 1831. Given the inclusive sympathies which he shared with other Oriel Noetics who desired to increase the comprehensiveness of the Church of England, he was to align himself as an opponent of Newman and the Tractarians.

company of the Whatelys, though they eventually disagreed politically and from 1829 drifted apart. Whately felt that Newman had already begun to move in a new circle of friends who were beginning to pursue their own agenda.[32] They were to become Newman's Tractarian colleagues, whose ecclesiological quest, from the perspective of Whately's very broad and inclusive view of the Church, appeared too disruptively controversial.[33] In the dispute of 1835-6 triggered by the appointment of John Hampden as Regius Professor of Divinity, Whately, who by this time had become Archbishop of Dublin, supported Hampden against the Tractarians, to whom he referred in correspondence to Lord Melbourne as "furious bigots."[34]

Despite the souring of their relationship, Newman nevertheless always looked back with affection on "dear Whately" as one who "opened my mind, and taught me to think and to use my reason." Certainly, Whately exercised a significant influence in Newman's early theological formation as his "gentle and encouraging instructor."[35] Very importantly, Whately actually employed Newman as a kind of research assistant to synthesize the manuscript of his own *Analytical Dialogues*. Between 12 June and 24 September 1822, Newman took his own copy and then, on behalf of Whately, effectively fashioned it into part of an article on logic for the *Encyclopedia Metropolitana*. When Whately later expanded this work in his *Elements of Logic* (1826), he acknowledged Newman's help as one "who actually composed a considerable portion of the work as it now stands, from

---

[32] *Apologia*, p. 10.

[33] Whately's desire for a non-controversial inclusivism in the Church is amply illustrated in his *Eight Sermons* preached before the University of Oxford in 1822, entitled "The Use and Abuse of Party-Feeling in Matters of Religion," (Oxford: University Press, 1822). Lecture VI entitled "Foolish and Unlearned Questions Avoid" (pp. 173-204) contains a typical expression of the Demea position in relation to "the scanty and indistinct conception" we have of unfathomable divine mysteries which are "unprofitable to discuss" (pp. 177-89).

[34] In a diary comment of 10 November 1860, Newman said, "There is scarcely anyone, whom in memory I love more than Whately even now," but he went on to observe that, "In 1836 he was most severe upon me in relation to the Hampden matter."

[35] *Apologia*, p. 7.

manuscripts not designed for publication, and who is the original author of several pages."[36]

As it turned out, both Copleston and Whately were self-conscious and uncompromising Demea theologians who, at the precise time that Newman was so closely associated with them, were aggressively promoting the work of William King, whose sermon entitled *Divine Foreknowledge Consistent with the Freedom of the Will* (1709),[37] is the classic historical expression of the fundamental theological position which Hume presents in very brief outline in the *Dialogues* through the mouth of Demea. Indeed, Whately published King's treatise in the belief that it contained the essential index to the right method of interpreting scripture, particularly in relation to the understanding of the nature of the Deity and His dealings with humankind. As it happens, this was published by Whately in 1821, just prior to Newman's election as a Fellow of Oriel.[38] Given Newman's close working relationship on matters of logic with his teacher, it is not insignificant that Whately, in the *Elements of Logic*, on which Newman actually collaborated, embraced and expanded upon some of the insights of King's *Sermon*, particularly relating to the analogical nature of religious discourse. Indeed, he actually quoted and discussed King's work at some length.[39] On its first appearance, Whately sent a copy of his *Logic* to Newman, who wrote in response on 14 November 1826 saying not only that Whately had taught him "to think correctly," and rely on himself, but that Whately "broke" him of his Calvanistic evangelical views.[40] It is important to appreciate that it was a distinctive set of theological insights as much as a capacity to think logically and independently that in Newman's case provided release from the religious tradition of his family upbringing.

[36] *Elements of Logic* (New York: William Jackson, 1834 edition), p. 6.

[37] Preached at Christ Church, Dublin, before the Irish House of Lords, on 15 May 1709. This treatise was the trigger of much controversy, causing it to be republished in seven editions.

[38] See Richard Whately, *The Right Method of Interpreting Scripture*, in what relates to the *Nature of the Deity, and His Dealings with Mankind, Illustrated in a Discourse on Predestination by Dr. King* (London: John Murray, 1821).

[39] *Elements of Logic*, op. cit., pp. 254-6. Note also the discussion of the category of "person" included in the Appendix on ambiguous terms of later editions (see pp. 289-301).

[40] See *Letters and Diaries*, Vol. I, p. 307.

At exactly the same time, King's line was closely followed by Copleston in his own approach to reconciling the apparent conflict between divine predestination and human free will in his *Enquiry into the Doctrines of Necessity and Predestination in Four Discourses*, which was also published in 1821. The republication by Whately of King's *Sermon* in association with Copleston's own work, which was so heavily dependent upon it, and the promotion of the distinctive set of views deriving from King by both Whately and Copleston, amounted to a programmatic approach to theology that gave Anglicans at Oxford at the time, including Newman, an alternative to the inherited option of the Calvinism of the period.[41] This opened the way for him to develop the fundamentals of a characteristic approach to God through the categories of mystery and conscience that were regularly to flicker to life in his sermons and other writings, and eventually to inform his mature theological work in the *Grammar of Assent*.

William King's thesis of 1709 about predestination and free will become seminal for subsequent Demea theologians, given that it was the vehicle for articulating a distinctive emphasis on the incomprehensibility and unknowability of God, as well as a way of understanding the nature of doctrine and the function of religious language. The basic thesis of King's famous *Sermon* was that no contradiction could be drawn between divine predestination and human free will precisely because humans are not given to have an intimate knowledge of the inner workings of the mind of God. Given that this remains from a human point of view an unknowable mystery, and that human beings do not really know what predestination is like in God in any exact sense, there is no way of knowing whether it is incompatible with human free will or not. All this is shrouded in mystery, for God is beyond all feeble but often over-confident rationalistic attempts at the precise conceptualization of his nature.

---

[41] As we shall see, William Ewart Gladstone was also touched by this theological movement.

Just as a person born blind can only imagine what colours might be like, so humans generally can only speculate about what it might be like for God to be God. Indeed, King pointed out that the workings of our own minds are by and large hidden from us and we speak of mental processes in what are often quite basic physical metaphors and analogies. We speak of "reflecting on" an idea or of "embracing an idea or weighing an argument." Such language, says King, actually tells us very little about the nature of these processes as they are in themselves, and it is only when we stop to think about it that we become aware of how figurative it actually is. Likewise, for the purpose of living our religious lives, we are obliged to work with fragmentary hints and glimpses and tentative analogical representations of the Divine. These, King argues, are sufficient for their pragmatic religious purpose without being clear and distinct or, indeed, in any unequivocal way informative.

In these insights of William King's, we have the essential kernel of the developed thesis of Mansel in the *Limits of Religious Thought* that Newman was to find so congenial. Mansel encapsulated the high orthodoxy of the Demea position by arguing that the surpassing mystery and otherness of God must entail that all humanly formulated religious truths are "regulative but not informative."[42] As Mansel understood the purposes of God, "He has given us truths which are designed to be regulative, rather than speculative; intended not to satisfy our reason, but to guide our practice; not to tell us what God is in His absolute nature, but how He wills that we should think of Him in our present finite state."[43]

In a letter to Professor Goldwin Smith in the course of the public discussion of the thesis of the *Limits*, Mansel actually acknowledged his dependence on William King, though the footnotes of the work itself reveal more reliance on the work of King's contemporary, Peter Browne, another Irish Bishop and

---

[42] For a discussion of Mansel's view of "regulative truth" see Don Cupitt, "Mansel's Theory of Regulative Truth," *Journal of Theological Studies*, N.S., Vol. xviii, 1967, pp. 104-26 and D. W. Dockrill, "The Limits of Thought and Regulative Truths," *Journal of Theological Studies*, N.S., Vol. xxi, 1970, pp. 370-87.

[43] *The Limits of Religious Thought*, Fourth edn. 1859, p. 94.

theologian of the Demea tradition.[44] Generally speaking, while King was concerned to underline the differences between the terms of analogical discourse when used in reference to God, Browne was committed to securing the elements of similarity despite acknowledged differences.[45] Either way, for Mansel the conclusion to be drawn in relation to any finite attempt to conceive the Infinite was that "in consequence of the inadequacy of the conception to express completely the nature of the objects," further adventures in speculative thinking were rendered precarious.[46] In the promotion of the Demea position by Copleston and Whately at Oriel in the 1820s, it was the work of King rather than Browne, however, which dominated the discussion.

Though Newman does not himself directly acknowledge the dependence of his own fundamental theological position on William King, it is impossible that he was not acquainted with the *Sermon* in the republished form edited by Whately in 1821. Indeed, it is most improbable that he had not in fact read the *Sermon*. Given that both Copleston and Whately were enthusiastically promoting the views of King at the time Newman arrived at Oriel, he could hardly have escaped being touched by the broad outline of its major ideas. Newman's many defences of the reasonableness of faith independent of a rationalistic temper of mind, and his many declarations concerning the practical usefulness of religious language, despite its acknowledged limited ability to provide clear and distinct information about the divine mystery, are unmistakable indicators of the fact that his thinking was very profoundly conditioned by the fundamental theological approach enunciated by King.

Certainly, Newman's expressed dislike of the design argument, and his conviction of the impossibility of coming to an understanding of the divine nature on the basis of it, is a clear

---

[44] *A Second Letter to Professor Goldwin Smith*, Oxford, 1862, p. 40. A contemporary of King, Peter Browne vigorously expounded the Demea position in his *Things Divine and Supernatural Conceived by Analogy with Things Natural and Human* (London, 1733). Indeed, Browne thought that King had taken his argument from his own *A Letter in Answer to Christianity not Mysterious* (ed. John Toland, Dublin, 1697).

[45] Something of the nuances between the thinking of King and Browne may be discerned in Mansel 's footnote xvii to p. 98; Limits op. cit., pp. 261-2.

[46] Ibid., Preface, p. xii.

echo of Whately, who had argued against Paley that God's moral qualities, his perfection and love, cannot be inferred from the mere inspection of the universe using processes of reasoning. Indeed, it was Whately in his commentary on King's *Sermon*, who, long before Newman, observed that if such a bare inspection were attempted, it would more likely than not lead to the conclusion "that the Deity was a being of a mixed or a capricious nature."[47] It is better to be soberly aware of our human limitations, and silent before the incomprehensible mystery of God who remains remote, sublime, and ultimately unknowable; after all, "it was the craving after forbidden knowledge which expelled our first parents from paradise."[48] To Whately's mind, humans must be humbly content with the representations of the divine that are given in the revelation of scripture, these being sufficient for all the practical purposes of religion.[49]

This pragmatic assessment of the purpose to which religious insights and concepts are put was spelled out by Copleston. He noted, by way of example, that when humans speak of the sea they use such words as "placid," "as cleansing with a priestlike ablution," "as now becoming restless, turbulent, furious, raging, and then abating in its anger—becoming peaceful, calm, tranquil, benign." All this, said Copleston, is analogical discourse whereby the sea is understood by reference to ourselves; the mood of the sea is interpreted through a kind of imaginative anthropomorphism. However, it leads to practical consequences, for if one speaks of the sea as becoming restless, then one begins to take in the sails, check the moorings, batten down the hatches. In other words, the imaginary language is sufficient to prompt us to action. Without explaining much about the sea and exactly why it is that a storm is about to break, it is sufficient to guide our behavior. Likewise, Copleston argued that we think of God

---

[47] *The Right Method of Interpreting Scripture*, op. cit., p. 121.

[48] Ibid., p. 125.

[49] A classic example of the Demea position, including its emphasis both on the mysterious incomprehensibility of much Christian doctrine and at the same time the practical usefulness of doctrine for making us "better men," is found in Newman's "Trinity Sunday" sermon, preached on 14 June, 1829 on "The Christian Mysteries" (No. 199 in Newman's numbering), *Parochial and Plain Sermons* (San Francisco: Ignatius Press, 1987 edn.), pp. 129-136.

in analogical terms. These are of limited value and relatively uninformative when it comes to transmitting a knowledge of God as he is in himself, but they are sufficient for the practical purpose of religious living.

This emphasis on the hiddenness of God, who remains a mystery even when revealed, entails that human images and analogical concepts of the Divine are representations which are accommodated to the limited capacities of finite human minds, and suited to the purpose of religious life and practical living, but which fall short of communicating a clear and distinct knowledge of God as God is in Himself. As in traditional fideistic negative theology, there is a gulf, an "infinite qualitative difference," between the human representations of the Divine such as we find in scripture and God's transcendent and absolute nature. The primacy accorded to faith over reason and understanding in turn generates a humble acknowledgement of the limitations of all human attempts to reach the Divine using reason and inference.

Very near the beginning of his preaching ministry, Newman himself articulated a classic expression of the representationalism of the Demea tradition in one of his first sermons at St. Clement's, Oxford in 1824.[50] In this sermon he combined talk of the "mysterious loftiness of God" with "the frailness and weakness of the human mind":

> While God is shrouded from my view in the obscurity of His incomprehensible essence, I may be told indeed and be convinced of His purity, wisdom and love, but such representations come with little force to my soul.—I go forward [and] He is not there—and backward but I cannot perceive Him (Job 23). The impression on my mind of His excellence is faint and weak—it is indistinct—He is so much above me that I cannot attain unto the knowledge of Him (Ps. 139).[51]

---

[50] In a Sunday Morning Sermon on 31 October 1824 (Number 29 in Newman's own sequential numbering of his sermons). See Placid Murray OSB, dd. *John Henry Newman, Sermons 1824-1834* (Oxford: Clarendon Press, 1991), Vol. i, p. 272.

[51] Ibid., p. 272.

In a sermon preached on 21 September 1828, we find a similar view:

> We cannot, My Brethren, understand the movements of the Divine Mind, and have no name even to denote in Him what in the case of men we call virtue and goodness. Yet surely, if we may dare accommodate earthly language to so high a purpose, there is no exalted grace or virtuous feeling which man can conceive, which is not shadowed out to us in the doctrine of the Incarnation of the Son of God.[52]

This approach to God from the initial premise of mystery and incomprehensibility in fact presented Newman with a Christological problem.

Some of his earliest sermons reveal that he had been attempting to integrate his inherited evangelicalism with the thought of Thomas Erskine in an exposition of the view that in Christ "the high and lofty attributes of the divine mind" are by revelation "brought down to the level of our understandings" so that "the rays of His glory which would else blind us, are attempered to the weakness of our vision—the infinitude of His counsels are traced out in legible characters as on a small tablet." [53] Christ in this way of thinking in a sense becomes the clear manifestation of the divine nature whereby the attributes of God are "rendered more intelligible." By the time he came to publish *Tract 73* in 1836, he had purged his views of this original reliance on Erskine by forsaking what he termed a Christology of "Manifestation" in favour of a more aggressive theology of "Mystery."[54] Newman came to see that the difficulty with the idea of "manifestation" was that it made the Infinite so intelligible and humanly available as to allow humans to have it on their own terms and to stand in judgment of it. By insisting

---

[52] Ibid., p. 211.

[53] Ibid., p. 272. See Thomas Erskine, *Remarks on the Internal Evidence for the Truth of Revealed Religion*, 6th edn., Edinburgh, 1823.

[54] See Newman's Tract "On the Introduction of Rationalistic Principles into Revealed Religion" in *Essays Critical and Historical*, Vol. I, pp. 30-90 (esp. pp. 31-71). The distinction between a theology of manifestation and a theology of mystery may be found on pp. 40-1.

that in His mediatorial role Christ points beyond himself, and that the Divine Mystery cannot be reduced to the proportions of finite mind, Newman came to argue more forcefully that the element of Mystery thus remains even when God is revealed. In this way he could retain an element of reverential awe in his approach to faith. Instead of thinking of Christ as the bearer of information concerning the Divine, about which theologians could then confidently engage in further speculative argument, Newman had come to see that doctrine is "Mysterious, because our information is *incomplete.*" And then, in a manner typical of Demea theologians, Newman went on to argue that we "are only informed so far on the subject, as bears upon *practical purposes.*"[55] Similarly, some years later, in a sermon preached a few months after the publication of *Tract 73*, he underlined the "singular practical effects" on the believer of accepting the mysteriousness of the God who in his dealings with his creatures is not obliged "to take us into counsel, and explain to us the reason for everything": "There is nothing according as we are given to see and judge of things, which will make a greater difference in the temper, character, and habits of an individual, than the circumstance of his holding or not holding the Gospel to be Mysterious."[56]

Indeed, by 1836 Newman's grasp of the importance of the category of "Mystery" was cited as "the badge or emblem of orthodoxy."[57] "To preach this is to preach the Gospel; not to apprehend it, is to be destitute of living faith."[58] A speculative rationalism in theology and religion that "would account for everything" was to be avoided at all costs, for "The Rationalist makes himself his own centre, not his Maker."

---

[55] Sermon 177 in Newman's numbering (21 September 1928), *Sermons* 1824–43, op. cit., p. 206.

[56] Sermon 411 on "The Mysteriousness of our Present Being," preached on 29 May 1836, *Parochial and Plain Sermons*, op. cit., 1987 edn. p. 912. See also Sermon 390, preached on 8 November 1835 on "The Gift of the Spirit": "…we shall unite conceptions the most lofty concerning His majesty and bounty towards us, with the most lowly, minute, and unostentatious service to Him" (p. 647).

[57] *Tract 73*, "On the Introduction of Rationalistic Principles into Religion," which originally appeared on 2 February, 1836. See *Essays Critical and Historical*, op. cit., p. 41.

[58] Ibid., p. 40.

It is at this point that we hear an unmistakable echo of the particular form of fideistic negative theology inherited from Whately who, in his commentary on King's *Sermon*, had pointed out in 1821 that Scripture "demands faith, implicit faith in mysteries which it does not attempt to clear up; and insists on faith as the fundamental point of religion."[59] In a way that anticipates Newman's constant criticism of liberalism, Whately exhorts all preachers of the Gospel to "shun those therefore who profess, by simplifying and explaining these mysteries, to make faith *easy*, and thus, in effect to destroy the very nature of it, considered as a *duty*…"[60] To Whately's mind there was no virtue simply in assenting to propositions that "can be satisfactorily and clearly demonstrated to the understanding."[61] As Newman himself was to put the point, grace is given "not that we may know more, but that we may do better."[62]

These are the particular emphases of a theory of religious belief which Newman expressed in a more sustained way in the *University Sermons* in which, in 1859 he himself detected the similarities with the thought of Mansel. The clear voice of Demea may be heard, for example, in the assertion in a sermon of 1831 to the effect that "Scripture communications…are intended for religious purposes" rather than for the purpose of providing exact or scientific information or dealing with "the determination of physical questions,"[63] and that "Reason" must not be allowed to become the "judge of those truths which are subjected to another part of our nature, the moral sense."[64] As he had said in another sermon: "Conscience is the essential principle and sanction of Religion in the mind."[65]

However, the significance of Newman's *University Sermons* is that they not only reveal Newman as a thinker who stands

---

[59] Op. cit., p. 125.
[60] Ibid., pp. 125-6.
[61] Ibid., p. 126.
[62] Sermon 199, "The Christian Mysteries," preached on 14 June 1829, *Parochial and Plain Sermons*, op. cit., p. 129.
[63] *University Sermons, Chiefly on the Theory of Religious Belief*, London, 1843, p. 59.
[64] Ibid.
[65] Ibid., p. 18.

squarely in the Demea tradition of Anglican theology and whose thinking is thus conditioned by it, but at the same time they represent Newman's first attempts to make his own original contribution to the development of that tradition. Insofar as in the *University Sermons* he grappled with the relation of faith and reason, and attempted to articulate a reasonable and coherent understanding of faith that was itself nevertheless independent of rationalistic inference and argument, Newman was making his first forays towards providing a systematic exposition of the more fideistic approach to religious faith of Demea that Hume had left so undeveloped. Newman was convinced that it was "absurd to argue men, as to torture them, into believing."[66] Instead of syllogistic processes, faith is based on "antecedent probabilities" apprehended by the believer as a moral conviction of the will, rather than as something strictly proved by inference.[67] For the decision of faith is not primarily the result of argument. Instead, as Newman was to contend in a sermon entitled "The Nature of Faith in Relation to Reason" (which he preached on 13 January 1839), "Faith is the reasoning of a religious mind, or of what Scripture calls a right or renewed heart, which acts upon presumptions rather than evidence, which speculates and ventures on the future when it cannot make sure of it."[68]

Faith in this sense, says Newman, is no different from other kinds of intellectual activity and the acquisition of knowledge generally where "we must assume something to prove anything, and can gain nothing without a venture."[69] Reason clearly has a part to play in the response of faith for Newman, but it is not the argumentative, over-confident reasoning of the expert in logic and philosophy so much as a reason that is common to all humans and that could be understood to distinguish them from the rest of the animal world. Reason in this sense is to be understood in association with the moral sense which operates

---

[66] Ibid., p. 63.

[67] See the sermon entitled "Faith and Reason, Contrasted as Habits of Mind" (1839) in which he questions the appeal to reason as an indispensable preliminary to faith, for faith is "independent of what is commonly understood by Reason."

[68] *University Sermons*, p. 195.

[69] Ibid., p. 207.

amongst lay people as much as amongst logicians, and thus becomes the ground of a faith commitment that is available to all.[70]

It is the capacity of the laity to come to faith through the grace of a moral sense that legitimately qualifies them to judge whether doctrinal definitions are to be received. Thus, in 1833 in his historical study of Arianism, he observed that it was the piety of the laity who were subjected to erroneous teaching that caused them to desert Arianising bishops.[71] The laity possessed the capacity to be "pre-eminent in faith" and the "champions of truth,"[72] for by acknowledging doctrines to be either compatible or incompatible with their faith, error was discerned and doctrinal authenticity and truth confirmed. Newman's particular understanding of the nature of faith as a judgment based on a moral sense common to all people rather than on the speculative reasoning of experts is what enabled him to conclude that lay people may appropriately be consulted in matters of doctrine.

Whately, in the *Elements of Logic,* had highlighted the ambiguity of the term "reason," by distinguishing its use to denote general intellectual powers such as the "Moral faculty, or power of distinguishing right from wrong . . . of which brutes are destitute," but which is in principle common to all human beings, from the use of the same term to denote the faculty of carrying on abstract logical processes of *reasoning.*[73] This fundamental distinction between different uses of the term underpins

---

[70] This abiding concern to articulate an understanding of faith that would be religiously available and recognizable to laity as well as to sophisticated theologians informed the writing of the *Grammar of Assent* as is evidenced in Newman's remark in correspondence to Mary Holmes. See footnote 13. See also *Letters and Diaries* Vol. xv, p. 381: The inner conviction wrought by "antecedent probability" is understood to be the way "you convert factory girls as well as philosophers."

[71] *The Arians of the Fourth Century* (London: Pickering, third edn., 1876), p. 357-8. When Newman first published the third edition in 1871 he supported a reference to Hilary, *Sanctiores sunt aures plebes quam corda sacerdotum,* by republishing a portion of *On Consulting the Faithful in Matters of Doctrine* as an appendix. See Note V: "The Orthodoxy of the Body of the Faithful during the Supremacy of Arianism."

[72] Ibid., p. 445.

[73] See entry under "Reason," *Elements of Logic*, pp. 302-3.

Newman's many attempts in the *University Sermons* to articulate an approach to faith that arises out of human reason, but reason understood as something common to all humans and thus shared by lay people in the Church, and independent of a reliance on the more rationalistic outcomes simply of the logical arguments of expert thinkers. Newman clearly wrestles with the contrast between an "exercise of Reason, so spontaneous, unconscious, and unargumentative" and reason as the "orderly and mature development of thought" of science and philosophy.[74]

Moreover, once again following Whately, Newman sought to blend Demea's scrupulously orthodox and apophatic approach to the divine reality through the concept of the sublime and incomprehensible mystery of God, with a concentration of attention on an inner awareness of the divine nature and will through religious sensibility. For Whately had pointed out that faith rested not upon the "presumptuous explanations" of reason, but upon "the natural and, as it may be called, instinctive principle of conscience."[75] The initial seeds of this position, originally expressed as though in passing by Hume's Demea,[76] were amplified in Newman's theology after a careful consideration of moral value and the operation of conscience with the help of Butler's *Analogy*. Following Bishop Butler, whom Whately referred to as "the great Butler,"[77] Newman understood conscience to be the inner pressure of the Divine Will, informed by the revelation of scripture, but natural to all humans. As he was to declare in answer to Gladstone's attack on papal infallibility in his *Letter to the Duke of Norfolk* in 1875: "Conscience is the aboriginal Vicar of Christ."[78] Thus, while still an Anglican, in a letter to Mary Holmes, he was able explicitly to say: "Religious truth is reached, not by reasoning, but by an inward perception. Anyone can reason; only disciplined, educated, formed minds

---

[74] *University Sermons*, "Wisdom, as Contrasted with Faith and with Bigotry" (1841), p. 279.
[75] Op. cit., p. 124.
[76] See p. 9 above.
[77] Op. cit., p. 124.
[78] *Certain Difficulties Felt by Anglicans in Catholic Teaching* (London: Burns & Oates), Vol. ii, pp. 247-50.

can perceive."[79] Years later, as a Roman Catholic in the *Grammar of Assent,* he continued to express essentially the same viewpoint: "My true informant, my burdensome conscience, gives me at once the answer to each of these antagonistic questions:—it pronounces without any misgiving that God exists:—and it pronounces quite as surely that I am alienated from Him. . . Thus it solves the world's mystery, and sees in that mystery only a confirmation of its own original teaching."[80] Newman's emphasis on faith and revelation, and his abiding disapproval of liberalism with its tendency to allow each individual the freedom, using an over-confident reason, to make up his or her mind and to believe that one private perception of truth was as good as another, and his suspicion of a natural theology that relied on reason to infer both the existence and nature of God from design, all flow from this fundamental position of high orthodoxy which places him essentially in the Demea tradition going back to the great Anglican theologian bishops of eighteenth century Ireland, William King and Peter Browne, and promoted in Newman's day by Copleston and Whately.

Something of the pervasive force of this tradition at Oxford at the time may be appreciated by observing that others were drawn into the same general approach for handling the apparent logical tension between Divine foreknowledge and predestination and human free will and responsibility. William Ewart Gladstone, for example, who, like Newman, had been brought up in a very strictly Evangelical household, also made the gradual transition to a more expansive position as a "Catholic Evangelical" and to what he called a more "traditional Anglicanism"during the course of the late 1820s.

For Gladstone, this quite momentous spiritual development occurred only after first grappling very seriously with the theology of baptism, notably with the question of whether it is to be understood primarily in terms of repentance or regeneration. The outcome of this study involved Gladstone in the rejection of the prevailing individualistic view amongst evangelicals of his day that baptism was merely an outward sign

---

[79] *Letter to Mary Holmes,* 8 March 1843.
[80] *Grammar of Assent,* op. cit., pp. 309-10.

of repentance. Apart from repentance, which Gladstone interpreted strictly as a turning, it involved the pledge of God's love, the objective working of Divine grace affecting human regeneration whereby all the baptized, including children, could be understood to have been embraced by God.

At around the same time, Gladstone found himself not just affirming the regeneration of all the baptized, but also rejecting the doctrine of predestination held by evangelicals of a more Calvinistic persuasion. During the period from 1829–1831, Gladstone wrote at Oxford a collection of "Papers…Chiefly Theological,"[81] including one on Calvinism and Arminianism, and three pages of notes have also been preserved from the same period headed "Predestination."[82] These clearly reveal that he was also heir to the basic approach of William King that had been so vigorously promoted by Copleston and Whately earlier in the decade. Indeed, it is clear that amongst the growing band of more Catholic minded Oxford scholars in the decade prior to Keble's Assize Sermon of 1833, including both Pusey and Newman, with whom Gladstone had certainly come into direct contact when he first went up to Oxford in 1828,[83] appeal was being made to the notion of divine mystery to answer over-confident and over-systematized Calvinist views of predestination that challenged a more generous appreciation of human free will in the response of saving faith and an associated preference for talk of divine foreknowledge as against predestination. Once again, the now standard Demea type argument ran that no contradiction could be drawn between the idea of divine decree and predestination on one hand and human free will and divine foreknowledge on the other, precisely because we do not know exactly what divine predestination and foreknowledge involve, this being an implication of the ultimate unknowability of God.

---

[81] British Library Add MS 44719, ff. 237-40.

[82] Peter Jagger, in his biography of the spiritual formation of Gladstone, points out that these appear to be those referred to by Gladstone in his diary as having been begun on 20 June 1830. See *Gladstone, The Making of a Christian Politician* (Pickwick: Allison Park, Penn., 1991), p. 128.

[83] Gladstone noted on a visit to Cuddesdon on 23 August 1828 that "Mr. Newman of Oriel, dined here." Another entry during this Cuddesdon sojourn reads. "An excellent sermon from Mr. Pusey."

Given this, it is no coincidence that Gladstone himself, who was consciously finding the more Catholic emphasis attractive, assumed the same broad approach. In dealing with the problem of the apparent difficulty posed by the tension between divine predestination and foreknowledge, Gladstone affirms the necessity not to probe the divine mystery. Indeed, in what is a classic expression of the approach espoused by Demea theologians, Gladstone wrote: "Rest therefore satisfied that as the foreknowledge and the decree are simultaneous in Him so are the predestination and the faith in us—and to inquire no further—for now thou seest that it is *impossible*, neither more nor less than *absolutely impossible* that the question should be answered either one way or the other—since it goes to make *two* of things which are *essentially and therefore indivisibly one*."[84] Then Gladstone, in words that are very reminiscent of Demea, goes on: "'It is not pretended that the question is *solved*—no, far from it—by this reasoning—but something is done if it be shown that (it) is necessarily insoluble' and thus removed to the realm of 'a difficulty to a *mystery*.'"

It is possible that Gladstone may have been recognizing the limitations of the argument of his appeal to insolubility.[85] It was not, however, just that Gladstone had been pressured by the Calvinist party and was opting out of controversy in favour of a quiet life; rather, he was expressing with some confidence the received, indeed, standard approach of the more Catholic party who appealed to the concept of Divine Mystery to disarm those who claimed an intimate speculative knowledge of the inner workings of the predestining mind of God so as to minimize the role of human free will in saving faith. In this Gladstone was in fact drawing upon the same orthodoxy as others, like Newman, who, in the Oxford of the 1820s, had been influenced—whether consciously or unconsciously—by Copleston and Whately,

---

[84] British Library Add. MS 44801, ff. 33-4. See *The Gladstone Diaries 1825-1854*, ed. M. R. D. Foot and H. C. G. Matthew (Oxford: University Press, 1968-74), entry for 20 June 1830.

[85] Peter Jagger makes this point in his biography, op. cit., p. 128.

informed by the original insights of William King.[86] The idea of the sublime incomprehensibility and unknowability of God was in the Oxford air of the time. As Gladstone was to apply it, such an issue as the apparent logical tension between the idea of Divine decree and predestination and human free will and Divine foreknowledge must be "deposited in the bosom of God who alone has perfect knowledge." Given the inscrutable mystery of God, and the limitations of human thought, there was no alternative; from the human perspective they must "there let it rest." "Let us implore the grace of God to keep us from troubling ourselves, or from being troubled by others upon it."

Newman was to make essentially the same appeal to the concept of "mystery" in his constant critique of an over-confident rationalism in a theology that would explain everything and only believe what could be explained. His aversion to this particular form of liberalism, as well as his emergence from an over-speculative Calvinism, became so definite and well defined precisely because, as a theologian passionately committed to the fundamental principles of the Demea tradition, he could see all the more clearly the sharp outlines of Cleanthes in what he understood to be a presumptuous reliance on human reasoning amongst other theologians of his day. This was the very opposite of what he himself understood to be the true and orthodox human approach to God. Certainly to recognize the voice of Demea in Newman's theology is to hold a most important key to understanding him.

---

[86] Gladstone writes, for example, partly as if to address himself: "Who art thou vain man, who hast engaged thyself in speculations which if their language be carefully examined is well nigh impious? Know these things and store them up in thine inmost heart forever that in the most High God, there is no precedence nor succession of ideas—for with him none of the relations of mind obtain—that in the most High God there is no order of intellectual perception and determination of will: for they are simultaneous, nay are they not identified." In a word, Gladstone's stress is on the radical difference between divine and human intelligence.

15

Love and Power: What Does Macmurray's Notion of Community Have to Say to the 'Devices of Politics' in the Contemporary Political Order?

Frank G. Kirkpatrick

Political philosophers, politicians, and religious ethicists are currently debating the nature of political community and the nature of human relationships. In the center of this debate among moral philosophers are two moral philosophies (liberalism and communitarianism) that are often set against each other. I would like to suggest a) that the differences between them are not as great as often portrayed in the literature; b) that a way through the debate for the religious ethicist within a theistic tradition can be provided by a moral ontology grounded in the intention and actions of a divine agent; c) that John Macmurray's understanding of both religious and political community provides a way of linking that moral ontology with the work of politics; d) that Macmurray's notion of community both goes beyond and incorporates key provisions in both the liberal and communitarian notions; and e) that the moral ontology on which his notion of community rests has the potential for contributing to the resolution of many of the issues now facing the societies and governments of the United States and the United Kingdom, both of which are seriously considering what has been called "devolution."

John Rawls and the Liberal Position

The classic statement of the moral dimension of a liberal vision of society is that of John Rawls, the moral philosopher whose seminal work *A Theory of Justice* (1971) has spawned an entire industry of scholarly studies and scholars' careers. Rawls' argument that justice is fairness presumes a view of society as "a system of cooperation designed to advance the good of those taking part in it. [It] is a cooperative venture for mutual advantage."[1] Any society requires a set of principles of social justice that will "provide a way of assigning rights and duties in the basic institutions of society and . . . define the appropriate distribution of the benefits and burdens of social cooperation."[2]

To generate these principles of social justice to which all can give their consent, Rawls engages in a thought-experiment (the "original position") that assumes that the parties to it are driven primarily by self-interest, that they have conflicting claims to the division of social advantages, that they may have no extensive ties of natural sentiment, and that they take no interest in one another's interests.[3] None of these assumptions may turn out to be true once they emerge from the original position, but the original position has to assume them in order to ground the most basic procedural principles for determining what everyone will ultimately agree is just once they "re-enter" society and "discover" who they really are. No one in the original position knows what his or her advantages or disadvantages in the real world are. Nor does anyone know what vision of the good he or she will hold in real life. But, given the reality of self-interest,

---

[1] John Rawls, *A Theory of Justice* (Cambridge, MA: Harvard University Press, 1971), 4.
[2] Ibid.
[3] Ibid., pp. 127-9.

no one has a moral reason to "acquiesce in an enduring loss for himself in order to bring about a greater net balance of satisfaction" for others.[4]

In the "original position" behind the "veil of ignorance," Rawls argues, rational people would come to accept two fundamental principles of justice: "First: each person is to have an equal right to the most extensive basic liberty compatible with a similar liberty for others."[5] The second, or difference principle, holds that: "social and economic inequalities are to be arranged so that they are both (a) to the greatest benefit of the least advantaged . . . and (b) attached to positions and offices open to all under conditions of fair equality and opportunity."[6]

There is no presumption that there will be any agreement as to the good to be pursued by individuals, nor that there will be any harmony between individual life-plans. In fact, Rawls believes that liberalism assumes that "there are bound to exist conflicting and incommensurable conceptions of the good."[7] Rawls insists that contemporary liberal cultures are diverse and pluralistic with respect to comprehensive religious, philosophical, and moral doctrines. Therefore agreement as to social principles must be made solely on the basis of individual rights, not on the basis of a common notion of the good. "Justice as fairness [is] the concept of right prior to that of the good."[8] It is based on the idea that persons must first agree to the principles of organizing their lives together before they begin to contemplate what is good for each of them individually. "We should not attempt to give form to our life by first looking to the good independently defined. It is not our aims that primarily reveal our nature but rather the principles that we would acknowledge to govern the background conditions under which these aims are to be formed and the manner in which they are to be pursued. For the self is prior to the ends which are affirmed by it."[9] The most we can hope for in a liberal, morally diverse society is an

---

[4] Ibid., p. 14. In this respect Rawls qualifies traditional utilitarian theory.

[5] Ibid., pp. 60–1.

[6] Ibid., p. 302.

[7] John Rawls, "Justice and Fairness: Political not Metaphysical," *Philosophy and Public Affairs*, 14 (1985), p. 245.

[8] Rawls, *A Theory of Justice*, p. 31.

[9] Ibid., p. 560.

"overlapping consensus" in the political realm as to what the rules of engagement are as individuals are given the greatest possible latitude to pursue their personal life-plans as they see fit.

This has the important implication that the political conception of justice "does not presuppose accepting any particular comprehensive religious, philosophical, or moral doctrine."[10] This kind of doctrine has no utility (and in fact is dangerous if applied coercively) for a liberal democratic political culture. Given the liberal post-Enlightenment assumption that people can never agree upon a single metaphysical or religious view of human beings in relation to some transcendent good, such a view cannot contribute to the principles of justice by which a society has to organize itself.

What liberalism does not consider, given its self-limitation of considering only principles of right, is the possibility that there is in fact (as construed by the Biblical, theistic tradition) an overarching intention for the fulfillment or flourishing of human beings, that that intention has been enacted and furthered in history by a divine agent whose intention it is, and that this intention can incorporate, without inconsistency, a wide variety of modes of expression without contradicting its underlying truth: namely, that persons are created in such a way that they can, ultimately, only achieve the fullest possible form of flourishing in certain kinds of community characterized essentially by mutual love. This possibility, however, is compatible with the creation of forms of impersonal association (societies) as providing the necessary means for and the conditions of the existence of smaller, more basic, more personally direct communities that alone can bring out in their members those qualities that lead to greater flourishing. In short, a community, in John Macmurray's sense, can rest on a societal base that meets the principles of justice as set forth by Rawls. But it can do so only if it can also sustain the fundamental insight of the communitarian critics of liberalism: namely, that persons are constituted by their

---

[10] John Rawls, "The Priority of Rights and Ideas of the Good," *Philosophy and Public Affairs,* 17 (1988), p. 252.

communal, historical, and cultural traditions, including visions of the good and the true.

For the liberal the purpose of the state is simply to ensure that all citizens have equal opportunity to advance whatever conception of the good they might individually happen to hold provided only that they do so without violating the two principles of justice. The liberal state need not insist that its citizens share a common metaphysical view of the truth about what constitutes the best end for all persons or about the essential nature and destiny of persons. Justice is a political, not a metaphysical, conception.[11] A liberal society must regard citizens as "independent from and as not identified with any particular conception of the good, or scheme of final ends."[12] The only conception of the person in the liberal society is a political one at the heart of which is the primacy of the individual's freedom to choose his or her own life-plan without unfair coercion by others. Liberalism "accepts the plurality of incommensurable conceptions of the good as a fact of modern democratic culture, provided, of course, these conceptions respect the limits specified by the appropriate principles of justice."[13] This clearly means that a society cannot embrace one religion's view of the good for all persons and enforce its acceptance by all the members of that society. The implicit assumption underlying these claims is, however, that any religion's view of the good entails its coercive imposition on others and unfairly restricts the freedom of persons to pursue equally valid, but ultimately incommensurable, visions of the good.

What is left unexamined is the possibility that there is a religious (metaphysical) option that locates the good of all persons in a divine intention that, by its very nature, supports human freedom as essential to flourishing but believes that ultimately all visions of the good can find fulfillment only if persons live in certain forms of community characterized essentially, though not solely, by mutual love in addition to justice.

---

[11] John Rawls, "Justice as Fairness: Political not Metaphysical," p. 223.

[12] Ibid., p. 241.

[13] Ibid., p. 249

The Communitarian Critique

Now some critics of Rawls' liberalism have objected that it leaves the human self in a naked, isolated, and radically untenable individualistic posture, cut off from the very others whose relationships with the self enable it to flourish. Such a view of the self, they argue, is not true to the fact of the self's embeddedness in a particular culture's traditions and views of the good. Michael Sandel was one of the first to dissect Rawls' assumption of what Sandel called the "unencumbered self." For the liberal, my essential identity can be distinguished from the ends that I choose. I am, essentially, a chooser, but not a chooser who is constituted by his choices. There are no "constitutive ends" that define the self prior to its choosing of any ends.

Sandel argues that this unencumbered self is capable of joining a "community" but what is denied to such a self "is the possibility of membership in any community bound by moral ties antecedent to choice; he cannot belong to any community where the self *itself* could be at stake. Such a community—call it constitutive as against merely cooperative—would engage the identity as well as the interests of the participants, and so implicate its members in a citizenship more thorough-going than the unencumbered self can know."[14] While acknowledging that this is a liberating vision, Sandel denies that it is true. We cannot, he argues, view ourselves as "independent selves, independent in the sense that our identity is never tied to our aims and attachments." To so view ourselves would be to remove our fundamental identity as persons from those "loyalties and convictions whose moral force consists partly in the fact that living by them is inseparable from understanding ourselves as the particular persons we are—as members of this family or community or nation or people, as bearers of that history, as citizens of this republic."[15] The self that is prior to its choice of "constitutive statements" is a self without character, without moral depth. "For to have character is to know that I move in a history I neither summon nor command, which carries consequences

---

[14] Sandel, "The Procedural Republic and the Unencumbered Self," in *Avineri and De-Shalit*, p. 19.
[15] Ibid., p. 23.

nonetheless for my choices and conduct." Whatever distance I can get on my encumberedness is always "precarious and provisional, [and] the point of reflection never finally secured outside [my contextual] history itself." The liberal self, however, is "beyond the reach of its experience, beyond deliberation and reflection. Denied the expansive self-understandings that could shape a common life, the liberal self is left to lurch between detachment on the one hand, and entanglement on the other."[16]

The truth, however, according to Alasdair McIntrye and other communitarians, is that "we all approach our own circumstances as bearers of a particular social identity. I am someone's son or daughter, someone else's cousin or uncle; I am a citizen of this or that city, a member of this or that guild or profession. . . The story of my life is always embedded in the story of those communities from which I derive my identity."[17]

Macmurray and Rawls

Now on first reading, it would seem that the communitarian claims of Sandel and MacIntyre track much more closely to John Macmurray's view of community as the condition for and the constitutive substance of the fulfillment of persons whose essential nature is interpersonal. But a closer reading suggests that Macmurray actually has the ability to accommodate much in the Rawlsian liberal tradition as well as the basis for an 'internal' critique of some of communitarianism's claims. In the process, Macmurray's understanding of society in relation to community provides him with some clear criteria for determining what political and economic polices are more conducive to human flourishing (more in conformity with God's intention for all humankind) than others. And with this determination, Macmurray can give us a way through the political debates about how societies can best serve the needs of their members, especially the disadvantaged, without diminishing the genuine, authentic flourishing of all, including the most advantaged. In the process, Macmurray gives us a moral ontol-

---

[16] Ibid., p. 24.
[17] Alasdair MacIntrye, *After Virtue* (South Bend: University of Notre Dame Press, 1981), p. 205.

ogy in which the reality of God's intention can become a decisive factor in a social ethic that does not betray the principles of justice but goes beyond them to a common vision of the common good and thus reconciles the concerns of both the liberals and the communitarians.

The Role and Reality of God

But Macmurray's understanding of community rests on his understanding of God. And one of the most striking features of contemporary moral philosophy is the absence of God. Belief in God is assumed to be one of the metaphysical illusions of the Enlightenment or a non-explanatory cognitive epiphenomenon, simply tacked on to an otherwise completely self-sufficient naturalistic explanation of the world. One of the reasons for this assumption is the conviction among many postmodernists that to believe in God is to believe in an ahistorical reality that can only ground absolute, unchanging, historically invariant moral norms that necessarily ignore the differences between persons, communities, and historical situations and do nothing other than reify and legitimate the unjust power relations between a dominant and a subordinate group. The possibility of a divine ground that is intimately involved in history and whose intentions include historical change, development, and the flourishing of diverse and unique others in different and particular communities, is simply not considered. But Macmurray's understanding of God as the Personal Other whose intention unifies history provides, I believe, just such a possibility and, as such, can help us to find a middle ground between the liberal and communitarian understanding of the political life of human communities without reducing community to (but also without eliminating the need for) the devices of politics.

Macmurray's philosophy can be made consistent with the theological claim of Biblical theism that God is at work in the world, both through an original divine act establishing the conditions of freedom and community as the necessary means for the fulfillment of human nature and through specific historical divine actions bringing to completion an intention that all persons flourish and find fulfillment in direct personal relationships of love in community.[18]

As Iris Murdoch has pointed out, modern thinkers who believe in no external reality, including the reality of God, "are left with a denuded self whose only virtues are freedom, or at best sincerity, or, in the case of the British philosophers, an everyday reasonableness."[19] Without a God whose purpose is a universal community we are left with the tragic shattering of the vision of "an ultimate community which will have transcended the distinction between the natural and the social, which will exhibit a solidarity that is not parochial because it is the expression of an ahistorical human nature."[20] Only an external reality capable of acting so as to bring about a community in which persons can be fully themselves can provide a reasonable alternative to this denuded self.

At the heart of Macmurrray's retrieval of God is the conviction that history (as well as nature) does yield itself successfully to a construal[21] that there is a purpose being worked out in it. That purpose reaches fulfillment only in the full flourishing of persons living in mutuality within the context of a loving community (or what the Bible calls the kingdom of God).

---

[18] I would admit that Macmurray's own treatment of the actions of God, and the nature of God as Personal Agent, is less than clear and sometimes downright ambiguous. I do believe, however, that taken in its entirety, his philosophy supports the belief in God as an historical Agent. See especially my recent book *Together Bound: God, History, and the Religious Community* (Oxford: 1994).

[19] Iris Murdoch, "On 'God' and 'Good'," in Stanley Hauerwas and Alisdair MacIntyre, eds., *Revisions* (South Bend: University of Notre Dame Press, 1983), p. 69.

[20] Rorty, "Solidarity or Objectivity?" in Richard Rorty, *Objectivity, Relativism and Truth: Philosophical Papers* (Cambridge: Cambridge University Press, 1991), p. 22. Rorty's reference to an "ahistorical" human nature is not consistent with a view of human agents in relation to a divine Agent working for the completion of a common intention in history, but clearly a vision of a universal community is consistent with it.

[21] The notion of a 'construal' is intended to suggest that any reading of history is something less than certain. Historical interpretation is always a provisional construal of what seems to be the best account of a series of events or actions given the available evidence at the time. There are enormous problems in any construal that the events of the past are in some sense God's. But without some such construal the Christian faith in God as an Agent who works in history for good would not be possible at all.

Community provides the fullest possible conditions for individual flourishing and individual flourishing provides the means for the flourishing of all the others who are the objects of the individual's love. Such flourishing presupposes direct personal relations between those who are bound together by mutual love. But it also presupposes that those direct relations have a material foundation that includes indirect relations between persons as well.

Society

Those cooperative indirect relations relative to the material foundation of community are what constitute a society. For Macmurray, like Rawls, the basis of any human society "is the universal and necessary intention to maintain the personal relation which makes the individual a person, and his life a common life."[22] But many societies are based on what Macmurray calls a negative motivation, namely fear for the self and therefore fear of the other, fear that the other is a threat to the material possessions and social status by which the self has come, falsely, to define itself. The unity of this kind of society is intended, for example, to advance the interests of "aggressively egocentric individuals" (as in Hobbes' conception). Society is the necessary evil that permits these "inherently isolated or unrelated" atomic units to live together. "They are united in a whole by an external force [the power of the State maintained through the sanctions of the Law] which counteracts the tendency of their individual energies to repel one another."[23] In such a society, because the self fears the other, its freedom to express itself fully is inhibited. It is afraid to open itself to others, to share its goods, to sacrifice some of its narrow interests for the sake of others because it fears that everything it gives away will diminish it and will entail a loss of self-identity and meaning. It can only assume that the others are just as negatively motivated toward it as it is toward them. In this kind of society, basic trust has been eroded, and with it the necessary conditions for supporting other-

---

[22] John Macmurray, *Persons in Relation* (New York: Harper and Brothers, 1961), p. 128.
[23] Ibid., p. 137.

regarding behavior. The result can only be the further disintegration and alienation of the society and its members in relation to each other.[24]

A community is distinguished from a society by the positive apperception of its members toward each other. If a society is held together by a negative bond of unity, the unity of a community is a personal and positive one. A community in its fullest possible sense has overcome the fear for the self and its correlative fear of the other. And in so doing it has opened up the possibilities of freedom for the other. "A community is for the sake of friendship and presupposes love. But it is only in friendship that persons are free in relation; if the relation is based on fear we are constrained in it and not free. Society is maintained by a common constraint, that is to say by acting in obedience to law. This secures the appearance of freedom, for it secures me from the expression of the other's animosity. But it does so by suppression of the motive which constitutes the relation."[25]

Now Macmurray does not believe that the negative (or egocentric) motive can, in societies of indirect personal relations, ever be entirely replaced by the positive (or "heterocentric") motive of love for all the others. It is utopian fantasy to believe that a society, especially one of the enormous size and complexity as a modern nation-state, can be turned into a community by the devices of politics. Nevertheless, it is crucial to acknowledge that societies cannot provide in and of themselves the substance of mutuality that constitutes the heart of authentic communities. Built as they are on indirect relations between persons, societies are only "potentially" communities. And because of this fact, the limitations of politics must be recognized as persons struggle to develop the conditions for full human flourishing, both for themselves and for others. But if we know what these conditions are, at least in a general kind of way (given our particular moral ontology in which the will of God plays a central role), then we have a fulcrum by which to critique and reform the structures

---

[24] This is the thrust of recent work being done by the African-American philosopher Laurence Thomas. See especially his *Living Morally* (Philadelphia: Temple University Press, 1989).

[25] John Macmurray, *Persons in Relation*, p. 151.

and institutions of society so as to best serve the purposes of community without replacing or becoming identified with them.

The crucial function of a society is to provide the material foundations on which the flourishing of individuals within communities must be built. Macmurray is fully in accord with both liberals and communitarians in regarding what Rawls calls the primary social goods as essential to a full, even spiritual life. These goods include rights and liberties, powers and opportunities, income and wealth, and self-respect.[26] The basic moral question for any society is whether these goods are fairly distributed in ways that permit all persons to flourish in the most just way possible. And this is the question of justice,[27] as Rawls has also argued.

Politics, for Macmurray, is the "maintaining, improving and adjusting [of] the indirect or economic relations of persons."[28] The institutional expression of politics is the state, "and its central function is the maintaining of justice." Justice, in this sense, is the minimum of reciprocity and interest in the other in the personal relation; it is a "kind of zero or lower limit of moral behavior." Justice is the negative aspect of morality but it is necessary to the constitution of the positive, though subordinate within it.

This view of justice fits nicely into Rawls' notion that the original position does not require the parties to be positively motivated toward the others. But it does require enough mutual interest in them so that they can all agree on a set of principles that will bind them together in a society in various forms of association, transaction, and exchange. Nevertheless, justice must insist that the others remain differentiated from me and from each other. Justice keeps morality from becoming sentimental or lapsing into what Macmurray calls "a minor mutuality which

---

[26] Macmurray does not question whether these goods carry over into non-democratic, non-liberal societies. Like Rawls, he seems to be working within the given framework of Western liberal society and assuming that its basic goods are those that, for the most part, constitute the foundation, if not the full meaning, of human flourishing.

[27] Rawls, *A Theory of Justice*, p. 62.

[28] John Macmurray, *Persons in Relation*, p. 188.

is hostile to the interests of the larger" society. The other must remain other, both in society and in community, and justice ensures that this will be the case in both. Locating justice within community keeps the latter from degenerating into a purely sentimental or totalitarian whole in which the rights of the individual get swamped by the imperatives of group solidarity. Justice acts as a block on forms of social unity that privilege ethnic, gender, class, racial, or other types of identity to the exclusion of individual rights. In this sense justice will be necessary even when genuine fellowship has been attained. For even then "the negative aspect would still be present, though completely subordinated to the positive, and functioning as a differentiating force within it . . . There must be no self-identification of the one with the other, or the reciprocity will be lost and the heterocentricity of the relation will be only apparent."[29] The equality of persons, with respect to their functioning within society, is necessary and it is one of the ends of justice. "My care for you is only moral if it includes the intention to preserve your freedom as an agent, which is your independence of me,"[30] in the sense of remaining an autonomous being whose decisions are her own, even if those decisions are ultimately fulfilled only in communal interdependence with me. Whether in community or in society, therefore, "I hope to secure justice in my dealings with [others] by limiting my activities for the sake of their interests, provided they will do the same in their dealings with me . . . We can consult together and come to an agreement about what is fair to each of us, so far as our separate courses of action affect one another and impinge on one another. This can be achieved by a common consent to general principles by reference to which each of us can determine what would or would not be fair to the other person if we did it. Such agreement is a contract between us, which . . . determines reciprocal rights and obligations which we engage ourselves to respect. It is a pragmatic device to secure justice in cooperation and to eliminate injustice."[31]

---

[29] Ibid., p. 189.
[30] Ibid., p. 190.
[31] Ibid., p. 191.

There is much in this lengthy statement that stands in close relation to (even echoes) Rawls' development of the principles of justice. It assumes society as a cooperative endeavor; that it is based on a contract; and that it protects the rights of individuals by limiting the activities of all for the sake of each. The parties to the contract must reach common consent (which is the purpose of the original position). Macmurray does not presume the veil of ignorance, but there is no reason to assume that he would be opposed to this hypothetical device (given an important qualification taken up below) because it does ensure that the common consent will not unfairly privilege some at the expense of others because they know their actual but contingent situation beforehand and will take steps to ensure the security of their advantages.

Macmurray would, however, also agree with much of what has been called the communicative ethics position, in particular its criticism that Rawls' original position runs the risk of obscuring the uniqueness of the concrete other, the individual person who cannot be reduced to a general, purely rational self. Seyla Benhabib, drawing on the discourse ethics of Jürgen Habermas, calls this position "interactive universalism."[32] Like Macmurray, she holds out for some form of ontologically based universal moral principles. Her stance is pragmatic and based on the actual discourse of persons in interactive communication with each other in a particular form of human association. It includes a "vision of an embodied and embedded human self whose identity is constituted narratively [the communitarian element], and the reformulation of the moral point of view as the contingent achievement of an interactive form of rationality [the liberal dimension] rather than as the timeless standpoint of a legislative reason [the Kantian factor]."[33] This interactive discourse ethic asks: "What principles of action can we all recognize or agree to as being valid if we engage in practical discourse or a mutual search for [moral] justification?"[34] This clearly tracks with both Rawls' and Macmurray's notion of con-

---

[32] Seyla Benhabib, *Situating the Self* (New York: Routledge, 1992), passim.
[33] Benhabib, p. 6. The bracketed words are my addition to her quotation.
[34] Ibid., p. 28.

sulting together to reach common consent about the principles of justice.

Consistent with her search for the universalization of moral principles (which Macmurray grounds in the will of God), Benhabib rejects the extreme claims of the cultural relativists. She denies, for example, their conviction that there is only a "radical incommensurability of conceptual frameworks." There is no reason, she argues, why we cannot engage other frameworks in dialogue, provided one is truly prepared to hear a different voice from one's own and to reformulate one's view as a result if the arguments are persuasive. Cultural relativists are simply too quick to assume no kind of conversation at all is possible with people in different cultures. But this assumption rests on "poor sociology and history." There has been much more interaction (and not always of the imperialist kind) between cultures than the "armchair philosophers of cultural relativism" have been willing to acknowledge. In the process they ignore the real, though incredibly complex, ways in which a common "humanity ceases to be just a regulative ideal and becomes increasingly a reality."[35] This last claim from a secular moral philosopher is hauntingly reminiscent of Macmurray's claim in *The Clue to History* that God's intention for the unity of humankind is increasingly becoming an historical reality.

Unlike the strict liberal proceduralists (who insist that procedures determining the right are more basic and universal than any particular conceptions of the good), Benhabib insists that discourse ethics entails strong normative assumptions about the moral status of persons within the communicative community, among them most centrally the "principle of universal moral respect" and the "principle of egalitarian reciprocity."[36] Both of these principles accord with Macmurray's notion of equality and the differentiation of the other as truly other in any genuine personal relationship. "We ought to *respect* each other as beings whose standpoint is worthy of equal consideration," and "we ought to treat each other as concrete human beings whose capacity to express this standpoint we ought to enhance by

[35] Ibid., footnote #48, pp. 62-3.
[36] Ibid., p. 29.

creating, whenever possible, social practices embodying the discursive ideal (the principle of egalitarian reciprocity)."[37] The
second principle requires us to engage in what Benhabib calls
the reversal of perspectives. We should be able to think from the
other person's point of view and see from within that view how
he or she judges others. Only if we can do this can we avoid
consigning others to a status of otherness that can be neglected
or treated with indifference in the interactive communicative
conversation.

Benhabib also insists that discourse requires the participants
to make sure that they have heard the voices of those others
who have traditionally been excluded from the conversation,
namely women and minorities. Benhabib criticizes Rawls on
just this point. She argues that Rawls, by "ignoring the standpoint
of the concrete other leads to epistemic incoherence in
universalistic moral theories."[38] The problem with the veil of
ignorance is that it tends to think from the point of view of
"the disembedded and disembodied generalized other."[39] From
this point of view "the *other as different from the self* disappears."
The self is abstracted from her concrete and specific identity
within the complex of human social relationships. And when
this happens the "voice" of the different and unique other is
effectively silenced. What remains is the old Kantian noumenal
self that is everyone in general and no one in particular. To
create the conditions for real community in which real persons
are real contributors, the concrete, embedded lives of different
concrete others must be included (what Macmurray calls the
heterocentric dimension of relationship). And the inclusion of
traditionally excluded "others" undercuts or deconstructs the
privileging of certain moral ideals, such as the "economic" or the
"political man," both of which seem to predicate the superiority
of the male autonomous morality free from the bonds of family
and personal and communal interdependence. But she argues
that there is no reason, once the voices of women are brought
into the conversation, why morality should be understood

---

[37] Ibid., p. 31.
[38] Ibid., p. 161.
[39] Ibid., p. 160.

primarily as the rational actions of impersonal agents in a field of indirect relations, such as economics and politics. Communicative ethics "projects a utopian way of life in which mutuality, respect and reciprocity become the norm among humans as concrete selves and not just as juridical agents."[40] Macmurray's insistence that a heterocentric ethic focus on the uniqueness of the other, and not on her usefulness for the egocentric self, suggests a similar support for treating others as concrete, and not simply as generalizable others.

One important implication of this view is that a society has a special obligation to empower all persons with the necessary material means to engage in the reasoned conversation from which a mutual consensus will be reached about the principles by which all those participating in the conversation agree to be governed. These conditions of empowerment go far beyond the negative liberty that conservatives and libertarians are so interested in, a liberty simply to be left alone by others in order to pursue one's private life-plan. Positive liberty is the provision of whatever is necessary to help people become free, equal, and competent moral agents. As Alan Gewirth has argued, there are certain "generic features and necessary conditions of all action" that must be provided in a just society. Freedom and well-being are the two chief such features. Freedom consists in "controlling one's behavior by one's unforced choice while having knowledge of relevant circumstances." And well-being is the "*substantive* necessary condition of action; it consists in having the general abilities and conditions needed for achieving one's purposes ... i.e., life, physical integrity, mental equilibrium ... not being lied to, not being cheated, not being robbed ... [and] additive well-being consists in having the abilities and conditions needed for increasing one's level of purpose-fulfillment and one's capabilities for action, it includes self-esteem, education, and opportunities for earning wealth and income."[41] If this means the provision of medical care, meaningful employment, economic justice, remedial education for the historically marginalized, aggressive

---

[40] Ibid., footnote #34, p. 60.
[41] Alan Gewirth, "Common Morality and the Community of Rights," in Gene Outka and John Reeder, Jr., *Prospects for a Common Morality* (Princeton: Princeton University Press, 1993), p. 36.

attacks on racial and gender discrimination, then such actions are morally obligatory on the part of the society itself for its members.[42]

Macmurray would probably support wholeheartedly the *Pastoral Letter* of the Roman Catholic Bishops in the United States dealing with economic justice.[43] The Bishops tie the effectiveness of human institutions, including the economic ones, to how well they protect human dignity. "We judge any economic system by what it does *for* and *to* people and how it permits all to *participate* in it."[44] This requires that the social and economic conditions of community be socially protected, that all persons have a right to participate in the economic life of society, that all members of the society have a special obligation to the poor and vulnerable, and that Christians are to make a fundamental "option for the poor," to strengthen the whole community by assisting those who are most vulnerable. This means that human rights are the "minimum conditions for life in community" and that these rights include not only civil and political rights but economic rights as well. The establishment and maintenance of these economic rights is perfectly consistent with Macmurray's understanding of the role of positive government and Alan Gewirth's commitment to human rights as the necessary conditions for moral agency. Positive government, in Macmurray's political philosophy, is one that exercises a "positive control of the material life of its citizens, [and] determines what use shall be made of the material resources of the nation . . ."[45] While acknowledging that socialist theory is committed to a doctrine of positive government, Macmurray's basic point (one that survives the failures of many socialist governments in

---

[42] For a fuller exploration of positive freedom, see Carol Gould, *Rethinking Democracy* (Cambridge: Cambridge University Press, 1988), "What Are Human Rights?" Gould argues that an adequate human rights theory must include "not only the minimal conditions for survival and civility that make human activity possible at all, but also the fuller conditions that are required for the free and self-developing activity that marks human life as distinctively human," p. 201.

[43] See *Economic Justice for All: Pastoral Letter on Catholic Social Teaching and the U.S. Economy* (National Conference of Catholic Bishops: Washington, D.C., 1986), passim.

[44] Ibid., p. ix.

[45] John Macmurray, *Constructive Democracy* (London: Faber and Faber, 1943), p. 18.

practice) is that we cannot separate the spiritual life (the life of love and mutuality) from its material base. "Without material resources we cannot live. Without adequate material resources, the personal life must remain stunted and undeveloped . . . The means of life are also the means of a good life. Freedom is the life blood of all culture and the condition of the good life . . . [and] whoever controls wealth controls the means of cultural development and personal freedom."[46] Positive government sees its duty as providing the "resources of the people for the welfare of the people."[47]

At the same time, however, Macmurray also holds that no political society should ever trespass into areas of personal life that depend upon the free exercise of one's reason and spiritual conscience. This means that Macmurray would resist some of the more extreme communitarian emphases upon the complete or thoroughgoing embeddedness of persons in their tradition, culture, history, or community. It is vitally important, he would argue, that persons retain a degree of transcendence over even the most powerful of constraining and defining conditions in order to be able to critique and reform them. He locates this area of transcendence in the religious life and denies the government any right to interfere with it. "There is a department of social life in which the political authority has no competence. It lies beyond the limits of the State's authority."[48] This State is "a material power and works by law and the sanction of law"[49] and has no place in determining the personal freedom and spiritual life of individuals. By implication this freedom can and ought to be used to determine how the power of law can be employed to serve the higher ends of freedom and the spiritual life, or, in short, the conditions for positively motivated

---

[46] Ibid., pp. 21 2.
[47] Ibid., p. 28. While Macmurray goes on to argue that the government "would plan and administer the economic life of the community" (p. 29), I do not believe that he would necessarily subscribe to all the details of a communist or socialist command economy. In fact, his whole argument on behalf of positive government is couched in the context of a defense of political democracy and the prohibition on government from entering into the spiritual and personal lives of its subjects.
[48] Ibid., p. 11.
[49] Ibid., p. 17.

community. And this means the ability to stand apart from one's political, legal, and cultural traditions in order to reflect critically upon how they might be altered (or better defended) in the light of the overarching purposes of genuine community to which they are or ought to be the means. And for Macmurray this standing apart is possible, in part, because one can appeal to the will of God as that which transcends all particular and his-torically contingent cultural forms even while being enacted in and through them.

This standing apart is also based on the assumption that, as Will Kymlicka argues in defense of liberalism and against some of its more extreme communitarian critics, "we *can* be mistaken about even our most fundamental interests, and because some goals *are* more worthy than others. Liberty is needed precisely to find out what is valuable in life—to question, re-examine, and revise our beliefs about value."[50] Freedom of choice is not the ultimate liberal value, but it is the value that is necessary for pursuing those projects, or life plans, that *are* in fact worth pursuing and fulfilling. "It is our projects and tasks that are the most important things in our lives, and it's because *they* are so important that we should be free to revise and reject them, should we come to believe that they are not fulfilling or worthwhile . . . Freedom of choice [is] a precondition for pursuing those projects and tasks that *are* valued for their own sake."[51]

This is what I take to be the heart of Macmurray's defense of religious and spiritual freedom from interference by the political sphere. It is within our religious lives that we discover the truly worthwhile form of life that is brought to completion in mutual community. And that form of life, for most religious people, depends upon an ontology that has a place for the intentions and actions of a divine agent both in establishing the ontological conditions of community and in moving history toward its fullest realization. Therefore, Macmurray, like Kymlicka,

---

[50] Will Kymlicka, "Liberalism and Communitarianism," *Canadian Journal of Philosophy*, Vol. 18, Number 2, June 1988, p. 185.
[51] Ibid., p. 187.

would reject the communitarian's claim that our identity is fully determined by our embeddedness in an historically contingent culture or tradition. There must be a sense in which the liberal is right that there is a self prior to its ends. It need not be a totally denuded self; it can be, as Benhabib has argued, a self in conversation and communion with others. It is impossible to view ourselves as totally without social embeddedness, but we can envisage ourselves without our *present form* of embeddedness. (If that were not possible, we would be nothing but the products of the forces that make us what we are.) Unless the communitarian can provide the self with the ability to reexamine its ends, he fails "to justify communitarian politics, for he's failed to show why individuals shouldn't be given the conditions appropriate to that reexamining, as an indispensable part of leading the best possible life."[52] But as long as we have the possibility of interactive conversation, and the social bonds that make it possible, we can enter the process of ethical reflection and compare "one 'encumbered' potential self with another 'encumbered' potential self." We can continually expose ourselves to other views of the good, "since we reserve the right to question and reappraise even our most deeply held convictions about the nature of the good life."[53] There must be a vantage point from which even the most rock-hard of such cultures can be viewed from beyond themselves by a reasoned conversation that opens up the vision of a human community that goes beyond (while remaining dependent upon) both society and its devices of politics. Only within the context of that reasoned conversation can the religious philosopher hope to ground his conviction that belief in the overarching intention for universal community of a divine agent makes the best sense (gives what Charles Taylor calls the best account) out of life in comparison to other construals and the source of means of fulfillment. But until that vision can be fully affected, law and the devices of politics remain necessary instruments for life in a just society.

In this delimited context, then, the law is to be judged by its "efficiency"; it is the "minimum of interference with the

---

[52] Ibid., p. 192.
[53] Ibid., p. 189.

practical freedom of the individual which is necessary to keep the peace" and "the means to justice in the indirect relations of the members of an association of persons cooperating for the production and distribution of the means of personal life."[54] These means include the material resources without which "we cannot live. Without adequate material resources, the personal life must remain stunted and undeveloped. The economic activities of a community are the indispensable basis for its cultural life. The means of life are also the means of a good life."[55] Now one of these means is freedom, which is the "life blood of all culture and the conditions of the good life." This is certainly in line with the liberal claim that freedom is among the highest priorities of any democratic culture and must not be unnecessarily starved by inadequate material conditions. And this means, for Macmurray, that the economic life of a society must come under the control of a democratic government (in what he calls positive democracy). Without that control, "there is no way by which the community can secure for all its members the means of realizing the cultural freedom which it is the purpose of democracy to make possible. The means of *exercising* the freedom that democracy assures to its members are distributed by the chances of economic success or failure in free competition. This means, in effect, that the realization of the good life depends upon relative wealth. Whoever controls wealth controls the means of cultural development and personal freedom."[56]

And this is precisely where Rawls' two principles of justice have their significance. They ensure that each person has an equal right to the most extensive basic liberty compatible with a similar liberty for others, and, in accord with the difference principle, that "social and economic inequalities are to be arranged so that they are both (a) to the greatest benefit of the least advantaged . . . and (b) attached to positions and offices open to all under conditions of fair equality and opportunity." And for Macmurray, a state, or society, is ultimately to be judged by how far it succeeds in "achieving and maintaining justice in

---

[54] John Macmurray, *Persons in Relation*, p. 194.
[55] John Macmurray, *Constructive Democracy*, p. 21.
[56] Ibid., pp. 21–2.

the indirect or economic relations of men ... The appeal must be to a sense of justice of all those affected, and the pragmatic evidence of this is a common consent."[57] And a common consent is best reached in a democratic society by an inclusive conversation among all the members, including those who have been historically disenfranchised by the unjust exercise of disproportionate power on behalf of economic, gender, and political elites. Thus Macmurray's commitment to justice is congruent both with Rawls' principles of justice and Benhabib's discourse ethics of communicative interaction.

And yet none of this denies the primacy of community as the context in which persons truly achieve their flourishing. The society that is maintained by common consent to the principles of justice is still, ultimately, in service to the community that is maintained by common consent to and ongoing practice of the principles of love and mutuality.

It is extremely significant that at the end of the day even Rawls, the arch-liberal, has room for such communities within his society of mutual cooperation. Critics and defenders have so focused on the liberal priority of the right in Rawls in theory that they have overlooked the importance he places on the virtue of life in community in practice. Roberto Alejandro has pointed out that Rawls has a strong sense of an encumbered self (quite at odds with the communitarian critique of him) that actually lives fully only in one form of community or another. Rawls admits that "there should be for each person at least one community of shared interests to which he belongs and where he finds his endeavors confirmed by his associates."[58] This notion of communal confirmation suggests that selves, ontologically and empirically, do not fully flourish until and unless they are affirmed and appreciated by others. This has parallels to Macmurray's claim that because it is "natural for human beings to share their experience, to understand one another, to find joy and satisfaction in living together, in expressing and revealing themselves to one another,"[59] it is necessary to enter a social

---

[57] John Macmurray, *Persons in Relation*, p. 203.
[58] John Rawls, *A Theory of Justice*, p. 442.
[59] John Macmurray, *Reason and Emotion* (New York: Barnes and Noble, 1962) p. 98.

union, or community. Thus for both Macmurray and Rawls a
goal of radical self-sufficiency is neither possible nor desirable.
One depends upon others "to confirm his sense of his own
worth."[60] In addition, the Rawlsian self, in Alejandro's words,
"develops sentiments and attachments, *not out of itself*, but out of
the influence it experiences in its dealing with other selves."[61]
Rawls goes on to say that some form of social union is necessary for the individual's powers to reach fruition. "Only in social
union is the individual complete."[62] This notion of personal
completeness in and through "social union" is clearly not too
distant from Macmurray's notion of community. It also suggests
that Rawls understands that society (the cooperative association) is not sufficient for the completion of the aspirations of
human beings. They require a tighter, more direct and personal
form of community and this fact opens Rawls up to a consideration of communal relationships that go beyond, without
replacing, societal principles of justice. And if this is true, Alejandro
is right in claiming that "for a Rawlsian, community is far from
being a mere attribute . . . it is constitutive of the individual's
identity," just as the communitarians claim. What Rawls does
not do is argue that any one particular kind of community or
social union is better than another. But Macmurray and the
Biblical theist would make such an argument, drawing on their
construal of God's intention for the fulfillment of human persons in and through mutual love. In this respect, Macmurray
keeps alive the importance of a moral ontology as the basis for
a full understanding of the relationship between society and its
devices of politics, and community with its mutuality of love.

---

[60] John Rawls, *A Theory of Justice*, p. 445.
[61] Roberto Alejandro, "Rawls's Communitarianism," *Canadian Journal of Philosophy*, Vol. 23, Number 1, March 1993, pp. 82-3.
[62] John Rawls, *A Theory of Justice*, p. 525.

16

Theomorphism

Benson Saler

In a book entitled *The Search for Transcendence: A Theological Analysis of Non-Theological Attempts to Define Transcendence,* William A. Johnson remarks, "The impulse to move from the ordinary dimension of life to the extraordinary is not one invented by the theologian but is one which appears to spring from the deepest levels of consciousness itself" (1974:1). Johnson's observation resonates with the experiences and opinions of many humanists and social scientists. Some of them, moreover, would add the human consciousness tends to be shaped and colored by culture, culture both in the sense of traditions and in the sense of processes unendingly negotiated and renegotiated in social transactions of diverse sorts.

Anthropologists, among others, have devoted some attention to the expression of culturally mediated impulses to move from more or less ordinary dimensions of life to the extraordinary, and they have done so in a variety of settings. Perhaps the most dramatic examples of those attentions are found in studies of "revitalization movements," a term favored by Anthony F.C. Wallace (1966:30) "to denote any conscious, organized efforts by members of a society to construct a more satisfying culture" (see also Wallace 1956). Those movements often take religious forms (e.g.,The Handsome Lake Movement among the Iroquois, or the Cargo Cults of Melanesia), and they often include some summons to a higher or extraordinary existential state. But, of course, we need not turn solely to the South Seas or elsewhere in the non-Western world for examples.There have been many revitalization movements in Western history. And, more particularly with respect to Johnson's observation, there have been numerous expressions in the West of desires to move from what are taken to be ordinary dimensions of human life to the extraordinary.

Perhaps the most salient of Western calls and aspirations to move to an extraordinary state are couched in theomorphic language. Theomorphism can be defined as the attribution of God-like qualities or capacities to objects that are not originally deemed divine.Theomorphism to some extent parallels anthropomorphism, the attribution of human qualities or capacities to objects that are not originally deemed human. But theomorphic language (the application to humans and to other creatures of language judged especially appropriate for speaking about God) is far less common in everyday speech than anthropomorphic language (the application of God and to much else of language deemed especially appropriate about humans). Furthermore, while anthropomorphism has received a good deal of scholarly attention (for a global and sophisticated perspective, see Guthrie 1993), theomorphism has been given less.

Theomorphism can be discerned in Christian traditions respecting the divinization of human beings. It is, however, theologically circumscribed in those traditions, a matter to which I return later.

In certain other Western traditions, theomorphic themes are sometimes less hedged or circumscribed by philosophical or theological consideration.That was the case among the ancient Greeks, and the pervasiveness of various theomorphic themes in Greek culture at different times underwrites Goethe's opinion that:

> The purpose and goal of the Greek is to deify man, not to humanize divinity. This is not anthropomorphism but theomorphism. (*Myron's Kuh*, quoted in Otto 1979:236).

The German poet, as Trevelyan (1981 [1941]:270) notes, supposed that the chief object of ancient Greek art and the hub of Hellenic spiritual activity was "*der schöne Mensch*," beautiful humanity. The Greek focus on beautiful humanity included a diversity of theomorphic elements. In the remainder of this paper, I explore some of them mainly with reference to the Greek epic tradition (particularly the *Iliad*), and then I briefly compare those examples of theomorphism to theomorphism in Christianity.

II

Theomorphism of a sort is associated with Euhemerus's claim concerning the origin of the Gods. The Sicilian Greek, who lived about 300 B.C.E., maintained that many of the Gods of Greek mythology, and particularly the Olympian deities, were once mortal men and women. Public recognition of their exploits invested them with heroic qualities, and appreciation of their benefactions facilitated their transformation into Gods. Sometimes, indeed, those mortals actively and adroitly advanced their reputations by establishing cults in their own honor (Lactantius, *The Divine Institutes*, I:22). Euhemerus also suggested that myths relating the adventures of divine personages are often based on real events, so that the analysis of myth might be directed to distilling history by boiling off exaggeration—a tenet that we call "Euhemerism."

Euhemerus, it should be noted, was neither the first nor the last Greek to propound the thesis that various divinities originated as flesh and blood people whose apotheosis was an honor conferred to them in gratitude for benefits received. Cultural understandings of that sort were of considerable antiquity and durability among the Greeks.

In the *Odyssey* (VIII:464-468), for example, Odysseus promises Nausicaa that if he returns home safely, he will honor her as he would a God because she saved his life. Hecataeus of Teos, who was born shortly before Euhemerus, is credited with the opinion that the Gods of Egypt are deified benefactors of their people. And Prodicus of Ceos, a contemporary of Socrates, and Persaeus, who studied with Zeno the Stoic, imagined that mortals who discovered new crops in their wanderings were honored as Gods because of the benefits that accrued to their fellows from their discoveries. Among the ancient Greeks, Charlesworth (1935:9) writes, "sacrifices, altars, precincts, etc., are a perfectly normal way of expressing gratitude for benefits and showing honor to a benefactor."

This and other theomorphic understandings can be found in the Homeric poems. Yet at the same time those poems express counter understandings. For epic poets and others of the Greeks, humans are often woefully distant from the God-like. Homer makes Odysseus aver that "[n]othing more feeble than man does the earth nurture" (*Odyssey* XVIII:130). And elsewhere in the Homeric poems we are given to understand that the Gods give us evil as well as good, that man himself increases his sorrows "*huper moiran*," beyond his portion, and that we are fated at birth to die. We are like the leaves, declares Glaucus, son of Hippolochus, for one generation replaces another (*Iliad* VI:146ff.).

Yet despite statements that recognize humanity's limitations and mixed lot, our human frailty, the Homeric poems on balance are fairly positive about the possibilities for a meaningful and even elevated existence. One of the most interesting things about those poems, in my opinion, is what they say about the possibilities of transcending what they take to be the ordinary human condition. They fall short of promising a Beatific Vision wherein the human mind will be elevated to a comprehension of mysteries hitherto revealed. Nor do they extol or otherwise recommend the relinquishment of all desire and the abandonment of self. They envisage transcendence, but they offer us neither Christian grace nor Theravada enlightenment.

The Homeric poems express three closely related but analytically distinguishable theomorphic themes: the divinization of valued traits or qualities, traits or qualities that we recognize as human, by associating them with Gods; the apperception of some mortals as God-like by virtue of their exhibition of valued qualities to an extraordinary degree, typically in consequence of divine favor; and the hero's often self-initiated triumph over his own mortality by means of his deathless reputation.

While these or similar theomorphics can be found outside of the Homeric corpus, I focus on that textual tradition, and particularly the *Iliad*. My reasons for doing so are multiple.

First, the Homeric poems remain foundational to Western culture, and they continue to be of interest to us.

Second, I suspect that many of my fellow anthropologists have had their ideas about "polytheism" shaped and colored by their understanding of Greek traditions about the Olympian deities, understandings traceable in significant part to the Homeric poems. While modern scholarship suggests that what is described in the Homeric texts differs in significant respects from actual on-the-ground Greek religion, the Homeric poems still dominate Western imaginings about the Olympian Gods.

Burkert notes (1985 [1977]:4), "The most important evidence for Greek religion remains the literary evidence," that the evidence includes "practically the whole of ancient poetry," and that for the ancient Greeks "religious texts in the narrow sense of sacred texts are scarcely to be found." Understandings derived from the Homeric texts, supplemented perhaps by understandings derived from Hesiod, constitute a prototypic model —the best or clearest exemplar (Saler 1993)—of what many anthropologists mean by polytheism. Those texts have thus been consequential for comprehending and comparing religions studied in the field. Anthony Wallace (1966:88), for example, makes "Olympian religion" the third of four major types of religion arranged on a typological scale (the others are "shamanic," "communal," and "monotheistic"). Wallace's illustration of the Olympian type is drawn from Dahomey in West Africa. But his prototypic model was almost certainly Hellenic.

Third, in exploring theomorphism rather than anthropomorphism in Homer, the *Iliad* is more immediate to my interests than the *Odyssey*. The former is the heroic epic par excellence, and it provides us with a clearer and more powerful expression of theomorphic themes. The latter, as many readers have noted, differs significantly from the former. Douglas Stewart cogently argues that:

> ...the *Odyssey* is not another epic weakly imitative of the *Iliad*, but a counterepic, a long hexameter poem on a figure who begins his career as a true hero, but in his later actions is energetically engaged in nonheroic and even antiheroic actions just to say alive (1976:21).

In the *Iliad*, Stewart points out, heroes publicly identify themselves and their pedigrees. In the heroic age it is customary for persons of their rank to do so. They take pride in acknowledging who they are. The central figure of the *Odyssey*, however, is careful in much of the poem to conceal his identity, not only from obvious enemies, but from others as well. His veritable obsession with false or empty identities, however effective as a dramatic element in the story, is decidedly subversive of the heroic ethos celebrated in the *Iliad*.

In the Homeric poems, the Gods sometimes conceal their identities: they take up disguises in order to accomplish their purposes, at times tricking humans in ways that we might judge to be cruel. They do so out of strength, however, and with no fear of death. When Odysseus misrepresents his identity in the *Odyssey*, he does so out of weakness. Directly or indirectly, he seeks to avoid death or, equivalently, to thwart other eventualities that would prevent him from returning home.

Iliadic heroes occupy something of an intermediate place between the Gods and the central figure of the *Odyssey*. They must face death, and they are inhibited by heroic values from doing all that they might to avoid it. Vulnerable to human frailties, and to the supreme frailty, death, they seek to transcend both their humanity and its termination. We can better appreciate their existential condition and their strivings, their frail humanity and their beautiful humanity, by exploring the three theomorphic themes mentioned earlier.

III

The divinization of valued traits or qualities. By divinization here I mean more than an intensification beyond the normally human of such traits or qualities as wisdom, strength, beauty and so forth, although such intensification is important. Associating valued traits or qualities with the Gods not only intensifies them, but it raises them above normal human capacities in another way: it renders them ageless and imperishable.

The Olympian deities described by Homer collectively excel mortals in many attributes the Greek admired. Each God, however, does not excel mortals in all particulars. As Ehnmark puts it:

> Each individual god does not possess all the human qualities brought to their highest perfection; on the contrary, the equipment of the gods is sometimes highly defective. It is true that nobody can rival a god in his own special sphere— nobody is more beautiful than Aphrodite, nobody wiser than Athene—but in other respects the gods may be inferior to men. Achilles is undoubtedly superior to Hephaestus in physical qualities and Odysseus is more cunning than Ares (1935:3).

Aphrodite well illustrates both the particularized excellence and the limitations of individual divinities. Not to her, Zeus declares, "are given works of war" (*Iliad* V:428). She is even called "coward" (*Iliad* V:331), an epithet that carried a highly negative valuation in the Homeric world.

The Cyprian's religious meanings are rich and nuanced. The anthropologist Paul Friedrich (1978:134) emphasizes her "liminality," understood in terms of the Greek system of religious categories; he maintains that "she bridges physical reality and metaphysical belief." On a perhaps more obvious (but no less important) plane of significance, the Goddess raises to the divine those physical traits deemed beautiful among mortal women, for Hellenic poets, sculptors, and others made her their paragon of feminine physical beauty. A statue of her by Praxiteles, though criticized by some of the artist's contemporaries because it showed the Goddess undressed, apparently captured ideals current in his day. We in our own time continue to be charmed by ancient stories to the effect that when Aphrodite first saw that statue, she exclaimed in amazement, "Where did Praxiteles see me naked?" (*The Greek Anthology* XVI:160, 162, 168).

There are many beautiful women in the Homeric poems. There is, however, a terrible and crucial difference between the beauty of most of them and that of Aphrodite. Their beauty (the Helen of the *Odyssey* seemingly excepted) will eventually fade while that of golden Aphrodite forever remains in bloom. It is not simply that laughter-loving Aphrodite is immortal whereas the human female is not, but that the Goddess is also ageless while the human female characteristically is not.

The crucial importance of coupling agelessness with immortality is illustrated by the sad story of Tithonus in Homeric Hymn 5, the Hymn to Aphrodite (218-238). Eos, Dawn, became enamored of the mortal Tithonus. She persuaded Zeus to grant him immortality, but she neglected to request eternal youth in her lover. In time poor Tithonus grew old, and though queenly Eos fed him ambrosia and supplied him with rich clothes, she avoided his bed. Eventually, "this seemed in her heart the best counsel": she locked the defective immortal away in a room where, we are told, "he babbles endlessly."

We can easily appreciate the pathos of that story (perhaps all the more so because of our growing tendency to consign the elderly to nursing homes). For the ancient Greeks, of course, the tale conveyed various bits of information, not the least significant of them being a reaffirmation of the importance of maintaining one's vigor. And the vigor of the God is imperishable.

Hellenes of different periods associated freedom from age and death with the Gods. Sophocles (*Philoctetes* 607), for example, intones that:

> The immortal Gods alone have neither age nor death!
> All other things almighty time disquiets.

Yet this was not consistently so in the Homeric poems. While the pair of horses that the *Iliad* (XVII:444) describes as "ageless and immortal" are of divine lineage, this was not apparently the case for the gold and silver dogs that guard the palace of King Alcinous (*Odyssey* VII:91-94). Those curious canines, described as "free from death and age all their days," are among a diversity of things cunningly wrought by Hephaistos.

In any case, a handful of exceptions aside, the Greek preeminently associated the conjunction of immortality and agelessness with the Gods. That the Gods are *athanatoi*, deathless, many classicists maintain, marks the crucial distinction between Gods and human beings. Not all classicists agree, however (e.g., Ehnmark 1935:2). In my opinion, though deathlessness and agelessness are clearly important, it is a conjunction of characteristics rather than one or two that sets the Gods off from humans. The Gods are not only ageless and immortal, but they possess particularized superiorities in attributes and powers (the wisdom of Athene, the beauty of Aphrodite, the skill of Hephaistos, etc.), and they possess collective capacities as focused in Zeus, including the power to make human beings God-like.

Now, when the Homeric Gods exhibit traits or qualities that remind us of positively valued human traits or qualities, do the divine manifestations closely resemble what we discern among human beings?

Faced with a similar question about *their* God, numbers of Jewish, Christian, and Muslim theologians have answered, "No, our God is so different in nature that our ordinary words, predicated of human beings, do not really apply to the divine essence." Some suggest that when we apply such words as "love" and "wisdom" to God, we do so by analogy, analogy that is weak and potentially misleading. Others argue that those words apply to God in unique ways, ways appropriate only to God and beyond full human understanding. And still others maintain that negative language is best when speaking about God because of our inability as finite creatures to appreciate the infinite: that while we might say what God is not, we are unable to say what God really is. In any case, and regardless of the particular solution that they prefer, these theologians generally agree that predicating wisdom of the monotheistic God is not the same thing as predicating wisdom of Socrates.

In the case of the Homeric Gods, however, predicates applied to God come much closer to resembling what we predicate about human beings. Those Gods do indeed exhibit qualities or traits found among humans, though sometimes intensified. Aphrodite's beauty, while exceeding that of mortal women, nevertheless corresponds—"ankle, thigh, and upper half"—to beauty in human females. And although the wisdom of Zeus and Athene is heightened by a certain prescience—which is why I qualified my "Yes"—the Olympians are not omniscient. To say that Zeus or Athene is wise is not all that different from saying that Odysseus is wise.

If we think of the Homeric Gods as manifesting traits or qualifies also found among humans, then a further link in our chain of reasoning is broadly theomorphic. Beauty, wisdom, strength, and other traits or qualities that we associate with men and women are not only writ large and rendered supernal through their association with the Gods, but they are made deathless and ageless as well. Though the Gods sometimes endure physical transformations or exercise their powers of metamorphosis, traits or qualities that they share with mortals transcend such alternations and oscillations and are ultimately durable. Those traits or qualities are divinized when attributed to the Gods. And, being intensified and rendered lasting, they are made wonderful.

When mortals exhibit such traits or qualities to an extent that surpasses the normally human—to an extent that is wonderful among men—the poet speaks of such mortals as God-like. Here the theomorphic element becomes even more palpable. Homer, the classicist Erland Ehnmark observes, "never speaks of human gods, but sometimes of divine men" (1935:3).

IV

The Appreciation of Some Mortals as God-like. Various mortals in the Homeric poems are described as resembling a God in one or another respect. Odysseus and Hector, for example, are said to be "the peer of Zeus" in artifice or counsel (*Iliad* II:169, VII:471). Talthybius is described as having a voice like that of a God (*Iliad* XIX:250), and the bard Demodocus is said to be "like the Gods in speech" (*Odyssey* IX:48). When mortals are credited with durable qualities that greatly surpass those exhibited by most human beings, such superiority is sometimes declared to be a gift from a God. Agamemnon, for instance, opines that Achilles's great strength is a divine gift (*Iliad* I:178), and Hector pronounces Paris's fair hair and handsome form to be gifts from Aphrodite (*Iliad* III:54-55).

The poet often awards the epithet "God-like" to mortals whose epic attributes distinguish them from common humanity. Trojans as well as Achaeans are so characterized. We read, for example, of "God-like Priam" and "God-like Paris." The regal stateliness of the one and the striking comeliness of the other are among their most important qualities.

In discussing those superiorities that distinguish some men from the common populace, Ehnmark (1935:5) argues that not all such features are equivalent or point to the same causal factors. Some are gifts of the Gods and betoken an element of the divine in human beings. Others are divine gifts without implying that their recipients are really like the Gods. And in still other cases the epithet "God-like" may have a more mundane significance: it may mean merely "eminent."

When, however, we encounter what amount to episodic superiorities occasioned by the purposeful intervention of the Gods, "it is possible," Ehnmark writes, "to ascertain the real significance. Man is invested with divine power and become undoubtedly like the gods" (1935:5). We are given a number of examples of this in the *Iliad* (e.g., V:183-185). Divine patrons inspire their favorites with epic courage and ardor, bestow on them extraordinary strength, render them wondrously terrible in appearance, and so forth.

Giving men such powers, Ehnmark (1935:8) remarks, "makes mortals really like the gods." Athene, for instance, gives Diomedes extraordinary power and lifts from his eyes the mist that prevents him from seeing Gods. So assisted, he wounds two divinities: Aphrodite, and, wonderful to relate, Ares, the God of War.

Ehnmark draws a theomorphic conclusion:

> . . . the expression 'godlike' *can* be something more than a mere metaphor. We are here concerned with the actual elevation of a man to a level where he becomes the equal of the gods. Man receives a share of divine power and accordingly of the divine itself. He can never achieve equality with the gods through his own unaided efforts. It is only when man's

own strength is reinforced by divine power that he attains to something like divine rank. Since this power proceeds from the gods and is not inherent in man as such, the superiority in man, which makes him godlike, is not a part of his human equipment, but is a divine quality (1935:9).

V

The Hero's Transcendence of His Own Mortality. In Book IX (410-416) of the *Iliad*, Achilles recounts what his mother, the Goddess Thetis, revealed to him about his own mortality. He must die, and either of two fates will bear him toward that doom. He can remain at Troy and die a warrior's death, forfeiting his chance to return home but gaining imperishable fame. Or he can return home and die peacefully in old age, though at the cost of lasting glory. The narrative relates that Fate allows Achilles to choose between these options. Yet while Achilles is credited with the power of choice, the option described is heavily biased by the poet's account of Achaean culture, and it is effectively foreclosed by epic conventions.

The heroic values celebrated by the *Iliad* weigh choices. Those values render it culturally grammatical for a person such as Achilles to choose imperishable glory. This, however, does not guarantee that Achilles will make that choice. In terms of Achaean culture as imagined in Homer, there is always the possibility that someone will act, so to speak, ungrammatically. But actual Greek epic conventions governing the *Iliad* (conventions celebrated rather less strenuously in that curious work known as the *Odyssey*) do effectively foreclose choice from the audience's point of view. And they do so despite the options granted Achilles in the narrative.

If Achilles were to forfeit imperishable glory, he would not be the best of the Achaeans, and the story of his wrath and its consequences would be an unlikely choice for bardic celebration. Indeed, were Achilles to opt for a long life at the cost of everlasting fame, he would repudiate the ancient prophecy that the son of Thetis will be greater than his genitor, a prophecy that induced the Gods to wed Thetis to the mortal Peleus, lest she bear a son to one of their divine company. Achilles must choose eternal renown, a type of immortality, in keeping with the teleological theomorphism of the epic handed down to us.

A warrior's death at Troy is the portal to poetic immortality for Achilles. In the bardic traditions that apply to Homer, it is the Muses who witness and remember all that transpires and who inspire the poets to recount what happened. Neither the Gods nor the mortal heroes in the epics have a full knowledge of all that occurs. Only the Muses do, and through their inspiration the bards and their audiences are given a global perspective. In the epic traditions relevant to Homer, the Muses confer "unfailing fame" on mortals who behave valorously or otherwise act exceptionally (just as they sometimes memorialize the disgrace of those whose conduct deviates from heroic norms).

Death, as the *Iliad* presents it, is a necessary step in the direction of immortality through an unwelcome termination of vigor. "The hero's death," the classicist Gregory Nagy (1979:9) writes, "is the theme that gives him his power—not only in cult but also in poetry." From Nagy's point of view, death, a natural process, is culturally negated both in the cult of heroes (an important complex in actual Hellenic religion) and in epic poetry. The hero reverenced at a local shrine after his death is given *time*, honor, as are the Gods, whereas the hero who is commemorated in epic poetry is the recipient of *kleos*, glory. "Unfailing honor" and "unfailing glory" suggest a kind of immortality for heroes, an immortality, says Nagy, "in the form of a cultural institution that is predicated on the *natural* process of death" (1979:1984).

Basic to that institution is lamentation over the hero's death. Not only is lamentation "an aspect of the hero-cult," but the incorporation of the hero into epic "is presented by epic itself as an external extension of the lamentation sung by the Muses over the hero's death" (Nagy 1979:184).

Nagy accepts the widely endorsed supposition that, "The cult of heroes was a highly evolved transformation of the worship of ancestors, within the social context of the city-state or *polis*" (1979:115). Hero cults, he points out, were based upon a fundamental idea found in ancient Greek religion: the idea that the power of a hero is concentrated in a particular place (Herakles is a conspicuous exception, for he was reverenced throughout Greece). The development of hero cults was well marked in the eighth century B.C.E. At about the same time, Nagy notes, the Homeric epic tradition emerged as a Panhellenic phenomenon, a form of "intensive intercommunication among the elites of the developing city-states" (1979:115).

The functions of the Homeric epics in bridging local loyalties and interests, Nagy argues, rendered it inappropriate for their central heroes to have "an overtly religious dimension in the narratives" (1979:116). That is, it would have proven dysfunctional to the promotion of Panhellenism had epic heroes been emphatically treated as actual or potential objects of cult, given the strong association in Greek thought between cult hero and local *cultus*.

The poet's failure to provide his heroes with a clear and consistent religious dimension, Nagy maintains, betokens "a restriction on the self-expression of the epic." This restriction notwithstanding, he continues, there are actually sporadic references in the Homeric poems to hero cults (for a different point of view, see Rohde 1925:25). While such references are neither frequent nor elaborated (and in those senses not emphatic), they must have been meaningful to the audiences that the bards addressed, or so Nagy supposes.

Thus, for instance, the funeral of Patroklos, described in Book XXIII of the *Iliad*, contains a number of elements associated with hero cults, e.g., wine libation, offering honey with oil, the singing of lamentations, and funeral games (Nagy 1979:116–117). Even more significant for Nagy's argument are references to a tomb for Achilles by the Hellespont, a tomb that in later Greek traditions flashed lights that comforted mariners. "The Achaeans of the future who survive Achilles," Nagy (1979:341) writes, are "Achaeans in ships." References to Achilles's tomb, he opines, are references to a time in the future outside of the narrative, and they:

> reveal Achilles as not so much a hero of epic but rather a hero
> of cult. The future of the narrative is the here and now of the

Homeric audience, and to them the tomb of Achilles is a
matter of religion, reflecting the era's marked preoccupation
with hero cult ...With his tomb overlooking the Hellespont,
Achilles manifests the religious aspect of his essence as hero
even within the epic framework of the *Iliad* and *Odyssey* (Nagy
1979:342).

Nagy also advances an interesting solution to the problem
of how a hero's bones can rest in the grave while myth relates
that the hero has attained immortality. Internment of the hero's
remains in a specific place is crucial to the hero cult of locality.
Yet myths about the immortalization of the hero imply a post-
mortem reanimation of the hero's body. "Accordingly," Nagy
argues, "the hero's remains cannot be pictured as being in his
grave *once he is immortalized,* and there seems at first glance to be
a conflict here with the requirements of cult ..." (1979:208). The
solution that he proposes is that *"the promise of immortalization
aims not at the here-and-now but rather as fulfillment in the hero's
future"* (1979:208, emphasis in original).

If this be granted, then, Nagy suggests, the ultimate afterlife
in both myth and cult would not be Hades but Elysium or
something comparable. Hades would represent a transitional stage
in the afterlife, when the *psukhe* separates from the body. Then,
in a place such as Elysium or the Isles of the Blessed, the body
and the *psukhe* could be reintegrated. From this interpretive
perspective, theomorphism played a role in integrating myth
and cult.

VI

The Homeric poems confront us with theomorphized
humans and anthropomorphized Gods. Although, according to
Nagy, the religious dimension is not stressed for either Gods or
men in Homer, that poetic corpus juxtaposes anthropomorphism
and theomorphism. Such juxtaposition, moreover, while
accomplished outside of an emphatically religious frame, has
parallels or analogies in various other Western traditions,
including some that we identify as pre-eminently religious.

Western religions, it is widely recognized, are colored by
anthropomorphisms. Yet in addition to describing deity in

anthropomorphic language, a number of Western religions also include theomorphic elements in their anthropologies. The conjoining of anthropomorphic theology with theomorphic anthropology is well marked in some members of the Christian family of confessions, particularly certain of the earlier members.

The theomorphic dimension is most clear in ideas after deification (*theosis, deificatio*). Compressing together various Patristic and later conceptualizations, suffice it for present purposes to say that deification, broadly conceived, refers to a transformative process whereby humans become more like God. While still remaining a creature, and never coming to equal his Creator, divinized man acquires God-like qualities: immortality, incorruptibility, and impassability. While these gifts bestowed by God are great, they are not in themselves the supreme reward of divinization. That reward, rather, is an increased intimacy between the creature and his Creator. Such intimacy permits humans to 'see' God without any intermediary; humans come to contemplate God with a clarity approaching (but never equaling) the clarity with which God knows himself.

That the word 'deification' has been employed as a multivocal term for expressing a complex of theological as well as soteriological ideas has been demonstrated by Donald Winslow with respect to the teachings of Gregory of Nazianzus (d. 309 C.E.). In Gregory's writings, Winslow argues, *theosis* amounts to a multi-faceted metaphor (1979:193). It is employed in an attempt to surmount the limitations of available language, limitations that render it difficult to talk about divinity, especially as divinity may relate to human beings (1979:198). For Gregory, Winslow writes, the relation between God and man

> was so intimate, both in its origin as well as in its future fulfillment, that he could speak of it in two complementary ways. When he sought to describe *God's* role in the relationship, he spoke 'anthropomorphically.' In the same way, when he attempted to describe what happens to *us* within the dimension of this relationship, i.e., theosis, he could well afford to speak 'theomorphically' (1979:199).

In discussing or alluding to deification, Christian writers stress the indispensability of God's salvific instrumentality. They particularize the instrumentality, moreover, with reference to the redemptive mission of Jesus Christ. Indeed, the theomorphic language of deification is characteristically coupled with the anthropomorphic language of incarnation. Thus Irenaeus (d. 202 C.E.) remarks that those who reject the Incarnation

> defraud human nature of promotion into God, and prove themselves ungrateful to the Word of God, who became flesh for them. For it was for this end that the Word of God was made man, and He who was the Son of God became the Son of Man, that man, having been taken into the Word, and receiving the adoption, might become the son of God (*Against Heresies* 3.19.1).

And in a famous text, Athanasius (d. 373 C.E.), after declaring that "through death immortality has come to all," goes on to say that the Word of God

> became man that we might become God; and he revealed himself through a body so that we might have an idea of the invisible Father; and he endured insults from men so that we might inherit incorruption (*On the Incarnation* 54).

The Christian emphasis on the indispensable and singular instrumentality of God for effecting the divinization of humans —"*solus Deus deificet*," God alone makes God-like, Thomas Aquinas puts it (*Summa Theologiae* 1a2ae.112,1)—has parallels in other Western traditions, however less emphatic or less explicit they may be. Some pages ago I quoted the classicist Erland Ehnmark on the subject of the investment of Homeric heroes with divine powers. In consequence of such investment, a hero, Ehnmark says, "becomes undoubtedly like the gods." "Man," to repeat more of the classicist's words,

> receives a share of divine power and accordingly of the divine itself. *He can never achieve equality with the gods through his own*

unaided efforts. It is only when a man's own strength is reinforced by divine power that he attains to something like divine rank (1935:9, emphasis added).

Now, though the understandings and sentiments expressed in the Homeric corpus differ in many important respects from those encountered in the writings of authors preoccupied with Christian doctrine, the theme of the elevation of human beings to the God-like in consequence of divine intervention, so marked in Christian traditions, is also found in ancient Greek epic. That this broad theomorphic theme plays a significant role outside of a clearly religious literature as well as within one suggests its importance to the evolving civilization that nurtured it.

In point of fact, theomorphic themes in one form or another (sometimes accompanied with warnings against theomorphic aspirations or pretensions) can be found in a diversity of Western traditions. Furthermore, they do not always require or imply divine intervention. In some cases they represent an extreme in humanistic optimism, for they suggest that human beings themselves have the capacity to effect their own transcendence.

In a famous case, now widely deemed a failure, it was held that by reallocating control over the means of economic production society could be transformed into a "celestial organism," and human beings, who have histories rather than fixed natures, would also be transformed for the better. Such thematic expressions are generally closer to epic than to religion, and while their theomorphism is relatively muted, it is there nonetheless. A powerful Western metaphor for these and various other theomorphic yearnings can be found in alchemy, whether they be voiced in magical or non-magical idioms. For just as base metal might be transformed into gold, so, too, might the sullied soul or the corrupt society be purified and raised to a higher state.

Yet in Western cultural traditions, the most elemental and salient manifestations of theomorphic longings go in tandem with expressions of the anthropomorphic and complement those expressions in interesting ways. Broadly put, anthropomorphic agencies make possible or otherwise facilitate the transcendence of the ordinary. The allowance that that might happen implies that a potentiality for transcendence is a fact of human existence.

Given, however, the great diversity of cultural themes respecting this matter in the history of the West (to say nothing of the non-West), we cannot insist that a theomorphic anthropology requires or is always accompanied by a vital anthropomorphic theology. Nor can we insist that an anthropomorphic theology requires or is always accompanied by a vital theomorphic anthropology. People may vest faith or interest in one without necessarily subscribing to the other. For the greatest part of its lifespan nevertheless, the West has tended to couple them.

17

Foundations, Philosophy and the Location of Socrates' Feet

Nino Langiulli

The following discussion attempts to make several interrelated points. The first is to offer the interpretation of a line in Plato's *Phaedo* as a response to Aristophanes' conservative view, i.e., philosophy undermines traditional views of reality and a *fortiori*, of morality, politics, and esthetics as well. The second is that the line is doubly ironic such that the second turn of the irony is Plato's reply to the ancient liberal view as represented by the Sophists—the view that reality, morality, and esthetics are solely matters of opinion and politics solely a matter of power since transcendent points of reference are impossible. Protagoras' dictum that "man is the measure: of the things that are that they are; of the things that are not that they are not" means that only immanence is possible. This is to say more specifically that truth and falsity cannot be known, only opinions possessed; goodness and badness cannot be achieved, only pleasures and pains can be; unity and sameness do not exist, only multiplicity and difference; justice and injustice are not possible, only the interests of the strong and the weak; beauty and ugliness cannot be discovered, only likes and dislikes.

The third point is a reply to the contemporary sophists, i.e., the anti-foundationalists or contemporary liberals.They, in order to affirm humanity and the human things, maintain that foundations do not exist and philosophy, as the attempt to uncover them, is either futile at worst or poetry at best.

The argument that foundations do not exist and that philosophy is futile is self-contradictory. The argument that philosophy is just poetry, and bad poetry at that, is Nietzsche's view. Unlike his liberal epigoni who are positive and optimistic about humanity, Nietzsche follows his argument of philosophy as poetry to its logical conclusion—to a negative and pessimistic humanism.

One important source for his argument is his interpretation of the _Phaedo_—an argument and interpretation with which those offered herein are in conflict.[1] That conflict will be treated at

---

[1] A recent book on the _Phaedo_—Paul Stern's _Socratic Rationalism and Political Philosophy: An Interpretation of Plato's Phaedo_ (Albany, State University of New York Press, 1993)—covers some of the same ground and even shares one of the conclusions reached here. Stern, however, has a different understanding of Plato's notion of the foundation for philosophy. Moreover, the line and its interpretation which are the point of departure for this discussion are not treated in the book nor is Plato's pun seen as a more profound response to Aristophanes than the one given in the _Apology_. Thus Stern misses the double irony as the vehicle whereby Plato indicates his deepest understanding of both political activity and political philosophy. Nevertheless on page 145 of his book, Stern reaches the correct conclusion: "The character of human existence itself moves us to seek explanations in that which transcends humanity. As the _Phaedo_ makes clear in its focus on death and immortality, human existence is characterized by an awareness of incompleteness, an awareness that confronts us most powerfully when we face our mortality." While Stern attributes this awareness to a non-dogmatic, thereby rational choice, the present discussion attributes it to the very act of philosophizing itself leaving intact the erotic, and thereby transcendent, character of the act—an act committed not only by Plato but by Nietzsche as well, his protestations and those of his epigoni notwithstanding. In attributing this awareness to "socratic rationalism" (an infelicitous anachronism), Stern seems to regard rationalism as an accomplishment in itself.The major difference between Stern's argument and the one offered here is that he locates the "ground" of Socratic philosophy in self-understanding (p. 180). This seems inconsistent with what he claims in the above-quoted passage from p. 145.A point of departure is not a ground. Consistent with what Stern writes on p. 145, Plato discovers the ground in the _order_ of the world (that order he calls divine) which is distinct from the self, but of which the self is a part. The result is a firmer and more stable awareness and appreciation of politics and humanity.

the end of this discussion wherein the true understanding and limits of humanity are disclosed most radically and most fundamentally in philosophy's search for a foundation.

In a remark near the beginning of the *Phaedo* (61d) that is arresting and slyly cryptic, Plato seems to make a joke about philosophy. Given its immediate context, it has an evident and not especially profound meaning. But it is its very obviousness that naggingly draws the curious reader beyond its surface triviality into the theme and core of the dialogue, namely, the relationship between philosophy, the soul, and morality. What is more, the sentence recollects others in the *Apology*. It may be that Plato is having a joke at the expense of Socrates, or even more interestingly, employing his irrepressible irony to make a joke about philosophy itself.[2] But the point—the connection, the joke, the irony—cannot be grasped unless and until the reader understands that the sentence *is* a response to Aristophanes' portrayal of Socrates in *The Clouds*—a portrayal addressed by Plato in the *Apology*. In the play Socrates is the character who, suspended in a basket in the air, represents for Aristophanes the corruption of Athenian religion and morality by means of scientific speculation and sophistry. This is to say that the gods are replaced by natural phenomena in the explanation of things and that traditional morality is challenged and undermined by clever, subtle though specious arguments. The young man, Pheidippides, by the end of the play denies the existence of the gods, beats his father, Strepsiades, and argues, moreover, that his parents *deserve* to be beaten.

In the *Apology*, Plato treats the character of Socrates in *The Clouds* as a caricature and alludes to it as his own. His Socratic character gives his first speech before his Athenian judges recalling the underlying bias against him.

> Socrates is guilty of criminal meddling, in that he inquires into things below the earth and in the sky, and makes the weaker argument defeat the stronger and teaches others to follow his example. It runs something like that. You have

---

[2] For some sense of Plato's use of irony, see *Phaedrus* (276d), *Republic* (536c), *Statesman* (268d), *Timaeus* (59c), *Laws* (685a). Then confer with Aristotle's *Politics*, 11, 6 (1265a6) and Kierkegaard's *Concept of Irony*.

> seen it for yourselves in the play by Aristophanes, where
> Socrates goes whirling round, proclaiming that he is walking
> on air, and uttering a great deal of nonsense about things of
> which I know nothing whatsoever (19 b–c).[3]

This caricature passing for a description is, as the character Socrates himself says (*Apology* 23d), the stock charge against all philosophers. They do not have their feet on the ground because their heads are in the clouds, asking questions about those matters which everyone else takes for granted or about things that are beyond ordinary human experience and thereby not worth knowing. They challenge the common-sense opinions in morals and politics, as well as the common opinions in religion, but wish at the same time to stand above and beyond the practical consequences of doing so. By means of these questions and challenges, they attract those young people who are eager for novelty and innovation and at the same time contemptuous of tired old views and manners, teaching them rhetorical and dialectical tricks which turn them into glib, not to speak of snide, smart-alecks ready to jettison God, family, friends, and country. Philosophers are, at best, impractical muddle-headed fools or, at worst, careless corrupters of youth. The philosophers' own distinctions between sophists, wise men, and philosophers are too subtle or arch to have any practical value or count very much when bodies are being counted for the showdown. Philosophers make no tangible contribution to human life. Professionals, such as physicians, lawyers, and teachers, do. So do priests, politicians and artisans as do persons engaged in agriculture and business. Poets and other artists may go unappreciated but the marks they leave are among the most characteristic and most lasting of cultural efforts. Even those other theoreticians or academics such as scientists, historians and mathematicians perform tasks which can be put to some good use in the human enterprise. But philosophers, committed as they are to the most theoretical of activities and therefore the most practically useless, should best be ignored and forgotten.

---

[3] All of the quotations from Plato's dialogues in this essay are taken from Plato, *The Collected Dialogues*, edited by Edith Hamilton and Huntington Cairns (New York: Pantheon, 1961).

Two of them, Richard Rorty and Jacques Derrida, have come in recent years to recognize and acknowledge this, despite their nostalgia for philosophy's past.

The tone of this expansion of the caricature may lead the reader to believe that the caricature should be dismissed. It *may* have been misapplied to Socrates, as Plato suggests, but sound political thinking requires that it not be dismissed altogether. It might not apply to the "genuine" philosopher who makes much of the difference between theoretical knowledge and practical wisdom and who, much more pertinently, *knows* not only the importance of ideas but the *danger* of them and *cares* about the danger. Now there is a kind of dealer in ideas, that obnoxious brand of human animal whom Eva Brann has shrewdly de-nominated a "monster,"[4] quite a few years before Paul Johnson's recent admonition,[5] namely, the intellectual. It is a feature of his monstrosity that he may frequently pass as a philosopher but one who wants to affect or change the world. It just might be that it is precisely this person whom Aristophanes portrays as the dangler from a basket. And who else could serve better the purposes of the play than that well known "pest," Socrates. The *Apology* is not nescient of the lack of ease in distinguishing the philosopher from the sophists (the ancient intellectuals). The character, Socrates, in his own defense, appeals to that which his judges, and most everyone else can understand, as a distinguishing mark: he charges no fee for his ideas. The fact that he has no "doctrine" is another distinguishing mark, but that is part of what is not so easy to understand.

In the *Phaedo*, however, Plato offers his retort to the caricature in the cryptic and seemingly negligible remark which is both the subject of this essay and the rubric for the theme of the dialogue—the relationship between philosophy, the soul, and mortality.

> And as he spoke he lowered his feet to the ground and sat like this for the rest of the discussion (61d).

---

[4] Eva Brann, "Commencement Address," *St. John's College Magazine*, (Annapolis: July, 1974). Cf. Aristotle's *Politics*, Bk. II, ch. 8, near the end of the chapter.
[5] Paul Johnson, *The Intellectuals* (New York: Harper & Row, 1989).

Not only does Socrates *not* have his feet dangling in mid-air, he has them planted squarely on the ground. The discussion in the *Phaedo* is, of course, concerned with the relationship of philosophy to human mortality. It is about what one does in the face of death (not only one's own but those of loved ones, a more significant trial) and what is the best kind of life, granting the ineluctability of death. This is no abstract and theoretical discussion for Socrates, inasmuch as he must suffer his own death shortly. As the *Phaedo* says:

> 'At any rate,' said Socrates, 'I hardly think that anyone who hears us now—even a comic poet—would say that I am wasting time and discoursing on subjects which do not concern me' (69c).

This remark is corroborated by Plato when, speaking of arguments in general and of the arguments for immortality in particular, he has Socrates say:

> We must not let it enter our minds that there may be no validity in argument. On the contrary, we should recognize that we ourselves are still intellectual invalids, but that we must brace ourselves and do our best to become healthy— you and the others partly with a view to the rest of our lives, but I directly in view of my death, because at the moment I am in danger of regarding it not philosophically but self-assertively. You know how, in an argument, people who have no real education care nothing for the facts of the case, and are only anxious to get their point of view accepted by the audience? Well, I feel that at this moment I am as bad as they are, only with this difference, that my anxiety will not be to convince my audience except incidentally, but to produce the strongest possible conviction in myself (90e-91b).

Socrates has his feet on the ground; he is discussing a question of the utmost relevance to himself and is deadly serious about it. It is a discussion of mortality and immortality in the face of his own execution.

The reader is then struck with a marvelously contorted and disconcerting irony. That he has come to expect such a thing from the masters of irony (Socrates and more so Plato) is only meager insulation when a new one blows in—especially if it is a compound irony. The point here must be made explicitly and it must be made clearly and distinctly. Although it is a mark of great writing to be subtle and even arch in exposition, it is not a mark of great teaching. Thomas Aquinas says of Plato, for example, that *"habuit malum modum docendi."*[6] For the sake of teaching, therefore, and at the risk of unsophistication, the irony can be untangled in the following manner.

Socrates has been accused of being an impractical theoretician with his feet off the ground, who also undermines with sophistry the common opinions on which civil society rests. But in the *Apology*, and in historical fact as well, according to Aristotle[7], Socrates is particularly concerned with the human things, the domain of morals and politics—the earthly things —the things that are his business. As the Athenian "gadfly," he is seeing to it that those conditions which make philosophy and indeed *human* life possible are pursued and preserved,

> . . . for I spend all my time going about trying to persuade you, young and old, to make your first and chief concern not for your bodies nor for your possessions, but for the highest welfare of your souls, proclaiming as I go 'Wealth does not bring goodness, but goodness brings wealth and every other blessing both for the individual and to the State . . .'
> It is literally true (even if it sounds rather comical) that God has specially appointed me to this city, as though it were a large thoroughbred horse which because of its great size is inclined to be lazy and needs the stimulation of some stinging fly. It seems to me God has attached me to this city to perform the office of such a fly (*Apology* 30b; 30e).

Pest though he may be, he is bothering about the human things and to that extent has his feet on the ground.

Now, in the *Phaedo*, to repeat the point made earlier, Plato responds to the stock caricature by asserting that Socrates, in his

---

[6] Thomas Aquinas, *In Aristotelis Librum De Anima Commentarium* (Turin: Marietti, 1948), I, VIII, 107, p. 31, "[Plato] had a bad method of teaching."

[7] Aristotle, *Metaphysics*, Bk. I, ch. 6, 1987b1.

discourse about the soul and mortality in the face of his own death, has his feet on the ground, keeping them there for the entire length of the discussion. But the irony of the matter is that *that* very discussion about the soul and the things which it is like—the "forms" or "ideas"—is about things which are, of course, not on the earth nor of the earth but "above" it. The discussion turns out to be not about the "human" things but about the "divine" things—not about the physical, moral or political realms but about the metaphysical realm.

> If all these absolute realities, such as beauty and goodness, which we are always talking about, really exist; if it is to them as we rediscover our own former knowledge of them, that we refer, as copies to their patterns, all the objects of our physical perception—if these realities exist, does it not follow that our souls must exist too even before our birth, whereas if they do not exist, our discussion would seem a waste of time (76e).

> Then let us return to the same examples which we were discussing before. Does that absolute reality which we define in our discussion remain always constant and invariable, or not? Does absolute equality or beauty or any other independent entity which really exists ever admit change of any kind? Or does each one of these uniform and independent entities remain always constant and invariable, never admitting any alteration in any respect or in any sense (77d)?

> But when it [the soul] investigates by itself, it passes into the realm of the pure and immortal and changeless, and being a kindred nature, when it is once independent and free from interference, consorts with it always and strays no longer, but remains, in that realm of the absolute, constant and invariable, through contact with beings of a similar nature. And this condition of the soul we call wisdom (79d).

> Now, Cebes, he said, see whether this is our conclusion from all that we have said. The soul is most like that which is divine, immortal, intelligible, uniform, indissoluble, and ever self-consistent and invariable, whereas the body is most like that which is human, mortal, multiform, unintelligible, dissoluble, and never self-consistent (80b).

It would seem that the discussion places Socrates' feet not only in the clouds, but "above" and "beyond" the clouds. Is it perhaps that Plato is *simply* confirming Aristophanes' caricature and thereby confirming the case not only against Socrates but also against philosophy itself—indeed against "foundational" or "onto-theological" philosophy as the current fashion will have it? And if this be so, then perhaps too we can understand another odd comment from the very writer and chief speaker of the *Phaedo:* "Plato was ill" (59b) and not present for the discussion, suggesting his separation not only from "dubious" arguments for immortality but also from high-flying philosophy.[8] Perhaps, but not so "simply."

On the one hand a discussion of mortality, immortality, and the nature of the soul would be perfectly appropriate for someone who is about to die. Such concerns in these circumstances are not the exclusive domain of philosophers. They might even be regarded as a mark of "realism" and "practicality"—of having one's feet on the ground. Yet the discussion *is* unmistakably about metaphysical things, i.e., the "divine" and not the "human." Hence the platonic irony. But there is another twist to it—the *final* twist. Just as with other things human, the irony cannot be endless, or else it could not be, or be understood.

If it be so that there exists a polarity and a tension between politics and philosophy, as the *Apology*[9] and other dialogues of Plato affirm, and if it be so that the proper business of philosophers is the inquiry into and investigation of everything and anything unto their ultimate grounds, even if the inquiry and investigation should conclude that no such grounds exist or that the very inquiry itself is futile or misplaced, then it follows that when the philosopher is concerned with metaphysics, he does have *his* feet on the ground; he is minding *his* own business. We must say here, again with our attention on the concerns and arguments of current anti-foundationalists, e.g., the later Heidegger, Derrida, Rorty and their followers, that the constitutive element of metaphysics is the *inquiry* itself. This is true of every period of the history of philosophy, whether it be the

---

[8] Ann Hartle, *Death and The Disinterested Spectator* (Albany: State University of New York Press, 1986), pp. 81-83.

[9] Plato, *Apology* (32a). "The true champion of justice, if he intends to survive even for a short time must necessarily confine himself to private life and leave politics alone."

ancient, medieval, modern or contemporary period. It also matters not whether the priority is ontological or epistemological.
For to begin with one is to reach the other. The even halfway
serious posing of the question that asks whether or not there is
a primary or fundamental sense of "reality" is deep into foundations. The particular *answer* that is proposed by any given
investigation is of secondary importance in determining whether
or not a foundational endeavor takes place. The fact alone, of
the inquiry seriously begun, is sufficient. The inquirer is most
faithfully the philosopher when he takes any question to its end
to find out whether or not the answer satisfies the question.

   Although the philosopher must consider the nature of political,
poetic or technical things, he must leave politics to the politicians,
poetry to the poets, and technical things to the technicians. This
is not to say, however, that because of his deflection from the
careers of politician, poet or technician, he cannot or ought not
"advise," "guide," or "teach" them. It is precisely because it is his
business to investigate these things, and to distinguish or
differentiate between them in the course of thinking about their
natures, that he can advise, guide, or teach.[10]

   Herein lies the *telos*, the end, of philosophy, a primal theme
which Plato illustrates in dialogues as the *Parmenides* and the
Sophist on the one hand and the *Apology* and *Phaedo* on the
other. A point throughout is the "wisdom" of Socrates, the only
wisdom to which he admits—most explicitly in the *Apology*
(21d; 23a–b) but operatively elsewhere. That wisdom, as Socrates
describes it paradoxically, is a knowledge of his own ignorance.
This means an understanding of the limits of his own knowledge
(and, by extension, of human knowledge as such), an understanding achieved through sustained inquiry into the differences
among opinions about things (and, by extension, among things);
thus the Socratic dialogue.

   The tensions between politics and philosophy lurk in every
corner of the *Apology* along with the crisscrossing contrasts among
politics, poetry, *"techne"* (the artisans) and philosophy, their
activities, ends, and presumptions. The politicians claim to know
what they do not know (*Apology,* 22a); the poets speak true things

---

[10] Plato, *Apology* (29c–31b).

but by virtue of a divine inspiration and not from knowledge (*Apology*, 22b-ϑ; and the artisans, who do know (as the "know how" of a craft) presume to speak on everything (*Apology* 22d). But the philosopher, in knowing the limits of politics, poetry, and "technology," as well as of philosophy, has, as it were, clipped his own wings, not leaving the ground of what he knows.

Plato speaks equally dramatically of the dangers of politics to philosophy in relating the risks to Socrates both from the democracy *(Apology* 32a-c) and from the oligarchy *(Apology* 32c-e). The danger from the oligarchy is particularly poignant inasmuch as its leaders had been "students" of Socrates.

The corruption of a philosopher's teaching in the hands of political activists, even among the most "faithful" of them, is not an uncommon complaint in the history of the tension between the actors and the ideologues. Most recently, what might be called "Marxian orthodoxy" has disengaged itself from the failed practices of the activist disciples (Lenin, Trotsky, Stalin, or Mao) by means of the distinction between pure and not yet applied Marxism on one hand and applied (e.g., in the Soviet Union) but hardly pure pseudo-Marxism on the other.

The complaint is self-serving and even puzzling in the face of Marx's own insistence in the *Theses on Feuerbach* (1845) that "the goal now is not to interpret but to change the world." The purists' interpretation of the changes which are imposed on the world (i.e., the several totalitarian and repressive socialist and communist regimes) is that, because they *were* so universally infelicitous, they could not have been "authentic." Non-Marxist, even anti-Marxist, adulterations must have been allowed to creep in.

Change has been integral to the agenda of much of the "modern project," from Descartes through the Enlightenment to Marx and Nietzsche—change in thought directed toward change in nature. The aim has been to change (or at least to dominate) nature, in the physical as well as in the moral realms; and the effort has not been unsuccessful—but at the cost of "authenticity."

Or, to put it another way, how much and what kinds of change are compatible with "authenticity"? Is the goal perhaps the actualization in this world of a New Jerusalem, completely secular, of course, and a monument to Marxist (or some other solely human) purity? A lesson in "feet upon the ground" might well be in order at this point.

Plato himself knew the temptation—and the price—of trying to make of philosophy more than a limit to thought, the enticements of a chance at last to really guide a ruler. His "Sicilian fling" or misadventure, his attempt to teach the tryant Dionysius some philosophy in order that he might govern well, was a bitter lesson for Plato (*Seventh Letter,* 345c-352a). It is not the role of philosophy to instruct princes or to plan cities.

For philosophy to be of any use to would-be politicians, poets, or "technicians," it is necessary for them first to desire to understand the limits to knowledge, the finitude of human understanding. Philosophy begins with the desire (a kind of *eros*) to know, but it ends as a love (thus the *philo*) of understanding, that is, as the ability to differentiate the natures and limits of things and opinions about them.

When the desire to know is clipped short, when the range of possible differentiations is pre-emptively hemmed in, to make it more accessible, then we get the stingy "understanding" found among contemporary literary theorists. Making use of the fashionable "method" of differentiating—that is, "deconstruction" —they arrive at no more profound "hegemonic structures" than race, sex or gender, and class for their universal categories or ultimate explanations. Unlike the poets in the *Apology*, these *literati* are hardly divinely inspired.

The "artisans" of time are just as puffed up and unaware of the moderating role of philosophy as were their counterparts in the *Apology.* Technology *is* a kind of knowledge and it *is* becoming ever more powerful, but it is not omniscience. The minds of technologists are filled with theories. Philosophy, as the criticism of theories, is the killer of their joy in ideas. On the one hand we have those pelagian optimists (for example, concerning environmental problems) who believe that more technology is the solution to problems brought about by technology—indeed scoffing at the very suggestion of human imperfectability. And, on the other hand (again in the context of environmental problems), we have the gnostic morticians who would "cut and run" before the battle is half-begun, in the pseudo-humble belief that "Nature" would be better off without the human species. In the first case we have the careless arrogance of conquerors of nature; in the second we have the presumptuous quietism of abject submission to it. The moderate voice of reason, with which philosophy speaks, is neither the voice of God nor the voice of doom.

The philosopher does have his feet on the ground when, among his many and sundry conversations, he discusses the "divine" things; for in so doing he profoundly understands his humanity. His search for God or the gods is an indication that he is not God or one of the gods. In understanding his humanity, he recognizes and acknowledges his mortality. The inquiry into the immortality of the "Soul," which like the "Forms" is universal and public, uncovers the radical "mortality" of the individual self.[11]

In the act of distinguishing the human things from the divine —the activity of making distinctions and therefore recognizing differences being its peculiar and specific work—philosophy resists the most tempting and dangerous of foundationalisms. I speak of that naked tempter—the individual ego, as the sole and ultimate arbiter of what is true and what is right and even what is pleasing.

With his feet on the ground and his mind on the "divine" or metaphysical things (dare we say on the "grounds" of things), Socrates is portrayed by Plato as the embodiment and coincidence of philosophy, humanity, and mortality.[12] In other words,

---

[11] An afterlife for the individual self is represented in the *Phaedo* in the form of a myth (107d–114d).

[12] The last lines of the *Phaedo* read as follows: "Such, Echecrates, was the end of our comrade, who was, we may fairly say, of all those whom we knew in our time, the bravest and also the wisest and most upright man" (115e). The theme of the *Phaedo* corroborates that very famous line in the *Apology* which has been incompletely and therefore incorrectly translated as "The unexamined Life is not worth living." The Loeb Library edition of the Greek text says, " ὁ δε ανεε, ε ταοτοζ βιοζ ου βιωτοζ ανθρωπψ" (The unexamined life is not worth living for a man) [38a 5–6]. Plato connects inquiry necessarily with being human. For God (or the gods) and beasts philosophy is unnecessary, indeed, it is absolutely useless. It is, however, useful and necessary in order to be human. Cf. Aristotle, *Nicomachean Ethics*, Bk X, Ch. 7–8, 1177a10–1179a30. *Non pace* to Pragmatists, Marxists, Darwinians, Freudians and the like who either deny theoretical inquiry or reduce it to the practical or the emotive.

it is in the act of philosophizing[13] that both the humanity and the finitude of human beings is discussed in the most *radical* way.[14]

---

[13] In Chapter 14 of *The Birth of Tragedy*, Nietzsche suggests another interpretation of the *Phaedo*, another interpretation of Socrates' life and death and consequently another conception of human nature. Man for Nietzsche is *homo faber*, man the maker—the maker of illusions, the constructor of paradigms, the creator of fictions. Those illusions or fictions are, of course, science, religion, history, mathematics, and indeed philosophy—fictions whereby human beings keep the absurdity and horror of nature at bay. Nietzsche suggests that in the face of death, Socrates, that "despotic logician," senses the limits of reason when voices in his dreams urge him to practice and cultivate the arts. The *Phaedo* reports that Socrates believes that he was already practicing the greatest art, i.e., philosophy, but that in order to clear his conscience and to obey the dream, he set himself the task of writing poetry by versifying some of Aesop's fables. Socrates points out that a poet who is worthy of the name ought to work on imaginative themes, not descriptive ones. He goes on to say that since *he was not good at inventing stories,* he made use of the already existing fables and versified them (60-61c). Nietzsche argues that this passage shows that both Plato and his character, Socrates, recognize that it is poetry, the creating of fiction, and not philosophy that defines human nature. Better yet, philosophy is just a sub-category of poetry with which one faces death by making existence appear intelligible and thereby justified. If, however, Nietzsche's argument is *sound*, then we *cannot* take it seriously. We must regard it as just another fiction. On the other hand, if we take his argument seriously, then we must regard his thesis, i.e., that humanity is defined by fictions, by illusions, by poetry, as unsound. (The prohibition against testing a thinker's thesis on his own thought, i.e., the prohibition against self-reference, does not *derive* [*pace* Betrand Russell] from the intrinsic course of an argument, but from an extrinsic wish to control or protect it by an *ad hoc* regulation.) For Nietzsche's own argument is not a poem; it is a philosophic statement, false though it may be.

Again, to say that poetry defines human nature is philosophizing, not poetizing. Furthermore, poetry, as Nietzsche himself claims, aims at domination of nature through the *creation* of fictions. The poet is a "fabricator" like the gods; philosophy, however, seeks to *understand* nature (and everything else—including poetry) in order to say something true about it. This is not to deny that philosophy has its own rhetoric. Philosophizing, i.e., inquiring about things in order to understand them, is at the same time a recognition of the finitude, the mortality, and the humanity of the philosopher.

Finally, what Socrates does in the face of death, as the *Phaedo* bears out, is not poetry but philosophy. The myths that supplement the arguments for immortality are not higher truths but ways of showing the limits of reason and, therefore, the limits of human nature.

Works Cited

Aquinas, Thomas. *In Aristotelis Librum De Anima Commentarium*. 3rd edition. Ed. A.M. Pirotta. Turin: Marietta, 1948.

Aristophanes. *The Clouds* in *Five Comedies*. Tr. B.B. Rogers. New York: Doubleday, 1955.

Aristotle. *The Basic Works*. Ed. Richard McKeon. New York: Random House, 1941.

Brann, Eva. "Commencement Address." *St. John's College Magazine*. Annapolis, July 1974.

Hartle, Ann. *Death and The Disinterested Spectator*. Albany: State University of New York Press, 1986.

Heidegger, Martin. "Discussion Between Martin Heidegger and Ernst Cassirer." Tr. Francis Slade. *The Existentialist Tradition*. Ed. Nino Languilli. New York: Doubleday, 1971.

Johnson, Paul. *The Intellectuals*. New York: Harper & Row, 1989.

Kierkegaard, Soren. *The Concept of Irony*. Tr. L.M. Capel. Bloomington, Indiana U. Press, 1965.

Nietzsche, Friedrich. *The Birth of Tragedy* in *The Birth of Tragedy and The Geneaology of Morals*. Tr. E. Golffing. New York: Doubleday, 1956.

Plato. *The Collected Dialogues*. Ed. E. Hamilton & H. Cairns. New York: Pantheon (Random House), 1961.

Stern, Paul. *Socratic Rationalism and Political Philosophy: An Interpretation of Plato's Phaedo*. Albany: State University of New York Press, 1993.

---

[14] Heidegger argues this same point in his discussion with Cassirer at Davos in 1929. Cf. "A Discussion between Ernst Cassirer and Martin Heidegger," tr. Francis Slade, in *The Existentialist Tradition*, Ed. Nino Langiulli (New York: Doubleday, 1971), pp. 192–203.

18

A History of the Doctrine of the Mean in Early Greek Thought: From Homer Through Plato

Marvin Fox

Aristotle's doctrine that virtue lies in a mean between the extreme vices of excess and defect dominated Western moral philosophy for many centuries. Even during the middle ages such eminent philosophers as Maimonides and Aquinas accepted the doctrine and gave it a place of central importance in the systematic structure of their own ethical theories.[1] Yet this same doctrine has been subjected to sharp and bitter criticisms by equally eminent philosophers. Perhaps the most famous attack was made by Kant who believed that he had shown conclusively the uselessness of Aristotle's doctrine of the mean. Kant argued that the doctrine is a tautology. It leads, in his opinion, to the absurd conclusion that we ought not be too virtuous, which

---

[1] These introductory remarks are based on the introduction to my paper, "The Doctrine of the Mean in Aristotle and Maimonides: A Comparative Study," in *Studies in Jewish Religion and Intellectual History Presented to Alexander Altmann*, (U. of Alabama Press, 1979); it also occurs as a short part of the introduction to Chapter 5 of my *Interpreting Maimonides: Studies in Methodology, Metaphysics, and Moral Philosophy* (U. of Chicago Press, 1990).

makes as much sense as saying that a circle should not be too round or a straight line too straight.[2] More recently Edward Von Hartmann attacked the doctrine, saying that it barely scratches the outer surface of morality and that it results in an "apotheosis of mediocrity." He adds, with irritation, "It is difficult to grasp how a Greek thinker with the acumen and far-sightedness of an Aristotle could have allowed his ethical theory . . . to be limited by such a trivially restricted horizon."[3] This claim that the Aristotelian mean makes virtue identical with mediocrity is a common complaint among Aristotle's critics.

Other writers have accused Aristotle of arguing in a circle or merely propounding as the most basic moral rule the principle that we should always be bound by moral convention. The doctrine of the man is held by them to be an empty formal principle which depends always on social convention for its identification of the middle way and the extremes. One must know the extremes to determine the mean and the mean to determine the extremes. "In order to determine that an action is a virtue or vice one must already have developed fixed moral principles. This involves us in a circle."[4] The fixed moral principles are not themselves derived from the mean, but serve instead to establish the mean. The only source for these principles is, according to this interpretation of Aristotle, the prudent man, the man of practical wisdom, and he turns out to be the man who has achieved a mastery of the conventional rules, values and expectations of his society. Aristotle, on this view, fails to show that the prudent man employs any principle other than moral convention. Should there be moral differences among

---

[2] *Cf.* Kant, *Die metaphysik der Sitten*, Cassirer edition, Vol. 7, pp. 244-5. Concerning the respected position of the doctrine of the mean, Kant says, "Wenn das die Weisheit ist, die zu erforschen wir zu den Alten (dem Aristoteles), gleich als solchen, die der Quelle näher waren, zuruckkehren sollen: virtus consistit in medio, medium tenuere beati, est modus in rebus, sunt certi denique fines, quos ultra citraque nequit consistere rectum, so haben wir schlect gewält, uns an ihr Orkael zu wenden."

[3] Edward Von Hartman, *Das sittliche Bewusstsein* (Berlin, 1886), p. 111. My translation.

[4] S. Schindele, "Die aristotelische Ethik," *Philosophisches Jahrbuch der Gorres—Gesellschaft,* Vol. 16, 1903, p. 150, My translation. Cf. Gomperz, *Greek Thinkers* (New York, 1912), vol 4, pp. 247-8.

societies, Aristotle has given us no way to resolve them, nor is it ever possible on his grounds to show that given social conventions are in moral error. Such is the direction of a second major line of criticism of Aristotle's doctrine of the mean.[5] The net effect of these criticisms is to deny both Aristotle's claim that ethical decision consists in choosing the middle way between the extremes of excess and defect, and his belief that this is a rational doctrine.

The present study intends to set the foundation for a full argument that will try to show that these criticisms rest on a misunderstanding of Aristotle. (This argument is made in the materials cited above in fn.1.) The doctrine of the mean was not Aristotle's invention. It had a long history in pre-Aristotelian Greek thought. To understand its specific Aristotelian form we must set the doctrine in the context of its historical sources and development. Moreover, we must recognize that it is not only an important principle in Aristotle's moral philosophy, but that he makes significant use of it in a number of other branches of his system. It seems clear that unless we grasp the nature and function of the mean in the rest of Aristotle's philosophy we shall not be able to come to terms with it in his ethics. A full understanding of the doctrine of the mean in Aristotle depends on a grasp of how this doctrine developed in earlier Greek thought. Aristotle did not emerge from a vacuum. He was the product of the long and rich history of Greek culture. Without that history as background we have only a bland and incomplete account of the way in which his teaching on this subject developed, and an inadequate basis for interpreting it. Our task in this study is to fill in that history by examining the ways in which the doctrine of the mean was understood and taught in the literature and philosophy of early Greece, beginning with Homer and culminating in Plato.

II

Classical scholars have regularly noted that Greek thought "is dominated everywhere by the omnipresent idea of the 'mean'"

---

[5] *Cf.*, George Grote, *Aristotle*, 3rd. edition (London, 1883), pp. 513-515.

(τὸ μέτρον)," and that Aristotle, in developing this doctrine, "reflects the general mind of Greece."[6] Aristotle's *Nicomachean Ethics* is seen by many as a culmination of Greek ethical thought, a work which has absorbed the results of centuries of Greek moral reflection and experience.[7] Gomperz, for example, speaks of "that law of moderation which played so eminent a part in the popular naturalistic morality of the Greeks."[8] In fact, Aristotle is thought to be **the** Greek moral philosopher, **par excellence**, because he grasped more clearly than any of his predecessors the central importance of the doctrine of the mean.[9]

The source of the doctrine is diverse. Some scholars lay the primary stress on the principle of the mean in Greek medicine. Bodily health was thought to depend on the achievement of a proper balance, measure, and harmony. Disease is understood as a disturbance of this harmony, an upsetting of the mean. Jaeger holds that the "ethics of measure or μέτρον rests on a transference into the mental sphere of contemporary mathematical views in medicine. The Aristotelian mean (μεσότης) is a conscious return to this point of departure, and carries the analogy through still more strictly."[10] Others see the main source in the folk-wisdom which arose out of efforts to till the soil successfully. Hesiod's advice to farmers is "observe thou measure: due measure is ever best."[11] This and similar bits of folk-wisdom are thought to express the view that in dealing with nature the farmer must avoid extremes and aim for the mean. His work must not begin too early or too late; he must not sow too much or too little; in short, he should follow the

---

[6] F.R. Earp, *The Way of the Greeks* (Oxford University Press, 1929), p. 42.

[7] R. Eucken, *Über die Methode und Grundlagen der Aristolischen Ethik* (Berlin 1870), pp. 9–10.

[8] Gomperz, op. cit., p. 257.

[9] Harald Schilling, *Das Ethos der Mesotes* (Tubingen, 1930), p. 11: "Das Mass ist die griechische Tugend, wie des einzelnen so des Staates, und weil Aristoteles so klar erkannt, so scharf erfasst hat ist er der griechische Ethiker, der griechische Staatsrechtlehrer par excellence." Quoted from Theobald Ziegler, *Die Ethik de Griechen und Römer* (Bonn, 1886), p. 134.

[10] Werner Jaeger, *Aristotle: Fundamentals of the History of His Development* (Oxford, 1934), p. 44, fn. 1; cf. A.E. Taylor, *Aristotle* (London, 1919), p. 105.

[11] μέτρα φυλάσσεσθαι. καίροσ δ' ἐπὶ πᾶσιν ἄριστος . Hesiod, *Works and Days*, p. 694.

mean if he is to be successful. From the limited sphere of agriculture the doctrine of the mean was then expanded to encompass all of man's life.[12]

Still another view connects the origins of the doctrine of the mean with Greek theology. One of the cardinal sins in early Greek thought was hybris, the state of excessive pride and self-assertion in which a man seemed to assert his superiority even to the gods. Such pride could easily arouse the wrath of the gods. A man who is too successful or too strong incurs divine resentment because he seems to have risen to a semi-divine status. The gods will destroy a man who has unrestrained confidence in the continuance of his own good fortune. To avoid divine retribution man needs to pursue a kind of moderation which testifies to his lack of hybris. Following the mean both in thought and action seemed to the Greeks a properly virtuous way of life, since this way, above all, was beloved to the gods.[13]

We shall attempt shortly to set forth detailed evidence of the extent to which the doctrine of the mean dominated pre-Aristotelian Greek ethical thought. It is important first, however, to understand that though Aristotle was a product of a long line of development he did not merely reproduce or summarize the thought of his predecessors. In fact, his own version of the doctrine of the mean barely mentions his predecessors. This is a point of some importance, since Aristotle normally introduces a topic by examining the opinions of earlier Greek philosophers. Though this is not the place for a full interpretation of this point I believe it is significant enough to require some preliminary attention. Basically, Aristotle is anxious to distinguish himself and his doctrine from the earlier Greek tradition. His achievement lies in the fact that while recognizing the validity of the well-established views concerning the mean, he was able to transform them from popular slogans into a philosophical principle. Aristotle was not merely a popular moralist who set forth the accumulated folk-wisdom and the cherished convictions of his people. He was a philosopher

---

[12] Max Wundt, *Geschichte der Griechischen Ethik* (Leipzig, 1908),Vol. I, p. 74; p. 215.
[13] *Cf.*, Earp, *op. cit.*, pp. 13, 16.

who frequently began with established views, but never ended with a mere repetition of those views.[14]

III

In the very earliest Greek writers the terms μέτριον and μεσότης do not occur in their later technical sense, i.e., referring to the mean as the morally right way. However, in Homer we find a stress on the importance of moderation and the mean though he employs other terms. Sometimes it takes the form of practical advice not to drink too much (i.e., beyond the right measure) or not to sleep too much. In the *Odyssey* Homer has Menelaus censure a man "who loves overmuch or hates overmuch; better is due measure in all things."[15] In a later passage Homer warns against the dangers of too much wine, drunk in large gulps and without moderation.[16] We noted earlier that Hesiod counsels that in his actions one should observe the proper measure, μέτρα φυλάσσεσθαι. Since he is advising farmers it seems likely that this is no more a technical usage than Homer's. Both seem to be saying that to get along in the world a man needs to be moderate and to do what is fitting in a way that is fitting. But from this early folk-wisdom there begins to develop a noticeable pattern in classical Greek literature. First, certain general slogans became widely accepted. The most prominent of these is, perhaps, μηδὲν, ἄγαν, "nothing to excess." This is frequently paralleled with the warning that the gods resent man's overbearing pride, that hybris brings about man's destruction. As Solon puts it in his plea for moderation, τίκτει γὰρ κόρος ὕββριν, "Excess produces hybris," the insolent pride which arouses the wrath of the gods.[17]

---

[14] *Cf.*, Michael Wittman, *Die Ethik des Aristotles* (Regensberg, 1920), pp. 61-62; *Cf.* also, Schilling, op. cit., pp. 12-13. The views which conflict with this interpretation of Aristotle will be discussed below in their proper place.

[15] Homer, *Odyssey*, XV, 65ff. ἀμείνω δ᾽ αἴσιμα πάντα. The word αἴσιμα derives from Αἴσα, the goddess of destiny, and refers to that which is appropriate or in due measure because it is in accord with the will of the gods.

In this and subsequent quotations from the Greek poets and dramatists I follow the text and translation of the Loeb editions, unless otherwise noted. In some cases I have made minor changes in the Loeb translations in order to emphasize the force of a particular word or phrase.

[16] *Ibid.*, XXI, p. 204.

[17] Solon, fr. 6.

In the writings of Theognis we find for the first time an explicitly formulated view which can be seriously considered as a direct forerunner of Aristotle's doctrine of the mean. To be sure, Theognis also exhibits the general approval of moderation which we noted in his predecessors. Like them he urges moderation in material possessions;[18] he also warns of the dangers of immoderate drinking.[19] At a second level we find in Theognis, as in most ancient Greek writers, the advice that nothing should be done to excess, μηδὲν ἄγαν.[20] Theognis, however, goes beyond this kind of generality. First, there are passages in which he explicitly ties together the good man and the man who achieves an appropriate measure in all things. "The good know how to keep due measure in every matter. (οἱ δ' ἀγαθοὶ πάντων μέτρον ἴσασιν ἔχειν)." "Of the men of our time the Sun can see none that is altogether good and observes due measure (ἀγαθὸν καὶ μέτριον)."[21] But, after, he goes farther in the direction which can be seen, in retrospect, to be leading to Aristotle. In Theognis we find one of the earliest instances of the use of the μέσον in an ethical sense. Initially it occurs in conjunction with μηδὲν ἄγαν, and seems to be a consequence of it. If one is to avoid excess, then he should pursue the middle way—not, as some might think, the opposite extreme. This can be seen in his advice to Cyrnus, "When thy fellow townsmen are confounded, Cyrnus, be not thou much vexed (μηδὲν ἄγαν) at aught they do, but walk the road, like me, in the middle (μέσην δ' ἔρχευ τὴν ὁδόν)."[22] Somewhat later he expresses the same idea, but he does not tic the mean to μηδὲν ἄγαν. He simply urges Cyrnus, "Walk gently, as I, in the midst of the way (ἥσυχος ὥσπερ ἐγὼ μέσσην ὁδὸν ἔρχεο ποσσίν)."[23] Finally, Theognis explicitly makes the connection between "nothing to excess," the mean, and virtue in a kind of foreshadowing of the

---

[18] Theognis, pp. 557-60. Cf. 693-4, where he notes how difficult it is to maintain "due measure when good things are to thy hand."

[19] Theognis, p. 475; 497; pp. 839-40.

[20] Theognis, p. 401; p. 657.

[21] Theognis, 614-616. Note that in both instances, the μέτριον, the mean of measure, is identified with the ἀγαθόν, the good man.

[22] Theognis, pp. 219-20.

[23] Theognis, p. 331.

subsequent development of Greek ethics which culminated in Aristotle. "Be not over-eager in any matter (μηδὲν ἄγαν σπεύδειν)— the middle-way is best in all things (πάντων μέσ' ἄριστα)—and thus shalt thou have virtue, Cyrnus (καὶ οὕτως, Κυρν', ἕξεις ἀρετην)."[24] Here we see how he moves from a folk-saying to the explicit formulation of the moral claim of the mean (μεσ' ἄριστα) and then views the mean as the way to virtue (ἀρετη). So far as I can discover this is the earliest instance in Greek literature where these connections are made explicitly and in the terminology subsequently adopted and formalized by Plato and Aristotle. That Aristotle knew the writings of Theognis is evident from the fact that he quotes him on a number of occasions. More significant is the fact that every single quotation from Theognis that Aristotle cites occurs either in the *Nicomachean Ethics* or the *Eudemian Ethics* and always in connection with a moral question.[25] Aristotle cites none of the passages in which Theognis propounds the doctrine of the mean as the way to virtue. However, it seems undeniable that he must have known these passages and that they constitute one important element in the complex of factors which influenced the development of his moral philosophy. Though there is a long way from the relatively unphilosophical moralizing of the early poet to the philosophical subtlety and sophistication of Aristotle, I shall try to show later that much that is obscure in the latter's doctrine of the mean can be understood if we set it in the historical line of development from which that doctrine emerged.

Some additional evidence for the early sources of influence on Aristotle's ethics can be found in a fragment of Phocylides, who was a contemporary of Theognis. In this fragment he gives unambiguous testimony to the desirability of the middle way:

---

[24] Theognis, pp. 335-6.
[25] *Cf.*, the entries under "Theognis" in Troy W. Organ, *An Index of Aristotle* (Princeton 1949), p. 165. The last entry should read 1243a17 instead of 1234a17. There are no additional citations in Bonitz's *Index Aristotelicus* which are clearly ascribable to Theognis.

"Many things are best in the mean; I desire to be a middle condition in my city."[26] This statement in quoted by Aristotle in his *Politics*, 1295b28, and it seems clear that he sees it as an instructive non-technical statement of his own doctrine.

In the next generation of poets and thinkers of ancient Greece we find the doctrine of the mean becoming more explicit. They tend to resort less to such general slogans as μηδὲν ἄγαν and concentrate instead on more specific moral advice. Thus, Pindar repeats the warning of his predecessors concerning the danger of excessive prosperity. Tantalus, though loved by the gods, aroused their wrath and "got himself an overpowering curse."[27] Moreover, such punishment is deserved, according to Pindar, since a man ought never allow himself to go beyond what is proper and fitting. Like the Aristotelian mean, the good way, says Pindar, has to be appropriate to the particular individual and the particular circumstances. Ixion, for example, was guilty of inexcusable hybris when he allowed himself to fall in love with Hera, "The allotted partner of the wedded joys of Zeus." Such insolence brings doom to a man, since he has forgotten that "it is ever right to mark the measure of all things by one's own station (χρὴ δὲ αὐτὸν αἰεὶ πάντος ὁρᾶν μέτρον)."[28] However, it is not only hybris that Pindar sees as morally unacceptable. He takes another step toward the later doctrine of the mean when he shows the danger, as well, of excessive humility. For, he says, "among mortals, *one* is cast down from his blessings by empty-headed conceit, whereas, *another*, underrating his strength too far, hath been thwarted from winning the honours within his reach, by an uncourageous spirit that draggeth him back by the hand."[29] Neither hybris nor self-depreciation are appropriate, says Pindar. In making our way in the world, when we search for gain, i.e. for our own best advantage, "it is right to pursue the due measure (χρὴ μέτρον θηρευέμεν),"[30] and this always includes a proper estimate of oneself, one's station and one's

---

[26] Phocylides, Fr. 12. I follow there Jowett's translation.
[27] Pindar, *Olympian Odes*, I:55f.
[28] Pindar, *Pythian Odes*, II;34.
[29] Pindar, *Nemean Odes*, XI:29 ff.
[30] Ibid., pp. 46–47

capacities. This proper estimate of oneself and acceptance of one's appropriate place is one form of the mean as Pindar views it. For, he says, "I am eager only for that which is within my powers. For of all the orders in the State, I find that the middle rank (τὰ μέσα) flourisheth with a more enduring prosperity . . ."[31] When he speaks in praise of Lampon, who pursues the mean in his heart and holds to the mean in action,[32] Pindar is lauding the same qualities. Lampon is a good man, because his thoughts, feelings and self-awareness, as well as his actions, follow the rule of due measure. In Archilocus, a contemporary of Pindar, we find the same belief that excess and defect are harmful to a man. He counsels, for example, that man should not rejoice excessively in victory, nor lament excessively in defeat, but should strive instead for that middle way which is appropriate to his human condition.[33]

In the great Greek dramatists of the fifth century, Aeschylus, Sophocles, and Euripides, we find further substantial evidence of the pervasiveness of the doctrine of the mean in pre-Aristotelian Greek thought. The theme of the danger of hybris and its evil consequences is common in Aeschylus. "For presumptuous pride(ὕβρις), when it has burgeoned, bears as its fruit a crop of calamity, whence it reaps a plenteous harvest of tears."[34] Similarly, we find general counsel to avoid the extremes. Thus, Athena urges that citizens should avoid both anarchy and tyranny, since both extremes threaten the welfare of the state.[35] And the chorus in *Agamemnon* proclaims that "glory in excess is fraught with peril."[36] Finally, we find all these themes coming together and explicitly connected with the μέσον , the

---

[31] Pindar, *Pythian Odes*, XI:51 ff.

[32] Pindar, *Isthmian Odes*, VI:71. μέτρα μέν γνώμα διώκων, μέτρα δὲ καὶ κατέχων .

[33] *Cf.*, Archilocus, fr. 66. Though none of the specific terms that refer to the mean are used in this passage the general direction of Archilocus' thought is, nevertheless, unmistakable.

[34] Aeschylus, *The Persians*, 821 f. *Cf.*, also Fr. 159 (Nauck). For other instances where he noted the danger of arousing the anger of the gods through human excess, *cff.*, *Prometheus*, 887 ff.; *Persians*, 362, 532ff, 724f.; *Agamemnon*, 378 ff., 921 ff., 947.

[35] Aeschylus, *Eumenides*, 696 ff.

[36] Aeschylus, *Agamemnon*, 468 ff.

fullest and least ambiguous of the mean. In *Eumenides*, the chorus, at almost the exact center of the play, says, "[A]pprove thou not a life ungoverned nor one subjected to a tyrant's sway. To moderation (παντὶ μέσῳ) in every form God giveth the victory . . . arrogance (ὕβρις) is in very sooth the child of impiety."[37] The extremes are to be avoided; the danger of hybris is ever-present; the one safe and desirable path open to a man is the mean. God is the forerunner of nature, who, like nature in later Greek thought, sets the framework in which human activity must be pursued. We can see here that the ancient folk-attitudes persist, but that they seem to be leading more and more toward a sophisticated version of the doctrine of the mean.

In Sophocles, as well, we find the general expression of the fact that the gods disapprove of excessive pride and applaud moderation. This is coupled with the dangers to human affairs that go with such unrestrained pride.[38] Even the desire for life itself should be restrained and moderate. As in all things, one should not want too much life, certainly not more than is fitting. A man is a fool if he "craves excess of days," because such craving means that he has "let go his hold of moderation (τοῦ μετρίου παρείς)."[39]

The principle of the mean is a basic and recurrent theme in the works of Euripides which is applied to a variety of circumstances and situations. In its most general expression it takes the form of metaphors which employ none of the technical terms later associated with the doctrine. So, for example, Menelaus urges Orestes to think of himself as a ship which makes no progress if its sails are completely slack, but which suffers the danger of keeling over if its sails are too taut. Just as the ship's captain must adjust the sails to exactly the right point between the extremes of slackness and tautness, so must a man order his actions and passions in accordance with the rule of the mean.[40] Part of this same general insistence on moderation

---

[37] Aeschylus, *Eumenides*, pp. 526–534.
[38] *Cf.*, Sophocles, *Ajax*, 127 ff., *Antigone*, 710 ff.
[39] Sophocles, *Oedipus at Colonus*, 1211ff. For the phrase τοῦ μετρίου παρείς I have adopted the translation proposed in Liddell & Scott under the entry παρίημι.
[40] Euripides, *Orestes*, pp. 682-710.

is the familiar caution against overpraise and its corollary, excessive pride. Euripides follows the tradition of his predecessors in his belief that excessive praise may arouse the anger of the gods, especially if it leads to unrestrained self-esteem. "Overpraise is odious,"[41] says Iolaus, and Clytemnestra repeats the same thought.[42] Both of them point out that a good man finds excessive praise intolerable. A man who is not offended by such excessive praise shows that he is insolently proud, and the gods punish men for such "overweening arrogance."[43] The same rule of the mean is applied to many other specific areas of human experience. It is best neither to grieve too much nor to rejoice too much, for men who have learned to temper these emotions are able to live their lives "in cool judgment self-reliant."[43] Neither can excessive anger or fear be approved for they also injure a man.[45] The same is true of eating and drinking beyond the proper measure. Gluttony and drunkenness are to be condemned.[46]

In many of the passages dealing with these topics Euripides uses the term μέτριον, one of the terms that subsequently became part of the technical language of the doctrine of the mean. We see it particularly when he speaks in praise of moderate material wealth. Too much gold is injurious, and too little makes life a burden. In facing trouble one might say, "Gold overbears all this, and wealth is sweet." However, the poet argues, "Would I clutch lucre—groan under its load, with curses in mine ears? Nay, wealth for me in measure sorrowless (εἴη δ' ἔμοιγε μέτρια μὴ λυπουμένῳ)."[47] Moderate wealth is not only most desirable for the individual; such moderation also makes a man the best kind of citizen. "For in a nation there be orders three:—The highest, useless rich, aye craving more; the lowest, poor, aye on starvation's brink, a dangerous folk, of envy overfull." Both classes threaten the well-being of the state. It is the middle-class, those of moderate material wealth, on whom society depends. "Of the

[41] Euripides, *Children of Hercules*, 202 ff.
[42] Euripides, *Iphigenia at Aulis*, 977 ff.
[43] Euripides, *Children of Hercules*, pp. 387-8.
[44] Euripides, *Iphigenia at Aulis*, 919 ff.
[45] Euripides, *Andromache*, p. 866.
[46] Euripides, *Suppliants*, 865. ff.
[47] Euripides, *Ion*, pp. 629-632: cf. *Ion*, p. 490.

three the midmost saveth states (τριῶν δὲ μοιρῶν ἡ 'ν μέσῳ σῴζει πολείς)."[48]

Even love which is unrestrained is undesirable, according to Euripides. An old woman, Phaedra's nurse, expresses it well; claiming to speak out of the experience of a long life, she says that ties of love which are too intense consume and destroy men. "Much have I learned by living a long time. Mortals, I know, should join with each other in loving feelings that are not excessive (χρῆν γὰρ μετρίας εἰς αλλήλους φιλίας θνητοὺς ανακίρνασθαι)."[49] She concludes the passage asserting that μηδὲν ἄγαν is the true counsel of the wise, which applies not only to love, but to all things human. And it is precisely this conclusion that the poet expresses (this time through the nurse of Medea's children) when he pays tribute to the mean as the highest principle of human behavior. "Sweeter name than 'The Mean' shall ye say not, and to taste it is sweetness untold. But to men never weal above measure availed."[50] All the specific rules of conduct in accordance with the mean are drawn together in this general pronouncement.

What is true of the poets and the dramatists is equally true of historians, the physicians and orators. Hippocrates employs the rule of the mean as a basic principle in medical practice. Herodotus in various places speaks in praise of those true heroes who met even the most challenging circumstances without deviating from the rule of right measure. Isaeus, Aeschines, Isocrates—all praise the men of moderation. There is no reason to give extensive and detailed examples from these sources. What is significant for us is that in none of these pre-Aristotelian instances has the mean reached the status of a philosophical principle or a technical rule of reason. In the writings of these men one can see ancient folk-wisdom coming to an ever higher level of explicit self-consciousness, moving from a general slogan

---

[48] Euripedes, *Suppliants*, pp. 238-245.
[49] Euripides, *Hyppolytus*, 252ff. I follow here the translation of Rex Warner (London 1949). *Cf.*, *Iphigenia at Aulis*, p. 552.
[50] Euripides, *Medea* pp. 125-130. Even in this strained translation the main point is clear enough.

like μηδὲν ἄγαν to the detailed and sophisticated formulations in Euripides. However, at its best it is, in these writers, little more than folk-wisdom, a kind of rule of thumb for dealing with nature, man and oneself. This approach to the mean is pervaded by two anti-philosophical elements—one is a regular appeal to practicality and the other to the all-encompassing fear of the gods. The former tends to be tied to individual circumstances, rather than general principles, while the latter, though general, involves elements of caprice and arbitrariness. Both inhibit the development of a moral *philosophy* as against mere moralizing or practical counsel. Our understanding of Aristotle's doctrine of the mean will depend on seeing how he retains the folk-elements while transforming the mean into a basic principle of his philosophy. But before we can turn to Aristotle we must study the development of the doctrine in the pre-Socratic philosophers and in Plato.

IV

The principles of the mean may be thought to be operative in the doctrine of those early philosophers like Empedocles who see the world as resulting from a combination of extreme elements. However, this is far too vague and generalized to be considered a significant and relevant source for the understanding of the Aristotelian mean. There are two pre-Aristotelian philosophers (apart from Plato) in whom the doctrine seems to have reached a conscious and sophisticated form, namely, Heraclitus and Democritus. In Heraclitus the mean is primarily a principle of nature while in Democritus it assumes the form of an ethical principle. One of the most cryptic fragments of Heraclitus deals with this subject. It is cited by Aristotle, who understands it as referring to nature as a harmony constituted out of parts which are opposed and contradictory. "Junctions are: wholes and not wholes, that which agrees and that which differs, that which produces harmony and that which produces discord; from all you get one and from one you get all."[51] This seems to suggest that the world exists as a kind of mean

---

[51] Heraclitus, fr. 10 (Diels) as quoted and translated in Oxford University Press edition of the *Works of Aristotle*, Vol. III, De Mundo, 396b20ff.

harmonizing and uniting contradictory extremes. In a more explicit statement Heraclitus sets forth appropriate measure as a condition of the existence of the natural world. "The cosmos," he says, "was not created by any one of the gods or of mankind." This suggests that it is not subject to the arbitrariness or capriciousness of gods or men. It is, rather, a fixed stable structure, which "was ever and is and shall be ever-living. Fire, kindled in measure and quenched in measure (ἀπτόμενον μέτρα καὶ ἀποσβεννύμενον μέτρα)."⁵² True measure is essential to the existence of the world and is fixed into its very structure. For without measure the world cannot exist. This, I believe, is what Heraclitus means when he says that, "The sun will not transgress his measure (Ἥλιος γὰρ οὐχ ὑπερβήσεται μέτρα); otherwise the Furies, ministers of Justice, will find him out."⁵³ Should the sun not observe that proper measure which is its mean, the Furies would exact their penalty, namely the destruction of the world. It is, perhaps, significant that though Heraclitus does not (in the fragments we have) deal explicitly with the mean as a moral principle, he connects it here with justice. In so doing he implies that the order which rules the natural world is a form of justice related to that which holds sway in the moral world, and both demand the observance of the μέτριον, the proper measure between destructive extremes. If the sun is too cold or too hot it will destroy the earth, and if man in his life fails to observe the mean he will destroy society. Such is the moral view which is suggested by the fragment we have quoted.

Some ground for this claim may be found in fr. 112, "Moderation is the greatest virtue (σωφρονεῖν ἀρετὴ μεγίστη), and wisdom is to speak the truth and to act according to nature, paying heed thereto." The term σωφρονεῖν, translated as "moderation," is not necessarily synonymous with the mean, but may be a kind of general expression for temperance. However, virtue and wisdom are joined in this statement, and wisdom, in

---

⁵² Heraclitus, fr. 30. In this and subsequent quotations from Heraclitus and Democritus I am following the Greek text and the numbering of H. Diels, *Fragmente der Vorsokratiker*, 6th edition, and the English translation of Kathleen Freeman, *Ancilla to the Pre-Socratic Philosophers* (Oxford 1952), unless otherwise noted.

⁵³ Heraclitus, fr. 94.

part, is action in accordance with nature. Since nature follows the mean, the human action which imitates nature should also be in accordance with the mean. From this it follows that Heraclitus' σῶφρον is not merely temperate in some undetermined way, but that he lives in accordance with the mean. This view is further strengthened by fr. 116 in which Heraclitus proclaims that every man can be a σῶφρον. If it is morally obligatory for every man to follow the mean, then it must be within each man's capacity. We see here that in some respects Heraclitus is anticipating Aristotle, basing both the philosophy of nature and moral philosophy on a common principle. This is a point which will assume great importance in our analysis of Artistotle.

In Democritus we find the mean dealt with in exclusively ethical terms. Some of the statements are of a general character that seem no further advanced than the early Greek folk-wisdom. So, for example, he says, "Immoderate desire is the mark of a child, not a man."[54] But even in this general statement Democritus already employs the term ἀμέτρως. It is evident that he connects lack of moderation with the absence of the appropriate measure which constitutes the mean. We can also find a significant step in the direction of Aristotle when Democritus deals with the mean as something other than a fixed point determined by simple calculation. Only a morally good man can be relied upon to know what action is appropriate in given circumstances. "Thrift and fasting are beneficial; so too is expenditure at the right time. But to recognize this is the function of a good man (γινώσκειν δὲ ἀγαθοῦ)."[55] Thrift (φειδώ) and expenditure (δαπάνη) are opposed; carried to excess they can easily become the extremes of miserliness or prodigality. But there is no fixed arithmetical mean which can be set down as a guide to the proper use of money in all circumstances. We are dependent on the practical moral guidance of the "good man" who is alone able to determine where the mean lies, i.e., what degree of expenditure or thrift is appropriate in any given situation. He alone can set forth the right measure.

---

[54] Democritus, fr. 70.
[55] Democritus, fr. 229.

This seems to be a significant foreshadowing of Aristotle's view that the mean is always relative to the particular person and circumstances. Democritus' ἀγαθός, the good man, is an early version of Aristotle's φρόνιμος, the man of practical wisdom. Though we can find in the fragmentary comment of Democritus little more than a hint, it nevertheless strongly suggests the doctrine which is fully worked out in Aristotle's ethical theory.

The progressive approach to a level of technical philosophic development can be seen in another statement of Democritus. "In all things equality is fair, excess (ὑπερβολή) and deficiency (ἔλλειψις) not so, in my opinion."[56] Not only do we have here a clear statement of the doctrine of the mean, but we have also the very terms ὑπερβολή and ἔλλειψις which Aristotle regularly uses for the extremes of too much and too little. Whatever the status of these terms in Democritus they achieve a fixed technical meaning in Aristotle's usage. Moreover, Democritus, anticipating Aristotle, affirms the dependence of happiness in life in accordance with the mean. Only by avoiding the extremes and following the middle way, says Democritus, can a man achieve that inner stability and serenity which is a condition of true happiness. "Cheerfulness is created for men through moderation of enjoyment (μετριότητι τέρψιος) and harmoniousness of life. Things that are in excess or lacking (τὰ δ' ἐλλείποντα καὶ ὑπερβάλλοντα) are apt to change and cause great disturbances in the soul."[57] The term for cheerful εὔθυμος, means literally "a good state of the soul." It is closely related to εὐδαιμονία , Aristotle's term which is usually translated as "happiness." Aristotle's "happiness" goes beyond Democritus' "cheerfulness," since it involves not only moral virtue which is achieved by living in accordance with the mean, but also intellectual virtue. However, Democritus makes clear that avoidance of the extremes is, at least, a necessary condition of happiness, if not a sufficient condition. Again we seem to have a fairly mature and sophisticated approach to the doctrine which Aristotle subsequently worked out in detail.

---

[56] Democritus, fr. 102.
[57] Democritus, fr. 191, 11.1-4, *Cf.*, fr. 233: "If one oversteps due measure, the most pleasurable things become most unpleasant."

While for Heraclitus the mean was primarily a principle of the operation of nature, for Democritus it seems to be exclusively a moral principle. These pre-Socratic philosophers continue the main lines of Greek thought which are already found in the early poets. Nature and morals were joined in the thought of Hesiod and separated by some of his successors. I have tried to show that in Heraclitus there is a suggestion of their being joined together again. In any case, we shall see that this is one of the keys to understanding the doctrine of the mean in Aristotle. Many of his interpreters are misled into thinking that the mean is only a moral principle for Aristotle. They ignore his extensive use of the mean as a principle of nature, and in doing so make it impossible to arrive at a proper understanding of the unified doctrine of the mean which operates in both Aristotle's philosophy of nature and in his moral philosophy. But before we can turn to Aristotle we must examine the most important of his predecessors, Plato. In Plato we shall discover additional dimensions of the doctrine of the mean and an additional major source of influence on Aristotle.

V

That Plato has a fully formed version of the doctrine of the mean can be established beyond any possible question. The large number and wide variety of texts in *The Dialogues* which set forth this teaching provide more than ample proof.[58] What is puzzling is that the doctrine has usually been associated with the name of Aristotle rather than Plato, despite the fact that Plato placed such importance on it. The mean is ordinarily thought of as a characteristic principle of Aristotle's moral philosophy, and is identified with Plato only infrequently. A.E. Taylor holds that even in so advanced and complex a dialogue as the *Philebus*, "Plato is giving reflective philosophical expression to the traditional wisdom of life which, from Solon on,[59] had

---

[58] There are more than thirty passages in nine of the Dialogues in which the doctrine of the mean occurs explicitly. I shall make some reference to most, if not all, of these passages, either in the text or the footnotes of this essay.

[59] I have tried to show above that the teaching of the mean considerably antedates Solon, and that it occurs as early as Homer and Hesiod.

preached the excellence of τὸ μέσον and is definitely form-
ulating the doctrine commonly known to us as the 'Aristotelian'
identification of the virtuous with the 'right mean' . . ."[60] He
goes on to say that the Platonic origin of the doctrine is clear,
but that it is ordinarily attributed to Aristotle by the modern
reader because we do not know our Plato well enough; while
"Aristotle in his *Ethics* usually treats allusions to the Platonic
dialogues as too easily recognizable by his auditors to need
documentation, much as Ruskin could still make constant appeals
to the text of the English Bible without express citation."[61] Taylor's
explanation may well be correct, so long as we grant his assumption that Aristotle's version of the doctrine of the mean is
substantially the same as Plato's. But if Aristotle's doctrine differs
from Plato's in significant ways then we need hardly be surprised
that it has usually been attributed to him rather than Plato.

Various scholars have argued exactly this point. Wittmann
takes the position that Aristotle is distinguished from all of his
predecessors, including Plato, by the fact that he alone elevated
the mean to the level of a general ethical principle. According
to Wittmann, earlier use of the mean was restricted. It was
thought to be descriptive of particular virtues, but not the
principle of all virtue. Plato, he claims, understood the mean as
relevant particularly to justice, but not to other virtues.[62] This

---

[60] A.E. Taylor, *Plato: Philebus and Epinomis* (London 1956), Introduction, p. 40.
[61] Ibid, pp. 40-41. Cp. also, A.E. Taylor, *Plato: The Man and His Work* (London
1949, sixth edition), pp. 269, 339, 415. In each of these passages Taylor strongly
affirms that in the *Politicus* and especially in the *Philebus* we have the "direct
source" of Aristotle's doctrine of the mean. It is interesting to note that Taylor
is not in agreement with other commentators when he offers a specific passage
as the Platonic source to which Aristotle alludes. In Plato, p. 415, he says that
Aristotle's allusion at *Ethica Nicomachea* 1104b12 is to *Philebus* 26de. Burnet in
his edition of Aristotle's *Ethica Nicomachea* interprets the passage as definitely
alluding to *Laws* 653a, with echoes of *Republic* 401e. W.D. Ross, in his notes to
the Oxford Aristotle edition, concurs with Burnet, as do Grant and Stewart in
their notes. It seems that Aristotle's allusions are not so easily recognizable,
even to scholars, and that choosing a particular passage in Plato as **the** passage
which Aristotle intended is a hazardous and uncertain business.
[62] Michael Wittman, *Die Ethik des Aristoteles* (Regensburg 1920), pp. 61-62:
"Nur in bestimmten Fallen hat man bisher vom Gedenken der rechten Mittte
Gerbrauch gemacht, nicht aber sollte das allgemeine Wesen der Sittlichkeit
erfasst werden ... So hat Plato Spezeill die Gerechtigkeit, Isocrates die Tapferkeit
als ein Vermeiden von Extremen dargestellt."

claim will be shown, subsequently, to be a complete error. Other more serious efforts have been made to distinguish Aristotle's doctrine of the mean from Plato's. It has been argued that Plato's ethics rely on measure rather than the mean as its basic principle. In substance this distinction claims that Plato was looking for a strict rule of mathematical measure which would apply universally to all men, while Aristotle gave up all hope of exactness and universality. Indeed he saw the mean as leading to gross determinations which are only roughly reliable and that vary with each individual and each set of special circumstances. Werner Jaeger is the most prominent scholar holding this view. He consistently differentiates between the early Aristotle, who was still pursuing the Platonic ideal, and the mature Aristotle who had abandoned this conception of moral principles. Thus, Jaeger holds that in the dialogue *Eudemus* Aristotle followed a completely Platonic line, "whereas Aristotle in his later ethics differs from Plato in that he seeks not for an absolute good but for the best of man (ἀνθρώπινον ἀγαθόν)."[63] Again in Aristotle's *Protrepticus* Jaeger sees evidence that "Aristotle's ethical inquiries were originally entirely dominated by Plato's problem of the measurability and measure of moral phenomena." He goes on to argue that "Aristotle's change consisted simply in rejecting the universal norms, and recognizing no measure but the autonomous conscience of the ethically educated person ('the good man'), a measure which can claim no 'exactness' in the epistemological sense."[64] This interpretation depends on viewing Plato's ethics as tied closely to his theory of Ideas and particularly to his conception of the Idea of the Good, while Aristotle's mature ethics is seen as based on a rejection and refutation of Plato's Idea of the Good. More generally this comes down to the claim that for Plato ethics is ultimately dependent upon metaphysical consideration, while for Aristotle ethics is a practical science devoid of all metaphysical foundations.[65] At first glance this seems to be a correct representation of the difference between Platonic and Aristotelian versions of the

---

[63] Jaeger, *op. cit.*, p. 48. Cf., Schilling, *op. cit.,* pp. 12-13, 14.

[64] Jaeger, *op. cit.*, p. 88, fn. 1.

[65] *Cf.*, Jaeger, op. cit., p. 396; Schilling, *op. cit.*, p. 3; Schindele, op. cit., vol 15, pp. 126-7.

mean. All that is attributed to Aristotle is supported by well-known passages in the *Nicomachean Ethics*. He does attack Plato's Idea of the Good and dissociates himself from it. He does say explicitly that in ethics we can only hope to find probable principles, not mathematical certainties. And he does introduce an element of subjectivity by making the mean dependent on the φρόνιμος, the man who has practical wisdom and moral sensitivity, while at the same time admitting that the mean will vary according to the characteristics of each individual moral agent and his particular circumstances. In our later discussion of Aristotle we shall see that these elements of his doctrine of the mean must be considered in the total context in which they occur, otherwise they can be readily misunderstood. Our immediate interest, however, is with Plato, and in what follows I shall try to show that the very characteristics which are supposed to distinguish Aristotle from Plato are found in Plato's version as well.

In Plato's works we find many general statements which caution against the dangers of excess. These statements introduce an atmosphere which places Plato solidly in the main tradition of Greek ethical thought. But they are only a small first step toward a more fully and philosophically formulated doctrine. In the *Menexenus* Socrates attaches himself firmly to the ancient tradition when he says, "of old the saying, 'nothing too much,' (μηδὲν ἄγαν) appeared to be, and really was, well said."[66] We have there nothing more than a repetition of an ancient slogan, but it is significant that this slogan merits the unqualified approval (assuming that the *Menexenus* is genuine) of the Plato who is popularly thought of as an absolutist. The statement in the *Menexenus* is paralleled by similar general praise of the middle way in other dialogues. One such instance is Socrates' appeal to Callicles to "change your mind, and, instead of the intemperate and insatiate life, choose that which is orderly (κοσμίως) and contents itself with what it has for its daily needs."[67] The term

---

[66] *Menexenus*, 247e. Unless otherwise noted all translations of passages from Plato are from the fourth revised Jowett edition (Oxford 1953). Greek quotations from Plato follow the version of the Oxford Classical Texts.
[67] *Gorgias*, 493c.

κοσμίως is not one of the specific terms used for the man, but it points to a general receptivity on Plato's part to the principle that there is a necessary relationship between virtue and right proportion, which right proportion is in many places clearly identified by Plato with the mean. In the very same discussion with Callicles, Socrates later on makes an even more explicit connection between the properly ordered or proportional life and the good. He argues that what "makes a thing good is its appropriate order (κόσμος) inhering in each thing ... and ... the soul which has an order of her own [is] better than that which has no order."[68] These brief preliminary general approaches to the mean are followed by Plato by far more extensive and less ambiguous statements.

Much has been written relating the ethical doctrine of the mean to the medical doctrine. It is well established that Greek medical theory rested largely on the principle that disease is an imbalance in the body, and that the task of the physician is to restore the body to its proper proportions Plato and Aristotle viewed the soul by way of an analogy with the body. To them health of soul, like health of body, requires the achievement of right measure or the mean.[69] This point is made very clearly by Plato in the *Timaeus* where he takes the view that, "Everything that is good is fair, and the fair is not without proportion (τὸ δὲ καλὸν οὐκ ἄμετρον)."[70] He goes on to argue that the healthy body must be properly proportioned, the healthy soul must pursue the mean, and the union of the body and soul requires right measure.

From this medical source Plato moves on to a general principle of the mean which is in no sense so narrowly restricted as some commentators claim. It is significant that the texts

---

[68] *Gorgias*, 560e, Cf., *Republic* 402e ff. for another instance where the ideal of κόσμος is set forth as parallel to the mean.

[69] Cf., A.E. Taylor, *Aristotle, op. cit.*, pp. 76-77, Jaeger, op. cit., p. 43 says, "This explanation of disease . . . as lack of symmetry was taken over by Plato from contemporary medicine, on which he based his whole sentence of ethics or therapy of the soul." Cf., also, R.C. Lodge, *Plato's Theory of Ethics* (London 1928), pp. 443-446.

[70] *Timaeus*, 87c ff Cf., also, *Timaeus*, 82a. Concerning the soul Plato says in *Timaeus*, 89e, "We take care that the movements of the different parts of the soul should be in due proportion."

concerning the mean occur primarily in the dialogues that were written from the time of the *Republic* to the end of Plato's literary career. At the height of his philosophical maturity Plato gave repeated expression to his conviction that the good life is one which pursues the middle way between the extremes. This was not merely an unreflective parroting of the poets and dramatists. It was the carefully and consciously developed position of a great philosopher. What clearer expression do we need than that contained at the very end of the *Republic*? In a kind of final summation of what constitutes the good life Plato's Socrates proclaims that a man can best shun evil if he will teach himself to "know how always to choose in such things the life that is seat-ed in the mean (ἀλλὰ γνῷ τὸν μέσον ἀεὶ τῶν τοιούτων βίόν αἰρεῖσθαι) and shun the excess in either direction, both in this world so far as may be and in all the time to come, for this is the greatest happiness for man (οὕτω γὰρ εὐδαιμονενστατος γίγνεται ἄνφωπος)."[71] Here, Plato introduces the technical term μέσον ; he sets forth the mean as having almost unlimited relevance to the good life; finally, he relates to its happiness (εὐδαιμονία), thus presenting us with all the elements of the doctrine with which we are familiar in Aristotle's version.

In the *Laws*, Plato's last major work this same note is sounded. As we shall see shortly, there are many specific applications of the doctrine of the mean in the *Laws*. However, our present interest is directed toward the clearest general statements of that doctrine which occurs in the *Laws*. All three participants in the conversation are in agreement "that true life (τὸν ὀρθὸν βίον —the right life) should neither seek for pleasure, nor, on the other hand, entirely avoid pains, but should embrace the middle state (τὸ μέσον) which . . . is a state which we . . . rightly ascribe to God."[72] This statement should not be seen as merely restricted to recommending a middle way between too much pleasure and too much pain. Since the desire for pleasure and the avoidance of pain are the main motives for ordinary human action, a rule concerning the pursuit of mean between these

---

[71] *Republic*, 619a. Translated by Paul Shorey, Loeb Classical Library edition.
[72] *Laws*, 792cd, 793a.

extremes is a rule with respect to all human conduct. This is substantiated by Plato's identification of such a life as true *imitatio dei*, a claim which could hardly be made for anything less than a complete moral life.[73] Finally, we can dispel any lingering doubt about Plato's commitment to the mean as a general moral principle if we consult his treatment of this topic in the *Statesman*. The Stranger and the young Socrates agree that we must "assert the real existence of excess beyond the standard of the mean (μέτριον), and of inferiority to the mean, whether in words or deeds." Moreover, "The chief difference between good men and bad [is] found in such excess or deficiency."[74] Here we have the principle of the mean announced without qualification or limitation. We are told clearly that good men are those who live in accordance with the mean, while bad men miss the mark, either exceeding the mean or failing to come up to it.

These passages seem to establish clearly that Plato, in his mature philosophy (as represented in the *Republic*, *Laws*, and *Statesman*), affirmed the doctrine of the mean as a basic principle of the moral life. I shall now try to show that he both follows his predecessors and goes beyond them. We shall see that there are numerous specific applications of the mean in Plato's works, and that they seem to be similar in character to the folk-wisdom which we discussed earlier; they strike us often as more nearly moralistic slogans than philosophic statements. Insofar, Plato could justly be said to be merely reflecting and reproducing the established traditions of Greek moralizing. When we see these slogan-like applications of the mean in their total context, however, they assume a different character. For they can only be properly understood if we remember that, unlike many of his predecessors, Plato elevated the mean to a general moral principle, and the particular instances of the doctrine which occur in the *Dialogues* acquire a new significance when they are understood as applications and exemplifications of this principle. Finally, the general principle itself will be shown to have far wider

---

[73] On the problem of *imitatio dei* as a principle to Plato's ethics, see Otto Apelt, *Platonische Aufsätze* (Berlin 1912), p. 109.

[74] *Statesman*, 283e. Translated by Harold A. Fowler in the Loeb Classical Library edition.

relevance than just to morality. The doctrine of the mean turns out to be a basic element in Plato's theory of truth and of being.

Let us turn first to a brief summary of the specific applications of the mean which are recommended by Plato. The very art of communication is best served, he holds, by observing the mean. Socrates quotes Prodicus approvingly to the effect that the principles of the art of rhetoric require "that a speech should be neither long nor short, but of a convenient length (ἀλλὰ μετρίων)—i.e., the right measure of mean."[75] But the largest number of practical applications are to be found in the *Laws,* since it is in that work that Plato sets forth detailed rules for the conduct of life in society. We find that the whole range of human activity is thought to be best when it is in accordance with the mean, up to and including death and burial. Thus, a son pays homage to his father by providing for him "the most moderate funeral," neither spending so much as to be ostentatious, nor so little as to be miserly.[76] Moreover, one should restrain his sorrow and his joy, allowing excessive expression to neither, but restricting both laughter and tears to their proper limits, i.e., that ordained by the rule of the mean.[77]

In marriage the advice of the wise is always to pursue the middle way. People of extreme temperaments or conditions should marry persons of opposite temperaments or conditions so that both they and their children will be properly balanced. A rich man should marry into a poor family; a man of honor and social position should marry his social inferior; a man of violent temper should marry into a quiet, calm family. Both the families concerned and society as a whole will gain from such alliances, "for the equable and symmetrical (τὸ ὁμαλὸν καὶ σύμμετρον i.e., the properly proportioned) tends infinitely more to virtue than the unmixed (ἄκρατος—the extreme)."[78] In dancing, as in all pleasurable activities, special praise is reserved for men of moderation, those who dance with restraint, observing due measure, even when they are celebrating their own prosperity.

---

[75] *Phaedrus,* 267b.
[76] *Laws,* 717dc.
[77] *Laws,* 732c.
[78] *Laws,* 773a-d.
[79] *Laws,* 816b.
[80] *Laws,* 955e. ff.

Such men are called "Emmeleiai," those who observe the proper order and achieve true harmony.[79] Just as we should be moderate in our own pleasures, so ought we observe the mean in our relations with the gods. Offerings to the gods should be strictly limited by the rule of right measure, for "a moderate man should observe moderation (ἔμμετρα τὸν μέτριον ἄνδρα) in what he offers."[80] Offerings of land, horses, gold, silver, ivory, copper and iron are to be prohibited, while gifts of wood or cloth are recommended, and even these are to be modest.

The mean is also the proper rule for economic activities. According to the *Laws*, retail trade is to be allowed to earn only a fair profit, which is to be determined by the guardians of the law in accordance with right measure.[81] The rule with respect to retail profits is only a reflection of a more general attitude toward property. The extremes of wealth or of poverty are injurious both to the individual and to the state. A virtuous man will avoid these extremes, as will a virtuous society. This rule applies to all our material possessions, even to the body itself. Here Plato stands against those tendencies in Greek culture which made a cult of bodily development. Many, he says, will disagree, but it is his view that, "Honor is not to be given to the fair body, or to the strong or the swift or the tall, or to the healthy body ... any more than to their opposites; but the mean states of all these habits(τὰ δ' ἐν τῷ μέσῳ ἁπάσης ταύτης τῆς ἕξεως)are by far the safest ..."[82] The connection is immediately made in this passage between the body and other material possessions. For he concludes with the admonition that the same rule of the mean applies to money and property. Excessive wealth or poverty also endanger the health of the state. Both in the construction of the ideal state in the *Republic* and in the legislation of an actual state in the *Laws*, Plato points out the dangers of economic extremes. "The community which has neither poverty nor riches will always have the noblest principles."[83] Consistent with this is the view that the size of the state should be severely

---

[81] *Laws*, 920c.

[82] *Laws,* 782cd.

[83] *Laws*, 679b; cf. *Republic* , 421e-422a. In *Critias*, 112bc, there is a picture of the ideal state of antiquity in which, again, one of the characteristics is the pursuit of a middle way between wealth and poverty, ostentation and meanness.

limited, following a middle course between the extremes of unlimited geographical expansion and reduction to a degree which is not viable.[84]

All these particular instances of the mean can be properly realized in a state which itself is formed in accordance with the mean, not only in its economic activities, but in its social and political structure. Extreme forms of government are evil and destructive. In spite of a widely-popularized picture of Plato as believing in a totalitarian dictatorship (albeit of the philosopher-king), the actual legislation in the *Laws* shows us a very different conception of government. Not a tyrannical dictatorship, nor an unrestricted democracy, but a state which is midway between these is the Platonic recommendation. "The mode of election ... is in a mean between monarchy and democracy, and such a mean (μέσον) the state ought always to observe."[85] This is identified by Plato with avoiding in the state the extremes of slavery or freedom, which are equally undesirable. In fact, he views the decline of the Persian state after Cyrus as due to the abandonment of the middle-way of political organization.[86]

From particular instances of the mean we move to a general rule of the mean in economic, social, and political organization. But this is insufficient. For ultimately the characters of the state and of its citizens depend on the laws by which they are governed. If, as we have tried to show, the mean holds a crucial place in Plato's moral and political philosophy, then it should be the key principle in legislation. That this is so is evident in a significant passage in Book III of the *Laws*, a passage which sets the tone for the detailed legislation which only begins in Book IV. If the state is to sustain itself and to make available to its citizens the highest opportunity for a truly good life, then the legislators must be guided by the understanding that, "If anyone gives too great a power to anything, too large a sail to a vessel, too much food to the body, too much authority to the mind, and does not observe the mean (τὸ μέτριον), everything is overthrown and, in the wantonness of excess runs in the one case to disorders,

---

[84] *Republic*, 423c.
[85] *Laws*, 756a-767a.
[86] *Laws*, 694a ff.

and in the other to injustice, which is the child of excess ...And
it requires a great legislator to know the mean and take heed of
the danger."[87] This will be the work of the truly great legislator:
that he knows the mean and sets down laws which institute the
mean as the rule of the individual and communal life in the
state. That Plato has given such a central place to the doctrine of
the mean seems to be established beyond any reasonable doubt.
We need to determine still whether he offered any philosophic
grounds for this principle or whether (as some contend) he
forgot his philosophy when he became a moralist and simply
relied on the established conventions of Greek society.

On the one hand, the mean may seem to be simply a result
of experience, trial and error, and shrewd observation of human
life. However, even in the contexts where this kind of explanation
seems justified, a careful reading will show that Plato had more in
mind. He moved consistently toward the understanding and
explication of the doctrine of the mean as a basic philosophic
principle. In a memorable passage in the *Republic* we can see how
Plato has drawn together and summarized his particular observations concerning the mean. He here expresses them in a general
statement which has elements both of common-sense experience
and philosophic insight. Explaining the rise and course of tyranny,
Socrates notes that in society extreme forms of behavior tend to
be self-destroying. An excess of liberty, unrestrained and undirected,
results in tyranny. Rulers act like subjects, and subjects like rulers.
Fathers are controlled by their children, rather than children by
their fathers. Even the animals in such a society are given unlimited
freedom so that it becomes difficult to know whether they are
ruled by men or rule over men. Such an excess of liberty destroys
itself, and from this extreme of so-called democracy tyranny arises.
From these observations Socrates is led to conclude that, "in truth,
my excess is wont to bring about a corresponding reaction to the
opposite in the seasons, in plants, in animal bodies, and most
especially in political societies."[88] Here Plato is affirming that the
mean is a principle of nature as well as of human society. All

---

[87] *Laws*, 691cd.
[88] *Republic*, 563e-564a, Shorey translation in Loeb Classical Library edition.
Cf., the entire passage beginning with 562b.

things—plants, animals, the very seasons, as well as man, are at their best when they observe the mean. Only in the right proportion, in accordance with due measure, do they find their fulfillment. The principle is rational, since, as he notes, excess brings about its own destruction. If this observation is correct, then a rational man seeking liberty will restrain himself to that measure of liberty which is viable. Too much liberty, like too little liberty, inevitably brings about the destruction of all liberty The same is true of every other excess.

What is especially significant is that Plato proposes here to view human action and human society through an analogy with nature. This may explain, in part, why the doctrine of the mean receives its fullest expression only in Plato's later dialogues. As he moves away from the direct influence of the teaching of Socrates to a growing concern with the natural world, he is led to see in the mean a basic principle of all existence. Whatever violates the rule of right measure destroys itself instead of fulfilling its nature. From this perspective the medical sources of the mean which we cited early in our discussion now take on new importance. For we have in them the first steps toward the generalized principle of the mean as a rule of both nature and man. The human soul must operate under the same principles of health as the human body, and health in the human body is only one instance of health or well-being which reflects the rule and the demand of the whole of nature.[89]

The mean, or right measure, is more than an empirical principle. It rests on basic claims that Plato makes with respect to knowledge and being. In one of the central passages of the *Republic* Plato discusses the qualities which are essential to the philosopher. What especially distinguishes the philosopher from other men is his devoted striving after truth. To be successful in this striving a man must be properly attuned to truth, and this attunement consists in right measure or the mean. Socrates reminds Glaucon, "Assuredly we should not say that the want of harmony and seemliness in a nature conduces to anything else than the want of measure and proportion." But in a philosopher

---

[89] *Timaeus*, 87c. ff., to which reference was made earlier, bears out the validity of this claim.

the absence of measure is critical since "truth is akin to measure and proportion."[90] The mean is not merely a convenient practical rule, not merely a bit of folk wisdom. In the center of one of his most important discussions of his most important topic, namely, the nature of the philosopher, Plato stresses that the truth is like right measure. And to be in harmony with truth, to be open to the opportunity of grasping the truth, the philosopher must himself be a man of harmony and measure, i.e., a man whose nature is in tune with the rule of the mean. To grasp true being, the Ideas, is the aim of the philosopher, and for this he must have "a mind endowed with measure and grace (ἔμμετρον . . . καὶ εὔχαριν), whose native disposition will make it easily guided to the aspect of the ideal reality in all things."[91] In the light of such an explicit statement it is impossible to accept the view that in Plato's thought the mean was never elevated to the status of a general principle. It is now clear that it is not only a general rule with respect to morality, but also a basic postulate of Plato's epistemology and metaphysics. We shall see subsequently that in his extensive application of the principle of the mean Aristotle was deeply influenced by Plato. In the case of both philosophers the doctrine of the mean cannot be understood only as a moral rule. I have tried to show in our discussions of Aristotle (referred to above) that most of the familiar difficulties in the conventional interpretation of his version of the mean arise from the tendency to deal with it in isolation from its metaphysical and epistemological setting.

But we need first to complete our discussion of Plato by considering his treatment of the mean in the *Philebus*, for it is here especially that moral and metaphysical considerations are brought together. Most scholars have recognized strong Pythagorean influence in the *Philebus*, particularly in the discussion of the πέρας and the ἄπειρον the limited and the unlimited. For our purposes there is no need to trace out these Pythagorean sources of Plato's teaching, since the main elements are clear enough in the text of the *Philebus*. Of prime significance

---

[90] *Republic*, 486d, Shorey translation. Ἀλήθειαν δὲ ἀμετρίᾳ ἡγεῖ ξυγγενῆ εἶναι ἢ ἐμμετρίᾳ; Ἐμμετρία.
[91] Ibid.

is the fact that in the discussion of a purely ethical problem, namely, whether pleasure is true good, Plato finds it necessary to introduce metaphysical questions. He approaches the moral problem by first dividing and classifying all things that exist (πάντα τὰ νῦν ὄντα),[92] and concludes that actual existence depends on measure, mediating between the unlimited and the limited. Each actual existent involves the imposition of limit on the limited, of a determinate form on the indeterminate. Unless this were done in accordance with the rule of right measure (i.e., the principle of the mean), the actual world would be intolerably grotesque. It is to measure and proportion (ἔμμετρον καὶ ἅμα σύμμετρον) resulting from the proper mixture of the unlimited and the limited that "we owe the seasons of the year and the rest of the blessings of life."[93] Without this element of measure there could be no ordered, intelligible, reliable world, nor a human society worthy of the name. In fact, Plato explicitly ties true being to this principle of measure. In his classification of existence, Socrates had introduced as his first two classes the unlimited and the limited. We have been discussing the third class, which is a mixture of the first two in accordance with measure. "And," says Socrates, "when I speak of the third class understand me to include under one name any offspring of these, being a birth into true being, effected by the measure which the limit introduces (γένεσιν εἰς οὐσίαν ἐκ τῶν μετὰ τοῦ πέρατος ἀπειργασμένων μέτρων)."[94]

We saw earlier that in the *Republic* truth is conceived as related to measure and proportion, and here, early in the *Philebus*, a similar relationship is established between being and measure. The threads are drawn together and joined at the end of the *Philebus*. The good is understood as a compound of truth, right measure and proportion, and beauty. Without truth it could have no reality. But truth depends upon measure and proportion. Finally proportion is the essential part of beauty. Measure stands quite properly at the center, for "measure and proportion . . . everywhere prove to be beauty and virtue."[95] For this reason

---

92 *Philebus*, 23c.
93 *Philebus*, 26ab, tr. by A.E. Taylor, *op. cit.*, cf. note 59 above.
94 *Philebus*, 26d, Jowett tr.
95 *Philebus*, 64e, Taylor tr. μετριότης γὰρ καὶ συμμετρία κάλλος δήπου ἀρετὴ πανταχοῦ ζυμβαίνει γίγνεσθαι.

Plato concludes in the *Philebus* that neither pleasure nor intelligence stands first in the order of goods. At the top of the hierarchy is measure, the mean, the fit or appropriate (μέτρον, μέτριον, καίριον) and whatever else is of this kind. Second are those things that are direct effects of measure, such as beauty and perfection.[96] Underlying this ranking is the same rationale which we noted in the *Republic*. Failure to achieve the mean is always self-destructive. Excess and defect destroy that which they are supposedly intended to realize. This is equally true in the world of nature and in the life of man. "Any blending that in any way fails of measure and proportion must inevitably spoil its ingredients and most of all itself. 'Tis no blend at all, but a veritable unblended confused mess that regularly brings confusion on its subject."[97] Here we have Plato's last word on the subject. Moral and metaphysical considerations, the study of nature and the study of man, all lead him to give first place to the rule of right measure.

Finally, we must recognize that in his views concerning the way in which the doctrine of the mean is to be applied to particular cases, Plato comes very close to what we find later in Aristotle. Early in our discussion of Plato we referred to interpretations which make much of the distinction between measure and the mean, assigning the former to Plato and the latter to Aristotle. The ethic of measure is supposed to be controlled by mathematically exact rules, while the ethic of the mean abandons all pretense of exactness. Moreover, the ethic of measure is thought to be objective, while the ethic of the mean has a strong subjective base, since it depends on the judgment of the man of practical wisdom. Like many of the other supposed distinctions between the Platonic and Aristotelian doctrines of the mean, this one is also unfounded. Plato understood clearly how difficult it is to give any exact determination of the mean in any particular moral situation. Like Aristotle, he also appealed to the judgment of the man of moral education and sensitivity.

Plato was keenly aware that there is a gap between legal ideals and moral actualities. The legal ideal is a code of law which is exact, specific, detailed and unambiguous. It should

---

[96] *Philebus*, 64ab.
[97] *Philebus*, 64de.

spell out exactly what the law requires, leaving no room for the frailties of individual human judgment. Ambiguity may be desirable in a poet, but it is unacceptable in a legislator. "The legislator must give not two rules about the same thing, but one only." If you are legislating about funerals, "you in the capacity of legislator must not barely say 'a moderate funeral,' but you must define what moderation is, and how much; unless you are definite, you must not suppose that you are speaking a language that can become law."[98] The legal ideal is well-stated, but Plato knows that the complexities of human life resist reduction to such precise rules.

In actual practice the legal and moral ideals are synonymous. The purpose of the law is to educate the citizen in virtue, i.e., to produce virtuous men. It is for this end alone that the state is properly governed by law.[99] But the very character of the moral life is such that few instances lend themselves to decision by way of the kind of exact rule at which the legislator properly aims. In the last analysis, Plato acknowledges that both moral and legal decisions rest heavily on the judgment of the best and most virtuous men. Neither the rule of the mean nor any other moral rule can be applied mechanically. "Now it is difficult to determine accurately the things which are worthy or unworthy of a freeman, but let those who have obtained the prize of virtue give judgment about them in accordance with their feelings of right and wrong."[100] This is a long way from being a mathematically exact, objectively determined rule of right measure. Even if we were to grant that Aristotle was more keenly aware of the problem, there is no ground for saying that Plato ignored the subtleties of moral choice in favor of rigid and mechanical rules. Nor was he unaware that relatively few men are endowed with the capacity either to know the mean or to abide by its rule. "The class of men is small—they must have been rarely gifted by nature, and trained by education,—who when assailed by wants and desires, are able to hold out and observe moderation (καρτερεῖν πρὸς τὸ μέτριον δυνατὸν ἐστιν)."[101] Because he knew this, Plato, like his pupil Aristotle,

---

[98] *Laws*, 719de.
[99] *Cf., Laws*, 630b-631.
[100] *Laws*, 919e., Cf., 658ef. and 663 cd.
[101] *Laws*, 918d.

depended on the law to guide and educate the citizenry and on wise and virtuous men to show by way of legal and moral rules (i.e., the principle of the mean) what was appropriate in each particular case. Plato elevated the mean to the status of a central philosophic principle, moral and metaphysical, but did not lose sight of the problems which arise when we move from abstract theory to the inexactitudes of practical decision. In this, as in many other regards, Aristotle followed in the lines set down by his teacher.

19

Political Action and Christian Faith

Glenn Tinder

The question I address is not whether Christian faith mandates political action. Surely it does, if political action be understood as consisting, not necessarily in activities so all-absorbing as seeking and holding office, but simply in responsible citizenship—in taking and defending positions, in such ways as circumstances invite, on major current issues. Political action in this sense is essential to being a member of society and hence to being fully human. Since Christianity might be described as a program for being fully human (with Christ understood as the gateway into humanity), Christianity must endorse whatever reason can show as being essential to our humanity, in this case political action. But the point can be put more strongly by using a central Christian concept, that of love. Love requires that we take thought, in some way, for all human beings; to ignore the human multitudes with which one shares the earth is contrary to the rule of love. Political action begins in the act of considering the general state of humanity and is thus a work of love. A Christian cannot in good conscience omit that work.

313

All of this I take for granted. The question I address is whether the political action commanded by the Christian ethic is subject to any important limitations. One strong reason for thinking that it might be is that both the Old and New Testaments contain many injunctions to wait, that is, *not* to act. "They who wait for the Lord shall renew their strength," is a typical utterance from Isaiah (40:31). "I wait for the Lord, my soul waits" is a familiar sort of refrain to any reader of the Psalms (Psalm 130:50). In the Gospels, Jesus repeatedly calls on his followers—not to act, but to "watch and pray." Indeed, a well-known Christian scholar has analyzed the drama of Jesus' passion in terms of waiting, giving his book on this subject the title *The Stature of Waiting.*[1] The authors of such lines, of course, were not thinking of politics but rather of the relations of humans with God. But it would be difficult to justify a politics of unhesitating action on the basis of things they said, for in a Christian universe one acts rightly only in response to God. A theology of waiting seems to require a politics of waiting.

What would such a politics be? What limitations on action would it entail? These are the questions I shall ask. The argument I shall advance is that, from a Christian standpoint, political action is problematic even though it is imperative. Faith and action do not fit comfortably together. This is due to defects of human understanding and character which impose limitations on our capacity for action—limitations that action tempts us to ignore, with severe spiritual costs. When we embark on action we are apt to repress our consciousness of the dangers and difficulties inherent in all projects of human mastery and in that way dim our awareness of our creaturely limitations and our moral faults. We are tempted to claim historical mastery of a sort only God can possess. During the two centuries since the French Revolution human beings have evinced great confidence in their powers of understanding and directing history. Today it is evident that such confidence has been misplaced. This is evident not only in the historical record—a record of steady failure in the most ambitious efforts to exercise historical sovereignty; it can be readily deduced from a sober appraisal of human nature.

---

[1] W.H.Vanstone, *The Stature of Waiting* (London: Darton, Longman and Todd, 1982).

In the following pages I shall try to sketch a theory reconciling political action with Christian principles. Such a theory must begin by taking into account the limits on human historical understanding and control.

Policy and Prudence

In an essay that will necessarily involve theological propositions, let us begin with a proposition that rests on common sense (as well as theology) and that almost everyone can accept, even though its consequences are not generally recognized nor universally accepted. This is that the framing of policy proposals and the conduct of government cannot be based immediately on revelation; rather they must be based on prudence. Their ultimate ground may be in revelation, or in theological principles that interpret revelation. This is arguably the case, for example, with the common maxim in liberal democracies that every human being should be treated as an end and not merely a means—a rule that may be less readily derived from reason than Kant believed. Nonetheless, a practical political program is never simply an inference from theology. It would have no prospects of success were it not for the faculty by which governing officials appraise prevailing circumstances and estimate what actions they allow and require. Refusing to consult prudence would be tantamount to abandoning politics in the normal sense of the word.

This simple fact places numerous obstructions in the way of Christian political action. One of these is that Christians often lack the seasoned judgment which underlies prudence. Not everyone is capable of prudence. People who know little about politics, either from personal experience or from reading, ordinarily are not, for they lack the knowledge of concrete reality on which sound practical judgment depends. Harry Truman was a prudent President partly because of long political experience and partly from extensive reading in American history. Such prerequisites often are lacking among Christians, particularly among members of the clergy. Hence one of the most common qualities displayed in the course of ecclesiastical forays into politics, both among Protestant clergy and Catholic Bishops, is naïvete. Christian leaders often pass judgment on matters of great complexity, such as the details of arms-control agreements, in which they are wholly wanting in professional competence. And they often betray a tendency to translate abstract moral principles into concrete policy recommendations without regard to prevailing circumstances or to perdurable human flaws. One of the most egregious mistakes into which this has led them is the supposition that governments which affirm noble aims can be relied on to act in furtherance of those aims. This has repeatedly affected their judgment of Communist societies.

Another obstruction which the need for prudence places in the way of Christian political action, at least in cases of action on the part of the churches, is the difficulty of consensus. Prudential judgments are debatable and indeed can cause deep party differences. Some of the most angry conflicts, such as that between supporters of free enterprise and of socialism, arise as much from differences of prudential as of moral judgment. In consequence, it is quite likely that the political initiatives of Church leaders will divide their followers. In response, someone might say that their theological pronouncements may also divide their followers. But within the major religious communities, the great theological issues are for the most part settled. And in any case, the responsibilities of Christian leaders are more theological than political. The splitting of a parish may be a risk which a pastor's theological responsibilities require. But how often is it a risk which his political responsibilities require?

The most serious obstruction which Christian clergy (although not most lay Christians) come up against when they enter into political action is the fragility of the authority of revelation. When debatable political proposals are bolstered with power and certainty purportedly drawn from revelation—which inevitably occurs whenever church officials take political positions publicly—the authority of revelation declines. This in turn jeopardizes the ability of the Church to perform its central spiritual function. In other words, when pastors and other church officials advance political arguments, and seek to lend those arguments persuasive force deriving from their ecclesiastical positions, they imply whether they mean to or not that their political arguments possess some or all of the authority of revelation. But many among the laity will know that the political arguments are debatable and some will feel sure that they are wrong. They will naturally infer that their theological underpinnings also are debatable or wrong. In this way, the Word of God is subjected to the hazards of political debate.

This obviously has happened repeatedly in recent decades. Pastors in their pulpits, Protestant leaders in the National Council of Churches, and Catholic leaders in the National Conference of Catholic Bishops—to say nothing of more extreme and controversial groups—have frequently entered into political controversies on the basis of platforms and principles widely viewed with doubt or hostility among the laity. Is it merely coincidental that during this time the mainline Protestant denominations have been losing members and that both the Catholic and Protestant laity have come to take rather lightly the moral and spiritual dicta of the clergy? There are numerous possible explanations of these developments, such as the secularity of modern society. An adequate explanation would probably be complex; but part of such an explanation might be that religious leaders have not been satisfied to assert religious authority but have asserted political authority as well. Failure in the latter effort has weakened them in the former effort. Viewed strategically, they have wasted limited resources. Viewed religiously, they have unnecessarily exposed the Word of God to the doubt and disdain called forth by the words of politicians.

The objection may be raised that there are political issues of such transcendent importance that church leaders would forfeit general respect by failure to speak clearly concerning them. Everyone, for example, deplores the acquiescence of the German clergy to Nazism. Their religious authority was destroyed precisely by their failure to assert political authority in the face of the Nazi onslaught. The validity of this objection must be granted. The event it is based on, however, suggests a rule for political action by churches and this rule indicates the exceptional nature of such action. As the distance between theology and politics narrows, the role of prudence shrinks, and the necessity for ecclesiastical action grows commensurately. Nazism was not just a political program. It was, tacitly, a theology, or counter-theology. For a Christian to know that it had to be opposed did not require seasoned practical judgment. A rudimentary knowledge of Christian theology could be translated directly—without the mediation of prudence—into consciousness of a political obligation. Of course the principle of separation of church and state presupposes a normal separation between theology and politics. To the extent, however, that they coincide, due to spiritual pretensions on the part of political leaders, political action on the part of the churches is not only permissible but obligatory.

If human beings were omniscient, no limits on political action would be appropriate. To begin with, we would not be dependent on revelation but would know God naturally. Further, our political judgments would not be debatable. The knowledge possessed by churches would be indistinguishably theological and political. As it is, however, to forget how far we are from omniscience is the essence of sin as Christians understand it, for it implies a denial of human limitations and of human dependence on God. It must be noted that this consideration does not weigh on individual Christians in the same degree as it does on churches; for individuals, the problems of consensus and of spiritual authority enter less prominently into the picture. But church leaders stand before the world as Christians whose obligation it is to clarify, especially for Christians but in some measure for everyone, the meaning of Christianity. They cannot meet this obligation, normally, when they attribute to Christianity a supposedly certain and unambiguous meaning with reference to partisan conflicts.

The basic principle here, it may be said, is that incomprehension implies political restraint. There is a second argument based on this principle.

Politics and Sin

The word sin has an old-fashioned look and is regarded by most writers today as unusable; it seems antiquated and overly theological. There is no word that can take its place, however. To begin with, to speak of sin is to speak of something scandalous, flagrantly contrary to the way things should be. Thus sin is not the same as selfishness, egoism, concupiscence, or any other like evils, although these will be seen, by anyone who believes in sin, as examples of sin. It is possible to say of such a quality as egoism that it is merely natural, the way people are. To speak of sin in such a fashion, however, would be to speak of something other than sin. The word points inevitably towards something starkly wrong—something utterly contrary to nature and contrary to the will of God. Further, it is a crucial characteristic of sin as such that it is non-objective.

By this I mean, first of all, that it issues from freedom and thus cannot be altogether causally explained. A sinful act may be exhaustively analyzed and may be related in numerous ways to accompanying social and psychological conditions. But no such analysis can reach an explanation of the act; if it could, then something essential to the notion of sin would have been excluded, namely, that someone bears responsibility for it. Objective analysis, therefore, can never go beyond "extenuating circumstances." The freedom underlying sin is equivalent to what we might call the mystery of sin, that is the mystery that evil arises from what is for the rational mind the abyss of human responsibility.

By the non-objective character of a sinful act I mean also that it affects not only the one who commits the act but also the one who analyzes it. When a psychologist studies a criminal deed, the psychologist does not become free of sin. And the sin of the psychologist affects adversely the inquiry which the psychologist conducts. Like finitude, sin renders perfect objectivity impossible; indeed, it might be said that sin intensifies our finitude. The standard of objectivity is appropriate in every sort of rational inquiry. To suppose that the standard has been reached, however, is to suppose that investigators have somehow divested themselves not only of finitude but of all wrongful bias, thus surveying reality as, according to Christian theology, God surveys reality. No doubt we can approximate perfect objectivity in studying things merely material—above all, inorganic realities—which do not arouse emotion. But in studying great human realities, like Nazism and capitalism, our capacities for objectivity are severely limited.

Sin of course is not the only human reality that surpasses objective comprehension; saintliness does so as well. Nonetheless, sin does evade comprehension. This is immensely important politically, for in evading comprehension, it evades assured control as well.

Political, or governmental, action is in large part an effort to deal with sinful acts. This is exemplified not only in the prevention and suppression of crime. A government that aims at achieving a fairer distribution of income must try to deal with the fact that some people claim for themselves far more than their fair share of wealth; a government that tries to protect the environment is necessarily concerned with people who are indifferent to the beauty and healthfulness of our common earthly home. If a government is dealing with sinful acts, however, it is dealing with acts which are not wholly comprehensible and which, therefore, it cannot assuredly deal with. Again and again governments and political commentators of varying persuasions propose arrangements which, they are sure, would resolve a problem facing society. Practically never do they fully come to grips with the fact that, because of sin, many people would find ways of evading those arrangements or of using them for their own sinful advantage. Reformers are particularly susceptible to such absent-mindedness—perhaps partly because they are more resolute than conservatives in facing social problems. Thus socialists for decades urged public ownership of the means of production, as though administrators would spontaneously shed their human flaws on taking up public responsibilities; others have seen education as the sovereign remedy for social ills, the plausibility of their viewpoint depending on the unstated assumption that wise and righteous educators can readily be found and empowered.

The modern faith in political action, evident most conspicuously among revolutionaries of all kinds, but evident also among reformers and even, in some degree, among conservatives, has been possible only because almost everyone has steadily and persistently ignored sin. It is a commonplace that religious belief has declined in recent centuries. So has sensitivity to sin—even though sin itself has, if anything, become increasingly conspicuous. Looking no longer to God as the ruler of history, modern peoples have entrusted that position to a supposedly virtuous class, race, nation, or political elite. Thus in the last half-century Western liberals have shifted their allegiance from Stalin to Mao to Castro to Daniel Ortega in an always-disappointed but never-ending search for a sinless leader capable of sinless action. And liberation theologians have for decades persistently averted their gaze from the record of communist and socialist failure and, although too sophisticated theologically to say so explicitly, have written as though sin would largely disappear once indigenous Latin America socialism replaced the rule of landowners and American imperialists. Perhaps the two reigning minds in the modern world have been Freud and Marx, and it might be said that the core truth for both is simply that there is no sin. There is only evil, and evil can be largely comprehended and brought under benign human control.

All of this may seem to imply that evil, in the form of sin, is irresistible. But this, of course, is not true—at least not from a Christian standpoint. Christianity has a quite unequivocal answer to the challenge of sin. It is the answer symbolized by the Cross, that is, suffering. Sin is overcome through suffering, and in no other way. Grace and self-discipline of course are needed too, but their work is accomplished in the fires of suffering. Such, at least, seems implicit in the centrality of the Crucifixion in the Christian mind. Action is not precluded, but it cannot accomplish anything except in subordination to the process of moral purification that comes about through suffering. The American Civil War may serve as an example. On the one hand, the Civil War was a vast action, carried out by governments and troops on both sides of the conflict. On the other hand, it entailed enormous suffering—suffering one can see written out, as it were, on the face of Abraham Lincoln. The War unquestionably accomplished something; the Union was saved, slavery was abolished, and in time national life was in some measure opened up to the former slaves, freed by the War. Could these things have been accomplished by the action alone, without the suffering the action entailed? If, somehow, the War could have been carried on without death and wounds, could the same results have been achieved? One who consults only evidence that is strictly objective might answer affirmatively. It can be argued, however, and there are signs the American people are coming to feel, that the nation was mysteriously ennobled by the tragedy of the Civil War. If that is so, then suffering played as definite a role as action in achieving the ends of the War. Lincoln's Second Inaugural indicates how this might happen—the tribulations of the War did something to cleanse the American people of the guilt and sin of slavery. Suffering created the moral groundwork which rendered the action effective.

My main argument in this essay is that Christian faith renders political action problematic. My argument in relation to sin might be summarized by saying that the religion of the Cross cannot be transformed into a religion of action. The Cross does not bar political action, but it places it in a context which complicates the problem of legitimizing it. I shall try to show at the end of this essay how this problem can be met.

Here, however, it should be noted that the ability of the Church to perform its spiritual mission is threatened by neglect of sin and the role of suffering no less than it is when the Word of God is identified with the political words of men and women. If sin is weak or nonexistent, as the doctrines of Marx and Freud imply, the life and death of Christ were pointless. If suffering is wasteful and unnecessary, as the technological societies of the twentieth century tell us they are, the Crucifixion was inconsequential. These are simple propositions, but they are scarcely open to doubt and their implications are plain. Churches which call themselves Christian but, encountering sin, ignore it and, faced with suffering, simply flee from it are doomed. They are engaged in a self-contradictory enterprise.

So far I have argued mainly from incomprehension. Of the things contained in revelation, we have only fragmentary knowledge; our political prescriptions are in the nature of highly debatable hypotheses; and while the fact of sin is a matter of clear awareness, the nature of sin is almost entirely beyond our understanding. Creatures thus limited in comprehension are clearly obliged to be restrained in action. There is one characteristic of political action, however, which deserves particular attention. That is its use of power.

Action and Power

We think of God as having power—overwhelming power, inconceivable in its vastness. Yet it is questionable whether God as understood in Christianity has any power at all in the sense that human beings have power. It is true that the Bible pictures God as able to accomplish whatever he intends, and we think of that as power. But sometimes, at least, and perhaps always, the God depicted in the Bible accomplishes his purposes through grace, rather than power. We do not understand in any complete and integral fashion what we mean when we say this. But we understand aspects of what we mean. Grace is always liberating, whereas power, however subtly and benevolently it may be used, always contains an element of coercion. When God creates the universe, it is not by power but by a liberating word—"Let there be light." When a human being uses power, it is by envisioning an end and by looking on other human beings as means to that end. This is true even if the end envisioned is the good of those regarded in relation to it. However provisionally and benignly, human beings are objectified and revitalized. They are treated with less than pure love, and this points to the difference between power and grace. In grace, love is in no way compromised or abridged. This is why grace is compatible with entire freedom in the one receiving grace, for love is simply full acceptance of the one who is loved.

The statement that human beings are incapable of bestowing grace would be misleading, although perhaps not literally false. They are capable of inspiring others through their words and acts, and in doing this it would seem that they can be at least channels of grace. The statement that human beings are only occasionally capable of inspired leadership, however, and that human inspiration often is used for evil purposes, would be entirely accurate. It follows that human government necessarily makes use of power. The history of civilization is in part a history of governments and this in turn is a history, occasionally, of inspiration, but also of craft, manipulation, deceit, threat, and violence.

The most important characteristic of political power is that it seldom weakens sin in those over whom it is exercised (as Paul argues, virtue is not attained by obeying the law) and often strengthens it in those who exercise it ("Power tends to corrupt, and absolute power corrupts absolutely"). The necessity of our using so crude an instrument may be called, in contrast to our incomprehension, our ineptitude. The fact of sin, which manifests itself naturally in social disorder and in exploitation of the weak, requires centralized power. But such power, in the hands of sober officials rather than impassioned revolutionaries, aims mainly not at eradicating sin but at controlling its consequences. Occasionally, no doubt, governments do eradicate, or at any rate weaken, sin. For example the imposition of punishments serves to mark some of the worst offenses and, by implication, some of the chief values, and in this way presumably sometimes has a salutary effect on the minds of citizens. But the idea that the main goal of government is virtue, rather than mere order, is dubious, even though it has been held by certain great thinkers, such as Aristotle and Rousseau. It presupposes a less-than-sober estimate of the uses of power. And from a Christian standpoint it is even worse. It is a pagan ideal, taking sin lightly and anticipating the union, on earth and within history, of virtuous men and women.

Hence the age-old axiom that society is properly under the rule of two swords, not one. Some things belong to Caesar and some to God. Many political and spiritual intuitions have no doubt been embodied in this ancient principle. But one such intuition is that governments are compelled to use means that cannot safely or fittingly be entrusted to spiritual authorities, such as priests. Another such intuition is that the eradication of sin, and the inculcation of spiritual qualities such as righteousness and wisdom, is not within the ordinary competence of those who employ such means. In short, human ineptitude, consisting primarily in our necessary and continuing reliance on power, renders the combination of spiritual and political authority in the same hands hazardous and unwise.

It is strange that people generally look favorably on action but suspiciously on power, for action and power are inseparable. Anyone proposing a program of action is proposing the systematic use of power. And any disadvantages inherent in the use of power are inherent also in any plan of political action. Christian reformers should be clear in their minds about this. A large-scale assault on injustice unavoidably involves a massive use of power and an effort to attain perfect justice entails not mere power, but totalitarian power.

The dualistic tradition is nearly unbroken in Christian history and is founded on the most elemental human traits—finitude and sinfulness. Yet Christian reformers repeatedly ignore that tradition and ignore also the guarded attitude toward power and political action which it embodies. Strangely, they often speak as though governments and party leaders could act with the same assurance and toward the same ends—peace, justice, and community—as God. They leave entirely out of account the ineptitude that distinguishes human beings from God. Do we need to be reminded yet again that many of the horrors of the twentieth century arose from confusing the human and divine?

Many, however, feel acutely dissatisfied with any doctrine implying that human action ought to be hesitant and limited. This may be partly because such a doctrine seems, by questioning the range and efficacy of human dominion, to derogate from human dignity. Probably more important, however, is that it seems immoral. Advocating limits on action is equated with advocating acquiescence in injustice. It is assumed that skepticism concerning those who propose to bring perfect justice on earth reflects indifference to justice. It cannot be denied that our sinful minds may sometimes work in such a way. That they need not do so, however, is indicated by a Christian figure such as Paul—at once unconcerned with political action but working for the alleviation of poverty, and markedly affectionate and compassionate in his personal relationships. And the notion that our duty is not only to behave justly toward our neighbors, and to do what we can to reduce the scale of injustice in the world, but to eradicate injustice entirely, is an illusion made more dangerous by the fact that it looks benign. It ignores both our incomprehension and our ineptitude. Granted, to urge restraint in action, and in that sense acquiescence in injustice, may open the door to an immoral indifference to the sufferings of the oppressed. On the other hand, to urge the swift and complete eradication of injustice may open the door to self-righteousness and totalitarianism. Sin is adaptable; it can flourish in either camp.

The principle that political action is problematic has consequences with respect both to the ends of politics and to the manner in which politics is conducted. Those consequences do not reduce us to political insentience or irresponsibility. To explain why they don't, in concluding this essay, may help clarify the thrust of my argument.

Political Ends

If man's ability to create a fully good and just society is in serious doubt, then surely it is reasonable to conclude that the first goal of politics must be that of providing every person with protection against the more or less evil and unjust societies that are likely to endure throughout history. The primary aim of politics must be freedom. Many of those who are acutely dissatisfied with arguments calling into question our powers of action regard the ideal of freedom with similar feelings. It is a limited ideal. There may be freedom at the same time that there is alienation and injustice. Freedom is compatible with serious social and economic evils; America today is illustrative. This is true, at least, if freedom is conceived of negatively—as mere absence of restraint. There is a positive concept of freedom, represented by thinkers such as Rousseau, according to which freedom is not mere absence of restraint but is rather the capacity to fulfill humanity's deepest potentialities. The positive concept of freedom does not aim at protection against an imperfect society but at participation in a perfect society. There is a certain logic in this view. But it is far from what common sense means by freedom, and in practice it leads in the direction of totalitarianism. Marx, too, had a positive concept of freedom. What I am proposing here, clearly, is the negative concept, and I find the fact that freedom so conceived is a limited ideal, a strong point in its favor. While modern history contains abundant evidence that humans cannot create just and good societies and that in trying to do so they invite disaster, it also demonstrates that humans can create societies in which there is widespread freedom. In striving toward freedom they do not overreach themselves.

Although freedom is compatible with alienation and injustice, however, it must be said that advocating freedom is not at all equivalent to unprotesting acquiescence in these evils. On the contrary, freedom is the primary condition required for overcoming them. Without freedom, the community which dispels alienation would be impossible, for the very idea of coerced community is a contradiction in terms. The idea of coerced justice is likewise internally contradictory, although not so obviously so. Granted, the notion of formally just order based on coercion is theoretically conceivable, even if practically impossible. But presumably the ideal of just order is that not just of formal justice, but of a society composed of just men and women. But to be a just man or a just woman is to be freely just. I readily admit that where freedom prevails, most people will probably not be altogether communal or altogether just; there will be much self-seeking and, in consequence, many social and economic derangements. Nonetheless, in making alienation and injustice possible, freedom also makes community and justice possible. And here we come to the point of freedom: not simply to protect individuals against the unpleasant things an arbitrary and overbearing government can do, but to make room for the things creative and communicative individuals can do.

It needs to be noted further that the idea of freedom is not inherently conservative, except for those, such as Leninists, who define conservatism as including every attitude opposed to a totalitarian assault on injustice. In the first place, freedom demands continual enlargement. There are always groups in a society whose freedom is less ample than that of the majority; this is exemplified in the position of blacks in America. Moreover, there are always conceivable freedoms—such as freedom to travel extensively, to experiment with new vocations, or to engage in advanced study in a field of interest—that few possess but that might be made more widely available without weakening the basic structure of liberties. Although there are basic freedoms, such as those of speech and worship, freedom is not a foreknown quantity which a society either possesses or lacks. For those who prize it in an unselfish fashion, it is a spur to political imagination.

Perhaps more important is that freedom allows people to do what they want to do, and the history of America and Western Europe shows that they almost always want to do things which dramatically alter society. Freedom means social change. True, such change is unplanned and often in some ways unfortunate. But what remedy is there for that? Not centrally-directed change, for that means the end of freedom—totalitarianism. The remedy must lie mainly in the sphere of non-political activity—art and literature, education, private charity, and religion—and with the groups that shape such activities. For Christians, the Church must be of first importance in rendering freedom constructive. Hence we need not conclude that social change under the conditions of freedom will be capricious and, from the standpoint of reform, valueless or harmful. This is particularly the case from a Christian standpoint. One of the three great Christian virtues, along with faith and love, is hope. An atheist may logically conclude that if humans cannot control history, disaster is certain. But anyone who trusts in God, or trusts simply, like Henri Bergson, in the spontaneous course of life, cannot entertain such a conclusion but rather must look on a free society as a place which calls upon us to live with hope.

It must be noted, finally, that freedom multiplies the sources of action. In this essay I have been concerned primarily with action by governments and churches. But of course action—political action—can be carried out by businesses, unions, and many other sorts of private associations. Such action is often selfish and misconceived, and it has little appeal to reformers of the kind, so common in modern times, who think of action as coming about under a corps of experts and professional administrators armed with the power of a sovereign government. Doesn't experience amply demonstrate, however, that action such as this invites not only arrogance but also the blindness and folly which arrogance (as an intensification of our finitude) necessarily entails? Essentially, the ideal of centralized, expeditious reform expresses the destructive conviction that human beings can take charge of history. Resisting injustice and seeking historical progress are not dependent on this conviction and do not cease to form political imagination just because freedom is assumed to be the first goal of politics.

Although the idea of freedom is not inherently conservative, it does suggest the acceptability of certain institutions often condemned by reformers. One of these is the American system of government. For reformers, it is a system which favors the wealthy, inhibits reformatory governmental action, and makes it difficult even to think in terms of the public good, to say nothing of seeking it in action. There is a good deal of truth in such a view. Indeed, the American government is nearly unworkable. Yet for over two centuries it has worked well enough to enable a widening majority of Americans to enjoy the basic liberties, and to do this in spite of the strains arising from a prolonged civil war and numerous international wars. Considering the political enormities that the world has seen during this time, that is a substantial claim to respect.

Capitalism is another institution, commonly repudiated by reformers, yet having a substantial claim to respect. As with the American political system, there is a great deal that can rightly be said in criticism of capitalism. Left to itself, it produces recurrent recessions, gross inequalities, and cultural disorder and vulgarity. Measured against the socialist dream, it is a very bad economic system. But measured against realistic human possibilities, it is a rather good system, and this is above all because it reconciles the imperatives of large-scale industry with widespread personal freedom. The fact that American capitalism came far nearer to realizing the communist ideal of material plenty, widely shared and freely used, than did communism itself is a familiar point but important enough to be worth recalling. Needless to say, it is not unchecked capitalism that deserves respect, but to use Michael Novak's phrase, *democratic* capitalism, which may be defined as capitalism in some measure restrained and directed by means of the political and cultural forms of a democratic society.

My argument throughout, it must be remembered, has been simply that action, rather than being always good or always bad, is problematic. It is an argument, not for inaction, but for action that is properly complicated and restrained. What does this mean?

Political Means

One who fails in action when constructive action is possible, fails in love—a rather simple rule. Nevertheless, Christians are not allowed the kind of simplifications endorsed by the ideologies. They are not allowed to be conservative, if that means being politically inactive and hostile to all social change. But neither are they allowed to be radical, if that means being exuberantly active, neglecting the double fact that humans are both finite and sinful, hence never fully competent in action. How is it possible to be neither conservative nor radical, neither committed to the established order nor committed to a program of change? Here we return to the Biblical theme noted at the outset of this essay—that of waiting.

Rather than being active or inactive, Christians are obliged by their faith to do what their Lord requires of them. They must wait for the leadership of God. How can they know where God is leading? Briefly, by assessing the historical circumstances they inhabit, in the light both of the moral law and of practical possibilities, and seeking with prayerful and inquiring minds to discover the course of action that presents itself to them as necessary in the sense of being absolutely incumbent on them. They must consult their consciences. This can be done, where common problems are at issue, only by listening and speaking. Awaiting the leadership of God, we make it possible for others to speak and we take time to hear them. And we ourselves speak. In political matters, conscience is a dialogic faculty. The rule of waiting is intended, not to cause indefinite postponement of action, but to ground action in the deliberative speaking and listening which allow our common conscience to be heard.

Waiting for the leadership of the Lord of history is a way of recognizing that we ourselves are not lords of history. A meaningful unfoldment of events is given to us when we are ready to receive and enact it but is not created by us. Many terrible things have occurred in our time, and most or all of them have come about when human beings were gripped by illusions of historical sovereignty. Humility has, to say the least, not been a conspicuous feature of political conduct since the time of the French Revolution. Yet, in view of our finitude and wickedness, humility befits us. It is not unreasonable, then, to connect the historical evils which have reached so terrible a climax in the twentieth century with the absence of humility. The concept of waiting is an invitation to humility. It is intended to help us recognize where historical lordship resides.

Is it intolerable to hesitate, prayerfully and reflectively, before acting, and sometimes not to act at all? Is it intolerable to be without a political program which would justify casting aside American constitutional democracy and capitalism? Only, it seems to me, if one is entirely without the trust in God which is hope or, to speak in terms Dostoevsky (perhaps the one great Christian prophet of our era) sometimes employed, without trust in the mysterious progress of humanly uncommanded and undirected life.

20

Skapelseteologi i Big-Bang-Hypotesens och Hugo-Forskningens Tid

Gunnar Hillerdal

Teologin, läran om Gud, är aldrig helt beroende av vare sig filosofisk kunskapsteori eller av nya rön inom naturvetenskaplig forskning. Ändå måste alltid första trosartikeln i kristen bekännelse ständigt relateras till den världs—och människobild varje generation får genom nya tänkare och forskningsresultat.

I denna essä skall jag framlägga aspekter på hur läran att Gud skapade världen och människan till sin avbild kan förnyas under hänsyn tagen till ny kosmosforskning och till de stora framstegen inom molekylär biologin.

1. Idén om Vår Herres fyrverkeri. En Big Bang teologi?

Jan-Arvid Hellström, ny biskop i Växjö och tidigare teologi professor i Uppsala, skrev sitt så kallade "herdabrev" till präster och kyrkfolk under temat "Bilder." [*I Om Vår Herre* (nr. 5/6 1993)] konstaterar han, kan vi endast tala i bildspråk.

I dag är det frestande att tala om Gud som en märklig och fantastisk sprängare. De fyrverkerier vi åstadkommer nyårsnatten är ett ingenting mot urexplosionen, som skapade stjärnsystemet i universum. Erinrar smågrabbarna, som älskar smällare, på sitt sätt om sin skapare, Vår Herre?

I ett temanummer av den kristna kulturtidskriften *Vår Lösen* försökte en svensk forskare, *Gunnar Welin*, sammanfatta vad som hände i begynnelsen vid "urexplosionen." Det engelska uttrycket "the Big Bang", från början ett slags glåpord av *Fred Hoyle*, tycks numera eljest ha blivit fackuttrycket över hela världen för den hypotes det är fråga om.

Ungefär en minut efter Big Bang, eller kvantbangarna, hade redan en del av energin 'kondenserats' till de vanliga subatomära partiklarna, elektroner, protoner och nuetroner. Så fösöker Welin kort sammanfatta. Under den närmaste halvtimmen slog sig protoner och neutroner samman till enkla atomkärnor. Den enorma hettan vid explosionen minskade successivt, och efter några hundratusenår var det svalt nog, bara 3000 grader eller så, för att atomer skulle bildas. "När fria elektroner fastnade i banor runt atomkärnorna blev rymden 'genomskinlig för strålningen', och denna har sedan dess genomkorsat rymden och når oss som bakgrundsstrålning med en temperatur tre grader over absoluta nollpunkten" (Welin).

"Nu lyssnar vi på skapelsens ögonblick." De senast citerade orden stod som rubric på ett reportage av *C. Atterling-Wedar* i svenska tidningen *Vår Kyrka* (dubblnumret 1, 2 1979). Hon hade gjort en intervju med *Arno Penzias*, en av 1978 års nolelpristagare i fysik. Denne fick jämte *Robert Wilson* utmärkelsen därför att de i ett viktigt hänseende bidragit till att verifiera Big-Bang-hypotesen.

> Vad de egentligen har gjort för att få Nobel-priset, kan i korthet summeras så här. De har lyckats identifiera de så kallade mikrovågorna som finns i rymdens radiobrus som en kosmisk bakgrundsstrålning . . . Det är radiovågor som härstammar från universums födelse, ett eko som varit på väg i alla miljoner år.

Arno Penzias, kunde man läsa vidare i reportaget, är av judisk konfession. Han "äter koscher även på nobelfester och upplever

Skapelsens Herre som en ganska personlig Gud." Så refererar C. Atterling Wedar sitt samtal med honom. Penzias gav också uttryck för en tro, som förefellar kunna läggas till grund för en Big-Bang-teologi. Hör här:

> "Man kan säga att universums materia var en enda komprimerad massa, som vi brukar kalla uratomen. Det var innan Gud sade sitt 'Varde ljus'. Sedan kom den stora skapelseexplosionen . . . Och så en dag, efter några tusen millioner år, kom Jorden till. Det är ju inte så konstigt . . . Vi brukar uttrycka det så att för Gud är en dag som tusen år . . ."

Finns då inte för Penzias en konflikt mellan tro och vetande? Tydligen inte, om vi får tro intervjun:

> "Jag brukar säga att om du inte kan motbevisa mig, så finns det ingen anledning att tro att jag har fel och du har rätt. Jag kan inte *bevisa* att det finns en Gud för att använda en nu vedertagen term, jag kan säga alltings upphov eller skapare om du vill.
>
> Jag kan inte bevisa det, men jag vill säga att jag har anledning att förmoda att alla de människor i olika kulturer som från olika utgångslägen, människor med stora kvaliteter, många stora tänkare, som har kommit till uppfattningen att det finns en Gud, de måste ha haft skäl för sin övertygelse . . ."

För varje gudstroende ljuder väl orden i reportaget som skön musik? Ändå skall i ärlighetens namn genast konstateras att denna livfulla "Big-Bang-teologi" liksom varje *gudsfilosofi* (för om en sådan är det egentligen fråga, en variant av den gamla idén om Gud som första orsak, *causa prima*) har sin begränsning och sin svaghet.

Redan *Immanuel Kant (1724-1804)* kom med avgörande invändingar mot det så kallade "kosmologiska gudsbeviset". Gud tänkes i detta vara alltings upphov, den första orsaken. Visst kan vi människor ha behov av en sådan tro (och personligen har vi rätt att hävda den som sannolik). Men filosofiskt är idén alls inte tanketvingande. Redan ett litet barn frågar vidare: "Vem var det så som gjorde Gud?"

Dessutom kan orsakskedjan böjas runt och formar som en cirkel. Det ar fullt tänkbart inom ny kosmologisk teoribildning att vi inte skall räkna med en "singularitet" (t.ex. en unik skapelse). Vi skall strax se hur *Stephen Hawking* resonerar! Som en första tes säges följande. *Gudstro, även skapelsetro, är något annat än en kalkyl kring en Skapare som gjorde världen ungefär som en mänsklig verktygsmakare gör sina verktyg.* Gud bör inte tänkas som ett slags övermänniska, oss överlägsen i intelligens och kraft. Det kan visserligen vara frestande att så göra, och eftersom vi har rätt att pröva olika bilder kan vi leka med tanken på Gud som sprängare av storfyrverkeriet (med en såvacker stjärnhimmel!). Men det kan aldrig få bli den viktigaste bilden!

2. Före Big Bang. Stephen Hawkings metaforer om Gud.

Kyrkofadern Augustinus (354-430) berättar att på hans tid cirkulerar en skämthistoria om vad Vår Herre gjorde innan han skapade världen. Augustinus ogillade den som halvhädisk, om jag förstått rätt. Enligt anekdoten frågar alltså någon: "Vad gjorde Gud innan han gjorde vår jord?" Svaret, tillskrivet en judisk rabbin, kommer blixtsnabbt: "Han inrättade Gehenna för alla som frågor såsom Du gör!"

Hur skulle emellertid vi människar kunna låta bli att fråga oss vad som fanns före Big Bang? *Stephen Hawking*—han får väl gälla som våra dagars *Einstein*?—är i varje fall inte tillfreds med en kosmosforskning som ändar i singulariteter (unika skeenden, en absolut första början och ett totalt slut). I boken *A Brief History of Time*—i svensk översättning med titeln *Kosmos. En kort historik*—avslutar Hawking sina resonemang med förhoppningen att det ska bli möjligt att framställa en fullständig teori för hur universum är tillräckligt för sig själv, utan singulariteter eller gränser. Lyckas det, sager han, får den nya teorin avgörande för konsekvensar för Guds roll som skapare. De allra sista orden i avsnittet "Slutsatser" har blivit berömt. Hawking använder formuleringar att det kan bli möjliget att vi "känner Guds tankar."

Man bör emellertid omedelbart inse, att Hawking här rör sig med en djärv metaphor. I en eftersinnande rolig essä om den nämda boken, publicerad i den svenska upplagan av essäsamlingen *Black Holes and Baby Universes and Other Essays*, konstaterar Hawking för övrigt att halva försäljningen av den tidigare boken, en best seller, kanske halverats de nämnda orden förutan.

Hawking leker rätt ofta med Gud. Han citerar för förtjusning Einsteins ord att "Gud spelar inte tärning" och vänder på dem: jo, det gör Gud, och ibland (i samband med resonemang om svarta hål) till råga på allt på sådant sätt att vi inte ser resultatet. En seriös lek, om uttrycket tillåtes med gudsbegreppet? Eller ett humoristiskt spel? Det må i så fall tillåtes. Ett extra nummer av *Judisk Krönika*, de svenska judarnas kulturtidskrift, förkunnade häromåret på första sidan att Vår Herre skapade humorn och löjet samma dag som Adam och Eva (numret kom ut när som den ena krissitutionen avlöste den andra i Israel). Kring den svenske ateistiske filosofen *Ingemar Hedenius*, som i boken *Tro och vetande* (1949) skarpt angrep svenska teologer och biskopar, skapades av någon ett i student-krestar halvt bevingat ord. "Det finns ingen Gud. Och Ingemar Hedenius är hans profet." Den lysande författaren och molekylärbiologen *Georg Klein*, framträdande cancerforskare, säger i en av sina böcker att han vara övertygad ateist. Blickande ut över världens ondska och erinrande sig den egna släktens öro—Klein är av judisk börd, invandrare till Sverige och förlorade sina anhöriga i Hitlers koncentrationsläger—säger han en gång: "Hur kan Gud vara så elak? Hans enda ursäk är att han inte finns."

Jag menar att Hawkings tal om Gud skall ses i liknande sammanhang: Gud blir en metafor, en bild. I sitt tänkande har han inte behov av någon Gud därför att han söker et fysikalisk teori just avsedd att eliminera singulariteterna, bl.a., den absoluta begynnelsen i Big Bang. Han räknar med den stora explosionen men vill söka sig bakom denna, så att saga till en tid före tidens början (om vi utgår från att tiden började med Big Bang). Med intentionen att visa att universum bara "är," alltid finns och har funnits, inför han i resonemanget "imaginär tid." Syftet är att finna en teori för ett slutet universum.

Jag kan här inte gå in på Hawkings intressanta resonemang om att universum utan kanter svarande mot att jörden är rund. (Ingen som reser runt den finner någon kant, sager han en gång skämtsamt). Nog sagt att tankegångarna är en utvidning av föreställningar om rummet som krökt. Den imaginära tiden ställs ut, för vår fortsatta föreställning, som en axel vinkelrät mot den tidslinje vi brukar rita horisontellt. Alltsammans syftar emellertid till att få fram den slutenhet som gör "Big Bang" till en icke, unik företeelse. Dé behovs ingen Gud som skapare!

Tilläggas kan dock, menar jag, att Hawking som flera andra stora företrädare inom kosmoforskningen ändå ändar i en form av gåta eller mystik. Den slutliga obesvarbara frågan gäller varför universum överhuvud finns!

Här kan emellertid skapelseteologen—förmodligen inte bara den som uppträder som kristen tänkare men andra må svara för sig—replikera att Hawkings slutstation kanske öppnar upp möjligheten för en ny dialog om vad som är "av evighet." Dock bör teologen därmed inte i första hand bejaka resonemangen om en "imaginär tid," som påminner om ett sätt att tänka så att säga en tid före känd tid. Evighet som *teologisk* term får ett kvalitativt innehåll, fyllt av en emotionellt laddad föreställning om en för människor ännu ofattbar men lockande dimension. Alltse något i grunden annorlunda än fysikens konstateranden och den teoretiske fysikens matematiska beräkningar!

Därmed är vi på nytt framme vid frågan vad skapelsetro egentligen är. Liksom varje annan form av gudstro är den en övertygelse förenad med starka känslor av förströstan och tillit. "Gud" må vara odefinierbar också inom skapelseteologin. Det är en gammal tanke I idéhistorien att man i största utsträckning tvingas arbeta med negátioner eftersom "Gud är annorlunda." *Gud är dock mer än en metafor, en realitet just för den som "tror" (med reell makt att påverka föreställningsvärld, känsloliv, vilja och beteende).*

Denne "Gud" i skapelseteologisk mening måste doch inte föreställningsmässigt vara knuten till en "singularitet" i fysikalisk mening. Gudstro går också att relateras till tanken att universum *inte* börjar med Big Bang.

Hawking frågar sig alltså varför universum tar sig besväret att existera. Skapelsetro i kristen teologisk mening grubblar inte med nödvändighet kring frågor om hur det kommer sig att världen finns. Den utgår från, i förtröstan och tillit, att det finns en mening med vår jord och hela universum.

3. Gud är storybyggare— men vad har han allt till?

Utan bilder kan vi inte tala om Gud. Jesus själv sade enligt fjärde evangeliet i sitt avskedstal: "I min Faders hus finns många rum" (Joh 14:1). I den nya kosmosforskningens tid är det frestande att tala om Vår Herre som storybyggmästaren av ett jättehus. Hur ser det egentligen ut i det väldiga kosmos? Hur många stjärnor finns—det talas ju om miljarder! Hur många Vintergatansystem, solar och planeter?

Universum fortsätter att expandera, tror nästan alla astrofysiker. Det är en följd av "Big Bang", konsekvenserna av urexplosionen. Det låter lite löjligt om man talar om Gud som storbagare. Emellertid har kosmos också liknats vid en jäsande deg. Den blir tillsvidare större och större. Russinen i den blivande kakan ligger förstås inne i degen. Då den fortsätter att jäsa, avlägsnar de sig längre och längre från varandra, alla stjärnorna!

Samma dag jag skriver dessa rader, i min sommarstuga inte långt från Göteborg på Sveriges västkust, kommer ett par barn och visar upp sin "flaskpost". Mycket riktigt: i flaskan fanns ett roligt brev med hälsningar och önskningar om kontakter från ett annat land, dock bara det närbelägna Danmark. Med de obemannade rymdfarkosterna Pioneer 10 och Pioneer 11 har vår lilla planets ledande astronomer försökt skicka motsvarande med rymdpost. I "rymdflaskan" fanns teckenspråksbudskap— för vem eller vilka förstår till äventyrs engelska, ryska eller esperanto på en annan planet? På en guldpreparerad aluminiumplakett "läser" man till vänster i ett diagram av vår position i Vintergatan. Underförstått: "Här bor vi." Vi som skickar bud. Till höger en man och en kvinna: "Så ser vi ut."

En och annan samtida filosof, t.ex. australiensaren *Peter Singer*, menar att vi människor är artpartiska, species-egoister, då vi förutsätter att vi är mer än djuren och har rättigheter utöver dem. Finns det liv i rymden på andra planeter och människor där? Eller helt andre varelser? Varför skapade Vår Herre ett så stort universum och fortsätter att utvidga det?

Är universums jättebygge Vår Herres stora äventyr? Vill Gud se levande varelser som lyckas fortsätta, var och en i sitt "hus", att bygga en varld, en vackrare, bättre?

För svenska läsare har utgetts ett samlingsverk *Här är vi hemma* (1982) med bidrag av flera forskare och författare. En mångsidig svensk *Rolf Edberg*—landshövding, politiker, delegate vid FN och nedrustningskonferens i Genève, författare m.m. —skriver i en inledande essä inledande essä bl a:

> Med den nya bild vi fått av universum måste vi tro att det finns otaliga världar på vilka evolutionen frambringat intelligent varelser. Säkerligen finns på miljarder världar civilisiationer som nått vida längre än vår. Vi leds att anta att intelligensen liksom livet finns inbyggd i universums struktur. När vi sedan försöker följa utvecklingen på vår egen himlakropp finner vi hur serier av tillfälligheter länkats till varandra för att göra just vår art till bärare av en intelligens som skulle nå därhän att den kunde färdas över ljusårens distanser och tränga in i varats innersta kamrar.

Forskarrön under senare tid—bl.a. existensen av betingelser för organiskt liv i nedfallande meteoriter—gör det mycket trolight att liv uppkommit på andra hall i universum. Om så är fallet, varför kan vi inte få säkra belägg därför—eller svar på rymdflaskposten sänd med Pioneer 10 och 11?

En svensk astronom och prisbelönad, författare *Peter Nilson*, har i boken *Solvindar* (1993) gett goda svar. Han erinrar först om den så kallade SETI-forskningen: med många teleskop jorden runt söker vi efter radiosignaler från andra varelser. Förkortningen betyder "Search for Extra Terrestial Intelligence." Så tar Peter Nilson ner oss på jorden igen. "Många öron lyssnar, men vad är det vi söker? Varför skulle någon skicka signaler just åt vårt håll genom Vintergatans ofantliga rymdöknar? Vem skulle ana att vi finns just här, vid denna lilla gula sol i stjärnmyllret?"

Värre än så. Peter Nilson konstaterar att igen civilisation i det expanderans universum kan var jämngammal med vår. Hela vår existens som människor är tillsvidare bara en kort episod— skall vi likna den vid en sekund?—i rymdhistorien. Jorden är ju en *ung* planet, förmodligen bara ungefär 5,000,000,000 år gammal (det är minst 15 miljarder år sedan Big Bang ägde rum). Slutsatsen Peter Nilson småningom drar är att om det finns fler civilisationer i universum kommer de inte att lära känna varandra.

De måste "i rymdmörkret vara lika ovetande om varandra som två fåglar på var sin sida av en ocean."

4. En snäll teologi för det expanderande universum.

Världs alltet blir alltså tills vidare—under hur många hundra miljoner år?—större och större. Big Bang-teorin förutsätter att universum expanderar. Vad kan en teolog säga om detta?

En barnafrom och snäll teolog kan förstås nöja sig med att bekänna att Gud är obegriplig i sitt majestät. Den allsmäktige Skaparen blir ett ofattbart mysterium, och storheten växer så att säga med astronomins nya rön. Räcker det då inte med tillbedjan?

Ett sätt vore att med den svenske psalmförfattaren Carl Boberg utbrista i lovsägalse. Jämför anslaget i sangen "O store Gud!" (nr. 11 i nya *Svenska Psalmboken*). "O store Gud, när jag den värld beskådar, som du har skapat med ditt allmaktsord ... Då brister själen ut i lovsångs ljud! O store Gud! O store Gud!" Just i det väldiga perspektivet finner sångaren det extra stort att Gud på vår jord sörjer också för fauna och flora. All omsorg ter sig som ett härligt bevis på Guds suveränitet som skapare och "fader".

Även Bibeln pekar strängt taget på stjärnhimlen som argument för Guds mäktiga omsorg. Det är, djupast sett, innebörden av uppmaningen i Första Moseboken till den barnlöse patriarken Abraham "Se mot himmelen, och räkna stjärnorna, om du kan räkna dem" (1 Mos 15:5). I varje fall har bibeltexten tolkats på det sättet av den svenska pingstväckelsens pionjär *Lewi Pethrus* i en sångtext som numera också ingår i svenska kyrkans psalmbok (2554:2): "Gör såsom Abraham gjorde,/blicka mot himlen opp! / Medan du stjärnorna räknar,/ växer din tro, ditt hopp."

5. Ett trotsigare utspel: varför är vi instängda på vår lilla planet?

Läser man den citerade texten i Första Moseboken jämte Lewi Pethrus' psalm får man närmast känslan av att stjärnor vinkar vänligt mot oss som Vår Herres bloss från en inte alltför avlägsen himmel ovanför molnen. Blir det emellertid inte annorlunda i ett universum med miljarder och åter miljarder stjärnor av vilke många—de allra flesta—ter sig avlägset kalla? I en tid då vi vet att "stjärnfall" inte kan ge oss tro på löftens infriande utan förmedlar associationer till nya fruktansvärda explosioner och till och med till uppkomsten av "svarta hål"?

Den ovan nämnde svenske författaren och astronomen *Peter Nilson* framför också tanken, att för den händelse vi upptäcker något alls beträffande liv på andra planeter, så kommer vi att finna att vi är råa barbaer i jämförelse med där existerande varelser. I varke fall ifråga om teknologi och vetenskap."Detta är ett sorgligt och förödmjukande faktum men egentligen självklart: en enkel sannolikhetskalkyl visar att det måste vara så."

Ungefär på same sätt, men i slutsatserna än mer brutalt, resonerar forskaren *Jacques Monod* i sin välkända bok "Slump och nödvändighet". Han sager att människan bör vakna upp ur sin tusenåriga dröm och erkänna sin fullständiga ensamhet. Mänskligheten på vårt klot kan, menar han, liknas vid zigenarna. Främlingskapet är fundamentalt, Universum är dövt för människors musik, också likgiltigt för både förhoppningar, förbrytelser och lidanden på jorden.

Om det finns en så väldig skapargud som ville något med oss människor, varför mäste han då vara så obegriplig? Den svenske skönlitteräre författaren *Lars Gyllensten* talar med rätta om vår "kreaturlighet", om människors instängdhet här på jorden. Är det inte en högst provocerande Gud som säges ha skapat människor till sin "avblid" men håller henne i total ovetskap om så mycket under i bästa fall en livstid på 70-80 år (Ps 90:10) på planeten Tellus, medan skapelse pågår i årmiljoner och åter årmiljoner? Är det inte nästan en oanständighet att hålla oss som små barn i ovetskap om vad som egentligen sker i stora stora världen?

Bibeln har som bekant också en trotsig Job och en argsint Jeremia som då och då går tillrätta med sin Gud. Dessutom den tredje patriarken som fick sitt nya namn, Israel, därför att han hårt i mörker brottades med en okänd (gud). Låt vara att denne

Jakob till sist utropade: "Jag släpper dig inte, men mindre du välsignar mig" (1 Mos. 32:26).

6. Vår Herre en farlig äventyrare?

Försöker vi en teologi för det expanderande universum finns anledning att pröva nya vägar, Särskilt om vi väger in vad fysiker-astronomer lär oss om att stjärnor "föds" och "dör", om "de svarta hålen" och liknande.

En ny skapelseteologi måste leta fram nya bilder. Är det någon form av jätteexperiment som pågår där ute i rymden, så farligt att vi för säkerhets skull inte få se så mycket av det? I så fall, vad är själva syftet med experimentet?

Handskas under alla omständigheter inte Vår Herre vårdslöst med sina sprängämnen och sitt byggmaterial? Varför mäste det i världsalltet vara som det står i Predikaren att "allt har sin tid". "Byrta ner har sin tid . . . Förvara har sin tid, och kasta bort har sin tid. Riva sönder har sin tid, och sy ihop har sin tid" (Pred. 3:2-7). Vad är det Gud håller på med i sin värld eller i sina världar (i pluralis, *Stephen Hawking* räknar med nya "spädbarns-universa" som föds ur strålning från de dödsbringande "svarta hålen")? Har Vär Herre själv klart för sig konsekvenserna av förintelsen i de svarta hålen? Varför måste hela stjärnor och kanske stjärnsystem bete sig som vätebomber i kubik??

Kunde inte Vår Herre vara lite mera av finsnickare och lättsam fixare, om nu något måste rättas till? Eller är Gud att likna vid en sjusärdeles reparatör, som förmår att återanvända allt? Skall profeten Jeremias ord tillämpas också på universum? "När kärlet som krukmakaren höll på att göra av leret misslyckades i hans hand, började han om igen, och gjorde av det ett annat kärl så, som han ville ha det gjort" (Jer 18:4).

"Se, jag gör allting nytt," laser vi på ett ställe i Uppenbarelseboken (Upp 21:5). Det är dock siarens vision inför ett slutscenario som där målas upp. Håller Vår Herre på att träna sig inför en grandiose final, eller vad pågår?

7. De svarta hålens teologi

Eller får vi en ny åskådlig undervisning om liv, död och förnyelse genom våra dagars astronomer och rymdfilosofer? Stjärnor slocknar och "dör", andra tänds, väcks till "liv". Partiklar, tror *Stephen Hawking*, kan falla in i svarta hål som sedan "avdunstar" och försvinner från vårt område av universum. Nya astonomiska visioner kan sätta igång vår fantasi. Måste vi tänka nytt och stort om död och liv? Vågar vi en teologisk nytolkning av den orimligt stora världsrymdens egendomliga processer?

Jag är inte säker på att jag vågar själv. Men jag vill hänvisa till en skönlitterär tolkning av den svenske författaren *Bo Beskow*, eljest mera känd som konstnär och målare (samme man som av FN:s generalsekreterare *Dag Hammerskjöld* fick uppdraget att utsmycka andakssrummet i FN-huset i New York). På gamla dager skrev Beskow flera romaner med gammaltestamentliga motiv. En av dem heter "Rösten är Jakobs" (efter 1 Mos 27:23). Beskow porträtterar patriarken som enligt 1 Mos 32:24-32 kom att ge namnet Israel ("Gud brottas") åt det folk som kämpat med gudsfrågor under sekler—och gjort så ställföreträdande för mänskligheten.

Den unge Jakob såg en gång—han var på panikartad flykt hemifrån—i en dröm i Betel en stege rest mellan himmel och jord (1Mos 28). I Bo Beskows roman återvänder Jakob många år senare till samma plats. Han är gammal redan, slår sig ner på en sten och mediterar medan han täljer en skål ur ett stycke skyomorträ. Då faller han på nytt i sömn och drömmer—eller vad är det som sker? Han förnimmer hur någon kommer med en vänlig vind och tar honom med på en underlig och underbar resa. Här ett utdrag:

> Så svindlande var aldrig min färd, så underbar aldrig min värld, så ofattbar stor och dock så välbekant.
>
> Jag kunde ju igenkänna de stjärnbilder vilka vi se från jorden, men dessa ha försvunnit bakom oss och vi möta andra stjärnehopa. Stundom färdas vi igenom myggsvärmar av små lysande, dansande stjärnor, vilka fastna som kardborrar och

diamanter i min mantel. I nästa stund gör vi vida undanflykter när vi möts av oöverskådligt stora himlakroppar som spärra vår väg, döda mörka himlakroppar . . .

Dubbelstjärnorna mötas i töckniga tunnlar och förenas i våldsam omfamning, avlande nya jordar och floder av eld i flammande sköten.

Genom alltsammans, genom de sju rymderna, rusa eldsvansade kometer av och en likt ivriga vallhundar i en fårahjord.

Dessa kometer tyckas driva stjärnhoparna, solarna och himlakropparna i ett bestämt syfte. Inför mina ögon bilda de en hög gestalt, större än något tänkbart, sträckande sig över sju rymders höjd och djup, höljd i dimmslöjor av stjärnstoft. Mitt i denna lysande stjärnskepnads sköte öppnar sig en mörk port.

Är detta porten till nya okända världar? Leder den till evighet eller intighet? Jag måste igenom den dunkla porten för att finna svaret.

Med bävande förväntan färdas jag in i detta svarta intighetshål för att få klarhet . . .

. . . och befinner mig i samma ögonblick åter sittande vid stenen i Betel, med ett stycke sykomorträ i mina händer.

Jag skakar stjärnstoft och iskristaller ur hår och mantelveck, och återtager det avbrunna arbetet med att skära i detta trästycke.

Bo Beskow är i Sverige känd som förnyaren av de medeltida glasmålningarnas svåra konst (främst i Skara domkyrka). I Växjös katedral har han gjort en väggmosaik med motivet "Det himmelska Jerusalem" (med bl a små guldfärgade bitar han i unga år köpte från överskottslagret då "Gyllene salen" i Stockholms berömda stadshus färdigställdes). Jag skulle önskat att Beskow före sin bortgång fått beställning att i en kyrka åskådliggöra sin vision av himlens stjärnor, vallhundarna och den höga gestalten vid svarta hålet!

Med ord hann denne förunderlige man likväl måla de svarta hålens möjliga budskap. Närmare än så kommer väl ingen idag en utläggning av stjärnrymden på naturliga teologins plan?

8. Big Bang, HUGO, slumpen—och Gud?

I Sverige lanseras för allmänheten kunskapen om den nya så kallade genomforskningen effektivt genom en skriftserie av Kungliga Vetenskapsakademien med det gemensamma temat "Människan och den nya biologin." Första numret i serien har fått det roliga namnet "Vem i hela världen är HUGO?" HUGO är förkortningen för det stora gx för många nationer gemensamma förskinings-projektet Human Genome Organization som syftade till att kartlägga bl a hela mänskighetens arvsmassa.

En vetenskapsjournalist vid namn *Peter Sylwan* för pennan för en expert-grupps räkning. På ett ställe i boken summeras det nya läget avseende "Vetenskapens världsbild." Inledningen är som följer:

> Det började med The Big Bang, Den Stora Smällen, när universum föddes. Och fråga inte vad som fanns före— tid och rum är relativa begrepp—men ur smällen föddes energin och kvarkarna, neutronerna, protonera och elektronerna. Deras fullständigt slumpvisa umgänge med varandra, energin och årmiljonerna, leder lika slumpmässigt till att det småningom uppstår en molekyl som kan kopiera sig själv. Ungefär som en ger ett avtryck i leran och avtrycket blir gjurtform åt en fot som ...Numera tror vi att den molekylen var rätt lik den molekylvi nu kallar RNA—en nära släkting till DNA.

Hela utspelet har intentionen att introducera grundtesen att allt liv har ett gemensamt historiskt—biologiskt ursprung. Under den journalistiskt valda nya rubriken "Senaste nytt" utformas på bara några få rader hela teorin. RNA:s förfader fortsätter att kopiera sig själv. Ibland gör han "slumpmässigt" misstag. Emellanåt visar sig dessa misstag funktionella, och så kan det nya som åstadkoms "göra fler saker än sin föregångare." "På den vägen är det"—fortfarande, menar Sylwan. "För ungefär 2 miljoner år sedan ledde detta till att de första människoliknande varelserna utvecklades på jorden."

Nästan lyriskt utvecklar vetenskapsjournalisten, å expert-gruppens vägnar, en framställning av "livets alfabet." Det sker med biblisk association och överton: "I begynnelsen var Ordet."

Den nya ärftlighetsforskningen har konstaterat att alfabetet har bara fyra bokstäver: A (svarande mot "basen" Adenin), C (Cytosin), G (Guenin) och T (Tymin), Naturen, säger Sylwan, har sitt eget knep att göra 64 tecken av de fyra (genom att "baserna" grupperas tre och tre, AAA, ACA, AGA etc). "Och med 64 tecken kan man säga det mesta. "Vi klarar oss (i svenska språket) med 28 bokstäver, Och Mozart skrev Trollflöjten med ett begränsat antal nottecken."

Det finns inte här utrymme för att repetera elementa om DNA-trådens uppbyggnad och om hur "generna" fungerar. I princip förutsätts att DNA sänder ut instruktion för hur celler skall byggas via en kopia med egen beteckning, den ovannämnda RNA.

Stephen Hawking lekte med tanken att kunna läsa Guds egna tankar. Den berömde svenske biologen och naturforskaren *Carl von Linné* har i ett minst lika berömt yttrande sagt att han I sina naturstudier "skådade Gud på ryggen." Kan HUGO gå ännu längre och finna så att sagaVår Herres hittills hemliga recept och utvecklingsmodeller?

I den nog så sekulariserade svenska forskarmiljön talar man emellertid i stället, såsom framgick av citat ovan, om "slumpen". Gud finns inte längre med i spelet, inte ens som metaphor. I en svensk debatt mellan en filosof och en teologie doctor *Christer Hedin*, tillika tidigare chef för der svenska riksradions vetenskapsredaktion, undrade emellertid den senare skämtsamt om Gud inte kan heta HUGO. Poängen var förstås att Gud ändå, trots tal om "slump", kan ha ett finger (och ett avgörande sådant) med i spelet. Debatten utspelades i ett reportage i SAS-tidningen Upp & Ner 1993.

9. Downs syndrome, Huntingtons sjukdon— Guds "trial and error"?

Den nya molekylärbiologin undervisar oss-vi som på det område det gäller är vetenskapens amatöres-om förbluffande ting. På det allra första stadiet, ägget, skiljer sig en blivande människa ytligt sett inte från andra encelliga organismer."Något senare", berätter *Peter Sylwan* i den nämnda HUGO-boken,"är det fortfarande mycket svårt att se någon skillnad mellan foster hos groda, gris och människa, kanin eller mus." Några gener hos oss "gör samma jobb" som motsvarande hos bananflugan. Och i ett berömt experiment har en forskare "botat" en "gensjuk" jästsvamp genom att inympa en motsvsrande gen från en människa.

Detta är en sak möjligen svår för de så kallade "kreationisterna" bland kyrkfolket och dess teologer. För andra kan väl utvecklingen som sådan accepteras vid eftertanke: skulle inte vår suveräne Herre få skapa på det sätt Han själv vill?

Svårare ter sig i stället att smälta de vetenskapligt fullständigt belagda rönen rörande ärftlighetens lagar för vissa sjukdomar, t. ex. Huntingtons, och irregulariteter som drabbar och ter sig synnerligen oönskade, t.ex. Downs syndrom (så kallade mongoloida barn). Den senare avvikelsen en "kromosomal sjukdom." Huntingtons sällsynta sjukdom drabber hårt bäraren av genen: i 30–40-årsåldern kramper som blir värre och värre, småningom nedbrytande av hjärnfunktioner.

Nu tycks rättviseproblemet, typiskt mänskligt men också av sådan beskaffenhet att vi tillvitar Gud en brist ("teodicéproblemet"), anmäla sig med hast. Hur kan Gud tillåta? Eller finns det någon mening i eländet? Eller lyckades kanske inte Vår Herre bättre?

10. Vad kan Gud då tänkas säga oss genom HUGO?

Skapelseteologi har definitivt också en mycket mänsklig sida: den handlar också om människors förväntningar om hur Vår Herre borde uppenbara sig genom naturen. Skapelseteologi är vidare mycket mänskliga funderingar om Guds avsikter med världen och med oss, om vår plats som människor här på jordklotet.

Vi förutsätter gärna att Gud ska vara god i den mening vi ofta inlägger i ordet, Vår Herre borde alltså vara generös, välvillig, rättvis (och helst ge alla ett lyckosamt och långt liv). Gud blir emellertid på det sättet snarast en projektion av julklappstomte och snäll trollkarl.

Det är således vårt mänskliga missnöje som skapar teodicéproblemet. Våra mänskliga anvisningar till Gud hur Han borde vara är den egentliga utgångspunkten. Det är ungefär som när en karta inte stämmer med terrängen: kan då kartan ändå användas? Det lönar sig inte att finna fel på Guds värld. Skapelseteologin måste utgå från den faktiska verkligheten.Vi må t. ex. ogilla att vår jord inte är fri från jordbävningar (som väl ändå inte kan vara beroende av vad vi människor ställt till?).Vi kan t.ex. tycka att det vore bättre—att Gud lyckats bra—om Los Angeles aldrig riskerade jordskred. Ett mera realistiskt sätt att gå till väga är att ställa frågan vad vi bör ta till för försiktighetsmått (flytta därifrån, bygga stabilare?) eller om vi är beredda att leva med riskerna.

Den som har gudstro och stalls inför HUGO tvingas fundera på åtskilligt. Mitt första och viktigaste intryck är att HUGO-forskarna, som själv gärna talar om "slumpen" i utvecklingen, gör oss vissa tjänster vilka i sista instans ter sig positiva.Vi tvingas för det första besinna hur vår tro på en skapargud kan relateras till deras resultat.

Min egen skapartro gäller *inte* en ofullkomlig gud. Gud är Gud, är som Han är. Om jag någon gång blir arg på Gud eller missbelåten med hans skapelse, beror ilskan och förargelsen på mig.Jag tror visst, attVår Herre om han önskat kunde begagnat flera än fyra bokstäver i "livets alfabet." Räcker de för honom, är de dock nog för mig.

Jag tror attVår Herre i sitt världsbygmästeri och jordklots-finsnickeri är sin egen arkitekt och verktygsmakare.Jag tror på en lekfull Gud som faktiskt, mänskligt bedömd, arbetar med en metod som liknar "trial-and-error". Jag räknar med en Gud som gläder sig över små finesser vi uppskattar (t.ex. en orchidé, en näktergal).Jag tror också attVår Herre är mycket seriös och själv önskar att något gott och meningsfullt skall komma av det som vi människor finner sorgligt i första omgången (t.ex. att barn föds med Downs syndrom).Det jag sålunda säger står ändå inte, i motsats till mitt intryck attVår Herre är en äventyrare i universum och på vår lilla jord.Vår Herres äventyr med oss människor på planeten Tellus består bl.a. i att Han överlåter till oss att reagera (t.ex., om människor i en ny tid med medicinsk teknik skall välja selektiv abort för av dem oönskade barn eller om de av fri vilja skall besluta att vårda ett sådant barn om det överlever födseln). Det finns anledning att utveckla några sluttankar om det dubbla äventyret, Vår Herres och vårt eget. Men först en sammanfattning av detta avsnitt.

Gud har här på jorden sitt finger med i HUGO därför att Han här i mycket arbetar genom av teknik och uppfinningar skickliggjorda människohänder—och genom forskare, också filosofer (och hoppas jag även teologer). HUGO-forskarnas utspel och filosofi tvingar oss att ta ställning till mycket, inte bara inom medicinsk etik utan t. ex., hur så kallade transgena växter kan användas för ökad livsmedelsproduktion (och därför kan utgöra ett hopp för försörkningen nästa sekel, något som faktiskt också påtalas av Kungliga Vetenskapsakademien i Sverige i en särskild skrift, "Nytt liv i Vår Herres hage"). Men framför allt får HUGO-forskningen liksom kosmos-forskarna, bl a Big Bang-fysikerna, oss att tänka over årmiljoner, vår korta stund på jorden och hur vi ska använda den (och i förlängingen på frågan om liv nyskapas efter döden, även vår egen död).

Själv mediterar jag garna over frågan om de svenska söta röda smultronen som gläder ungarna här hemma i Sverige verkligen tillkommit av en slump. Jag tror det inte. Jag tror i stället—med en tro nu i betydelsen av tillit och förtröstan—att det finns en Gud som ville barnen väl.

11. Vår Herres märkliga delegationsbestämmelser: vårt mänskliga äventyr

Skapelsteologi är främst "naturlig teologi" och bör därför inte i första taget åberopa skriftord. Nu, i slutomgången av min essä, är det likväl synnerligen frestande att citera några rader i Bibelns skapelseberärttelse:

> Och Gud skapade människan till sin avbild, till Guds avbild skapade han henne, till man och kvinna skapade han dem. Och Gud välsignade dem. Gud sade till dem:
> "Var fruktsamma och föröka er, och uppfyll jorden och lägg den under er. Och råd över fiskarna i havet och över fåglarna under himmelen och over alla djur som rör sig på den" (1 Mos 1:27).

Den som inte är "kreationist" läser förslagsvis texten som en underfundig och rolig baklängesprofetia. Människan är ju faktiskt—den tidigare nämnde australiensiske filosofen *Peter Singer* må säga vad han vill—herre över fauna och flora. Stanner vi upp vid 1 Mos. 1:27 är delegationen total. Människan har fått jorden, planeten Tellus, i uppdrag. Faktiskt, reallt, fungerar det så idag (vad man än vill saga om senare "uppenbarelse" avTio Guds bud med mera). Det nästan befängda är att vi dessutom tagit det allra första uppdraget, att "uppfylla jorden" på så blodigt allvar som om vi vore kreationister. Lite dråpligt blir det också—kunde Vår Herre ha menat så?—att erinra sig genomforskningens experiment bl.a., med transgena djur ("konstgjorda") och därutöver all lyckad växtförädling. (Vem motsätter sig nya slags rosor och mycket effektivare jordbruk med genmanipulerat utsäde och ogräsbekämpning?)

Tillåter Vår Herre att mänskligheten inte bara har en (nog så blodig) historia utan fortsätter att lägga planeten under sig (Antarktis, kanske också vår planetsatellit månen i nästa omgång?)? Uppenbarligen, enligt en strikt tolkning av delegationen. "Varldsligt regemente," sade *Martin Luther*, drivs med "ratio", förnuftet (fast mänskliga emotioner ofta driver oss till oförnuftiga gärningar).

En rimlig skapelseteologisk tes är—detta upprepar jag— att mänskligheten på Tellus är Vår Herres äventyr. Måhända har Gud, i sitt väldiga universum, andra äventyr och experiment för sig? Människornas historia på jordklotet är en del i det stora äventyret. Samtidigt är detta äventyr just människornas, folkens, kollektivens.

Detta är emellertid inte allt—fråga är om det ens är det viktigaste. Det sagda utesluter nämligen inte att varje liten mänsklig grupp, t.ex., en familj, har sitt eget livsäventyr. Och i sista instans varje individ!

Fråga är emellertid också hela tiden om mänskliga livsäventyr inför och genom och i (eller välj andra propositioner som Luther gjorde för att uttrycka Guds närvaro i "konsubstatiationen" i nattvarden, t.ex., "med" och "under") Gud. Då *Paulus* för kristendomen till Europa försöker han inför Atens filsofer ett stycke naturlig teologi. Han talar förtröstansfullt om att alla skapats av en enda Gud. "I honom är det vi lever, rör oss och är till, som också några av era egna skalder har sagt:Vi har vårt ursprung i honom" (Apg 17:28). Det betyder att den ende Guden har ett ärende till och ett uppdrag till var och en. Delegationen gäller mänskligheten men också, nedbruten från kollektivet, den enskilde. Denne eller denna, man eller kvinna, medverkar i det stora uppdraget och äventyret—och har samtidigt sitt eget.

Är delegationen då verkligen total? Ja, i så måtto som människan är utrustad med förnuft och fri vilja. Hon är verkligen i jordiska ting fri (att hon sedan genom misstag står i skuld till medmänniskor och sin skapare och i det stycket är ofri, oförmögen att själv lösa sig från skulden, är en annan sak som inte gäller första trosartikeln och skapelseteologin). Människan är också fri att välja det goda, vad hon med sitt moraliska förnuft finner rätt, i livsäventyret. Detta bekräftar åter igen "uppenbarel-seteologen" Paulus då han i brevet till Rom utförligt diskuterar "hedningarna som inte har lagen" (det vill säga den uppenbarade judiska lagen) och som ändå "av naturen kan fullgöra lagen" (Rom 2:14) eller bryta mot dess innebörd. "Om det vittnar också deras samvete och deras tankar när tankarna anklagar varandra och försvarar sig" (2:15).

Är detta resonemang rikitigt—och vem vill bestride denna mänskliga frihet, betygad likaväl av missionären Paulus som t.ex., av existentialisten-ateisten *Jean-Paul Sartre*—ingår i det stora äventyret att fälla avgöranden nu och för framtiden. I äventyret, mänsklighetens och Guds på planeten Tellus, ingår politikers och ekonomers ansvar. Också läkares och teknikers. Även ditt och mitt, hur vi hanterar ekonomi, arbete (eller eventuell arbetslöshet vi drabbas av), hälsa och sjukdom (som vi ibland ådrar oss, ibland ändå i detta liv kanske alldeles oförskyllt drabbas av—*där* väljer vi inte alltid fritt), vår fritid, våra telationer (även t.ex., de sexuella). Fortfarande gäller dock "den naturliga lagen," säg detta faktum ätt vi är människor med moraliskt förnuft med tankar som kan "ankalaga varandra," "försvara sig" (åter Rom 2:15).

Så fortsätter äventryret, Vår Herres på planeten Tellus och mänsklighetens. Vart går utvecklingen? Det kan ingen nu förutsäga—men mänsklighetens äventyr är även Guds. Så säger i varje fall en teolog som funderar över första artikeln. Han tillägger att det egna livsäventyret och andras inte heller kan överblickas, vad gäller slutet. Men skapelsetron innebär att det är ett äventyr inneslutet på något sätt i Gud hand. Det är tilliten och förtröstan som får sista ordet, utgör finalen.

12. Vår Herres genskrift

En av Sveriges mera originella kristna förkunnare just nu är stockholms-prästen *Lars Collmar*. I sin bok, *"Den leendes Guden"* (1994), berättar han hur han en gång bad Gud att få bli fullständigt fri från allt som band honom. Han tänkte därvid inte bara på sitt förflutna utan på det personliga arvet, som tycktes honom vara en belastning. Var det inte en blandning av en fars neurotiska plikttrohet och en mors ibland lite alltför glada lättsinne?

I det läget hörde han emellertid som vore han en aktör i et drömspel Vår Herre muttra: "Vad jag har skrivit, det har jag skrivit."

Till vårt personliga livsöde, tillika Guds skapelseverk, hör vissa förutsättningar: generna, arvet. Det är dessa vi skall förvalta, fritt utveckla. En mera trösterik än förfärande tanke: vem om inte Gud gav oss förutsättningarna? Vi är i Vår Herres hand, dock inte bara brickor i ett stort spel utan människor fria att utvecklas och att delta i mänsklighetens och Vår Herres stora äventyr på jorden.

21

The Threat of the Religious Right

Balfour Brickner

(A presentation on the occasion of recciving the 30th George Brussel, Jr. Award from The Stephen Wise Free Synagogue, New York City, Erev Shabbat, March 12, 1993, by Balfour Brickner, Senior Rabbi Emeritus, Stephen Wise Free Synagogue.)

President Ashen, Rabbi Youdovin, Cantor Math, distinguished past presidents of the congregation gathered on this bima, your honor, Mayor David Dinkins, thank you. Thank you from the bottom of a very full heart. I am deeply grateful to be the recipient of such an honor. I think all of you know how humbled and proud I am to be the 30th beneficiary of this treasured award. I have been involved personally in lobbying for about one-third of those who have preceded me as your honorees, and I can remember being here for the ceremonies when many of my friends stood where I stand now:

Al Vorspan, my beloved colleague and dear friend, Rabbi Eugene Lipman, Mary Iemma and Margaret Jenkins, with whom I worked for many years as we built the housing that still stands at the top of the East Side of our city in a project know as The Upper Park Avenue Community Association (UPACA), Mayor John Lindsay, Clarence Mitchell. It is indeed a most distinguished group whose ranks I now proudly join.

But, in truth, none of this would have been possible without you, this wonderful congregation of ours. You not only allowed and authorized the creation of this award given to one "for exceptional devotion to the causes of individual freedom and social justice, in the spirit of the Hebrew prophets," you encouraged everything for which it stands. You wanted, and, I believe, still want this sacred space to lead Jews and others down the path of righteousness. You want this institution to pioneer, to be in the vanguard of religiously motivated social involvement and to have that leadership articulated from both pulpit and pew; first, through the forceful voice of your rabbis Stephen Wise, Ed Klein and now Ira Youdovin, as they interact with their communities, and secondly through an active committee of laypersons involved, in the congregation's name, in the repair of our fractured society. I am proud, very proud that this is a place where the rights, concerns, and needs of gays and lesbians can be heard and met. I am proud that here the homeless can find shelter, the hungry, substance; where Palestinian and Israeli, Arab and Jew can meet; where Christian and Jew, Black and Jew can find one another beyond the enmity, the differences, the disagreements. I am proud that this is the place where the unthinkable can be thought, the politically cruel and selfish, exposed; where the tradition of a free pulpit and a pew free to respond is not only expected but zealously cherished, nay demanded; where if we do not think and act on the exciting cutting edge of social change and challenge, you are disappointed. It is that spirit that drew me here. Simply put, there is simply no other place like the Stephen Wise Free Synagogue, the place where you can expect the unexpected and find it. And all that is because of you. As a congregation you are still one of the remaining bastions of openness: a congregation of people who understand God as a driving force for justice, inclusive not exclusive, the antithesis of the authoritarian or the autocratic.

All this seems so obvious, so normal that it hardly merits our mention. Yet, today, the matter is not so clear. Throughout our country and the world, God is being demonized. Religion has become a force of divisiveness, mayhem, madness and now murder. In the name of God, misguided spiritualized energy is being transformed into a death force bristling with intolerant doctrines, and reinforced with assault guns. Hindus and Muslims kill each other in India. Islamic fundamentalists murder in Egypt, Algeria. Jewish fundamentalist become vigilantes on the West Bank. Serbs re-enact the Holocaust in Bosnia Herzegovina.

At home, God only knows what motivated those who blew apart the World Trade Center while what, for years, we warned might happen in the escalating "war of choice," has now tragically occurred. A demented "Christ-fascist" shot to death a dedicated physician for no other reason than that he mercifully performed abortions. Sickening as is that act, even more disgusting is the response to that act, even more disgusting is the response to that murder by those who embraced this sick soul, encouraged him, propagandized him, washed his feeble brain. Hear the response of one Randall Terry, "leader" of Operation Rescue, when asked to comment on the murder of Dr. Gunn: "While we grieve for him and for his widow, we must also grieve for the thousands of children he has murdered." This act, the proliferation of terrorists who, in the name of "life," destroy it, these authoritarian know-nothing bigots, have come to power as a direct result of being tolerated, coddled, encouraged, by the administrations of Ronald Reagan and George Bush. They deliberately refused to use the offices of police protection and civil rights enforcement at their disposal to prevent this army of compulsory pregnancy vandals from violating the law, as they have before in family planning clinics all over America. The book Leviticus admonishes us: "You shall not stand idly by the blood of your neighbor" (Lev 19:16). In a very real sense the blood of Dr. Gunn stains the hands of these two past presidents. They need to know that and they must live with that knowledge for the rest of their lives.

This is what happens when religion turns right. It thinks and acts wrongly. By "right" I mean authoritarian and by "wrong" I mean compulsory. I am beginning to be frightened by people who call themselves religious. And why not? The Jewish right disgusts me no less than the Christian right angers me. I am embarrassed by a Jewish religious right that props up a sick old rabbi in front of a mob of his frenzied fanatical disciples and lets them rant of this man that he is "melech, ha-mashiach," "The

King, Messiah." I am humiliated when I see who the people of Israel have allowed to become the Ashkenazic chief rabbi, while his counterpart from the Sephardic community is no better.

There must be more and better religious social activism than a Cardinal who can hardly wait to mount his pulpit to praise those of the Board of Education responsible for jettisoning one of the finest chancellors of education this city has ever had, an action in which we now know the offices of the archdiocese were deeply involved. There must be more and better religious social activism than the prattle of a Robert Simonds, founder of a new San Diego based organization, "Citizens for Excellence." In 1985 this good Christian published a 65-page booklet entitled "How to elect Christians to public office." This same devout soul is also the author of this sentiment: "The separation of church and state is a socialist myth perpetrated by the American Civil Liberties Union." Simonds is only the latest in a battalion of right-wing Christian fundamentalists about whom, from this pulpit, we have been trying to alert people for the past decade. Now, as "stealth candidates" they threaten to steal our local communities and that could happen here in New York City.

We cannot ignore the current dynamics operative in our city. We live in an increasingly polarized place where the gap between rich and poor is growing obviously and dramatically. As this happens, we hear with increasing loudness the rising voice of anger and frustration of the disenfranchised, those who see themselves as powerless. Little wonder that hate radio is growing in popularity. It is the one place where the unempowered feel they can be heard. Those who have created these media work that rage from the dark confines of their radio studios, cynically manipulating that anger for a buck, all at the expense of the city's social atmosphere. The radical right, religious and secular, feeds on this atmosphere of disgruntlement. They encourage fear, mistrust, distrust of "the haves," "the liberals," "the educated elite." They feed on suspicion of "the outer boro wealthy" by "the inner city poor." The school board is only one facet of their efforts to exploit class tensions. Their obsession with sex is even more of a problem. Witness their almost hysterical opposition to sex education in the public schools, to

AIDS education, to teaching about birth control, to the distribution of condoms in our public schools, even to the institution
of school based clinics. And what are we to make of their general homophobia? They have politicized sex and drawn into
their activities the normally conservative from our cities' ethnic
and racial groups.

Stealth candidates are ubiquitous. They struggle to gain
control of all local structures, from school boards to local
community boards to PTAs. Not even fire or police departments
are immune. It is estimated that they now occupy over 18,000
positions on local bodies nationwide. This is the fulfillment of
Pat Robertson's promise. America is facing a massive CHARGE
OF THE RIGHT BRIGADE and we need to be aware. People
say I am overly concerned. Besides, I am told the right has the
right, nay the duty, to try to influence public opinion. That is
their vocation. It is a valid argument. Religious groups do have
the right, the obligation, to make their views known. In fact
Judaism has always been involved in this endeavor, one I have
long called "the politics of God." Too frequently the forces of
organized religion have just stood by watching people die at
the hands of ruthless tyrants. We have a responsibility to bring
to bear our truth on their political power. Didn't Nathan do
that before King David? Didn't Amos do that at Beth El when
he thundered, "Jeroboam shall die by the sword?" Didn't
Matathias continue that tradition at Modin? In fact, it has never
ceased. The remembered giants of religion are remembered
precisely because they championed justice, struggled to affect
social change. But there is an enormous difference between
their style and the approach of today's sheikhs and self-proclaimed
messiahs. The Martin Luthers, and Stephen Wises, and the Martin
Luther Kings advocated a finer public morality, not a specific
religion for all. They sought to persuade, not impose, to influence,
not coerce. While motivated by theology, they never connected
their efforts to imposing on the populace a specific brand of
religion. It is at this point that groups like the Moral Majority
and newly alive Christian Coalition, Concerned Women for
America, The Family Forum and the Eagle Forum, the
Lubavitcher Chassidim and some parts of the Roman Catholic

hierarchy became allied, and parted company from religious civil libertarians.

My concern is not that organized religion seeks to influence the public atmosphere. Nor is my fear that those with whom I disagree seem all too influential. If they are, it is a crying commentary on us and what we have allowed to pass for religion in this society, not on them for what they have tried to sell us. My concern is that too few from the ranks of America's mainstream religious communities seem willing or able to confront the religious radical right in the public square, which I believe deserves to remain naked, devoid of both the substance and trappings of sectarian religion. What worries me is the tiredness of liberals, our willingness to accept defeat seen as compromise. What worries me is our too heavy reliance on secular organizations, or the executive and judiciary branches of government, to defend our rights. If President Clinton, with a stroke of his pen, restored many rights protecting choice for women and has tried to introduce sanity into America viz its attitude toward homosexuals, it is equally true that the Supreme Court can no longer be counted upon to protect privacy or defend religious rights. The Smith case in Oregon ought to convince us of that new reality. Prohibiting the use of peyote in religious worship is just the first step. Maybe the abolishing of Kiddush wine will be the next one. We seem to be tiring of all these struggles. But, tiredness is a luxury we cannot afford. It is what those who would rob us of our freedoms hope will happen to us. Advocacy still demands our response. There is a Religious Freedom Restoration Act that still awaits passage in Congress. Similarly with the Freedom of Choice Act. The president's plans for economic reform and the reform of our health care system will need our careful review. And in the area of service, the blight of homelessness, poverty's by-products, inadequate health and housing, and the woes of our environment will continue to demand our creative, caring response. That response is what gave and gives us our uniqueness.

For God's sake, we have a reputation to maintain. If we have earned people's enmity by our brashness, we have earned their grudging respect by our reach.

I know that social action is not the be all and end all of this congregation's life. But, it is the heart that drives the spiritual blood through our worshipping, educational, social veins and arteries. It is what gives us our life, our color, our vitality. Please God, let us keep it flowing.

Mayor David Dinkins:

Thank you and good evening all. It's both an honor and a pleasure to come back to the Stephen Wise Free Synagogue and particularly when we're here this evening to pay tribute to a leader, a champion of causes, a wonderful human being and a dear friend of mine, Rabbi Balfour Brickner. I extend my warmest greetings to his bride and to the senior rabbi of this beloved congregation, Rabbi Ira Youdovin, to Frank Ashen, distinguished president of the Stephen Wise Free Synagogue, to Dr. Stephan Lynn, esteemed chair of the Temple's Social Action and Social Service Committee, and to Barbara Joeson Fife, who plays a key role in my Administration as Deputy Mayor for Planning and Development, also a member of this congregation. Reflecting upon Rabbi Brickner's numerable achievements, I can think of no finer leader who has added so much to our city, to our country, indeed to the entire world, through his passionate embrace with the most important issues of our time, especially civil and human rights. It's no accident that we share a professional and personal bond because we share an underlying ideology. I believe that Rabbi Brickner's philosophy of life can perhaps be summed up best in the words of Reverend Doctor Martin Luther King, Jr., who wrote from a Birmingham jail: "Injustice anywhere is a threat to justice everywhere." Some of you may not know this, since Rabbi Brickner is an extremely modest individual, but he was incarcerated in Birmingham with Dr. King for demonstrating on behalf of integration and the rights of African-Americans. So I know that these words of Dr. King's have a particularly powerful resonance for Rabbi Brickner. Indeed, he has toiled along freedom's road. He has been a foot soldier in the cause of social justice, and tonight, I have the privilege of joining and presenting Rabbi Brickner with this

great honor: The *George Brussel Memorial Award*, in recognition
of the generous gifts he has given us through his four decades of
good work. Perhaps more than anything else, Rabbi Brickner
is driven by a deep belief in community, a blessed community
on which Dr. King so eloquently focused. Everything he has
accomplished is rooted in furthering tolerance and bringing
people together, here in New York City and in other parts of
the world. He has traveled far and wide, sharing his moving
message. He has addressed special sessions of the United Nations on human rights. He was responsible for conducting
human rights missions in Saigon, Vietnam and Nicaragua. He
has traveled to Japan to speak at a meeting with the World Conference on religion and peace. He has even brought teams of
inter-faith clergy to Israel for archeological digs—one of the
many ways he has expressed his abiding belief in the importance of inter-religious connections. But since he made New
York his home some 32 years ago, Rabbi Brickner has energetically embraced the challenges of our multi-cultural society,
and dedicated himself to finding innovative solutions. As co-
founder of the Upper Park Avenue Community Association, he
was instrumental in creating low income housing in East Harlem.
He developed an assembly program at Martin Luther King High
School here on the Upper West Side to help ease tensions between African-Americans and Jews. And during the unrest in
Crown Heights, Rabbi Brickner recognized the futility of escalating dissension and publicly spoke out as a voice for calm and
reason. He has continued to serve as a key liaison between City
Hall and the Jewish Community and has a healing and calming
influence, particularly when tensions flair. Robert Kennedy
told us that it is from numberless diverse acts of courage and
belief that human history is shaped. Each time a man stands up
for an ideal or acts to improve the lot of others, or strikes out
against injustice, he sends a tiny ripple of hope, each increasing
the other from a million different centers of energy and daring;
these ripples build a current, which can sweep down the mightiest
walls of oppression and resistance. Clearly, Rabbi Brickner has
met that call, sending forth a message of hope and compassion
and understanding to millions, and helping shape the course of

human history that will bring peace and love to the generations that follow us. There are so many other endeavors upon which Rabbi Brickner has placed his indelible signature that it would not be possible for me to mention all of them. But I would be remiss were I to overlook his tireless advocacy on behalf of the pro-choice movement, the Inter-religious Coalition for Healthcare, Parents and Friends of Lesbians and Gays and the American Israel Civil Liberties Coalition. In this synagogue alone, he was responsible for launching an early childhood day care center, a shelter for the homeless and an AIDS momentum project. This invaluable work, through the years, had everything to do with him being named a New York City Human Rights Commissioner in 1991. The *George Brussel Memorial Award* conferred annually by the Board of Trustees of the Stephen Wise Free Synagogue is given for exceptional devotion to the causes of individual freedom and social justice in the spirit of the Hebrew prophets. Rabbi Brickner, your being named as a recipient of the 30th annual *George Brussel Memorial Award* calls to mind the words of Voltaire, the immortal writer and philosopher—if I may be permitted a bit of poetic justice with Voltaire, let me say that if Rabbi Brickner did not exist, it would indeed be necessary to invent him.

22

Leo Strauss and Relativism: The Critique of Max Weber

Alan Mittleman

One of the most penetrating critiques of Max Weber's "value free" sociology came from the political theorist Leo Strauss. The entire second chapter of Strauss's *Natural Right and History* is devoted to the argument against Weber, whom Strauss called "the greatest social scientist of our century."[1] Strauss was obliged to confront Weber not only because of the latter's greatness, but because he seems to conflict at every point with the substantive position that Strauss apparently wants to defend. Strauss argues that it is at least possible to defend the view that there is a culturally invariant, universally knowable standard of right inherent in nature. Weber seems to argue, in contrast, that nature discloses no such standard; that there is, furthermore, an unbridgeable distinction between "facts" and "values" and that values, therefore, are essentially without foundation in anything other than human will. If Strauss sets out to defend (or at least to open up some critical doubts about the modern presentiment against) natural right, Weber, on Strauss's reading, is the champion

[1] Leo Strauss, *Natural Right and History* (Chicago: University of Chicago Press, 1965), p.36. (*NRH*)

of an historicism that, in its acute modern form, most starkly rejects natural right. Strauss sees Weber then as the last historicist. A man of the highest probity, Weber is the one who carried German historicism to its logical limit and who, with courage and despair, stared unblinking into the abyss that historicism uncovers.[2] Strauss treats this "greatest" of social scientists then as a kind of philosopher. He reads Weber's sociological studies as existentialist texts, as records of a solitary confrontation with meaninglessness.[3]

But all of these claims are controversial. Strauss, quite arguably, practiced a form of writing no less esoteric than the great thinkers whose presumed esotericism is integral to Strauss's own

---

[2] NRH, p. 38. For Strauss's concept of intellectual probity, cf. his *Philosophy and Law*, Fred Baumann, trans. (Philadelphia: Jewish Publication Society, 1987), p. 18: "This new bravery, understood as the readiness to hold firm while gazing upon the abandonment of man, as the courage to endure fearful truth, as hardness against the inclination of man to deceive himself about his situation, is called probity."

[3] The greatest pathos of some of Weber's classic lectures, such as "Science as a Vocation" and "Politics as a Vocation," lends support for such a reading. The scope and power of Weber's studies would undoubtedly have established him as a master and founder of sociology, but the element of pathos and the tragedy of his own personal history certainly contribute to the perenniel interest in him. Strauss's contemporary and correspondant, Karl Löwith, joined him in reading Weber as an existentialist. Cf. Karl Löwith, *Max Weber and Karl Marx*, Tom Bottomore and William Outhwaite, eds. (London: George Allen & Unwin, 1982), p. 22. Löwith follows Karl Jasper's earlier assessment of Weber in this matter. On the other hand, Weber's own friend and colleague, the philosopher Heinrich Rickert, emphasized that Weber did not see himself as a philosopher. Given Strauss's oft stated commitment to understanding writers as they understood themselves, this is an important datum. Rickert, however, while picturing Weber as a sociologist who was not interested in philosophy for its own sake, nonetheless argues that Weber was a kind of Socratic thinker who made an enormous contribution to philosophy. Following Rickert, I take issue below with Strauss's specifically existentialist reading of Weber. Cf. Heinrich Rickert, "Max Webers Stellung zur Wissenschaft," *Logos*, Vol. 15:1926, pp. 222-237. On a more general sense in which Weber is a philosopher, cf. NRH, p. 76.

hermeneutic.[4] Depending upon how esoteric Strauss is thought to be, his critique might, to some degree, mask a substantial measure of agreement with Weber. Perhaps Strauss criticizes Weber less for his alleged relativism and nihilism than for his unreserved publicity of those sad insights.[5] *Natural Right and History* is a convoluted and inconclusive book.[6] Perhaps it, in its totality, and Strauss, in the totality of his works, arrive at no more ultimate a foundation than Weber's apparent formulation of a radical and unresolved pluralism of ultimate values, of com-

---

[4] For some of Strauss's own statements about the centrality of esotericism in philosophical expression, cf. especially Leo Strauss, *Persecution and the Art of Writing* (Westport, Conn.: Greenwood Press, 1952). Perhaps the most radical reading of Strauss as an esoteric writer is Shadia Drury's *The Political Ideas of Leo Strauss* (New York: St. Martin's Press, 1988). Drury sees Strauss as a Nietzschean for whom natural right establishes only the superiority of the *übermenschlich* philosopher to dominate, at least covertly, the human herd. Any implications of the natural right tradition for justice are subsidiary to that tradition's alleged authorization of the philosopher's will to power. For sharp critiques of Drury, cf. Robert Pippin, "The Modern World of Leo Strauss," and Jurgen Gephardt, "Leo Strauss: The Quest for Truth," in Peter Graf Kielsmansegg et al, *Hannah Arendt and Leo Strauss: German Emigres and American Political Thought After World War II* (Cambridge: Cambridge Univeristy Press, 1995).

[5] Cf. Drury, *The Political Ideas of Leo Strauss*, p. 123. On her view, Strauss vigorously criticizes Machiavelli less for what he says than for his less than esoteric way of saying it. The betrayal of esotericism is tantamount to the abandonment of natural right. Insofar as natural right reveals the conventionalistic character of the "truths" by which humans live, that is, insofar as it reveals that every social order is sustained by salutary fictions, its disclosure fundamentally threatens society and the philosopher's place within it. If the philosopher does not veil his insight he imperils himself and his fellow citizens. Removing the veil therefore indicates, if not a suicidal bent, a misplaced faith in the reason of the many. It assumes that the many can live with the abysmal truth, that is, it assumes that the many can be philosophers. Philosophers are, however, precisely those men whose superior nature (i.e., they are superior by nature) distinguishes them from the many. The betrayal of esotericism from Machiavelli on is a theme in Strauss's overall critique of modernity. Cf. "Introduction" in Leo Strauss, *The Rebirth of Classical Political Rationalism*, Thomas Pangle, ed. (Chicago: University of Chicago Press, 1989), pp. XXIff.

[6] An attempt to read *NRH* as a partly esoteric work whose significance is, to a degree, disclosed by its structure is Richard H. Kennington's "Strauss's Natural Right and History," in Alan Udoff, ed. *Leo Strauss's Thought: Toward a Critical Engagement* (Boulder, CO: Lynne Rienner, 1991), pp. 231-33.

peting gods and demons.[7] However this may be, it is at least
clear that Strauss does try to undo or, minimally, to criticize
historicism from within—no naïve return to the ancients is
possible—and therefore, Strauss perforce shares some common
premises with Weber.[8]

At least on the surface, Strauss rejects Weber's putative
nihilism in the name of natural right. But I shall argue that
Strauss, who may, after all, share in this nihilism, had a deeper
argument with Weber. Strauss sees Weber, albeit in a highly
ironic way, as a "religious" thinker. Strauss's problem is not only
or primarily that, *pace* Weber, values lack foundation, but that
the only source of authentic values is, for Weber, religious

---

[7] One of Strauss's thrusts against historicism and therefore against the alleged
impossibility of philosophy as knowledge about the eternal things runs: "In
particular, the 'experience of history' does not make doubtful the view that the
fundamental problems, such as the problems of justice, persist or retain their
identity in all historical change, however much they may be obscured by the
temporary denial of their relevance and however variable or provisional all human
solutions to these problems may be. In grasping these problems as problems, the
human mind liberates itself from its historical limitations. No more is needed to
legitimize philosophy in its original, Socratic sense: philosophy is knowledge
that one does not know; that is to say, it is knowledge of what one does not
know or awareness of the fundamental problems and, therewith, of the
**fundamental alternatives regarding their solution that are coeval with
human thought**" (*NRH*, p. 32, emphasis added): Strauss's essential skepticism,
his Kantian predilection for sketching out the logical conditions for the possibility
of a view rather than substantive argument in favor of a view, his acquiescence—
e.g., in the above citation—in a minimalistic possibility of philosophy as
knowledge of enduring, fundamental (and perhaps irreconcilable) alternatives
all strongly echo Weber. The theme of ultimate conflict between competing
fundamental alternatives is particularly strong in Weber.
[8] *NRH*, p. 33. Cf. also Gadamer's comments in Hans-George Gadamer, *Truth and
Method*, Joel Weinsheimer and Donald G. Marshall, trans. (New York: Continuum,
1994), pp. 532-41. Strauss distinguished between the scholar and the philosopher
(Pangle, ed., p.29). Historical scholarship, in Strauss's sense, provides a way back
into the world of "natural understanding," that is, into the conditions within which
the fundamental philosophical problems appeared to the great philosophers of
antiquity. We need to regain the "cave" of natural understanding; that is, to regain
a politically situated point of view on the perennial problems. To do so we need,
minimally, to understand the great thinkers as they understood themselves. Cf.
Jurgen Gephardt, in *Hannah Arendt and Leo Strauss*, pp. 98-102. This insistence on
a Verstehen–based hermeneutic which exposes the coherent rationality of a unique
historical subject as a goal of scholarship is certainly shared by Max Weber. As we
shall see, Weber, like Strauss, advocates an understanding that frees us from our
own subjective, historically conditioned preoccupations.

consciousness.[9] Weber, although personally faithless, stands as a man of faith in the sense of an apologist for faith. It is his longing, no less than the nihilism that accompanies it, which Strauss rejects.

On Weber's side, one must ask what was the range and point of his commitment to the fact/value distinction, with its implication of the foundationlessness of values. Is it justifiable to expand this methodological observation into a comprehensive Weltanschauung, as Strauss does? Was Weber, in fact, an existentialist in Strauss's precise sense of the term ("existentialism is a reaction of serious men to their own relativism")?[10]

Let us first explore the problem of the fact/value distinction and its implication that values lack foundation. Strauss's critique of the "nihilistic" Weber is the culmination of an attack on historicism. Strauss distinguishes two types of historicism: a naïve historicism, which he calls conventionalism, and the radical, philosophically-informed historicism of modernity.[11] Conventionalism claims that there can be no natural, immanent standard of right because history is, if the anachronism may be excused, "multicultural." History presents us with infinitely diverse and mutable conceptions of justice. Yet Strauss claims that, far from defeating the quest for natural right, this awareness of an open-ended pluralism is the basic condition, the incentive, for the emergence of the quest.[12]

Conventionalism, which is after all the classical, sophist position, is distinguished from modern historicism in that conventionalism, like its ancient opponent, Platonism, assumes that, in the face of diversity, the fundamental distinction is still that of *nomos* and *physis*. It holds that *physis* continues to have a higher dignity than human custom but that right cannot be located there. Right belongs only to custom: justice is a matter of human agreements with no natural, meta-conventional basis. Modern historicism, by contrast, rejects both Platonism's and

---

[9] For a representative citation see Weber's "Science as a Vocation," in H.H. Gerth and C. Wright Mills, trans. and eds., *From Max Weber: Essays in Sociology* (New York: Oxford University Press, 1978), p.155.

[10] Pangle, ed. *Classical Political Rationalism*, p. 36.

[11] Kennington, "Strauss's Natural Right and History," p. 233

[12] *NRH*, p. 10.

conventionalism's ascription of normativity to nature. The distinction between nature and custom loses its fundamental status or, at least, its fundamental point: Nature is not the source of norms. Human creativity, based on freedom, is itself the source of norms. But insofar as this free, creative "world-construction" activity takes place within history, it can never rise to a vantage point beyond history. It can never leave the Platonic cave. Philosophy, as the attempt to rise above opinion and ascertain truth, is not possible. The attempt to achieve knowledge of eternal things, of a world beyond the cave, must be viewed as delusion or myth. There are no eternal things to be grasped or, more minimally, there is no way of grasping them.

Strauss tells us that historicism did not emerge full blown in this form. Historicism has, of course, a history. It begins, as is generally acknowledged, in reaction to the natural right teaching of the eighteenth century that informed the revolutionary movements. Against a teaching that elevated the self-evidence of universal individual rights as an endowment of nature, historicism founded norms upon the historical experience, the ancient conventions, of distinct, unique *Volker*.[13] It was local, parochial customs and practices, not abstract "rights" that made human beings at home in the universe. Yet in arguing against absolute, inviolable norms of natural right, 18th and early 19th century historicism did not understand itself in as existentialist or nihilist a way as its radical successor did. Early historicism continued to live under the "protecting atmosphere" of religious and metaphysical beliefs.[14] Thinkers such as Herder held that history was a benevolent process, guided by Providence. The particular values of Englishmen or Germans may differ, but they all come from an ultimate divine source. Diversity is the veil of providential harmony. The 19th century German "Historical School" replaced divine Providence with the State and its destiny as the leitmotif of history, but a faith in the moral purposiveness

---

[13] *NRH*, p. 16. For a more conventional history of the historicist movement that parallels Strauss's in significant ways, cf. George Iggers, *The German Conception of History* (Middletown, CT: Wesleyan University Press, 1968), esp. chapter 2.

[14] *NRH*, p. 26.

and meaningfulness of history remained.[15] Beliefs such as these, which Weber in the name of "value free" social science eventually rejected, mitigated the nihilistic force implicit in historicism's basic denial of natural right.

But historicism became its own undoing. The metaphysical and religious assumptions which sheltered it at its origins both collapsed from within and failed to withstand the growing positivism of the 19th century. Internally, its grandiose assump tions were ill-suited to historicism's own inherent commitment to a critical, empirical study of the past. Critical study of history shows only what persons and cultures believed. It does not and cannot show whether their beliefs were valid. Nor can any empirical study demonstrate the validity of the metaphysical or moral assumptions about Providence or the State which historicists from Humboldt, Ranke and Droysen to Rickert continued to hold.[16]

Externally, historicism's response to a natural science-inspired positivism was to strengthen its own claim to scientific status on the basis of a renewed methodology. Historicism had always rejected a conception of history as lawful in a mechanistic way. History had to do with freedom, with unique individualities and unrepeatable events. By the late 19th century, historicism increasingly invested in *Verstehen*, the "sympathetic under-standing" of historical agents, as its unique contribution to science. Now, with no universal standards remaining, with no approach to other minds than a non-judgmental empathy possible, historicism could discover no reason why the human actors and cultures it studied held the values they did other than sheer willfulness alone. *Verstehen* allowed one to appreciate the commitment of other ages and agents to their values. It allowed one to study how others rationalized this commitment, but it did not permit one to engage the other's reasons as reasons. Reasoning could only become rationalization. Having denied that persons hold values because they can base themselves on meta-historical, rational standards, historicism could find no reason for holding values other than a leap of faith.

---

[15] Iggers, *The German Conception of History*, p. 36.
[16] Ibid., chap. 6.

> To the unbiased historian, "the historical process" revealed itself as the meaningless web spun by what men did, produced and thought, no more than by unmitigated chance—a tale told by an idiot. The historical standard, the standards thrown up by this meaningless process, could no longer claim to be hallowed by sacred powers behind that process. The only standards that remained were of a purely subjective character, standards that have no other support than the free choice of the individual. No objective criterion henceforth allowed the distinction between good and bad choices. Historicism culminated in nihilism.[17]

By "nihilism," Strauss does not mean indifference to values nor does he mean skepticism about values. Skepticism is coeval with human thought as such. Skepticism is impressed by our uncertainty, by the irrefragibility of our ignorance. Historicism, by contrast, claims that knowledge of history is possible, that we can determine what actually took place and why. Its goal was to understand events "wie es eigentlich gewesen." Nor is historicism skeptical about the possibility of absolute moral truth or natural right. It is certain that there are no such things. It is certain that philosophy, in a Platonic sense, is impossible.[18]

The certainties of historicism generate a contradiction which occasions its nihilism. Historicism claims that all knowledge and belief are dependent on and relative to the historical situation. Yet historicism exempts its own root conviction from this judgment. Its own conviction of the historical nature of all truth is, it believes, an absolute, metahistorically valid insight. Even though this conviction was produced at a certain point in the historical process, in the history of historicism, it is a final truth. If a future age were to abandon this truth—a possibility no historicist could deny—it would not render the truth untrue. It would simply represent the descent back into delusion.

Strauss argues that historicism copes with this contradiction by seeing its own final truth not as an achievement of a self-transcending theoretical reason, but as a deliverance of fate, the fortuitous disclosure of an absolute moment.

---

[17] *NRH*, p. 18.
[18] Ibid, p. 20.

> The final and irrevocable insight into the historical
> character of all thought would transcend history only if that
> insight were accessible to man as man and hence, in principle,
> at all times; but it does not transcend history if it essentially
> belongs to a specific historic situation.[19]

The decisive insight of historicism was uncovered at a given time as an "unforeseeable gift of unfathomable fate."[20] That is, with all clarity, thought has now come to realize its own absolute dependence upon fate. That is the content of the historicist revelation: there is no thought that transcends fate. This is not a theoretical insight that needs to be defended by rational argument, thus embroiling historicism in a logical contradiction. Rather, this is a revelation of Being: the historicist has turned from reason to Being, abandoning a belief in the intelligibility of reality for a radical participation within it. Ultimately, the historicist must show a "contempt for reasonableness and [a] praise of resoluteness."[21]

Human beings are fated to be born into cognitive and moral frameworks, relative to their historical situation, which they had no part in choosing. We are "thrown" into this circumstance of framework relativism. We cannot see anything without a framework, yet the very framework by which we see conditions and limits our sight. And as history shows us, there are innumerable frameworks, each as legitimate as any other. Yet fatalism, Strauss implies, is not determinism. While fate has fixed our circumstance and our options, a thin sliver of choice is left to us. Within the limits of our thrownness, we can, indeed, we must choose a framework and truly make it our own. Yet there is, ultimately, no rational guidance for this choice.

> Our choice has no support but itself; it is not supported
> by any objective or theoretical certainty; it is separated from
> nothingness, the complete absence of meaning by nothing
> but our choice of it. Strictly speaking, we cannot choose

---

[19] *NRH*, p. 28.
[20] Ibid.
[21] Pangle, p. 30. The harvest of historicism, Strauss strongly implies without explicit statement, is Heidegger. Cf. Kennington, p. 235.

among different views. A single comprehensive view is imposed on us by fate: the horizon within which all our understanding and orientation take place is produced by the fate of the individual or of his society...Yet the support of the horizon produced by fate is ultimately the choice of the individual, since that fate has to be accepted by the individual. We are free in the sense that we are free either to choose in anguish the world view and the standards imposed on us by fate or else to lose ourselves in illusory security or in despair.[22]

Having to choose on the basis of nothing constitutes nihilism, in Strauss's terms. Nihilism signifies, therefore, the impossibility of philosophy; the impossibility of the quest, on the basis of reason alone, for a rightly guided life.

If reason alone cannot guide us, then a serious life requires a meta-rational form of guidance. For centuries, this has been provided by revelation. Revelation, like existentialism, denies, albeit non-nihilistically, the possibility or, more precisely, the necessity of philosophy as the "one thing needful." Strauss's early work on Spinoza and Maimonides was predominantly concerned with rejoining the debate between philosophy and "orthodoxy" on its original footing.[23] He discovered that, contrary to our modernist prejudice, philosophy, in its Enlightenment

---

[22] *NRH*, p. 27.

[23] E.M. Sinclair, trans., *Spinoza's Critique of Religion* (New York: Schocken, 1965); Fred Baumann, trans. *Philosophy and Law* (Philadelphia: Jewish Publication Society, 1987). Revelation does not deny the possibility of philosophy, nor is it obligated to. Indeed, revelation qua holy Law in Judaism and Islam can even afford to authorize the pursuit of philosophy as the quest for scientific knowledge of God's world. Philosophy, far from being a scandal for revelation, is legally grounded by revelation, according to Strauss. But can genuine philosophy accept such authorization? For philosophy to be permitted by revelation assumes the priority of revelation over philosophy, thus robbing philosophy of its own sense of radical sufficiency. If philosophy "cannot refute the possibility of revelation [then it] is fatal to the rationality of the choice of philosophy" (Kennington, p. 238). Revelation constitutes a permanent scandal insofar as it robs philosophy of its self-understanding as the one thing necessary for a rightly guided life. Cf. *NRH*, p. 75. While the early Strauss seems still to have been moved by a religious project to revisit the debate, he later shifted ground. The possibility of a return to Socratic philosophizing as a way of overcoming the Enlightenment removed the urgency of overcoming the Enlightenment from the point of view of revelation. Cf. Kennington, ibid.

form, did not win the debate. It mocked and derided orthodoxy, but it did not defeat it. The Enlightenment was able to argue for the unknowability of miracles, but not for their impossibility. Neither was it able to establish the absolute truth of atheism. Insofar as the Enlightenment could not overcome the possibility of an omnipotent God, it could not exclude the possibility of miracles or of revelation. God was not yet dead, because we had not quite killed Him.

Strauss turns to Weber, as suggested above, for the forcefulness of his nihilism. Weber stands, in Strauss's demonology, as the classic statement of the foundationlessness of all values. But there is also this additional dimension: although Weber's task is ostensibly that of the methodologist and sociologist of religion, his language always gives away a deeper struggle: "Follow God or the Devil as you will, but, whichever choice you make, make it with all your heart, with all your soul, and with all your power."[24] On Strauss's reading, Weber locates himself at the center of the old struggle between reason and revelation. Weber's thesis that there is ultimate, irresolvable conflict between values, that no hierarchy or harmoni zation of values is possible, revisits the conflict between reason and revelation in a secular mode. Why?

Weber, like existentialist nihilism, denies that reason can arrive at natural right, i.e., that philosophy can achieve insight into a rightly guided life:

> The fate of an epoch which has eaten of the tree of knowledge is that it must know that we cannot learn the *meaning* of the world from the results of its analysis, be it ever so perfect; it must rather be in a position to create this meaning itself. It must recognize that general views of life and the universe can never be the products of increasing empirical knowledge, and that the highest ideals, which move us most forcefully, are always formed only in the struggle with other ideals, which are just as sacred to others as ours are to us.[25]

---

[24] Quoted in *NRH*, p. 45.
[25] Max Weber, *The Methodology of the Social Sciences*, Edward A. Shils and Henry A. Finch, trans. and eds. (New York: Free Press, 1949), p. 57.

Reason attains only to clarity about the ultimate, insoluble conflict between values which are themselves created by assertions of human will. Yet our ideals are nonetheless "sacred" to us. They have their source in the experience of the sacred known to demagogues and mystagogues. In the West, these experiences have been formalized as prophecy and revelation. Prophetic charisma channels experience into socially usable ideas and ideals. Weber is studiously agnostic toward whether such experiences are genuine, but, his non-reductionist stance notwithstanding, he clearly believes that revelation and prophecy have become, as a consequence of our "disenchanted" modernity, unavailable to us. Their light reaches us, in the night of modernity, like the light of long dead stars. Weber's Protestant upbringing and sociological research led him to the belief that all values and ideals originate in religious consciousness. Yet, it is precisely this that modern men and women of science recognize as foundationless, i.e., as products of "mere" consciousness, rather than as the authentic communication of a god.[26]   Having excluded the possibility of reason as the source of norms, and having emptied faith of its substance (but not its social function) Weber is left with nothing but the hollow, self-destroying rationality of nihilism. Weber thus becomes a (most ironic) protagonist of revelation for Strauss. Strauss's critique of Weber is a philosophical critique of the claims of revelation, formulated, surprisingly, by an opponent who has no faith in the revelation he despairingly thinks is necessary. Strauss attacks Weber, therefore, not only for his nihilist modernism, but for his ostensibly "traditional" advocacy of the necessity of orthodoxy!

Strauss's view that Weber is a "religious" thinker emerges in his consideration of Weber's conviction that there is an ultimate, insoluble conflict between values. We have already seen that Weber thinks we cannot rise above our foundationless value commitments. How does he reach this view? Weber was con-

---

[26] *NRH*, p. 70. Weber's belief that religion is the ultimate source of ethical values is evident, for example, in the following: "Only positive religions—or more precisely expressed—dogmatically bound sects are able to confer on the content of cultural values the status of unconditionally valid ethical imperatives" (Max Weber, *Methodology of the Social Sciences*, p. 57).

vinced that individuals alone make history and confer significance on facts and actions. Weber belongs to the crisis of
historicism. His insistence on value-free inquiry derives from
his realization that the German Historical School indulged a
number of metaphysical, value-charged assumptions that are,
from a scientific point of view, illicit. In addition to providence
and its secularization, historicism believed in the integral character of nations, the existence of Volk-minds and the general
intelligibility of history. Weber reacted to these grandiose but
gratuitous assumptions sharply, contending that the historically
real is always individual.[27]   Historicism erred in deriving the
individual from an alleged whole, a Volksgeist, for example. But
if only individuals are real, then there are no mysterious forces
moving them. The only meaning history has is the meaning
individuals ascribe to it. And individuals are evidently motivated by irreducibly plural and conflicting ideals. Yet Weber, no
less than Strauss, rejects naïve conventionalism. Weber does not
think that the difference of views between individuals or cultures proves the subjectivism of views.[28]

Strauss advances two interpretations of Weber's "insolubility
thesis." The first is that Weber's position is entailed by his tragic
view of life. Weber is impressed by the constant tension between
ethics and politics: an effective political actor must often incur
moral guilt. The insolubility thesis is "a part, or a consequence"
of the comprehensive view according to which human life is
essentially an inescapable conflict."[29]   If the conflict were
avoidable, guilt need not be incurred. But the conflict is
unavoidable and even the best of politicians outrages ethics and
incurs guilt. No hierarchy, synthesis or harmonization of values
is possible. Values are all at the same rank.

We are unable to rank values, because no point of view
external to our situation, that is, no perspective on the whole, is
available which would allow us to adjudicate among ultimate

---

[27] NRH, p. 37.
[28] By subjectivism, Weber seems to mean privacy or inconsequentiality. At
any rate, the multiplicity of values is more than a numeral matter of diverse
cultures. Max Weber, The Methodology of the Social Sciences, p. 12.
[29] NRH, p. 65.

values. It is possible to say, for example, within our current situation that sexual love within marriage occupies a higher rank than prostitution. But from the point of view of radical asceticism, sexuality per se must be rejected. Perhaps prostitution is even to be preferred because it makes no moralistic apology for what it is. From Weber's point of view, there is no way of adjudicating between the ideals of sexual love vs. asceticism.[30] A conflict of gods and demons prevails. Human dignity is defined by the probity with which we confront the irresolvability of our situation. A shallow life is one where probity is evaded and conflict avoided. But the man of dignity accepts this conflict as his own. The war of value against value in the world cannot be denied its place within the microcosm of one's own soul.

Strauss's second interpretation considers the insuperable conflict, for Weber, within ethics as such. As all students of Weber know, he distinguished between the ethic of absolute ends (*Gesinnungsethik*) and the ethic of responsibility (*Verantwortungsethik*).[31] That Kant would have us speak the truth to a would-be murderer in hot pursuit of his victim, demanding that we tell him where the victim is hiding rather than lie, is an example of the former. The *Gesinnungsethiker* understands himself to be possessed of a truth close to its source in revelation. It is a truth that resists rationalization and disenchantment: it scorns adjustment to the ways of this world. It refuses to justify itself by its consequences. Its inherent rightness is its only criterion. This sort of other-worldly orientation toward moral purity Weber finds completely unfit for this-worldly decision-making, particularly in politics. Yet *Gesinnungsethik* cannot be denied its dignity or place, nor can it be refuted by a more consequentialist, teleological orientation. "One cannot prescribe to anyone whether he should follow an ethic of absolute ends or an ethic of responsibility, or when the one and when the other."[32]

Weber is a "religious" thinker, in Strauss's view, insofar as he finds in *Gesinnungsethik* the purest articulation of values and insofar as an ethic of absolute ends has its source in revelation.

---

[30] *NRH*, p. 63.
[31] Cf. e.g., "Politics as a Vocation," pp.116ff.
[32] Gerth and Mills, *From Max Weber*, p. 127.

Those who import a *Gesinnungsethik* into politics in our times are demagogues, secular prophets of revelation-like ideologies.[33] Yet how does Strauss explain Weber's clear rejection of the ethic of absolute ends for the ethic responsibility? Since Strauss has argued that values lack both foundation and rank for Weber, he must deprive Weber of any rational basis for his preference. "[W]hat he said about the moral commands is not much more than the residue of a moral tradition in which he grew up and which, indeed, never ceased to determine him as a human being."[34] Weber's "preference" is either an artifact of his upbringing, that is, a product of fate or the result of an irrational leap of faith, a resolute commitment for commitment's sake.[35] It matters little whether Weber arrives at his view through submission to fate or sacrifice of intellect, that is, whether Weber is primarily a nihilist or a "theologian." In either case, he rejects the possibility of reason alone penetrating the foundation of values and ordering them by rank.

Strauss is surely accurate and justified in much of his critique. Whether one agrees or disagrees with Strauss that natural right is possible or desirable, his analysis of Weber's thesis that values are both foundationless and in insoluble conflict remains

---

[33] In Weber's usage, "demagogue" is not a pejorative term. In his *Ancient Judaism* and his *Sociology of Religion*, he routinely refers to the prophets as demagogues. What separates religious demagogues from secular-political ones is the former's willingness to endure the consequences of their absolute commitments, e.g., Jesus's unconcern with the consequences of his renunciation of wealth. The *Gesinnungsethiker* who brings "ultimate concerns" into politics, by contrast, inevitably compromises his own absolutism. Salvaging absolutism through rationalization further corrupts the *Gesinnungsethiker*. Cf. ibid., p. 122. Weber's criterion for distinguishing the "true" prophet from the mere demagogue is thus eminently moral. Whether Weber believed in the possibility of genuine or authentic revelation as a more substantive criterion is hard to determine. He practiced a methodological agnosticism and refused to speculate about the ultimate source of prophetic charisma.

[34] *NRH*, p. 43, cf. also p. 48.

[35] Strauss argues that, given Weber's thesis on value, the value of science must perforce be culture-bound and relative. To orient oneself toward knowledge therefore requires a leap of faith: cultivation of intellect demands the sacrifice of intellect. "He tried to remain faithful to the cause of autonomous insight, but he despaired when he felt that the sacrifice of the intellect, which is abhorred by science or philosophy, is at the bottom of science or philosophy" (*NRH*, p. 76).

penetrating and profound. Weber did not understand himself to be a relativist, largely because he did not see himself as a philosopher. He restricted his inquiry to the methodological problems of the social sciences.[36] But Strauss does not let him get away with this evasion. He simply follows Weber's assumptions all the way down in good, unrelenting Weberian fashion. In this he is not alone. All serious students of Weber have found in his methodology a substantial philosophical position. Even his friend Rickert dismisses Weber's own protestations and portrays him as an old-fashioned Socratic, prizing conceptual clarity as the highest good.

In my view, however, while it is fair to read Weber as a philosopher, it is unfair to dismiss Weber's own rejections of the charge of relativism. Strauss fails to do justice to Weber's deep-seated moralism, which, I would argue, informs his theoretical no less than his practical political purposes. A normative agenda orients Weber's project, providing a "protective atmosphere" which tempered his own perception of the threat of relativism.

Why does Strauss misjudge Weber's normative orientation? Arguably, Strauss underestimates the moral purpose lying behind the fact/value distinction in the first place. Strauss believes Weber to hold prima facie that an unbridgeable gap divides fact from value and that, therefore, values arise as assertions of the human will rather than as consequences of the nature of things. But then Strauss shows how Weber's work routinely violates its own canon of ethical neutrality (*Wertfreiheit*). Weber cannot simply attend to the facts; in order to analyse and explain the value-laden phenomena of social life on their own terms, as he is committed to doing, he must make evaluations of his own. From this, Strauss draws two conclusions. The first is that Weber is seriously incoherent. The second is that the fact/value distinction must not be as fundamental for Weber as it first seems.

> The true reason why Weber insisted on the ethically neutral character of social science as well as of social philosophy was, then, not his belief in the fundamental opposition of the Is and the Ought but his belief that there cannot be any

---

[36] Rickert, "Max Weber's Stellung zur Wissenschaft," pp. 230-31

genuine knowledge of the Ought. He denied to man any science, empirical or rational, any knowledge, scientific or philosophic, of the true value system: the true value system does not exist; there is a variety of values which are of the same rank, whose demands conflict with one another and whose conflict cannot be solved by human reason. Social science or social philosophy can do no more than clarify that conflict and all it implications; the solution has to be let to the free, non-rational decision of each individual.[37]

Strauss claims that Weber rejects a logical or categorical opposition between fact and value in favor of an agnosticism toward knowledge of true value. Strauss therefore tells us to disregard the significance of the fact/value distinction for Weber. But rather than following his own advice and leaving the distinction alone, he continues to write as if it were crucial for Weber. Much of Strauss's critique is devoted to showing how extensively Weber engages in evaluation, thus contradicting his own rule. Is Weber really so naïve or confused? Perhaps the incoherence is more on Strauss's side than Weber's. I would argue that Strauss misrepresents, to a degree, the point of Weber's distinction in the first place; Weber never considered the opposition between fact and value to be so categorical.

While interpreters such as Rickert refer to the "deep gap" (immer eine tiefe Kluft) between understanding and evaluation, fact and value, Weber himself spoke of the distinction as a "hairline."[38] Weber is less interested in "facts" and "values" per se, than he is interested in the processes by which they are discerned, evoked and measured. That is, "fact" and "value" indicate for Weber the practices of scientific understanding (*Verstehen*) and evaluative judgment. Weber, therefore, saw the distinction in normative, pragmatic terms rather than logical, categorical ones. As one active in both politics and science, Weber was concerned to bring the fruits of social science to politicians and policy makers. He was equally concerned to keep science free of partisan pressures. He neither wanted universities to discriminate,

---

[37] *NRH*, pp.41–42.
[38] Rickert, ibid., p. 230. Weber, *The Methodology of the Social Sciences*, p. 110.

in hiring, for example, against candidates of politically unpopular personal views, nor did he want any professor to play the prophet or demagogue from the lectern. These positions, powerfully expressed in his "Science as a Vocation," reveal the normative context for the fact/value distinction: That distinction arises not from an abstract consideration of concepts or linguistic usage, but from participation in the worlds of science and politics, of theoretical knowing and practical judging as distinct, yet related activities. The act of distinguishing between fact and value is a value–oriented action. There is, therefore, a normative dimension inherent in the distinction. Weber treats the distinction not as an ethically neutral observation about the nature of reality, but as indicative of a task, a duty.

If we understand the fact/value distinction in purely logical terms, it suggests that we can simply bracket out our own values and attend to the facts qua facts. Our value-laden starting point is an embarrassment to the pure knowledge of the facts and their causal relationships which we hope to achieve. Strauss returns again and again to the value-ladenness of Weberian method in order to embarrass him. But far from seeing our own value-laden presuppositions, Weber embraces them gladly. There is no presupposition less knowing for him. Our value-orientation allows us to understand culture—the human conferral of meaning and significance on some portion of the infinite, meaningless world-process—as a human thing. When we analyze the social reality of an historical group, we, as beings seeking the significance of some portion of reality, reach out to beings who have constructed a significant, intelligible world. It is our interest in meaning which alone opens us to the historically embedded meanings that constitute culture.[39] Social facts always conceal values. Or to put it more precisely, social values become facts for the researcher. Weber is only incoherent if the fact/value distinction is a logical or categorical one. If, however, he uses the distinction to make another kind of point, he is neither embarrassed nor incoherent.

The Weberian tool for *Verstehen* is the ideal type. Ideal types are internally consistent models of the values significant to the

---

[39] Weber, ibid., p. 78.

subjects under study. As models of value, ideal types represent the orienting presuppositions of cultures in purer form than they are likely to actually occur. One abstracts from the thought and life of a Christian group, for example, to find what the ideal type of "Christianity" meant to them. How did they orient their conduct in terms of this ideal? Ideal types are, therefore, not only " models of" but "models for" in Clifford Geertz's sense.[40] They not only crystallize some configuration of values, they are also templates for action.

Ideal types are conceptual links which allow the social scientist to enter into the mentality of the historical subject. Weber is empathetic, however, that ideal types are no more and no less than conceptual tools. They are not pure inductions which correspond in some positivistic way to discrete events in the world. Weber views the ideal type as Kant views the categories. They are means by which the understanding creatively masters and structures the data of experience in order to create intelligibility. Weber's hermeneutic approach to scientific knowledge anticipates the paradigm theory of Thomas Kuhn:

> But these concepts are shown to be obviously in-
> appropriate as schema into which reality could be completely
> *integrated*. For none of those systems of ideas, which are
> absolutely indispensable in the understanding of those
> segments of reality which are meaningful at a particular
> moment, can exhaust its infinite richness. They are all attempts,
> on the basis of the present state or our knowledge and the
> available conceptual patterns, to bring order into the chaos of
> those facts which we have drawn into the field circumscribed
> by our *interest*. The intellectual apparatus which the past has
> developed through the analysis, or more truthfully, the
> analytical rearrangement of the immediately given reality, and
> through the latter's integration by concepts which correspond
> to the state of its knowledge and the focus of its interest, is in
> constant tension with the new knowledge which we can and
> *desire* to wrest from reality. The progress of cultural science
> occurs through this conflict.[41]

---

[40] Clifford Geertz, "Religion as a Cultural System," in his *The Interpretation of Cultures* (New York: Basic Books, 1973), p. 93.
[41] Weber, The Methodology of the Social Sciences, p. 105.

The ideal type is a product of the researcher's will and imagination. It captures not only, to continue the above example, what some subjects thought Christianity was, but also what the researcher isolates as enduringly interesting and valuable in Christianity. Thus the user of ideal types runs a calculated risk. He must do his homework and try to grasp what and how his subjects thought, but he cannot altogether exclude how he thinks.[42] The line between fact and value, understanding and evaluation is a "hair-line."

Presuppositions are therefore not an embarrassment. Our presuppositions accompany us every step of the way. Our task is to become acutely aware of our own inevitable tendency toward evaluation. We can neither indulge it, nor banish it. Weber's approach is to try to channel our propensity toward evaluative judgment into judgment of a certain sort: the researcher must determine whether his subjects acted in a manner consistent with their own values. Did the subjects live up to the ideal implicit in the ideal type? This sort of judgment, Weber believed, minimized the importation of our contemporary, "foreign" values into the world of our subjects. On the other hand, it does *judge* the data by a criterion of rational consistency. Weber did not believe that we can avoid judgment altogether, nor did he believe that we could only judge on the basis of standards which emerge "from the subject matter itself."[43]

The sort of judgment he was after aimed at a balance of understanding and critique. To achieve such judgment, the researcher must practice "the elementary duty of scientific self-control."[44] The fact/value distinction, in my view, derives its significance from the duty of scientific self-control. Comprehensive understanding requires a refined kind of evaluation. We must forbear from imposing some but not all of our judgment

---

[42] Ibid., p. 98.
[43] Ibid. Weber writes contemptuously of the "modern relativistically educated historian who on the one hand seeks to 'understand' the epoch of which he speaks 'in its own terms' and on the other still seeks to 'judge'it, [and who] feels the need to derive the standards for his judgment from the subject matter itself…"
[44] Ibid, p. 98.

on the data. The attainment of such understanding is a normative ideal. This ideal is not unattainable or illusory, but it does require *agon*. And the *agon* is driven by desire: the desire to achieve clarity. Rational, that is, communicable clarity, shared with the community of researchers, is the product of the struggle. When clarity is achieved, objectivity is achieved. The thin edge of objectivity obtrudes from the thick wedge of desire, interest and private judgment which supports it.

This observation does not undermine Strauss's contention that values ultimately lack ontological foundation for Weber. But it does suggest why Weber did not view the problem of his own thought in as dire a manner as Strauss. Weber saw the opposition of fact and value, and therefore the non-factual basis of value, under the aegis of a normative program, suffused by a value orientation. He was able to reject the charge of relativism because the point of his fact/value distinction was not to claim that values lack foundation, but that certain values ought to prevail in the conduct of science and that we have a duty to orient our scientific conduct toward those values. It is of course true that Weber is unwilling to embed this conviction in an argument that the life of science is the highest form of life, the life authorized by nature, that is, the life that is naturally right.

If the foregoing observations are correct, then it makes more sense to view Weber as a moral thinker than as a "religious" one. This casts some doubt on Weber's alleged existentialism or nihilism. Since Weber did not view himself as a relativist, his work was not a reaction of a "serious man to his own relativism." Weber's work was, rather, the response of a serious man to the relativism of his times. *Verantwortungsethik*, the centerpiece of Weber's essays on politics and science as vocations, is presented as the most reasonable moral orientation for an age in which reasonable persons ought to be wary of political and religious certainties. For all of Weber's theoretical interest in extreme, sectarian positions, politically and morally he eschewed extremes. He found the religious and romantic absolutism of *Gesinnungsethik* subversive of civil society. Civil society requires the moderation of righteous passion and the promotion of a sober consequentialism. On the other hand, Weber recognized that politics is made with both the head and the heart. He saw some integration of the two types of ethic as the human ideal.[45]

Strauss's depiction of Weber as both a "religious" and a nihilistic thinker surely captures important dimensions of Weber's work. But it just as surely distorts the vibrant and activist moralism that underlies that work. Perhaps Strauss undervalues this ethical dimension because he sees Weber retrospectively through the lens of Heidegger to too great a degree. Or perhaps Strauss has simply responded to Weber's own failure to give a more foundational account of his deeply held moral convictions.

---

[45] "[A]n ethic of ultimate ends and an ethic of responsibility are not absolute contrasts but rather supplements, which only in unison constitute a genuine man..." in "Politics as a Vocation," p. 127.

23

Preachers and Professors on Jews and Judaism: A Look at the Second and Twentieth Centuries

Robert S. MacLennan

I. The Anti-Jewish and Anti-Judaism Use of the New Testament by Modern Scholars and Preachers

1. Introduction

The theological anti-Judaism and the cultural- social anti-Jewish USE of the New Testament in Christian scholarship **and preaching** did not disappear in the last decade of the twentieth century. In the second century of the common era Christian writers on Jews and Judaism such as Tertullian (*Answer to the Jews*, 196 C.E.), Barnabas (*Epistle*, 117 C.E.), Justin (*Dialogue with Trypho the Jew*, 160 C.E.), and Melito (*Pascha Homily*, 180 C.E.) introduced anti-Jewish ideas that still permeate modern scholarship in the University and the Church. Scholars and preachers in the last decade of the twentieth century still perpetuated hostility toward Jews and Judaism through their putative scholarly and thoughtful writings, lectures and sermons. It seems that little has changed even though we are living in the post-Holocaust age.

This anti-Jewish and anti-Judaism use of the New Testament in theological and homiletical works can be found in the subtle and not so subtle writings of Christian scholars and preachers throughout the Americas and Europe today.

Professor William Johnson has always insisted that scholars and preachers learn from each other as they do their work in the University and Church. In his chair of Philosophy, Judaism and Christianity at Brandeis University and other colleges and universities in the United States and Europe, as well as from the pulpits of his various parishes, Dr. Johnson has inspired many to never forget the connections between work in the University and the Church. He has given us an example of good scholarship and excellence in the pulpit by working in both places at the same time. I have benefitted from his friendship and scholarly example.

Yet, as I have investigated the topic I wish to discuss in this chapter, I have discovered that sometimes both Church and University do not benefit from each other and may even perpetuate bad habits. The subject of this essay is an example of that. Anti-Judaism and anti-Jewish teachings have flourished in both institutions and have occasionally come to the aid of each other in creating a climate of hostility toward Jews in Western culture that has prevailed since the second century of the common era.

There are reasons why anti-Judaism and anti-Jewish attitudes in the University and Church exist today. To get at those reasons I have looked at the use made of the New Testament in general and one text in particular. The text is Mathew 27:25, a notoriously useful verse for those who would look for a biblical basis for demeaning Jews and Judaism. In the second part of this chapter I will introduce a second century preacher's view of Israel. Melito of Sardis is credited with being the source of anti-Judaism in Christian scholarship and preaching. In each section I will draw some conclusions and make suggestions for getting beyond this anti-Jewish quagmire in scholarship and preaching.

2. The Shift in the Scholarly Understanding
of Jews and Judaism of Late Antiquity

As a preacher, teacher and scholar who has worked in the church and the scholarly guild since the 1950's, I am aware that there has been a shift in the way Christian scholars and serious students speak about Jews and Judaism as they are found in the New Testament. It is also clear that this shift has not affected many contemporary preachers, teachers and scholars of the New Testament here in the Americas and Europe.

The dramatic shift has come in our understanding of Jews and Judaism during the development of Christianity and Judaism in the first three centuries of the common era.

With the discoveries of the *Dead Sea Scrolls*, the *Nag Hammadi* library, and renewed interest in the study of rabbinic literature, so-called *Old Testament Apocrypha,* and *Old Testament Pseudepigrapha,* and the works of Philo and Josephus, our understanding of Jews, Judaism and Christianity has changed. The change is that we now realize that both Judaism and Christianity are more complex in their origins and trajectory. No longer can we talk about monolithic Judaism or Christianity with a straight line of development from Moses to Jesus and beyond.

Now we have evidence from archaeology and new literary discoveries (*Dead Sea Scrolls, Nag Hammadi* texts, work in the *Pseudepigrapha,* and the *Apocrypha*) that demonstrate a more complex picture of this development in the Eastern Roman Empire and the Persian world of late antiquity. Now we know that Christianity and Judaism emerged out of a similar context in Palestine and emerged into several kinds of Judaisms and Christianities. So instead of talking about a monolithic form of Judaism or Christianity, we now must study the various forms of Judaism and Christianity. We now think in terms of Judaisms and Christianities.

There is also more evidence from Israel in general and Galilee in particular that suggests that the world Jesus lived and taught in was far more diverse and urban than we previously knew [see

J.A. Overman, "Recent Advances in the Archaeology of the Galilee in the Roman Period," *Currents in Research I* (1993), pp. 33-57]. Galilee was under Roman rule during and after Jesus' time, and as an occupied region, the Galilee had its own set of social, economic, religious and political problems, not the least of which was sectarian tensions between various groups of Jews.

Some of the writings of the New Testament and especially the Gospels reflect these conflicts of Jews with each other. Matthew presents us with vivid examples of this struggle. Matthew wrote about Jesus and his disciples, but he composed his story after the destruction of the Temple in Jerusalem in 70 C.E. In his story, Matthew reflects on the social and political tensions and sectarian struggles of Galilee in the late first century.

Although scholars and preachers benefit from this information about the writer and his times and are able to understand the formative Judaism and emerging Christianity reflected in this writing, there is still a gap between these insights and what is actually taught in seminaries, churches and the universities. Respected teachers and scholars continue to perpetuate an anti-Judaism, anti-Jewish, and anti-Semitic teaching, preaching and writing.

To illustrate what I mean we can look at one well known and misappropriated verse in Matthew and read what commentators still say about it. The verse is Matthew 27:25.

3. Interpreting Matthew 27:25 in an Anti-Jewish Way

I have suggested that Matthew 27:25 is often used by scholars and preachers to support an anti-Jewish, anti-Judaism, and anti-Semitic program in the University and Church. The text reads as follows:

> *(24) So when Pilate saw that he could do nothing, but rather that a riot was beginning, he took some water and washed his hands before the crowd, saying, "I am innocent of this man's blood; see to it yourself." (25) **The people as a whole answered, "His blood be on us and on our children!"** (26) So he released Barabbas for them; and after flogging Jesus, he handed him over to be crucified"* *[NRSV, 1991].*

Most commentators from the second century to the present use Matthew 27:25 to support the idea that Jews brought the pain and suffering they have endured through the centuries on themselves. The reason for their plight may suggest that they have killed their Messiah and have committed *Deicide*: the killing of God. Matthew 27:25 is a way that many commentators justify their anti-Jewish tirades. Jewish suffering throughout history is often viewed as self-inflicted.

Modern commentators may not be so obvious in the way they point the finger at Jews, but they do indulge in the same reasoning, even though it is much more subtle. There are several ways in which modern commentators perpetuate the myth that Jews bring suffering on themselves.

First, the text is viewed as a theological statement and the historical or social conditions of the community to whom the text was written are not taken seriously. An example of this is found in the recent commentary by Douglas Hare, a seminary professor, who has contributed some helpful insights on Matthew in the commentary series, *Interpretation: A Bible Commentary for Teaching and Preaching* (1993). But in his comments on Matthew 27:25 he writes:

> *In any event, it is theologically important to the Evangelists to transfer as much responsibility as possible from Pilate to the Jewish leaders.* Matthew contributes to this ongoing project by adding several verses to the narrative he receives from Mark 15:6-15... Pilate announces to the crowd, "I am innocent of this man's blood... It is your responsibility!" (v.24, NEV). In verse 25 this responsibility is willingly accepted by "the people as a whole" (correctly translated by the NRSV). Again this is "theological" rather than a historical note. Matthew does not mean merely "the whole crowd" (TEV) that happened to be present; in that case he would have used his favorite expression, "the crowds" (see v. 20). For him, *laos* ("People") is a term reserved for Israel, *God's special people in the old dispensation (see 2.6). Israel as a whole assumes the guilt of Jesus' death with the ominous declaration, "His blood be on us and on our children!" (v.25).*

This statement and the ones that follow may sound positive toward Jews and Judaism, yet they actually have a theologically anti-Jewish and anti-Judaism edge to them. The commentary continues:

> Since this text has been so sinfully misused in Christian history by those who cried "Christ killers!" and murdered and pillaged as "avengers of Christ's death," it is imperative that we **understand Matthew's intention.** *He surely does not mean the words as a self-curse, as if Israel were collectively declaring: "We acknowledge that we are accursed murderers and that all our descendants should be treated as murderers."* **This statement gives voice rather to the theological conviction that Israel as a whole has rejected its Messiah in a final and definitive way and in consequence deserves to be deselected as God's special people.** *Understood in this way, verse 25 is to be viewed less as an attack on Jews as an apologetic for the Gentile mission and* **for the church in which Gentiles now predominate** *(cf. 21.43). Nevertheless the "left hand" of this apologetic is inevitably polemical.* **Matthew's anti-Judaism** [emphasis mine] *must be countered with the more positive appreciation of God's irrevocable relationship to Israel articulated by* Paul *in Romans 11." (317-318).* [This is a bit anachronistic, since Matthew was written in 85 and Paul in 60 something].

Hare suggests that Matthew is speaking theologically and as such is anti-Jewish. By turning Matthew into a theologian, Hare seems to dismiss the fact that the writer of Matthew was a Jew speaking with Jews in the Galilee during a particularly difficult time for his own people there. The social and political realities caused Jews living in late first century Galilee to be in conflict with each other. Matthew was not speaking theologically, but politically and socially. Hare seems not to take these conditions seriously in his interpretation of Matthew 27:25 and so presents an anti-Jewish case and uses the mouth of Matthew to do so.

Here we read more about Hare's view of Jews and Judaism than we read Matthew's view. It is Hare who translates the Greek word for *people,* **laos,** as "God's special people in the old dispensation, Israel as a whole assumes the guilt of Jesus' death..." Matthew is not so explicit. I wonder how Matthew would translate **laos**? Hare's comments on *laos* are not simply a translation of a Greek word. He is making his own theological comments about Jews and Judaism: they are "God's people in the old dispensation."

Hare also gives his view of Israel when he suggests that Matthew 27:25 is a statement that "...gives voice rather to the theological conviction that Israel as a whole has rejected its Messiah in a final and definitive way and in consequence deserves to be deselected as God's special people." Where does Hare get this interpretation, if not out of his own conceptions and understanding of Jews and Judaism?

Another way commentators use Matthew 27:25 in an anti-Judaism and anti-Jewish way is to suggest that this verse highlights the struggle between Jews and Christians.

Again, Hare's reasoning suggests that on one side of the struggle are Jesus and the church, and on the other side are **the** Jews, the enemy of Jesus, Christians and the church (see Hare, p. 318). This dichotomy appears in many Protestant and Catholic commentaries on the New Testament.

In the *New Century Bible Commentary* (1972) on Matthew, for example, David Hill writes:

> *Verse 25b may be understood, from Matthew's point of view, as a prophecy of the judgment which will fall on **the** Jews in the future, by reason of their rejection of the Messiah (p. 351).*

Who are **the** Jews in this account? And who are the ones who have accepted Jesus as the Messiah? This suggests a way of viewing Jews and Christians as two different groups. One will be judged as a "messiah rejecting people" and the others as a people who chose to follow Jesus as the Messiah of God. It is interesting to note that often when categorizing or generalizing about Jews in scholarly writings it is always preceded by the definite article, as in *the* Jews.

Even in Daniel Harrington's excellent commentary on Matthew in the *Sacra Pagina Series* (*Matthew* 1991, pp. 392, 393) we read the following about the Jews:

> *... Matthew [in 27:25] meant more than the small group of Jews who gathered around Pilate's judgement seat at Passover time in A.D. 30. That **group** fulfilled a representative function vis-à-vis*

> **Jesus and the Christian Community.** Harrington continues,
> *"Given Matthew's concern for Christian identity within Judaism,*
> *it seems likely that for him 'all the people' represented **the Jewish***
> *opponents of **the Church**...Why have not all (indeed most) Jews*
> *accepted the gospel?...Matthew 27.11-26 (especially 27.25) is*
> *a major text in the history and present reality of Christian-Jewish*
> *relations."*

It seems that "Christian identity within Judaism" is more Harrington's concern than Matthew's. It is not clear that Matthew is concerned about "**all (indeed most) Jews**"; rather the main point of Matthew's gospel when it relates to the opponents of Jesus and the disciples is referring to the specific group of Scribes and Pharisees. It is important to find out who they are and what they represent in Matthew's context in upper Galilee in the latter part of the first century.

Even though Harrington goes on to give some very helpful comments about the work of preachers and teachers in making sure that they do not blame Jews today and to see the earliest conflicts recorded in Matthew as an inner Jewish one (393), the overall effect is still to perpetuate the idea of a conflict between Jews and Christians. He continues to talk about *the* Jews and *the* Christians, as if this is what Matthew wanted to convey. Clearly, Matthew is not building a case for Christians against Jews. It would be anachronistic to say that Matthew was defending a developed form of Christianity or even the church.

Eduard Schweizer's commentary on Matthew (*The Good News According to Matthew,* translated by David E. Green, John Knox Press, Atlanta, 1975) is clearly describing a conflict between Jews and Christians when he writes:

> *Now, however, **the people of God's** own covenant call on him*
> *to bring judgment down upon them, so terrible is their blindness...*
> *The only thing that makes the verse defensible is Matthew's repeated*
> *warning to **the Christian community** not to go the same way...*
> *he takes quite seriously the possibility that **the Christian***
> *community, too, could fall victim to God's Judgement...*(pg. 509).

This statement is typical of the way many scholars treat the New Testament writings. Jews and Christians, these commentators suggest, are in conflict with each other, with the New Testament being a record of that conflict.

Further, the not so subtle reference to a *blind people* (the Jews) is reminiscent of years of anti-Jewish rhetoric in the church, an anti-Judaism that is captured by the central doors of the Notre Dame Cathedral in Paris. There one can see the statue of the blindfolded synagogue in the form of a woman, standing with a broken staff in her hand, while confident lady church stands with an unbroken staff in her hand.

Dale Bruner, a college professor, wrote a commentary (*The Churchbook,* 1990) on Matthew that is unapologetically in praise of "the words of God, seeking to learn what concerns the Creator of us all" (xii). He is not subtle, but states many times throughout his commentary the idea that Matthew is defending Christians against Jews. He writes on Matthew 27:25:

> *Matthew's Jesus thus turns at the end of the Gospel toward the main enemies of the Church* (808)... *Matthew means this as Israel's self-indictment* (1033)... *This verse gives Matthew's aetiology of Israel's demise, put in a scene; here Israel makes its formal decision not to be the people of God anymore... [the destruction of Jerusalem in 70] was God's judgement on his Messiah-rejecting people in A.D. 30. Matthew did not mean that the suffering of all future Jews is traceable to this day's deed* (1033).

Bruner continues:

> *In all evangelism of the Jewish people we must be sure to apologize...* (1034).

I find it difficult to understand how anyone can be so sure about what "Matthew means" about "Israel's self-indictment." It is not clear that Matthew knows that Israel has made a "formal decision not to be the people of God anymore." But it does seem clear that Bruner views the text and the self-understanding of Israel that way. I am not sure what we have to apologize for on behalf of Matthew, instead it seems more appropriate to apologize for the way we have read and used Matthew's writings against Jews and Judaism.

The older *International Critical Commentary* series (Allen, 1957, p. 232) suggests that Matthew uses the Greek word *ethnos* [often translated "Gentiles" or "Nations"] to mean "the conception of the Christian society," as if the author of Matthew already in the late first century knew of a "Christian society." This is an anachronistic way of thinking about Matthew at the very least, but Allen's comments also show how Christian commentators perpetuate a "we-they" view of Jews against Christians or visa versa. Both Bruner and Allen characterize the anti-Jewish, anti-Judaism and anti-Semitic teaching of the Church.

Further, D. Hill (1972, p. 351), in his commentary on Matthew in the *New Century Commentary,* and E. Schweizer in his 1975 (509) commentary on Matthew both assume the separation between Jews and Christians. It is interesting that they can make this distinction because Matthew does not use either the word Jew or Christian to designate the groups that are in conflict in his gospel.

Probably the most obviously blatant form of anti-Jewish and anti-Judaism commentary on Matthew 27:25 comes from a well-meaning statement by Dr. Bruner in his commentary on Matthew where he suggests that:

> **We know** [emphasis mine] *that the Holy Spirit wants this verse to be interpreted only in the limited, historical sense that Israel's rejection of her Messiah meant Israel's rejection of her first century safety. For it is a historical fact that when Israel chose the Zealot-liberation option of her leader ("Barabbas"!) and sought to overthrow Rome in 66 A.D., when she rejected the teaching of the other Jesus, she dug her own grave...[and on and on]* (vol II, 1034).

Again, how can anyone be clear about what the Holy Spirit wants? In this statement by Bruner we read more about the twentieth century view of Jews and Judaism than we do of Matthew's view of them.

Finally, some scholars have tried to suggest that the way around the anti-Jewish or anti-Judaism use of the New Testament is to suggest that the writings of the New Testament itself are full of anti-Jewish sentiments. Some refer to Paul, as J. Becker does in his *Paul, the Apostle to the Gentile,* Westminster Press, 1993, p.

33: Paul "*divides his life into two halves on the basis of his calling, and the Christian Paul has almost entirely disposed of the Jewish period of his life... the Jewish portion of his life is seen as dark background and as harshly drawn contrast to the beginning of his second, real life*" as their evidence for dismissing Judaism or that Jewish portion or *dark background* of their life. In claiming that the New Testament is itself an anti-Jewish book, they do not deal with the sectarian nature of the New Testament writings. But the fact is that the New Testament is a Jewish book. No one ever suggests that the Jewish *Dead Sea Scrolls* are anti-Jewish or anti-Semitic. Everyone has accepted the fact that they are Jewish sectarian writings.

Hare writes: "Matthew's anti-Judaism must be countered..." (318). In this phrase Hare echoes a pervasive problem among scholars of the Bible. Like Hare, many commentaries suggest that it is our job to counter the anti-Judaism in the text. This seems to suggest that we are actually encountering self-hating Jews among the New Testament writers.

4. Conclusion and Suggestions

A way out of the quagmire of an anti-Jewish or anti-Judaism use of Matthew 27:25 and the rest of the New Testament might be facilitated by looking at this Jewish book from a different perspective and context.

For example, in commenting on Matthew 27:25 we must first of all acknowledge that the debates between Jesus and his opponents, as presented in Matthew's gospel, are not unique to Matthew or Jesus but were part of the social, political, and economic turmoil of first century Israel. Many groups resented and rejected Jewish leadership during this period, so the debates and hostilities that we find in Matthew are typical of certain groups who were feeling betrayed to the Roman occupiers by their brothers and sisters. As J.A. Overman observes in *Matthew's Gospel and Formative Judaism* (Fortress, 1990): "*Certain disturbing and offensive passages within Matthew, such as 21.43; 27:25; or chapter 23 must first of all be read and interpreted in terms of his wider setting and horizon of the sectarian nature of Judaism*" *(151).*

A footnote (n. 3, 151) in Overman's book is worth quoting in full:

> *Concerning 27.25 particularly, this is a typical accusation by sectarian communities. A common means of discrediting the leadership is accusing them of shedding "innocent" or "righteous" blood. . . Matthew, like other sectarians, also tries to implicate these leaders in the death of other righteous persons in Israel's history. . . Note also concerning 27.25 the striking parallels in 1 Sam. 26.9 and 2 Sam. 1.16. Both of these are the words of David, who declares that the guilt (I Sam 26.9) or the blood (2 Sam 1.16) is upon the head of the one who "kills the Lord's Christ." To my knowledge the connection here has not been explored. These explanations and the wider context in which this disturbing passage must be placed in no way excuse or explain the unfortunate abuses and history associated with this verse.*

The difference here is that Overman is using the material and literary evidence of first century Galilee to understand Matthew's statements. Matthew is seen as a leader of a community that lived in a particular time and place and held certain assumptions about the world. Some of those views were compatible with his fellow Jews in Galilee, some were not. Those who disagreed were the named opponents.

Further, an appropriate interpretation of Matthew 27:25 makes no attempt to see this statement as a way of describing a putative conflict between Christianity and Judaism. There is no mention in Matthew of what the Holy Spirit or God wants or wanted, but only an examination of what the text tells us about the tensions that exist between members of formative or sectarian Jewish movements. This way of looking at the text makes all the difference in the way one understands what is being conveyed by the author. In other words, it is possible to read Matthew 27:25 as a text discussing the struggles of a particular community at a particular time and place, and not as theological or confessional document that is trying to show the superiority of Christianity or Judaism, even in the first century.

It is instructive too, as Overman points out, that the literature we might read in order to understand something of Matthew's community and point of view would not be "articulated by

Paul in Romans 11" (Hare, 318) or "Luke 19.41-44" (Bruner, 1034), but 4 Ezra (late first century), 2 Baruch (early second century) I Enoch (second century B.C.E. to first century C.E.) and the Psalms of Solomon (first century B.C.E.). In this pseudepigraphal literature the sectarian movements are well articulated and thus the modern reader can get an idea of the issues and struggles of the first century sectarian Jewish communities.

When we place Matthew 27:25 in the context of its own time, place and circumstance, we then read the text as a typical sectarian writing that conveys the tension of late first century occupied Galilee. In doing this we then stand within the context of an intra-Jewish struggle and not an anti-Jewish polemic. This leads us to conclude that any anti-Jewish or anti-Judaism use of Matthew 27:25 is mostly in the mind and passions of the scholar and not the text itself.

II. A Second Century Source for the Anti-Jewish Use of the New Testament: Melito's Sermon

1. Introducton

One source for the anti-Jewish and anti-Judaism use of the New Testament in modern scholarship may be traced to Melito of Sardis, a second century preacher whose anti-Judaism grew out of his struggle for the emergence of a Christian community in Sardis. Melito's sermons add another dimension to our understanding of how anti-Jewish and anti-Judaism attitudes and actions first emerged. Jon Levenson, in his essay "Is there a Counterpoint in the Hebrew Bible to the New Testament Antisemitism?" [*Journal of Ecumenical Studies,* 22.3 (Spring 1985): 245], wrote:

> *There is a tragicomical irony here, that a tradition which sets such great store on love and reconciliation should have canonized literature, in part, from a situation of hatred and strife. However,*

*read against their historical context, the New Testament documents exemplify a truism of human nature: We are rarely generous with our competitors, especially when the competitors have **prima facie** first claim upon the status to which we aspire. If we are to replace them, we had better show that they deserve to be replaced, and, if we dare not boast that we are better than they, then let us at least portray them as worse than we.*

I do not agree with Jon Levenson's analysis that the New Testament portrays "our competitors" as "worse than we" since, as I have said above in the Matthew sections, the New Testament is about an intra-Jewish or a Jewish sectarian struggle and are not anti-Jewish. But I do agree with Levenson's notion that we try to replace our competitors by attempting to demean them. Melito of Sardis tries to diminish the importance of Jews in Sardis through his passionate and eloquent rhetorical poem on the Passover by demonstrating that Israel's history is the history of failure. Melito is actually the first Christian preacher who introduces the idea that Israel killed God.

In the last two decades of the second century, Melito of Sardis, known as the Bishop of Sardis (Eusebius, *Ecclesiastical History—HE, LCL I*, 4.26.1), a eunuch caught up in the Holy Spirit (*HE*, 5.34.2-6) and a prophet (Jerome, *De viris illustribus*-PL 23.678), wrote a sermon in masterful rhetorical style known as *Peri Pascha*, that caused one scholar, Eric Werner (Werner, "Melito of Sardes, The First Poet of Deicide," *HUCA*, 37,1966), to describe Melito as the first poet of deicide. In fact, Werner viewed Melito, Bishop of Sardis, as the source for the theological concept of deicide and the main source, *fons et origo*, of the theological concepts and the anti-Jewish writings that would follow him in the church (Werner, 199).

What is important about *Peri Pascha* is that it is an early, second century example of a view of Jews and Judaism (although, Melito avoids using the word Jews and Judaism throughout his poem, he substitutes Israel) that has persisted to the present time. Melito's message in the poem, which follows Jon Levenson's view of what a competitor does, is that Israel has given up her position as the people of God to the Church. And, if that were not terrible enough, Israel has murdred Jesus "in the middle of Jerusalem" (72; 79.565; 93.692) and essentially *murdered God* (*PP*, 96.715). These words have influenced Eastern and Western Christian writers throughout the history of the Church.

But, I am not sure that simply by saying that Melito is the *fons et origio,* the source for the anti-Jewish and anti-Judaism concepts in the church, we get at the problem behind Christian theological thinking and emotions against Jews and Judaism. We have to ask what is in what he says and thinks that has become so endemic in Christian scholarship and preaching to the present.

2. Melito as a Preacher to an Emerging Church

Melito, as a preacher and, according to Eusebius, the Bishop of Sardis (around 166), and one of the great luminaries of Asia, a eunuch, "*who lived entirely in the Holy Spirit, who lies in Sardis, waiting for the visitation from heaven when he will rise from the dead* ..."(*HE* 5.23.5), greatly influenced not only his own community but the whole of the emerging Church. One of the most avid supporters of Melito was the well known John Chrysostom, who also demeaned the Jews through his writings and preaching.

Melito lived in the city of Sardis which today is a well known archaeological site of late antiquity (G. M. A. Hanfmann, *Sardis from Prehistoric to Roman Times,* Harvard, 1983). It boasts a large synagogue that occupied the center of the city and was attached to the Roman bath there. Sardis was a prominent city in western Asia Minor (see S. Mitchell, *Anatolia* II, Oxford, Clarendon Press, 32ff, for a description of Jewish communities in Anatolia and Sardis). Archaeologists have confirmed over the last ten years that Jews in Sardis were intimately involved in the life of the city during the time Melito wrote his *Peri Pascha.* This is a very significant fact to remember as we read the *Peri Pascha.* In the homily Melito talks about the ancestors of the people who occupied a prominent position in his town where he was reputed to be the Bishop.

We know from Melito that he left Sardis for a while and visited Palestine (*Melito of Sardis, On Pascha and Fragments,* Trans, S. Hall, Oxford, Clarendon Press, 67, *Fragment*):

> *I was zealous to do such a thing, recognizing your zeal for the faith and studious application to the word, and that you prefer these things more than any in your love to God, as you strive for eternal salvation. So, going back to the east and reaching the place where it was proclaimed and done, I got precise information about the books of the Old Covenant, of which I now send you a list* (HE 4.26.3-4). [Here follows the earliest list of Old Testament books.]

Melito's visit was probably the first visit of a western pilgrim to the east, "*the place where it was proclaimed and done* . . . ," which is an early paradigm for what the *land of Israel* was to become for Christians throughout the centuries. It is a land of pilgrimage and the source of the Christian traditions. It has *become* the Holy Land for the Church. As the *new* Israel the church claimed property rights on their land. The Church, according to Melito, had replaced the *old* Israel in Palestine. This actually took place in the later Roman period (after 325). The *competitor*, as Levenson suggests, was being replaced in his own land.

This visit to the land where the gospel was first preached was used by Melito to establish his authority. It is amazing what a trip will do to establish one's credibility when he returns home. Melito used this visit to establish his authority with his followers (and perhaps, in his mind, among the putative venerable Jewish community) in Sardis. Obviously, if he could have a first hand experience of the "land" and recover the essential texts of the "Old Covenant" and establish what those texts are (Melito's list of OT books nearly agrees with the canon fixed at Yavneh between 70 and 100 C.E.), he would be able to build his arguments against his competitors in Sardis, as he saw it, on much more substantial grounds.

3. The sermon against Israel: Peri Pascha

The *Peri Pascha* is a 105 stanza poem about the history of Israel beginning with the Exodus. In these verses Melito carefully establishes that fact that Israel, the competitor with the emerging church, was a failure:

> *The scriptures from the Hebrew Exodus had been read*
> *and the words of the mystery have been plainly stated,*

> how the sheep is sacrificed
> and how the people is saved
> and how Pharaoh is scourged through the mystery,
> Understand, therefore, beloved,
>   how it is new and old . . . (1-2.7)

He continues:

> *The people [Israel] then was a model by way of preliminary sketch,*
> *and the law was the writing of a parable;*
>   *the gospel is the recounting and fulfillment of the law,*
> *and the church is the repository of the reality (40).*

And failure:

> *It is he that has been murdered.*
> *And where has he been murdered? In the middle of Jerusalem.*
> *By whom? By Israel (72).*

> *O lawless Israel, what is this unprecedented crime you committed,*
> *thrusting your Lord among undprecedented sufferings . . . (81).*

After reviewing the archaeological evidence for second century Sardis, it is possible to surmise that Melito wrote what he did about Jews in Sardis to a church that was probably overwhelmed by the venerable Jewish community there. No wonder Melito wrote with such passion. He was probably trying to keep his people from leaving the Church and becoming part of the more significant Jewish community. In other words, the evidence from archaeology and from the sermon itself suggests that Melito, like Chrysostom later in the fourth century, was concerned that his followers were not as loyal as they once might have been with what he was teaching. It is also possible that they were not clear about the difference between the Judaism of Sardis and the "Christianity" they were experiencing. The ritual life of Jews in Sardis may have been seen by the emerging church as plenty adequate for a person interested in scripture (which Melito called the "Old Covenant"). There was no New Testament at the time, even though Melito refers to a number of its writings.

The message of *PP* focuses on the issue of replacement; Israel is to be replaced by the Church. Israel has not done what he was supposed to do and has lost his part in the greater work of the gospel and, therefore, is to be replaced by the church.

> *The model then was precious before the reality,*
> *and the parable was marvelous before the interpretation;*
> *that is, the people was precious before the church arose,*
> *and the law was marvelous before the gospel was elucidated.*
> *But when the church arose*
> *and the gospel took precedence,*
> *the model was made void, concerning its power to the reality,*
> *and the law was fulfilled, concerning its power to the gospel.*
> *(41-42).*

4. Melito's Congregation: The Audience

Melito's congregation was a group of people who struggled with their own identity in the context of a well established and venerable community of Jews, Romans, Pagans and others. In this cosmopolitan and venerable mix it would have been difficult for those preaching the message of Jesus to get a hearing, not to mention a following. Therefore I suggest that Melito had to turn up the volume and the vehemence. It appears that when one looks at the social context of Melito's community that he wrote his *Peri Pascha* out of a sense of inferiority and inadequacy.

Further, Melito had to deal with the appeal of Judaism to his own people. His problem was that he was using texts that were also part of Israel's self-understanding and identity. Melito was arguing from the Hebrew canon that he called the "Old Testament." He uses those texts to develop a story about the inadequacy of his opponents. At one point in the poem (47) Melito goes back to the beginning (Genesis) to show how all history from the beginning pointed to *Christ* (65).

Melito certainly worked hard to show that Israel had been replaced. This still leaves us, though, with the question of what happened to the relation between Melito's people and the community of Jews in Sardis. Nothing is known about that relationship except possibly this little glimpse through the *Peri Pascha*. There is no record of a great church in Sardis. I would not think that Melito, Bishop of Sardis, would be a welcomed guest at the annual *Yom Kippur* service, nor would be asked to deliver his bible studies in the great hall of the central synagogue in Sardis . . . or would he? Perhaps they thought what he said was interesting and beautifully written, but weak. Little did they know the havoc his "weak argument" would cause throughout the history of the relations between Jews and Christians and others in Europe in the next two thousand years, as Christian preachers and teachers listened to and used Melito in their arguments against Jews and Judaism.

5. Conclusion and Suggestions

I conclude by restating the suggestion made by Jon Levenson about a truism of human nature that *"we are rarely generous with our competitors, especially when the competitors have prima facie first claim upon the status to which we aspire. If we replace them, we had better show that they deserve to be replaced, and, if we dare not boast that we are better than they, then let us at least portray them as worse than we."* Melito does this in his *Peri Pascha.*

I suggest that Melito and every non-Jewish commentator of the New Testament in and outside of the Church has tried to make Jews and Judaism look bad. But it is not necessary to continue this trend. There are ways to get beyond anti-Jewish and anti-Judaism use of the New Testament. One way is to see the New Testament as a Jewish book with a Jewish message and not an anti-Jewish tract.

Another important task is for us as preachers and teachers of the New Testament to read it as we read the *Dead Sea Scrolls* or any other Jewish sectarian literature of the first century. Reading it this way forces us to back off from the need to demean Jews and Judaism as a dead people and religion. It also prohibits us from viewing the history of Israel as one of failure to live up to God's way in this world. It is important to read the New Testament as literature that describes one of several first century Jewish communities struggling for its own identity.

Finally, if there are apologies to be given they are not for the New Testament views of Jews and Judaism, or for the struggles Jesus and his Jewish disciples were having with their fellow Jews, but they should be given by those scholars and preachers, in the University and Church, who use the New Testament in an anti-Judaism or anti-Jewish way. Perhaps one way the teaching of the New Testament would be best served is if it were taught in our university and college departments of classics and social history of religion.

24

Face to Face: Towards an Organic Jewish-Christian Dialogue

Michael Paley

And Jacob was left alone. And there wrestled with a man until the breaking of the dawn. And when he saw that he prevailed not against him, he touched the hollow of his thigh and the hollow of Jacob's thigh was strained as he wrestled with him. And Jacob was left alone. The word in Hebrew is *vayevahtar,* to be left alone, but not just alone, but to be abandoned without another. Alone in every fiber of your being. Who is Jacob at this moment? We are told he had just descended from the mountains of his father-in-law Laban, where he has become wealthy once again, but not without a sense of trickery and magic. He has left his family for the second time, under tense and difficult circumstances. He is on the edge of confronting his brother from whom he stole both birthright and blessing. Esau, the hunter, the first born, the strong man, the twin. Jacob, at a moment in which he cannot turn back to the past, is afraid of the future. He is alone between the times.

Suddenly a figure appears. A man wrestling him, hugging him, intertwining and knotting with him. They become one.

Jacob prevails and then as the dawn nears, he turns the man over and gazes into his face. There is a *midrash*, a rabbinic understanding, that says when Jacob turned the man to vanquish him, he saw his own face; the man bore the face of Jacob.

One evening, ten years ago, I walked up the hill in Hanover, where I was the Jewish Chaplain at Dartmouth College. It was a cold, damp November night, with a full moon beaming down. I was a bit late and a bit winded, and I breathed out heavily into the night. Suddenly, I saw on the vapor of my breath, my own face. I dissipated it and breathed it out again. It was not a clear picture, only an abstraction of who I was. I was alone, and yet there was another there with me. Jacob has discovered that to see the face of the other, he must see his own face first.

Jacob demands from this moment of encounter, a blessing. He has changed. He has become *Yisrael*, Israel, which means one who strives with God. He calls the place Peniel, and says, "For I have seen God face to face and my life is preserved." Jacob has now discovered that to see the face of God on the other he must first see the face of God on his own face. In the next verse, we are told that Jacob lifted up his eyes, and there was his own face. In the next verse, we are told that Jacob lifted up his eyes, and there was Esau, armed and strong and angry. As Esau ran toward him, Jacob looked at him in a new way. They embraced, knotted up, and became intertwined. They kissed and wept. What has happened? Jacob expected to be devoured but was embraced!? Esau expected that his moment of triumph over his twin had finally come, only to be disarmed by the new look on Jacob's face. Esau has discovered the face of God in Jacob's face and realized that he must bear the face of God as well.

We are told in Genesis that these two boys had struggled even within their mother's womb. Esau the red man, the cunning hunter, the man of the field. Jacob the plain man, the dweller in the tent. Here they are, grown with children, together again. The key moment is the wrestle. It is Jacob with himself. When he is alone, and agitated, he is able to catch for an eternal moment a glimpse of himself as other. He sees deeply into his own face, with its wounds, its strength, its hope and its dignity. When he crosses the river to meet his brother, he gazes upon his face and, for the first time, sees the family resemblance in his twin. They look alike. They are organically related. They have taken different paths, and neither path has succeeded completely. They embrace each other because they recognize the face of God on each other. After a long and difficult time, in that moment they are friends, at peace.

I am asked to speak on the Jewish-Christian dialogue endowment and "to foster new connections of knowledge and understanding between the Christian and Jewish faiths." I have been asked to speak at a complicated time of the year and at a complicated time of our history together. For most of the year, Jews and Christians spend their time in gentle ignorance of the liturgical calendar of the other. At Christmas time we certainly know what's going on. You catch our attention and we respond weakly. Let's admit it, Hanukkah was never much, and even eight nights of trying to buy off our children doesn't convince them.

But this time of year, the springtime, is the location of our festivals, of birth and rebirth, of liberation and redemption. It is these festivals of Passover and Easter that link us so closely together. Closer than siblings. So close that we can't escape the memory that long ago we were one. My question to you and to myself is that if we could truly have been one at that moment in history, if we could have sat around the table at the supper, whether it was the last supper of slavery or the last supper of corporeality, and seen the grace of God and the image of God on the faces of our family, can we recapture that? We have spent the last two thousand years working out the flaws in our respective stories, and much blood has been spilled because of those flaws. Can we, at this moment in history, hope to come together again?

My tradition spends this time of the year on its seven-week journey from redemption to revelation. It is an odd direction for a journey. One would certainly think that revelation would have come first. It makes more sense that if we stood at the foot of Mount Sinai and received the Torah, then we would proceed to carefully follow its prescriptions and laws until fulfillment and redemption were granted. Why does the tradition carefully count the 49 days, the Omer, between Passover and Shavuot (or Pentecost), when we recollect receiving the Torah? The reason for this counting is to underline that revelation—not redemption—is the ultimate human aim. Revelation cannot simply be Torah or Testament or Scripture. Revelation must be *our participation in revealing the presence of God in this world and on each other's face*. This is an important distinction. If it were redemption that was the end of all religious life, then we would, and we did, bicker about whose plan for that redemption is better and who is holding back the redemption from coming. Who is the Jonah among us that must be tossed overboard, so we can get on with it? If redemption is granted first, then the human journey to revelation is the great mission. Then we would have to look at each other and admit that none of us can do it alone, not Jacob, not Esau, and certainly not us.

I do not want to stand here and blink at the past. No self-respecting Rabbi can stand at the beginning of the twenty-first century, throw open his arms and say bygones are bygones, let's start fresh from here. Our seven-week journey from Passover to Shavuot contains two recent and one ancient holy days. The ancient one is Lag B'Omer, and it recalls the Roman persecutions of the Rabbis in the second and third centuries. The recent ones are Yom HaShoah, the Day of Holocaust Memorial, and Yom Ha-Atzmaut, Israeli Independence day. History, both old and new, intrudes on our meditation.

These images of destruction and regeneration are deeply rooted in the journey from Passover to Shavuot. We are commanded to count each night from the second night of Passover to the eve of Shavuot, 49 days—a week of weeks. Passover is the festival of love. When we sat at the edge of liberation with our loved ones, we ate together as families. In freedom, we were able to declare privacy and experience intimacy. On the Sabbath of Passover, we chant the romantic love poem, "The Song of Songs." On Shavuot, we stand at the fiery mountain. There is a Midrash that tells us that when we received the revelation, the mountain itself was uprooted and held over our heads. In the eighth chapter of "The Song of Songs," we find that "love is as strong as death is" (*The Song of Songs* 8:6). This part of the year has both. Jewish tradition tells us that on this journey we will observe seven circuits of weeks, like a bride in love, dancing around her groom at a Jewish wedding. But we are also constrained like mourners from public celebrations and joyous festivals. The movement from redemption to revelation is pressed between love and death. In the 21st century, both Christians and Jews experienced unprecedented periods of love and death. I believe these periods have pushed us to a new realm—a realm where we can see each other and see the face of God.

This is a complicated time of our history together. We have had a hard century. In our nation, we have seen the terror of families bereft of their children and on the news each night we are exposed to one killing field after another. It seems that this is the last moment to proclaim the possibility that we could reveal the presence of God and see the face of God on the other. But I am hopeful. My teacher, Rabbi Irving Greenberg, has taught the difference between hope and fantasy. Fantasy is a tale that you tell yourself to keep yourself going, but with no real hope that it will ever come true. In fact, it may be worse if it does come true. It's better planted in the safe spaces of the mind. Hope is the persistent belief and set of actions to make one's vision come to reality. I want to speak not of fantasy, but of hope, in Christian-Jewish dialogue. It may take an eon for that fulfillment, but one must truly believe it is possible, and plan toward that possibility.

For nearly two thousand years, Jews and Christians have been like Jacob and Esau. We have struggled over birthrights and blessings, and at dark moments, one did not even offer a pot of soup to the starving brother. In this century, relationships have changed. The Holocaust that annihilated Jews attacked not only Judaism, but the Bible, the Christian tradition and consciousness as well. It was a movement that tried to dissolve the relationship between humankind and God so that some mortals could proclaim themselves the kings of all kings. It was a pagan assault on the sacred. It ushered in a tear-filled awareness of what Abraham Joshua Heschel, paraphrasing John Donne, called, "No religion is an island." Religious communities affect and are affected by each other. This century has accomplished the global mentality, but it has also brought with it those that wanted to control that entire globe. Some, and only some in the religious communities in the post-Holocaust world, realized that all religions were becoming minorities, and that they would have to work together in an unprecedented way.

I believe that our story of Jacob and Esau contains the critical image. Our second reading from the Book of Numbers tells of the Gentile prophet Billam and his attempt to curse the children of Israel on their trek through the desert. He is told by God that he is not allowed to curse them and so as he gazes on their encampment, he says, "They are the people who dwell alone, they are not reckoned among the nations." The Jewish people, over the past millennia, have lived alone and in fear. They have as a community, although not as individuals, experienced the ethics of powerlessness. The ethics of powerlessness confront the perspective that power corrupts and absolute power corrupts absolutely. If that perspective is true, then the only moral alternative is powerlessness. The Jewish community has seen itself as the ever-dying people, the victims of history, chosen only to survive as a sign among the nations. But in the last fifty years, the Jewish community has changed radically. Powerlessness almost cost us our people. Even though it was a moral alternative, it was not an option for life. And so the Jewish community entered the realm of power, not just in the State of Israel, but also in America, the global economy, the Academy and elsewhere. The community made great strides and Jews were allowed and then even welcomed into the entire society. A Jewish boy from Brooklyn could even dream of becoming the Dean of St. Paul's Chapel of Columbia University, a position I was proud to hold for seven years!

There was another crucial change. Religious communities and society in general began to see themselves in separate pieces. No one was quite secure enough to claim their truth as the truth. Each community had to wrestle with itself and no community was spared. In the last fifty years, the Jewish community has lost the innocence of powerlessness. We have seen what it means to be a majority, to make decisions and to exert influence. We have truly become the powerful Jacob, with all of the twists and turns that brought him to that moment of meeting. We have breathed out heavily into the cold, and we have swiped at our own image. We have become startled by what we have seen. For all these centuries, we were sure we were different. We were the people who dwelled alone! Not reckoned among the nations; but now we saw our face, in the haze of the late twentieth century. The dawn came and the mist fell from before our eyes.

The Christian community has also had a hard century. As if the Enlightenment, secularism, fundamentalism, and ecumenicism weren't enough, now there are the Deconstructionists. When I was a graduate student, I studied Patristics, the works of the Church Fathers. This was a wonderful time for me because it was theologically stimulating and it provided an absolute treasure trove of nasty anti-Semitic quotations that I could mention in dialogue with my Christian colleagues. Graduate school was also the first time in my life that I studied closely with Christians. It was a spiritually delicate time for me and I experienced great inner conflict. At that time I was deeply supported by my Christian friends in two ways. First, they were very serious about God and one's personal relationship with God. This was at a time when you could barely raise the topic of God in the Jewish community. And second, they approached those Patristic texts with great candor and criticism. My teacher was the great Paul van Buren, and I found that he was courageous enough to explore every corner, to uproot assumptions and revisit fundamental questions of faith.

All religious struggle is private. Faith waxes and wanes in its strength, and exposing it to others endangers its enterprise. It is a long pursuit and it leaves you vulnerable. Belief in interfaith can become an easy substitute for one's own search. It is tempting to trade authenticity for compromise, and one needs a guide to help you persist. My teacher, The Rev. William Johnson, was my guide, and vigilant in his care for me. There was something about his Christian commitment to the impossible that allowed him to demand that I stay on my own path, while being challenged by his. One year he taught at Bryn Mawr College and I would travel out to see him and study modern Christian thought. After our study we would have a baseball catch. Johnson had been a real baseball player in the '50s. We would throw back and forth, my wobbly tosses and his pinpoint returns. Our catch turned us towards each other and we needed to trust the different ability of the other to deliver and receive if the level of our play was to work. As our combined but separated confidence grew, we fell into a more authentic rhythm. Finally, we achieved a level where we could give it all we had and still remain together. Aristotle, in the *Nicomachean Ethics*, Book IX, speaks of three levels of friendship. Friends of utility and pleasure are the two lower categories. The highest friendship is a friend who is committed to the good and who attracts you toward the good. The Rev. William Johnson encouraged me to give my spirituality all I had, while providing a firm and dependable foundation as the "other."

Growing up in a majority Christian culture, I had never imagined that Christians could feel alone and abandoned, like Christ on the cross. But I saw it, and I was changed by it. Some years later when I was at Columbia, a student came in to see me, and reported to me that she was off to Africa to work for the next two years in a refugee camp. "Why?" I asked, having pegged her for Wall Street. "Because I am a Christian, and my pastor told me that if I was lucky, I would have the chance to serve." As she turned to leave, I couldn't help but notice a hint of the divine clinging to her face.

For most of you, these images of Christianity are ones that you know. But most in the Jewish community have only rare access to Christians at the level of faith and action. It only occurs in late-night dormitory conversations or graduate student lounges, outside of structured conferences. In our generation, and only in our generation, this has begun to change. We have seen the Christian community, in public ways, search for its center. We have seen them struggle for words. As the Jewish community re-understood itself, it began to see the Christian community with more clarity. This is not a finished moment. There are many angry voices that cloud that understanding. And the temptation to turn back must be great. But there is a suspicion that turning back is to follow the example of the wife of Lot, who turned to salt as the price for her nostalgia.

And so at the beginning of the twenty-first century, we have both spent some time alone. And we have found out much about ourselves. We are stronger because we are less secure; we see that the world around us needs us both. We live at a time when the power of humankind is unprecedented. Our industrial plants can manufacture plagues to match those rained on Egypt, and our medical schools are edging towards the miracle of life and the revival of the dead. We are, as a species, feeling our power in the physical realm, without new images to temper them in the spiritual realm. It once might have been a true and appropriate dream that all humankind would celebrate together in one voice, with one language. But now, we must see that the plan of the divine is working itself out in such a way that many different images, stories, communities, traditions and memories are needed.

The French phenomenologist philosopher Emmanuel Levinas speaks of the image of the face. He says that gazing on the face of the other is the first ethical imperative. When I look at your face, I am changed from a being preoccupied by self, to a person responsible for the other. Years ago, I once sat in a meeting with Rev. Peter Gomes of Harvard. He was holding forth on one topic or another, when his comments turned to the Jews. I was the only Jew in a room of Christian ministers, and I was the youngest person there. He turned to me and fixed my eyes and spoke to me from his heart. I had every right to be intimidated and defensive. But his look was broad and true and responsible. Because of this look, I was able to respond with my whole being. I was changed by his look. We spoke back and forth for some time. It was a memorable occasion and we have been friends ever since.

Our friendship has a distinctive quality to it. My friend and I find ourselves on different sides of many of the issues of the day. There is very little chance that we could enter into a political coalition. It may be that this is why our dialogue works well. In the first stage of the Jewish-Christian dialogue, it was the Liberal political coalition that fueled the conversation. During

the Civil Rights Movement and the Vietnam war, Jewish and
Christian clergymen (I think they were all men), led by Abraham
Joshua Heschel, Martin Luther King, Jr. and his students, among
others, came together to confront the evils they saw in the society.
    Even the Second Vatican Council produced a theological
document, *Nostra Aetate*. Most of the collaborations were
political. There was a great need in America for the liberal
agenda to be articulated. And the religious community came
together to fulfill that mission. I only mention them to say that
that was the rallying point, the realm in which the conversation
was acted out.
    In a different way, we see the same phenomena at work
today. In November 1999, I stayed up through the night to
watch a political drama unfold. Around two or three in the
morning, New York Governor George Pataki stood to declare
his victory. Behind him was a curious array of religious leaders:
black-hatted ultra-Orthodox, a well-known New York Evangelist,
and some Catholic priests. They had come to cheer the success
of the new inter-religious coalition. This coalition supports
school vouchers, community control and other aspects of the
new Conservative agenda. I remember saying to myself that I
was hopeful that they had had a wonderful Jewish-Christian
dialogue on the status of the Divine law, or the impact of love in
the kingdom of God, but I don't think so. Real dialogue, the
sharing of hearts, is more difficult than political action projects,
but ultimately it is more significant and fruitful. This is not to
say that the religious voices are not critical in the public square,
or that I have given up hope in the Liberal agenda. I strongly
believe in community against the individualism that grows before
our very eyes, and I certainly still believe that taking care of and
serving "the least among you" is a religious obligation. But the
contribution of the religious communities speaking to each other
of learning how to share their voices, faith and imagination has
a higher goal.
    My hope is that our religious traditions can look at each
other in a new way, a way that preserves the separateness of
each, but engages openly enough to learn, and responsibly
enough to challenge. We must encounter each other pressed

between love and death with its risks and illuminations. We must teach each other with the intention that they learn about themselves rather than hope that they will become us. In this way, the traditions will move past simply acting together and approach the moment when their engagement with the "other" will reveal the presence of God in our world. This will produce a revelation, which we will find on each other's faces and will serve as a foundation for a new ethic in our spiritually hungry human society.

We must reenvision God as one who can hear many voices, and who wants us to develop the same capacity. This capacity will become, if we are sincere, critical, as we build this new foundation in a world where human power is expressed and can be abused. We must learn anew. We must learn what James Laney called "An Education of the Heart". Levinas observed that once you are able to see the face of God in the face of the other, you are never the same. Because once one sees the face of God in the face of the other, then one cannot escape the reality that revelation is not only possible, but commanding. But you cannot look lightly. We must learn to look with our whole being, with the ability to take the other's faith seriously. Can I *really* look across the table at my colleagues and feel and understand and be amazed by their religious commitments?

I do not think we have been able to do it before now. But I have hope of the revelation, not just a fantasy of it. The project of seeing the face of God in the other, of knowing that there are other realms to which we might aspire, and to know that even though it seems like a remote possibility, it could happen, is part of the great plan for humankind. It is a hope and not a fantasy because I believe that this enterprise was designed to last for millennia. And it was not a one generational leap. We have all become Jacob. We have all had time alone to conjure and dissipate our self-perceptions and false mirrored images.

Jacob was alone. And there he wrestled until the breaking of the dawn. And Jacob saw the face of God. And because he saw that face, he prevailed. And Esau, the hunter, came over the hill and saw Jacob anew. And they fell into each other's arms and kissed and wept. We are all Jacobs now. And we have had our time dwelling not among the nations. It is time to come back with intellect, imagination and commitment—to bring a new realm of meaning into this kingdom of God.

25

Can Christianity Shed Its Anti-Judaism?

by Krister Stendahl

For a Christian theologian, the issue of Christianity shedding anti-Judaism is a serious question—one infinitely intensified after the Holocaust. The record of anti-Judaism is clear and overwhelming and allows for no excuses. I shall not rehearse it here. Perhaps I could refer to Marc Saperstein's *Moments of Crisis in Jewish-Christian Relations*, which actually grew out of our joint seminars at Harvard Divinity School on "The Perception of the Other," a course I offered at Brandeis University.

Two things make the record of Christian anti-Judaism especially serious. While bigotry and hatred always exist as an underbrush, Christian contempt for the Jews in its most virulent form is found among some of the greatest figures of the Christian tradition: John Chrysostom, Augustine and—worst of them all, Martin Luther—from whom I have learned such great insights in other respects.

In a time when many churches have taken serious steps to face up to this record and make amends in thought and deed, the virus of anti-Judaism in Western secular culture plays havoc, unchecked by the theological critique that has begun in the churches. Ever since Voltaire, Christian anti-Judaism has been transmuted into "enlightened" secular contempt for the Jews.

How to account for this venomous tradition? How did it begin? What happened in the decades before and after the fall of Jerusalem's Second Temple in the first century of the Common Era?

These were years of great religious diversity among Palestinian Jews—not to speak about the Jewish Diaspora. The Dead Sea Scrolls have confirmed and sharpened our understanding of the wide spectrum of Jewish thought from intense apocalyptic expectations to the first steps of the consolidation of Judaism that becomes codified in the Mishnah, the central part of the Talmud.

Similar to the ethos of the Qumran community of the Dead Sea Scrolls, both the movement around John the Baptist and the ministry of Jesus from Nazareth were closer to the apocalyptic end of that spectrum—with the expectations of God's Kingdom, the Messianic Age, around the corner.

As a part of that wing of late Second Temple Judaism, Jesus spoke the musty language of an eschatological messenger, in the style of the prophets of old. It is in the teachings of Jesus, not of Paul, that we find the words about "Gnashing of teeth in hell" and "Ye brood of vipers," and heavy words about Satan and the Devil. Even so, his cutting and scathing critique of the foibles of his people and their leaders does not reach quite the decibels of some other groups. But the discussion is all within Judaism. As the prophets of old, their lambasting of the people is from within the people, identifying with Israel.

Think of the famous lament of Jesus over the city: "O Jerusalem, Jerusalem, killing the prophets and stoning those who are sent to you! How often would I have gathered your children together as a hen gathers her brood under her wings, and you would not! Behold, your house is forsaken and desolate" (Mt 23:37). It was spoken within and it was first heard within Israel, Jesus identifying with Israel in the spirit of the prophets.

But when Church and Synagogue had parted ways, words like that were hurled like missiles from a mainly gentile Church toward the Synagogue across the street, from which now those Jews who followed Jesus had been excommunicated. And by that shift Christian anti-Judaism was born. The gentile Church inherited the language and sentiments of an intra-Jewish conflict and projected it on "the Jews," once the identification with Israel was lost. As Christianity gathered political power, name calling grew into contempt, and contempt into pogroms and worse.

Much has been written and more can be said about why and how that parting of the ways happened. No one factor was decisive. No one action or doctrine did it. As only a small number of Jews but an ever-increasing number of gentiles joined the Jesus movement, the outcome was Christian Churches, which, for all practical purposes, were gentile communities.

At the same time, Judaism, having lost its center in Jerusalem and its temple, found a new identity in the leadership of its sages and their interpretation of Torah. Major parts of the literary works of Judaism from the time of the Maccabees to the time after the fall of the Temple became part of the Christian tradition rather than of Rabbinic Judaism. Jewish writings like *Ben Sira*, *Wisdom of Solomon*, *Enoch, 4 Ezra, 2 Baruch, Testaments of the Twelve Patriarchs*, etc., became part of the Christian tradition and reached posterity through the Church's transmission. The Rabbinic consolidation of Judaism and the increasingly gentile constituency of Christianity transformed what had begun as a division within the Jewish community into two distinct communities, the Synagogue and the Church.

Once established, these two entities felt the necessity to define themselves by sharpening their differences. These differences appeared even greater once the Greek-speaking Jewish communities all over the Roman Empire partly died out and partly were absorbed into Christianity, while at the same time the language and thinking of Christianity was enlivened by Greek and Roman culture. Yet it was when Christianity became the official religion of the Roman Empire in the fourth century that Christian anti-Judaism first became a serious threat to Jewish existence. Political power plus religion was and is a dangerous brew.

But enough of description and of the shameful miseries of the past. What can be done? Can Christianity free itself from anti-Judaism? I said there are really no excuses. The most common form of excuse is perhaps to declare Christianity blameless and put the blame on imperfect Christians who did not live up to the ideal of loving their neighbors. But that analysis underestimates the problem and forgets that, for example, St. Augustine saw love as the motivation for his recommendation of chastising yet not killing the Jews in the Roman Empire. The Christian contempt for Jews and Judaism has to be faced more squarely.

The first Christian theologian who perceived and was horrified by the specter of Christian anti-Judaism was the apostle Paul. The first of all major Christian theologians saw it coming and tried to counteract it. In his letter to the Christians in Rome in the late 50s C.E. only 25 years after Jesus' last Passover, he addresses gentile Christians in Rome who display contempt toward Israel and feel superior in their Christian faith and status (Rom 11:11-36). In a series of metaphors and in a style that shows he is agitated, he tried to quench that sentiment. Finally he says: "I'll tell you a secret lest to be conceited: the whole of Israel will be saved..." He does not say how, he does not say that they will accept Jesus as the Messiah. His only aim is to counteract the contempt that gentile Christians seemed to have shown already toward Israel. And it upsets him: Paul, the great missionary, had discovered how religious zeal could lead to attitudes and actions alien to God's will and purpose. Actually he had been burned once. It was out of religious zeal that he once had persecuted the Christians (Acts of the Apostles 8:3). And he was not to let it happen again. But it did and it has. Oh, that we had heeded his warning.

Paul's warning actually implies a critique of the most common habit of thinking about other religious communities: we seek our identity by stressing how we differ from others. *They* say—*we* say. Definition by contrast has been the rule of the game. The more distinct the difference, the stronger our convictions. But how would it be if we defined ourselves and our tradition by what makes us glad, by what nurtures and energizes us? It is not as important to be different as it is to be right. And it may be possible to be right together with others, not only in sharp contrast to others. Of course our egos may feel prouder if we and no one else is right. But that may be why religious divisions sometimes are more important to human pride than to God.

"I will tell you a mystery..." said Paul. In contemporary language, he might have said: religion is not governed by the rules that apply to zero-sum economics. To recognize the beauty and the truths of another tradition does not deduct from my own faith. I need not hate all other women to prove that I love my wife. Therefore one way for Christians to shed their anti-Semitism is to practice the three rules of all religious dialogue:

1. Let the others define themselves. We all tend to define or describe the other in negative contrast to ourselves. Hence our descriptions of the other often are a breach of the commandment, "You shall not bear false witness against your neighbor."

2. Compare equal to equal. If you compare the ideal of your own with the average of the other, not to say the best of your own with the worst of the other, you will score false victories and truth will suffer. Christian love and Christian crusades both have their analogues in all religions.

3. The highest and indispensable stage of dialogue is what I like to call Holy Envy: to see something in the other that one finds beautiful, but it is not one's own; to want to learn; to want the other to tell more about it, tell us so that we get enriched, warmed, fascinated.

Perhaps one could add a fourth point. Once there is sufficient trust and mutual respect between partners in dialogue, not least between Jews and Christians, there comes the time when Jews can tell what troubles them in Christianity and Christians feel free to ask their questions. For Christian anti-Semitism will never be overcome just by repentance but by building new relationships. And relationships mean mutual esteem. When I come to Brandeis, I come for that conversation that will engender Christian conversion from contempt. I believe it can be done. I know it must be done. The apostle Paul already told me that it must be done. He even hinted how: by a deeper understanding of God's mystery rather than by self-serving theological definitions.

26

Invocation at the Dedication of the United States Holocaust Memorial Museum

O God hidden and revealed
Be present with thy creative
Power of life

Be present in this place, this
Memorial of the obscenest of deaths

Be present as thy Spirit,
thy driving wind, thy breath of life once
hovered over the chaos and the void
on the first day of the world

By thy presence may this Memorial,
this Yad vaShem, work in each of us who come here
that most specific resolve for what must be

his next step – her next act
By thy most holy and creative presence
let the work we dedicate today not have been in vain

In thy presence let there be much silence

Silence for each and everyone to hear
and to respond honestly, decisively.

I for one as a Christian
pray that we in the churches
be rudely and finally awakened
to our age-old complicity in the
ultimate crime of the Holocaust

Be Present O God to us all
and bring us together in the
one resolve against all hatred

And let the words of thy prophet, his cry, his lament
be heard for generations on the Mall of this Nation:
"Is it nothing to you, all ye that pass by?
Behold and see if there is a sorrow like unto my sorrow,
which is done to me..."

So we say: Never again – ever. Amen.

(Invocation given at the Holocaust Memorial Museum in
Washington, DC, on April 22, 1993 by Bishop Krister Stendahl.
The words of the prophet Jeremiah are from the Book of Lam-
entations 1:12.)

27

God and Evil: A Unified Theodicy/Theology/Philosophy

David Birnbaum

100.00 THE EPICENTER OF THE DIVINE

Holy potential is at the epicenter of the divine.

100.01 The Divine Name

And Moses said unto God:

"Behold, when I come unto the Children of Israel, and shall say unto them:

The God of your fathers hath sent me unto you: and they shall say to me: What is his name? what shall I say unto them?"

And God said unto Moses:

I-WILL-BE-THAT-WHICH-I-WILL-BE; and He said: "Thus shalt thou say unto the Children of Israel:

I-WILL-BE hath sent me unto you."
—Exodus 3:13-14[1]

The name of the God of Israel first proclaimed to Israel—
Eheyeh Asher Eheyeh, "I-Will-Be-That-Which-I-Will-Be"—is
in effect a declaration that the holiest state of the holy is the
God of Potential. God is the actualization of potential in its
conscious holy form. All that we know of God's universal name
is that which it stands for: holy potential within potential within
potential *ad infinitum.* For the entire God of Israel is a God of
willed potential.

Holy potential is more than human potential writ large.
"To whom will you liken Me that I shall equal?" (Isaiah 40:25
cf. 46:5). Holy potential transcends time, space and the cosmos.
Holy potential tracks to the forward wave of the cosmos, to the
forward wave of time. Embedded within it are thus potentialities
rippling infinitely forward, embedded within infinite concentric
circles cycling outward to infinity.

> Has it not been told you from the beginning? Have you
> not understood the foundations of the earth? It is He that
> sits above the circle of the earth . . . That stretcheth out the
> heavens as a curtain, And spreadeth them out as a tent to
> dwell in.
> —Isaiah 40:21-25 (cf. 44:24, 45:12)

100.02 The Primordial Divine

The infinite potentials/Potentials of the Divine, including the potentials to create the universe, within which God

---

[1] The phrase *Eheyeh Asher Eheyeh* is commonly translated in the present tense,
I-AM-THAT-I-AM. Note, however, that the literal and simple translation
(*peshuto*) is future tense; as we translate it, Onkelos maintains the future tense,
and Rashi's translation is clearly future-oriented—"I will be with them during
this travail, as I will be with them in future travails." The main thrust of Nehama
Leibowitz's explanation (in *Studies in Shemot,* p. 60) is also future-oriented.
She cites Psalms 91:5, "I will be with them in trouble."

would create man to strive for his own munificent potentialities,[2] are inherent in the eternal Divine.[3]

> Who calls the generations from the beginning,
> I, the Lord, First
> And the Last, I am He.
> —Isaiah 41:4 (cf. 44:6, 45:11)

> the Holy seed
> shall be the stock thereof.
> —Isaiah 6:13

---

[2] See below for citations regarding linkage of God's potential to man's potential.
Note that T.B. Hagigah 11b admonishes against inquiry into origins or futures.
However, the works of Maimonides and other medievals, aside from the
kabbalists, stand as clear counterweighs to its admonition.

[3] See Isaac the Blind, "God beheld in Himself these essences, which would
manifest themselves at the creation of this world." As cited in Scholem, *Origins
of the Kabbalah*, p. 281. Scholem's footnote 172 says: "As quoted in *Sefer ha-
Emunah weha-Bittahon*, chap. 18, and in a somewhat better text, in the old
miscellanies preserved in Old Ms. Christ Church College 198, fol. 25b."

Isaac the Blind, son of the Rabad, Provence, France, is referred to by Scholem
as "the central figure in the oldest Kabbalah" (Ibid., p. 252).

Cf. Isaac the Blind's commentary on the beginning of *Midrash Konen*, as
cited in Scholem, ibid., p. 287.

Cf. Ibid., p. 451, citing a text of the kabbalists of Gerona. "Before God
created the world . . . all things were mixed together and all essences were
hidden, for He had not yet brought them forth from potentiality to reality,
like a tree in whose potency the fruit is already present." Scholem footnote
205 says, "Thus in Ms. British Museum, Margoliouth 752, fol. 36a. A very
similar passage also in *Kether Shem Tob* in Jellinek, *Auswahl kabbalistischer Mystik*,
p. 41."

Cf. Abraham Ibn Ezra in his commentary on Daniel 10:21. "And man alone
is the foundation of the sublunar world and it is because of him that the world
was created, his soul being linked to the Upper Soul." As cited in Stitskin,
Eight Jewish Philosophers, p. 120.

Cf. Saadia Goan, *Beliefs and Opinions* 4:1. "Although man is not the largest
of the creatures, by virtue of his soul he encompasses the entire universe."

Cf. Bosker, *Abraham Isaac Kook*, p. 379.

Cf. Kant's argument in favor of the "principle of plenitude" (the principle
that whatever can exist must somewhere actually exist, since otherwise the
creative capacity of God would not be fully realized): "It would be absurd to
represent the Deity as bringing into action only a small part of his creative
potency." From Kant, *Allgemeine Naturgeschichte und Theorie des Himmels* (1755),
pt. II, chap. vii, as trans. In A. O. Lovejoy, *The Great Chain of Being*, p. 140. Cited
in Passmore, *The Perfectibility of Man*, p. 216.

> ... who shut up the sea with doors,
> When it broke forth,
> And issued out of the womb?

—Job 38:8

> Out of whose womb came the ice?
> And the hoar — frost of heaven,
> Who hath gendered it?

—Job 38:29

Independent of time, matter, and energy, and indeed, independent of a universe, existed Holy Divine Potential— the primordial Divine.[4] At the eternal origins of out-of-time: Holy Potential within potential ... *ad infintum*—tracking to the forward edges of time.[5]

At the embryonic stage of holiness, deep in the womb of nothingness, deep at the core or out-of-time, hinged on an indefinable and infinite circularity, there was an ascending holy metaphysical fire:Yearning, imploring calling forth into the void.[6]

[The concept of a primordial Divine has clear and direct precedent in the concept of the *En Sof* of Kaballah.[7] See section 100.03 below.]

---

[4] We find it easier to posit Infinite Holy Potential as eternally preexisting all, as opposed to positing the classic God of Israel—an entity—as preexisting all.

Cf. Scholem, *The Origins of the Kabbalah*, p. 348.

Later in the text (section 200.00) we call *Holy quest for potential* the underlying 'dynamic.' Subsequent to the First Printing, Haim Cohen, Former Justice, Supreme Court of Israel, suggested that the term 'abstract dynamic' or 'dynamic abstraction' might be closer to the intended mark. I agree, in particular, for the embryonic stages of *Holy quest for potential.*

[5] See *SeferYesirah* (1562) fol. 63a, as cited in Ibid., p. 341. "Before anything at all was created, God was unfathomable and limitless, alone and unique, capable of subsisting by Himself in the potency of existence."

Cf. Ibid., pp. 282-283, 441.

Cf. Hirsch, Chapters of the Fathers, on Avot 5:1. "However, in this world ... all the things that were made first were contributing factors in the creation of what came after them, and were, in fact, completed by the latter ... All things sustain and are sustained in their turn."

[6] See Matt, *Zohar*, p. 24.

Traversing the Bridge

And as nature abhors a vacuum, Holy Potential abhors nothingness. This is a cosmic axiom.

Simultaneous with the eternal origins of out-of-time, an equilibrium of nothingness was thrown into disequilibrium by its own Holy Potential. Exploding and imploding. Echoing through this day and racing towards infinite time, Holy Potential screamed forth.

Genesis

Flowing from the Essence of the Divine, the infinite holy potential of the Divine demanded more expression.[8] Among these elements were the potentials for the creation of the universe, and within the latter the potentials for man to quest for his spiritual potential,[9] as well as others, including mercy, love, truth, justice, beauty, and harmony.[10] The holy potential core of the Divine demanded more than just potential.[11] For the potentialities of Divine creation are inherent in the eternal Divine origins and in the Divine Essence itself.[12]

---

[7] See Scholem, *Origins of the Kabbalah*, pp. 281-284, 438, 443.

Cf. Ibid., pp. 431-432. "Asher ben David, too expresses himself clearly in a theistic and personalistic vein, identifying '*en-sof*' with the personally conceived supreme primordial cause."

Asher ben David was the nephew of the aforementioned Isaac the Blind and grandson of the Rabad. He "carried on the traditions of his father and uncle during first half of the thirteenth century in Provence and at the same time served as one of the most important links with the mystical centers newly forming in northern Spain, above all in Gerona." Ibid., p. 252.

[8] See Hirsch, *Timeless Torah*, p. 16.

[9] See Hirsch, *Chapter of the Fathers*, on Avot 5:1. "Man is the final work of creation, the goal and summit of the whole, in whom all creation culminates."

[10] Note also the statement of the Sages. "For the sake of Israel, Moses, [and the precepts of] challah, tithing, and first fruits, was the world created." See also Hirsch, *Timeless Torah*, p. 5.

[11] The possible argument, alluded to by Maimonides, that every potentiality needs an agent to actualize it, is inapplicable to our context for at least three reasons differentiating our case: (1) infinite potential, (2) potential within potential ad infinitum, and (3) holy potential.

[12] Maimonides notes *(Guide 2:26)* in particular from *Rabbi Eliezer.* "Whence were the heavens created? He took part of the light of His garment, stretched it like a cloth . . ."

At the eye of the primal cosmic storm, warping from out-of-time towards time, unzipping the cosmic void into positives and negatives, the infinite Divine blaze leapt forth. A creative supraconscious dynamic, transcending time, space, and eternity. Focusing its holy metaphysical force. Genesis.[13]

> And God divided the light from the darkness.
> —Genesis 1:4

A holy dynamic flows forth through this day, tracing its origins to the inner core of the Divine. Beneath the eddies and swirls at the surface of the cosmic stream, beneath the deep and powerful major cosmic currents, from out of the epicenter of the holy, flows the deepest primal current—questing, beseeching, and indeed, screaming—for ultimate potentiality.[14]

★

"At the beginning" . . . there was a "separation," a primal tear. The almost-void divided into its potentialities. A separation of unity into polarities. A separation beyond pain.

Separation—for the purpose of ultimately experiencing an ultimate re-unification. Or, to put it simply: all this for a little romance down the road.

The cosmic womb separating. A cosmic attempt at simultaneous daring, and eventual return-to-the-womb. The cosmic womb.

In order to experience the drama of ultimate love/fulfillment, the cosmos had to first separate. Into opposites, polarities.

---

[13] See "The Creation of Elohim," in Matt, *Zohar*, pp. 49–50.
   Note in particular the "radical" position of the *Zohar* at the conclusion of the chapter:
   With the Beginning
   The Concealed One who is not known
   Created the palace
   The palace is called *Elohim*
   the secret is:
   "With Beginning _____ created *Elohim*"
   (Genesis 1:1).
[14] See Greenberg, *Perspectives: Voluntary Covenant*, p. 2.

Whether male/female; positive/negative; good/evil, yin/yang. All this for the drama of the teenage boy looking for his dream girl; for the cosmic drama of falling in love.

The cosmos attempts to achieve simultaneously that which by definition is not achievable simultaneously: "Daring" simultaneous with "Bliss." The drama of a daring quest for infinity, simultaneous with the bliss-closure of the womb. Its agent is love, careless love. In love, we—and the cosmos—attempt to square-the-circle. That is the cosmic drama. The cosmic conundrum. That is the extraordinary and excruciating infinite spiral. That is love's draw, its awesome, cosmic power.

100.03 Kabbalistic Parallel

Lurianic Kabbalah can be refocused in the light of this formulation. Indeed, if one takes the liberty of stripping Kabbalah of its majestic imagery down to its very core, it would seem that the major elements of kabbalistic doctrine were groping or heading in this very direction.

We would draw the following parallel and relationship:

Infinite Holy Potential	*En Sof*
Cosmic Quests for Potential	*Sefirot*

A neo-kabbalistic variation of "infinite holy potential" would posit that the *En Sof*—the infinite, the root of the *Ten Sefirot*, "the Root of all Roots"[15]—demanded greater expression. Within the obscurity of mystical doctrine, one factor is clear. The *En Sof* — the Primal/Infinite Divine—had "neither qualities nor attributes."[16]

Our neo-kabbalistic development would posit that the kabbalist's Ten *Sefirot*, the next level of Divine emanation, demanded more tangible expression.[17] The Ten *Sefirot* are variously described as the Ten Spheres, Regions, Faces, Manifestations, Crowns, Stages, Garments, Modes, Branches,

---

[15] See Scholem, *Major Trends in Jewish Mysticism*, pp. 207, 208, 214.

[16] See Ibid., p. 207, Cf. Maimonides, *Guide* 3:20. Cf. Matt's "introduction" to Moses de Leon, in *Zohar*, p. 33.

[17] See Hirsch, *Chapters of the Fathers* on Avot 5:1. "By ten utterances was the world created . . ."

Powers, Emanations—of God.[18] The Ten *Sefirot* are "the ten spheres of Divine manifestation in which God emerges from his hidden abode."[19] They are most commonly enumerated as follows:

KETER ELYON	"Supreme Crown"
HOKHMAH	"Wisdom"
BINAH	"Intelligence"
HESED	"Love/Mercy"
GEVURAH	"Power"
RAHAMIM	"Compassion"
NETSAH	"Everlasting endurance"
HOD	"Majesty"
YESOD	"Foundation"
MALKHUTH	"Kingdom of God"[20]

One interpretation, which converges with our study, is that they are "the ten stages of the inner world, through which God descends from the inmost recesses down to His revelation in the *Shekinah.*[21] We would recast *Sefirot* as primal quests for potentiality which enable Infinite Holy Potential to "traverse the bridge" from "emptiness" to "Somethingness" and mandating Creation. They are the "transition from *En Sof* to creation."[22]

There is, indeed, a significant current in kabbalistic doctrine which links the *Sefirot* with the concept of potentiality.[23]

---

[18] Note Agus, *The Evolution of Jewish Thought*, p. 287.

[19] See Scholem, *Major Trends in Jewish Mysticism*, pp. 213–214.

[20] See Ibid., pp. 213–214.

[21] Ibid., p. 214.

[22] Matt, *Zohar,* p. 34.

[23] See Scholem, *Origins of the Kabbalah*, pp. 81–84, 437.

Cf. Ibid., p. 450. "In their conception of the emanation, the kabbalists of Gerona unite the two motifs of the emergence from potentiality to actuality on the one hand, and of the maturation of the organic process, on the other."

Cf. Azriel of Gerona, *Commentary on Talmudic Aggadoth*, p. 110 (lines 13–14 in particular), and idem, *Perush Eser Sefirot*, p. 4 (sec. gimel).

On a very closely related track the Book of Bahir deals with the aeons, or powers, of God. Scholem notes: "Each *middah* [aeon] is a particular spiritual potency." Ibid., p. 82.

> Every *Sefirah* is transformed from a general attribute of
> God into what the Kabbalists call a *Partsuf,* a "countenance"
> of God, which means that all the potentialities implied in
> every *Sefirah* are now brought under the influence of a
> formative principal.
>
> —Vital[24]

100.04 Buttress and Elaboration

> Gods's life-giving powers flow from the very highest
> degree of Holiness—from His Own Presence—down to the
> flesh-and-blood, cause-and-effect world in which we human
> beings live.
>
> —Scherman[25]

Leviticus 12:1-4 presents the rule that when a woman gives
birth she descends in purity.[26] Moreover, when a woman gives
birth to a daughter she descends twice the level of purity that
she descends when she gives birth to a boy. The Or HaChaim
explains that this perplexing formulation teaches us that during
pregnancy a woman achieves a higher level of holiness, since she
is carrying another life.[27] The conception of a daughter, who will
maintain within herself a greater creative potential, raises her to
a higher level of holiness. After the potential leaves her womb,
her level of purity descends. Inasmuch as a female fetus represents
a higher level of potentiality, upon the birth of a girl the mother's
level of purity descends doubly. For potential creation is indeed
holy. And the level of creation potential is directly related to the
level of holiness.

The cosmic fate is interlinked with the fate of God, the
universe, and man.

> Remember the former things of old:
> That I am God, and there is none else;

---

[24] Hayim Vital, *Ets Hayim* (Warsaw, 1891), XI, 7, p. 107, as cited in Scholem,
Major Trends in Jewish Mysticism, p. 269, n. 76.

[25] Scherman, "An Overview: Kaddish," p. xii.

[26] Specifically, when a woman gives birth to a male she becomes "impure" for
seven days; to a female, fourteen days (Leviticus 12:6).

[27] Or HaChaim, Leviticus 12:2.

I am God, and there is none like Me;
Declaring the end from the beginning
And from ancient times things
That are not yet done.

—Isaiah 46:9-10

Soloveitchick notes:

> ... the Jewish people see their own fate as bound up
> with the fate of existence as a whole ...When the historical
> process of the Jewish people reaches its consummation and
> attains the heights of perfection, then (in an allegorical sense)
> the flaws of creation as a whole will also be repaired. 'He
> bade the moon renew itself for those who were burdened
> from birth, who like her will be renewed and will extol their
> Creator on account of the name of His glorious kingdom'
> [from the blessing over the new moon].[28]

God is represented in *Tanach* as a many-faceted deity. It is
for this reason that He is known by many Names.[29] We postulate that the primal essence of God is potentiality, i.e., a
supradimensional metaphysical intangible. Potential is implicit
through God, and through God, the universe and man.[30]

---

[28] Soloveitchik, *Halakhic Man*, p. 107.

[29] See Agus, "The Meaning of Prayer," in Millgram, *Great Jewish Ideas*, p. 235.
"The tetragrammaton (YHVH), whatever its original meaning and
pronunciation, is understood to be a formula, combining the future, the past
and the present."

Cf. Hick, *Readings in The Philosophy of Religion*, p. 72, "that His true name is
He that is, or in other words, Being without restriction, all Being, the Being
infinite and universal."

[30] See Whitehad, "Process and Reality," in Alston and Nakhnikian, *Readings in
Twentieth-Century Philosophy*, p. 151. "Viewed as primordial, he [God] is
unlimited conceptual realization of the absolute wealth of potentiality."

Cf. Berkovits, *Major Trends in Modern Philosophies of Judaism*, p. 21. "God is
m'huyab hamziut, He is absolute and exists of his own uncreated intrinsic
necessity."

The essence of God is eternal, timeless and infinite.[31] The Primal Essence inexorably quests after its own infinite potentiality.[32]

> Creation finds its expression in man's fulfilling all of his tasks, causing all of the potentiality implanted in him to emerge into actuality, utilizing all of his manifold possibilities, and fully bringing to fruition his own noble personality. The power stored up within man is exceedingly great, is all-encompassing, but all too often it slumbers within and does not bestir itself from its deep sleep. The command of creation, beating deep within the consciousness of Judaism, proclaims: Awake ye slumberers from your sleep. Realize, actualize yourselves, your own potentialities and possibilities, and go forth to meet your God. The unfolding of man's spirit that soars to the very heavens, that is the meaning of creation.
> —Soloveitchik[33]

If a man's future potentialities are crucial, with his existence and striving for spiritual and intellectual achievement energizing the universe, it would seem that the cosmic order itself might

---

[31] See Berg, *Kabbalah for the Layman*, p. 72.

[32] See Bokser, *Abraham Isaac Kook*, p. 4. "Rav Kook saw the whole universe stirred by the pulsating energies emanating from the divine source of all existence."

Cf. Steinsaltz, *The Thirteen Petalled Rose*, p. 39. "All these Sefirot are infinite in their potency, even though they are finite in their essence."

Cf. *Shem Olam*, p. 41, as cited in Agus, *The Evolution of Jewish Thought*, p. 285. "The primal man consists in his turn of ten *sefiroth*, which were conceived as being both God and not-God. 'For that which is infinite and boundless could not make that which is finite and definite; therefore, it was necessary to postulate ten *sefiroth* in the middle, which are both finite and infinite.'"

[33] Soloveitchik, *Halakhic Man*, p. 132. (Soloveitchik cites Maimondes, *Guide* 2.32. "Prophecy is a certain perfection in the nature of man. This perfection is not achieved in any individual from among men except after a training that makes that which exists in the potentiality of the species pass into actuality.")

Cf. Ibid., p. 132. "In truth, Greek philisophy was also familiar with the notion of a process of development from relative nothingness to a perfect existence. What is more, this problem is practically the central issue in Greek ontology. The dispute between Heraclitus and Parmenides concerning the nature of being—whether it is perpetual development and movement or fixed, perfect existence—still made itself felt in the analyses of Platonic and Aristotelian schools and their successors.

be jeopardized if man annihilated himself. Thus the imperatives of potential do not exceed the limits necessary for survival.[34] On the other hand, if potential is at the essence of the Divine, we indeed have grounds for optimism. For only an awesomely positive potential down the road could dynamize all.

> Radiant is the world soul,
> Full of splendor and beauty,
> Full of life,
> Of souls hidden,
> Of treasurers of the holy spirit,
> Of fountains of strength,
> Of greatness and beauty.
> Proudly I ascend
> Toward the heights of the world soul
> That gives life to the universe.
>
> —Kook[35]

★

He hangs the world upon nothingness.

—Job 26:7[36]

---

[34] See Lamn, *The Face of God*, sec. 5, comments on "Survivalist Hester."

[35] Kook, "Light of Penitence," in Bokser, *Abraham Isaac Kook*, p. 376.

[36] To draw a parallel with architecture: Aristotelian philosophy concerning the origins of the universe can be compared to a classic structure: the upper structure, i.e., the universe, is supported by the foundation—God. Our formulation can be compared somewhat to an infinitely expanding geodesic dome—with all elements supporting each other. (A geodesic dome, often employed as a roof for large stadiums, is composed of a framework of light, straight-sided polygons in tension. It was originally conceived by Buckminster Fuller.)

Our conception adheres to classic Jewish doctrine of a spiritual and conscious God of infinity.[37]

The question then arises: Is spirituality at the beginning of the process or at its culmination? We are comfortable with the notion that it is at both the beginning and the end, a continuum. This is congruent with traditional religious thought. We add, however, that elements of circularity of time, God, or time/God can be theorized to buttress the concept of a cosmos dynamized by potentiality.[38] In the primordial realms of the infinite, potentialities and circularities reign supreme.

Somewhat in parallel to the construction of a geodesic dome, where all parts support one another, so too in creation, the potentialities of all creation support each other as well as the holy actualization spark. Thus, where the overwhelming thrust of classic Western philosophy is linear (i.e., A caused B caused C), our formulation is circular, with embedded potentialities providing the crucial supports and linkages.

100.05 Man—and the Quest for Potential

Man's ultimate quest for potentiality is a primary imperative of the universe.

---

[37] See Agus, *The Evolution of Jewish Thought*, p. 74. "In the Hellenistic world there was current the Stoic conception of *anima mundi*, the soul of the world, which pictured the Deity as the sum and substance of the laws prevailing in the universe. The rabbis did not think of God as the world's soul, in the sense of being the expression of the totality of its powers and functions."

Cf. Ibid., p. 87. "Philo rejected the Aristotelian concept of the Deity as the unmoved mover, since it implied the eternity of the world and denied the miracle of creation. Similarly, Philo repudiated the Stoic view of God as a material principle, immanent in physical nature, revealed in reason and expressed in the laws which govern all events in the universe. The Stoics believed the fundamental energy of the universe to be a quasi-rational logos, conscious, inflexible, and benevolent . . . Scripture emphasizes the spiritual character of God's being and his difference from the material world."

[38] Stephen Hawking, a physicist, observes: "It may be that the universe really did not have a beginning. Or maybe the 'space-time' forms a closed surface without an edge like the surface of the earth but in two more dimensions." From WNET's production "The Origin of the Universe" (approximately 5478 on standard-speed VHS tape).

Soloveitchik notes:

> Man initially is receptive, is pure potentiality. But creation, by
> definition, means spontaneity, actuality, action, renewal,
> aspiration, and daring.[39]

> With respect to the very first reference to man in Genesis
> (1:26) 'let us make man in our image,' Ibn Ezra comments:
> "Now I shall explain something you should know, namely,
> that the entire act of creation was for the purpose of man in
> accordance with the commandment of God ... Accordingly,
> since man's rational soul never dies it is comparable in its
> eternity of God ... And, therefore, the prophet states that 'he
> saw the Glory of God as the appearance of a man.'"[40]

The portions of the Torah (Pentateuch) and Prophets read
on the first day of Rosh Hashanah, the Jewish New Year, focus
on the belated conception of a child by Sarah and Hannah. The
focus is not on the creation of the world, which would seem
the natural selection. The focus is, rather, on the problem of
conception faced by two important personages in Jewish history.
Why this focus on Rosh Hashanah? Thus we might reinforce
our notion that a biological conception parallels the creation of
the universe. For the potential of Sarah to conceive Isaac and
the potential of Hannah to conceive Samuel are implicit in
creation, which is itself predicated on holy potential. Thus the
conception of Isaac and Samuel, each of whom would bring
cosmic potential a significant step closer to fruition, are indeed
events quite relevant to the anniversary of creation. The pain of
the childless mother reflects the pain of the ultimate Creator
who yearns for ultimate fulfillment of the goals of creation.

Thus, while creator potential is not the only potential, it is
essential for the achievement of manifold other potentialities.
(*Peru urevu,* "Be fruitful and multiply," is the first *mitzah* [Divine
precept] and is categorized, by some *mitzvah rabbah,* a great
mitzvah.) Other potentialities, including spiritual and intellectual

---

[39] Soloveitchik, *Halakhic Man*, p. 131.
[40] Stitskin, *Eight Jewish Philosophers*, p. 120.

attainment, are dependent on it. Consequently, creator potential receives a sanctity distinct to itself.

100.06 Linkage: Linkage of God's Potential to Man's Potential

I, even I, am He
that blots out your transgressions
for my own sake.

—Isaiah 43:45

And by Israel [the Lord] will be glorified/beautified.

—Isaiah 44:23

I will place salvation in Zion,
For Israel, my glorifier/beautifier.

—Isaiah 46:13

I was wroth with My people,
I profaned Mine inheritance [Israel].

—Isaiah 47:6

An already infinite God inexorably seeks His own potentialities, as difficult as this concept may be for the finite to comprehend. To an "infinity" one can add. This does not detract from the infinite aspect of the original infinity. Divine perfection is Divinely enhanceable. This does not detract from the original perfection.

It is for this reason that the potential of the Deity is linked to, and influenced by, man's striving for potential[41] and by man's ascent. The greater man's freedom and consequent ascent, the greater the cosmic potential.[42]

---

[41] See Genesis Rabbah, chap. 30, on the verse ". . . walk before Me, and be wholehearted" (Genesis 17:1)—"in the view of Rabbi Johanan was need His honor; in the view of Rabbi Simeon ben Lakish He needs our honor." As cited in Heschel, *Man Is Not Alone*, p. 243.

[42] See Soloveitchik, *Halakhic Man*, p. 91. "Halakhic man cannot be cowed by anyone. He knows no fear of flesh and blood. For is he not a creator of worlds, a partner of the Almighty in the act of creation?"

Cf. Berkovits, *Faith After The Holocaust*, p. 60. "Man, according to his own strength, continues the work of creation and becomes, urged on by God's call, a humble associate of the Creator."

Inasmuch as the cosmic Divine potential is intertwined with that of man, one must come to the conclusion that while man is totally dependent on the Divine, God is also somewhat dependent on man, to whatever small degree.[43] That elements of a dependency exist is recognized in Jewish tradition.[44]

The Midrash makes this point:

> When the Israelites do God's will, they add to the power of God on high. When the Israelites do not do God's will, they, as it were, weaken the great power of God.[45]
>
> "Ye are My witnesses, saith the Lord, and I am God (Isaiah 43:12). That is when you are my witness, I am God, and when you are not My witnesses, I am, as it were, not God.
>
> —Midrash Rabbah, Psalms 123:1[46]

---

[43] See Bokser, *Abraham Isaac Kook*, pp. 27-28. "As long as the striving for divine ideals and their effectuation in the course of a continuous historical existence does not manifest itself in the nation, the divine Presence is in exile, and the life-force released by the service of God is in a state of weakness" (Ikve Hatzon, "Daat Elohim," in *Eder Hayakar*, pp. 130-141).

[44] "Of course, man needs God, 'in the fullness of His reality,' needs man. He who says 'Thy will be done,' may say no more, but truth adds for him 'through me whom Thou needest .'" (Martin Buber, *I and Thou* [New York: Charles Scribner's Sons, 1958], p. 83. "God thus responds to a man's dealings with the beings and things of the universe by pouring His divinity into all of nature. In this sense, it is man who 'turns the world into a sacrament.'" Idem, *mamre* (Melbourne University Press, 1946), p. 105. As cited in Schulweis, *Evil and the Morality of God*, p. 99.

Cf. Gordis, *A Faith for Moderns*, p. 260.

Cf. Soloveitchik, *Halakhic Man*, p. 99. "The dream of creation is the central idea in the halakhic consciousness—the idea of the importance of man as a partner of the Almighty in the act of creation, man as creator of worlds."

See also the contemporary discourses of Rav Shlomo Chaim Hakohen Aviner in *Tal Hermon: Iyunim BaTorah,* editor A. Kleinspitz, privately printed in Jerusalem by Ateret Kohanim. See section on *Bereshit.* Translation of selected segment follows:" . . . All that God created needs completion by us, as is written '*asher ba-rah Elohim la-a-sot,*'" "It is possible to say that all we do is a continuation of . . . '*na-a-seh ha-adam.*' We complete the creation of man."

[45] Midrash Rabbah, Lamentations 1:6.

[46] See Fackenheim, *God's Presence in History*, p. 23.

Genesis 1:26 states: "And God said, 'Let us make man in Our image . . .'" The Zohar responds to the question of why the plural "us" by explaining that man is a partner (*shutaf*) with the Divine in the creation of man.[47] The rabbinic/kabbalistic concept of *tikkun olam* ("perfecting/completing the world") further complements the theme of man's partnership with the Divine.

> Were it not for My covenant, day and night, the laws of heaven and earth I should not have ordained.
> —Jeremiah 33:25

> God is in need of man for the attainment of His ends.
> —Heschel[48]

> When Israel performs the will of the Omnipresent, they add strength to the heavenly power; as it is said: "To God we render strength" (Psalms 60:14). When, however, Israel does not perform the will of the Omnipresent, they weaken—if it is possible to say so—the great power of Him who is above; as it is written, "Thou didst weaken the Rock that begot Thee."
> —Pesikta[49]

100.07 Focus: Potential and the *Mitzvot*

The first directive to man in the Torah is not what one might expect in a divine text. It does not focus on interaction between God and man, nor on fraternal interaction between man and man. Rather, the first directive to man is *peru urevu*, "Be fruitful and multiply" (Genesis 1:26). The first directive to

---

[47] There is a midrashic concept that there are three partners in the creation of a child—man, woman, and the Divine.

[48] Heschel, *Man Is Not Alone*, p. 241.

Cf. Ibid., p. 242. "God is a partner and a partisan in man's struggle for justice, peace and holiness, and it is because of His being in need of man that He entered a covenant with him for all time."

Cf. Heschel, *God in Search of Man*, p. 413. "To be is to stand for, and what man stands for is the great mystery of being His partner. God is in need of man."

[49] Pesikta, ed. Buber, XXVI, 166b, as cited in Heschel, *Man Is Not Alone*, p. 243.

Noah after the flood is the same (Genesis 9:12). Fulfillment of creator potential is a holy thrust of the cosmos, flowing directly from the core of the Divine essence.

★

We can now also begin to unravel the perplexing aspect of the two *mitzvot,* each noted twice, whose affirmative performance, according to Scripture, is rewarded with long life: (1) "Honor thy father and mother" (Exodus 20:12, Deuteronomy 26:17), and (2) *shiluach ha-kan,* the requirement to send the mother bird away prior to taking her young (Deuteronomy 22:6-7). For the link between creator and potential is sanctified and protected. Honoring the link is obligatory.[50] Destruction of the link in the mother's presence is profane. Divine potential flowing through life potential was the original source of life; and thus, symmetrically, sanctification of potential is rewarded by long life.

Nachmanides, in his commentary on the *mitzvah* of *shiluach ha-kan,* declares: "Scripture will not permit a destructive act that will bring about the destruction of a species, even though it has permitted the ritual slaughtering of that species for food."[51]

We are directed not to boil a kid (goat) in its mother's milk (Exodus 23:19, 34:36; Deuteronomy 14:21).[52] This thrice-stated directive becomes the basis of the demanding kashruth laws of separating milk and meat. We are also directed not to sacrifice or kill an ox or ewe and their respective young on the same day (Leviticus 22:28).

Perhaps the psychic ground of the vast body of law permeating from these directives is the Divine sanctification of the link between creator and potential which in no way must be profaned. While the partaking of the goat's meat, its kid's or its milk individually is certainly permitted, the use of one of a

---

[50] See below on this section on the Torah's tolerance of the consumption of animals.

[51] Ramban, *Commentary on the Torah,* vol. 2, p. 448.

[52] Inasmuch as the boiling of a kid goat in its mother's milk was apparently a pagan rite, the thrice-cited proscription of this practice is also taken in some quarters as a general injunction against paganism.

creator's (life-giving) potentialities to complete the termination of another of its (life-giving) potentialities is thrice-forbidden. While the killing of an ox or its offspring is certainly permitted individually, the killing of both on the same day, whether for mundane or holy purposes, is forbidden. The sanctity of the creator link is clearly established and protected. Jewish law expands the kid/milk directive into the voluminous laws requiring the separation of meat and milk products. The link of potential is thereby sanctified every day at every meal.

★

The *mitzvah* of bringing first fruits (*bikkurim*) as an offering to the Divine is cited three major times in the Pentateuch (Exodus 23:19, 26; Deuteronomy 26:1-11; also see Number 18:13). Even the face value of the *mitzvah* may be interpreted as a celebration/sanctification of holy potential[53]. As the Divine is the cause behind all new fruit, we are instructed to bring a holy offering of the first of the new fruit.

The particulars of this directive are amplified by the last tractate of the Mishnah order of *Zeraim*. The Mishnah clarifies that if the vine from which the first fruits have been plucked has withered prior to the actual offering in Jerusalem, the offering is still brought, but no invocation[54] is made—*niktzatz ha-ilan, mevi ve-eino korei*. The potential of the mother vine has an effect on the holiness of the first fruits.[55] Inasmuch as *mitzvat bikkurim* is a celebration/sanctification of holy potential, the de-potentializing of the mother vine lowers the holiness of the fruit sufficiently to disqualify it from the invocation of *bikkurim*.

★

Potential becomes a salient element elsewhere as well. The proscription of *neveilah* (Deuteronomy 14:21), i.e., the prohibi-

---

[53] The usual explanation is *hakaras ha-tov*—acknowledgment of God's good. Our interpretation would be a further refinement of this general explanation.
[54] "*Arami oved-avi . . .*"
[55] See also T. B. Berachot 40b.

tion of eating of a carcass which has died, as opposed to having been properly slaughtered, may be related as well. Having entered a state of "nonpotentiality" by nonritual means, its purity level has been lowered to unacceptable levels.

★

An examination of the textual placement of these directives provides fascinating juxtapositions. The directive of kid/milk is stated three times. In its first two (Exodus 23:19, 34:26) it appears in the same verse as, and exclusively with, the directive of *bikkurim*. The third occurrence (Deuteronomy 14:21) appears in the same verse as, exclusively with, the proscription of *neveilah*. The verse immediately following contains the directive of tithing. The underlying motif is not so obscure, after all.

★

Newtol Press, Professor of Biology at the University of Wisconsin, observes that the laws of kashruth, with regard to permitted and prohibited animals, have the clear effect of conserving the earth's energy and the survivability potential of vulnerable species.[56] In particular, the most vulnerable of the vertebrates, carnivorous animals, are protected by forbidding them as a source of food. Of the mammals, only herbivores that are also ruminants (e.g., cows), i.e., which can digest even plentiful grass, are permitted. This subset of vertebrates has the greatest chance of finding sufficient food, and it is this subset alone which is permissible as food. Aside from any other reasons for it, kashruth has the effect of preserving the ecological potential of planet earth.

Ideally, the Torah would have preferred vegetarianism, and indeed, this was the Torah position before the Flood. As a concession to mankind, the Torah permitted the slaughtering and consumption of animals. Within this context, the Torah then maximizes potential, as noted above.

★

---

[56] Newtol Press, "Kosher Ecology," *Commentary* 79, no. 2 (February 1985).

While man is clearly given dominion over the earth (Genesis 1:26, 9:2-3), he is also given the responsibility for preserving the earth. He must protect life-giving potential even in military contexts. Deuteronomy (20:19-20) directs that only non-fruit-bearing trees may be cut down for siege works. The rabbis further extended this prohibition to proscribe shifting the course of a stream for the military purpose of drying up trees,[57] condemned the stopping up of wells,[58] and proscribed the killing of animals unnecessarily.[59]

The laws of kashruth, the rabbinic injunctions against *bal faschit* (unnecessary destruction), the laws of *shmitah* (fallow fields during the seventh year) and land redemption upon jubilee (Leviticus 25:23-24), have, aside from their more obscure metaphysical rationales, the ecological effect of first preserving, and then increasing, the world's physical potential.

★

Life and death have I placed before thee, the blessing and the curse. Mayest thou choose life, that thou mayest live, thou and thy descendants.
—Deuteronomy 30:19 (cf. 30:35, 11:26)

200.00 THE UNDERLYING DYNAMIC

Holy quest for potential is the underlying core dynamic of the cosmic order.

Holy quest for potential—our parallel to the kabbalistic *En Sof*—is the "primal scream of the cosmos." Holy Potential, emanating through and from the Divine Essence, radiates through the universe-questing, pulsating, exploding, reaching, energizing, expanding in time and out-of-time.[60]

---

[57] Sifrei, Shoftim, sec. 203.

[58] Pesachim 56a.

[59] Chullin 7b; Tosefot Baba Kamma 115b, based on Avodah Zarah 30b.

[60] See also Leibniz, who posits that the universe as a whole must display a "perpetual and very free progress . . . such that it advances always to still greater improvement." Translated in Weiner, Leibniz; Selections, p. 354, as cited in Passmore, *The Perfectibility of Man*, p. 215.

It is at the core of the holy/natural drive of the cosmos. It is the primal engine of cosmic existence.[61]

200.01 General Quest for Potential

200.01a Natural Order

And all the goodliness of God is as the flower of the field.

—Isaiah 40:6

God, as the cosmic ruler, is beheld in His boundless majesty reigning supreme over creation. His will crystallized in the natural law, His word determining the behavioral patterns of nature.

—Soloveitchik[62]

The Spirit of God hovered over the face of the waters and over the void. And God said, Let there be light.

—Genesis 1:2-3

From there on through this day the majesty of creation seeks its maximal potential.[63] Life is daring.[64] The cosmos strives not just for survival; it quests for its maximal potential.[65] Long

---

[61] See Book of Bahir, excerpt from sec. 64-67, as cited in Scholem, *Origins of the Kabbalah*, p. 77. "The potency of one is [also] in the other . . . all thirty-six potencies are already found in the first . . . and the potency of each one is found in the other."

Cf. Ibid., *Origins of the Kabbalah*, p. 462. citation from *Megillath ha-Megalleh*.

[62] Soloveitchik, *The Lonely Man of Faith*, p. 31.

[63] See Scholem, *Origins of the Kabbalah*, p. 289. "The divine power spreading from the sefiroth in Creation . . . also descends below the human domain to living beings of a lower order, even to plants."

[64] "That they may know from the rising from the east, and its setting westward, that there is none beside Me; I am the Lord, and there is no other" (Isaiah 45:6).

[65] See Kant, *Idea of a Universal History,* First Proposition, as cited in Passmore, *The Perfectibility of Man*, p. 216. "All the capacities implanted in a creature by nature, are destined to unfold themselves, completely and conformably to their end, in the course of time." "Who can fail to discover that the hand of the Lord is behind all this!" (Job 12:9).

before Prometheus stole fire from the gods to give to man, God grasped life from out of the void and created fire and man.[66]

200.01b Mortal[67]

Man inevitably seeks out the highest mountain, literally and allegorically. He girds himself and summons the guts, energy, and means to challenge it. Sometimes quixotically, sometimes daringly. Sometimes a fine line.[68]

Man will construct gossamer cathedrals with spires reaching heavenward, and project space probes to the far ends of the cosmos.[69] Man stands questing, hands lifted heavenward.[70]

---

[66] See Soloveitchik, *The Lonely Man of Faith*, p. 32 (citing Bereshit Rabbah 59): "Our sages said that before Abraham appeared, *majestes dei* (the glory of God) was reflected only by the distant heavens and it was a mute nature which 'spoke' of the glory of God. It was Abraham who 'crowned' Him the god of the earth, i.e., the god of men."

[67] See Scholem, *Origins of the Kabbalah*, p. 339, expounding on the views of the "Gerona circle" of Kabbalists. "In this view, primordial man is . . . only a configuration of the supreme potencies."

[68] See Schulweis, *Evil and the Morality of God*, p. 129. "Akiba, the rabbinic sage, is asked by Tinneius Rufus, the pagan, 'Whose works are greater, those of God or those of man?' Akiba replies that the works of man excel, and as evidence places before him sheaves of wheat and dishes and cakes. Akiba regards the latter as greater not because he would denigrate God. For Akiba God and the human being are not contending forces. The sheaves represent the nonhuman givenness—the product of seed, water, soil and the sun; the cakes represent the transformation of that givenness, the actualization of the potential for the sake of the sustenance of humanity. It is bread and wine, not sheaves and grapes, which are sanctified in praise of the transaction which with human hands brings the natural process of controlled perfection. The ideals are not the final reality already extant in some realm of being. Rabbinic wisdom expresses the faith which calls for transformation. 'Everything needs to be acted upon. The lupine must be soaked, the mustard seed sweetened, the wheat ground, and man must be perfected. Everything requires repair.'"

[69] According to Herder, men of different ages are linked by a "golden chain of improvement." Herder, *Ideas*, bk. IX, chap. 1 p. 231, as cited in Passmore, *The Perfectibility of Man*, p. 223.

[70] See the discussion of Soloveitchik in Peli, *On Repetenance*, p. 14.

Cf. ". . . a man's reach should exceed his grasp,/Or what's a heaven for?" Browning, Andrea del Sarto.

Soloveitchik describes "Adam the first"[71] as "aggressive, bold, and victory-minded. His motto is success, triumph over cosmic forces. He engages in creative work, trying to imitate his Maker *(imitatio Dei)*."[72]

200.01c Universal

The universe seeks its maximum and optimal-potential—inexorably.[73] For this, we postulate, is its *raison d'etre*. We can only speculate on the precise hierarchic standing of various potentialities, but we suspect that spirituality is near the apex.[74]

For those philosophers who are of the opinion that God fashioned the world out of primeval matter, or that random combinations of primeval matter evolved into the universe, ultimately the question narrows down to: Where did the smallest subatomic particle come from? Ultimately they must bridge the gap from "nothingness" to "somethingness."

For all those who postulate eternal God or gods, the question remains: In what sense is eternity to be understood?

In Jewish philosophical tradition only the kabbalists face the issue. And their solution is the obscure *En Sof.* We propose a parallel solution: that the infinite holy quest for potential—the core of the Divine—bridged the gap.

---

[71] There are two places where a Scripture relates creation of man. The first is near the end of Genesis 1; the second, in Genesis 2. There has been considerable discussion on the differences in wording and nuance between the two chapters. See Soloveitchik's classic *The Lonely Man of Faith.*

[72] Ibid., p. 15.

[73] See Herbert Spencer, *Social Statics.* Ed. Cit., pt. I, chapter II, #4, 65, as cited in Passmore, *The Perfectibility of Man*, p. 241. "Progress ... is not an accident, but a necessity."

See also Stephen Hawking, *A Brief History of Time*, p. 121. "Why did the universe start out with so nearly the critical rate of expansion that separates models that recollapse from those that go on expanding forever, so that even now, ten thousand million years later, it is still expanding at nearly the critical rate? If the rate of expansion one second after the big bang had been smaller by even one part in a hundred thousand million million, the universe would have recollapsed before it ever reached its present size."

[74] Faith is described as "the queen of virtues" by Philo, *On Abraham*, XLVI, 270 (Loeb ed., vol 6 p. 133), as cited in Passmore, *The Perfectibility of Man*, p. 61.

The perception that dawns on a person to see the world
not as finished, but as in the process of continued becoming,
ascending, developing — this changes him from being "under
the sun" to "being above the sun."

—Kook[75]

The universe is not static, it is on the march to the future.

—Gordis[76]

Now, things desire their perfections.

—Aquinas[77]

History, therefore, is moving toward a final perfection.

—I. Greenberg[78]

... the full worth of reality is found not in its actual, but
in its potential value.

—Berkovits[79]

The creative act is an escape from the power of time
and ascent to the divine.

—Berdyaev[80]

In contrast, classic Aristotelianism does not focus on potentiality in general in any significant way. According to the classic
position, a potential is actualized only by some actually existing
thing as its cause. It is the "Prime Mover" who actualizes potentialities.[81]

---

[75] Bokser, *Abraham Isaac Kook*, p. 229.
[76] Gordis, *The Book of God and Man*, p. 147. Cf. idem, *A Faith for Moderns*, p. 208.
[77] Aquinas, *Summa Theologiae*, vol. I, q. 6, a.1, p. 110.
[78] Greenberg, *The Third Great Cycle of Jewish History*, p. 1.
[79] Berkovits, *God, Man and History*, p. 81.
[80] Berdyaev, *The Destiny of Man*, p. 136.
   Berdyaev elegantly straddles the Aristotelian position of creation out of primal matter, and the position of those (including traditional Jewish thinkers) who posit creation ex nihilo ("out of nothingness").
[81] In Aquinas' *De Potentia Dei*, potency (power) and act are important principles; however, Aquinas' meaning, emphasis, and thrust are different from ours. For summary, see article on Thomas Aquinas in *Encyclopedia of Philosophy* (New York: Macmillan, 1967), vol. 8, p. 110.

In our system, however, "Holy Potentiality" is a thoroughly overarching dynamic, emanating from the infinitely holy through creation to the far reaches of the cosmic order. Soloveitchik notes: "He is the Lord of the hosts, who resides in every infinitessimal particle of the creation and the whole universe is replete with his glory."[82]

The infinitely holy potentialities themselves, embedded within eternity, are inherent in the eternal origins of the Divine. This is one of our crucial divergences from the Aristotelian line of approach.[83]

200.02 Spiritual Quests for Potential

200.02a Cosmic

At the Genesis Point, a Divine spark leapt forth. The spark initiates a cycle of becoming, creation and rebirth. It is the core of this spiritual blaze of potentiality whose ultimate perfect achievement is a primal cosmic end. It is this transcendental flame which directly continues the spark of life which the Divine infused through Primal Man.

200.02b Mortal

Man is a creature with the ability to undertake a search for the Tree of Knowledge. He is a creature with the ability to undertake a long-term spiritual quest. With dominion over the earth, man as a species is not burdened with a battle for survival with nonhuman creation.

---

[82] Soloveitchik, *The Lonely Man of Faith,* elaborating on the verse "Holy, holy, holy is the Lord of hosts; the whole earth is full of His glory" (Isaiah 6:3).

[83] To our knowledge, the Aristotelians, while considering, at least peripherally, the concept of potential, do not seem to have proffered or developed the concept of holy potentiality, specifically: Holy Potential within potential within potential . . . *ad infinitum.*

Man's restless spirit seeks to transcend its limits.[84] Man must dare to reach down into the depths of his spirit and find his essence;[85] this is his spiritual quest.[86]

By prayer, study, piety, contemplation, solitude, abstinence, penance, sacrifice, charity, purity, and love, man approaches his goal. This is a resolute and continuous assault, day after day, century after century. Man seeks to draw the Divine near. Man seeks to grasp the Divine.

200.03 Ultimate Quests for Potential

200.03a Cosmic

The cosmic thrust for potential is man-centered. Within this constraint, the cosmos seeks its own perfection. The quests for spirituality and perfection, and the attendant quests for freedom, harmony, and beauty find their source in the metaphysical spark which actualized the cosmos. It was the origin of this quest of quests which bridged the gap from "nothingness" to "Somethingness."

200.03b Mortal

Man always seeks to raise himself to a higher level.[87] This quest is in effect an extension of a primal cosmic thrust. Judaism attempts to channel and consecrate this imperative. Quests for fame, fortune, power, and security, to whatever extent their

---

[84] See also Merton, *The New Man*, p. 31, and his footnote on p. 56: "In the Biblical concept [as opposed to the Nietzschean], man is raised above himself by supernatural gifts for which his nature has a passive and obediential potency, gifts by which these hidden potentialities receive a supereminent realization."

[85] See also Ibid., p. 27.

[86] Rabbi Kook, in his introduction to his commentary on the *Siddur Olat Riyah*, writes that "man's soul is continually in a state of worship. It expresses the soul's yearning for inner fulfillment from a state of potentiality to actuality." Stitskin, *Studies in Torah Judaism*, p. 86.

[87] See Herder, *Sammtliche Werke*, ed. B. Suphan, 33 vols. (Berlin 1877-1913), vol. 5 p. 98, as cited in Barnard, *J. G. Herder on Social and Political Culture*, p. 28. "The essence of life is never fruition, but continuous becoming."

However, note that Herder also seemingly posits in the opposite direction in *Ideas for a Philosophy of the History of Mankind*. Bk. VIII, chap. IV, as cited Ibid., p. 304. "Everything that exists strives towards self-preservation; from the grain of sand to the solar system it strives to remain what it is."

extensions are employed to the ultimate ends of the universe, fulfill this overriding cosmic thrust.[88]

Mankind is probing, alert to potential advance. While a significant segment of humanity idealizes the past and/or the status quo, a dynamic segment is always tugging it forward, from the day on which a first voice rang out, crying to mankind slumbering on the raft of Earth, "We are moving! We're going forward!"[89]

Mankind sanctifies its explorers, especially its successful ones. For mankind is also an explorer expedition—with its own scouts way up in their cold, wet, and lonely crow's nests. Sweeping the skyline end to end with their lucky eyepieces. Scanning for new land mass. Ah, there! Peeking over the horizon! There it is! —or was it only a midshipman's mirage?

---

[88] Adherents of Ayn Rand take note!
[89] Teilhard de Chardin, *The Future of Man*, p. 11.

28

After 20 Years,
A Hostage Reflects

Moorhead Kennedy

As January 20, 1996 approached, the media remembered
that it was the fifteenth anniversary of my release, along with 51
others, from Iranian hostage captivity. In a truly contemporary
way, CBS showed me hunched over my laptop, tapping
comments onto the Internet. I was 'speaking' to an AOL 'Forum'
on the significance of my captivity.

Was this event, which had so engrossed public attention,
still significant? If so, how? For example, shortly after my return,
the paraplegic leader of a Viet Nam veteran's organization had
called me to thank the hostages for having made patriotism once
again respectable. I am quite sure that it did. But I had
hoped that, in contrast to *bombing Qum (the Ayatollah's Vatican)
into a parking lot*, and other less edifying 'patriotic sentiments,'
the experience would have a more profound effect on the American
people, as it had on me.

The experience held a mirror up to our society, so that we
might see ourselves more accurately. In our renewed national
self-confidence, we might have realized that not everyone accepts
American leadership. We might have realized that America can

be strong only to the extent that it is prepared to be humble, to listen to others, even to those who do us wrong.

So I retired from the Foreign Service, and, through speeches, op-eds, TV appearances, books, and sermons, I became a kind of unlicensed lay preacher and began to spread my message.

My captors, Muslim militants, or, as they called themselves, *Students in the Path of the Imam*, had their own message to spread, not entirely unrelated to mine. To illustrate , as I was blindfolded for the first time, and with my hands tied, led down the main staircase of the Embassy to begin my captivity, my guard whispered in my ear, *Viet Nam!*, *Viet Nam!* My captors saw themselves as surrogates for the Third World, the avengers of Viet Nam, the spokespersons for the Poor and the Oppressed.

The takeover would, they thought, bond the Poor and the Oppressed together to rise against the Rich and the Powerful. Some of my captors carried in the hip pockets of their captured fatigues a paperback book, in English, about their Fellow Oppressed. It was called *Bury my Heart at Wounded Knee*. Before long, they had allied themselves with a militant Native American group. I even helped my captors to draft a rallying message to the Penobscot Indians, on their island near Orono, Maine.

Unfortunately for my captors, neither the Penobscots, nor the Poor and the Oppressed generally, rose in their support. When the Iranian delegation showed up at the UN General Assembly, they found, to the contrary, that their fellow Third World governments did not approve of diplomatic representatives, of which they had plenty of their own, being held hostage. Oppression, as we hostages pointed out to our captors, is not remedied by oppressing others.

Many of the policies, and the power structure, that my captors had found so offensive remain in place to this day. Anger against the West, against its presumptions of superiority, its perceived disdain for the welfare of much of the world, also remains, to be expressed through acts of violence and destruction. Noteworthy was the first attack by Muslim militants on the World Trade Center in New York.

Others began to copy them, most visibly in the demolition of the Murrah Federal Office Building in Oklahoma City. The public jumped to the conclusion that Muslim militants were responsible for the Murrah explosion as they had been for the first attack on the World Trade Center. After all, wasn't the explosive material used in both demolitions the same? And, of course, how much easier to pin the blame on strange people from the Middle East!

But, in the process of facing that our kind, Americans affiliated with right-wing fringe groups, *were* responsible, the public lost sight of an important reality. The two separate explosions, one by a native-born Gulf War veteran or one by recently immigrated Muslim fundamentalists, were not only chemically, but also conceptually related. Both are expressions of shared anger.

I remember asking one of my guards in 1980 why they were antagonizing the United States when the Soviet Union was right on their border, and invading Afghanistan. He replied, *The Soviets are an enemy, but you Americans are the real enemy.* The real background was not military, but religious and cultural.

When Muslim militants blew up the main building of the American University of Beirut in 1991, they resolved their anger by picking a target that was emblematic of the Western influences that many considered had failed them, that was antithetical to their beliefs, cultural patterns, or vision of the Middle East they want.

Paranoia and Powerlessness

For Terry McVeigh and his colleagues, the distant authority figure, the Federal Government, represents power over them, one that they could not control. Some militia-type groups, for this reason, reject all central authority. They will not recognize authority above the county sheriff. This leads to paranoia about not only the Federal Government, but also the UN, which is even more beyond their control. Hence the fear of the black helicopters, the invasion threats, and so forth.

When the embassy in Tehran was taken over in 1979, some of our new captors asked where the *tunnels* were that were supposed to run to the various Iranian ministries, and through which the United States was exercising power and control. I suggest that whether the control is thought to be exercised from above, from helicopters, or from tunnels 'undermining' from below, the fear is similar.

Revenge Against the Authority Figure for Perceived Injustice

The Double Standard

Oklahoma City commemorated and was in revenge for the second of two misplaced federal assaults on the Branch Davidian compound in Waco, TX. The federal Government was declared by Branch Davidian sympathizers to have practiced a double standard, using in Waco an unreasonable degree of force, which it would not have used in other situations.

Of all the areas in which our world society, since my release, has failed to make progress, indeed has gone backward, it is in our inability to handle shared anger, at home and abroad.

If the problem of shared anger in this country is not confined to Arabs, Iranians, and other Muslims, still less is it confined to eccentric white Americans who join militias. We may be seeing more of it among the downsized, those from the educated middle class, whose loyalty to the system and to individual employers is perceived to have been betrayed. To cite a series in *The New York Times*, how does a plant manager feel when he is downsized and cut loose six months before his pension rights are to vest?

Shared anger can turn easily into organized anger, into terrorism. Always bearing in mind the possibility of their spreading into other groups, let us look at two, Muslim militants and militias. What are the causes of these violent reactions?

Disappointment with the Authority Figure

One explanation given for Oklahoma City, offered by the sister of the alleged culprit, Terry McVeigh, is that the American Dream is not working out. On this level, the Federal Government had failed them. The values of the Beltway are not those of the heartland.

Muslim terrorism, too, is a reaction of disappointment, against the West exemplified best by the United States, a West that to the Middle East had held out such promise. Starting from a position, real or perceived, of inferiority, the Middle East has been trying to come to terms with the West, and not all that successfully. Its coping device was imitation, perhaps evident in Western-style nationalism and the evolution of national states, complete with ideologies, parliaments, anthems, and flags. The Shah of Iran had tried to make his country a western industrial state, modeled after the United States.

Our Iranian captors contrasted the world's indignation over the taking of American diplomats with our own past violations of Iranian sovereignty, about which no international protest had been made. In such circumstances, it is easy to feel disrespected, and powerless, angry and prone to violence.

The Insult

As a result of Western superiority, as perceived by Westerners, there has been a reluctance in the West to take Islam seriously. Because Muslims are 'strange,' they have been ridiculed. Remember *The New Yorker* cartoon, *Hey, Mac, which way to Mecca?* Epithets like 'camel jockey' or 'rag head' are used by those who would never dare to refer to other ethnic groups in a similar way.

A most spectacular reaction, since it took the form of a *fatwa*, or judicial opinion, from the Ayatollah Khomeini himself, was the death sentence passed on the Anglo-Indian author, Salman Rushdie, for his *Satanic Verses*. A chapter was perceived as a sacrilegious insult to the Prophet Muhammad. Reacting to this chapter, people were killed in riots in Pakistan.

Without in any way agreeing with the *fatwa*, we might ask whether some responsibility does not rest with Rushdie's British editors, who failed to take into account the offense, anger, and bloodshed likely to result from publication of this perceived insult. It was, to cite Mr. Justice Holmes' famous limitation on freedom of speech, like shouting **Fire!** in a crowded theater. The need to be taken seriously, and not to be made fun of, can result in the taking over of embassies, the blowing up of trade centers or federal office buildings, or death sentences.

The Statement

Explosions and similar terrorist events are also *statements*. They are correctives to the feeling that others don't know or care who you are, or what you stand for. You may have thought that you were invisible. Make an effective statement, however, and others will listen. A major demolition is like a wake-up call.

But there are other means. On the fifth anniversary of my takeover, my wife and I were invited to take part in an *ABC Nightline* program with Ted Koppel. Also featured, coming in by satellite from his office in the Iranian Foreign Ministry, where he is in charge of terrorism, was my former chief captor, Hossein Sheikholislam.

I asked him what he hoped to gain by taking over the US Embassy in Tehran, and he replied, "*When I was a student in the United States, no one knew where Iran was. But now they know what Iran says, what Iran stands for...*"

Powerlessness

As their anger and frustration builds up, a group begins to understand that had they enjoyed power, no one would have dared to treat them unjustly. Blowing up a building is an exercise of power, a further corrective to feelings of powerlessness. And, in organizing and planning 'The Deed,' running the risks, facing the prospect of trial and punishment, while generating publicity for their cause, the group is further bonded, emerging stronger and more dedicated. This is a further corrective to feelings that they are invisible, powerless, subject to ridicule, and don't count.

What Can We Do About These Angers?

I was not the only hostage to argue that we had lessons to learn from our experience. About a year after our return, my colleague in captivity, Barry Rosen, organized a panel at

Brooklyn College of six of us former hostages, to discuss lessons learned.

Afterwards, a retired schoolteacher stood up and berated us. *What's all this about understanding those bastards? And their motives? Look what they did to you! Put you through mock executions! Lined you up half-naked against the wall! Poked weapons in your necks! You guys ought to be angry! Really angry! What's the matter with all of you?*

As a panel, we had suggested that unless we can get our own angers under control, to do our best to try to understand angers on the part of others and do something about them, then we are bound to encounter that anger again. Unless we examine why and how we can offend, we will become victims of the anger we provoke.

In my own view, we have to learn to love our enemies. That does not mean to *like* them—Jesus did not impose *that* commandment upon us —but rather to try to understand them, and to act in such a way that, in time, they will cease to be enemies. And there are times when we must take responsibility for angers not of our own making. It is not enough to say, for example, that Bosnian angers go back hundreds of years, that ethnic cleansing was practiced during the Balkan wars, that we have no strategic interests in Bosnia.

For if we walk away from these angers, and their appalling consequences, then we will only be acting like the America complained of by my captors in conversation after conversation, a country ultimately concerned only with itself and its material well-being, unconcerned with the plight of the Poor and the Oppressed.

29

Two Prisoners

Robert Satter

Bill Davis and Ben Reid were each convicted of murder. Bill was sentenced to natural life imprisonment without hope of pardon or parole. Ben was sentenced to death. I did not represent either at his criminal trial. But I helped both get pardoned from their severe sentences, released from prison, and readmitted to society.

I reached out to them as human beings in dire trouble. I also elevated them into symbols to validate my faith in the rehabilitation of prisoners and my opposition to capital punishment.

Over a span of more than thirty years I have been entangled in their lives and they in mine. Each marched to his own inner drum beat. Each fulfilled his own destiny. Each touched me and my family in his own separate way.

Bill Davis was convicted in 1953 of killing a beautiful, thirty-year old woman named Penny Evans. She was a Westport socialite and former actress and dancer; he was a handyman and gardener on her estate. They were lovers. On the day of the murder, both drunk, they quarreled over money he claimed she owed him. She threatened to call the police. He flew into a rage, hit her with his fists, stabbed her with a dull knife, and finally strangled her with an electric clock cord. Apprehended the next day, he readily confessed in a twenty-six page recitation in which he expressed deep remorse for what he had done. At the trial he defended himself on the ground of temporary insanity, claiming her mention of the police made him lose his head because of his blind fear of policemen; he had once seen them ruthlessly beat up a man in Philadelphia. The jury did not buy his defense, found him guilty of first degree murder, but recommended mercy. The judge sentenced him to prison for life under a statute that prohibited his ever being pardoned or paroled. This meant Davis was doomed to spend the rest of his days behind bars.

My first contact with Davis was a letter he sent me from prison in 1963 when I was a state representative. He requested that I introduce a bill repealing the natural life sentence law.

Shortly after that, I went to see Davis at the state prison. He was a short, chocolate-complexioned man, about thirty-five years old, wearing a neatly cropped mustache and horn-rimmed glasses. He had an agreeable, if slightly fawning manner. His prison uniform was pressed, his posture erect, his gaze steady. I liked him instantly.

After that meeting, I was even more delighted to work hard for the bill repealing the law under which he had been sentenced. My elation over its final passage abated several months later, when a Superior Court judge questioned whether the newly enacted measure applied retroactively to those, like Davis, already sentenced under the old law. In the 1965 legislative session I again sponsored and successfully pressed for passage of another bill that repealed the natural life sentence law retroactively. The ambiguity eliminated, Davis became eligible for release when the pardon board and parole board gave their approval.

Whenever I went to the prison to see clients, I always stopped by to see Bill. His joy at seeing me raised my own spirits. Every Christmas morning, especially, I made it a ritual to visit him and bring along a small present. I used to take along my oldest daughter, Mimi. We drove up from our home in Newington to Somers, gaily chatting in a holiday mood. After our visit, we drove back, sobered by seeing men confined behind stone walls and steel bars.

In November 1965, after Bill had been in prison for thirteen years, I started representing him before the board of pardons in the hope of getting him pardoned from his life sentence. The board met at the state prison in Somers. Its five members consisted of two lawyers, a physician, a state Supreme Court justice, and a retired Wesleyan College professor whom I knew slightly. I could make out a good case for Davis. He had a perfect prison record with no bad conduct reports whatsoever. He had completed high school courses for an equivalency diploma, trained himself to work as an X-ray technician in the prison hospital, played the organ for prison church services, and typed books for the blind.

"If discipline is to work in the prison," I argued to the board, "rewards must be given for exemplary conduct. If a model prisoner like Bill Davis is not pardoned, the message is sent that a prisoner's conduct does not matter. If a model prisoner like Bill Davis is not pardoned, both the prison disciplinary system and the pardon system fail. Most significantly, Bill Davis is completely rehabilitated. His prison record, his self-education, his service to others proves that. He should be pardoned because he deserves it."

Each time, however, my earnest pleas to the board failed.

In November 1967, I planned to make another attempt. At the breakfast table the morning of the hearing it suddenly occurred to me to ask Mimi, then a senior in Newington High School, if she wanted to go with me. She said, "Sure, Dad." As we started out that gray morning, I had another thought. "You know, Mimi, Davis was convicted of killing a young woman. If you feel that you know him well enough from our Christmas visits to make a plea for him, it could be helpful."

"I'll think about it," she said. We rode to the prison in silence, I reflecting about the argument I would make that morning. When we arrived, Mimi said she would say something on Bill's behalf.

Hearings before the board of pardons go on all day, case after case. When Davis's name was called in mid-morning, he emerged from a locked door into the hearing room. His khakis were neatly pressed, his expression was grave. He smiled, however, when he saw Mimi was with me. I gave essentially the same speech I had given before. It appeared to have little effect. At the end of my remarks, I said, "One other person wants to speak on behalf of Mr. Davis, my daughter Mimi Satter." The board members shifted in their chair impatiently. They had a host of cases yet to hear.

Mimi stood up. She made a short, eloquent plea in succinct, completed sentences: "You can kill a person in two ways. You can kill his body. Or you can kill his spirit. Mr. Davis has proven by his record in prison that he is fully rehabilitated and deserves to be released. If you keep him in prison any longer, you will kill his spirit. You should not do that to anyone."

She smiled and sat down. The Wesleyan professor on the board smiled back.

On the drive home I told Mimi that she had spoken magnificently. At supper time we got a call from Jerry Demeusey, a *Hartford Courant* reporter. He shouted through the phone, "Bill Davis was pardoned. Your daughter wowed the board members. That's all they talked about. She did it! She did it!"

I clasped Mimi. Both of us had tears in our eyes. God, I was proud of her!

In July 1968, Davis was released from prison. He went around personally thanking everyone who had helped him: legislators who had voted for the bill repealing the natural life sentence law; the defense lawyer at his trial who had stood steadfastly by him; a devout church woman who had visited him regularly and restored his religious faith. He expressed enormous gratitude to Mimi. On the day he left prison she helped clean and ready the apartment into which he moved.

Bill took a job as an X-ray technician at Day-Kimball Hospital in Putnam and then at Norwich State Hospital. Later he worked as a counselor at Long Lane School, the state juvenile correctional facility. There he reached out to the youngsters ten to fifteen years old, being confined after their first brushes with the law. When he discovered the kitchen help was stealing the bacon and ham purchased for the inmates, he arranged for the boys to make their own breakfast so they got what was due them. He often took the older lads home with him on weekends and sought, by example of his life, to guide them in the right direction. They came to swear by Bill. He once told me that none of "his boys" ever attempted to run away. He was proud of that.

After a severe heart attack in 1978, he had to take an easier job as chief X-ray technician at Mansfield State Hospital, where he worked until he retired in 1981.

While in prison, Bill's wife had occasionally visited him. After his release, their relationship faltered and I represented him in the divorce. A year or so later Bill fell in love with a white parishioner at the Putnam Baptist Church where he played the organ. Their wedding was held in our living room. I officiated. Ruth and our girls were members of the wedding party and prepared the wedding supper.

Bill and Marge went to live on a lake in northeastern Connecticut, where Ruth and I visited them many times. Marge cooked sumptuous meals and we four always had pleasant chats before a roaring fire. Bill sometimes talked about his time in prison, calling it his "college experience." He took pride in playing the organ at a local church and in serving as chairman of his town's housing authority. In 1984 he was voted Volunteer of the Year for transporting and providing companionship for the elderly of his community. He wrote me:

> Dear Friend,
>   I want you to know that my volunteer work continues each day. I know that no amount of good work can erase my sins of the past but I am certainly doing my best. I am Vice President of our Senior Center and I am on the Board of Directors of the Area Agency on Aging which funds many programs in Eastern Connecticut.
>
>   Best,
>   Bill Davis

Ruth and I always invited Bill and Marge to the gatherings at our home when we celebrated our important wedding anniversaries and the marriages of our children. Our friends would inquire who they were and be fascinated by their story. The link between Mimi and Bill remains important. At Mimi's wedding party in June 1984, Bill made a toast expressing his gratitude to Mimi that brought tears to people's eyes. On her part, Mimi always credits her participation in Bill's release with motivating her to go to law school and, as a labor union lawyer, to defend the underdog.

I am twice blessed. Bill vindicated my faith in the redemption of prisoners; he also shaped my daughter's career as a fighter for social causes.

In his Christmas card of 1994 was a letter saying he had had a spell of bad health: his right leg had been amputated because of poor circulation and he was on dialysis ten hours a night. I called immediately to arrange to see him. During the holidays my wife and I drove out to his home. Bill was in a wheelchair, grayer and frailer than the last time I had visited, his right trouser leg now dangling. We greeted each other warmly. He told of his recent ordeals, ardently praising his wife, Marge, for saving his life. Over and over he spoke of her as "his angel." He said he was looking forward to a prosthesis so he could walk again.

The four of us went out to dinner. The conversation flowed freely and cheerily among us. At one point I said to Bill, "What do you feel best about in your life?"

"Oh, that's easy," he answered, "The things I did for those kids at Long Lane. I'm sure I helped some of them straighten out. And the help I've given the elderly of this area in Connecticut."

Near the end of the meal I asked him, "How do you keep up your spirits, Bill? You're incredible."

He reflected a moment and then said, "When I was in prison, I returned to praying as my mother had taught me. Even when I was under a sentence prohibiting pardon or parole, I had faith someone would get me out. Then you and Mimi came along and vindicated that faith. Even with all that has happened to me recently with my health, I still hold on to it. And I have Marge, my angel."

That bought tears to my eyes. I felt a surge of enormous love for this beautiful, indomitable man.

In 1985, the Connecticut legislature again passed a law authorizing natural life sentences for murderers. Bill Davis is a living refutation of that law.

★

On the morning of January 16, 1957, the frozen, battered body of Florence McCluney was found by Hartford police in the back seat of a parked car. She was a 47-year old black woman who worked as a housekeeping aide at a local hospital. Two thousand dollars in cash were sewn into her underclothes. The cause of death was eight blows by a blunt instrument to her head.

Based on a neighbor's tips, suspicion centered on Ben Reid, a 19-year old derelict who had been a ward of the state for most of his life. When confronted by the police, he confessed: hungry, homeless, destitute, he had accosted McCluney, a friend of his mother, because he knew she carried money on her person. He intended only to rob her, but when she resisted, he struck her repeatedly with a hammer. After stuffing her body in a car, he panicked and fled. He never found the money in her clothes.

Reid came to trial on the charge of first degree murder in a Hartford Superior courtroom adjacent to the one where Joseph Taborsky and Arthur Culombe were also being tried for first degree murder. Taborsky, a notorious criminal, had spent four years in death row, been released when the state Supreme Court reversed his murder conviction, and then enlisted Culombe, a dull-witted drifter, as his accomplice in a series of brutal killings which had sent tremors of fear throughout central Connecticut. Their pattern was to rob lonely package stores or gas stations at night, force the attendants to kneel, and shoot them in the head. "Mad Dog Killers," the newspaper headlines screamed after each murder. When finally apprehended, their trial attracted huge crowds. The Hartford courthouse palpitated with rage towards them.

As the Taborsky-Culombe trial came to its climax, Reid's case started. Nobody attended but his mother. His court-appointed lawyer sought to keep the jury from hearing Reid's confession on the grounds it was illegally procured. When that failed, while not conceding Reid's guilt, he presented some evidence of Reid's disadvantaged background in an effort to avoid imposition of the death sentence.

Reid's trial lasted three days. The jury was out little more than an hour. On the same day, the Taborsky-Culombe jury also rendered its verdict. Both verdicts were the same: guilty of first degree murder without recommendation of mercy. Nobody was surprised at the outcome of the Taborsky-Culombe trial.

Even the prosecutor was shocked that the jury did not recommend mercy in the Reid case. Because it did not, the judge, following the law, immediately sentenced Reid to death.

Reid was confined to death row in the state prison. His cell measured seven by seven feet. An unshaded light bulb burned day and night. He remained in that cell five years while the legal process followed its methodical course.

The automatic appeal to the state Supreme Court failed. Reid's counsel then sought a writ of habeas corpus in the federal district court, claiming the trial court erred in admitting the confessions into evidence. There he was successful. The federal judge held Reid's confession had been obtained illegally because he had not been informed by the police of his right to counsel. This was particularly egregious because, as the opinion noted, Reid was "a dull normal mentality on the borderline of mental deficiency." The federal judge ordered that Reid either be retried without the use of the confessions or be released. The state appealed to the Second Circuit Court of Appeals. The court reversed the trial court, and reinstated the conviction. The United States Supreme Court refused to hear the matter. That was four years before the Supreme Court decided *Miranda vs. Arizona* which would have freed Reid because that case required the police to inform persons in custody of their right to remain silent and their right to counsel before obtaining a confession.

Reid's only hope now lay with the board of pardons. It was a slim hope. Since 1951, when the law was changed to allow juries to spare persons convicted of first degree murder by recommending mercy, the board had not commuted a single death sentence. It had the grisly practice of holding its pardon hearing on the day a condemned man was scheduled to be executed. The day fixed for Reid was June 25, 1962.

Months earlier a vigorous campaign had been initiated in Hartford to save Reid. It was sparked by a brilliant article by William Styron in *Esquire* dramatizing the injustice of Reid's predicament, and organized by William Johnson, professor at Trinity College, and George Will, his student, now a national columnist, and by Albert Holland, vice president of the college. Holland was particularly dedicated because he had been in the shadow of death as a Japanese prisoner during World War II. He asked me to join the drive because of my reputation as an ardent opponent of capital punishment.

On the day of the hearing, the sun shone brightly in a blue June sky. Reid had been kept apprised of all the efforts on his behalf. One can only imagine the mixed emotions he felt on awakening that morning. Did he feel a surge of hope that his ordeal would be over, that he would be pardoned and allowed to live? Or did he feel cold dread that he would die that night in an electric chair already measured for him by the executioner several days before?

A pleasant breeze blew through the open windows of the large room on the second floor of the state prison in Wethersfield that morning. The five board members, all men, sat on a raised judicial bench. Reid sat in a wooden arm chair to their left, behind a low wooden enclosure. Dressed in freshly pressed prison khakis, shirt open at the throat, he was a muscular young black man, his face impassive and expressionless. The fact this might be his last day on earth concentrated attention and heightened the drama in the room.

Holland opened the proceedings by presenting in a direct, but deeply sincere manner, the facts of Ben's impoverished, uncared-for life. He then called on me to speak. I reminded the board of the unfortuitous connection between Reid and the notorious Joseph Taborsky, and contended the public furor and vengeful outcry attending Taborsky's trial had infected Reid's own nearby courtroom and similarly sealed Reid's fate.

"You may recall the conclusion of *Moby Dick*," I said, "how, as the ship Pequod sinks beneath the waves, the arm of a sailor appears from the depths to hammer a pennant against the mast. Just as the nail is being driven home, a gull flies by and its wing, interposing itself between hammer and mast, is nailed fast to the spar, so that the final glimpse of the doomed ship is this bit of fluttering life being dragged with it into the deep."

I paused and then pointed toward Reid. "If Benjamin Reid dies tonight, his life, like that of Melville's gull, will be sacrificed just as surely as if the arm of Joseph Taborsky had reached from the grave to drag him down."

Still pointing: "If Benjamin Reid dies tonight, his death will be Taborsky's last grim legacy. Taborsky has killed enough. Ben Reid should not be yet another of his victims. This board should revoke the death penalty and spare Ben's life."

When I finished, there was a long silence in the room. Holland then introduced others who spoke movingly about Reid's blighted upbringing. One was a middle-aged white woman who had been a nurse at the Hartford County Home during the eight years Reid had lived there as a child. She read passages of Ben's letters sent to her from prison: "I do not want sympathy, I just merely want a chance to show everyone that I have reformed and repented of my wrong that was done thoughtlessly, senselessly."

Reid's mother, badly crippled, shuffled before the board to say, "I ask you, would you grant him life, please?" Reid himself, erect in his pressed khaki uniform, pled in a barely audible voice for mercy. The last speaker for clemency was Reid's prosecutor who had since become a judge. Tall, patrician, Douglass Wright said the trial had been fair, Reid was guilty of the crime, but after much reflection, he had reached the conclusion Reid's execution would be an injustice.

In response, state's attorney John Labelle did not cry out for vengeance. A man of great professional and personal integrity, he said to the board this was a classic case of first degree murder; guilt was clear but the decision to pardon was up to the board. "Whatever you do isn't going to upset our office one bit."

The hearing over, we waited on the shaded lawn in front of the prison for a decision. Children playfully rode their bicycles across the street, unaware that the life of a man hung in the balance. Walking off by myself, I thought, "How can men decide to kill another man under such a lovely sky?"

Finally, word came down: Ben was spared. His sentence was commuted to life imprisonment.

After that I used to visit Ben, as I did Bill Davis, whenever I went to the prison. On Christmas morning Mimi and I brought presents for both of them. Ben had an engaging personality, a warm smile, and intelligence that belied the characterization of him as mentally defective. Ben was also a superb athlete starring in football and baseball at the prison. He listened avidly to the Red Sox games on his radio and delighted in telling me the batting averages and pitching records of the Boston players.

Others who had helped Ben get pardoned also remained in contact with him over the years. They included Bill Styron, Bill Johnson, Bert Holland, faculty and students of Trinity College.

When Ben had been in prison ten years, I started to appear before the board of pardons annually to urge that he be pardoned from his life sentence. On the fifth try, in November 1973, the board agreed. All Ben then needed for his release was approval of the parole board. But just before the first hearing before that board, Ben got into an inexplicable fracas with a guard, resulting in his parole request being turned down.

In the meantime, the group of Reid believers were preparing for his seemingly inevitable release after the next parole board meeting in two months. While in prison Ben had obtained his high school equivalency diploma and taken some college courses. Trinity people proposed to enroll Ben as a special student in the college summer school. Styron agreed to let him stay in the studio next to his home in Roxbury, as a sort of halfway house, until a permanent place for him could be found near Trinity. Then just a week before the parole board meeting, Ben walked away from a prison work detail and into the woods.

His whereabouts were unknown for two days. Ruth thought he was heading toward our house, and nervously locked the doors. But Ben was captured in Holyoke, Massachusetts. His actions exceeded our worst fears.

After leaving the prison, Ben had wandered all night through the woods, eluding state police dogs. In the morning he was behind some homes in Longmeadow. Observing a man get into a car with his golf clubs, Ben crept up to the back porch, knocked, and, when a woman answered, forced his way into the house. He brandished a steel antenna as a weapon. Getting the woman and three young children into a car, he made them ride up and down the Connecticut River valley for most of the day. At one point, when they were in a state park, he had sexual intercourse with the woman. Later, after she had driven him to Holyoke, he boarded a bus for New York City. Waiting for the bus to leave, he was spotted by an off-duty prison guard and quickly arrested.

We who had stood by Ben were devastated. We had watched him grow in prison and demonstrate, by his letters and conversations, qualities of self-awareness and strength. We had put our trust in him. We also projected our hopes that he would prove that our opposition to the death penalty was justified.

But Ben marched to the tune not of our hopes, but of his own fears. His escape, within weeks of the time when, in all probability, he would have been legally released, could only be explained by his dread of being free. Possibly, plans of the Trinity people to enroll him in college had scared him. But the more likely reason for his act was he could not face leaving prison, the only home he knew.

Recounting the turn of events at supper with Bill Styron and his lovely wife, Rose, some weeks later, we could not suppress the thought of what might have happened if the plans for Ben to stay at Roxbury had been carried out.

Despite my disappointment, I represented Ben on the charge of rape in Springfield, Massachusetts, Superior Court. At first he pleaded not guilty, and asserted to me his innocence, claiming the woman had consented. The trial was scheduled for the Wednesday before the Super Bowl game in Miami. The prosecutor boasted to me he had tickets. Sensing his eagerness to avoid a trial in order to get to the game, I negotiated a favorable plea bargain: a guilty plea by Ben in exchange for a recommended sentence of ten to fifteen years. When I told Ben that if found guilty by a jury, he could get life imprisonment, he readily agreed to the bargain.

So Ben went off to the Massachusetts state prison. He wrote to me occasionally and I replied. After ten years, Massachusetts released him, and he returned to Connecticut to serve a three year term for the prison escape. In January, 1983, as the time for his parole board hearing approached, I, now a judge, urged prison authorities to transfer Ben to Whiting Forensic Institute for psychiatric evaluation and treatment. Up to then Ben had received no rehabilitative help during the twenty-six years he had been in prison.

While he was at Whiting, the date for his parole hearing was set. I advised him to ask for an adjournment because he had not completed the treatment, but he insisted on going ahead. Whiting discharged him for lack of cooperation and returned him to the state prison at Somers. On the day of the hearing before the parole board, he set fire to his bunk mattress, almost asphyxiating his cellmate. Of course, his application was denied.

When I went to see him after the incident, he was contrite. This time I let him have it. "Ben, I'm not interested in your words, only your actions. Every time you are up for release, you do something to assure it won't happen. You've let down everyone who has tried to help you. It's clear you don't ever want to get out of prison."

He lamely denied it.

Ben was returned to Massachusetts, under an interstate compact, to continue to serve his Conneticut time. Whenever he wrote to me, he always mentioned how he was going to "show" me how he was improving.

At about that time a Boston lawyer named Fred Corneel and Bert Holland's widow, Eva, who lived in Wellesley, assumed responsibility for Ben. Fred paid for a psychologist to visit Ben in prison and help him adjust to the prospect of freedom. Eva offered to take him into her home if he was granted weekend leave. Fred, Eva and I met several times to plan for his being freed.

Massachusetts prison authorities undertook a progressive program of minimum security placement which led to Ben, for the first time, living in a halfway house and working at a job outside of the prison. In December 1985 he wrote me:

> Dear Judge Satter,
>
> I'm working with the Mentally Retarded Adults, at a daycare clinic. It's hard and sad, yet it's rewarding, in that these people have no basic living skills and must be taught to feed, toilet train themselves etc. This is survival and the time and effort I give is greatly appreciated. I feel good about this and it humbles me. I am glad this was my first job in Boston. Thank you Judge Satter for everything and I am grateful to you always.
>
> Sincerely,
> Ben

In 1987, Ben was finally released. The next summer I took him to a ball game at Fenway Park. I knew he had listened to Red Sox games during his years in prison and loved the team. When we met at the gate, he was thinner than I remembered him and now gray around the temples. He walked into the park and looked about like a novitiate entering Saint Peter's in Rome for the first time. He gazed lovingly at the neatly raked dirt of the infield, the manicured green grass of the outfield, the white chalk lines stretching from home plate to the foul poles. He pointed to the high fence in left field and said with a smile, "The Green Monster."

We had seats in far right field but he didn't mind. He followed the game intently, commenting on every play. He knew his baseball. When a vendor came by, I asked Ben if he wanted a hot dog.

"No," he said, "they're not kosher."

"What?" I exclaimed.

"I'm attending an orthodox synagogue now and I only eat kosher."

"Ye Gods!" I said to myself.

Later I asked him if he wanted a beer. He said, "I don't drink."

Between innings he told me he lived in a single room off Massachusetts Avenue. "A nice building," he said, "very secure."

He worked as the manager of a variety store near Boston University, supervising five clerks, handling the cash register, and depositing the day's receipts in the bank. The owner knew of his past, he said, and trusted him.

The main problem he faced on his job was shoplifting. When he caught a kid or student, he severely chastised them but never turned them over to the police. "I see myself in them when I was young and tempted to steal," he said. "I tell them it is wrong and they can get into trouble. They listen and don't do it again, at least in my store."

We had a splendid time together, parting with a hearty handshake. We have repeated our baseball outing several times.

But Ben's path has not been straight. He lost the job at the variety store, got another in a cafeteria, lost it, got another as a bellhop at a hotel. Fred Corneel, the Boston lawyer, regularly gives him money to help him make ends meet.

1994 was a bad year for him. He lost his job, fell behind in his rent and was evicted, lived on the street for a time and then sought out a church shelter for the homeless. Despite hitting bottom, the heartening thing is he never turned to crime.

More recently he landed a job as a clerk in a delicatessan, earning $250 a week, and rents a room in a rooming house. He gets along — but barely.

How do I feel about Ben? I felt betrayed when he raped the Longmeadow housewife, and let down by each of the stupid acts that kept him in prison. In 2000 he was sixty-two years old. The demons within him seem to have subsided and he seems to have attained a measure of maturity. I believe he does not now present a danger to anyone. And yet his thirty years in prison may well have damaged his capacity to live successfully on the outside.

Why do I persist? Because I have known Ben for more than thirty years, and cannot abandon a friend. Because Ben is a human being who has achieved a measure of redemption. Because I hold to my opposition to the death penalty and want to prove that even with Ben I am right.

Two prisoners—both murderers—both reformed—one a sterling citizen in his community; the other still struggling to make his way. The only connection between them is in my mind, because I was involved in their lives and they in mine. Their stories reveal the cruel dilemma of society dealing with crime and punishment and applying general rules to specific people.

30

The Cathedral of
Saint John the Divine

Paul Moore, Jr.

Bill Johnson was a canon of the Cathedral of St. John
the Divine for twenty-five years. He loves the place and has
made a major contribution to its life. He established there the
Institute of Theology, which had at its heart a devoted community
of Christians whose worship has centered in the 9:15 Eucharist
at the Cathedral. He has also participated in many of the great
events which have taken place there and has articulated the
kind of Anglican theology, liberal, catholic, intellectually honest,
searching for truth in an atmosphere of freedom, for which the
cathedral stands. The following "tour" of the cathedral, therefore,
seems an appropriate addition to the *festschrift*.

As the Eucharist spells out in liturgy the heart of the
Christian faith, so, in its way, does the Cathedral of St. John the
Divine spell out that same faith in action: in its acceptance of
all peoples; in its involvement in every aspect of the life of the
city; in its seamless life of worship, education, social action, and
the pastoral ministry of compassion. In Europe, two styles of
cathedrals were built in the Middle Ages; the one, typical of the
British isles, was set apart upon a hill or in the midst of a large

479

close, complete with lawns and gardens; the other, typical of the Continent, was placed in the very center of the city, where all the activities of society could take place, from mothers nursing their babies, to political rallies, to the rollicking fiestas of the great holidays. One represented a theology that sensed God as apart from life, to be reached in quiet meditation, the other as God in the very center of hustle and bustle, the joys and tragedies, the filth, and the beauty of everyday living. The National Cathedral in Washington typifies the former, the cathedral in New York, the latter.

When I came to New York and looked out the window at the massive pile of stone, I wondered if it would be possible to give life to the largest cathedral in the world in the modern metropolis of New York.

Despite its glorious history, the cathedral, in recent years, had become quiescent except for a regular liturgical life under the inimitable leadership of Canon Edward West, the acting dean; some ground-breaking conferences set up by Canon, later Bishop, Walter Dennis; a boys' school; and occasional great services like the first performance of Duke Ellington's jazz Mass. When I asked for advice, one of my friends, Bob Potter, said half-jokingly, "Sell it." Even the building itself was in trouble: a recent engineering study declared that the central dome was unsafe and would have to be rebuilt. This would have wiped out whatever endowment was left. We faced a crisis not only of direction but of survival; I needed someone with the competence to be steward of a great monument. I needed someone who cared passionately about the city and one who shared my liberal, catholic theology. Most important, I needed someone with enormous energy and courage.

The first and only person who came to mind was James Parks Morton. Jim Morton studied for a career in architecture at Harvard. On a visit to Cambridge in the early fifties, I met Jim and had something to do with his changing course to the priesthood. After seminary, he joined our team in Jersey City. He and his wife, Pamela Taylor, lived and worked with us for five years. He later ran the national urban program of the Episcopal Church and then became the director of an ecumenical urban training center in Chicago. He was known to take risks, sometimes at the expense of sound financing.

In due course, I nominated him to the trustees to be the dean of the Cathedral, and he was confirmed with great enthusiasm. This choice with that of Bill Johnson was the most important appointment I have ever made. Under Jim's chaotic but brilliant leadership, the cathedral has become one of the great religious institutions of the world.

Come and stand on the northwest corner of Central Park and look at it. Its great bulk towers on the cliff of Morningside Heights. It watches over the deep poverty of Harlem, can be seen from the gleaming skyscrapers of midtown. Behind, stand the cultural institutions of the Heights: Columbia University, the Jewish Theological Seminary, Union Theological Seminary, St. Luke's Hospital, the Bank Street School, Barnard College, the Convent and School of the Community of the Holy Spirit. Although some New Yorkers think of the location as way uptown and wish it were in midtown, the trustees chose the site so that the cathedral would be near what they thought would be the intellectual center of New York, a modern Acropolis. As the city developed, however, its location on the edge of Harlem became a different blessing and shaped the kind of place it was to become, a spiritual home for all the people of New York and a sign of hope for the poor.

Come up the stone steps and stand before the great bronze doors, depicting scenes from the Bible. On each side of them, stern sculptures of Old Testament prophets guard the entrance. Their words of justice and peace often sound forth from the pulpit. Each Easter, dressed in a gold cope and miter, the bishop knocks on the doors with the ornate crozier of the bishop of New York. As the doors swing open, he cries, "He is risen Alleluia!" And a thousand voices reply, "The Lord is risen indeed! Alleluia!"

One morning during this ceremony, in the early seventies, it was picketed by three different groups: one claiming that our choir was not integrated, as it filed past with several black faces; another that we were being unfair to the squatters across the street, even though we had provided them with a furnace; and thirdly, that somehow I was keeping a local settlement house, over which I had no jurisdiction, from being run by the local residents ... life in New York! Being picketed from the left was especially painful; my right side was tough, the left sensitive.

When the doors of the cathedral open and your eyes become accustomed to the gloom, you immediately are confronted on one side by a larger than life cross, where hangs a strong and suffering Christ, and before which red vigil lights are burning. Directly in front of you is an iconostasis, on which glisten images of Christ the King, Mary Theotokos, God-bearer, and other icons of Saints revered by the Orthodox. Both Dean Morton and Canon West were deeply influenced by Orthodox spirituality. Thus, as you enter, you see two great Catholic symbols of East and West, the icons and the crucifix. Looking up through the opening in the iconostasis, the largest Gothic nave in Christendom stretches before you, and your eyes pass through this nave and the chancel to the distant high altar, the heart and soul of the place.

The original architects of the cathedral, Heins and LaFarge, designed the sanctuary and choir in Romanesque and Byzantine style, but a later bishop decided the nave should be Gothic. Ralph Adams Cram declared it his greatest work. In between the nave and chancel, the unfinished crossing with its huge round Roman arches of unfinished blocks of stone lend the building a crude strength reminiscent of Durham Cathedral. I rejoiced in the unfinishedness of the central space, for it symbolized the restless unfinished city that surrounds it and forms an appropriate setting for the variety of productions, some quite secular, others, from a different faith, which are part of the cathedral's life.

As you walk through the iconostasis, you see on your right an altar, made from an enormous, handsome slab of walnut, designed by the well-known Japanese-American artist Nakashima and dedicated to peace. In recent years, peace has been a major concern of our life here. On the afternoon before the great march for peace at the time of the "freeze" movement, the cathedral was filled with several thousand people, representing every faith imaginable: the Hiroshima maidens, still bearing the scars of the atomic bomb, were there; Japanese Buddhist monks, Hindu holy men, rabbis, bishops from the Anglican, Orthodox, Methodist, Lutheran, and Roman Church, leaders of the black churches, an ancient Native American chief intoning an eerie chant for peace. There were orphans of war from all over the world who spoke of their loneliness and terror. As each person prayed, it was as if the whole world were screaming to the one God of all to help us, help us cease the murder and the horror of war and to protect us from atomic annihilation. Never have I felt so proud of that dear place.

Behind the peace altar, on a pillar, is a small bronze bas-relief depicting a moment in the struggle for women's ordination. I had been active in this crusade for many years and had written a book about the details of that saga. The book opens with the scene depicted on the bas-relief: several women in the diocese had been made deacons but were not yet allowed to be ordained to the priesthood. They wished to demonstrate at the service in which the male deacons were to receive priests' orders. I was happy to have them do so, and Eddie West, with his accustomed aplomb, arranged the demonstration with liturgical dignity. I was seated in my chair, having just ordained the men, when the women came forward and knelt before me. I so wanted to ordain them that I could hardly keep my hands from going forward to touch their heads. Since canon law prevented me, I felt as if my hands were literally tied behind my back. The bronze, sculpted by a woman member of the diocese, depicted that symbolic moment. Now we have well over a hundred women priests in the diocese carrying out all the functions of priesthood, and the Church already has two women bishops. Many of them have been ordained at the cathedral. The issue, of course, created a major furor in the Church, but the rapid acceptance of the women proved the Church was ready. Even those parishioners who were adamantly against the idea of women priests came to receive the ministrations of a particular woman and found themselves respecting and growing fond of her.

Across from the altar of peace, stands a large cross depicting the agony of the people of Nicaragua, created by a Nicaraguan artist, Carlos Sanchez Arias, known as "Kalo," a cartoonist and billboard artist. The corpus is a woman. At its center, a blade pierces the figure, and the blade is adorned by the stars and stripes. My son George, an artist who had lived in Nicaragua, arranged for the cross to be lent to the cathedral. I visited Nicaragua twice and became a friend of Miguel D'Escoto, a priest who was the foreign minister of the Sandinista regime. He had carried this huge cross on his back in a pilgrimage of peace. It also was part of a demonstration in front of the U.S. Embassy. The first time I ever heard of Nicaragua was when I asked my Marine Corps drill sergeant what his campaign ribbon represented. He said, "Nicaragua." This was the campaign in which Augusto Cesar Sandino gave his life when leading the guerilla opposition to the United States. It was after him that the Sandinista movement was named.

On either side of the nave are bays commemorating various aspects of the life of the Church, each with its own window. The stained glass shows doctors, nurses, lawyers, sportsmen, soldiers, athletes, artists, architects, authors and so on. From its very start, this great building has recognized the vocation of the laity, and Canon Johnson's Institute of Theology provided the laity and the clergy with superior theological education.

The acquisition of the most recent window provides an amusing morality tale of the importance of good manners. One day, Canon Jonathan King was giving a guided tour to some tourists. A tourist in a Harry Truman tropical shirt asked, "How much does a window like that cost?"

"Thousands of dollars."

"If I wanted to give one, who should I write?"

The other tourists giggled, but not the Canon. He politely gave the gentleman the Dean's address. The call was made. The dean flew to Miami with a sketch of the only remaining uncompleted window under his arm, nervous that the old gentleman would not want to give a window honoring sportsmen. The dean was ushered into a palatial front hall, adorned with the heads of elk, antelope, a lion's skin, and other mementos of Col. Robert Pentland's life. The Cathedral was given a window and a bequest of a million dollars when the old man died.

The windows are permanent, of course, but some of the bays express contemporary subjects. The first bay on the right memorializes the suffering of the Holocaust with a sculpture of a corpse twisted in an agony of death. In the next bay stands a huge cross of burnt timbers, at the base of which lies a fireman's helmet and glove. This is a memorial to the men who died in the most costly fire in the history of the city.

Underneath the window, depicting the medical profession, is the AIDS memorial, a book in which one can have the name of a person dying of AIDS inscribed in handsome script. Vigil lights are lit there by those who offer a prayer for their departed lovers, friends, and relatives. I will never forget the dedication of this shrine early on in the epidemic when so much shame and fear was attached to the disease that it was often hard for the families or friends even to find an undertaker or a church where they could have a funeral. This shrine was to symbolize God's love for those who died and to lend them a dignity in their death of which they were deprived in their dying. The evening of the dedication, we celebrated a Eucharist at the crossing and processed down the darkened aisle to the shrine, which was shining with candles. After the prayers of dedication were said, the names of those who had died of AIDS were solemnly recited in the silence, each echoing through the darkened gothic arches as if up to heaven: "John, Harry, Bruce, Matthew…" At the conclusion, members of the congregation came forward for a blessing. We clergy laid hands on them, one after the other. I remember whispered requests that I pray for Ralph or Daniel; tearful words that the person himself had AIDS but had not dared tell his family who did not know he was gay. Another sought absolution for the guilt he felt, another stood up after the blessing and asked, "Please hug me." He just wanted me to hold his shaking body. This service has become an annual event, now an interfaith service. The giving of the blessing of dignity and love to those involved in this epidemic is the most important thing we can do for thousands of people, mostly young, who feel rejected even by God at the moment when they most need love.

Nor was the tragedy of AIDS something happening outside the diocesan family. Early on in the epidemic, one of our clergy, Mills Omaly, came to me and told me, in the strictest confidence, that he was HIV positive and that he already was having symptoms of AIDS. He was a splendid priest, and had just been called to a new parish where he was enjoying a vigorous and popular ministry and where, he said, he was happier than he had ever been in his life. He and I agonized over when he should tell his people. Mills courageously took the matter into his own hands. A couple of months after our conversation, our annual diocesan convention took place. A resolution urging compassion and support for people with AIDS was presented. I saw Mills coming up to the microphone; my heart sank. Being a quiet person, he had never spoken before in convention. I was anxious, because the diocese had only recently calmed down after the uproar of my ordaining a lesbian to the priesthood. Mills spoke powerfully to the resolution, paused, and said, "I am especially moved by the resolution because I have AIDS." The great hall was silent, motionless, stunned. I looked out at the delegates and saw shock and confusion on their faces. Finally, someone rose and began to clap. Then another and another, until the whole convention gave him a standing ovation, surrounding him, hugging him, comforting him, with tears streaming down their faces. Of all the years I presided at the convention, I think that was my proudest moment. Love had overcome fear and hostility. The painful conflict over homosexuality, which had torn us apart, had been worth it. The anger and pain had been redeemed. Mills died a year later. His leaving the parish was a difficult business, but in that moment in convention he knew he was loved. He was buried from the cathedral.

The next bay after the AIDS memorial celebrates the ecological movement. A great bronze wolf, sculpted by a member of the cathedral family, stands guard, as it were, for endangered species, and a huge fossil sea shell stands there as a reminder of our stewardship of the ocean. Jim Morton has been a leader in the ecological movement and was one of the first people to bring the Church's attention to ecology as a theological issue: he chaired a conference on the subject in Moscow that included the Dalai Lama, Mikhail Gorbachev, and Mother Teresa, among others. Most of the great leaders of the movement have preached from the Cathedral pulpit.

As you reach the Crossing, you will see a plaque dedicated by the Queen Mother, a friend of Bishop Donegan, to commemorate her visit.

Pause now at the crossing and look back at one of the most glorious rose windows in Christendom, a deep blue. In its center is depicted a life-sized Christ, who looks tiny in the context of this great circle. Then turn and see the blazing red of the east window symbolizing images from the book of Revelation, the author of which gave his name to the Cathedral of St. John the Divine.

Underneath this window is the high altar, on either side of which stand two menorahs, given in gratitude by Alfred Ochs, the publisher of *The New York Times*, for work by Bishop Manning on behalf of the Jewish community. Beyond them, two majestic blue vases, from Emperor Hirohito of Japan, adorn the retable. Mussolini gave two silver candlesticks by the bishop's throne. We are proud of these gifts from the people of Japan and Italy, despite what their leaders later did. President Benes of Czechoslovakia donated a crystal chandelier, which hangs nearby in the ambulatory, and President Ataturk of Turkey gave the rug that leads up to the high altar.

The crossing is the largest of any Gothic cathedral and here great moments have been witnessed. Up the long aisle to the crossing comes the procession of the beasts on St. Francis Day for the blessing of the animals which includes a horse, a camel, a bowl of algae, a golden eagle, a parrot, a tree, a python, and an elephant, followed, of course, by two men with shovels. We thank God for these animals and bless them as they lumber into the sanctuary, for in New York, animals give grace to lonely lives and companionship to children who unconsciously long for nature. I remember putting my little finger into the hole of a small cardboard box to bless Jeremy, a white mouse.

Here, during an especially tense time in the Middle East, came two mayors of Palestine. They had been conducting a protest fast at the U.N. and had told the secretary general that they would only break their fast if it could be done in a religious setting. He called the dean, who drove down to the U.N. in his vestments and brought them to the Christmas Midnight Mass. When the time came for the Kiss of Peace, the rabbi who had chanted the Old Testament lesson from Isaiah met them in the midst and they exchanged the Kiss of Peace.

There, in the crossing, I was ordained a deacon in the Church of God in 1949. And there, over the years, the bodies of the great and humble have been brought for a last farewell. The liturgy for Jim Henson, the beloved creator of Sesame Street, included Big Bird and the song by Kermit the frog about how hard it is to be green. We cried. It was there that I conducted a memorial service for our friend John Belushi and heard his brother tell tales of taking a bath with him when they were boys. John hated the act he was asked to perform, from time to time, in which he dressed up like a bumble bee. He and Dan Akroyd had a pact that whoever survived the other would dance it at his funeral. So the bumble bee dance took place after the reminiscence of the bathtub. I fantasized, in my homily, that John was playing his electric guitar with the heavenly harpists. There were those who disapproved of our having a service for him because he died of an overdose, but I thought it highly appropriate that somehow the cathedral could welcome his friends and family and pray that despite the agonies of his last days, he could rest in peace.

In the crossing, too, each Good Friday, the Passion of Christ is acted out. On Thanksgiving Day, Native Americans and their culture are honored. The Pilgrims take a back bench.

Here, then, truly, is the crossing of the sacred and the profane, the holy and the broken. Here the incarnation of Christ in the world is displayed for all to see, his compassion, his power to redeem, his love.

Climb the steps into the chancel and see, towering above you on either side, the great granite columns that hold up the arching ceiling, each weighing 130 tons.

One windy day in March, I took my grandchildren on a tour of the mysterious upper regions of the cathedral, climbing up an endless, circular stone stairway, which begins at the entrance to the chancel. We climbed and climbed and eventually came out on a balcony overlooking the nave. Far below, I spied a gaggle of tourists and could not resist the temptation of bellowing down at them in my most thunderous voice, "God is looking at you!"

In the clerestory, we went past the studio of Philippe Petit, who attained fame as the acrobat who walked on a wire between the summits of the Twin Towers. His punishment was to give a free exhibit for children by walking a high wire across the pond in central Park. When we laid the cornerstone for the new east tower, Philippe danced across Amsterdam Avenue ten stories in the air: he stood on the roof of the old people's home, dressed in gleaming white knickers, purple socks, and a purple sash and, taking a silver trowel from his sash, the trowel used to lay the original cornerstone of the cathedral, flashed it in the brilliant sunshine, walked half way across, genuflected, to everyone's horror, and proceeded to reach the parapet of the cathedral. There, he presented me with the trowel to lay the cornerstone of the tower, which I did, as my cope blew behind me in the high wind.

I took the grandchildren to the very top that day, and discovered that above the false ceiling of the nave is a roof. Between the ceiling and the roof is an enormous barn-like space where scores of pigeons fly back and forth to their nests. However, the greatest thrill of all, that afternoon, was stepping outside and seeing the whole city of New York spread before us.

There is an ambulatory around the back of the chancel and sanctuary, along which are set the Chapels of the Tongues. The first architects carried out in this way the theme that the cathedral was for all the people of New York, by having each of the ethnic groups then living in the city represented by a chapel, designed in the architecture of their native land, and named for their patron saint: St. James for the Spanish, St. Martin for the French, and so forth. Each chapel is an exquisite bit of architecture in its own right. I particularly love St. Martin's, where the sacrament is reserved as a silent place for individual prayer. Here, every other week, I celebrated the Eucharist for the diocesan staff before we came together to plan for our work. I believe these gatherings were one of the reasons we remained a relatively dedicated and happy group. It is hard to maintain a hostile attitude to one with whom you have just exchanged the Kiss of Peace. A brief homily at each service gave me a chance to emphasize again and again what we were about.

Moving behind the high altar and along the north side of the chancel, you come upon the baptistery, a small, high-vaulted octagonal space of Gothic design, perfect in every detail. On one side is the columbarium, where ashes are placed with dignity and grace. Here is the beginning and the end of a Christian's life.

The ambulatory and the north wall of the crossing are appropriate places for art exhibits. The most notable had to do with the celebration of Christian women and their contribution to the life of the Church down through the ages. One sculpture within that exhibit depicted a woman on a cross. The artist, Edwina Sands, a granddaughter of Winston Churchill, was attempting to show, through a flight of artistic fancy, that God took on the flesh of women as well as men when God became incarnate and that women as well as men have borne the suffering of the cross down through the ages. The exhibit, opening in Holy Week, caught the attention of the media, some of which incorrectly stated that the female crucifix was on the high altar. On Easter afternoon, I had flown to a Trappist monastery for a retreat with which to begin a sabbatical. Monday morning, a monk came shuffling into where I was having a quiet breakfast and put the local paper in front of me. On the front page was a photograph of the sculpture. The article said that both my suffragan bishops had made statements to the press condemning it as heretical.

I was both bemused that so many people failed to get the point and angry that my two suffragans had made statements without notifying me. As with most controversies, it provided a fine teaching moment to elaborate on the incarnation and on the equality of the ministry of women in the Church.

Before leaving the east end of the cathedral, I want you to visualize what it was like to stand behind the high altar, looking out over the faces of thousands of people, and realizing that their hopes, their fears, their joys, their pains have been laid out upon the altar and that in lifting up the bread and wine you were offering their lives to Almighty God. Sometimes celebrating the Eucharist was such an intense experience that I could hardly utter the words of consecration.

There were other great moments in the sanctuary: the Maundy Thursday service commemorating the institution of the Last Supper; the quietness, the imagining of that last warm but tragic time Christ experienced with his disciples, his washing their feet, symbolized in the cathedral by everyone in the congregation coming forward and giving their hands to be washed; the sweet, timid, young hands of children, the wrinkled, fragile hands of old women, the calloused hands of manual workers, black hands, Asian hands, the caring hands of doctors and nurses, the hands of priests.

After the austerity of the remembrance of the Passion on Good Friday came the Easter Eve service of baptism and confirmation, where sometimes as many as fifty people were baptized in front of the altar amidst the joy of the first Eucharist of Easter, being born anew with the risen Christ. Sometimes more water splashed on me than on the baptizands, as we dealt with lively, squirming children. But I was always deeply moved by the adults who came forward, often shaking with emotion, and bent over the font, presenting their gray hair to be wetted in the waters of baptism, presenting their wrinkles to be born again. After the baptisms, I would move to my chair in front of the altar and lay hands on many more in the rite of the gift of the spirit in confirmation. Babies of all colors, presented by parents from all walks of life; men and women, old and young, rich and poor took part. The ceremony was always a bit chaotic, with infants crying and people becoming confused as to what to do, but the very chaos gave a vitality to the wonder which was occurring, whereby God was indeed entering their lives forever.

We walk down from the altar through the chancel, back to the crossing, where, on the north side, stands the great marble pulpit from which is preached the word of God. Technically speaking, unless the speaker is an ordained clergy person, what he or she says is an address, not a sermon. An ordained person vows at ordination to preach the word of God and has theological education to assure the people, as far as humanly possible, that what they hear from him or her is within the teaching of the Church. No such assurance is present when a lay person speaks, but both the dean and I feel strongly that lay persons who are experts and experienced in various important fields of human endeavor speak words we need to hear, words that represent the presence of God in the world. Thus we have had secretaries general of the U.N., Vice President Gore on ecology, Carl Sagan, Leonard Bernstein, Marian Edelman of the Children's Defense Fund... and many others speaking from their hearts of the hurts and dangers facing God's people.

We also ask religious leaders of other faiths. I remember particularly the first time the Dalai Lama spoke there of the sufferings of the people of Tibet. He is a humble and whimsical man, a holy and courageous man. Someone must have told him that in America every speech begins with a joke. And so he began by speaking of frustration he had experienced. He said, "It was like a man who buys a beautiful car from a dealer and on the way home it stops and he cannot fix it. It makes him throw up!" A stunned silence preceded some nervous laughter. No one could believe that this great holy man would tell such a silly joke, but you know, it made his later profound remarks the more believable. He did not exalt himself, but was earthy and spoke to us as a humble person. On another occasion, Jesse Jackson preached on the subject of the homeless, preceding a great rally and march starting at Columbus Circle.

Housing was a subject very close to me, beginning in 1950, when I became chairman of the Jersey City NAACP committee on housing. We were concerned with poor conditions and overcrowding, but massive homelessness did not exist then. Homeless people came to us only once in a while...chronic alcoholics or families left on the street after a fire. By the time I arrived in New York, however, the numbers of homeless began to grow, and as the cuts in federal funds for housing increased and the state emptied its mental hospitals without providing shelter for the discharged patients, the problem grew and grew. Early on, I preached a sermon that said New York would become the Calcutta of the North, where we would step over bodies in the street and not think a thing about it. This was thought to be a rhetorical overstatement at the time, but the prediction became true all too soon. In the morning, in Grand Central Station, commuters in their three-piece suits, carrying shiny briefcases, stepped over bodies on their way to work. Even the best intentioned "pass by on the other side" to quote the parable of the Good Samaritan, because there were so many bodies that coming to the assistance of every one you saw would be impossible. It seems to me that a modern interpretation of the parable would urge political action on homelessness. I once tried to start a movement to include having shelter as a basic human right. Someday this may occur. Until then we have to work for short-term solutions. Certainly, in this country, if you do not have an address you are deprived of rights afforded other citizens.

The cathedral began a housing initiative, shortly after Jim Morton became dean, called Urban Homesteading Assistance Board, U.H.A.B., which encouraged local people to rehabilitate empty buildings and move in. This was called "sweat equity," since their equity in the building was their work, not their cash, for they had no cash. The city cooperated with guaranteed mortgages, and our staff taught the builders about the paperwork and administration involved. Over the years thousands have found homes this way. I used to say to those who stated that homelessness was a most complicated problem, that indeed it was simple. Provide homes, as the government used to, and homelessness would disappear. The point is that the private sector cannot or will not provide houses cheap enough for those beneath the poverty line, and ever since the Reagan-Bush years, the government has held back on subsidy.

I go into this in some detail, because it illustrates how we not only preached but acted on the social difficulties surrounding us.

Perhaps the best known sermon I preached there was when New York was on the edge of bankruptcy in the early seventies and businesses began leaving the city seeking pleasanter and cheaper surroundings in the suburbs, usually in a location near the residence of the CEO. Jim Morton and my wife, Brenda, broached the idea to me a couple of weeks before Easter when I had the flu. The last thing I wanted to do was think about a sermon, but they insisted. We decided to call Peter and Ellen Strauss, who owned a radio station and were old New Yorkers. (Ellen was a Sulzberger of *The New York Times* family) and also call Osborne Elliott, then the editor of *Newsweek*. They were quite surprised when I asked them to help me prepare my Easter sermon. Ellen suggested I call her aunt, Iphigene Sulzberger, who was still the power behind the throne at the *Times*, and ask her assistance. The result was a front page spread and the whole sermon printed in the financial section (a first, I think). I said that these corporations owed their very existence to the people of the city and that even if they moved to Darien, they would still be benefiting from New York. Therefore, it was totally irresponsible to desert the city in a time of need. It was like rats leaving a sinking ship. This caused a major reaction. My brother, William H. Moore, the CEO of the Bankers Trust Company, told me that his friends would call each other Brother Rat as they drove through the Lincoln Tunnel. Businessmen called me and explained why they had to leave the city. Others called to say they were staying. It established sort of a "good guy, bad guy" dynamic. I was asked to speak on the subject. We held rallies. It had an effect in other cities: the issue of a corporation's responsibility to its community was debated. Unfortunately, the power of the bottom line has overcome this brief period of ethical questioning, and businesses are once again deserting the cities that give them life.

That ornate marble pulpit was a splendid place from which to preach the word of God, never more moving than on Christmas Eve, when, in the darkness, thousands of candles twinkled, held in the hands of thousands of unknown persons, each of whom had come to find God, in thanksgiving, or praise, or forgiveness, or healing; into this dark and wonderful mystery of the body of Christ I was privileged to preach the word of God.

Going down the side aisle, we pass the figure of Bishop Manning, who once erected a tenement at the door of the cathedral so that all who entered were made aware of the slums of New York. Further down, you come to the Poets' Corner, where, year after year, we dedicate a memorial to an American writer. At these quiet, beautiful ceremonies, a well known current literary figure reads from the writings of the person we are remembering and a new plaque is dedicated with a quotation inscribed upon it.

The action of the cathedral does not stop on the steps. Underneath, in the great crypt, two basketball courts are used by the cathedral school and neighborhood children; an office runs a program of meals for shut-ins, and another assists homeless persons, who may be staying in our shelter, to find jobs. A counselor for teenage vocations is kept busy finding work for young people. In a room adjoining the building, a tapestry repair workshop takes care of ancient, precious tapestries, including the cathedral's own collection of Barberini tapestries designed by Raphael. An ensemble specializing in the playing of old instruments practices next to the cathedral ballet troupe's studio.

In the Cathedral House each Saturday, Canon Johnson held classes of theology for the laity at The Institute of Theology. There too, with the aid of Canon Johnson, the Institute Pastoral Hispano began to train Latino Church persons for the ministry within the context of their own culture. In the Synod Hall, next to my office, the Big Apple Circus was born.

Strangely enough, the most publicized activity of the cathedral was the building of the unfinished towers. During the financial crisis of the seventies, when the people of the city were losing the self-confidence, even arrogance, which has always been the mark of a genuine New Yorker, Jim Morton conceived of beginning a building program toward the completion of the cathedral towers. The nave had been dedicated on the Sunday before Pearl Harbor, and no new stone had been laid down since that time. During the urban crises of the sixties, Bishop Donegan declared, rightly I think, that no more building would occur until the conditions of the city improved. For this reason, I was initially against Jim's idea. But one of his great qualities is a stubbornness of purpose. Instead of forgetting his plan, he sought to combine the building of the tower with a social purpose, which would remove the stigma of spending money on bricks and mortar when so much poverty surrounded us.

Within a year, men and women from the city were beginning
their training as stone masons. People were excited by the idea,
and money was raised. The image of minority youths being
trained by an old English artisan who had last worked on the
façade of the Liverpool Cathedral was appealing. Furthermore,
we declared the project to be a sign of hope for the city, especially
that part of the city. I remember talking about it with an old
taxi driver one day. He said, "I remember when I was a kid
during the Depression and the cathedral was being constructed,
my Dad told me that as long as Big John was a-building there
was hope for our town."

One of the first apprentices was a former Hispanic gang
leader whom we had come to know through the urban
homesteading project. Another was a black woman who became,
as far as we know, the first woman stone mason. This training
was not just romanticism, for working with stone had become
more and more important as the restoration movement gained
momentum in the cities of America. And so slowly, stone by
stone, the cathedral continues to rise and lives rise with it.

We have been criticized again and again by so-called
orthodox Christians for what they feel are secular activities taking
place in God's house. Others are enraged that the Dalai Lama,
who is not a Christian, speaks from the pulpit. Images like a
female crucifix deeply offended many because they are
misunderstood. However, in the inclusiveness of our life there is
TRUE catholicity. I believe we symbolize the outstretched
wounded hands of our Lord welcoming all of the God's people
into his house of worship. But we have been scrupulous in
maintaining Anglican teaching and liturgy, lest we lose our own
identity in welcoming the identity of others.

The cathedral's transcendent beauty, catholic inclusiveness,
vitality, identification with the City, and plain human warmth
has an effect on many people who are not religious in any formal
way. A college professor I know was brought back to the faith
by a visit there; James Taylor, the popular singer, speaks of it as
his church; a long skeptical agnostic friend of mine was
overwhelmed by a mystical experience during the Easter
Eucharist. Many Jewish persons feel at home with us, more

than in their own synagogues. This is the people's Church. Our goal has been to create in the life of St. John's a mirror of the medieval cathedral through which the whole life of the city flows and whose towering beauty symbolizes the hopes and dreams of the people of God.

The life and work of the city goes on within and without those giant walls, and those who walk down the great stone steps hopefully carry with them into the world the love of God and God's longing for justice and peace.

31

Beauty and Bands:
Eleven Years in Rome: 1970-1981

Harry Reynolds Smythe

Early in 1969, in the course of a period of rest from my parochial and academic duties, I was startled to receive a letter from the primate of Australia, archbishop of Melbourne, putting before me the prospect of taking up a position of world significance in Rome as director of the Anglican Centre. This had been founded in 1966 as an Anglican response to the second Vatican Council of the Roman Catholic Church and for some four years had been under the guidance of an Englishman, Canon John Findlow, who was about to retire. I was happy in my parish of St. James's, East St. Kilda, and in my teaching in Trinity College within the University of Melbourne, and I had no desire to leave. On enquiry, however, I learned that the archbishop had submitted my name already to the archbishop of Canterbury, having anticipated, no doubt, my opposition. In these circumstances it seemed wise to wait and see what the outcome might be.

Nothing happened for some weeks. I had begun to feel a sense of relief until, suddenly, my little pattern of commitments and interests changed its perspective, when a letter reached me in my retreat at Mt. Eliza on the bay of Melbourne bearing a

London postmark. It was signed by Bishop Ralph Dean, who was then entitled "Executive Officer of the Anglican Communion" and based in London at Lambeth Palace. The letter bore an invitation to meet the bishop in Manila in the Philippines and, much to my surprise, an offer to be responsible for the payment of my fare from Melbourne and return. I agreed, without further commitment, to make the journey, as the visit appeared to be merely exploratory. I could not have been more mistaken.

The long flight took place within the month. As my plane descended over the airport at Manila, I observed troops lining the runway, a long red carpet unfolded from the terminal building, and further detachments of military guards at the entrances and exits of the airport. Surmising that it was a little early for such a ceremonious welcome to be prepared for me, I discovered with relief that Madame Marcos and the cardinal archbishop of Manila were expected on their return from Rome. Bishop Ralph Dean met me, but we were both obliged to take refuge immediately against the wall of the terminal building as the huge crowd pressed forward to greet President Marcos, who came to meet his wife. They drove off in a flourish of wealth and power. We found ourselves a taxi and were conveyed more modestly to the bishop's hotel on the northern outskirts of the city. We dined pleasantly together, and deferred serious discussion until the morrow in view of my long journey from Melbourne.

On the following morning at 9 a.m. I called on the bishop in his suite. He talked with me until mid-day about the Anglican Centre in Rome, its foundation and history, its difficulties and its expectations, especially the hopes cherished for it by Dr. Michael Ramsey, archbishop of Canterbury, who had made an unprecedented visit to Rome in 1966, when he was received with warmth and understanding by Pope Paul VI. I listened with close attention, thankful to be briefed with this detailed analysis. Toward mid-day, however, I began to look furtively outside the bishop's windows towards a swimming pool surrounded by palm trees, so that I realized that my capacity to absorb information was waning rapidly. In a pause in the bishop's exposition, I commented somewhat nonchalantly: "It must be very interesting for you, my Lord, to be traveling the world like

this, interviewing candidates." "What do you mean?" the bishop
exclaimed rather sharply. "Well," I replied, "you have told me
that you have come from India and that you are traveling to
North America. You have invited me from Australia. I assume
that you have been interviewing candidates in different countries
for the position in Rome." "You are the only one," the bishop
replied. I was stunned by this answer. It appeared that the
archbishop of Canterbury had invited all the primates of the
Anglican Communion to submit names for consideration for
the post in Rome. Only the primate of Australia, archbishop of
Melbourne, had replied, nominating me as a candidate—without
my knowledge or consent! This disclosure of strategy induced
in me, nevertheless, a subdued happiness. Later I asked the bishop
about his diocese in Canada. Because of his residence in London
he was able to visit it only infrequently. He reassured me, however,
when he said: "Of course, they can always see me on television!"

Later in the afternoon, to escape the stifling heat and humid-
ity, we went swimming in the pool of the American Officers'
Club. At this stage, in the bar, the bishop told me that he would
recommend to the Archbishop of Canterbury that I should be
appointed to Rome with the new, if fulsome, titles of "Representative in Rome of the Anglican Communion and Director of the
Anglican Centre." This double title was important, if cumber-
some. As I discovered later, it had to be translated with care in
Italian, so that the phrase "in Rome" would be placed immediately after the noun "Representative." Canon John Findlow, my
predecessor in office, had been "Personal Representative of the
Archbishop of Canterbury and Director of the Anglican Centre
in Rome." The wider reference of the title to be conferred on
me was designed to make clear the commitment of the whole
Anglican Communion to a major and particular ecumenical
project. It was not to be a representation of the Church of England only. For this reason, it was explained to me, an Australian
in office in Rome was being preferred to another Englishman.
The function of representation was designed to have an Anglican
rather than a specifically English character. Fittingly, likewise, I
was to be succeeded in due course in 1981 by an American, so
that the same principle might be observed.

Quietened in spirit, I returned to Melbourne musing on the momentous responsibility to be offered to me, and, within a short while, the letter of appointment arrived from the archbishop of Canterbury, offering to me the post in Rome. I resolved, after consultation with the archbishop of Melbourne and my churchwardens and other friends, to accept the invitation, and arranged to leave my parish, with deep regret, on Easter Day, 1970.

In the meanwhile, when my leave came to an end in August 1969, I resumed my parochial duties in East St. Kilda, and took up with vigor the further challenge of completing the building of the parish church before my departure. I had cherished the hope of this enterprise for some years. I had received most loyal and informed support from my churchwardens, from the vestry, and from the whole congregation. Owing to the untimely death of our architect, one churchwarden, himself of the same profession, took over responsibility for the work. The vicar's warden, William Sampson, was also a man of taste and sensibility, who assisted me in my determination to create something both beautiful and unique. We had collected for some years cast-iron columns in the Corinthian style, window frames in heavy wood, tiles and stained glass from the several large Victorian mansions in the parish and nearby. These were being ruthlessly demolished to make way for blocks of flats. We had stored the relics from the past carefully, and we now found ourselves delighted with the effects when they were incorporated into the building. Some of the new and most striking glass was designed by an artist who had already done fine work in the chancel and the Lady Chapel, Dr. Dismas Zika. The overall effect of these changes wrought by shapes, new spaces, and colour proved overwhelmingly beautiful. An atmosphere of spaciousness and elegance was created, with the result that, as I had planned, none could enter the building without being touched with a feeling of awe. Of special importance was a collection of metal columns in the Corinthian style, which I had collected over the years. These, too, were skillfully incorporated, so that one of the noteworthy features of the church became the contrast between the ornateness of individual parts of the decoration and the simple background of classical arches of early Christian Roman architecture. My churchwarden, Bill Sampson, and John Beaumont, the people's warden, and all members of the vestry and of the congregation did a splendid job of co-operation, so that I saw fulfilled in materials and shapes and colours the dream which I had some years earlier when, seated in my stall, I lapsed into sleep while an aged visitor was preaching! A dear friend, Mrs. Marea Meyers, called at a critical moment when funds were running low and made a substantial donation of some $5000. In a sense, however, the largest donation came to me at the hands of an old lady who, after evensong, pressed into my hand the thirty shillings of her old age pension as her total gift. I saw completed, therefore, the work which I had begun, but for three days only; the builders removed the screens and scaffolding on the Thursday in Holy Week of 1970 in preparation for the visit of the archbishop of Melbourne on Easter Day. At the parish communion the archbishop dedicated the completed work and blessed me for my task in Rome. I left immediately from the newly built narthex and was driven to the airport by my sister. It was a moment of both fulfilment and of termination, as one phase of my life closed in order to allow another to open. Ten very full years of pastoral commitment concluded with the goodwill of the people and the archbishop's blessing. There were many rich memories for me and a deep thankfulness for the support of the people whom I had endeavoured to serve. Only shortly before my own departure my friend and colleague, the Reverend Dr. Barry R. Marshall, chaplain of Trinity College, had been called to the principalship of Pusey House, Oxford. We had taught together at Trinity College for some years, but we were not to meet again. I had scarcely arrived in Rome when he met with a tragic accident by falling from a ladder to his death. Ultimately both our lives were changed by this traumatic event.

The first stop on my flight to London on Easter Day, 1970, was Auckland, New Zealand. Again in Fiji I called on friends both Indian and Fijian. Thence, via Los Angeles and the North Pole, I reached London. I stayed briefly at St. Edward's House, Westminster, which allowed me to make calls on Canon and Mrs. Bernard Pawley, who knew Rome and the Anglican Centre well; on Canon Jeffrey at the office of Bishop John Howe, successor to Bishop Ralph Dean and the newly appointed secretary general of the Anglican Communion. I traveled to the north of England to meet Bishop John Moorman by whose initiative the archbishop of Canterbury had been persuaded to found the Anglican Centre in Rome. I lunched at Lambeth Palace with Archbishop and Mrs. Ramsey. This proved a cordial and supportive occasion. After luncheon the archbishop introduced me to Canon John Findlow, who had been director of the Anglican Centre from the time of its foundation in 1966.

Canon Findlow looked extremely tired. I attributed this to the circumstances of his departure from Rome, not all of which were known to me at that time, but in effect he had been the casualty of a "palace revolution." For some time, behind his back, he had been subjected to a large amount of personal criticism for his alleged laziness, but no one took the trouble to seek for the cause of this condition. A critical move against him was made by the bishop of Ripon, the representative of the archbishop of Canterbury on the Council of the Anglican Centre in Rome, and by influential American members of the council. These members of the council approached the archbishop of Canterbury, without John Findlow's knowledge, and complained about the director's "laziness." They led the "putsch" which lost him his job, so that when I met him at Lambeth Palace, he and his wife and daughters were being housed by the archbishop as refugees in a tower upstairs. No one knew at that stage that John Findlow was suffering from a rare tropical virus which he had contracted unknowingly while on the archbishop's business in Africa. This condition was misdiagnosed in Rome, but, on returning to England, John Findlow died. This tragedy occurred within three weeks of my meeting with him. The archbishop presided at his requiem, together with many other dignitaries. He received high praise in death.

I flew out to Rome to find the Anglican Centre housed on the fourth floor of the magnificent Palazzo Doria Pamphilj at via del Corso 303. This site is in the very center of the historic city, close to major Roman Catholic religious and educational institutions. The prestigious position was due to the initiative and generosity of Don Frank and Donna Orietta Doria Pamphilj, who made the large suite of rooms available at a very low rental. I was welcomed by Miss Christine Slatford, the English secretary to whom I remained indebted for many years of faithful and skillful service. She spoke fluent Italian and proved an invaluable assistant. Most members of the Council of the Anglican Centre were resident in Rome. They also were welcoming and generally supportive of my work. The many initiatives which I presented to them were approved with enthusiasm.

One of my first duties, however, was to learn Italian. To achieve this I took lessons from Professoressa Ginepro, an Englishwoman who was married to an Italian. She had been a resident in Italy for many years. Curiously, although expelled from Italy during the war of 1939-45, she had remarried a fervent supporter of Il Duce Mussolini and had even retained some fascist loyalties and opinions. I discovered this to my surprise when I knocked over a book from the table from which I was reading my lessons to her, and a photograph of the dictator, mounted on his parade horse, fell to the floor. As I recovered it with an apology, Professoressa Ginepro exclaimed to my surprise: "My hero!" The focus of my interest in the language was, at outset, the mastery of its grammatical constructions, although, at an early stage, I found myself in the course of my duties at a large public meeting in Rome where no one spoke English. My replies to well developed questions (in the Italian manner) tended to be monosyllabic! A little later in that first year I found myself together with Brother Michael Fisher of the Anglican Society of St. Francis at a large meeting of students of the University of Perugia in Umbria when we contrived, more by charm than by linguistic skill, to avoid a situation of mutual incomprehension.

I made a visit to Assisi not long after my arrival to Rome. I had been there only once before, but memorably, in 1948 when I myself was a student at Oxford. I had retained an image of unforgettable beauty and tranquility. On this new occasion I noticed an attractive small house to let in Via Dono Doni no. 2 immediately adjacent to the Cathedral of San Rufino. After a few enquiries I took possession of this house, found some simple, attractive furnishings for it, and began to use it on weekends when I had no special duties in Rome. In the summer, when Rome swelters in the heat by day and by night, I found my refuge in Assisi very welcome. It was my private responsibility. It allowed me to make many effective contacts with the citizens and religious authorities of this small provincial city and, in a general and informal way, to promote Anglican-Roman Catholic understanding. I called on all the religious communities and on Monsignor Niccolini, bishop of Assisi, who was a Benedictine and aged some 96 years. I was received everywhere with interest and kindness. The bishop of Assisi set aside an ancient church in the city for Anglican worship and, in due course, five Anglican bishops, including the bishop of Exeter who had conferred Holy Orders on me, celebrated the Holy Eucharist together in this church, in the presence of the Roman Catholic religious and civic authorities, and of a very large congregation which consisted mostly of local people.

In Rome, during the first months after my assumption of office, I made myself known to as many persons of authority and influence as was practicable. These included H.E. Johannes Cardinal Willebrands, head of the Secretariat for Promoting Christian Unity, and members of his staff. At that time, and throughout my 11 years in Rome, I was received at the secretariat, as elsewhere in the Vatican, with unfailing courtesy. Every support was given to the furthering of my particular ministry of reconciliation. Canon W.H. Purdy, his cousin Miss Margaret Orrell, Father Pierre Duprey, Father Basil Meeking, and other members of staff became friends as well as informed and much valued counselors. It was often due to their initiative that I was able to meet other people of influence within the Vatican. I never at any time encountered discourtesy, indifference, or antagonism.

At the same time I began to meet some of the ambassadors accredited to the Holy See and to the Italian State. Such occasions, whether in the form of calls initiated by me or in social circumstances arranged by them, offered attractive opportunities to make the function of the Anglican Centre known at the highest level of international activity and relationship. The work of Christian reconciliation had reached a high point in the seventies, and was prompting a spirit of initiative and expectation.

Only later did it become apparent that those who were committed to Christian unity on the Anglican side by a process of information, recognition and exchange were not really supported in depth by many Anglicans in positions of ecclesiastical authority, who remained inward-looking and sometimes obsessed with past controversies of theological opinion. This was true of groups of Anglicans in England, in Ireland, and in Australia where a mentality obsessed with the notion of infallibility of the Holy Scripture precluded intelligent discussion. In the United States the Episcopal Church was well disposed generally to the prospect of reconciliation with Rome, and led by presiding bishops who had a firm grasp of Anglican principles of faith and order, and were supportive personally of the Anglican-Roman Catholic dialogue. They were all supportive of the Anglican Centre in Rome, and, after the Church of England, supplied the second largest funds for its maintenance and mission. In my opinion it was a tragedy of a major kind which overwhelmed the Episcopal Church when it allowed itself to be deflected from this ecumenical enterprise with Rome into the altogether different and contradictory path scorched for it by the proponents of the ordination of women. The Church of England, despite deep internal opposition, has now followed this same path. For a time in the early seventies the presence of Michael Ramsey as archbishop of Canterbury provided a critically intelligent and stabilizing influence on all ecumenical initiatives and expectations. Now, however, that whole enterprise, which so many Christians accepted as well pleasing to God, lies in ruins. It has often been taught to the people that the Roman Catholic Church was responsible for the corruption and collapse of historic Catholicism at the period of the sixteenth century Reformation, with a consequent breakdown of European civilization into warring nation-states and empires. Whatever an informed understanding of the complexities of history may make of this simplification, no one may claim that the Roman Catholic Church of the twentieth century has been responsible for the breakdown of ecumenism. Other Christians have resolved to elect for themselves other alleged priorities, camouflaged, at worst, under the claims of "justice."

An important step forward which I was able to initiate in Rome was the establishment of an Anglican professorship in Anglican studies at the Pontifical Gregorian University. This move was supported willingly by the Secretariat for Promoting Christian Unity and by the archbishop of Canterbury. The costs involved, largely expenses of travel and accommodation, were defrayed by the Council of the Anglican Centre. Under the care of the Society of Jesus, the Gregorian is the principal educational institution, among several other distinguished academic ecclesiastical bodies, in Rome. It was training some 1200 ecclesiastical students from almost 100 countries of the world. I began my responsibilities of teaching with a course of lectures, 24 in all, on the theme of "Anglican Theology Today." and, later, on that of "Anglican Spirituality Today." I preferred the latter as being more positive and practical in content. Some well known Anglicans of international reputation took part in these series. These guests included academics and several bishops both English and American. Throughout my years of teaching at the Gregorian I received much kindness and hospitality from my brother-professors, with a touching occasion of good will and good wishes at the end.

In this field of endeavor initiated by the Anglican Centre, a curious episode took place in 1976. I received word from the university that it was no longer possible "for non-Catholic professors or teachers to lecture in the university." I made several enquiries locally before referring the matter to the archbishop of Canterbury. Eventually I called by appointment on the Rector Magnificus of the University, Father Carlo Martini, who is now cardinal archbishop of Milan. He expressed dismay and sympathy, informing me that he had received the instruction from the Vatican, but that he had pursued the matter zealously by a personal visit to the Vatican without being able to detect its ultimate source. He had consulted in vain Archbishop Giovanni Benelli, the under secretary of state, who was credited with the two divine attributes of omniscience and omnipotence. I knew that Archbishop Benelli was well disposed to me personally, but even he, according to Father Martini, confessed himself at a loss to identify the source of antagonism. Father Martini concluded his interview with me by saying: "I have done all that I can to resolve this matter, but I have failed."

The issue remained unresolved while I remained at my post in Rome. Several suppositions surfaced as speculation, but none had the dignity of supportive evidence. One surmise was that "bishops from a large Catholic country" (supposed variously to be Spain or South American) had said to the pope in *ad limen* audience: "How can we send our ecclesiastical students for training in Rome when even the Pontifical University is riddled with Protestant teachers?" This explanation carried little weight in view of the fact that a distinguished Waldensian biblical scholar had been teaching for years at the Pontifical Biblical Institute next door to the Gregorian University. Having drawn attention to the whole issue at the Secretariat for Promoting Christian Unity, I resolved to raise it at the highest level in audience with H.H. Pope Paul VI. Alas! At this stage Pope Paul was extremely frail in health. It seemed possible that he could have been influenced to make a decision in this matter by people ignorant to the facts or ill-disposed or both, but the truth or otherwise of these suppositions perished with his death in 1978.

On several occasions I raised the issue with H.H. John Paul II. His Holiness expressed very emphatic approval of the Anglican professorship, and, on more than one occasion, he uttered his dismay that he had been unable to resolve the question of the responsibility taken to obstruct it. At my final audience with His Holiness at Easter 1981 I did not consider it appropriate that this issue should be raised by me. His Holiness, however, initiated an exchange on this theme and said most emphatically: "Knowing that you were coming to see me today, I called for the papers on the question of the Anglican professorship at the Gregorian University"—a surprisingly thick pile of documents lay before him on his desk—"and I have insisted that this matter be set right, and I will so insist. It is in full accord with the decrees of the Second Vatican Council. I do not in the least understand why any such difficulty should have arisen." It interested and dismayed me at the same time that the will of the most powerful personage in the Roman Catholic Church could have been thwarted by an undetectable person, whose activity contributed to our common loss.

Early in my ministry in Rome, Pope Paul VI said to me: "You may have access to me at any time for matters concerning the Anglican Centre and the Anglican Church."This was a quite exceptional privilege. Ambassadors accredited to the Holy See informed me that they would normally be received at the beginning of their tour of duty and at the end, unless some unusual circumstances should intervene. As a rule a private audience would be arranged in my case by my request to the Secretariat for Promoting Christian Unity through whose good offices the matter would be put forward. Alternatively, on one occasion, I wrote directly to the private secretary to His Holiness. My requests were received always with the utmost courtesy.

On one occasion during the reign of Pope Paul VI, when civil life in Italy was darkened by much political turmoil and terrorist violence, I had an unexpected opportunity to make Pope Paul laugh.The audience took place at a time when His Holiness had been speaking in public, saddened and visibly depressed by the civil unrest. I chose to inform him of the many very happy occasions in my own recent experience when I had been traveling across the world to address large numbers of Anglican and Roman Catholic young people. "Many young people in conference or as individuals have requested me," I said "to convey to Your Holiness their most respectful and affectionate greetings." The pope was visibly pleased. "Even here in Rome," I continued, but I was interrupted immediately by the look of surprise on the pope's face."Even here in Rome," I persevered, "there are many graffiti" . . . again I was forced to pause as His Holiness exclaimed with an emphatic gesture of horror: "Molto cattivi!" "Indeed," I replied, "Your Holiness is correct. There are many wicked ones. Some, however, are scribbled on the walls near to where I live in the Doria Palace which express towards Your Holiness sentiments of profound respect and affection." "How can that be?" the pope exclaimed. I continued: "On walls near the Gregorian University close to my residence there is a large scribble which reads: Evviva Paolo VI! Paolo Sesto Superstella!"

This exchange took place when the film "Jesus Christ Super-star" had appeared in Rome. The audience was ending. We were speaking in Italian without the presence of an interpreter. The pope burst out laughing. "I never thought," he said, "that I should ever find myself as a superstar!" Normally such an audience closed as I requested his blessing, but, on this occasion, His Holiness continued to laugh as I withdrew. I bowed to him and left the open door into one of the vast throne-rooms where I encountered two cardinals talking between themselves as they waited to be received. They looked up as I emerged, puzzled by the pope's laughter, which was audible, and I bowed to them as I passed on my way, daring to surmise that I may have given a blessing inadvertently on this occasion rather than received one. The British minister to the Holy See said to me later: "Harry, you have succeeded where we have failed; you have made the pope laugh!"

In August of my first year in Rome, my sister, Gladys, accompanied by a friend of hers, flew from Melbourne to join me for their holidays. I had not told them of my renting of the house in Assisi, as I wished to keep this as a surprise. Signora Claudia Conti, my housekeeper in Rome, traveled ahead to Assisi to prepare for my guests who, on their arrival from Rome with me, by train, on a day of intense heat, were delighted to be welcomed by Signora Claudia and to find themselves in a quiet private house instead of a hotel. Later we traveled on to Cortina d'Ampezzo in the Alps, and thence to Innsbruck and Oberam-mergau and to a tiny village near Berchtesgaden. All our plans were fulfilled pleasantly. I missed my sister very much on her return to Melbourne.

Other visitors joined me from time to time in the house in Assisi. These included the British minister to the Holy See, Mr. Desmond Crawley, and his wife, Daphne; the Bishop of Ripon and Mrs. John Moorman; the archbishop in Jerusalem and his wife, and many others. All were invariably pleased to have the opportunity of experiencing the life of the tiny Umbrian hillside town after the noise and bustle and splendor of Rome. There were often opportunities of introducing my guests to local personages, and to the several religious communities with which I had become friends. I myself found much peace of mind in

Assisi, especially at times of strain in my work or in personal relationships. The tranquility and beauty of the Umbrian countryside and the opportunities to pray undisturbed in shrines hallowed by the faith of many thousands of fellow Christians from the time of St. Rufino in the late Roman Empire, through St. Francis and St. Clare, were a source of solace and quiet inspiration. Occasionally, when weather permitted, I would walk to the summit of Monte Subasio, on the slopes of which the little town of Assisi stands, gaze with wonder at the immense prospect in all directions, and descend via Spello. This is the Roman city of Spellium mentioned by Livy at the time of its siege by Hannibal. On one occasion in an ancient church in Spello which I had thought deserted, I was confronted with a moving and unusual outburst of piety when I came upon an aged peasant woman kneeling before the glass coffin which held the body of a local saint. The old lady, on her knees, and with emphatic gestures of disapproval, was reprimanding the saint aloud, and in no uncertain terms, for his failure to concede to her prayers of request. Is the "invocation of Saints" to be dismissed, I wondered, as the 39 Articles of Religion of the Church of England claims, as "a fond thing vainly invented . . . grounded upon no warranty or scripture, but rather repugnant to the Word of God"?

Bishop John Howe, secretary general of the Anglican Communion, who visited me regularly in Rome and oversaw all my work, was always supportive and understanding (rather than inquisitive) when I needed these phases of retreat and rest. In 1973 I suffered an acute attack of pneumonia which proved dangerous in its effects. These were tiresomely prolonged and could have been mortal. With Bishop Howe's knowledge and sympathy I was glad to withdraw to Assisi for the summer to regain my strength. During the early months of this surprisingly long and exhausting illness I had received much kindness of hospitality and nursing from members of the Focolare Movement at Loppiano near Florence and at Monte Cavo near Rome. One of the members of the Movement, Annunziato Barbato, was assigned to nurse me. Curiously, at a later stage, his work was continued by an Australian friend who, at that time, happened to be in Istanbul, but who sensed there, without any word from me, that I was seriously ill. He appeared without notice at the door of the Anglican Centre in Rome and continued to nurse me back to health. Perhaps not all "saints" need verbal invocation in order to be inspired to act? On my recovery Pope Paul VI received me very kindly in audience. In the autumn of the year 1973, I was able to resume my duties in Rome. These now included the teaching which I had undertaken at the Pontifical Gregorian University. Much interest was then being shown in the phenomenon of Anglicanism which, from its inception, in the sixteenth century as a national movement with a large admixture of political factors, had become an international religious "communion." It had become also less English in character and more specifically "Anglican." It seemed to commend itself to some thoughtful and discerning Roman Catholics as agreeable both with the Gospel and with some at least of the principal insights of the Second Vatican Council. I endeavoured to further this growing knowledge and interest in Anglicanism by additional talks and lectures at the Anglican Centre, close to the Gregorian University. A wide range of participants took part in these, including visitors from overseas, and Mr. Terry Waite, who at that time was resident in Rome as advisor to the superiors of major religious communities within the Roman Catholic Church. From time to time I myself was invited to visit Pontifical institutes, universities, seminaries and religious communities in Rome, Naples, and especially in Siena, and in Florence, where I had made happy links of personal friendship first with Cardinal Florit and later, more extensively, with Father Aldinucci, abbot of San Miniato al Monte, a person of immense good will, and with Cardinal Giovanni Benelli, whom many expected to succeed Pope Paul on the throne of St. Peter.

A large number of visitors came, often unannounced, to the Anglican Centre. Some few expected it to be open every day, including weekends, at hours convenient to themselves. Many bishops and other clergy made welcome visits from the different provinces of the Anglican Communion. I tried to maintain contact with them by means of a newsletter which gave information on the activities of the center and on the progress of the Anglican/Roman Catholic dialogue. For a short time I found myself an observer at the meetings of the Anglican/ Roman Catholic International Commission, where I was made welcome by all members except one. At times I regretted the exclusive pre-occupation of the commission with theological problems. These were dealt with very thoroughly, and eventually three remarkable consensual Agreements of Principle were achieved. Unfortunately, however, in the meantime, the Anglican Communion allowed itself the luxury of other priorities. One of these was the issue of the ordination of women. I regretted this reversal of commitments very deeply and, with others, foresaw the tragedy of distrust and "discommunion" which would follow. When this distasteful word was introduced into Anglican international conference, however, it was disallowed by the archbishop of Canterbury himself; for many Anglicans, and many faithful clergy among them, it has now become a tragic fact. Who will bear the guilt and shame of these lost priestly and lay vocations? It is frequently alleged by those who wish to extenuate their responsibility for the loss of clergy and lay people which has resulted from the changes introduced in recent years that "only X hundreds" have left or resigned. These were usually, however, well-informed members of the Church, faithful in their vocations. It has seemed to me a form of sacrilege to set their ministry, whether lay or clerical, at naught, or to make it impossible for them to discharge their office conscientiously.

One issue of my Anglican Centre newsletter was devoted to the question of the ordination of women, as it alarmed me to have noted that some Anglicans continued to consider this matter in isolation from both historic Christian tradition and, in particular, from the solemn commitment made between Pope Paul VI and the archbishop of Canterbury in the Common Declaration of 1966. This precluded *unilateral* action in matters of significance *on both sides*. It was constantly alleged by Anglican proponents of change in the historic position of Anglican teaching that the Roman Catholic authorities, especially those in the Vatican, were being consulted and kept informed. The Anglican/Roman Catholic International Commission, however, deferred any study in depth of this issue until the prior concern of the doctrine of the priesthood could be resolved. Meanwhile Anglicans, even Anglican bishops, actually initiated the critical change by ordaining women to the priesthood, or, as some would have it, by professing to do so. The issue was carried through piecemeal all over the Anglican Communion by majority opinions rather than by a common and patient search for truth. Truth, whatever it may be, is always the first casualty of religious controversy. In my opinion it was open to the Anglican Communion to explore the issue of women's ordination to the point of agreement, if such agreement could be achieved, *but not act alone* in view of the Agreement of 1966 between the archbishop of Canterbury and Pope Paul VI. The fact that it did act alone and in its own, not dishonourable, piecemeal method has understandably sown the seeds of massive distrust, and played into the hands of some very conservative and rigidly doctrinaire Roman Catholics who obviously regretted deeply the whole Roman Catholic ecumenical enterprise.

On one occasion, I overheard a representative of the Episcopal Church of the United States, who was on his way to an Anglican Consultative Council Meeting in Dublin, say: "Let us go ahead and ordain women and show the Roman Catholic Church the way ahead!" How much arrogant insensitivity is bound up in this exclamation! I listened to such statements with dismay. On another occasion when I was speaking privately with a bishop of the Episcopal Church of the United States, and under the delusion that we were merely exchanging private opinions, he exclaimed: "I don't see how anyone who holds your position as representative of the Anglican Communion could entertain your views on the ordination of women." Such naïvete can be very damaging. It fails, as in this instance, to distinguish between privately held opinions and the represen tative and impersonal character of an ambassadorial office. It does not indicate any profound reflection or charity or episcopal pastoral care, but the same anti-intellectual liberalism to which modern insights, however bizarre, are considered self-authenticating. This particular bishop, although well disposed at a personal level, lacked any understanding of the distinction between private opinion and the impersonal character of representative functions. His view on this matter, now shared by many, is really a concealed form of tyranny. He would have been outraged as a liberal had I had the temerity to point this out!

There were other Anglicans, of course, prepared to leap on the feminist horse (scarcely a stallion!) in order to be carried to positions of influence and power. They were happy, seemingly, to contrive their own future. A friend of mine from my own early years of training, who had become a well known bishop and had served as a diocesan, was told by his fellow bishops "to conform and ordain women or get out." As an Anglican faithful to the tradition which he had received, he got out. The proponents of novelty, advocates of radical and unilateral change, rarely seemed aware that their views required substantial and positive proof. When they failed to persuade, they took refuge in tyranny, rather like hard-line communists of the old-fashioned doctrinaire kind. Before I left Rome for the Lambeth Conference of 1978, I received a visit from a young priest of the Church of Sweden, accompanied by his wife. They both besought me to make known to the bishops of the conference that unhealed distress which the matter had introduced to their Church since 1952. I did this, unavailingly.

The issue was bedeviled by intrigue at the Lambeth Conference even before it came to the vote. On the night before the debate was due to take place I overheard a group of bishops and others, known supporters of the ordination of women, discussing tactics for the public debate in conference. "Make sure," one speaker said, "that you all bunch up around the microphones, so that you can leap up to support our speakers immediately." Obviously, for such people, no issue of Christian truth was involved. I reported this matter at once to the chaplain of the archbishop of Canterbury who, annoyed at the unseemly tactical ploy, took immediate and effective measures to counteract it. To my surprise I found myself invited to speak!

On another occasion at the same conference I was speaking with a Bishop when he was joined by several of his fellows who were discussing the issue of women's ordination between themselves. They made much of respect for conscience, especially in favour of those who accepted the novelty. I enquired, politely I hope, what provision they intended to make for a person like myself who had struggled to remain faithful to the vows of ordination when, at the time of death, he asked to receive the sacrament of the Eucharist. Would there be in every hospital and hospice both a male and a female priest so that no conscience would be afflicted? "I suppose," an English bishop replied, "you would have to make a spiritual communion." I decided that, if this were the best the Church could do for its clergy in *extremis*, I would prefer the lenient regime of an ayatollah! The Anglican Communion now embodies no longer the historically traceable shape of a reformed Catholicism, but, at the vital point of Eucharistic communion, has become a sect, having introduced a twentieth century novelty which has no historic precedent except in paganism. I cannot accept that intrigue and partisanship have any rightful pace in the thoughtful construction of Christian doctrine. They belong to the deformations of truth characteristic of sectarianism, not to the Catholic faith. My convictions, however, did not prevail in this controversy, and the policy of the Church has gone even more markedly against them since the Lambeth Conference of 1978. Many hundreds of clergy and lay people have been effectively unchurched by their own side.

In 1975, 1977 and 1979, I made extensive tours overseas from Rome to England, the United States including Hawaii, Fiji, New Zealand, and Australia. I found myself delighted to be received everywhere with a most generous hospitality, joy and enthusiasm. This was especially true of the many young people whom I met and talked with, both Anglican and Roman Catholic. I was invited to preach in several cathedrals, parish churches and religious communities. I met many Anglican and Roman Catholic religious leaders, including several primates in the Anglican Church and three cardinal archbishops of the Roman Catholic Church. These journeys, and others which I undertook in Austria, Germany, Belgium, and Denmark, helped me to realize how important it was to have a representative of the Anglican Communion stationed in Rome who could refer back to the people of God, in person, the insights and issues which were being clarified in discussion within the Anglican/ Roman Catholic international dialogue. Local support, in my experience, was always forthcoming readily and joyfully. This was specially true of meetings with clergy and lay people, where good will always prevailed, often with a very moving enthusiasm.

The patient work of the Anglican/Roman Catholic International Commission furthered the process of theological renewal, and hence of reconciliation, between both the Churches then committed to it. The scandal of division, theological and ecclesial, had persisted unhealed for four centuries. Many matters needed reform and renewal on both sides of the formal ecclesiastical divide, and the over-riding task was to determine how to restore communion. It was unfortunate, in my opinion, that the work of the commission gave the impression to some observers of being confined exclusively to intellectual problems. True, moral and practical issues had been set aside for lack of time. This attitude gave the impression, however false, to some observers that only those who hold correct theological opinions may be accepted as communicants. The subsequent 'revision' of the commission's thought process and decisions by the Vatican Office for the Doctrine of the Faith confirmed this impression, and, in effect, evacuated the commission's work of its meaning in favor of a traditionalist hard-line Romanism.

Early in 1978, before the Lambeth Conference, Dr. Ronald Coggan, archbishop of Canterbury, made arrangements to be received in Rome by H.H. Pope Paul VI. The archbishop enjoyed the hospitality of the Venerable English College throughout his visit, receiving in this way the courtesy extended to his predecessor, Lord Ramsay. The English College had a splendid tradition of hospitality of which I myself was a not infrequent, and always appreciative, beneficiary.

I met the archbishop at the airport, together with other dignitaries, and accompanied him to his lodgings in the college. He and his suite of bishops and counsellors were received with courtesy and kindness. I found it a new experience to move about in Rome in a large convoy of official Vatican and police cars with out-riders forging ahead of the procession, re-directing the traffic, and any unwary pedestrians, with an imperious ruthlessness. This made a sharp contrast with my normal progression on foot or by 50 lire bus rides! One heavily laden bus was forced shuddering onto the foot-path as we sped from the Vatican to a luncheon with the abbot primate of the Benedictine Order on the Aventine. I found this aspect of power and position rather disconcerting. It seemed very different from an occasion recorded in the life of Pope John XXIII, when he found himself trapped in traffic in central Rome behind a crowded bus, but ordered his driver to wait. "These people," he said, "are uncomfortable, tired of standing and hungry. I prefer to wait."

On the evening of the day of the archbishop's arrival a dinner was held in his honour by Cardinal Johannes Willebrands in the Casa del Clero near Piazza Navona. Before the dinner began I found myself exhausted. I was moving along the table hoping to find myself assigned a seat at the very end where I would have no guest on my right, avoiding thus at least some proportion of the courtesies of conversation. While thus seeking my place, I heard a voice behind me saying: "Dr. Smythe, please come here." I turned to confront our host, Cardinal Willebrands, who was seated at the side in an armchair chatting with the archbishop of Canterbury, his principal guest, and accompanied by two other cardinals. I became involved in their exchanges of conservation and, as a result, I had no opportunity to find my own place at table. When we moved to the table, therefore, I looked again rather longingly towards the far end of the table, but discovered to my great surprise that I was placed close to the center opposite Bishop John Howe, and with Monsignor Jean-Francois Arrighi on my right and Archbishop Giovanni Benelli on my left. The archbishop of Canterbury, who was seated at the center opposite our host Cardinal Willebrands, was engaged in conversation by Archbishop Benelli, then credited with being the most powerful man in the Vatican. In due course Archbishop Benelli turned to me. Here, I thought, is the man who knows everything about the Vatican as under secretary of state and is conversant with the business and the politics of the

Church throughout the world: what can I possibly say of interest to him? I began to speak, however, of how the Anglican Church cares for lepers in Fiji where I had served briefly in 1965. I told of the work of Sister Betty Slader, who had devoted her life to this ministry. It made a very moving story, and Archbishop Benelli was visibly touched by it. As we took leave of each other after the meal was ended, the archbishop drew me aside and said: "Dr. Smythe, I want you to know that, as a result of our conversation, as long as you remain at your post in Rome, the resources of the Secretariat of State will be at your service." We became friends from that time. Later I was the archbishop's guest on several occasions when he became Cardinal Archbishop of Florence. Once, to our mutual joy, we attended together a meeting, and addressed together, a vast group of 1000 young Christians. The archbishop was especially kind to me when I called on him during my pilgrimage begun from Rome in 1981. I reached Florence only to be informed of the tragic and imminently mortal illness of my only and much loved sister in Australia. The archbishop counselled me to meet the claim of charity by returning to my sister in her distress, but not to give up the pilgrimage on foot from Rome to Canterbury which, he said, "is very important to God in the interests of Anglican/Roman Catholic reconciliation." It was a most tragic loss to all Christendom when, in the following year, he died suddenly.

On the morning after the arrival of the archbishop of Canterbury in Rome, the archbishop and his suite were received in private audience in the Vatican. At one stage Bishop John Howe, secretary general of the Anglican Communion, and I were waiting outside the audience chamber in a very long and magnificent room which contained several enormous vases well over man-size and supported on elaborate stands. Bishop Howe proceeded unthinkingly to lean against one of these, until I ventured to point out to him that he might well go down in history as the man who brought ecumenical expectations crashing to the ground! Much attention was being devoted in the private audience meanwhile to the proposed text of the Joint Declaration which was to be signed the following day. Eventually, however, pope and archbishop agreed to all aspects of it and the final wording was approved. We were then driven very fast across the city for the luncheon with the abbot primate at San Anselmo on the Aventine.

In the afternoon of the same day, the archbishop of Canterbury dedicated two large bronze doors at the west front of the American Episcopal church of St. Paul within the Walls on Via Nazionale. He preached a sermon in the presence of Cardinal Willebrands and the members of the secretariat for promoting Christian unity. This address caused some offence, because the archbishop chose to introduce the issue of sacramental intercommunion, mentioning how many times he had encountered this phenomenon in the course of his travels across the world. He seemed to regard it as a positive contribution to Christian Unity, or at least as indicative of a desire for change on the part of many Christian people imprisoned behind denominational boundaries. After the service I found him in serious exchange with Cardinal Willebrands in the vestry, and it was some time, despite the anxiety of the police escort, before we were free to drive down to the Doria Palace. From that stage of the evening the archbishop was my guest, and I was responsible for him.

With the gracious and generous permission of Don Frank and Donna Orietta Doria Pamphilj, I had arranged a reception in the palace for some 450 guests, all of whom were connected in some significant way with the work of the Anglican Centre. The setting was, in biblical language, "exceeding magnifical." As the archbishop entered, the footman, Mario, bowed and led us past the Throne Room. The archbishop turned to me and said: "Do you live in this splendour all the time?" I considered it discreet to answer, "No, Your Grace, in more modest quarters upstairs!" We were welcomed by Don Frank and Donna Orietta, who were standing outside the ballroom with their son and daughter, Jonathan and Gesine. There followed the long line of my guests whom I received and presented to the archbishop. I am rather pleased to recall that I made the presentations of 450 people without need to refer to the list which I held in my hand. Several cardinals and Archbishop Benelli, under secretary of state, were present. Donna Orietta had said to me: "Harry, your party will be made if my cousins the Colonnas come, but we must see to it that they are properly recehed." Princea Colonna is the head of the Roman aristocracy, but to this respect, which I was urged to show for the order of social precedence, fell victim to the vagaries of circumstances. I had had a charming note from Prince Colonna accepting my invitation, but expressing his regret that his wife would be assisting the sick, as her custom was, on a train to Lourdes. He enquired whether he might be accompanied by his mother instead. In the midst of the reception of the guests, Prince Colonna and the Princess Isabella, his mother, entered the palace downstairs by the wrong door, found themselves in the kitchens, and reached the ballroom by the service lift. They appeared quite undismayed by the failure of protocol. At the other end of the table a social precedence, as it were, appeared: my friend Signora Ida, who had stood for years at her flower-stall at the corner of Piazza Venezia and the Vicolo Doria. Princess Orietta Doria Pamphilj had gone in person to urge her to accept my invitation to be present. She curtsied to the archbishop and presented him with a posy of flowers. There were several ambassadors and their wives among the guests, all of whom had assisted me in various ways with my own work. I invited also the one poor man whom I knew in Rome as a friend, hopeful that his presence might be noted as evidence in my favour at the Last Judgment.

After some time I withdrew from the gathering with the archbishop and Bishop John Howe by means of a secret lift which gave access to the floor on which the Anglican Centre is housed. We were joined by Don Frank and Donna Orietta for an excellent dinner prepared by Signora Claudia and served with the assistance of a waiter hired for the occasion.

While we were still at table I heard the telephone ring in my study. I had told Signora Claudia that I would not take any calls during dinner, but she stood outside the dining-room in my line of sight, making empathic gestures to attract my attention. The caller was Bishop Ramon Torrella, vice president of the Secretariat for Promoting Christian Unity. He asked apologetically to speak with the archbishop of Canterbury. I declined this request, but called Bishop Howe to the telephone. He re-appeared after some time, looking rather annoyed. I refrained from asking questions. When our guests had taken their leave, the archbishop expressed the wish to walk back to the Venerable English College on the Via Monserrato. We did this together, accompanied by Bishop Howe. The unusual spectacle offered to the citizens of Rome of seeing two *porporati* on foot accompanied by a priest in a black cassock offered an object lesson in simplicity after the heavily guarded movements of the day.

On the following morning, immediately before the grand reception of the archbishop in Sistine Chapel, another curious incident occurred when the archbishop was called to the telephone before we left the English College. The British minister to the Holy See, Mr. Dugald Malcolm, himself privy to the issue involved, asked me not to enquire about it. I respected this advice, and it was only later that Bishop Howe informed me of what happened. It seems that, after the private audience of the archbishop with the pope on the previous day, at which the final text of the Joint Declaration had been agreed word by word, line by line, some person unnamed had intervened with the pope to insist on a change in a part of the wording. The document was to be signed in public after the solemnities in the Sistine Chapel were concluded. The responsibility for this untoward intervention was ascribed by some to the pope's Jesuit theologian, although the identity was a matter of speculation. Far more alarming was the fact that some person had the influence to intrude into a delicate situation and to insist on an alteration of a text already agreed by the signatories. The archbishop was well aware of the significance of what had happened and he let this be known in a clever, discreet way. The Anglican bishops in his entourage, together with Bishop Alan Clark and Cardinal Willebrands, seemed annoyed at the intervention, but agreed that the substances of the Joint Declaration had not been notably weakened.

First, however, there was a magnificent reception of the archbishop of Canterbury in the Sistine Chapel where two thrones of equal dignity had been set before the altar. Members of the Vatican were seated to the left of the high altar and members of the archbishop's suite to the right facing, all of us.

the Last Judgment of Michelangelo. It was from that position that I was invited to read the liturgical lesson. Above us all, prelates, princes, and people, loomed the immense and majestic fresco, reminding us of the ultimate implications of every human action. Pope Paul appeared very frail in health. The archbishop of Canterbury assisted him at the end down the steps of the sanctuary as they withdrew with their advisers into the Cappella Paolina. Here were set two chairs and two desks, each of which was surrounded from behind by a small group of the counsellors. The press and television crew were confined to the far end of the vast room. First, Monsignor William Purdy of the Secretariat for Promoting Christian Unity was asked to read the text of the prepared Joint Declaration in English. The pope and archbishop, seated, studied the document before them attentively and, at one point, to the astonishment of those present, although unnoticed by Pope Paul VI, the archbishop of Canterbury picked up the pen in front of him and appeared to make an alteration in the text! It was only afterwards on enquiry from Bishop Howe that I learned that the archbishop had noticed the omission of citation marks before a biblical text being quoted in the document and that he had inserted them. Perhaps it was his subtle and kindly comment on the unwelcome intervention overnight from the other side?

Despite the efforts of Archbishop Robert Runcie and Archbishop George Carey, the visit of Archbishop Donald Coggan in 1978 may be viewed, in my opinion, as the last serious and unambiguous commitment of the Anglican Communion to the goal of corporate reconciliation and unity with the Roman Catholic Church. The later visits of archbishops of Canterbury, however well intentioned, could not succeed because of the growing commitment of the Anglican Communion to the ordination of women. This unilateral move was allowed to develop, seemingly without check or warning on the Anglican side, despite the fact that it had no detectable support in the ancient common traditions of the Church. In the New Testament, moreover, the imperative of unity is stated unequivocally as the basis of an effective evangelism. Only an attitude which is basically sectarian could allow the issue of the ordination of women to take precedence over the explicit urgencies of the Gospel.

As the time drew near for the conclusion of my ministry in Rome, I consulted Bishop John Howe and others on my own future. No solution to this issue was offered. "You should be looking round yourself for a job," Bishop Howe expostulated. The most that I considered myself able to do, however, was to ask advice from those well-qualified by office and responsibility to give it, and I replied to Bishop Howe's statement by saying, rather chillingly, that I had not "looked round for a job" at any time in Holy Orders. "Had I done so," I added, "I would not have chosen to be ordained. If I had merely been 'looking round for a job,'" I said, "I could have been president of the Chase Manhattan Bank or something by now, but I have always waited on the counsel of those set over me, trusting to find there evidence of God's will." Perhaps I should have added to this outburst: "Despite the facts!" The bishop and I did not discuss the matter again, and I found it difficult to believe the folly of what was being allowed to happen in full view of the most highly placed authorities of the Roman Catholic Church to whom, in Pope Paul VI's words, I had been accredited as "the Anglican ambassador." In the time which remained to me in Rome it happened not infrequently that officials of the Papal Court, members of the Curia ambassadors to the Holy See and to the Italian State, and, on two occasions in audience, the pope himself, asked me about my future. One does not betray the incompetence of one's own side, so that I always replied: "This matter rests with the archbishop of Canterbury by whose authority I was appointed to my present office." It did rest there, unresolved for two years, despite the archbishop's goodwill.

I believe now that God had another plan for me which may not have found fulfillment had the ministers of his Church acted on my behalf in a manner which seemed to me at the time so clearly their duty. One night in 1980 in Rome in my sleep, in a kind of auditory experience in which I saw nothing, a voice said to me: "Why not walk?" In due course, therefore, once the interpretation of my "vision" became clear, I did exactly that, walking from the Tomb of St. Peter to the Throne of St.

Augustine in Canterbury. It took 10 years in all and included a traumatic personal family tragedy and a broken leg, but I arrived in Canterbury on July 3, 1991. At the invitation of Bishop John Taylor, sometime bishop of Winchester, I laid my pilgrim's staff on the high altar before the Throne of St. Augustine. The long journey was offered, as it had been daily, for the unity of the Anglican and Roman Catholic Churches according to the will of God. The motive remained unspoiled by the ever increasing evidence to the contrary. The toil and tears and sweat of my work and my journey are held in reserve, I believe, in that place where good things wait upon God for their purification and perfection.

32

The Challenge of European Union to the Churches of the United Kingdom

John S. Nurser

Introduction

It was not only the Germans who, by the 1930s, felt that the 1919 Treaty of Versailles was vengeful to a degree that had made subsequent peace between the nations of Europe improbable, and an economic slump almost inevitable. While working together, representing their countries in the Reparations Commission preparatory to the Treaty, an Englishman, John Maynard Keynes, a Frenchman, Jean Monnet, and an American, John Foster Dulles, had been led to the same conclusions. It is hard to think of three men who made a more creative contribution to the post-World War II world on the basis of that earlier experience. Keynesian theories of demand-management and Monnet's advocacy of economic institutions under joint European Community (rather than national) control were dominant ideas in seeking stable peace and prosperity. As for Dulles, three of his concerns in the 1940s have their roots in the

Versailles experience. First, he saw that any personal Christian belief of the men who made the post-World War I treaties had no discernible effect on the manner or content of their peace making, partly because no mechanism existed by which an informed and consciously Christian position could be fed into the process. Out of that perception came the Commission of the Churches on International Affairs in 1946. Second, he saw the practical as well as Christian wisdom in offering a hopeful future to defeated nations, and from that came his role in the peace treaties, especially with Japan. Third, like many Americans, he found it irritating that endemic quarrels between the sovereign nation-states of Europe should—twice in a lifetime —drag America into global armed conflict; and from that came his determined support (shared by Winston Churchill) for ever closer union in Europe, and for a post-war global order of diminished sovereignties.

Even ten years ago, it would have appeared absurd, even perverse, to link these great matters with the concerns of Christian congregations. A violence and hatred that money will not bribe to "be good" has, at least in Northern Ireland and the former Yugoslavia, shown that reconciliation has to be built on changed world-outlooks *inside* local communities if it is to be built at all. Such change is not normally welcome or easy. A faith-tradition can easily lose its sense of what Christians call sin, especially of its own. Yet, as Hans Kung keeps on saying, without peace between faith-traditions, there will be no peace. If the European Union has the potential to further peace and justice, and in doing so needs its constituent folk-communities to change—even repent— then it is important to look at how local churches—even if only in one state, the United Kingdom—might respond.

Looked at from the perspective of the year 2000 and beyond, it is remarkable that, almost alone of the major public institutions in British life, the Christian churches have welcomed the growth of trans-national European institutions in this last half-century.[1] This is in spite of the profoundly national character of British church traditions. What, however, these formal church speeches

---

[1] *Inter alia, Christians and the Common Market* (for the British Council of Churches), SCM, London, 1967. *Reports to the General Synod of the Church of England:* GS95 (1972), GS (Misc.) 340 (1990), GS1135 (1994). Similarly, for other denominations and nations.

and papers conceal is, first, the lack of priority given to Europe in the international concerns of the churches as institutions; second, the confined constituency of church leaders among whom these concerns are active; and third, the almost total absence of any consciousness either in public life or among the local population (whether church-going or not) that the issues with which "Europe" is connected in the media have any points of contact with Christian faith, action, or baptismal membership.

In the UK there are relatively few institutions for the study of contemporary church history, and discussion of "Christianity and the future of Europe" questions takes place at a level very different from that of the institutes that exist in mainland Europe. A network of academically resourced conversation among churches in Europe needs to be established. It is encouraging that the Conference of European Churches (Protestant, Orthodox, Anglican) is working closely with the Council of European Bishops' Conferences (Roman Catholic). The practical weight of high-level statements from these trans-national groupings, and especially those emanating from the different sources within the British churches, needs to be nuanced and discerned. Similarly, for a rooted and fruitful dialogue between fellow European Christians it is important that there be sufficient practice in hearing each other use our national and ecclesiastical languages, so that we can recognize the very different spins that national myths give to value-concepts and words that as Christians we seem, at first glance, to share so heart-warmingly and straightforwardly across Europe. That is a salutary lesson, already experienced (even within the same Europe-wide party) by members of the European Parliament coming from different histories and cultures.[2]

There are, too, misunderstandings of matters of fact that can be quite widespread and unquestioned—we only need

[2] The British co-chair (Mr. Armedèe Turner, QC, MEP) of negotiations for union between the British Conservatives in the European Parliament and the mainland European People's Party (Christian Democrat) in the early 1990s is an Anglican. It was his insistence on the practical importance of including the religious element in looking at this problem of language that led the group of Christianity and the Future of Europe (CAFÉ) to call an inter-disciplinary meeting at Westcott House, Cambridge, in 1993, whose work has continued at the German Evangelical Academy at Bad Segeberg and at the European Parliament in Brussels.

look at current British media perceptions of EU's Social Chapter. Even educated mainland Europeans have misconceptions about the history of Christianity in Britain: e.g., (i) that not only the Church of England but the worldwide Anglican communion is self-evidently Protestant, (ii) that "England," "British Isles," and "United Kingdom" are interchangeable terms, and (iii) that the established churches of Britain are financed by the state. All these perceptions are false. It is therefore useful, as a preliminary, to give a brief historical survey.

The Nations of the British Isles and Their Churches

Since 1922 there have been two sovereign states, equally members of the European Union, in the British Isles: the Republic of Ireland, and the United Kingdom of Great Britain and Northern Ireland (consisting of England, Wales, Scotland, and Northern Ireland).[3] The ecumenical organisation Christians Together in Britain and Ireland (the successor to the British Council of Churches, but now including the Roman Catholic Church), operates across the boundaries of these sovereign states. This fact of two sovereignties is even now not always grasped in Britain. Past imbalance of power (though it is important to recognise the remarkable economic growth of the Republic since entry into the European Union [EU]) and a common English language make it easy for English churchmen to subsume Irishness in "Britishness" in their minds. As politically dangerous in the last generation (because so resented by their churchmen) has been the English tendency to subsume Scottishness as well as Welshness in "Englishness," within the one island of Britain. The Act of Union (1707) between England (then including Wales) and Scotland found it necessary to assert the establishment of the Reformed church in Scotland.

---

[3] There is a deep division, to some extent party-political (formally, the British Conservative party also calls itself the *Unionist Party*), between those in the United Kingdom who see their nation as England, Scotland or (to a lesser extent) Wales and (Protestant) Ulster, and those who refuse to concede my variety of national status to be distinguished among holders of the UK passport, available to "subjects of the Queen."

The republic of Ireland's constitution refers to the special standing of the Roman Catholic church. The identity of Northern Ireland in its political adherence to Britishness is explicitly bound up with its Protestant (and in particular Scots Reformed) colonisation in the seventeenth century. The Anglo-Welsh Tudor settlement of church and state in the 1530s (there is still no written constitution in the UK to supersede it) included the "establishment" and "reformation" of the church, whose only clear-cut features were the cutting out of any jurisdiction from outside (especially that of the papacy, but also the ghost of holy emperors), the exaltation of scripture as the touchstone of doctrine, and the use of the vernacular English language in the liturgy of the Anglican Churches of England (including Wales) and Ireland. At least until the late seventeenth century this was a factor in alienating the Celtic-speaking peoples of Wales and Ireland—even Cornwall—from the Elizabethan settlement. The non-conforming Protestant chapels (Reformed and Baptist) and the Roman Catholic Church became respectively the bearers of Welsh and Irish folk nationalism until the mid twentieth century. Indeed, it remains a question whether the Irish Republican Army may still be described as the "Catholics" into the third millennium, however strongly the Catholic church leadership distances itself from that organisation.

From the time of the Union of Scotland and England at the accession of the Scottish king to the English throne in 1603, there have been in the British Isles two separate national cultures (legal/educational/religious systems) in Scotland and England, plus two "nations," the Welsh and the Irish, subjugated by England with very varying degrees of local effectiveness. It is now customary (or at least politically correct) to speak of "four nations" of the United Kingdom of Britain and Northern Ireland, plus, of course, the independent Republic of Ireland (of which half of the population of *Northern* Ireland might prefer to consider themselves citizens). So these five "nations," now working together in churches in Britain and Ireland, have very different church-state traditions.

Financing the Churches

Naturally, too, there are different traditions of financing church life. In Ireland and Wales the clergy of the Henrician Reformation inherited the endowments of the medieval church, both ownership of lands and rights to levy traditional tithes. Since the clergy of the established churches was not recognized as *their* pastors by the bulk of at least the peasant population, this caused chronic social unrest and antagonism. When those Anglican churches were disestablished a century ago, they had to rebuild on an economic basis provided by members' giving, and they lost their financial as well as their social salience. The post-Reformation churches of Protestant Welsh and Catholic Irish nationalism depended, and still depend, on the giving and devotion of their congregations. Now no longer the bearers of national feeling, the Welsh free-church chapels are much reduced, and even Irish Catholicism feels the pinch.

In Scotland and England there were different stories. We have to recall that the British Isles never experienced the traumas of 1789 and then of Napoleonism as did France. Church buildings have not been destroyed. Clergy never became salaried by the state, even in the centuries when they were the public officials responsible in their localities for the keeping of records of e.g., births, deaths, and marriages, for education, and for the relief of poverty. So while the levying of tithes and church rates on land for local clergy stipends and church buildings was unpopular (and it continued in vestigial form until the 1930s), there was a sufficiently broad-based affirmation of the two established churches by the population (especially if influence was weighed as well as bodies counted) for them to continue as the dominant partners alongside the congregationally funded and anti-hierarchical chapels. It used not to be altogether unfair to describe the Church of England as "the Tory (Conservative) party at prayer."

It has been well said that the Church of England was the only territorial church of medieval Christendom to escape "reformation." The systematic dismantling of the anomalies of medieval church life at the Council of Trent had no impact on any part of Britain or Ireland. In the same way that a medieval king was thought to be under obligation to "live of his own, so the Church of England inherited a structure in which endowments (some of them still lands of which there is record of having been donated by Anglo-Saxon lords) were attached to identified clergy posts and parish churches or cathedrals. In substantial part, that was still the way in which the endowments of the Church of England were applied until the 1970s (I myself, as the incumbent of villages in Suffolk from 1974 to 1976, had in person to collect rents from land bequeathed to a predecessor by a local knight who had gone off on one of the Crusades). The endowments of the Church of England have now been brought together and are managed centrally, but they are still held in trust for the sole purpose of providing pastoral ministry to the population of parishes (in sum, the total territory of England) in the care of individual priests.

The consequence of this until the 1920s was that there was (in theory) no way in which the Church of England could develop a national policy, deploy clergy, or direct and discipline their energies. Even less, however, has it been possible for the *state* to do any of those things. The Church of England, and certainly the Church of Scotland, are no longer state churches, if we define the state as the apparatus of government. We do not have a government minister responsible for religious matters or, as for example in Denmark, for the internal administration of a national church.

Thus, religion is state-specific. Europe-wide agreements often do not fit. For example, in its preamble, the 1984 Council of Europe Convention on Culture defines religion as one of the integral elements of culture. For the UK government, this convention came on to the desk of Lord Gowrie, then Minister for the Arts, who had absolutely no administrative or policy responsibility for the Church of England in particular or religious bodies in general!

The British Crown

Often overlooked is the role of the monarchy in Britain. It is there, however, that the Church of England has its connecting point to the political constitution. The royal family seems divorced from power, merely theatrical (as the Victorian political theorist Walter Bagehot called it), and in the past decade its traditional mystery no longer protects against intrusion by the tabloid press. Rupert Murdoch, the owner of the tabloid *Sun* as well as *The Times*, and the colossus of world Sky television, is an Australian-American who is a self-confessed republican (and also ardently anti-European).

Yet the coronation of the monarch (the "supreme governor" —*not* the "head"—of the Church of England) is the locus in the absence of a written constitution of important symbolism about political power in Britain. The coronation itself is performed by the archbishop of Canterbury on behalf of the trans-generational nation. The current year's moderator of the Church of Scotland has also recently been given a liturgical role, to proclaim the Bible's authority over national life. The ritual of coronation symbolises an implicit contract under God between the people and their traditional political/ecclesiastical/legal institutions on the one hand, and the new king and those who are correctly his ministers and government on the other. Or at least this is what it used to symbolise. It will be interesting to see how the order of coronation of the next king will be shaped. Will his successions require a church coronation in Westminster Abbey at all? And surely there will have to be a role given to non-Christian faiths that are now so important in Britain, but were virtually absent last time, in 1953.

It is at this symbolic level that the Church of England is very fragile. The Prince of Wales has let it be known that he will wish to translate the sixteenth century royal title Defender of the Faith into that of the protector and patron of faith in general— in his own case, perhaps, of an ecologically sensitive Christian humanism—but equally of Islam, Hinduism, Judaism, Buddhism and, of course, Catholicism. Traditionally, the king has been an Anglican in England and a Presbyterian in Scotland. But never, *never*, a Catholic in Ireland. In practice, although Queen Victoria was famous for her personal predilection for Scotland and Scotland's religion, British government has spoken in the accents of southern England. Power has been located in the "home counties," those adjacent to London.

It is of great importance that Henry VIII, when king of England and wishing—in Parliament—to reshape the organized (and endowed) church, but not its doctrine, used the word empire. In its origin, the claim that "this England is an empire"[4] brought echoes of the major controversies that divided medieval schoolmen (Christian and Catholic clergymen, of course) between papalists and imperialists. One could think of the imperial role of Constantine (born at York) within his contem porary church of Christ, and the relation between Byzantine emperors and patriarchs through the following centuries. England had never fallen within the outreach of Charlemange's renewed Empire of the German Nation. The 1533 Reformation statute's actual assertion was that no external human body whatsoever, personal or corporate, was to have authority of any kind within the borders of the realm of England and, of course, of its dependent territories, whether in Wales and Ireland then, or further afield later.

Every subsequent century, the borders of the king of England's realms were pegged further outward. By 1930, after 400 years, a vast proportion of the surface area of this planet was coloured pink-for-Britain on the map. Over it, the king (still crowned by the archbishop of Canterbury) was in some sense sovereign through a rich variety of elected parliaments and appointed governors. Its *lingua franca* and its law was English. "This England" of 1533 had become an empire in a sense of undreamed of by medieval emperors.

The English language

From 1947, this has all unraveled. But no one should underestimate, even in the twenty-first century, the real influence both of Queen Elizabeth II and of her Commonwealth of Nations, the forum that still gathers together the once-constituent dominions and colonies and the sub-continental Indian raj. For one thing, all speak English, as does the great North American dominion, the one that got away. As the United States exercises

---

[4] Act in Restraint of Appeals, 1533.

pre-eminent technical and media power globally, so airline pilots and television stations speak English everywhere.

Linguistic xenophobia is one of Britian's dominant traits. For most of the UK, access to the public world is via TV and the popular press, so anything that is not in English, e.g., in elections to the European Parliament, does not exist. There is no social advantage to be gained by knowing a foreign language. Warsaw is a city in a European state, but there is no comparison with, for example, San Francisco in its significance for British consciousness of the world. The USA and Australia are much more visible than mainland Europe.

In Britain, the Europhiles come from the educated middle classes. Their annual holidays are in France or Italy. They often own second homes in the Dordogne or Umbria. There they may speak the local language. But they are not electorally significant. At election time, media debate about Europe is tuned (very scientifically) to age-groups (e.g., pensioners) or classes (e.g., semi-skilled workers) that are deemed crucial to swinging key seats. These groups tend to be more nationalist and less well educated. So political debate on Europe in national elections (even to the European Parliament) is either populist or willfully (and undemocratically) obscure.

The question must arise whether these language considerations are also true for other post-imperial peoples. Does Santiago de Chile seem more real than Helsinki in the Spanish mind? It is as important for their church identity as for their national identity that some Europeans, most evidently the Spanish, Portuguese, Russians, French and British, have also an extra-European linguistic and cultural world to inhabit.

These facts are so self-evident and straightforward that it is easy not to give them their proper weight in discussion of national—and in particular British—attitudes to Europe. The British Protestant churches have to an unusual degree lived in an English-speaking world (though, over the past century, *academic* theologians have normally have found it necessary to study at the great German universities). Present-day parish clergy rarely know even Greek, Latin or Hebrew. The global Anglican Communion of churches is virtually confined to those parts of the world once settled, governed, or traded with by Britain. The great English Reformed denominations, the Congregationalists and the Baptists, defined themselves by their dissent from the Elizabethan church settlement. The Methodists defined themselves in protest against the lack of evangelical zeal among eighteenth century Anglicans. But in all cases (including the Quakers) they are within their English religious tradition—now grown world-wide.

This is, from the other end of the ecclesiastical spectrum, also the premise of High Church Anglicans. Their understanding of what happened at the break with Rome was that the Church of England put off accretions of post-Patristic error in *renovatio* as the one holy and apostolic catholic church. But only for the English nation. There was in this picture (understandable in the sixteenth century) no understanding of a Christianity that was other than territorial and European. The Church of England wished other nations well, as they chose to be Roman Catholic, Lutheran, or whatever, but it was "none of our business." As a governing idea, this has remained until very recently the justification for keeping the Anglican presence in mainland Europe as a chaplaincy strictly confined to English speakers, to resident English-speaking aliens. Outside Europe, Anglicanism has had to find a very different—and now normative—self-understanding. This has been hard for English Anglicans to understand. Until World War II, an element in traditional apologetic for the Church of England was that it was a form of Christian religion shaped for the unique and God-given peculiarity of the English temperament. If not Henry VIII, then Elizabeth I was pictured (not wholly convincingly—but she did breathe the same air as Shakespeare) as a benevolent ruler who saw what was needed to acculturate the Christian religion to her people.

The Effect of Overseas Empire

It was the overseas Empire that made Britain more than the name of an island.[5] Once abroad, members of the four (and even the five) nations described themselves as British. This has had important consequences for the post-World War II immigrant

---

[5] Linda Colley, *Britons: Forging the Nation 1707-1837*, New Haven, 1992; Daniel Jenkins, *The British: their Identity and their Religion*, London 1975.

populations from South Asia and the Caribbean who likewise define themselves as British rather than, for example, Welsh. These so-called ethnic communities, now third generation, have almost no sense of Europe as their continent. It is conceivable that British Muslims (from Pakistan and Bangladesh) will establish a primarily European common Muslim identity together with Turkish Germans and Maghreb French and Indonesian Dutch, not to mention indigenous Bosnians—but not yet.

The global British Empire was yesterday, however. A real question—experience as *tremendum et fascinosum*—now presents itself as the European Union is seen to be replacing that former dominant political, social and economic reality; will the four nations now find their *own* individual and differing relationships within the continent of Europe? These relationships have a great deal to do with a pre-modern history in which church and nation were inseparably bound up with each other. That same question is being asked in other states of the European Union, such as Spain.

Ireland

In shorthand, the indigenous Irish were the first victims of English imperialism. They were branded as a lower race. Medieval Irish resistance to English hegemony changed its character in the sixteenth century when the imposition of Protestant Reformation created a Roman Catholic Irish nationalism. The Anglican Church of Ireland was from the beginning more Calvinist than the Church of England. For over 300 years, Irish Roman Catholic priests were educated in the seminaries of Latin Europe, and came back to Ireland as the recognized social and political leaders of their communities. Any enemies of England who landed in Ireland were welcome. In the seventeeth and eighteenth centuries French (and therefore Catholic) invasions represented real danger to England, and real hope for Ireland. The enthusiasm of the Irish Republic for the European union was able to grow from this sense of the Latin mainland as a political counterweight to England, and as the home base of their religious culture. The Irish have found world-wide vocations within the Roman

Catholic Church, and have been conspicuously successful in international organisations.

Above all, the Irish have travelled—been blown about the world like thistledown. In the sixth century St. Brendan is said to have rounded Scotland in a coracle. Scots-Irish Protestants poured into American through Philadelphia in the eighteenth century. Catholic Irish "freedom fighters" as well as thieves were numerous among the first generations of convict settlement in Australia after 1788. Then, before, during, and after the great potato famine of the 1840s large populations of uneducated and almost medieval rural poor flooded west to the USA and eastwards into the industrial conurbations of both England and Scotland. The consequences for British Roman Catholicism as a whole have been very great, as a large number of parish priests, teaching sisters, etc. have been drawn in each generation directly from rural Ireland.

Scotland

The character of religion in Scotland has similarly been influenced by the Reformed Kirks' having to carry so much of national identity, although the Roman Catholic now approximates in size to the Reformed, and formally recognized, Church of Scotland. When the influx of Catholic Irish arrived in the Glasgow area, it joined less numerous but significant indigenous group of Catholics displaced by poverty and the clearances from the Celtic/Gaelic highlands and islands of West Scotland. Some of these clans had remained Catholic after the Reformation. However, there was not a *religious* enmity (as in Ireland) toward the English, but rather rivalry with the lowland Scots. The highland regiments with their kilts and bagpipes have been and are an integral part of the elite military tradition of the British army. Glasgow was home port and shipbuilder to the merchant marine of the British Empire; its engineers, doctors and administrators found distinguished careers under the British flag. The practical horizon of Scotland since the mid-eighteenth century was across the oceans to the west.

What has happened now in Scotland is a sharp break with what—in the years of empire—had been a practically advantageous marriage with England. Suddenly Europe is welcomed. Scotland stretches as far north as Oslo, and for centuries, Norway to the east had been Scotland's most significant "other." As the English began to threaten Scottish identity, c. 1300, the "auld alliance" with France was forged, and has remained part of national self-consciousness. The Scots Reformation was directly linked to the international web centered on Calvin's Geneva. In the golden age of the Scots' intellectual life in the 18th century there were especially close links with their fellow Reformed in the Netherlands. In the twentieth century Scots or Scots-Americans have been in the front rank of the World Alliance of Reformed Churches and of the World Council of Churches. The Reformed religious community founded in the 1930s on the island of Iona has played a leading role in Scottish religious life—active in social work among the excluded poor of industrial Glasgow, cultivating a Celtic spirituality, prophetic of a virile peace and a healed creation, rebuilding the old abbey on Iona as a pilgrimage center, and anxious to assert the identity of Scotland-in-Europe. Ecclesiastically the Scottish Reformed Church, of all the British churches, belongs most unambiguously to an international and Euro-positive tradition.

The down-side of this is that they are also the heirs—together with their Catholic antagonists—of the sectarian polarisation that is common in mainland Europe. It has not been an unfamiliar cry that the pope is anti-Christ. In 1927, the powerful Church and Nation Committee of the Church of Scotland called for the regulation of Irish Catholic immigration in strong language. In its words, we can recognize the practically universal racism of European Christianity of that decade:

> The Church of Scotland, whose interests in the past have been so intimately associated with those of the Scottish people, has clearly an obligation to defend Scottish nationality such as no other organisation or institution has....If ever there was a call to the Church of Scotland to stand fast for what men rightly call dearest— their nationality and traditions—that call is surely sounding now when our race and culture are faced

with a peril which, though silent and unostentatious, is the greatest with which the Scottish people have ever been confronted.

The Committee continued to report to the Assembly on this "Irish Menace" right up until 1939: the Irish (who were judged of the "inferior sort") were seen as threat to the Scots' racial and cultural purity, their jobs and welfare resources.[6] When, in the 1980s, the theological faculty (also the Reformed seminary) of Edinburgh University appointed—amid much dissent—a married Irish-Catholic ex-priest to the chair of theology, it was the defining moment of a new age. The holder of this post had traditionally been expected to exercise the Reformed equivalent of church *episkope*.

For the two major Scottish churches the ever-closer union of the Europe project is nothing but welcome. This is especially important as Scots' identity has had, since the Act of Union (1707), to rely on culture. Its political and economic lives have been merged with England's in the Westminster Parliament and the British government. The concept of subsidiarity, with its Reformed origins and modern-day Catholic advocacy, offers the Scots a way to reclaim some of the national identity they feel they have lost. Perhaps they can see a future like Bavaria's among the "lände."

The 1999 policy of the UK Labor government for constitutional change was more radical than anything in the twentieth century. Wales in 1999 had elections to its own Assembly, and Scotland to its own regional Parliament and government. Similarly, perhaps, Northern Ireland might be given space to find peace in a Europe of the Regions where political sovereignty is less either/or than it has been. The comprehensive Council of the Isles, where the Republic is a foundation member too (and, it is said, even contemplates some form of association with the British Commonwealth), was an integral element in the Northern Ireland Good Friday Peace Agreement and met for the first time in December 1999.

---

[6] W. Storrar, *Scottish Identity, a Christian Vision,* Handsel, Edinburgh, 1990, pp. 218–19.

England

England is quite another story. It is important first to note the overwhelming preponderance within the UK of England's population in the southeast, and the extraordinary centralised character of British government, media, finance, and economics in London, a megalopolis which effectively stretches 80 km in every direction. To include England within these new levels of decentralised government is more difficult.

London has attracted immigrants over many generations— Flemings, Huguenots, Jews, Scots, Welsh and Irish; and since the mid-1950s, Afro-Caribbeans, Bangladeshis, Indians, Pakistanis, and West Africans. It is not only this necessary multiculturalism of a world city that has led to a national self-image which claims to be tolerant of differences. A frequently quoted and generally approved dictum of Queen Elizabeth I is that she had "no wish to make windows into men's souls." Her successor, James VI of Scotland and I of England, worked tirelessly for the reunion of Christendom.[7] One of the very greatest contributions that the English churches can make to the project of European Union is a long experience of living quietly within a spectrum—rather than an either/or—of religious conviction.[8]

In the decade before the events of the 1968 student revolutions, an unusual number of British people had experience of living and working as partners in development among members of the other world faiths in other continents. A seldom-remarked (and under-researched) fact is the sudden drying up of public promotion of overseas mission-as-conversion within local congregations around 1960, when it was already clear large numbers of Hindus, etc., lived only a bus ride away. Equally sudden was the packing away of school textbooks telling the classical Whig story of English liberties—speaking of "our incomparable liturgy" (1662 Book of Common Prayer), the unwritten constitution secured by the "glorious revolution" of

---

[7] W.B. Patterson, *King James VI and I and the Reunion of Christendom*, Cambridge, 1997.

[8] Though it has to be confessed that it was only during World War II that Catholics were accepted as full members of the cast of "our (English) island story."

1688, and the deeds of the heroes of war and overseas expansion. A dramatic change had occurred.

Fifty years later, it is no longer possible to speak publicly of England as a Christian country, let alone a Protestant country. The importance of this transition can hardly be overestimated. But the first half of the twentieth century's easy-going and unde-manding companionship between the state and a family of churches has left England with some precious inheritances. Pan-Protestant bible study has been replaced by a professional teacher's introduction to religion itself and to world faiths, but religion is still a formal element in the national school curriculum. Biblical theology in state-financed universities continues to find a place, but as complemented by, and included in, the secularised discipline of religious studies. For the moment, religion is still included as a department in its own right within the programming of radio and TV.

The sensitivities of the post-World War II period were de-terminedly anglophonic. It was marked on the one hand by technological self-confidence and economic self-doubt (in which the USA was model, rival, bailer-out); and on the other hand by a moral obsession with race. Again, it was the USA, after the 1954 Supreme Court ruling on school segregation, and then Martin Luther King, that scripted the drama of how black immigrants' experience in Smethwick (Birmingham) or Notting Hill (London) was perceived by the professional classes, the young, and many church leaders. Increasingly, the churches saw the establishment of apartheid in South Africa as *the* cosmic issue, played out to the counterpoint of NATO and nuclear weapons. Very little energy was given—it was resented as a di-version— to the recovery of a democratic Germany, the building of trans-national structures that could not easily be unscrambled in a common European Iron and Steel (armaments industry) Community, or to the astonishing moment when ratification of a European Convention of Human Rights actually gave indi-vidual British citizens the means to seek redress against their own sovereign state. That was surely when self-understanding of "this England" as an Henrician empire was finally contra-dicted.

Attitudes to the Europe Project

Why was Europe so little regarded in the 1950s in Britain? It is well known how careless and negative the UK delegation to the meeting of European governments at Messina in 1955 had been; that it judged any coming together in an Economic Community was unlikely to succeed and was inherently alien to Britain's national interests. English church leaders of the 1930s and 1940s like William Temple, William Paton, and George Bell —Europeans of the first rank – found no successors in the 1950s.[9] Sir Winston Churchill's speech at Zurich in September 1946 proposing a new sense of European political identity was in stark contrast to the attitudes of the governing Conservative Party in the 1950s, which constantly sought to claim Britain's right to a reserved seat of its own at any global top table. It poured scorn on a future for Britain—like Sweden's, it was said —as a medium sized country within the European Continent. It was in 1962 that Dean Acheson, the US Secretary of State, made his famous remark that Britain had lost an empire but had not yet found a role.

The Labor Party, with its traditional dependence on the trade unions, contained many who regarded those building the European Communities as agents of a capitalist boss' plot; and probably a Catholic plot, too. A cabinet minister from the Cooperative tradition, A.V. (later Lord) Alexander, was eloquent in his opposition. There was intense suspicion of Catholic activists among trade union leaders (which, in Australia, led to a splitting of the Labor Party).

Traditional English (as opposed to Irish) Catholics were normally Conservatives. They were not enthusiastic for European political entanglements. In principle, their religious world was Euro-centric, but the one charge they could not permit was lack of patriotism. The story of papal commissioning of the Spanish Armada (1588) and of English Catholic "gunpowder, treason and plot" to blow up King and Parliament in 1605 (whose frustrations are still only thinly overlain in an English child's year on November the 5th as the occasion for bonfire and fireworks)

---

[9] J.A. Zeilstra, *European Unity in Ecumenical Thinking 1937-1948*, Utrecht 1995.

was at the root of the rhetoric of Catholic exclusion from English society until the 1820s.

The prospect of structural consolidation of France and Germany in a European Community also struck chords of alarm within the unbroken traditions of British diplomacy. The aggression of medieval English kings to west and north had been designed to close off European mainland access to England's back door. The particular game which the British learned to make their own was the balance of power. To preserve openness to trade across the sea and to maintain the freedom of the British, safe on their islands, to make alliances as the current situation dictated; these remained the two requirements of policy. This even had its analogue in the self-image of the Church of England as a "bridge church," equidistant from, and apart from, Geneva, Rome, and Constantinople. Such have been used against enduring institutional rapprochement with Protestants.

What emotionally, perhaps, the British have never quite grasped was that the experiences (quite unparalleled in British history) of the two twentieth century "people's wars" against Germany were directly a consequence of balance-of-power habits. Sending small professional armies abroad, plus subsidizing the ally of the moment, had worked against Louis XIV and Napoleon. But world wars are a new context. Apartness is not a receipt for the avoidance of suffering. It was balance-of-power diplomacy that delivered a whole generation to slaughter on the Somme and in Flanders. Even after two world wars in a lifetime there has not been the same sense in Britain as in France and Germany that it is urgently necessary — if as Christians we intend to obey Jesus' command to be peacemakers—to replace the shifting alliances of sovereign state in Europe by a trans-national structure of ever closer union.

This special dynamic toward the prevention of fratricidal war in Europe has figured very strongly in Franco-German attitudes to the European project. It has shaped the *acquis communitaire* of the European Union so far. This is often in tension with the dynamic that drives other, later, incomers to the Union and, in particular, of Britain. *Their* dynamic—at least for the moment—is overtly economic.

The attitudes of the church to a policy for peace and unity are likely to fall into different categories of energy and conviction from those to a policy based on calculations of relative national prosperity. The churches (in Britain at least) are ascribed a far greater part to play in discussion of generally moral choices than numbers of regular worshippers would indicate. If, therefore, the churches can come to see the European Union as relevant to reconciliation, human rights, and world development, this could have a major impact in changing the terms of the public debate.[10]

Can the English Learn to Love Europe?

The Irish, Welsh, and Scots churches have all expressed warm endorsement of the widespread feeling in those "nations" that they should participate wholeheartedly in building Europe. The English churches have to take account of a different national sentiment. What is striking is the great gulf between words and deeds: between what has been said, often with passionate conviction, by leading figures (especially in the Church of England), what synods and assemblies have resolved at the national level, and any observable consequences. There is at present an almost brutal refusal—even among believers—to allow the churches the right to speak in the public square.

Christianity and the Future of Europe (a "body in association" of Churches Together in Britain and Ireland) asked M. M. Tolstoy to investigate attitudes to the European Union in congregations of different denominations in Cambridge.[11] The initial findings were of the suffocating apathy that is characteristic of English society's response to Europe generally (with the exception of the Quakers, who are eloquently and impressively Euro-conscious). Europe is not, it is thought, a topic that deserves to occupy the time or study (even prayers) of practical men and women active in local church life. There is a level "up there" where "someone" should discuss such questions seriously. But they are at least granted theoretical importance. Dr. Tolstoy writes:

---

[10] G. Davie, R. Gill and S. Platten (eds.), *Christian Values in Europe*, Cambridge, 1993.

[11] M. M. Tolstoy, "An exploration of attitudes to the European Union in different faith communities" (unpublished, Cambridge, 1996).

I have learned that... the time to establish contact and trust is not wasted time, so everything takes much longer than is anticipated initially. The European Union is not a topic that has been discussed in any of the church communities I have worked with, apart from the Quakers. The clergy do not see it as part of their responsibility to bring it up for serious discussion not necessarily because they are not interested, but mainly because, as they can only see it in terms of party politics, it is considered to be a private matter that does not belong in the church.

The clergy do not seem to be familiar with documents that various church bodies have produced. It is a non-subject, because they do not feel competent to deal with it in an impartial manner. It has become abundantly clear that Reports that were written in this country on the topic of Church and Europe are not received and/or taken notice of.[12]

What she says of her conversation with the parish priest of the Catholic congregation is particularly interesting, that it:

reminded me of what some people have called the protestantisation of the church, i.e., his thinking was mainly concerned with the Roman Catholic Church in Britain. He had not read or taken notice of any of the public pronouncements by the pope on Europe and was entirely puzzled as to why I would want to talk about it. But when I started to talk to him about the wars that had been in Europe this century, about the ever present danger of nationalism as well as of the ways in which banks and businesses were interdependent, about the freedom to move within the European job market etc., he began to warm to the subject. It had obviously never struck him in any way whatsoever. He had no idea what people in his congregation thought about it.[13]

In England, if one occasionally comes across a real sense of local engagement, it is grounded either in successful experience of church involvement in a civic or diocesan twinning or in the enthusiasm of a minister to make a personal study, e.g., via a

---

[12] Ibid., p. 4.
[13] Ibid., p. 17.

sabbatical, of some aspect of mainland European church life. Parishes do not remember the neighbouring cities and regions of mainland Europe, the political and religious leaders of the nations of Europe, or the officers of the European Union in their regular weekly intercessions—whereas it is routine (at least in the Church of England) to include remote dioceses and even individuals working, e.g.,in Melanesia or Ghana. Europe has not been included (as has, e.g.,Latin America) in the world of discourse of university theology. It has played no formal part in ministerial formation.

There are two striking exceptions to this general failure among the English churches to see the relevance to Christian faith of what is being attempted in Europe. There are the (largely middle-class) Quakers. From the beginning there has been a tendency to the universal in Quaker theology—the doctrine of a common and immanent spark of divinity in every human being. William Penn in 1962 was the first to speak of the desirability of a united Europe—a true Philadelphia. English Quakers have made a serious contribution to the building of international organisations from the League of Nations on. In 1979 they founded Quaker House in Brussels as a presence, a kind of embassy to the institutions of the European Union.

Also, there is the tradition represented by the Industrial Mission Association. This was set up in direct continuity with the Anglican chaplaincy to workers in munitions factories during World War II.[14] As with the Mission de France, it was a response to the fact that wartime experience had revealed that the normal parochial ministry of clergy had almost no contact with the urban working class. By 1960, most Anglican dioceses had detached a team (often functioning ecumenically) to minister in the world of work. In England—uniquely in Europe—they encountered almost no anti-clerical hostility, and in their heyday they depended upon being invited into a work situation both by management and trade unions.

What soon became very obvious to them was the global character of modern economic life, and international links were

---

[14] P. Bagshaw, *The Church beyond the Church: Sheffield Industrial Mission 1944: 1994,* Sheffield, 1994.

established (now the European Contact Group). That was the power of multi-national corporations, and that the pursuit of social justice required Christians to engage together at a matching (and certainly a European) level. These concerns contributed to the founding in the 1960s of what became the European Ecumenical Commission for Church and Society (a Protestant/Anglican group) working in relation to the European Union and the Council of Europe. This has now (1999) been incorporated, as its Commission for Church and Society, into the Conference of European Churches at Geneva.

In parallel with the development of the European Union since the Treaty of Rome in 1956, there has been gradual but inexorable decline in church attendance in the mainline churches, with their ministers unable to maintain regular contact with their national flocks. Church attendance in England is low. On an ordinary Sunday there are roughly equal numbers in church of Catholics, Anglicans, and non-conformist churches—together under 10% of the population. The charismatic/evangelical congregations—those least likely to have any element of natural law theology— have most vigour, most young people and include many black-majority churches. There is a diminishing penumbra of non-practising adherents of all churches. It is not much that consciousness of belief has changed overnight; rather that over the generations there were no longer reserved spaces for public worship on a reserved day. So folk-religion becomes unvisited, and in time, alien. The car and TV are universal. Sabbatarian prohibition of shopping and sport has disappeared. Contact with children and young adults is no longer a salient aspect of many congregations' worship.

Perhaps most important, there is a collapse of deference to clergy, as having recognised qualifications to teach religious truth and morals, and as officers of the community. Vocations to ministry as a career and the finance to pay their professional salaries are declining. The supermarket and the car have replaced the High Street and the bicycle. It is therefore quite unusual for the sluggish church attender to have the chance of casual personal conservations with his or her local minister. It is unlikely any mainline congregation's minister will be under 45.

In general, clergy work largely with the over-50s and the socially excluded, they live and work locally in a way few other professionals now do; they are exhausted by the demands of the immediate, and they have no experience of the Europe-wide collegiality of work that is now commonplace for academics and business people, many of whom are Christian. Dr. Grace Davie has described our religious situation as "believing without belonging."[15] In a mobile society the result is that the language of belief, when it is divorced from community exercise and from the leadership of a personally known and accredited local minister, can become locked into a private, unexamined, backward-looking, and essentially irrational mode—an offshore archipelago of rocks of tribal identity, as for example in Northern Ireland.

As in the rest of Europe, where there is a resurgence of histories of anatagonism and grievance, nearly all with a church identity dimension, the lack of educated religious vocations and of living religious practice as a factor for danger. It is from the past that there comes the survival of a deep wish for English cultural and religious apartness, and of steretypes of Catholicism as a particularly threatening ("organised," "autocratic," "unscrupulous") form of the general danger presented by "the continent" across the Channel. The English-speaking world outside Europe, on the contrary, provokes no such anxieties.

Are there positive indicators within the British religious scene for a constructive engagement with the project of European Union? As M.M. Tolstoy's project in Cambridge indicates, it is possible by personal engagement to press through to a recognition that Europe is important for "us." But congregations are unwilling to relate their faith not only to Europe, but to any questions of work, politics or environment. It was therefore an event of considerable significance that the Catholic bishops of England and Wales under the late Cardinal Hume decided to publish a position paper before the 1997 general election. They declared the church's teaching of social ethics to be as binding as its teaching of personal ethics on the consciences of Catho-

---

[15] Grace Davie, *Religion in Britain since 1945*, Blackwell, 1994.

lics.[16] This call was at once endorsed by the Anglican archbishop of Canterbury.

One opportunity for moving out of the "church-as-building" is participation by congregations (together, for example, with local Muslim groups) in twinning with comparable civic communities abroad. It is in such meetings, especially between members of different Christian denominations, that we can discover that we share what is still potentially a plausible faith-language across nations and histories, and that we can delight in complementing each other's discipleship in Christ. One example of such an initative is the link, since 1981, between the Catholic dioceses of Bruges (Belguim) and Nottingham (England), and the Anglican diocese of Lincoln. Many of the practical issues, for example, family breakdown, unemployment, racism, ecology, are part of the experience of all Europeans. Taize and Iona are only two of many pilgrimage places that have shown young Europe at common prayer.

In recent years, our politicians have had to pay attention to public anxiety about the decay of civil order. In the autumn of 1996, parents of gunned-down primary-school children in Dunblane (Scotland) and the widow of a London headmaster murdered by teenagers outside his own comprehensive school were granted licence, by their suffering, to call for a more morally educated society. A strong case was made for day-by-day teaching of a common curriculum of social ethics, human rights, and citizenship in the classes for adolescents in ordinary schools across Europe. The Christian churches (and humanists and other world faiths, too) have an irreplaceable contribution to make. It is perhaps only in this way that our populations will be given a vocabulary of concepts and stories to use routinely to rehearse public values. Politicians are dependent, for good or ill, on such stories. The European Union, if it were no longer perceived solely as a matter of free trade and national advantage, could develop the responsibility to promote and safeguard "our" common language of a "good society." It was a comparable need that lay behind the determination of the American Federal

---

[16] *The Common Good and the Catholic Church's Social Teaching*, London, 1996.

Council of Churches in 1945—as John Foster Dulles put it—
to see human rights as the "soul" of the new United Nations
organization. Jacques Delors, President of the Commission of
the EU, fought (against stubborn opposition) to establish as
European Union policy that a program be set up in 1994 to
develop a "soul for Europe."[17]

At the heart of the Europe project is a vision of the common
good that, as expressed in regional policy and subsidiarity, gives
space for moral personality at every level of community. Good,
well-trained clergy will be necessary. Because volatile identities
are in question, this can be dangerous. Identities have problem-
potential both in acts of war and marriage.

It may be useful to cite a commonplace experience in the
present-day Church of England, when necessity forces a "marriage" of six or seven village communties under one priest.
Diocesan office wisdom says, enquire beforehand whether the
proposed new group identity will have to include memories of
emnity from the seventeenth century civil war, when village A was
for King and village B for Parliament! Collective memory of the
other can be positive, but in Europe it is always a factor, and it
always includes religion.[18] So present-day religious leadership
needs to be there, to "make love, not war." The education of
religious leaders of all faiths should be required by law to include participation in an approved trans-frontier program in,
for example, Northern Ireland or Bosnia. This should include
training in leading their people in public prayer for "the other,"
and particularly for the traditional enemy. A member state of
the European Union should have as much concern for this limited
area of training of ministers of religion as it has for common
standards in the training of medical professionals.

Finally, we should not underestimate how rapidly, particularly
among young people, the matter-of-fact workaday realities of
the European Union are becoming accepted as normal. When,
in November 1996, a fire in the Channel Tunnel shut down what
in twelve months had become a main artery of communication

---

[17] D. Schwarzer and W. Lenz, eds, *A Soul for Europe—Ethics and Spirituality in
the Process of European Integration,* Tübigen, 1998.
[18] D. Johnston and C. Sampson, *Religion, the Missing Dimension of Statecraft,*
Oxford, 1994.

with mainland Europe, there was a sudden consciousness that Britain had lost a "good thing"—an element in something more than economic life. Christian ministers should take that "something more" as the beginning of a vocation, an opportunity both for prophecy and inculturation. It will not be easy and will require much patience.

Whether they succeed is perhaps more important for the European experiment and for world peace in the twenty-first century than is commonly allowed. Contrary to expectation, the local British churches may well play their part.

33

Swedish Experiences in Relation to Drunk Driving

Hans Klette

Summary

1. The drunk driving problem is a social problem that relates to both alcohol problems and traffic problems, e.g., alcohol policy and traffic policy.

2. Drunk driving must be studied from both the actor's perspective and the structural perspective.

3. Studies on the effects of drunk driving laws must include the interactions of three processes: (a) the legislative or political decision making process, (b) the criminal justice decision making process, and (c) the legal influence process.

4. The criminal justice approach to drunk driving must always be supplemented by the public health approach.

5. The legislative efforts in relation to drunk driving are formed in a political struggle between powerful groups as a compromise based on basic goals or values, basic public interests and special group interests and their perception of reality.

6. The alcohol and vehicle producers' responsibility for the negative consequences of their products must be increased.

7. We have sufficient knowledge of the effects of the most important countermeasures to suggest effective programs on drunk driving but political determination is lacking.

Alcohol and Traffic as Social Problems

The traffic system is a major subsystem of the larger social system with the main function of providing transportation—mobility being one of the features of modern society. We demand that the subsystem function efficiently and that it provide transportation which is readily available, comfortable, inexpensive, and rapid, while maintaining an acceptable degree of safety. These aims and demands are often in conflict.

The control of the traffic system involves large numbers of important subsystems and has become deeply enmeshed not only with most of the major industrial systems but also with major agencies of the society. All these groups have vested interests, their own needs to satisfy instead of the needs of society, and they are often in conflict about the proper way of controlling safety problems.

In relation to alcohol the vested interests are at least as great as in relation to traffic, for instance the great economic interests involved in the state alcohol monopoly and the private alcohol industry. The state can be said to have four kinds of interests in relation to alcohol, i.e., fiscal interests, interests of industrial policy, interests of public order and interests of social policy.

If we combine the two areas of alcohol and traffic we understand that drunk driving must be seen as a social problem in the broadest economic, political and social context and that conflict occurs about the proper way of controlling the problem.

Satisfaction of Basic Needs
by Driving and by Drinking

The principle function of driving is to provide a change of location. But driving can also satisfy other needs such as: (a) The affiliation and acceptance need—related to the individual's role within the structure of the group. A person strives to have meaningful relations with others. The car often gives young people their first chance to get away from home and meet friends. In the car they can be part of their own group and create meaningful group relations. (b) The need for esteem—both self-esteem and recognition from others. Satisfaction of this need produces feelings of self-confidence, prestige, status, power and control. Driving can give a feeling of freedom, power, a sense of superiority and being master of all.

Drinking alcohol seems mostly to be closely associated with important social functions, while drinking to fulfill an individual need usually seems to be an additional function. Among these needs are: (a) In relation to physiological needs, alcohol satisfies the taste and adds calories to the diet. (b) Concerning safety and security needs, alcohol can help the individual to feel free from fear and physical danger, and concern for the future. (c) In relation to affiliation and acceptance needs, alcohol can often play the important role of making relations among people in various groups easier. (d) Regarding the need for esteem, alcohol is often used to produce feelings of self-confidence, prestige, power and control. When we have found out what kind of needs are satisfied by alcohol and by driving, we have to find alternative means of satisfying these needs.

The Politics of Drunk Driving

In studies on the legislative decision making process in relation to alcohol and traffic or the social factors determining the form and content of this legislation, a combination of the actor's perspective and the structural perspective should be used, which can be summed up as follows:

(1) The most important groups of actors in the field of alcohol and traffic are the political parties, the interest organizations, the legal and administrative authorities, the experts and the mass media. These groups act mainly according to their group interests, their perception of reality or which factors they perceive as important in causing the drinking and driving problem, and their positions of power.

(2) The social structure with its economic, social and political substructures sets a limit to the groups of actors trying to influence the legislation.

(3) There is a dialectic relation between the social structure and the behaviour of the groups of actors.

(4) The goals or basic values of the society and the public interests are often in conflict and the balance is formed as a compromise between these values and public interests but also special powerful group interests and their perception of reality.

Thus, how we perceive these conflicts has much to do with which perspective we take and our perception of social reality. The way that dominant members of society look at things is supposedly the way things actually are, but behind these views are value judgments with ideological assumptions to the question concerned. The concept of the politics of reality becomes important in this relation. It refers to the fact that different individuals and social groups have stakes, both political, ideological and material, in certain definitions of what is true. Another concept, the hierarchy of credibility, also becomes important in an area where there are many experts. It refers to the fact that some people have more power than others in defining what is true.

The Symbolic Function of Law

Legislative decision making in relation to drunk driving and its sanctioning system is a good example of what can be called the symbolic function of law. This function relates to the need for compromise in the legislative assembly, turning legislative form into a means of resolving group conflicts. Part of the function of law is to give recognition to ideals different from established conduct. Most of its complications arise from the necessity of pretending to do one thing while actually doing another. The legislator very often moves within a social reality very narrowly circumscribed by his political duties to party ideology and not to scientific truth. The formulations in the debates often serve the function of restoring peace and harmony in a situation, where opposing interests might tear apart politicians and others.

Definition of Drunk Driving

Every amount of alcohol increases unnecessarily the risk of a traffic accident. As other factors like inexperienced driving, inexperienced drinking, nighttime driving, driving at a high speed are involved in combination with drunk driving especially among young drivers, a 0.02 % BAC can be seen as an indication of significant impairment of driving ability by alcohol and the point where the relative dangerousness of drunk driving starts to be a significant social problem that needs to be socially · controlled by the criminal law.

General Prevention

An important Swedish contribution to drinking-driving countermeasures is the experience based upon the idea of the Uppsala School of Legal Philosophy, that criminal law can be used to educate or create morality. This view considers law primarily as a tool of general prevention or long-term general deterrence in contrast to simple deterrence or short-term general deterrence practiced and advocated by most Anglo-Saxon countries.

In Sweden, imprisonment has been used less as a form of punishment or retribution but more as means to create morality and to stress the importance of protecting social values in relation to drinking and driving, e.g., not to kill or harm another fellow-human-being by driving drunk and even not to combine alcohol and traffic at all.

The Swedish Government—very consciously and very slowly, step by step—stiffened the drinking and driving law starting with fines and disqualification of the driving license in the 1920s. The criminal law was then put in the center by introducing mandatory jail—usually one month—in the early thirties, and compulsory blood tests were introduced in the mid -thirties. A persé law of 0.08% BAC was established in 1940, with fines between 0.08% and 0.15% and jail above 0.15%; a lowering of the legal limit to 0.05% occurred in 1957 and to 0.02% in 1990. Random breath tests were introduced in the mid-seventies, and vehicle forfeiture at the end of the eighties. In 1994, jail was introduced in cases above 0.10% BAC.

The criminal law approach has been supplemented by a public health or treatment approach since the end of the 1960s by using probation with supervision and treatment of alcohol problems in cases above 0.15% BAC. In the 1980s, contractual treatment outside and alcohol treatment courses inside the prisons were introduced. Since 1991, different tests have been used to check alcohol dependence in cases above 0.15% BAC before regaining the driver licence.

The introduction of breath tests as the main evidence for DWI in 1989, and with blood tests as a supplement, raises questions in relation to legality and equality as three "reductions" exist in testing, namely relating to (1) the accuracy of measurements, (2) the elimination of alcohol in the body and (3) the blood-breath conversion factor. Thus, 0.02% BAC de jure corresponds to 0.05% BAC *de facto.*

During the seventy years of the Swedish program against drunk driving, other factors were used in combination, especially information, education, alcohol policy factors like price, availability constraints and sales age, and traffic policy factors.

Important things take time and the Swedish experience emphasizes that it takes several decades to create effective, long-lasting countermeasures in a democratic society.

Although the Swedish approach seems to have been relatively effective in relation to drivers in general, who usually separate drinking from driving, it appears to have failed with the young drivers and drivers with alcohol problems.

In this connection it should be noticed that effective general deterrence seems to be achieved only when the perceived certainty of punishment exceeds a certain threshold level. My belief is that the risk of detection cannot be raised to the level where the legal threat provides a long-term effect at a politically bearable cost. This seems to be especially true in relation to the two most important groups of risk takers among the drunk drivers —young males and those with alcohol problems.

The most important drunk driver is the heavy user of alcohol, who regularly exceeds 0.10 – 0.15% BAC. He uses alcohol as a drug often together with legally prescribed drugs of different sorts. The important question to ask is what kind of basic need he satisfies by the consumption of alcohol and/or drugs and driving, and then try to find alternative satisfactions.

The criminal justice approach and the public health approach should be able to supplement each other. By using the first approach we try to teach the new generations of drivers not to combine alcohol and driving. By using the second approach we try to reach drivers with alcohol problems. Unfortunately, most legislators do not understand that a high BAC implies a high probability of having an alcohol problem and are not willing to put up adequate resources to secure effective countermeasures.

Basic Findings

1. In relation to social control, four thresholds must be reached before sanctions will have any essential and lasting impact on the behavior of drinking-and-driving in our democratic societies. These four thresholds relate to: (a) awareness or basic knowledge of the law; (b) perception of the law as legitimate or fair; (c) early detection of the offence and immediate correction of the offender; and (d) satisfaction of basic needs related both to the drinking and to the driving.

2. In relation to the political process we must notice—besides the economy—a) the main goals or the basic values of the Western democratic societies, e.g., democracy or participation, liberty or freedom, justice or equality, and security; in the small homogeneous Swedish welfare society, "solidarity" must be added; (b) the most important public interests in relation to drinking-driving, e.g., traffic safety, criminal policy, public health, alcohol policy and environmental policy; and (c) the goals or values and the public interests are often in conflict and the compromises made between or among them differ across societies.

Policy Recommendations

Based upon the scientific findings of social control and in relation to the political process, especially the public interests and the social goals and values, the following recommendations concerning the social control of drunk driving should be made:

1. In relation to law and criminal justice:

(a) A "zero alcohol" drunk driving law *de jure,* which corresponds to approximately 0.02% BAC *de facto.*

(b) Police enforcement by random breath tests—using passive screening devices—and extensive advertising.

(c) Immediate road side adjudication and sentencing using immediate driving license suspension and fines (the ticket system) as first sanctions and educational information.

(d) Later additional criminal sanctions in cases above 0.10% BAC (compulsory treatment and short prison sentences, and vehicle forfeiture for multiple offenders).

(e) The installing of ignition interlocks with breath testing devices—also effective against car theft—for multiple offenders.

2. In relation to alcohol policy:

A minimum drinking age of 20.

3. In relation to traffic policy:

(a) Licensing age at 18—training to drive from 16.

(b) Graduated licenses from 18 to 20 or the first two years with driving restrictions progressively removed as the driver advances without any accidents or offences; the restrictions should include zero BAC, a licensed adult supervisor, no passenger, no nighttime driving, no driving above 80 km/hour.

4. In relation to car production:

(a) As the usage problem is very serious—the nonuse of safety belts being very high even with mandatory use laws —passive or automatic restraints, especially automotive seat belts and air bags, must be part of all cars.

(b) The most important countermeasure to drunk driving is the installation of "Alcolock" in all cars at the production line. The producers' responsibility and legal liability for the negative consequences of their products are continuously increasing and as "Alcolock" would save many lives, compulsory "Alcolock" in all cars is a fair and rational approach to make drunk driving countermeasures most effective.

34

A Possible Relation Between Levodopa-induced Dyskinesias in the Treatment of Parkinson's Disease and Neuroleptic-induced Tardive Dyskinesia

Lars M. Gunné

Glutamate antagonists were recently shown to be potentially useful in the treatment of Parkinson's disease. Using primate models, mostly based on systemic administration of the dopamine-specific neurotoxin 1-methyl-4-phenyl-1, 2, 3, 6-tetrahydropyridine (MPTP), it is possible to induce a syndrome that closely resembles Parkinson's disease, with slowness of movements, muscular rigidity and tremor (1-3). Studies of regional firing (4), and regional 2-deoxyglucose (2-DG) uptake (5) have demonstrated characteristic transsynaptic rearrangements of neuronal activities within the basal ganglia as a result of the interrupted dopaminergic neurotransmission. Some inhibitory GABA-ergic pathways were chronically downregulated, due to tonic inhibition, while others were disinhibited and unregulated. A glutamatergic pathway, originating from the subthalamic nucleus, is also disinhibited in this chain of basal ganglia neurons and the resulting increased glutamate neurotransmission can be modulated by receptor anagonists. It was found that glutamate antagonists, active on AMPA or NMDA receptors, can potentiate levodopa effects in models of parkinsonism (6-8).

In the present paper we suggest an alternative use of glutamate antagonists in the prevention of levodopa-induced dyskinesias during the treatment of Parkinson's disease. Our hypotheses are based on long-term studies of a related phenomenon: neuroleptic-induced tardive dyskinesia.

Tardive Dyskinesia

For the last two decades our research group has studied the neurobiochemical background of tardive dyskinesia (TD), a movement disorder caused by long-term neuroleptic drug administration during the treatment of schizophrenia and related disorders. It is a major concern in the psychiatric clinic that most antipsychotic drugs produce a substantial number (around 20-30%) of TD cases, with persistent or even irreversible movements in the face (grimacing or tongue protrusion), extremities or trunk (chorea).

We managed to set up an animal model for this condition, using 27 South American Cebus apella monkeys, which received chronic neuroleptic drug treatment for up to five years. After between three months and three years, fifteen of these animals had developed typical signs of TD in the tongue, perioral area or extremities. The brains of these animals were subject to an extensive neurobiochemical mapping, focusing on changes within monoamine (dopamine, 5-hydroxytryptamine and noradrenaline) and GABA (gamma-amino butyric acid) synthesis, storage and release, together with studies of 2-DG uptake as a measure of regional synaptic activity. The brains of dyskinetic animals were compared with chronically neuroleptic-treated monkeys without TD and with untreated controls (9).

In the early 1970s, when these studies were initiated, the dopamine receptor supersensitivity hypothesis represented the prevailing explanation of TD: neuroleptics block the dopamine receptors and this caused parkinsonism, with a reduction of movements. But a compensatory dopamine receptor supersensitivity would later give rise to the opposite: hyperkinesias and TD (10,11). During our work, increasing interest was focused on transsynaptic rearrangements within inhibitory GABA and excitatory glutamate neurons caused by the chronic blockade of dopamine receptors. This long-term blockade produces a predictable pattern of activity rearrangements, called the "disinhibitory zig-zag" (12), with downregulation of neuronal activity within certain GABA-ergic pathways and disinhibition with unregulation in others. The key site for the production of the hyperkinetic movements of TD seems to be the medial globus pallidus (GMP), where a glutamatergic pathway from the subthalamic nucleus (STN) terminates (13). This STN-GPM pathway is chronically upregulated as long as the dopamine neurotransmission is impaired by daily neuroleptic doses (14).

Fig.1 shows the regional uptake of C14-labeled 2-DG in two groups of chronically neuroleptic-treated monkeys four months after drug discontinuation. The fairly high uptake of 2-DG in the GPM area of non-dyskinetic animals (left) probably reflects the high glutamate release and high synaptic activity, resulting in an increased glucose utilization in this area. In contrast the dyskinetic animals (right) show little synapse activity in GPM, possibly due to a regional excitotoxic lesion from the chronic glutamate release. The next neuronal link, a GBA-ergic pathway from GPM to the ventral thalamic target area, showed the same differences in thalamic glucose utilization between dyskinetic and non-dyskinetic animals (15). In a healthy unlesioned brain this GMP-thalamic pathway is unregulated as long as striatal dopamine receptors are blocked by neuroleptic drugs, resulting in an inhibitory effect on cortical motor centers, via the cortico-basal ganglia-thalamo-cortical loop. Our observations may open up a new possibility to protect the GPM nucleus by administering a suitable glutamate antagonist with the neuroleptic treatment, in order to prevent the occurrence of TD (16). It may be of interest in this context that clozapine, the only antipsychotic drug that seems to be virtually free of TD-related side effects, has been reported to have glutamate antagonistic properties (17).

The finding that the chronically upregulated GPM-thalamic GABA pathway had become dysfunctional may account for the switch in movement pattern, from parkinsonian hypokinesia to the hyperkinectic movements of TD. The disinhibitory zig-zag pattern within chains of GABA neurons changes direction when an upregulated pathway becomes underactive, and this could be a likely background to the behavorial change from parkinsonian hypokinesia to dyskinetic hyperkinesia (16).

However, as mentioned above, TD and tardive parkinsonism may often coexist in the same patient, where the basal movement pattern becomes slow and restricted, interrupted only now and then by the involuntary choreic movements of TD. The parkinsonian element may be due to malfunction in other GABA-ergic pathways, which have been chronically downregulated through inhibition during neuroleptic treatment. We found evidence for such long-term dysfunction, with low activities of glutamate decarboxylase (the enzyme that synthesizes GABA in the nerve terminals) and low GABA levels in three different areas (18). These were all terminal areas of chronically inhibited GABA neurons and their normal function had not been restored even after four months of drug discontinuation. Such malfunctions within downregulated neurons may tend to preserve the symptoms of parkinsonism long after drug discontinuation and may account for the basal movement pattern of tardive parkinsonism that coexists with outbursts of dyskinetic movements (16).

After the brain GABA neurons have become dysfunctional both within upregulated and downregulated neuron systems, this results in a decreased ability of the brain to buffer swings in striatal dopamine function. Such a reduced buffer capacity appears to be a common feature both of TD and Parkinson's disease.

Parkinson's Disease

The symptoms of Parkinson's disease are due to a failing brain dopamine system and the transsynaptic rearragements within GABA and glutamate neurons are similar in Parkinson's disease and chronic neuroleptic treatment. The upregulation of certain GABA-ergic and glutamatergic pathways and downregulation of others have been extensively studied in animal models for Parkinson's disease, using both regional firing and 2-DG uptake techniques (6, 14).

Clinically, the manifestations of Parkinson's disease are dominated by reduced movements, tremor and rigidity. Following levodopa administration, to compensate for the loss of dopamine, the movement pattern is initially restored to normal for several hours. After a few years of levodopa treatment, however, this interval with normal movements becomes shorter and various movement disorders, well known from neuroleptic treatment (dyskinesias, dystonias and akathisia), may complicate the picture (19-21). In the late management of Parkinson's disease, levodopa-induced dyskinesias may become a major problem that is even described as more disabling than the parkinsonism itself (22). In order to improve the treatment results at this stage various combinations of levodopa with dopamine receptor antagonists and protacted release preparation of levodopa, or even prolonged IV pump mechanisms have been tried (23, 24).

Some recent reports have discussed the possibility to potentiate levopoda by the addition of glutamate anatagonists in order to modify the effects of the upregulated subthalamofugal pathways. In primate models of Parkinson's disease certain glutamate antagonists produced an additional symptom-reducing effect when given together with small doses of levodopa. If such a treatment is introduced in the clinic, most patients would probably have to wait for it until the first good results of levodopa are failing after three to five years. Against a background of our studies of TD it would be a mistake to wait, while the high glutamate release may produce irreversible excitotoxic lesions to the STN-GPM and the GPM-thalamic pathways.

Are levodopa-induced dyskinesias and "on-off" fluctuations related to an induction of levodopa metabolizing enzymes with increasing variations in plasma levels, or do they merely result from a reduced neuronal buffer capacity caused by impairment of the dopamine transmission? A study by Sacks in a group of severely dopamine-lesioned post-encephalitic cases seems to indicate that a dyskinesia-producing lesion had occurred in these patients before any treatment was instituted. They had acquired their dopamine lesion during the epidemic of encephalitis lethargica in the 1930s, and they had very severe (98%) brain dopamine reduction. When they were started on levodopa in the 1960s, they developed dyskinesia-related problems very early during their treatment. Despite their severe parkinsonism, some of them had to abandon this treatment, due to their marked degree of dyskinesia. Observations like these would suggest that the duration and degree of the underlying dopaminergic deficiency plays a major role for the appearances of dyskinesias.

Our research group is focusing on the preventive treatment in animal models of Parkinson's disease and TD, using glutamate receptor antagonists to protect the postsynaptic neurons from chronic glutamate-induced depolarization and excitotoxic damage. Crossman *et al* (5, 6) found an increased uptake 2-DG in the GPM area in a monkey model of Parkinson's disease. We are hypothesizing that these signs of high synapse activity may later be succeeded by a low 2-DG uptake in GPM, particularly after the animals have begun to develop levodopa-induced dyskinesias. In support of our view there is evidence of a disappearance of glutamate receptors in GPM in patients with Parkinson's disease, and it was speculated that this may render glutamate antagonists less effective in late stages of the disease (25).

In conclusion, glutamate antagonists might be useful in the concurrent long-term treatment together with neuroleptics to prevent TD and in the long-term treatment of Parkinson's disease to prevent the occurrence of levodopa-induced dyskinesias.

REFERENCES

1. Davis CG, Williams AG, Markey SP, et al. Chronic parkinsonism secondary to intravenous injection of meperidine analogues. *Psychiatry Res* 1979;1:249-254.

2. Burns RS, Chiueh CC, Markey SP, Ebert MH, Jacobowitz DM, Kopin IJ. A primate model of parkinsonism: Selective destruction of dopaminergic neurons in the pars compacta of the substantia nigra by N-methyl-4-phenyl-1, 2, 3, 6-tetrahydropyridine. *Proc Natl Acad Sci* USA 1983; 80:4546-4550.

3. Langston JW. MPTP: insights into the etiology of Parkinson's disease. *Eur Neurol* 1987; 26 suppl 1:2-10.

4. Miller WC, DeLong MR. In: *The Basal Ganglia II.* Carpenter MB, Jayaraman A, eds. Plenum Press 1987; pp 415-427.

5. Crossman AR, Mitchell IJ, Sambrook MA. Regional brain uptake of 2-deoxyglucose in n-methyl1-4-phenyl-1, 2, 3, 6-tetrahydropyridine (MPTP)-induced parkinsonism in the macaque monkey. *Neuropharmacol* 1985; 24:587-591.

6. Brotchie J, Crossman AR, Mitchell IJ, Duty S, Carroll C, Cooper A, Henry B, Hughes N, Maneuf Y. Chemical signalling in the globus pallidus in parkinsonism. In: *Progress in Brain Research* Vol 99. Arbuthnott GW, Emson PC, eds. 1933; pp. 125-139.

7. Greenamyre JT, Eller R, Zhang Z, Ovadia A, Kurlan R, Gash DM. Antiparkinsonian effects of remacemide hydrochloride, a glutamate antagonist, in rodent and primate models of Parkinson's disease. *Ann Neurol* 1994: 35: 655-661.

8. Löschman PA, Lange KW, Kunon M, Retting KJ, Jähnig P, Honore T, et al. Synergism of the AMPA antagonist NBQX and the NMBA antagonist CPP with l-dopa in models of Parkinson's disease. *J Neural Transm* PD sect. 1991; 3: 203-213.

9. Gunné LM, Häggström JE, Johansson P, Levin ED, Terenius L. Neurobiochemical changes in tardive dyskinesia. *Encephale* 1988; 14:167-173.

10. Klawans HL. The pharmacology of tardive dyskinesia. *Am J Psychiatry* 1973; 130 :82-86.

11. Tarsy D, Baldessarini RJ. The pathophysiologic basis of tardive dyskinesia. *Biol Psychiatry* 1977; 12:431-450.

12. Gale K, Casu M. Dynamic utilization of GABA in substantia nigra: regulation by dopamine and GABA in the striatum, and its clinical and behavioral implications. *Mol Cell Biochem* 1981; 39:369-405.

13. Smith Y, Parent A. Neurons of the subthalamic nucleus in primates display glutamate but not GABA immunoreactivity. *Brain Res* 1988; 453:353-356.

14. Delong MR. Primate models of movement disorders of basal ganglia origin. *Trends Neurosci* 1990; 13:281-285.

15. Mitchell IJ, Crossman AR, Liminga U, Andrèn P, Gunne LM. Regional changes in 2-deoxyglucose uptake associated with neuroleptic-induced tardive dyskinesia in the Cebus monkey. *Mov Disord* 1992; 7:32-37.

16. Gunné LM, Andrèn PE. An animal model for coexisting tardive dyskinesia and tardive parkinsonism: a glutamate hypothesis for tardive dyskinesia. *Clin Neuropharmacol* 1993; 16:90-95.

17. Lidsky TI, Yablonsky-Alter E, Zuck L, Banerjee SP. Anti-glutamate effects of clozapine. *Neurosci Lett* 1993; 163:155-158.

18. Gunné LM, Häggström JE, Sjöquist B. Association with persistent neuroleptic-induced dyskinesia of regional changes in brain GABA synthesis. *Nature* 1984; 309:347-349.

19. Marsden CD. Parkinson's disease. *J Neurol Neurosurg Psychiat* 1994; 57:672-681.

20. Sage JI, Mark MH. Basic mechanisms of motor fluctuations. *Neurology* 1994; 44 suppl 6:S10-S14.

21. Kuno S. Dilemma in the treatment of Parkinson's disease with L-dopa. *Eur Neurol* 1994; 34 suppl 3:17-19.

22. Nutt JG. Levodopa-induced dyskinesia: review, observations and speculations. *Neurology* 1990; 40:340-345.

23. Poewe WH. Clinical aspects of motor fluctuations in Parkinson's disease. *Neurology* 1994; suppl 6:S6-S9.

24. Nutt JG, Woodard WR, Hammerstad JP, Carter JH, Anderson JL. The "on-off" phenomenon in Parkinson's disease. *N Engl J Med* 1984; 310:483-488.

25. Ball EF, Shaw PJ, Ince PG, Johnson M. The distribution

of excitatory amino acid receptors in the normal human midbrain and basal ganglia with implications for Parkinson's disease: a quantitative autoradiographic study using 3H-MK801, 3H-glycine, 3H-CNQX and 3H-kainate. *Brain Res* 1994; 658:209-218.

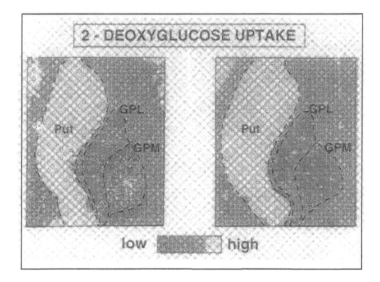

Fig. 1: Autoradiograms showing C14-2-deoxyglucose uptake in basal ganglia of chronically neuroleptic-treated monkeys. Left: combined autoradiograms from three monkeys without TD. Right: combined autoradiograms from four monkeys with TD. Put=putamen; GPL=lateral globus pallidus; GPM=medial globus pallidus.

35

Assisi

Marvin Barrett

1. Assisi is rather like Taormina, where Mary Ellin and I chose to spend the first six months of our marriage thirty years ago. Less restless, less raffish, but with the shops, the transients (more pilgrims than tourists, more Italians and Americans than Germans and Danes), even the restaurant bars. But it certainly is not the "Las Vegas of the pious," as one friend who scratched it from his itinerary suggested. So far I am pleased with my choice of a place where lumps might be forgotten or obliterated. The hotel is without bustle or swimming pool. None of those hungry eyes in the lobby seeking you out, trying to place you, or out by the pool in their long chairs observing behind their dark glasses.

Was Mary Ellin right to pass, to say that we couldn't both afford the trip; that after all that had gone on maybe a rest from each other, a substantial rest, would do us both good? However much she loved Italy, would like to recapture our youth, she could wait. I had my experiment to make, a few weeks in peaceful, sanctified surroundings, a complete change. Better to conduct it alone.

I am not sure. Maybe two weeks in Assisi would have put her back on track. Given her the shove she needs toward starting a new novel. We'll never know.

According to the *Rome Daily American*, I missed by one day a large anti-American rally organized by the Communists here in Assisi to celebrate Saint Francis's birthday. Saint Francis is patron saint to everybody.

Out of my window I can see two churches and Mount Subasio. Under the window is a table for my typewriter.

2. The drive to Todi, the birthplace of Jacopone, the lawyer turned mystic poet, is by back roads through vineyards and fields of tall plants that could be tobacco—at least they were harvesting leaves, from the ground up, that didn't look edible and binding them into grayish green bales. Outside of Foligno long lines of wagons are parked, heaped with purple and yellow grapes. In the distance I spot Bevagna, Montefalco, and finally Todi, bright on its hill. The day is perfect. Cooler than yesterday, but not too cool, and clear.

I go directly to the main square without a hitch or false turn although I have to thread my way through a maze of narrow streets and alleys to reach it. At one end is the cathedral; at the other, the ancient town hall; cars parked solidly between. I circle and finally find a place. But I can't get the car into reverse to come at it straight; indeed I have been going forward ever since I left Rome. I know where reverse is—to the extreme right and down, hard— but each time I put the gear where it should be, the car moves forward closer and closer to the shiny red Fiat in the next place. We actually touch. Not hard but hard enough to scratch the perfect paint, to make a small dent.

In the glorious, sun-drenched square of Todi (two stars in the Michelin), halfway from the cathedral to the Palazzo del Popolo, with all the male population congregated to take advantage of the sun, the midday break, I have reached an impasse. I can move neither forward nor back. I will never escape. I should never have accepted the foolish, over-sized car; a subcompact would have done very nicely, fitted into the space perfectly. Greed alone had prompted me—something for nothing, more than I paid for. I had only myself to blame. I should never have come to Italy, attempted to escape among strangers, forget my stomach, my heart. I sit there sweating, grunting, trying the gear yet again.

Finally the group of Italian youths who have been watching the whole performance with narrowed, critical eyes—I can see them in my rear view mirror: "What will the stupid American do next?"—come toward me in a pack like something out of *West Side Story*, not exactly snapping their fingers, but with an air of menace, circling. I wait for them to act, to pull me from the front seat, separate me from the ridiculous car that I am obviously incompetent to drive. Now they are examining the car next to me, the bright red one with its new dent. They are bending over it, lifting it, moving it six inches to the right, out of my way, motioning me into place. I do as I am told.

They move on. Eventually I get out of my car, ignore the cathedral, the municipale, the church where Jacopone is buried, and go off in search of the Ristorante Umbria—one button in the Michelin; "the best in the province" according to *Let's Go Europe*.

By the turn-off for Montefalco—"the balcony of Umbria" or, as my local guidebook says, "the railing of Umbria"—I am sufficiently recovered to try again. Another town square, high up, sleepy. A single black sedan with a lady crocheting in the backseat. She tells me to go to the church of San Francesco—every town has one—where, if I hurry, I will be able to see the Benozzo Gozzoli frescoes lit.

An old gentleman in a black suit is showing them to two backpackers with red knees and beards. Saint Francis holding up Arezzo. Saint Francis stripped. Saint Francis zapped with the stigmata, laser style. Saint Francis preaching to the birds. A whole wonderful Gozzoli world, sweet and bright. Umbria as it used to be, possibly never was.

Back at the car a middle-aged man in shirt sleeves summoned from the bar across the square waits to take me up the Torre Comunale. There is no refusing. Everyone who comes to Montefalco goes up to the Torre Comunale. We begin the climb, flight after flight, narrower and steeper. What am I doing up here with my faulty heart, my defective stomach, risking my life, what's left of it, keeping up with this fellow half my age who makes his living climbing towers?

And there, finally, at the top, the reason for the climb—spread indeed as beneath a balcony, over a balustrade, all of

Umbria, as it is today—Todi, Bevagna, Foligno, Spoleto, Spello, Assisi, and far in the distance, slightly blurred, Perugia.

At dinner I read the following paragraph from Evelyn Underhill propped in front of me:

> And so we get such an astonishing scene when we reflect upon it, as that of the young Francis of Assisi, little more than a boy, asking all night long the one question which so many apparently mature persons have never asked at all: "My God and All, what art Thou and what am I?" And we realize with amazement what a human creature really is—a finite center of consciousness, which is able to apprehend, and long for, Infinity.

And what would young Francis of Assisi, longing for infinity, have thought of me on my querulous pilgrimage through that familiar countryside? What would he have made of me sitting in the corner of my hotel dining room, reading my pious book, while I inadvertently ordered, and then ate, two pathetic, wizened, overcooked little birds?

3. To see Pinturicchio frescoes in the Baglioni chapel in Spello, you insert your hundred-lire note (or your dollar bill) into a slot in a wooden box with a glass top, and as it flutters into a nest of hundred-lire notes at the bottom, the lights come on and there they are: the Annunciation, the Nativity, the Dispute in the Temple, the child Jesus with the eyes of an old man, standing on the tessellated marble of a Renaissance square, sibyls looking down from above, the artist himself, observing from a niche to the right, all are put there to honor Perugia's first family—yeggs and bullies, murderers and tyrants, every one, who used their own cathedral across the valley for a barracks, who laid waste to the countryside between and turned the peasants into "plundering, murdering savages," like themselves. The evil bribing the talented to evoke the good. In the midst of chaos.

And here am I with my American money bringing it miraculously back. Five minutes and the lights go out.

Then onto the valley floor where another act of devout obliteration has been performed—Santa Maria degli Angeli squatting like a huge masonry toad over Porziuncola, Francis's cunning little church, where it all more or less began. Two scales: one small, living, authentic; the other big, bombastic, after the fact, diluting, blowing things out of their original properly human proportion.

Not quite. The edifying presence still haunts those hollow, pompous vaults. If we say it big and loud and often enough, how can we forget what once happened here? The carryings on.

So here I am, headquartered in my cozy hotel room surrounded by all these witnesses, these examples, good and bad, making my pious little tours to the Hermitage, San Damiano, working back in scale to the small, the dark. What am I looking for? Waiting for? Trouble? A cure? Do I really think in the time I have allotted—praying, reading my devotional books, making my pinched little interior comments, sightseeing in this place with its echoes of genuine holiness—do I think I can back out of the dead end I have stumbled into, turn myself around, get this saint with all his documented miracles, His Lord, His God, to haul me out, diminish those lumps that I've never felt nor believed in, actually make them vanish?

4. "In that time and by God's will there died my mother, who was a great hindrance unto me in following the way of God; soon after, my husband died likewise, and also my children. And because I had commenced to follow the aforesaid Way and had prayed God that he would rid me of them, I had great consolation of their deaths." Thus wrote the blessed Angela of Foligno—a not very attractive town that I have no intention of visiting. "The holiest woman," according to her contemporaries, "in the whole vale of Spoleto."

Our thirty-first wedding anniversary. I talked to Mary Ellin at 11:15 a.m., 6:15 her time. None of my mail has gotten through. Little Mary Ellin is not feeling well. Nothing to worry about, she hopes. A doctor's report today. How am I doing? Fine. A nice room. A nice view. Beautiful country. Nothing about the cold sweat I woke into, the three unpleasant dreams I left behind, my depressing reading, blessed Angela and her unfortunate family. "Get rested up. Everyone asks after you. You are missed."

5. Today I took my excursion to Urbino, along the old Roman Via Flaminia. A handsome town—a rich beige; a handsome palace. Somewhere in its bare halls was Piero's Flagellation—the figure of Christ tiny, blurred, but the right, the only tolerable size. Three lounging figures forward on the right, bigger, no one knows who exactly they were supposed to be, standing there, paying no heed. Pilate in the back on the same plane with Christ, staring at him bleakly across an unbridgeable gap, but not really at him, or at the man with the whip. A small world filled with space; timeless—time stopped.

Who is the figure on the pedestal to which Christ is bound? Naked golden, his right hip cocked, a staff in one hand, an orb in the other. There is no one there to tell me.

6. A Sunday drive through Umbria and Tuscany to Borgo San Sepolcro to look again at what Aldous called "the greatest picture in the world. " It has been thirty years since I first saw Piero's Resurrection with Mary Ellin on our wedding trip, sixty since Huxley wrote about it, and its impact has not diminished. There is Christ, the captain of the winning water polo team, and I do mean winning, rising out of the tomb as from an invigorating plunge, flapping his banner above the sleeping figures in the foreground. "They are, you are, you sleepers out there as well," his expression and posture seem to say, "in for a rather nasty surprise. " No frozen time, no extra space in this picture ten times the size of the Flagellation in Urbino. A gelid urgency. Huxley, still a fashionable young agnostic when he wrote his deception, saw little religion in it. But I, three times his age, have no difficulty in finding in that lowering figure the essential Christ, the triumphant challenger— different from most Renaissance Christs, more like the Christ Pantocrators of Cefalu and Monreale, with their vibrating glare painstakingly built of a thousand shiny bits of stone and glass. Perhaps the eyes are cold, or perhaps they are just looking beyond you, around you, through you at what is holding you back, at what has yet to be done. Not hostile. Not melting. Not really relating to any look I have ever seen on any face that has ever been turned toward me. Unique.

7.   There are no beggars in Assisi. I have been here for a week and not seen one. I did see a lot of old ladies looking out of the window in an old-folks home on the way to the basilica, but Assisi seems remarkably free of society's obvious problems. A young punk kid at the band concert last night looking bewildered. Some backpackers, but of the clean-cut sort. No evidence of drugs. Do you suppose Francis's war on poverty, if that was what it was, has succeeded first here? Was that his intention? To embrace poverty and, by embracing it, eliminate it, make it invisible? I rather think not. At any rate, a town whose most famous son's principal love was poverty, has its own hidden away.

Piero's resurrected Christ keeps coming back to me; Irving got something of that steady, absolutely honest, truthful, all-seeing, head-on glare in a collage I call the Tin Angel: small pieces of pasted paper adding up to that hovering, beetling presence, Hopkins's "Grandeur of God;" and behind the glare, bright wings. It is the face we'll meet one way or another, sooner or later—the unavoidable, excruciatingly beautiful glare of God that means what our lives tell us it means—better sooner than later.

8.   To Bevagna for lunch. Another beige town—lower, smaller, poorer. One restaurant open. I consume two more pigeons. This time I know exactly what I am ordering, but I don't want to eat pig. It is not on my diet. Bevagana is where Francis preached to the birds.

After lunch an excursion into the hills to Sassovivo Abbey. "In a lovely setting overlooking a small valley, the Benedictines in the 11 c. founded their abbey," says the guidebook. "A beautiful Romanesque cloister remains, its semicircular arches supported on slender twin columns. Coloured marbles and mosaics from the decoration….Come out by the Tolentino road. After a half a mile take a little road on the right (sign post) and bear left."

I follow the directions and drive up into the hills. After a mile or two there are a group of parked cars, a path off to the right, a locked shed. "Buon giorno," I say to a young man. He stares back at me, saying nothing. There is a dark grove behind him, no small vall ey, no cloister. A gun club? Some sort of clandestine meeting? Terrorists? Salvationists? A hunt for white truffles? The residue of the rally in Assisi a week ago Sunday? I drive on. Another young man on a midget motorbike roars round me and up the hill. There is a hiker climbing in the hot sun. Wide views of mountains to the east and west.

Around the bend a large ochre building behind a metal gate. I stop to investigate. A sign on a wall: "The Commune of Jesus." It is locked tight. Blank windows and a sense of being observed from behind them. I back away. The road narrows and climbs between ploughed fields. I drive among muddy farm yards and dirty white stucco buildings up a ridge. The car is too big. I get out and walk until I come to the top, another mountain to the north, a town, no small valley, no eleventh-century abbey. Coming back, below me and the deserted buildings, I see a dozen people—men and women in dark clothes, kerchiefs, heavy shoes—crouched against the earth harvesting a crop I cannot make out.

A wasted afternoon. But in Umbria, on my particular errand, there can be no wasted afternoons.

I saw my first roller skaters in Italy—two boys in the piazza in front of San Rufino. Roller-skating on the cobblestones of Assisi below the ageless pink-gray façade of its duomo is almost as bizarre as roller-skating in the Seventh Avenue subway—the black kid, orange satin hot pants, six foot if he was an inch, six foot ten in his boot-skates, rolling off the train and swooping, left foot, right foot, great swallowlike swoops, down the tunnel toward Eighth Avenue.

9.   Now that they are drawing to an end, what have the two weeks in Assisi meant? A coherent stretch of time set apart from what came before, quite distinct, as I intended it to be. Beyond that, what? The religious element in the environment is separated from my experience, and I haven't been able to make a bridge. Maybe it is because Francis's religion is a young man's religion. I see very few antique Franciscans either in the choir of San Francesco in the morning or in the streets during the day. Middle-aged, but vigorous middle age, and many, many young men in habits. The pilgrims are from a different world too—in large shepherded groups, sometimes American, more

frequently not. Even the churches are somehow remote, apart—
no matter how beautiful and moving. I do admire San Francesco,
am amazed by it, and the façade of San Rufino, but it is difficult
to relate them to my spiritual experience.

Here and in Rome, Catholicism still appears a closed, alien
world. I don't belong, and it is important to belong. Nor has there
been a religious insight or experience, a therapeutic blast or radiance
that might have swept away all those ambiguities that the doctors at
St. Luke's and Mount Sinai revealed and then gave up.

However there is a gentleness about the atmosphere here
including the religion that has, I believe, served a purpose.

The concierge told me I was "un uomo tranquillo"—the
calmest guest in the house. I would live to be 150. The last
time someone said that was at Trabuco. And shortly thereafter,
the rumble and the slide began.

So if Francis's is not an old man's religion, whose is?

10. Awake at two, in a sweat, my ears ringing, out of a
strange dream—a variation on the usual air-raid dream which
terminates in a blinding flash. This time the planes flying over
saw nothing, dropped nothing. I came out from my shelter and
realized that by simply avoiding being seen I had somehow
achieved a sort of peace, for others as well as myself. The two
warring factions were reconciled. *A contested border was resolved.*
My doing. Il uomo tranquillo.

At six I opened the shutters and curtains. There was a clear
sky and the morning star over Mount Subasio; and to the west,
the moon.

Uomo *tranquillo* or not, there is some sort of desperate
struggle going on inside me which could, I suppose, explain the
sweating and the ringing ears, if not the dream. I am obviously
trying to come to terms with something—a conflict that has
been there always and that I've always glossed over, a conflict
under a conflict under a conflict. I become frightened and
stubborn. I would seem to prefer to die rather than give in, and
I am not really certain of what I am fighting for or against. Or
if I know, I refuse to admit it. Something has settled in for a last
ditch stand and is determined to take everything with it. And
something, thank God, seems to be resisting.

I lit a candle in the chapel of Saint Peter of Alcantara at San Francesco for the family, big Mary Ellin, little Mary Ellin, a good report from her doctor. It is the same chapel where Saint Joseph of Copertino used to take off, praying to the Virgin and suddenly shooting up from the floor of the main church, through the roof, and off into the blue, out of sight. Then just as miraculously back in place, praying. The Virgin is still there.

Could it be this abyss over which we seem suspended does not exist, that, whatever our subjective sensations, we are always being borne up, and that Icarus fell in place? No drop, no deadly impact for Phaethon, for any of those noted plummetters, for Lucifer himself. All fleecy clouds above, below. And the levitators—Saint Joseph, Milarepa, Francis himself—the same?

Biography of
William Alexander Johnson

Addresses:	27 Fox Meadow Road, Scarsdale, NY 10583
	44 Pascal Avenue, Rockport, ME 04856
Born:	August 20, 1934. Brooklyn, New York
Father:	Charles Johnson, born in Sillerud Parish (Varmland), Sweden (Deceased)
Mother:	Ruth Anderson, born in Masthug Parish, Gothenburg (Vastergotland), Sweden (Deceased)
Married:	Carol Genevieve Lundquist. June 11, 1955
Children:	Karin Ruth, born June 22, 1956
	Karl William, born December 18, 1959
	Krister Frederick, born July 24, 1963

EDUCATION

B.A. (Philosophy) 1953,Queens College of the City University of New York, *Cum laude*

B.D. (Systematic Theology, Philosophy of Religion) 1956, Drew Theological Seminary, *Magna Cum laude*.

Teol. Kand. (equiv. to B.D.) 1957, University of Lund in Sweden

M.A. (Philosophy) 1958, Columbia University

Teol. Lic. (equiv. to Ph.D) 1958, University of Lund in Sweden, *Cum Insigniore Laude Approbatus*

Ph.D. (Philosophy of Religion) 1959, Columbia University
  Thesis: *The Religious A Priori: A Study of the Philosophy of Religion of Anders Nygren with Particular Reference to his Dependence upon Schleiermacher*

Teol.Dr., 1962, University of Lund in Sweden
  Thesis: *Nature and the Supernatural in the Theology of Horace Bushnell*

FURTHER STUDIES

  1958, Oxford University, Magdalen College

  1959, The University of Basel, Faculty of Theology

  1965, The University of Copenhagen, Faculties of Philosophy and Theology

ORDINATION

  1955: Deacon in the New York East Conference of the Methodist Church

  1958: Elder in the New York East Conference of the Methodist Church

  Priest, March, 30, 1968, in the Episcopal Church, Christ Church Cathedral, Indianapolis

PROFESSIONAL POSITIONS

1952-1954: Director of the Boys' Club, Salvation Army, Jamaica, New York

1954-1956: Minister, Mt. Hope and Teabo Methodist Churches, Wharton, New Jersey

1957: Assistant in Instruction (Philosophy), Columbia University

1958: Assistant in Instruction (Christian Ethics), Union Theological Seminary, New York

1957-1959: Minister, Immanuel Methodist Church, Brooklyn, New York

1959: Minister, Union Methodist Church, Brooklyn

1961-1962: Lecturer in Philosophy and Theology, Hartford Seminary Foundation, Hartford, Connecticut

1959-1963: Instructor, Assistant Professor of Religion, Trinity College, Hartford

1963-1966: Associate Professor of Philosophy and Religion, Chairman of the Department, Drew University, Madison, New Jersey

1966: Visiting Lecturer in Philosophy of Religion, Union Theological Seminary, New York

1966: Research Professor in Philosophy and Religion, New York University

1966-1968: Visiting Professor of Philosophy and Religion, Princeton University, Princeton, New Jersey

1967–1971: Professor of Philosophy and Religion, Chairman of the Department, Manhattanville College, Purchase, New York

1970: Visiting Professor of Christian Ethics, General Theological Seminary, New York

1969–1975 (winters): Visiting Professor of Protestant Theology, The North American College, Vatican City

1970–1973 (summers): Priest-in-Charge, St. Paul's Within the Walls, American Episcopal Church in Rome

1971–1995: Albert V. Danielsen Professor of Philosophy and the History of Ideas, Brandeis University, Waltham, Massachusetts

1972: Visiting Research Fellow, Princeton University

1973–1999: Canon Residentiary, and Canon Theologian, Director of the Institute of Theology, Cathedral Church of St. John the Divine, New York

1974: Visiting Scholar, MIT Humanities' Seminar.

1974–1995: Director of Graduate Studies, Philosophy and the History of Ideas Department, Brandeis University

1976: Visiting Professor, Bryn Mawr College, Pennsylvania (Roian Fleck Prize, Resident of Religion)

1978 (summer): Priest-in-Charge of the Church of England Chapels, in Strasbourg, France; Heidelberg and Stuttgart, Germany

1979 (spring): Visiting Professor, Rikkyo/ St. Paul's University, Tokyo

1979 (spring): Visiting Professor, University of Gothenburg, Gothenburg, Sweden

1980 (spring): Visiting Professor, Rikkyo/St. Paul's University, Tokyo

1988 (spring): Visiting Professor, Rikkyo/St. Paul's University, Tokyo

1988 (spring): Missionary and Instructor, The Arthur Turner Training School, Pangnirtung, Baffin Island, Northwest Territories, The Canadian Arctic

1989: Missionary, Interim Priest-in-Charge, The Protestant Episcopal Church, Ajijic/Chapala, Mexico

1994-1995: University of Copenhagen (American Scandinavian Fellow)

1995-1997: Visiting Professor, University of Western Australia, Perth

1997-1998: Lecturer, Royal Viking Sun and Vistafjord *The Greek Isles, Land of the Midnight Sun*

2000: Visiting Professor, Murdoch University, Curtin University, Perth

2001: Professor Emeritus, Brandeis University

2001: Senior Honorary Canon, The Cathedral Church of Saint John the Divine

LECTURED AT

Universities in: Sweden, Denmark, Finland, Norway, Russia, Iceland, Great Britain, Scotland, Ireland, Germany, Switzerland, Italy, Portugal, Spain, Greece, Yugoslavia, Czechoslovakia, Hungary, Egypt, Sudan, Israel, Jordan, Syria, Lebanon, Iran, Laos, India, Pakistan, North and South Vietnam, Hong Kong, Thailand, Taiwan, Japan, Okinawa, Guam, South Korea, the Philippines, Cambodia, Hawaii, Alaska, Canada, The High Arctic, Puerto Rico, the Virgin Islands, and Mexico.

About 250 universities in the Continental United States.

AWARDS, FELLOWSHIPS, ELECTION TO ACADEMIC SOCIETIES

1952: All-American baseball player

1953: All-American soccer player

1953: Graduate Honors in Philosophy, Queens College of the City University of New York

1954: Morrow Memorial Fellowship, Drew University (Awarded to the student in the middle year "who demonstrates greatest potential as pastor and preacher")

1954-1956: University Fellow, Drew University

1956: Daniel Delaplaine Fellowship, Drew University (Awarded to the outstanding senior for graduate study abroad in theology)

1956: Scandinavian-American Foundation Fellowship.

1957-1958: Fulbright Scholar, University of Copenhagen

1958: Dempster Graduate Fellowship of the Methodist Church

1959: Kent Fellowship of the National Council on Religion in Higher Education (now the Society for Values in Higher Education)

1959: Rockefeller Brothers Fellowship for Graduate Study

1958-1959: University Fellow, Columbia University

1960: Phi Beta Kappa (elected a post-doctoral member)

1962: Pi Gamma Mu (National Social Science Honor Society)

1963: Phi Sigma Tau (National Philosophy Honor Society)

1964: Harbison Award, Danforth Associates Award, the Danforth Foundation (awarded nationally on the basis of skill to "the professor of the year in the U.S.A.")

1964: David F. Swenson-Kierkegaard Memorial Award, for postdoctoral studies in Denmark, 1964-65

1964: One of the "Outstanding Ten Young Men in America," chosen by the Junior Chamber of Commerce

1970: Post-Doctoral Fellowship for Cross-Disciplinary Study, The Society for Religion in Higher Education

1971: Research Fellowship of the American Philosophical Society

1972: Guggenheim Fellowship, for study in Rome

1973-74; 1974-75: Danforth Foundation Experimental Learning Project Grants

1976: Roian Fleck Prize, Resident in Religion, Bryn Mawr College, Pennsylvania

1977: The Hale Lectureship, Seabury-Western Theological Seminary, Evanston, Illinois

1977-present: Consultant for Public Programs, National Endowment for the Humanities

1975-1977: National Science Foundation Grant (with Professor S.S. Schweber), for the course "Science and Ethics," Brandeis University

1977: Ford Foundation grant

1978: The Distinguished Alumnus Lectureship,Faculty of Theology, Lund University

1978 (summer): Rockefeller Fellow of the Aspen Institute for Humanistic Studies, Aspen, Colorado

1978: National Endowment for the Humanities Grant (with Professor Marvin Fox), for the course "Modern Jewish and Christian Religious Thought," Brandeis University

1980: Distinguished Alumnus Award, Queens College of the City University of New York

1981: Arthur Vining Davis Foundation grant for Theological Education, Institute of Theology, Cathedral Church of St. John the Divine

1982: Trinity Church grant, for project in "Christianity and Anti-Semitism"

1982: Elected Chaplain of the Venerable Order of the Hospital of St. John of Jerusalem

1982: Fellow of the Aspen Institute for Humanistic Studies, Jerusalem, Israel

1983: Examining Chaplain, Diocese of the Arctic, Northwest Territories, Canada (The Rt. Rev. John Sperry, Bishop)

1983: Special Commendation from the Institute of Theology, Cathedral Church of St. John the Divine

1984: Trinity Church grant for Theological Education, Institute of Theology

1984: Research Fellowship, The American Scandinavian Foundation in New York City: "Swedish Immigration and the Establishment of Swedish-American Churches in the U.S.A."

1984: The Tauber Award, Brandeis University, for research on Jewish-Christian relations: "Saint John's Gospel and the Origins of Christian Anti-Semitism"

1984: Elected Trustee, Queens College of the City University of New York

1984: The Hiatt Lecturer, Holy Cross College, Worcester, Massachusetts

1984: Elected to National Board of Directors, The Raoul Wallenberg Foundation

1985: Research Grant, The American Philosophical Society

1985: *Newsweek*: "One of the 10 Best Preachers in the U.S.A."

1985: Grant, National Endowment for the Humanities

1986: Board Member, The Westchester Institute of Psychoanalysis and Psychotherapy

1986: Honorary Fellow, Trinity College, Dublin

1986: Appointed Advisor, Council of International Understanding, New York

1987: Editorial Board, *Journal of Religion in Intellectual Life*

1988: Elected member, Explorers Club, New York

1988: Elected member, The Lotos Club, New York

1988: Elected Professor of Near Eastern and Jewish Studies, Brandeis University

1988: Research Grant, The Endowment for Biblical Research, Boston

1988: The John Biaz Lectureship, Calvary Episcopal Church, Pittsburgh

1990: Elected member, The Century Association, New York

1990: Appointed Academic Advisor, The Lotos Club, New York

1991: Elected Vicar of the Korean-American Congregation, Cathedral Church of Saint John the Divine

1998: Appointed Academic Advisor, The Century Association, New York

1998: American Scandinavian Fellowship to Copenhagen

2003: Appointed member of the U.S.A. Committee for UNESCO

PROFESSIONAL AND FRATERNAL SOCIETIES

American Academy of Religion

American Friends Service Committee (Past member of Executive Committee, College Division)

American Philosophical Association

American-Scandinavian Foundation

American Society of Christian Ethics

American-Swedish Historical Foundation

Asia Society

Authors Guild (of the Authors League of America)

The Australian-American Society

The Century Association

Church Society for College Work

The Coffee House

Columbia University Faculty Club

Danforth Associates (Senior Associates, 1968 to present)

Danish-American Society

Ecumenical Foundation for Christian Ministry in the City of New York (Past member of the Executive Committee)

English Speaking Union

Episcopal Churchmen for South Africa

Episcopal Radio and T.V. Foundation (Trustee)

The Explorers Club

The Hume Society

Institute for Scientific Humanism (Fellow)

International Platform Association

Japan Society

The Jerusalem Society

The Lotos Club

Medieval Academy of America

Metaphysical Society of America

Metropolitan Opera Club

MIT Humanities Seminar (Visiting Scholar)

New Haven Theological Discussion Group

Northern Student Movement (Past member of Executive Committee)

Parents' Committee, Wellesley College (1973-1976)

Parents' Committee, Trinity College (1981-1985)

Phi Beta Kappa

Scandinavian-American Heritage Society

Shakespeare Society of America (Academic Advisor)

Society for Religion in Higher Education

Society for the Advancement of Scandinavian Studies

Society for the Scientific Study of Religion

Society of Anglican Theologians

Society for Christian Ethics

Society of Christian Philosophers

Swedish Pioneer Historical Society

University Club, New York

Vasa Order of the United States

Venerable Order of the Hospital of St. John of Jerusalem (Chaplain)

Willa Cather Pioneer Memorial Foundation

World Ship Society

LISTED IN

The American Registry of Outstanding Professionals

The American Biographical Institute Medal of Honor

Anglo-American Who's Who

Book of Honor (Third Edition)

Clerical Directory of the Episcopal Church

Community Leaders of America (Tenth Edition)

Contemporary Authors

Current Biography

Dictionary of International Biography

Directory of American Philosophers

Directory of the American Philosophical Association

Directory of American Soldiers

Directory of Distinguished Americans

Directory of Rockefeller Brothers Fellows

Directory of the Society for Christian Ethics

Directory of the Society for Religion in Higher Education

5,000 Personalities of the World

International Book of Honor

International Scholars Directory

International Register of Profiles

International Directory of Philosophy and Philosophers

International Educator of the Year

International Health Professional of the Year

International Man of the Year

International Who's Who in Community Service

International Who's Who in Distinguished Leadership

International Who's Who in Education

International Who's Who of Intellectuals

Men of Achievement

Men and Women of Distinction

National Registry of Prominent Americans

Notable Americans

One Thousand Great Americans

Outstanding Intellectuals of the 10th/21st Century

Outstanding Young Men of America (1964-65), Junior Chamber of Commerce

Personalities of America

Personalities of the Americas

Personalities of the East

Personalities of the 20th Century

The Twentieth Century Award of Achievement

Two Thousand Notable Americans

Who's Who in America (39th Edition)

Who's Who in American Education

Who's Who in the East

Who's Who in Religion

Who's Who in the Twenty-First Century

Who's Who in the World (5th Edition)

Who's Who (Namenstexte der Prominenz aus Poltitik, Wirtschaft und Kultur)

BIBLIOGRAPHY OF WILLIAM ALEXANDER JOHNSON

BOOKS

1. *The Philosophy of Anders Nygren*, Lund: Lund University Press, 1958.

2. *Sermons from a College Chapel*, Hartford, Connecticut: Trinity College Press, 1960.

3. *Christopher Polhem: The Father of Swedish Technology* (translation from Swedish into English), containing preface by William A. Johnson, completely revised by William A. Johnson, published by the Trustees of Trinity College, 1963.

4. *Nature and the Supernatural in the Theology of Horace Bushnell* (Studia Theologica Lundensia 25), C.W.K. Gleerups, 1963.

5. *On Religion: A Study of Theological Method in Schleiermacher and Nygren*, Leiden: Brills, 1964.

6. *Problems in Christian Ethics*, Hartford, Connecticut: Trinity College Press, 1965.

7. *Swedish Contributions to Modern Theology*, (with Nels F.S. Ferré), New York: Harper & Row, 1966.

8. *The Search for Transcendence*, New York: Harper & Row, 1974.

9. *Invitation to Theology*, New York: Oxford University Press, 1977.

10. *The Christian Way of Death*, New York: Seabury Press, 1977.

11. *Philosophy and the Proclamation of the Gospel*, (The Hale Lectures for 1977), Evanston: Seabury-Western Theological Seminary, 1978.

12. *The Gospel and the Jews*, (The Hiatt Lectures), Worcester, Massachusetts: Holy Cross Publications, 1984.

13. *Christianity and Terrorism* (with Moorhead Kennedy), New York: Morehouse-Barlow Press, 1987.

14. *The Story of the Scandinavian Immigration to the United States*, American Scandinavian Foundation, 1988.

15. *O Boundless Salvation: Swedish Immigration and the Churches They Established in the United States*, Swedish Historical Society, 1990.

ARTICLES, REVIEWS, CONTRIBUTIONS TO BOOKS, ETC.

1.   Translation: "The Message of John Wesley and the Modern Man," Harald Lindström, *The Drew Gateway*, Summer 1955.

2.   "En pastors äventyrliga resa till Sverige" (About my
        experiences in the Stockholm-Andrea Doria collision),
        Svensak Sänderbudet, September 27, 1956.

3.   "Resume of Per Erik Persson's Thesis," *Sacra Doctrina*:
        Translation, Gleerup, Lund, 1957, pp.306-316.

4.   Sermon abstracts, *New York World Telegram and Sun*,
        1957-1959.

5.   Review of Malcolm L. Diamond's *Martin Buber: Jewish
        Existentialist*, *Christian Advocate*, November 24, 1960.

6.   Review of Richard Mathison's *Faith, Cults and Sects of
        America*, *Hartford Courant Magazine*, February 5, 1961.

7.   Review of Robert S. Paul's *The Atonement and the
        Sacraments*, *Union Seminary Quarterly*, Vol. XVI, No.4,
        May 1961, pp. 423-425.

8.   Review of Morris Keeton's *Values Men Live By*,
        Christian Advocate, September 28, 1961.

9.   "The Decline and the Fall of Christendom," sermon
        on WTIC Radio Station, Hartford, Connecticut, April
        1, 1962.

10.   "Mystical and Revealed Religion in Hathan
        Söderblom," *Lutheran Quarterly*, Vol.XIV, No.2, May
        1962, pp.150-164.

11.   "What is Existentialism?," *Alumni Reading Program*,
        Trinity College, June 1962.

12.   "Religion Majors Don't All Aim for the Ministry," with
        Alice Moldenhauer, *New York World Telegram and Sun*,
        July 7, 1962.

13.   Review of Etienne Gilson's *The Philosopher and
        Theology*, *Hartford Courant*, July 22, 1962.

14.   "Guilt according to Freud and Kierkegaard," *Hartford
        Seminary Quarterly*, Vol.II, No.4, Summer 1962, pp.40-
        54.

15. "Tillich's Religious Symbol: An Analysis and Critique," *Encounter*, Vol.23, No.3, Summer 1962, pp.30-48.

16. "Love Came Down at Christmas," *The Y.W.C.A. Magazine*, December 1962, pp.4-5, 33.

17. "The Life of Jesus,"TV Series *We Believe*, WTIC-TV, Hartford, Connecticut.Text of script published by the Greater Hartford Council of Churches, 1962.

18. "Methodist and Swedish Immigrant: The Life of Olof Gustaf Hedström,"*American Swedish Historical Foundation Yearbook*, 1962, pp.46-49.

19. "A Dying Way of Life: Critical Analysis of James E. Sellers' *The South and Christian Ethics*," *Christian Advocate*, January 17, 1963.

20. "The Case of Benjamin Reid,"*The Churchman*, January 1963, pp.6-7.

21. Contribution to the book *Masterpieces of Christian Literature* (Ed. Frank N. Magill), Harper and Row, 1963. Articles on Martensen's *Christian Dogmatics*; Brunner's *Dogmatik* (Vol. I-III); Bucer's *De Regno Christi*; Troeltsch's *Religious A Priori*; Billing's *Our Christian Vocation*; and Söderblom's *The Living God*.

22. "The Modern Cultural Milieu in Theological Perspective," *Metabagdad: Report of the Chicago and New York Conferences on Metropolitan Planning*, The National Council of the Protestant Episcopal Church in the U.S.A., January 1963, pp.1-12.

23. Review of Jaroslav Pelikan's *The Light of the World*, *The Journal of Bible and Religion*, Vol. XXXI, Number 2, April 1963.

24. Review of Jacob Neusner's *A Life of Rabban Yohanan Ben Zakkai* (CA 1-80 C.E.), *The Connecticut Jewish Ledger*, April 25, 1963; and *The Hartford Courant*, April 21, 1963.

25.   "Students for the Defense," *The Intercollegian*, June
        1963, pp.306–310.

26.   Review of *The Letters of James Agee to Father Flye*, *The
        Drew Gateway*, Spring 1963.

27.   Review of Roy Pearson's *The Believer's Unbelief* and
        M. Holmes Hartshorne's *The Faith to Doubt*, *Christian
        Advocate*, July 4, 1963.

28.   "The Case for Civil Disobedience," *The Southern Patriot*,
        Summer, 1963.

29.   "Luther's Doctrine of the Two Kingdoms," *The Lutheran
        Quarterly*, Volume SV, No.3, August 1963, pp.239–250.

30.   "Metaphysics and History according to St. Thomas,"
        The Anglican Review, Volume XLV, No.4, October 1963,
        pp.345–357.

31.   "Of Catholic Interest" (Review of 15 books dealing
        with contemporary Roman Catholic thought), *The
        Christian Century*, November 13, 1963, pp.1404–1407.

32.   "Spiritual Healing and the Biblical Witness," *The
        Christian Advocate*, November 21, 1963.

33.   Review of Peter Day's *Strangers No Longer*, *The Pulpit*,
        December 1963, pp.28–30.

34.   "The Impact of Religion on a Pluralistic Metropolis,"
        *The Report of the 1963 San Francisco Conference on
        Metropolitan Planning*, The National Council of the
        Episcopal Church, New York, 1963.

35.   "Problems in Christian Ethics," TV series, 12
        half-hour programs, ABC-TV, Spring 1964.

36.   "Important Theology: a Review of C. Michalson's *The
        Rationality of Faith*, H.P. Van Dusen's *The Vindication of
        Liberal Theology*," *The Christian Century*, March 11, 1964,
        pp.337–339.

37. Contributions to the book *Machines* (by Robert O'Brien and the Editors of Time, Life Inc.), New York, 1964.

38. "Modern Culture in Theological Perspective, The Report of the Omaha Conference on Metropolitan Planning," Omaha Conference on Metropolitan Planning, National Council of the Episcopal Church, 1964.

39. "It Was a Long, Hot Summer in the North, Too," *Intercollegian,* October–November 1964.

40. Review of Stephen Neill's *The Interpretation of the New Testament, The Christian Century,* Novemer 1964.

41. "Recent Books in Church-State Problems," *Union Seminary Quarterly Review,* November 1964, pp.85–89.

42. "You Can't Go Home Again," sermon, The American Youth Foundation, St. Louis, Mo., September, 1964.

43. "Horace Bushnell Revisited: A Study of the Development of his Theology," *The Drew Gateway,* Autumn 1964.

44. Review of Kenneth Hamilton's *The System and the Gospel,* and Review of Edward J. Jurji's *The Phenomenology of Religion, The Drew Gateway,* Autumn 1964.

45. "Religion Course Deals with Realities," with Elenore Lester, *The Sunday Star Ledger,* December 6, 1964, Newark.

46. "On Being a Christian," *The Methodist Teacher,* Summer 1965.

47. "The Theology of Horace Bushnell," *Encounter,* Vol. 26, No.1, Winter 1965, pp.65–74.

48. Review of Richard R. Neibuhr's *Schleiemacher on Christ and Religion, The Christian Century,* April 7, 1965. pp. 439–441.

49.   Review of William Robert Miller's *Non-violence: A Christian Interpretation*, *The Drew Gateway*, Volume XXXV, No.3, 1965.

50.   "Preaching and the Death of God Theology", *Pulpit Digest*, February, 1966.

51.   Review of Thomas Ogletree's *Christian Faith and History*, *The Christian Century*, May 1966.

52.   "Protestant Biography," TV series, 5 half-hour programs, ABC–TV, Fall 1966.

53.   "Modern Culture in Theological Perspective," *Report of Prarieopolis Conference of the Church of Canada*, Brandon, Manitoba, November 1966.

54.   "Swedenborg as a Modern Thinker: His Influence upon American Thought," *American Swedish Historical Foundation Yearbook*, 1966.

55.   "A Wife in the Rectory," *Jubilee*, January 1967, pp. 12–20.

56.   "White Backlash and Black Power," *Jubilee*, February 1967, pp.30–41.

57.   "Nygren and Schleiermacher on Religion," *Union Seminary Quarterly Review*, March 1967, pp.243–254.

58.   "National Service: An Alternative to Selective Service," *Motive*, February 1967, pp.22–27.

59.   "Liturgy and Social Action," Sermon, St. James Episcopal Church, New York, 1967.

60.   Review of *Horace Bushnell* (Ed. H. Shelton Smith), *Journal of Religion*, January 1967; *The Drew Gateway*, Autumn–Winter 1965-66.

61.   Review of *The Reality of God*, by Shubert Ogden, *Union Seminary Quarterly*, March 1967.

62.   "Is There an Alternative to Selective Service?" *Hi Way*, May 1967.

63.   "Toward a Theology of Urbanization," *Newsletter of the Urban Training Center*, Chicago, Spring 1967, pp.27-35.

64.   "A Brief Encounter with the Discipline of Religious Education," *New York University School of Education Bulletin*, Spring 1967, pp.1-17.

65.   "Baccalaureate," Sermon, Manhattanville College, Purchase, New York, June 1, 1968.

66.   "Brethren Theology: a Review of *Kierkegaard and Radical Discipleship*, by Vernard Eller," *Christian Century*, Vol. LXXXV. Number 23, June 1968.

67.   "Christopher Polhem: The Father of Swedish Technology," *The American Scandinavian Review*, Summer 1968. (Also appeared in Winter, 1964.) pp.162-175.

68.   "New Themes in Christian Philosophy," *Religious Education*, July-August 1969, pp.333-334.

69.   "Alumnae: Asking Questions, Calling for Answers," *Manhattanville Alumnae Review*, Summer 1969.

70.   Review of *Theological Ethics; Politics, Helmut Thielicke*, *Christian Century*, No.48, November 26, 1969, pp.1521-1522.

71.   "Swedenborg," *American Swedish Historical Foundation Yearbook*, 1969-1970.

72.   BOOK REVIEWS:
        Choice Books for College Libraries, 1964 to 1970.
        Bibliography of Philosophy, 1960 to 1970.
        Review of Metaphysics, 1965, 1967 to 1970.

73.   "Bonhoeffer," TV program, CBC, New York, December 1970.

74. "The Anthropology of Søren Kierkegaard", *Contributions to Kierkegaard's Presence in Contemporary American Life: Essays from Various Disciplines* (Ed.Lewis A. Lawson), Scarecrow Press, Metuchen, New Jersey, 1970. Originally appeared in the *Hartford Quarterly*,Vol. IV, No. 4, 1964.

75. "The Relationship between The Rev. Joseph H. Twichell and Mark Twain in Hartford between 1871 and 1891,"*American Philosophical Society Yearbook*, 1972, pp. 622-623.

76. BOOK REVIEWS:
The Bibliography of Philosophy, 1971, 1972, 1973.

77. Review of *Experiential Religion* by Richard R. Neibuhr, *Anglican Theological Review*, Vol. LV, No. 1, January 1973.

78. "Pentecost III,"Sermon at the Cathedral Church of St. John the Divine, New York, 1973.

79. "Confessionalism and the University," Church Society for College Work, Boston, December 1973.

80. "The Christian and the University," *Functions of Faith in Academic Life* (Jews and Christians in Higher Education, Special Edition), May-June 1974. Also appeared in *Journal of Religious Education*, Spring 1974, pp. 584-599.

81. "A Christian's Affirmation of Israel," *Reform Judaism*, April 1974.

82. "The Philosophy and Theology of Anders Nygren," *Journal of the American Academy of Religion*, June 1974, pp. 374-376.

83. "Agenda for Reform in the Church: Review of Richard P. McBrien's *The Remaking of the Church*," *The Review of Books of Religion*, September 1974, Vol. 4, No.1.

84.   "The Search for Transcendence,"TV program with Dr. David Read, WPIX-TV, New York, March 28, 1975.

85.   "The Search for Transcendence," Tapes: 12 hours of lectures at International Christian University, Tokyo, Spring 1975.

86.   "Institute of Theology Reflects Concerned Community," *The Episcopal New Yorker,* April 1975 (with Betty Gray).

87.   "Korea to Guam," *The Episcopalian,* May 1975.

88.   "Report of the Study Commission of the Ministry to The Military,"The Executive Council of the Episcopal Church, July 1975, 15 pages.

89.   General Editor of *Undercurrents,* the Journal of the Institute of Theology of the Cathedral Church of St. John the Divine (Vol. 1, Spring 1975; Vol. 2, Spring 1976).

90.   BOOK REVIEWS:
        Bibliography of Philosophy, 1974, 1975, 1976.
        Anglican Theological Review, 1976.

91.   "Hope in the Church," *Selected Sermons,* Seabury Press, May 16, 1976.

92.   "Readings in Christian Spirituality,"*The Episcopal New Yorker,* Winter 1975.

93.   "Process Management: Bad Theology in the Service (?) of the Church," *The Christian Century,* July 1976.

94.   "There's No Thanking God for his Musical Friday," *The Episcopalian,* October 1976.

95.   Review of *God, Secularization and History: Essays in Memory of Ronald Gregor Smith* (Ed. E.T. Long), *The Anglican Theological Review,* October 1976.

96.   "Christian Education: Tackling Today's Problem", *Sign of the Times* (Newsletter of the Cathedral Church of St. John the Divine), Vol. 1, No. 10, December 1976.

97.   "Hard Times in South Korea," *Brandeis University: The Justice*, February 22, 1977.

98.   Review of Bernard and Margaret Pawley's *Rome and Canterbury Through Four Centuries*, *Church History*, Spring 1977.

99.   "Column Left," with the Rt. Rev. Clarence E. Hobgood, *The Episcopalian*, June 1977.

100.   "A Theology for Critical Situations,"Cassette Tapes: 12 hours of Lectures at St. John's University and Seminary, Tokyo, Spring 1977.

101.   "The New Religious Consciousness," *The Christian Century*, September 14, 1977.

102.   "The Discipline of Philosophy and the Proclamation of the Gospel," Cassette Tapes: *The Hale Lectures*: "How to Avoid Making Mistakes in Theology," "Theological Truth and Language Games," "What Philosophers can Preach About," Seabury-Western Theological Seminary, Evanston, Illinois, 1977.

103.   "The Semper Fidelis Story is Told—and Told Very Well," *The Episcopalian*, December 1977.

104.   General Editor, *Auschwitz: Beginning of a New Era* (Reflection on the Holocaust), The Cathedral Church of St. John the Divine, 1977.

105.   *Bibliography of Philosophy*, 1977, 1978.

106.   Cassette tapes published by The Christian Educational Tape Network, New York, 1978, of courses given at the Institute of Theology, Cathedral of St. John the Divine:

Biblical Theology (I-II-III), 30 hours of lectures given during academic year 1975-1976.

Theology of Death and Resurrection, 20 hours of lectures given during Fall and Winter semesters, 1976-1977.

Moral Theology, 12 hours of lectures given during Spring semester, 1977.

Major Figures of the Christian Church (I-II-III), 30 hours of lectures given during the academic year 1977-78.

107. Reviews of Anders Nygren, *Essence of Christianity*, and *The Common Catechism:A Book of Christian Faith,The Anglican Theological Review*,Vol. LX, No. 1, January 1978, pp.112- 117.

108. "Faith and Proclamation: Principles of Preaching," Cassette Tapes, 12 hours of Lectures, Tokyo, January 1978.

109. "Jesus: Lord and Christ—Lectures in Christology," Cassette Tapes, 12 hours of Lectures, Berchtesgaden, Germany, March, 1978.

110. *EVIST Resource Directory*, "Science and Ethics" course taught at Brandeis University 1975-1978 (with Professor S.S. Schweber).

111. "Science vs. Ethics: Humanity's Dilemma as Technology Grows" (with Robert E. Wood), *Brandeis University Bulletin*, May 1978, p. 10.

112. "And Which of Them Would be the Greatest?" Ordination Sermon, Cathedral Church of St. John the Divine, June 3, 1978.

113. "Some Reflections on American Political Religion" (lecture given at the Aspen Institute for Humanistic Studies), *The Aspen Times*, July 27, 1978, pp. 11-12B.

114.   Review of Paul L. Holmer, *C.S. Lewis: The Shape of His Faith and Thought*, and John Cogley, *A Canterbury Tale: Experiences and Reflections* 1916-1976; *Historical Magazine of the Protestant Episcopal Church*, Vol. XLVII, No. 3, September 1978, pp. 355-359.

115.   "Caring for the Vulnerable Family Member: The Moral Issues," *Proceedings* of the Florence B. Heller Graduate School Conference; "Caring for the Vulnerable Family Member", Brandeis University, November 1978, NEH Grant, pp. 1-33.

116.   *Bibliography of Philosophy*, 1979.

117.   "Encountering the 'Other,'" *The Christian Century*, October 10, 1979, Vol. XCVI, No. 32, pp. 984-985.

118.   *Bibliography of Philosophy*, 1980.

119.   "Biblical Humanism and the Challenge of Technology," *The NICM Journal*, Winter 1980, Vol. 5., No. 1, pp. 37-38; 52-68.

120.   Review of Robert Rankin (ed), *The Recovery of Spirit in Higher Education, The NICM Journal*, Spring 1981, Vol. 6 No. 2, pp. 90-93.

121.   Television programs (2 hours), FEN Network, Japan, "The Christian World of C.S. Lewis," January 1982.

122.   "Reminiscence of Karl Barth," *NYU Alumni Journal*, 1981.

123.   Response to Arthur Waskow's *A Time to Renew, The NICM Journal*, Winter 1981, Vol. 7, No. 1, pp. 29-32.

124.   "Theology of the Eucharist," *The Episcopal Church Quarterly*, February 1982, 8 lectures given in Tokyo, reproduced on cassette tapes, Christian Education Tape Network, New York.

125.   Sermon outline, Human Rights Sunday (Advent II), December 5, 1982, Human Rights Office of the National Council of Churches (nationwide distribution).

126.   "Dill," "Parsley," "Vanilla," articles for distribution by the East Asiatic Company, Copenhagen.

127.   *Institute of Theology Newsletter*, Autumn 1982, Spring 1983.

128.   Review of J. Robert Moskin's *Among Lions, The Definitive Account of the 1967 Battle of Jerusalem, The Christian Century*, November 10, 1982.

129.   "Learning the Faith at the Institute of Theology" (with Jan Maas) *The Episcopal New Yorker*, January 1983.

130.   "The Catechism of the Episcopal Church," *The Episcopal Church Quarterly*, February 1983,10 lectures given in Tokyo, Japan, reproduced on cassette tapes, Christian Education Tape Network, New York.

131.   Review of *The Polite Escape, On The Myth of Secularization* by Harry J. Ausmus, *The Christian Century*, March 9, 1983, pp. 222-223.

132.   Review of *The Rabbi's Life Contract* by Marilyn Greenberg, *The Christian Century*, October 26, 1983, pp. 971-972.

133.   Review of *Living Issues in Ethics* by Richard T. Nolan and Frank G. Kirkpatrick, *The Christian Century*, November 9, 1983, p. 1025.

134.   "New Programs for Theological Education," *Report to the Arthur Vining Davis Foundation*, Autumn, 1983.

135.   Various reviews in *The Bibliography of Philosophy, The Anglican Theological Review, Review of Metaphysics, Episcopal Radio and TV Foundation Review*.

136.   "Why Brandeis Works," *Capital Campaign*, Brandeis University, 1984.

137.   "Reflections on Preaching," *The Christian Century*, November 1984, pp. 23-26.

138.   Book reviews in *The Bibliography of Philosophy, The Anglican Theological Review, Review of Metaphysics, The Episcopal Radio and TV Review, Institute of Theology Newsletter*.

139.   "The Theology of the Episcopal Church," *The Episcopal Church Quarterly*, February 1983 (10 cassette tapes of lectures given in Tokyo).

140.   Review of The Fire of Your Life: *A Solitude Shared* by Maggie Ross, *The Christian Century,* December 19-26, 1984, pp.1203-4.

141.   "On Death and Dying," *The Episcopal Church Quarterly*, January 1985 (seven lectures given in Tokyo, reproduced on cassette tapes, Christian Education Tape Network, New York).

142.   "Hope in the Church," *Selected Sermons*, Episcopal Parish Supplies, May 5,1985.

143.   Review of *How Can We Know?* by A.N. Wilson, *The Living Church*, October 27, 1985, p.14f.

144.   Review of *Springs of the Spirit* by Harry Reynolds Smythe, *The Living Church*, November 24, 1985, pp. 18-19.

145.   "19th Century Immigration and American Assimilation," *American Philosophical Society Yearbook,* 1985.

146.   Review of *Evangelicals on the Canterbury Trail* by Robert Webber, *The Living Church*, March 30, 1986, p.13.

147.   Review of *Systematic Theology:Ethics* by James W. McClendon, Jr., *The Christian Century*, September 24, 1968, pp.815-816.

148.   Review of *The Creation of Patriarchy* by Gerda Lerner, *The Christian Century,* November 5, 1986, pp.983f.

149.   Review of *Community: A Trinity of Models* by Frank G. Kirkpatrick, *The Living Church*, December 14, 1986 p.5ff.

150.   Articles on A.J. Ayer, Stephen Toulmin, *Encyclopedia of World Biography* (1986 Edition), pp. 79-81.

151.   "Jesus and the Canaanite Woman," *Selected Sermons,* 1986, Episcopal Church Parish Supplies.

152.   Study Guide: "Christianity and Terrorism" for the Episcopal Radio-TV Foundation, with Moorhead Kennedy, Council on International Understanding, The Myrin Institute, 1986.

153.   Review of *Caring and Curing: Health and Medicine in the Western Religious Traditions,* edited by Ronald L. Numbers and Darrel W. Amundson, *The Christian Century,* October 7, 1987, p. 864f.

154.   Review of *The Book of Uncommon Prayer,* by Kenneth Swanson, *The Episcopal New Yorker,* vol. 153, no. 3, p.36 (1988).

155.   Review of Joseph M. Kitagawa, *The History of Religions: Understanding Human Experience, The Living Church,* October 9, 1988, pp. 15-17.

156.   Review of Marvin Barrett, *Spare Days, The Christian Century,* September 28, 1988, p. 850.

157.   Review of Eric James, *A Life of John A.T. Robinson, The Living Church,* October 23, 1988, p. 13.

158.   Review of James Carpenter, *Nature and Grace: An Integral Perspective, The Christian Century,* February 15, 1989, pp. 181-182.

159.   "The Problem of Evil—Why We Suffer" (5 lectures given in Tokyo, reproduced on cassette tapes, The Episcopal Church Foundation, New York, January 1988).

160.   Contribution to volumes, *From Ancient Israel to Modern Judaism: Intellect in Quest of Understanding* (Essays in Honor of Marvin Fox): "Antisemitism in John's Gospel," 1989 Vol. I, pp. 149-170.

161.   Study Guide, "Brandeis Briefs," *Philosophy of Religion: the Existence of God*, Brandeis University National Women's Committee, 1989.

162.   Review of Sissela Bok, *A Strategy for Peace: Human Values and the Threat of War*, *The Christian Century*, November 1, 1989, pp. 993-994.

163.   Review of Edwin Robertson, *Dietrich Bonhoeffer: The Shame and the Sacrifice*, *America*, October 7, 1989, pp. 220-224.

164.   Article, "The Jews in Saint Mark's Gospel," *Religion and Intellectual Life*, Vol. VI, No. ¾, 1989, pp. 182-192.

165.   Review of Lawrence Perlman, *Abraham Heschel's Idea of Revelation*, *The Christian Century*, April 25, 1990, pp. 439 ff.

166.   "Lay Leadership," *The Living Church*, May 27, 1990, p. 10f.

167.   Review of David Birnbaum, *God and Evil*, *The Christian Century*, October 17, 1990, p. 942 ff.

168.   Review of Marvin Fox, *Interpreting Maimonides: Studies in Methodology, Metaphysics and Moral Philosophy*, *The Christian Century*, January 23, 1991, p. 87ff.

169.   Article, "A Christian's Response to the War in the Persian Gulf," *Publications of the Cathedral Church of Saint John the Divine*, New York, January 27, 1991.

170.   Review of "Søren Kierkegaard and the Christian Faith," *The Institute of Theology Publications*, New York, February 1991 (p. 24).

171.   Article, "The Person and Ministry of Jesus Christ," *The Institute of Theology Publications*, New York, March 1991 (p. 20).

172.   Article, "The Meaning of Life", *The Meaning of Life* (*in Chinese*), New York, *Platinum Press*, 1991.